Systems Approach Applications for Developments in Information Technology

Frank Stowell
University of Portsmouth, UK

Information Science
REFERENCE

Managing Director:	Lindsay Johnston
Senior Editorial Director:	Heather A. Probst
Book Production Manager:	Sean Woznicki
Development Manager:	Joel Gamon
Acquisitions Editor:	Erika Gallagher
Typesetter:	Jennifer Romanchak
Cover Design:	Nick Newcomer, Lisandro Gonzalez

Published in the United States of America by
   Information Science Reference (an imprint of IGI Global)
   701 E. Chocolate Avenue
   Hershey PA 17033
   Tel: 717-533-8845
   Fax: 717-533-8661
   E-mail: cust@igi-global.com
   Web site: http://www.igi-global.com

Library of Congress Cataloging-in-Publication Data

Systems approach applications for developments in information technology / Frank Stowell, editor.
    p. cm.
  Includes bibliographical references and index.
  ISBN 978-1-4666-1562-5 (hbk.) -- ISBN 978-1-4666-1563-2 (ebook) -- ISBN 978-1-4666-1564-9 (print & perpetual access) 1. Management information systems. 2. Computer software--Development. 3. System design. 4. Systems analysis. 5. Information technology. I. Stowell, Frank A.
  T58.64.S94 2012
  658.4'038011--dc23
                          2012012682

British Cataloguing in Publication Data
A Cataloguing in Publication record for this book is available from the British Library.

The views expressed in this book are those of the authors, but not necessarily of the publisher.

Table of Contents

Detailed Table of Contents

Section 1
Information System Provision

Chapter 1

> *Manuel Mora, Autonomous University of Aguascalientes, Mexico*
> *Miroljub Kljajić, University of Maribor, Slovenia*

In this short article, we present an e-interview to a well-recognized system scientist Barry G. Silverman, who is Professor of Systems Science and Engineering at the University of Pennsylvania, and Director of the Ackoff Collaboratory for Advancement of the Systems Approach (ACASA) in the same university. In this e-interview, Professor Silverman, teach us on the origins, and still applicability and need of the Systems Approach, but now focused on the present complex social systems. A Systems Approach must and can provide a white-box research approach and advance on the limitations of the reductionist black-box research approaches. Professor Silverman, also alert us on the scarcity of PhD academic programs covering these systems approaches and makes a call for continuing the "difficult missionary effort" of teaching and doing research on the Systems Approach.

Chapter 2

> *Yves Wautelet, Université Catholique de Louvain, Belgium*
> *Christophe Schinckus, Facultés Universitaires St-Louis, Belgium*
> *Manuel Kolp, Université Catholique de Louvain, Belgium*

This article presents an epistemological reading of knowledge evolution in software engineering (SE) both within a software project and into SE theoretical frameworks principally modeling languages and software development life cycles (SDLC). The article envisages SE as an artificial science and notably points to the use of iterative development as a more adequate framework for the enterprise applications. Iterative development has become popular in SE since it allows a more efficient knowledge acquisition process especially in user intensive applications by continuous organizational modeling and requirements acquisition, early implementation and testing, modularity,... SE is by nature a human activity: analysts, designers, developers and other project managers confront their visions of the software system they are building with users' requirements. The study of software projects' actors and stakeholders using Simon's bounded rationality points to the use of an iterative development life cycle. The later, indeed, allows to better apprehend their rationality. Popper's knowledge growth principle could at first seem suited for the analysis of the knowledge evolution in the SE field. However, this epistemology is better adapted to purely hard sciences as physics than to SE which also takes roots in human activities and by the way in social sciences. Consequently, we will nuance the vision using Lakatosian epistemology notably using his falsification principle criticism on SE as an evolving science. Finally the authors will point to adaptive rationality for a lecture of SE theorists and researchers' rationality.

Chapter 3

Theresa A. Kraft, University of Michigan, USA
Annette L. Steenkamp, Lawrence Technological University, USA

Companies invest significant sums of money in major Information Technology (IT) projects, yet success remains limited. Despite an abundance of IT Project Management (ITPM) resources available to project teams, such as the Project Management Institute (PMI) Body of Knowledge, IT standards and IT governance, a large percentage of IT projects continue to fail and ultimately get scrapped. Recent studies have shown an average of 66% IT project failure rate, with 52% of the projects being cancelled, and 82% being delivered late. The purpose of this research was to provide a way for uncovering potential causes of IT project failures by utilizing a systemic and holistic approach to identify critical success factors for project management. The holistic approach has enabled the development of an ITPM conceptual model, which provides a method to evaluate the critical success factors of a given project, and their alignment with each other. The adoption of the systemic methodology and its implementation increase the potential for IT project success, and alert project leaders of potential problems throughout the life of the project.

Chapter 4

Miroljub Kljajić, University of Maribor, Slovenia

The relationship between industrial and scientific knowledge and systems methodologies is discussed in this paper. As the measure of the former on the macro level, Gross Domestic Product (GDP) is assumed to be the consequence of systems' Research and Development (R&D), which is estimated indirectly by the number of articles published in academic journals in the last 40 years. It is assumed that Production, Management and Information Systems (IS) can be considered suitable main representatives of the quality of organizational processes and that GDP is their consequence. In turn, the Systems Approach (SA), Systems Engineering (SE), Operational Research (OR), Information Systems Development (ISD) and Simulation represent the methodology set for coping with organizational complex processes. We looked for the articles containing the aforementioned variables as topic keywords in core scientific databases. Results show a sufficient correlation between the number of publications and the GDP.

Chapter 5

Walter Hürster, Private Researcher and Independent Consultant, Germany
Thomas Wilbois, T-Systems, Germany
Fernando Chaves, Fraunhofer IITB, Germany

An integrated and interdisciplinary approach to Early Warning and Risk Management is described in this paper as well as the general technical implementation of Early Warning and Risk Management Systems. Based on this systems approach, a concept has been developed for the design of an Integrated System for Coastal Protection. In addition to this, as a prototype implementation of a modern environmental monitoring and surveillance system, a system for the Remote Monitoring of Nuclear Power

Plants is presented here in more detail, including a Web Portal to allow for public access. The concept, the architectural design and the user interface of Early Warning and Risk Management Systems have to meet high demands. It is shown that only a close cooperation of all related disciplines and an integrated systems approach is able to fulfil the catalogue of requirements and to provide a suitable solution for environmental monitoring and surveillance, for early warning and for emergency management.

Information Systems as a discipline has generated thousands of research papers, yet the practice still suffers from poor-quality applications. This paper evaluates the current state of application development, finding practice wanting in a number of areas. Changes recommended to fix historical shortcomings include improved management attention to risk management, testing, and detailed work practices. In addition, for industry's move to services orientation, recommended changes include development of usable interfaces and a view of applications as embedded in the larger business services in which they function. These business services relate to both services provided to parent-organization customers as well as services provided by the information technology organization to its constituents. Because of this shift toward service orientation, more emphasis on usability, applications, testing, and improvement of underlying process quality are needed. The shift to services can be facilitated by adopting tenets of IT service management and user-centered design and by attending to service delivery during application development.

Composite applications integrate web services with other business applications and components to implement business processes. Model-driven approaches tackle the complexity of composite applications caused by domain and technology heterogeneity and integration requirements. The method and framework described in this paper generate all artefacts (workflow, data, user interfaces, etc.), required for a composite application from high level service oriented descriptions of the composite application, using model transformation and code generation techniques.

An important feature in collaborative environment is coordination, defined as the act of managing interdependencies between activities performed to achieve a goal. These interdependencies can be the result of loosely integrated collaborative activities (the use of coordination processes within the collaboration activities is not required) or tightly integrated collaborative activities (sophisticated coordination mechanisms are necessary). The existence of both activities along with the dynamic nature of these environments adds a greater complexity to the coordination that has not been taken into account in traditional collaborative systems. In this work, the authors present a partially Services Oriented Architecture (SOA) that defines and maintains dynamic coordination polities in collaborative systems based on coordination models.

Chapter 9

Zongjun Li, Government of Ontario, Canada

Annette Lerine Steenkamp, Lawrence Technological University, USA

The Mobile Enterprise is a new form of enterprise in the contemporary mobile era. Although several well-known enterprise architecture frameworks are used by enterprises, it is apparent that there is no industry standard available to enable an enterprise to transform its business processes to incorporate mobile technologies to advantage. This paper presents a conceptual Mobile Enterprise Architecture Framework and supporting methodology and process model which can aid enterprise decision makers to evaluate the business values, and analyze the risks and other critical business and technical factors for enterprise mobile initiatives and mobile transitions. The framework covers both the enterprise and mobile enterprise architecture domains that represent the Enterprise, Business, and Mobile Adoption levels. The goal at the Enterprise Level is to obtain a mobile enterprise and the technologies adopted at the Mobile Adoption Level are the different mobile technologies to be incorporated. Each level contains some important components impacting the mobile enterprise transformation. The methodology and process model cover the Strategy, Analysis, Design, Implementation, and Maintenance stages for each mobile initiative, and were validated in a research project against some Ontario Government mobile initiatives.

Chapter 10

Matthew L. Smith, International Development Research Centre, Canada

Theory testing within small-N research designs is problematic. Developments in the philosophy of social science have opened up new methodological possibilities through, among other things, a novel notion of contingent causality that allows for contextualized hypothesis generation, hypothesis testing and refinement, and generalization. This article contributes to the literature by providing an example of critical realist (one such new development in the philosophy of social science) theory development for a small-N comparative case study that includes hypothesis testing. The article begins with the key ontological assumptions of critical realism and its relation to theory and explanation. Then, the article presents an illustrative example of an e-government comparative case study, focusing on the concept of trust, which follows these ontological assumptions. The focus of the example is on the nature and process of theory and hypothesis development, rather than the actual testing that occurred. Essential to developing testable hypotheses is the generation of tightly linked middle-range and case-specific theories that provide propositions that can be tested and refined. The link provides a pathway to feed back the concrete empirical data to the higher level (more abstract) and generalizable middle-range theories.

Chapter 11

Giuseppe Conti, Fondazione Graphitech, Italy

Raffaele De Amicis, Fondazione Graphitech, Italy

Stefano Piffer, Fondazione Graphitech, Italy

Bruno Simões, Fondazione Graphitech, Italy

The management of a territory is a complex process, involving a number of different operators, administrators and decision makers. Territory management requires accessing and processing a wide range of heterogeneous and multi-dimensional GI (GI). Within a typical scenario, the process involves departments at public administrations responsible for urban planning, environmental control, infrastructure planning and maintenance. Additionally units such as civil protection, fire brigades also play a vital role when dealing with emergencies. Data to be managed range from alphanumerical information, stored within enterprise-level databases, to satellite imagery, vector data and information coming from on-site sensors. It is acknowledged that creating an infrastructure capable to provide access to such a range of information requires, an integrated system approach, both from a technological and from a procedural point of view. This article illustrates the benefit of adopting a system approach which makes use of Service-Oriented Architectures (SOA) and 3D geobrowsers to provide an answer to the aforementioned shortcomings. To do so the article presents the client-server platform designed to support decision makers and experts from local or regional administrations in the process of managing their territory. The infrastructure developed allows a large number of concurrent applications to access geographical data in a fully interactive way, within a 3D environment, thus providing support to territorial and environmental management tasks. The work illustrates also the results of the application of the infrastructure within a real-life scenario, thus providing the chance to discuss of implications of adopting such an approach.

When vocational student teachers communicate on a virtual platform in a combined campus and web based university course they focus on the contents of teaching and learning. However, in communicating professional teacher knowledge they implicitly express their personal values too. Without giving it much thought, they embed values in their verbal entries and they assess embedded values in their peers' texts. This article introduces a soft systems model for categorizing the influence of values on web based interactions.

Recent research suggests that a strong link exists between business innovation and service oriented IT architectures: modern IT architecture enables business to quickly create new services. However, the relationship between IT capabilities and business performance is not always straightforward. How does SOA support fast innovation in practice, and under which conditions is it effective? In this paper, the authors investigate these issues and ask: How can a SOA architecture like the Enterprise Service Bus support business innovation? This paper investigates this question through a case study at an airline company. Analyzing the relationship between innovation and IT architecture in the company over time, the authors offer the following conclusion: ESB gives strong support to business innovation, under two conditions. First, the implementation of ESB has to be comprehensive, that is, it should include the core processes of the business. Second, the top management (and partners) need to understand the principles of ESB.

The specifications of automated learning scenarios can lead to advantages for virtual learning environments and important benefits for organizations, although research in this e-learning area has not addressed this issue. To achieve this goal, one requirement is to have an infrastructure able to support the execution of specifications of learning scenarios. This paper presents an open service-oriented architecture based on the Open Services Interface Definition (OSID) specifications proposed by the Open Knowledge Initiative (OKI) and other normative specifications. The architecture is used as a technological infrastructure in a virtual learning environment with more than 40,000 students enrolled and has been tested as the infrastructure of a tool to automate specifications of learning scenarios. A case study has been used to test the suitability of the architecture and describe such a tool for the future.

As websites increase in complexity, locating needed information becomes a difficult task. Such difficulty is often related to the websites' design but also ineffective and inefficient navigation processes. Research in web mining addresses this problem by applying techniques from data mining and machine learning to web data and documents. In this study, the authors examine web usage mining, applying data mining techniques to web server logs. Web usage mining has gained much attention as a potential approach to fulfill the requirement of web personalization. In this paper, the authors propose K-means biclustering, rough biclustering and fuzzy biclustering approaches to disclose the duality between users and pages by grouping them in both dimensions simultaneously. The simultaneous clustering of users and pages discovers biclusters that correspond to groups of users that exhibit highly correlated ratings on groups of pages. The results indicate that the fuzzy C-means biclustering algorithm best and is able to detect partial matching of preferences.

Section 2
Security and Privacy

Many citizens rely upon online services, and it is certain that this reliance will increase in the future. However, they frequently lack a solid appreciation of the related safety and security issues, and can be missing out on an essential aspect of awareness in everyday life. Indeed, users are often *concerned* about online threats, but it would be stretching the point to claim that they are fully *aware* of the problems. Thus, rather than actually protecting themselves, many will simply accept that they are taking a risk. This paper examines the problem of establishing end-user eSafety awareness, and proposes means by which related issues can be investigated and addressed. Recognising that long-term attitudes and practices will be shaped by early experiences with the technology, it is particularly important to address the issue early and improve awareness amongst young people. However, the problem is unlikely to be addressed via the approaches that would traditionally be applied with adult users. As such, the paper examines information gathering and awareness-raising strategies drawing from qualitative methodologies in the social sciences, whose pluralistic approach can be effectively applied within school contexts.

Chapter 17

Zbigniew Kwecka, Edinburgh Napier University, UK

William J. Buchanan, Edinburgh Napier University, UK

Investigators often define invasion of privacy as collateral damage. Inquiries that require gathering data from third parties, such as banks, Internet Service Providers (ISPs) or employers are likely to impact the relationship between the data subject and the data controller. In this research a novel privacy-preserving approach to mitigate collateral damage during the acquisition process is presented. This approach is based on existing Private Information Retrieval (PIR) protocols, which cannot be employed in an investigative context. This paper provides analysis of the investigative data acquisition process and proposes three modifications that can enable existing PIR protocols to perform investigative enquiries on large databases, including communication traffic databases maintained by ISPs. IDAP is an efficient Symmetric PIR (SPIR) protocol optimised for the purpose of facilitating public authorities' enquiries for evidence. It introduces a semi-trusted *proxy* into the PIR process in order to gain the acceptance of the general public. In addition, the *dilution factor* is defined as the level of anonymity required in a given investigation. This factor allows investigators to restrict the number of records processed, and therefore, minimise the processing time, while maintaining an appropriate level of privacy.

Chapter 18

Nikos Vrakas, University of Piraeus, Greece

Costas Lambrinoudakis, University of Piraeus, Greece

The convergence of different network types under the same architecture offers the opportunity for low cost multimedia services. The main objective has been the high quality of the provided services. However, considering that older equipment with limited processing capabilities may be present in such environments, a tradeoff between security and service quality is inevitable. Specifically, low resource enabled devices cannot utilize state of the art security mechanisms, such as IPSec tunnels, integrity mechanisms, etc., and they simply employ HTTP Digest authentication. The lack of integrity mechanisms in particular raises many security concerns for the IMS infrastructures. Attacks such as Man in the Middle (MitM), spoofing, masquerading, and replay that can be launched in IMS environments, have been pinpointed in bibliography by various researchers. Moreover, an internal attacker may utilize his legitimate security tunnels in order to launch spoofing and identity theft attacks. This paper presents a cross-layer spoofing detection mechanism that protects SIP-based infrastructures from the majority of the aforementioned attacks without requiring an additional cryptographic scheme which would inevitably introduce considerable overheads.

Chapter 19

Emmanouil Magkos, Ionian University, Greece

Current research in location-based services (LBSs) highlights the importance of cryptographic primitives in privacy preservation for LBSs, and presents solutions that attempt to support the (apparently) mutually exclusive requirements for access control and context privacy (i.e., identity and/or location), while at the same time adopting more conservative assumptions in order to reduce or completely remove the need for trust on system entities (e.g., the LBS provider, the network operator, or other peer nodes). This paper surveys the current state of knowledge concerning the use of cryptographic primitives for privacy-preservation in LBS applications.

Chapter 20

Ioannis Mavridis, University of Macedonia, Greece

Access control technology holds a central role in achieving trustworthy management of personally identifiable information in modern information systems. In this article, a privacy-sensitive model that extends Role-Based Access Control (RBAC) to provide privacy protection through fine-grained and just-in-time access control in Web information systems is proposed. Moreover, easy and effective mapping of corresponding components is recognized as an important factor for succeeding in matching security and privacy objectives. Such a process is proposed to be accomplished by capturing and modeling privacy requirements in the early stages of information system development. Therefore, a methodology for deploying the mechanisms of an access control system conforming to the proposed Privacy Improved Role-Based Access Control (PIRBAC) model is presented. To illustrate the application of the proposed methodology, an application example in the healthcare domain is described.

Preface

The chapters contained within this text reflect the value of Systems Thinking in the design and development of Information Technology (IT). Its contents also reflect the growing range and number of contributions that the *International Journal of Information Technologies and the Systems Approach* (IJITSA) attracts. The chapters cover a diverse range of topics such as Software Engineering, Knowledge Management, Surveillance, and Privacy. Readers will forgive me, I hope, for the rather crude grouping of these fine papers. I have taken the position that this text is devoted to the use of Systems Ideas in the development of Information Technology in its variety of forms. Rather than repeat the editorials for each of the relevant editions, I have instead written an overview of the use of Systems Ideas within the context of particular applications published in IJITSA. To this end, I have divided the book into two sections. The first section is concerned with information provision and the second with security and privacy.

The text is composed of papers from the 2010 and 2011 editions of the IJITSA. In general terms, the first section deal with ways of attempting to overcome the difficulties of IT provision through the examination of current design methods and how they can be improved. In some instances, these papers show a distinct move from a technically-based approach to what might be called a soft approach. That is to say one that takes into account the social systems in which IT resides. For this reason, we briefly explore the difference between a computer system (or data processing system) and an Information System (IS). It is important to do so as we reflect the methods of design. The text then moves on to the chapters that address the benefits and the dangers of IT supported security systems. It is here where we consider if technological surveillance, ostensibly there to protect its citizens, might have unwanted effects upon individual privacy and freedom, but first we begin with information technology provision.

INFORMATION TECHNOLOGY PROVISION AND FAILURE?

There are few that would contest the assertion that information is the most important commodity we have. Moreover, it stands to reason that the way in which we design these systems will have a significant impact upon those who use them. Yet over the past decade, there is evidence that large information systems fail. The end-user, or client, is often unconsciously considered by the designer as a component of a data processing system, rather than viewing technology as a resource within a network of human communication. We find that the reductionist paradigm that underpins these design methods is often found to be lacking when confronted with modern information system requirements and the complex processing that characterises human decision-making. To ignore the customs and practices of the intended users is to invite trouble and will lead to failure. For example, a manager is reported as saying he had not seen one successful project in 25 years, which he put down to politics and lack of alliances of the technical competent. He continued by saying that "...the problem is not technical but dismal management and shoddy methods" (Caulkin, 2004). Cross (2005) echoes this contention by pointing out that large and complex projects cut across different agencies creating management difficulties. He points out that most government projects start with the intention of using off-the-shelf software that inevitably ends up being customised for the users. A recent report states that "A plan to create the world's largest single civilian computer system linking all parts of the National Health Service (in the UK) is to be abandoned by the Government after running up billions of pounds in bills. Ministers are expected to announce next month that they are scrapping a central part of the much-delayed and hugely controversial 10-year National Programme for IT" (Wright, 2011).

Of course failures are not confined to the UK, as IT projects have a poor record throughout the world (see Kraft and Steenkamp [2010] in this text, who make a similar point). In 2005, Cross reported that 70% of projects in the USA failed to meet their timetable or budget or come up to specification. OECD reported only 28% of all IT projects in the US were successful in 2000 (OECD, 2001). The reports give several reasons for this lack of success, including differences between public and private sector projects, project size, project isolation, government interface with IT industries, market and technical dominance of IT companies, modernity of equipment, and the extent to which government retains IT expertise. It is clear from these reports that the failure is rarely of a technological nature but arises from a combination of lack of clarity in objectives, poor management, naivety, and unrealistic expectations (Computing, 2003).

Failure, then, results from a mixture of things, and there is scant evidence of a failure of technology. One conclusion that can be formed is that reported failure is the result of human error and not failure of the technology. We should remind ourselves that any enterprise information technology is used as an aid to decision taking and policy-making. Once installed and operating, the technology rarely fails, and yet the Information System that it supports is often reported as failing. It was estimated that in 2004 IT spending in the UK hit £23Billion (£12 B from public sector) and yet only 16% of British projects are successful, and it is not much better in the USA, which is at 28-34% (OECD, 2001; Computing, 2004).

The likelihood of avoiding future failures is doubtful, as there is little to suggest much has been learnt from the recent past, but what is an IS Failure? Because of the considerable investment in Information Technology to improve business efficiency, it is not surprising that computing power and efficiency are considered by many to be synonymous. Attempts to define IS failure often tend to focus on a failure to the take up the technology and its associated software, but success and failure are not as easy as this to measure as the take up of the technology may relate to the lack of consideration given to the needs of the end user (e.g. Myers, 1994; Stowell, 2010). Fortune and Peters (2005) characterise IS failure as a "...product of outputs which are considered to be undesirable by those involved." They cite Vickers (1981) who perhaps proves a richer and more experiential definition as "A human system fails if it does not succeed in doing whatever it was designed to do; or if it succeeds but leaves everyone wishing it had never tried."

Clearly, a failure can be caused for a variety of quantifiable reasons such as being over budget, technology breakdown, and so on, but the implications of Vickers's definition is that it is the impact upon the users and intended consumers that causes the greatest problems. Whilst the specific cause of failure differs with each information system, what they have in common is economic and social calamity. The failure of a large public IS affects not just those who operate the IS or use it as a management tool, it also frustrates the sponsors, the designers, those who managed the project and, increasingly, the general public.

There are numerous reports of IS failure (see Fortune & Peters, 2005), but the puzzle is why do they continue? Lyytinen and Robey (1999) suggested that many information systems departments appear unable or unwilling to adjust their practices even when they fail to produce beneficial results. It would seem that lessons about failure are not being learnt and research into design methods are not taken up. This is a situation that one commentator described as being "…like a computer virus, endlessly replicate the mistakes of the past" (Caulkin, 2004).

If we accept Caulkin's premise that the problem is not technical, then the problem of failure does seem to lie outside the technology. The Dunleavy and Margettes (2004) report places great emphasis on the relationship between government and IT companies. They suggest the politics of Government operation and technical expertise as being key factors in success. These are all points of great importance, but they are focused on procurement of technology and not the failures following implementation. It is natural that as a digital processor is at the heart of most information systems it is often the acquisition and use of the technology that is cited as the success or otherwise of the Information System (Lynch & Gregor, 2004; Bisson, 2004). Many of the chapters in this text are concerned with this area (*e.g. Conger, Software Development Life Cycles,* and *Methodologies*).

INFORMATION SYSTEMS DESIGN

It is not uncommon for the methods of design adopted for information systems to be lacking in some respect. They are often methods whose origins are from the early days of computing where it was assumed that the computer would carry out the tasks that a human did not need to do, and the human activities would fit around the technology. Traditional Data Processing, as it was once called, is not concerned with information because it produces data that are used to guide routine activities without being explicitly interpreted to the activity. Human actors are informed by the data. That resulted in a profusion of data, which Ackoff (1978) referred to as an irrelevant abundance of data processing. With more powerful and easy to use technology, the modern day designer needs to take all aspects of the communication system into account, both human and technological.

We now recognise that although an information system, or system of information (Stowell, 2010), comprises a variety of technological devices, these are aids for human decision-making and not autonomous technical systems. They operate in the service of humans and not the other way around. Notwithstanding this, these significant failures in information systems continue (e.g. Wright, 2011). The prime reason for failure seems that IS development is undertaken as a technological project and not thought of as a system of information where, combined with the technology, it supports the system to be served (Wynter, et al., 1995). Because of this, there is a tendency to focus on the technology at the expense of engaging the end-user, or client, in the development and consequent ownership of the IS itself. This is not a new assertion, and similar observations could be found in the literature some decades ago, e.g. "An IS fails when it cannot fulfil the expectations and this incapability calls for stakeholder action" (Lyytinen, 1988). The difficulty has been, and still is, how the user, stakeholder, client, call it what you will, can engage in something as complex as IS development? IS development necessitates specialist knowledge of problem solving, technology, working practices, and some degree of clairvoyance.

When my colleague, Daune West, and I published our text (Client led Design, 1994), we were criticised because it was felt that non-technical clients did not have the skills to lead such a development programme. Yet since that time, a significant number of researchers have attempted to find ways in which the client can have greater involvement and control over the project (e.g. Champion, 2001; Cooray, 2010; and chapters contained within this text). Our reasoning at the time, and still is, is that computers need to identify data objects, but people are interested in identifying and understanding what that object means. IS provision is about a total system of information, and as such, we need to consider the whole, that is all components, including human and technical.

Information Systems are formed from interrelated information units and relations between them. Our primary task then is to understand the purposeful actions of those that make up the system of interest and with the clients describe the information system that enables it. In other words, our first task is to consider the *'system to be served'* and conceptualised in some way before the *'serving system'* can be considered (Checkland & Scholes, 1990; Wynter, et al., 1995). Together with the clients, we can then envisage how the technology could be assimilated into their information system. It is only then that we are in a position to specify the technological support. It is what might be called a *Voluntaristic* theory of action (Parsons, 1949; in Burrell & Morgan, 2005, p. 84). This no trivial undertaking given the rate of change taking place within the global economy and the multi-relationships that the modern enterprise needs to maintain in order to survive.

OVERCOMING FAILURE?

The number of IS failures has prompted a variety of attempts to include the clients in development. In Software Engineering (SE), the more advanced approaches of IT development do show an awareness of the importance of user involvement. For example, the XP development cycle starts promisingly with "…end user stories that are used to estimate development time and define a plan for the release of applications… it makes it easier to get feedback from users as the whole application is developed" (Bisson, 2004). But the approach soon lapses into technology driven criteria for success as the satisfaction of the customer is measured by the delivery of software—"…satisfy them through early and continuous delivery of valuable software" (Agile Alliance Europe, 2004). Wautelet et al. ("Towards Knowledge Evolution in Software Engineering: An Epistemological Approach"), contained within this text, acknowledges that user requirements have been poorly taken into account partially because the modelling methods used have their origins in programming concepts rather than those more suited to human actors. They argue that Software Engineering "…is by nature a human activity… confront their visions of the software system they are building with users requirements." They suggest a framework for SE based upon iterative development. In the special edition of IJITSA (Vol 4, no 1, 2011), Steencamp and Gonzalez explored the range of approaches related to Service Oriented Computing, in particular the use of a systems approach in the development process. These papers, which explore the use of IT to support collaboration and contribute to business transformation, are included within this text as distinct chapters. A variety of ideas are explored in this section that look at the ways in which easier integration between systems can be achieved as a means of providing a better foundation for adding new applications. Conger ("Software Development Life Cycles and Methodologies") points to the fact that despite the number of research projects that have failed, SE still suffers from poor quality applications. She says that moving towards the development of usable applications embedded within organisational services requires some changes. Conger argues for more emphasis on usability, applications, testing, and improvements, and a shift to user involvement in design. The constantly changing nature of business and the need for the businesses' IT structure to follow suit is the topic in the paper by Karakostas and Zorgios ("Model Driven Engineering of Composite Service Oriented Application"). They propose a unifying framework in which workflow, data, and user interface are modelled. The ideas expressed in the special edition have some resonance with the Champion et al. (2005) paper in which the researchers explore the relationship between using soft ideas (e.g. SSM) and Object models to 'navigate the gap' between client requirements and technical support. The key consideration is how the users' requirements can be successfully translated into an information system that meets their needs.

Despite the advances in software architecture and data mining, there is still a way to go before we can be confident of its value to IS provision. We find that the primary measurement of success is still in terms of working software. On the face, it is as good a measure as any, but we must ask ourselves is it good enough criteria for assessing the usefulness of an *information system*?

What seems to be overlooked are the intended clients who are best placed to define their Information System before we think about the data processing system part of the equation. IS development is usually technically biased because a computer system needs a concise specification and one that can be validated. The alternative of involving non-technically skilled clients in IS development is problematic. Aside from the time factors and costs involved, there is a certain level of technical understanding required. Attempts have been made by researchers to develop ways of involving the user, that is to say ways in which the end user, or clients, might take responsibility for the development of their information system.

The chapter by Kraft et al. ("A Holistic Approach for Understanding Project Management") is an account of an investigation of the problem of IT project failure. These researchers also point out that the projects become problematic because of the mixture of technical, social, and economical endeavours. They use what they describe as a holistic approach in which Soft Systems Methodology (Checkland, 1999) plays and important part in the development of a conceptual tool, which they say will assist project leaders in recognising potential difficulties throughout the life of the project.

In the Hurster et al. chapter ("An Integrated Systems Approach for Early Warning and Risk Management"), they describe how they adopted an integrated approach in which the involvement of all related disciplines succeeded in providing a solution in the development of an early warning system for risk management. They involved all relevant stakeholders in their project as a means of meeting and defining their requirements, including the specification of communication links with the corresponding interfaces. These chapters (and others within) share a similar view that stresses the importance of engaging with the clients.

In his interview for IJITSA (Vol. 3, No. 2, 2010, pp. 57-63), Professor Silverman's reply to the question about the future development of DSS has many similarities to the developments in Information Systems methods. Professor Silverman says that "...modelling social systems and societal dynamics is only possible by dragging onto the modelling stage, all of the exoteric information, and knowledge about the stake holders in a given social technical systems." So there seems to be a general acceptance by SE and IS researchers and practitioners that modern IS provision is about enabling client participation. The consequence of this is a move towards methods that enable the client to take responsibility for the definition and consequent development of *their* IS as a whole, but how this is achieved is a more difficult proposition.

DEFINING INFORMATION SYSTEMS

IS design and development methods are predicated on satisfying a technical need because a computer and associated software needs a concise and verifiable specification. Given this situation, it is not unreasonable for the major actor in the design process to be a technical expert, and as a consequence, the design approaches employed are technically oriented. As we can see from many of the chapters contained in this text, several researchers, from Software Engineering and Information Systems, agree that we have to find ways of embracing the needs of the clients.

There is no doubt that attempting to define the IS without the full engagement of the clients can lead to difficulties during implementation and operation. Cooray (2010) undertook research in which she attempted to model the information systems requirements for a city library. Her approach, following Champion et al. (2005), Champion (2001), and Guo et al. (2000), used conceptual models used as part of SSM (Checkland, 1999) and AIM (Stowell & West, 1991; Stowell, 2012) as the basis for developing relationship models and class diagrams. These were quasi-technical models that she used to promote discussion with the clients as a precursor to the technical specification. Cooray's work contributes to attempts to combine the soft aspects of IS provision with the technical elements in one unified approach.

However, client-centred approaches have been developed over the years, for example, Information System Engineering (e.g. Jackson Methodology, 1975), SSADM (1990), multi-view (Avison & Wood-Harper, 1986). Although these have improved the IT design, they have been less successful in providing a sound basis for Information Systems development. The continued level of IS failure suggests these ideas have had little impact. One problem is that the clients are not truly in control. This is because despite best efforts, these methods are still driven by technology and end up modifying the clients' needs to satisfy the technical requirements. In their text, *Client-Led Design*, Stowell and West (1994) advocated IS provision be *Client-Led* rather than *Client-Centred,* but the difficulty here was in finding the method that moved the client from an everyday language definition of their information needs into a technical specification. Stowell and West used a conceptual model into a data flow diagram to achieve this, but this was only moderately successful, as it still meant a 'leap' from a non-technical to a technical description. Champion (2001) suggested an answer to this difficulty by suggesting that the client should 'navigate' from one to the other. This was developed further by Cooray (2010) in her research in IS provision in a city library, but one difficulty in involving the non-technical client and the technical expert is that one will see the information needs and one the technical potential. Following a less than satisfactory outcome to one publically funded project, the chairman of the public accounts committee stated, "One of the major problems was the 'horrible interface' between civil servants, who understand all there is to know about…. a system but know little of how a computer works, and technicians who just know the reverse." He went on to say that, "…they don't spend enough time at the start of the project explaining where they are both coming from" (Morris & Travis, 2001).

Because Systems is a meta-discipline, it can offer an alternative approach. In a paper printed in IJITSA in 2008 (Vol. 1, No. 1, pp. 25-36), we questioned if we were right in thinking in terms of information systems or if we should think more about systems of information. What we meant by this was that thinking in terms of Information Systems tends to place it in the same arena as information technology. Information Systems then become thought of as a physical artefact rather than in terms of the information that we need to make our way in the world. We ventured that we might be better thinking in terms of 'systems of information' that we need in order to function, whether it is in our daily private lives or in our working capacity.

By thinking about the systems of information we use, or need, we can separate those activities that are better undertaken by a human, such as activities that require tact and understanding, from those that are relatively routine, such as simple financial transactions. A system of information that encompasses the relationship between the computer, data processing, and human conversation into information and organization is proposed by Langefors (1995), called an integrated information system. Perhaps assimilation is a more appropriate description of the aim of the designer. The advantage of thinking how technology might be assimilated into the information system means that consideration of aspects of the wider system and issues such as decentralisation and IS strategy and activities that will influence the behaviour and form of an organisation are taken into account.

However if we accept this proposal, it follows that the methods we use to enquire into the systems of information are different than those that are primarily concerned with IT. An important distinction to be made is that the method of design should be *client led* not *client centred*. The client, rather than the technical expert, should take responsibility for the outcome of the design, but the difficulties of client involvement are many. For example, the association created by the form of the data may well affect interpreting the data. A sentence is conveyed to a third party who has the knowledge to receive it as a fact and no more. Information is more intimate and relies upon a shared understanding and synergy. We need to distinguish between facts obtained though interpretation and information obtained through inference drawn from conveyed factual knowledge. Langefors (1995) suggests that interpretation depends upon a clearly restricted set of knowledge whilst Inference involves a much more complex knowledge (and maybe these can be infinite).

INTEGRATED SYSTEMS

From a design point of view the IS professional is concerned with finding ways of defining that information system as a whole. The process can be broken crudely into the technical and non-technical requirements, bearing in mind that the former must be assimilated into the latter. Kljajic ("The Importance of Methodologies for Industrial and Scientific National Wealthy and Development") reports attempts to combine methods and concludes that Simulation and a Systems approach (it is not clear which) should be fused with what is referred to as one holistic methodology. Like many who have gone before have discovered, attempting to combine methodologies has its own problems, e.g. conflicting epistemologies.

Langefors refers to the main task of the IS professional being concerned with the external properties of the IS, and the technical specialist, on the other hand, is concerned with the internal details. This separation of roles implies a division which is not compatible with assimilation; we would suggest that the solution is that the IS Professional acts as the navigator (Champion & Stowell, 2005), guiding the client from problem definition to satisfaction.

The process of modelling external details enables the client to say what they want their information system to be, leaving the *navigator* to describe how the information system is constructed. The notion of external properties as a means of describing the system of interest has some resonance with the black box notion in engineering and used as a modelling tool in Systems (Stowell & Welch, 2012). By considering, with the client, the output requirements of their notional system and then the inputs necessary to achieve them, the IS they want can go through a process of *authentication* (Champion & Stowell, 2002).

For Langefors, the idea of External Property definition is refined by describing two attributes, Functional and Interface. Functional, he suggests, is concerned with what the system will do for the clients and users, and the way in which this is described is in everyday language. The Interface, on the other hand, has to do with how an object interacts with other objects and is of the technical kind and understood by software engineers. Importantly, there is a clear relationship between everyday description and specification, but the problem is how to do it whilst retaining client involvement. The papers in this section provide us with some interesting attempts to address these problems and much to stimulate our thoughts.

We now turn to the second section of the text, in which we have chapters relating to Security and privacy.

SECURITY AND PRIVACY

There are not many who would challenge the need to collect data relevant to matters of our security. Few would argue with the wish to have advanced warning of actions that might threaten our personal lives or the population. In modern times, we have found the need to increase security in order to protect us from those who wish to cause harm. To this end, there is an ongoing increase in security systems introduced to protect us from those who would 'steal' from us. Our increased use of technology to carry out transactions that hitherto would have been done through personal visits to shops and other businesses means that a new area of theft has opened up. Furnell et al. ("Prevention Actions for Enhancing Online Protection and Privacy") draw our attention to our dependence upon on-line services and how our lives are dominated by email and mobile communications. Magkos ("Cryptographic Approaches for Privacy Preservation in Location-Based Services") points out that just as the 'system' needs protecting against unauthorized access so too does the users' data need protecting from unauthorized access.

These technologies have opened up new areas of crime, not the least, but perhaps the most disturbing, is that of identity theft. Many complain of the way in which our privacy is infringed through the way in which our use of the Internet is monitored and used as a tool for marketing, or worse. Professor Tsudik ("Interview with Gene Tsudik") makes a valid point that many in our society have enthusiastically embraced a public forum for their personal feelings, such as blogs and social networks, yet complain of invasions of privacy. He goes on, "…increasing use of digitalization has led to some real concerns about privacy that weren't there a decade ago. This includes medical and employment records…."

The growing dependence upon on-line communications has not been matched by citizens' awareness of eSafety. Identity theft, financial losses, and failures to protect personal data have given rise to a growth in IT security. Although unwelcome, these systems of protection are seen as a necessary development by most private citizens, but have we got the balance right? The use of technology as an integral part of security is an area that the population has tacitly allowed to flourish (Katos, et al., 2007).

Alongside the increase in cyber crime, we are increasingly made aware of the rise of what is called cyber warfare. The Shorter Oxford Dictionary (2007) defines cyberwar as "…the use of computers to disrupt the activities of an enemy country, esp. the deliberate attacking of communication systems." The attacks include official websites and networks, disruption or disabling of essential services, stealing or altering classified data, and crippling financial systems. The security firm McAfee surveyed 200 IT executives working for utility companies in 14 countries who reported Internet-based attacks on critical systems such as gas, power, and water. The report suggests that "… eight out of ten … networks had been targeted by hackers during the past year" (BBC News, 2011). In a separate report, the BBC news service reported, "Government networks receive around 20,000 malicious e-mails each month, around 1,000 of which are deliberately targeting them." There are reports that the Defence firm Lockheed Martin, which makes weapon systems that are sold around the world, was the latest to be hit. The same report announced the UK's National Cyber Security Programme as part of the Strategic Defence and Security Review (BBC News, 2011).

Increasing surveillance also threatens individual privacy and the freedom of information (e.g. Dandeker, 1994; Whittaker, 1999; Lyon, 2004; Stowell, 2007; Kwecka & Buchanan, 2011). It is difficult to keep a watchful eye over those things we wish to protect without an invasion of privacy. If we think about data collection, often undertaken in a crude and anonymous manner, it may be used in any one of a number of ways without our knowledge. As one security expert declared, "If you can't find the needle, you have to take the haystack" (Harris, 2006). The increase in the use of technology in this way adds to individuals' feelings of powerlessness and loss of privacy. For example, the monitoring of data collection points, e.g. cctv and loyalty cards, are, to some degree, anonymous, but the individual has little, or no, idea how the data will be used. Dandeker (1994) made the point that the change in bureaucratic systems of administration shifted control of surveillance from personal to the indirect. As a consequence, surveillance became depersonalised, making it more difficult to identify who is behind the surveillance.

Most citizens are unaware what personal data is held on them or how accurate it is. The State is in the position of observing its citizens, but we are unable to tell when we are being observed. In some respects, the use of technology in this way can be viewed as a new form of Bentham's (1787) notion of the Panopticon or even in terms of a "superpanoptican" (Poster, 1989). In this case, technology replaces the physical prison but retains the key feature of observation of the subject who is unaware of being observed. Integrated networks mean that data can be collected about each individual in a variety of ways; some are explicit, some less so, with the potential of infringing on what most citizens consider to be their inalienable right to privacy; we need to protect the rights of the accused as well as the offended. Kwecka and Buchanan, in their chapter ("Minimising Collateral Damage: Privacy-Preserving Investigative Data Acquisition Platform"), consider the problems involved in protecting the privacy of all those involved in a cybercrime. They propose an approach that they suggest provides a balance between privacy of the alleged perpetrator and the victim.

SURVEILLANCE AND POWER: TECHNOLOGY THE MODERN BOGEYMAN?

To claim that technology is neutral is to ignore history. Technology can be used to monitor those who use it and how they use it. Access to the data that is available to us through the Web has both the potential to free and to enslave. ICT has the potential to enable citizens to gain a greater awareness of the society in which they live and improve life chances. It is now part of our culture, and it influences social behaviour and cannot be stopped. Kranzburg and Purcell (1967) reminded us that we have a responsibility here because although the process cannot be stopped "…nor the relationship ended … we must try to understand it and direct it to … goals worthy of mankind."

In their paper ("Quis Custodiet Ipsos Custodies?") Katos et al. (2007) question whether ICT's are being used by Governments to control the population rather than protect it? They point out that information provides a significant source of power for those that have access to it, and the task of governing depends increasingly upon having access and the means of controlling information about individuals. The data might be collected with their knowledge, e.g. applying for a credit card or opening a bank account, or without their knowledge, e.g. cctv images or the linking of apparently independent data such as loyalty cards and marketing data (Wilson, 2007). So we may ask, "Where does privacy of personal data end and interference begin?" Foucault saw power as always being in the hands of a powerful minority, "... because they presented themselves as agencies of regulation, arbitration, and demarcation as a way of introducing order..." (Gutting, 1996, p. 100). We think that we would all agree that information is a source of power, and the way that it might be used is a means of exercising power. Giddens (1981, pp. 172) suggests that Foucault's argument produced a "...too negative view of bourgeois freedom," but the developments in technology coupled with fears of extremist actions have provided a reason for increased surveillance of the general population. We need to ask ourselves if there is a stage where there are too many measures of security, and does the collection and holding of personal data in whatever form exceed that required to make us secure?

Katos et al (2007) remind us of an important point, raised by Dandeker (1994), who said that the state cannot survive without a minimum line of consent, but legitimacy rests on the recognition that its acts are legal; and as such, it can adopt any policies that reflect that. It follows that legislation hurriedly brought following anti-social acts can lead to a threat to individual freedom. Indiscriminate and general collection of data under the policy of improving security also provides a means of ensuring that those with power exercise control over the population. Mavridis ("Deploying Privacy Improved RBAC in Web Information Systems") points out that "Privacy awareness is increasing from the practice of modern organisations that utilize Web applications to collect, store, and process private information of users, usually gathered from monitoring their behaviours in order to provide more personalized and competitive services." If business enterprises do it, one must assume the same applies to government agencies. As Dandeker (1994, p. 27) suggests, the control and surveillance of antisocial behaviour in all its forms provides an opportunity for policing and general surveillance of the population, and we suggest, unchecked, 'Security' becomes a new form of social control.

A document entitled "A Report on the Surveillance Society" (COM, 2006; Wood, 2006) indicates that, at times, a form of social segregation takes place without the knowledge of the citizen. For example, data obtained for individuals travelling by air is collected and analysed for reasons of security. Although this is understandable and few challenge its use, the way that it is used is undemocratic and the result of the way that 'security' is put into practice. It is likely most citizens, especially those travelling by air, are happy to accept such monitoring and control, but how much is too much? Privacy is about balancing individual needs with societal interests and a matter of self-protection, but, as Lyon (2004, pp. 193) continues, privacy is a privilege. This argument raises important issues about human rights and when and how we should decide that the monitoring and control of data affecting us all is sufficient?

Dean (1998) pointed out, "Government concerns the shaping of human conduct and acts on the governed as a locus of action and freedom. It therefore entails the possibility that the governed are to some extent capable of acting and thinking otherwise." Katos et al. (2012) question if the checks made upon us nowadays are all necessary. They ask if they go beyond security. ICT provides a way of enclosing the population within what Dean refers to as "apparatuses of security" (Dean, 1998). The question we must ask is where does security finish and population control begin?

If we assume that the purpose of surveillance is to exercise control over a situation it monitors, e.g. crime reduction and terrorist activities, then we must take into consideration both the subject and the means of monitoring that subject. How much monitoring is too much? How do we know when we have gone beyond the use of technology for security into harnessing its use for social manipulation? Katos et al. (2012) put forward the argument for Ashby's Law of Requisite Variety (LRV). LRV says that in any situation "...if a certain quality of disturbance is prevented by a regulator from reaching some essential variables then that regulator must be capable of exerting at least that quantity of selection" (Ashby,

1978, pp. 229). In other words, the variety in the controller must have as much variety as that which it seeks to control. In order to bring about effective control over any situation, the control mechanism must be capable of addressing as many different outcomes as it is possible for a situation to develop. In practical terms, this means the more complex the system the more difficult it is to predict its behaviour and the more difficult to exercise control. As a reminder of the practical difficulty, Sir David Pepper, the recently retired Director of GCHQ (the UK's surveillance centre), said, " You would have to have so many people involved in the security services I am not sure what anybody else in the country would do" (Pepper, 2009).

SUMMARY

The majority of chapters in this text apply Systems ideas as a means of understanding a variety of problems within the general heading of IT. The many applications of the ideas provide examples of the way in which Systems Thinking is being used in Information System and Information Technology development. In this preface, we have attempted to add ideas to those contained within in the hope that it will encourage others to explore the use and appreciate the value of Systems Thinking and Practice.

We hope that you will enjoy reading this text.

Frank Stowell
University of Portsmouth, UK

REFERENCES

Ackoff, R. L. (1978). *The art of problem solving*. New York, NY: John Wiley and Sons.

Ashby, R. (1978). *Design for the brain*. London, UK: Chapman and Hall.

Avison, D. E., & Wood-Harper, A. T. (1986). Multiview: An exploration in information systems development. *The Australian Computer Journal, 18*(4).

Bentham, J. (1995). *Panoptican letters*. M. Bozovic, (Ed.). London, UK: Verson. Retrieved from http://cartome.org/panopticon2.htm.

Bisson, S. (2004, April 11). Taken to extremes. *The Guardian*.

Burrell, G., & Morgan, G. (2005). *Sociological paradigms and organisational analysis*. Aldershot, UK: Ashgate Publishing Company.

Champion, D. (2001). *Navigating the gap between purposeful action and a serving information system*. Unpublished PhD Thesis. Milton Keynes, UK: De Montfort University.

Champion, D. (2002) PEArL: Establishing the authenticity of action research filed studies. *Systemist: Special Conference Edition*, pp. 36-43.

Champion, D., & Stowell, F. A. (2003). Validating action research field studies: PEArL. *Systemic Practice and Action Research, 16*(1), 21–36. doi:10.1023/A:1021928511690

Champion, D., Stowell, F. A., & O'Callaghan, A. (2005). Client-led information systems creation (CLIC): Navigating the gap. *Information Systems Journal, 15,* 213–231. doi:10.1111/j.1365-2575.2005.00191.x

Checkland, P. B. (1999). *Systems thinking systems practice, 30 year retrospective.* Chichester, UK: Wiley.

Checkland, P. B., & Scholes, J. (1990). *Soft systems methodology in action.* Chichester, UK: Wiley.

COM. (2006). A strategy for a secure information society, dialogue. *Partnership and Empowerment, 251.*

Cooray. (2010). *End user driven development of information systems –Revisiting Vickers notion of appreciation.* Unpublished PhD Thesis. Portsmouth, UK: University of Portsmouth.

Cross, M. (2004). *Why government IT projects go wrong?* Retrieved October 20th 2005, from http://www.itweek.co.uk/computing/features/2072199/why-government-projects-wrong.

Cross, M. (2005, October). Public sector IT failures. *Prospect,* 48-53.

Cyberwar. (2007). Definition. In *Shorter Oxford English Dictionary.* Oxford, UK: Oxford University Press.

Dandeker, C. (1994). *Surveillance, power and modernity.* Oxford, UK: Polity Press.

Dean, M. (1998). *Governmentality, power and rule in modern society.* London, UK: Sage Publications.

Dunleavy, P., & Margettes, H. (2004). *Government IT performance and the power of the IT industry: A cross national analysis.* Paper presented to the Annual Meeting of American Political Science Association. Chicago, IL. Caulkin, S. (2004, May 2). Why IT just doesn't compute: Public sector projects even more likely to fail than private. *The Observer,* p. 9

Fortune, J., & Peters, G. (2005). *Information systems, achieve success by avoiding failure.* Chichester, UK: John Wiley & Sons.

Giddens, A. (1981). *A contemporary critique of historical materialism (Vol. 1).* London, UK: Macmillan.

Guo, M., Wu, Z., Stowell, F. A., & Cowell, J. (2000). AM/OO modeling. In *Proceedings of the 5th UKAIS Conference,* (pp. 312-321). Cardiff, UK: UKAIS.

Gutting, G. (1996). *Foucault.* Cambridge, UK: Cambridge University Press.

Jackson, M. A. (1975). *Principles of program design.* San Diego, CA: Academic Press.

Katos, V., Stowell, F. A., & Bednar, P. (2007). Quis custodiet ipsos custodies? *Systemist, 29*(2), 96–105.

Katos, V., Stowell, F. A., & Bednar, P. (2012). (forthcoming). Macroeconomics of privacy and security for identity management and surveillance. *Kybernetes.*

Kraft, T. A., & Steenkamp, A. L. (2010). A holistic approach for understanding project management. *International Journal of Information Technologies and Systems Approach, 3*(2), 17–31. doi:10.4018/jitsa.2010070102

Kranzburg & Purcell (Ed.). (1967). *Technology in western civilization.* Oxford, UK: Oxford University Press.

Kwecka, Z., & Buchanan, W. J. (2011). Minimising collateral damage: Privacy-preserving investigative data acquisition platform. *International Journal of Information Technologies and Systems Approach, 4*(2), 12–31. doi:10.4018/jitsa.2011070102

Langefors, B. (1995). *Essays on infology*. Lund, Sweden: Studentlitteratur.

Lynch, T., & Gregor, S. (2004). User participation in decision support systems development: Influencing system outcomes. *European Journal of Information Systems, 13*, 286–301. doi:10.1057/palgrave.ejis.3000512

Lyon, D. (2004). *The electronic eye*. Cambridge, UK: Blackwell.

Lyytinen, K., & Robey, D. (1999). Learning failure in information systems failure. *Information Systems Journal, 9*, 85–101. doi:10.1046/j.1365-2575.1999.00051.x

Morris & Travis. (2001, February 16). Straw calls halt to £80m IT system. *The Times*.

Myers, M. D. (1994). Dialectical hermeneutics: A theoretical framework for the implementation of information systems. *Information Systems Journal, 5*, 51–70. doi:10.1111/j.1365-2575.1995.tb00089.x

News, B. B. C. (2011a). *Report*. Retrieved from http://bbc.co.uk/news/technology-13599916.

News, B. B. C. (2011b). *Report*. Retrieved from http://bbc.co.uk/news/technology-13122339.

Parsons, T. (1949). *The structure of social action*. Glencoe, IL: Free Press.

Pepper, D. (2009, June 8). *Who's watching you?*. [TV Programme]. London, UK: BBC Two.

Poster, M. (1989). *Critical theory and post-structuralism: In search of context*. Ithica, NY: Cornell University Press.

SSADM. (1990). *SSADM version 4, reference manuals*. Oxford, UK: Blackwell.

Stowell, F. A. (2007). The knowledge age or the age of ignorance and the decline of freedom? *Systemic Practice and Action Research, 20*(5), 413–427. doi:10.1007/s11213-007-9076-2

Stowell, F. A. (2010). A question for research: Do we mean information systems or systems of information? In Paradice, D. (Ed.), *Emerging Systems Approaches in Information Technologies: Concepts, Theories, and Applications* (pp. 25–38). Hershey, PA: IGI Global.

Stowell, F. A. (2010). Information systems or systems of information? *International Journal of Information Technologies and Systems Approach, 1*, 25–36. doi:10.4018/jitsa.2008010102

Stowell, F. A. (2012). (in press). The appreciative inquiry method - A suitable candidate for action research? *Systems Research and Behavioral Science*.

Stowell, F. A., & Welch, C. (2012). *A managers guide to systems thinking*. Chichester, UK: Wiley.

Stowell, F. A., & West, D. (1991). The appreciative inquiry method: A systems based method of knowledge elicitation. In Jackson, M. C., Mansell, G. J., Flood, R. L., Blackham, R. B., & Probert, S. V. E. (Eds.), *Systems Thinking in Europe* (pp. 493–497). New York, NY: Plenum. doi:10.1007/978-1-4615-3748-9_70

Stowell, F. A., & West, D. (1994). *Client led design: A systemic approach to information systems definition*. London, UK: McGraw-Hill.

Vickers, G. (1981). The poverty of problem solving. *Journal of Applied Systems Analysis, 8*, 15–22.

Whittaker, R. (1999). *The end of privacy*. New York, NY: The New Press.

Winter, M. C., Brown, D. H., & Checkland, P. B. (1995). A role for soft systems methodology in information systems development. *European Journal of Information Systems, 4*, 130–142. doi:10.1057/ejis.1995.17

Wright, O. (2011). NHS pulls the plug on its £11bn IT system. *The Independent*. Retrieved from http://www.independent.co.uk/life-style/health-and-families/health-news/nhs-pulls-the-plug-on-its-11bn-it-system-2330906.html.

Section 1
Information System Provision

Chapter 1
Interview
The Systems View from Barry G. Silverman: A Systems Scientist

Manuel Mora
Autonomous University of Aguascalientes, Mexico

Miroljub Kljajić
University of Maribor, Slovenia

ABSTRACT

In this short article, we present an e-interview to a well-recognized system scientist Barry G. Silverman, who is Professor of Systems Science and Engineering at the University of Pennsylvania, and Director of the Ackoff Collaboratory for Advancement of the Systems Approach (ACASA) in the same university. In this e-interview, Professor Silverman, teach us on the origins, and still applicability and need of the Systems Approach, but now focused on the present complex social systems. A Systems Approach must and can provide a white-box research approach and advance on the limitations of the reductionist black-box research approaches. Professor Silverman, also alert us on the scarcity of PhD academic programs covering these systems approaches and makes a call for continuing the "difficult missionary effort" of teaching and doing research on the Systems Approach.

INTRODUCTION

Barry G. Silverman is Professor of Systems Science and Engineering at the University of Pennsylvania where he is also Director of the Ackoff Collaboratory for Advancement of the Systems Approach (ACASA). He holds the BSE ('75), MSE ('77) and PhD (also '77) all from the University of Pennsylvania. The focus of his research has largely been on aesthetic and cognitive engineering of game-theoretic software agents that can help humans improve their learning, performance, and systems thinking in task-environments. Barry is the author of over 130 articles, 12 books/proceedings, 100 technical reports, 7 copyrighted software systems, a boardgame, several research and teaching excellence awards, and is a Fellow of IEEE, AAAS, and the Washington Acad. of Science.

DOI: 10.4018/978-1-4666-1562-5.ch001

This interview offers systems researchers and practitioners a conceptual enrichment on the foundations, origin and modern relevance of the Systems Approach, from a Social System Science side. We thank Professor Silverman his willingness for this interview, which continues as follows:

Q1. IJITSA

To start, we would like to know your conceptualizations for the terms Systems Approach, Systems Thinking or Systems Paradigm ? Are the same but are used differently in the literature?

Professor Silverman

Systems thinking is quite old – probably dating back before the Egyptian pyramids. The ancient Chinese, Egyptians, Greeks, and Romans all had to be systems thinkers. Their governments, projects, and armies, among other things, were products of big picture thinkers. The Athenians and Romans, in particular, invented systems of governance (i.e. Republics) that fed off of increasing individual freedoms. The invention of permitting individuals to strive for their own goals, to be purposeful, led to citizens wanting to protect the collective. A remarkable feedback cycle. The Greeks applied it to their own citizens, while the Romans used it to enfranchise an ever-widening circle.

Formalisms like the Systems Paradigm, theory, and approach are much newer, and most versions are traceable to the work of a number of notable post-industrial revolution era scientists in the 1900s. I see these concepts a bit like worldview, design, and methodology, respectively. Specifically, I tend to see the Systems Paradigm as all-important and in contrast to the Scientific Method. Synthetic vs. reductive. Within the systems paradigm, however, there are a number of methods or approaches – design inquiry approaches, soft systems methodology, mess formulation, systems engineering, and so on. There is no one agreed

upon standard about how to conduct investigations and problem solving within the Paradigm.

Q2. IJITSA

Based in his extensive research career and as a key system thinker, could explain us why is still useful the Systems Approach as a scientific methodology and paradigm in the modern world (e.g. for the everyday more complex research situations than ever in the past based on Bar-Yam's ideas on complexity) ?

Professor Silverman

Social systems are so complex and rapidly changing, that many people are giving up on trying to understand them, on inquiry into how and why they function as they do. The purposefulness of each of a social system's parts is often thought to be impenetrable. We thus see the warnings of the end of science and the end of theory. In the systems age where everything is interconnected and rapidly and continually changing in complex, unexpected ways, it is harder and harder to justify or take the time for reductive scientific method. Social science is inherently fragmented into sub-disciplines, positivism is passé, and reductive inquiry seems unable to answer the large social system questions of our era. Instead, with the rise of big computing genomics and the "Googlification" of the world, there seems to be little need to reflect and understand theories, causality, or mechanism. Big pictures and trends can simply be derived. Indeed, without understanding what is in these results we are able to compare them and model their trends – just as is done with DNA. This has many benefits, but it is also another temptation to give up on understanding. The greatest consumers of black box modeling may be those producing the volatility forecasts and financial portfolio performance estimates that guided traders, banks, and investors. Once instruments are bundled for investors (e.g., mortgages, credit card loans, etc) it seems that few investors bother to check the situations and intentions of the actors actually involved (e.g, homeowners, student loans, etc.). Instead the frenzied attention seems to focus on the volatility and statistical properties of the price when the market reacts to and trades those securities. Since they are absent any theory of the true mechanisms or underlying dynamics about those who must pay off the debt, such models are incapable of predicting watershed events not covered in the lagged variables they regress over. Also, even when they work, they can only predict but not explain social phenomena. Such black box modeling seems to foretell the end of social science. After all, who needs explanatory theories and mechanism investigations when we can predict and profit from the likely outcomes and trends in social systems? (Well at least most of the time.)

But failure to understand mechanism, at best, dooms one to having to be lucky to avoid mistakes. Failing to explore causality enslaves one to unexpected effects for any action undertaken. The current financial imbroglio and entering the Iraqi situation blindly are but two examples. An inability to penetrate beyond the surface may encourage one to do nothing since without greater insight, more often than not, further interventions will worsen the situation. It thus seems to me that we need the systems paradigm now more than ever before. Synthetic thinking and the systems approaches and design analyses are well suited to counter these trends.

Q3. IJITSA

Based in –also- his long career as business consultant for business and governmental organizations could explain us the benefits from having used the Systems Approach as a management and engineering conceptual tool in real business and governmental settings ?

Professor Silverman

The approach I am taking to counter this affront to reflection is what I call "systems social science". This is a variation of design inquiry that re-opens the dialog for inquiring into the design of social systems and for investigating it within a computational sphere. Fight fire with fire. The modern reflective approach, what I shall call **Systems Social Science (SSS)** can best be supported by computer simulation investigations that attempt to implement many theories into an open process (white box) where scientists, subject matter experts, and analysts can inspect designs, mechanisms, cause and effect, and operation-outcome explanations. If the social genomics are producing large, rapidly changing trend pictures, then systems social scientists need to delve into those big pictures with large computer arrays and computational science that easily support studies of the dynamics cutting across many reductive sub-disciplines in the social sciences. Thus they can potentially come to grips with synthesizing mechanism answers underlying big pictures and with exploring the current and future designs of a given social system.

In this view, computational social science is a systems or design topic. It's not just a black box statistical approach, but instead, a computer-based investigation of the synthesis of theories, expert knowledge, social genomic pictures and trends, and all other evidence and models. Of vital importance to this approach is (1) adopting best-of-breed theories from the social sciences (those that are descriptively valid); (2) keeping an openness to the wide array of systems methodologies and tools, whatever works best for implementing each theory (eg, adaptive agents, operations research, knowledge management systems, etc.); and (3) a design inquiry approach aimed at learning about a given social system. The point of such a synthesis is to better understand what unexpected effects emerge as a result of policy interventions in network-centric worlds where the social system is complex and poorly understood. This cannot be reliably done in the absence of social science, and not solely with social genomes and black box models. The point is that systems design is the methodological glue that can and must shift the fundamental science in this field.

This is a claim that how we approach the fundamental, underlying social sciences requires a paradigm shift, similar to the metamorphosis happening over the past half-decade to systems biology. However, it is not a claim that systems models that work in biological (or even mechanical) systems will work in social systems. In general, re-applying such models is a badly conceived idea and they won't work for long since social systems are fundamentally different from mechanical or even biological systems. They deserve their own form of causality and mechanism modeling.

Q4. IJITSA

It was about 60 years from the beginnings of Bertalanffy's General System Theory and world view systems methodologies derived from it (from 1951 reference). What is your opinion, from today's perspectives, on the Theory of Systems' curriculum for management and business administration, and engineering schools for graduate and undergraduate levels? Are sufficient course taught by level and sufficient research conducted in PhD level at present? Do elements of System Theory, Cybernetics, and System Dynamic should be taught in primary and secondary education levels in order to understanding complex phenomena?

Professor Silverman

The field of Systems Science and Engineering (SSE) flourished in the first few decades following GST, particularly in the 60s with the boosting of Systems Analysis in the US military, and on into the 1970s. This was true in engineering and business schools. Since then, there has been re-trenchment, general loss of status, and a diaspora for many of us in the SSE disciplines. Very few Systems Engineering departments remain in the USA, and often those are cobbled together with other departments, as is my current Electrical and Systems Engineering (ESE) home department. This is unfortunate and often a sign that the home institution does not place a priority on synthesis, and it thinks the hypothetic-reductive paradigm seems more stable, accreditable, and mature, in a scientific sense. It is often also a sign of insecurity, an inability to move to the future. In the socio-technical systems arena, I often see engineering schools shying away from synthesis and favoring traditional disciplines that can pass accreditation by old-school evaluators. In B-schools a recent trend that may counter this effect is that toward design and team collaboration as opposed to emphasis on individual competition.

Interestingly, I find the field of anthropology to be the boldest and most systemic. A close second might be the field of history. After all, anthropologist and historians are faced with social systems they must explain. Broad-ranging systems dynamics they must profile and account for. Of course, those fields are famously lacking the computational and mathematical bases that the SSE field so often seeks to add. That is a paradox of sorts – the more mathematical or computational a field, the less it focuses on systems science. This does not need to be so. Extending the SSE curriculum into primary and secondary educational venues is a major but very significant challenge for those of us in the SSE fields. This implies difficult missionary effort of the highest priority

Q5. IJITSA

We know that a specific theme of research and application for you has been DSS, Expert Systems, and a present KMS. On such themes, could you express your opinion on the future development of DSS, ES, KM Engineering and SE as a methods and tools for decision support in complex systems.

Professor Silverman

Yes of course. For those of us in the computational SSE disciplines, this is a renaissance era where there is cornucopia of approaches one can place in one's toolbox. There are top-down approaches such as, among others, systems dynamics (sets of difference equations) if one knows the equations of the system. There are also many bottom up approaches, collectively called agent based modeling and simulation, if one only knows the micro-decision making and wants to study what will emerge. The bottom up approaches are what I tend to pioneer, though I use a mix of all approaches in my toolbox, as a good tool-smith should. Within the bottom up approaches there are numerous techniques and camps. Let me simplify these to two camps, for the sake of brevity in this interview:

1. **'Rational' Actors**: Presumed normative as in early economic theory and intro game theory classes - perfectly informed, purely logical, and motivated by self-interest to maximize their material payoffs. All actors have identical payoff functions. Closed form analytical solution is generally possible. These are also referred to as rationally-*consistent* actors, as in discussion of the neoclassical, post-World War II economics approach to rationality which cleansed itself of any reference to psychic concepts. These actors are emotionless geniuses.

2. **Descriptive agents**: Following the new field of human behavior modeling, these agents are characterized by descriptive rather than normative models. I like to profile real world individuals with best-of-breed social science instruments - specifically, a synthesis of personality profile instruments, bounded rationality (coping styles depending on stress level), prospect theory, hyperbolic discounting and other forms of perceptual myopia, biases (mirroring, confirmation,

etc.), emotional construals, and grievances, among other models. Aside from material payoffs, these agents attend to moralistic payoffs; and even when they do consider material payoffs, they may commit errors and use biased heuristics. The idea of descriptive agents is to realistically model these *non-consistent* behaviors.

It strikes me that descriptive behavior agents are the future, despite many proponents of rational actor mathematics. I think that modeling of social systems and societal dynamics is only possible by dragging onto the modeling stage, all of the exoteric information and knowledge about the stakehoders in a given socio-technical system. Only then can you accurately model and simulate purposefulness, intent, and situations with reasonable accuracy and validity. Only then can policy analyses be successful, can decision support and design inquiry take effective form. Barring this, all you have is mathematics for mathematics sake.

Q6. IJITSA

As a close collaborator of the eminent scientist Professor Russell L. Ackoff (passed away in 2009 year) could you let us know on his main Systems ideas that have impacted your research, and any additional insights on the state of the art of Theory and Practice of Systems Science in a global world?

Professor Silverman

I miss Russ' presence. I work in the exact building he started in and live in the county he lived in. So I walk around spaces all the time where I interacted with him directly, It is something I have not yet got past – that I cannot talk to him anymore.

He was not a computationalist, as I am sure you know, and I am a devotee. But one of his last books was surprisingly algorithmic and computationally oriented – On Purposeful Systems (2006) -- even though he never thought of it that way. In fact he was often apologetic about how terse and algorithmic it was.

I recently completed a paper on "Systems Social Science (S3)"for *Intelligent Decision Technology journal*. This will appear in 2010. This paper traces the origins of the pragmatist school of philosophy starting with EA Singer, Jr., and continuing through the life's work of Churchman and Ackoff. As the paper explains, I view my own research on social systems as extending what all three of them set out to do. Dr. Singer grew ill and never completed his attempts to "sweep in" many social sciences. Dr. Churchman set out a vision for the field of Design Inquiry, but never completed a computational implementation. And Dr. Ackoff, set out to alter systems thinking in management with great success in the business sector, among others. I hope that my S3 research is able to make a small addition to each of their towering contributions.

IJITSA

Thanks very much for sharing your knowledge and wisdom with us and the IJITSA readers (system researchers, academicians, PhD students and practitioners)

Professor Silverman

Well, I appreciate your interest. And I appreciate your efforts to position a journal in this space of IT and the systems approach(es). That is not easy to do and avoid the pressure to focus on sub-specialties. But much needed. So, hats off to you and the editors.

Hence, main lessons extracted from this interview can be summarized as follows: (i) a systems approach have been used (intuitively at first and with initial systems engineering procedures) from old civilizations for city planning and building designs (pyramids, bridges, castles, etc) but explicitly as formalisms until early the 1900 century; (ii) in particular, the systems paradigm

(with different specific methods) is relevant for designing and researching the modern complex social systems through a white-box approach in contrast with the most accepted reductionist black-box approaches; (iii) a Systems Social Science (S3) approach based on white-box simulations is viable due to the new computational capabilities at present, and the richness of the available intelligent system frameworks (for instance, the descriptive agents simulation approach); and (iv) there is a scarcity of systems paradigm formal academic programs in USA (and by consequence in the rest of other developed countries). Furthermore, Professor Silverman recognizes that his research is based on the extensive works from E. Singer, W. Churchman, and R. Ackoff, with the challenge of making explicit (through the available computer tools) the theorized underlying mechanisms (like generative subsystems) present in every system.

In this IJITSA issue, we are pleased to inquiry Professor Silverman—an Honorary Editorial Board member of IJITSA—on his system view which has been developed through a vast scientific, academic and consulting career from endings in the 1970s. We are also sure that his answers will help us to enrich our knowledge on the Systems Approach. Thanks to Professor Silverman.

REFERENCES

Ackoff, R. L., & Emery, F. E. (2006). *On purposeful systems*. New Brunswick: Aldine Transaction.

Churchman, C. W. (1972). *The design of inquiring systems: Basic concepts of systems and organizations*. New York: Basic Books.

Silverman, B. (1995). Knowledge-based Systems and the Decision Sciences. *Interfaces*, *25*(6), 67–82. doi:10.1287/inte.25.6.67

Silverman, B. (in press). Systems Social Science. *Intelligent Decision Technologies*.

Silverman, B., Bharathy, G., Nye, B., & Eidelson, R. (2007). Modeling factions for 'effects based operations': part I – leaders and followers. *J. Computational & Mathematical Organization Theory*, *13*(4), 379–406. doi:10.1007/s10588-007-9017-8

Silverman, B., Bharathy, G., Nye, B., & Smith, T. (2008). Modeling factions for 'effects based operations': part II – behavioral game theory. *J. Computational & Mathematical Organization Theory*, *14*(2), 120–155. doi:10.1007/s10588-008-9023-5

Silverman, B., Johns, M., Cornwell, J., & O'Brien, K. (2006a). Human behavior models for agents in simulators and games: part I – enabling science with PMFserv. *Presence (Cambridge, Mass.)*, *15*(2), 139–162. doi:10.1162/pres.2006.15.2.139

Silverman, B., O'Brien, K., & Cornwell, J. (2006b). Human behavior models for agents in simulators and games: part II – gamebot engineering with PMFserv. *Presence (Cambridge, Mass.)*, *15*(2), 163–185. doi:10.1162/pres.2006.15.2.163

Singer, E. A. (1959). *Experience and Reflection*. Philadelphia: University of Pennsylvania Press.

This work was previously published in the International Journal of Information Technologies and Systems Approach, Volume 3, Issue 1, edited by Frank Stowell and Manuel Mora, pp. 57-63, copyright 2010 by IGI Publishing (an imprint of IGI Global).

Chapter 2
Towards Knowledge Evolution in Software Engineering:
An Epistemological Approach

Yves Wautelet
Université Catholique de Louvain, Belgium

Christophe Schinckus
Facultés Universitaires St-Louis, Belgium

Manuel Kolp
Université Catholique de Louvain, Belgium

ABSTRACT

This article presents an epistemological reading of knowledge evolution in software engineering (SE) both within a software project and into SE theoretical frameworks principally modeling languages and software development life cycles (SDLC). The article envisages SE as an artificial science and notably points to the use of iterative development as a more adequate framework for the enterprise applications. Iterative development has become popular in SE since it allows a more efficient knowledge acquisition process especially in user intensive applications by continuous organizational modeling and requirements acquisition, early implementation and testing, modularity,... SE is by nature a human activity: analysts, designers, developers and other project managers confront their visions of the software system they are building with users' requirements. The study of software projects' actors and stakeholders using Simon's bounded rationality points to the use of an iterative development life cycle. The later, indeed, allows to better apprehend their rationality. Popper's knowledge growth principle could at first seem suited for the analysis of the knowledge evolution in the SE field. However, this epistemology is better adapted to purely hard sciences as physics than to SE which also takes roots in human activities and by the way in social sciences. Consequently, we will nuance the vision using Lakatosian epistemology notably using his falsification principle criticism on SE as an evolving science. Finally the authors will point to adaptive rationality for a lecture of SE theorists and researchers' rationality.

DOI: 10.4018/978-1-4666-1562-5.ch002

INTRODUCTION

Software engineering (SE) is by nature a human discipline. In huge software projects hundreds of analysts, designers, developers, project managers, potential users, etc. are involved in the process of creating a software application aimed to fulfill services easing the everyday work and life of thousands of individuals. To deal with such a process the traditional waterfall model in which requirements are collected once for all at the beginning of the project life cycle is nowadays too limited. Researchers have led to the definition of advanced modeling languages as well as to more elaborated life cycles using the concept of iterative development. Their success come from the fact that requirements elicitation is no more a standalone task at the beginning of the project but rather a continuous process using feedback loops allowing to better apprehend needs on the basis of prototypes.

In this article we propose a modern epistemological reading of SE as an evolving science as well as software project knowledge evolution. As a first basis, project actors' reasoning context is studied. Indeed, actors involved in a software project have a limited vision inherent to their bounded rationality. At first sight Popperian theories could be used to describe the evolution of software engineering theoretical frameworks. Due to the nature of SE belonging also to social sciences we will show that this vision is abusive. The Lakatosian falsification principle will be used to demonstrate the complexity of getting a crucial experiment in SE. Adaptive rationality will be used to characterize SE theorists and researchers' expertise field vision.

This article is organized as follows. Section 2 presents the context of the research, the followed approach and justifies the utilization of the epistemologies used in the article and their combination. It also points to the article contributions. Section 3 proposes an epistemological reading of software processes and on the evolution of knowledge in SE as a discipline as well as within a particular project. To this ends we used Herbert Simon's bounded rationality, the Popperian knowledge growth theory nuanced by the Lakatosian falsification principle and finally adaptive rationality. The implications are then overviewed in section 4 while conclusions are summarized in Section 5.

PROBLEM STATEMENT

This section presents the research context i.e. software engineering and more particularly software development life cycles; the research approach, i.e. the framework developed for applying different epistemologies at different level of a defined software development system. It then turns to the epistemological trends where the application of the particular epistemologies are justified and finally point to the main contributions of the article.

Research Context

Software Engineering (SE) is an engineering discipline concerned with all the aspects of software production. Following Arlow and Neustadt (2002), a SE methodology[1] is made of a *modeling language* and a *software development process*.

The modeling language is the syntax made of concepts associated with visual icons used to build models (see for example the *Unified Modeling Language* (OMG, 2007; Rumbaugh et al. 1999; Booch et al. 1999)). The modelling language can be:

- Graphical when it uses diagrams with a couple of formalized symbols – representing concepts – linked together through relationships with eventually other graphical artefacts representing constraints;
- Textual when it uses standardized notations with parameters for computer interpretation.

The software development process defines the WHO, WHAT, WHEN and HOW dimensions of software development. A software development process can generally be split up into four disciplines (often called phases):

- The analysis discipline focuses on defining the problem (*what the problem is*) independently of any solution that is why it is said to be problem-oriented. Its two main purposes are:
  - To model stakeholders' (end-users, managers, engineers, etc.) requirements by providing models allowing the software development teams and stakeholders to agree on what the system should do;
  - To build a domain model i.e. a representation of all the relevant concepts or real-world entities in a particular domain of interest.
- The design discipline is concerned with the elaboration of a solution to the problem described during analysis. It is a system-oriented discipline focusing on *how to solve the problem*;
- The implementation phase is concerned with the component building from scratch or by composition. On the basis of the models developed during the previous disciplines, the team should build exactly what has been requested even if there remains place for innovation and flexibility;
- The testing phase is concerned with the evaluation of software correctness, completeness, security and quality. Many approaches to software testing exist but effective testing of complex products is essentially a process of investigation rather than creating and following well defined procedure.

Following Royce (1998), a System Development Life Cycle (SDLC) is "*a conceptual model used in project management to describe the stages involved in a system development project from an initial feasibility study through maintenance of the completed application*". Several SDLC have been proposed over the years. Depending on the project, some SDLC appear to be more adequate than others, best known are:

- The waterfall model (Royce, 1970) describes a development process based on a series of phases (often called disciplines) that are fulfilled one after another in a linear/sequential way. This type of SDLC can only be successful when a series of assumptions (see (Boehm, 2000)) are met at the same time. Otherwise, risks are introduced in the process;
- In the *incremental model* the phases of the waterfall model are repeated using an iterative prototyping philosophy. The incremental process model is iterative by nature; it focuses on the delivery of an operational product with each increment. Early increments do provide capability that serves the user and also provide a basis for user evaluation;
- The spiral model is defined in (Boehm, 2000) as "*a risk-driven process model generator used to guide multi-stakeholder concurrent engineering of software intensive systems. It has two main distinguishing features. One is a iterative cyclic approach for incrementally growing a system's degree of definition and implementation while decreasing its degree of risk. The other is a set of anchor point milestones for ensuring stakeholder commitment to feasible and mutually satisfactory system solutions*". Using an spiral SDLC implies that

risk is considered during the early stages of the project not at the late ones as in a process fully driven by sequential activities (see (Boehm, 2000)).

Modern software development processes as the Rational Unified Process (IBM, 2003), eXtreme Programming (Beck, 2005) and other Agile Modeling techniques (Ambler 2002) apply the principles overviewed into the incremental and spiral models in every day software applications development. In this perspective, the reader should keep in mind the principles of SDLCs in software development rather than the details of the nowadays used methodologies. In the rest of this article, when we will reference iterative development we point to software development in an iterative manner with no unique analysis, design, implementation and test stage but rather an iterative repetition of these stages allowing to enrich the produced artifacts on the basis of the feedback obtained by users.

Research Approach

This article defines a system to study knowledge evolution when engineering software from an epistemological point of view. The focus is thus mainly on knowledge acquisition techniques: modelling languages and software development life cycles. To be consistent with this goal, we distinguish two levels of knowledge evaluation:

- The macro-level is concerned with the study of the knowledge about the theoretical frameworks used to guide software development. Indeed, nowadays software developments can be very complex, involve tens of individuals and be of critical importance, facing such a context, one need advanced and mature modelling languages and development life cycles;

- The micro-level is concerned with the evolution of knowledge in the software project itself i.e. the knowledge on user requirements, stakeholders expectations, business processes, the organisational setting in which the system will be deployed etc.
- A feedback loop i.e. each software project is another experience for testing the applied theoretical frameworks; the experience provides guidance for their evolution.

Figure 1 proposes a system view of the two levels we propose here to study knowledge evolution in SE.

In the system defined above, micro-level characteristics (the knowledge of project actors) have a strong influence on the macro-level theoretical framework (the way knowledge is collected and formalized) adoption and evolution. Consequently, section 3.1 will adopt a micro level approach and enlighten useful conclusions for the comprehension of the macro-level. The macro-level approach of section 3.2 directly envisages the evolution in the software project knowledge acquisition frameworks (modelling languages and development life cycles).

Epistemological Trends

The article envisages the instantiation of a series of epistemological frameworks to the micro or/ and macro levels exposed above. These frameworks are:

- Herbert Simon's bounded rationality principle: a theory addressing human problems;
- The poperian knowledge growth model: a theory addressing natural problems subject to refutation in case of empirical failure;
- Lakatosian falsification and adaptive rationality principles: theories developed for quasi empirical sciences envisaging adaptability in case of empirical failure.

Figure 1. A system for studying knowledge evolution in software engineering

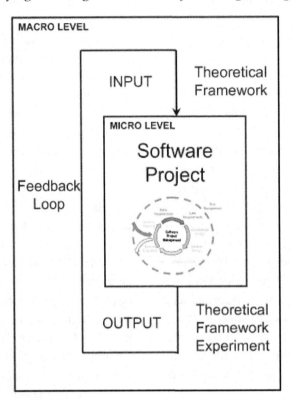

(Wautelet, 2008) has developed a framework for evaluating software development life cycles of defined software engineering methodologies (applications can be found in the thesis). This framework includes both engineering and project management concepts. We choose here to adapt this framework not for evaluating a development methodology but rather an epistemology's applicability into this particular area. Indeed, our goal is to give a genuine vision of software engineering using a couple of epistemological trends. To evaluate the applicability of those epistemologies onto knowledge in SE, the criteria enlighten into that framework are particularly well indicated since its goal is to evaluate a development methodology in terms of SDLC and modelling capabilities (for a full justification of those criteria see (Wautelet, 2008)). We will thus use the criteria not for the evaluation of a particular development methodol-

ogy but to evaluate how a particular epistemology envisages the criteria. However the framework is a little too detailed for what we want to evaluate and we will retain the following criteria:

- **Engineering concepts:** How does the epistemology envisage a development life cycle? This will be evaluated in terms of:
  - **Process cutting**: Could the epistemology envisage a life cycle divided into phases, views, disciplines?
  - **Covered stages**: Could the epistemology envisage a life cycle not covering all of the known software development stages (analysis, design, implementation, test, etc.)?
  - **Stages scope**: Could the epistemology envisage a life cycle where stages are poorly covered?

- **Modeling language:** Does the epistemology envisage the use of a modelling language? This will be evaluated in terms of:
  - **Models representation:** Could the epistemology envisage a modeling language only representing partially of the problem?
  - **Models coverage:** Could the developed models cover only a part of process disciplines?
- **Project management concepts:** How does the epistemology envisage a project management perspective to drive software development? This criterion can be evaluated in terms of:
  - **Process description**: Could the epistemology envisage a non exact description?
  - **Project management**: Could the epistemology envisage human practices to conduct a software project?
  - **Software metrics:** What is, following the particular epistemology, the status of metrics giving a quantitative aspect of the developed software application?

Table 1 summarizes the instantiation of the criteria to the epistemologies, main lessons that can be taken when evaluating epistemologies at the light of the exposed framework are:

- Simon's bounded rationality principle addresses human empirical problems; framework's criteria at the light of the theory is not from particular interest since the epistemology studies human behaviour rather than scientific theories. That is why the framework is adopted at micro level – where human actors are dealing to develop a software solution – rather than at macro level – where theoretical frameworks are developed.

- Popperian knowledge growth model addresses natural problems and theories should be refuted in case of empirical failure. When applying these software engineering criteria, the epistemology appears to be "radical" for the development process characteristics i.e. the proposed theoretical framework should be exact, capture all of the problem complexity at once, cover the whole of the known modelling and SDLC aspects and propose exact realization workflows.

- Lakatosian falsification and adaptive rationality principles address quasi-empirical problems and theories are adaptable when facing empirical failure. The criteria's application show that Lakatos is less "radical" that Popper since the development methodology is seen as a partial guidance rather than as an exact solution.

We choose to apply Simon's rationality principle at micro level because the theoretical framework is particularly well adapted for characterizing the human behaviour when building a software solution. The popperian epistemology is the basic reference to study science evolution especially in hard sciences, its adoption on SE was thus a first step for such a study. As will be shown in next section, its radicalism was not completely in line with the studied field that is what led us to the application of a less radical epistemology, the Lakatosian one.

We decide to apply different epistemologies, Simons' bounded rationality on the one side, Popperian knowledge growth model and Lakatosian falsification principle and adaptative rationality on the other because (i) micro and macro levels address different kind of problems having their own characteristics so that they can hardly be studied on the basis of the same epistemology (ii) Popper and Lakatos have their own – partially divergent – vision of science evolution, the study

Table 1. Used epistemologies through SE methodologies evaluation framework

	Simon's bounded rationality principle	Popperian knowledge growth model	Lakatos falsification and adaptive rationality principles
Nature of the problem	Human	Natural	Quasi-empirical
Nature of the theory	N/A	Not subject to empirical failure	Adaptable in case of empirical failure
Engineering concepts			
Process divided into disciplines	Acceptable	Should include all dimensions	Conceivable
Covered stages	Can be partial	Should be complete	Can be partial
Stages scope	Can be partial	Should be complete	Can be partial
Modeling Language			
Models representation	Can be ad hoc	Should be complete	Can be partial
Models coverage	Can be partial	Should be complete	Can be partial
Project management concepts			
Process description	Basic	An exact workflow	A convenient workflow
Project management	Can be "ad hoc"	Should be exact	Formalized
Software metrics	Subject to interpretation	Should be exact	Acceptable guidance

of software engineering frameworks evolution at the light of the ideas of the two philosophers.

In a word, engineering software is a complex activity requiring a pluralist approach for an accurate evaluation. In the same line, other theories will be refereed to (for example behavioural economics) into the analysis but are considered as secondary in the context of the article so that they are not included in the table above. Finally, we preferred avoiding all new (post-modern) epistemologies (as (Lyotard 1979; Latour, 1988, Rorty, 1990)) because these are embedded in the linguistic dimension of knowledge. We decide to consider SE as quasi empirical science rather than a simple "language game".

Contributions

Basili (1992) defines Software Engineering (SE) as "*the disciplined development and evolution of software systems based upon a set of principles,*

technologies and processes". These theoretical frameworks are expected to solve practical problems by proposing software solutions. SE is a practice-oriented field (where empiricism often plays an important role) and constantly evolving; however, one must dispose of a framework to build common (and preferably best) practices for software quality improvement. Kaisler (2005) points out that "*We develop more experience, we not only continue to learn new practices, but we refine and hone the practices that we have already learned*". SE is the genuine discipline that emerged from this interconnection between practices and software solutions. Today's software development has become a very complex task and no one has the required skills or time to resolve a sophisticated problem on his or her own. Software development phases need the input from lots of people having to use concepts and ideas for which they share a common understanding. This can be referred as SE's key role: providing some common theoretical entities to allow specialists to develop software solutions.

Few articles in specialized literature point to an in depth questioning of SE knowledge evolution. As Kaisler (2005) emphasizes, the literature is mainly technical or practical and focused on the software design processes. Research methodologies, however, need to be conscientiously built to favour the development and improvement of software solutions. To this end, an epistemological analysis is of primary importance as pointed out by (Basili, 1992), "*The goal is to develop the conceptual scientific foundations of software engineering upon which future researchers can build*".

The idea is to demonstrate that the roots of software development – especially those implying users intensively – can be found in social sciences and not only in exact ones with a profound consequence on the evolution towards an adequate knowledge acquisition process in software engineering. The proof of concept is based on the study of the project involved actors' knowledge evolution (micro level) towards a whole software project. Rationality evolves progressively to them into enterprise software projects, so that an iterative development life cycle – by nature including this postulate – is better adapted for this type of developments. On the same way, SE theoretical frameworks (macro-level) evolutions especially in the field of modelling languages and development life cycles also evolve progressively by adapting existing ones rather than by defining completely new approaches; micro and macro levels are envisaged in the form of a system.

This study is a contribution to the philosophy of computer science and like most philosophical treatises it neither addresses itself to any practical problems, nor does it solve them. It however provides a new (nuanced) vision of a well known discipline: SE as a quasi-empirical discipline rather than a hard science. This is an interesting reference for researchers and other SE practitioners (see section 4, implications).

A STUDY OF KNOWLEDGE EVOLUTION IN SE

This section details the practical application of different epistemologies on the micro and macro levels defined earlier.

Micro-Level Approach: A Study of Project Actors' Rationality

This section evaluates knowledge evolution into software projects (micro level) at the light of Simon's bounded rationality principle, conclusions are then brought to the development life cycles (macro level).

Bounded and Perfect Rationality or the Quest for a Satisfactory Solution

Herbert Simon (Nobel Prize in economics, 1978) proposes the concept of *bounded rationality* (Simon, 1983) to characterize the human reasoning and behavior in uncertain situations. This concept illustrates the idea that human beings have limited abilities to analyze all the parameters and implications of the solutions they could deploy to a given problem they face. According to Simon, the rationality of human beings is related to the present and to the psychological biases. The rationality suggested by Simon is much broader than the perfect rationality which would allow one to be able to evaluate all the present and future parameters of a particular solution. This idea of perfect rationality is often used in economics and whereas the concept of bounded is more often used in management sciences, Simon has won a Nobel Prize for his work.

The concept of perfect rationality is extremely useful to solve some theoretical problems (Arthur, 1994). Perfect rationality presupposes that individuals have much higher computational abilities than they have in the real world. Indeed, beyond a defined level of complexity, the logical abilities of people are not sufficient to evaluate the situation. Moreover, in complex situations implying interactions between people, an individual, who would have perfect rationality, would have to guess the behavior of other people (this leads by bounded rationality). So human behavior is always determined by bounded rationality and this rationality does not depend only on the ability to evaluate a situation but also on the interactions with other (non-perfectly rational) people. Let us remind that human relations are partly driven by subjective beliefs which complicate the rational evaluation of a particular situation. We could say that the complex interactive situations can be seen as undefined problems. To face such problems, Arthur (1994), in accordance with the behavioral economics (and with the bounded rationality principle), proposes to think the human mind as a "problems simplification machine". This simplification is possible thanks to internal patterns developed by people. Each actor has a collection of internal beliefs which materialize in a particular evolving behavior. Indeed, actors improve their behaviors and learn which of their internal belief is adapted to face a complicated and undefined situation. We can then observe a kind of iterative improvement of human behavior. The principle of bounded rationality results from a particular *conservative incrementalism* materialized in a careful attitude always concerned by feedbacks provided by human interactions (Kaplan & Kaplan, 1982).

This vision of rationality can be used to characterize an organization behavior as a team involved in the process of engineering a software product. Indeed, given the uncertainty and the complexity of the real world and the technological progress, there is no universal and optimal software solution which would be rationally superior to the other possible solutions. Because software engineering is a human practice, the perfect software solution driven by a perfect rationality does not exist. The illustration on Figure 2 shows the multiple actors' visions of a software product. When building a software solution several actors (and models) bounded rationalities intervene, for instance:

Figure 2. A multi vision representation of software development

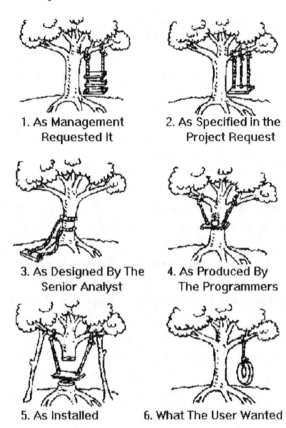

1. As Management Requested It

2. As Specified in the Project Request

3. As Designed By The Senior Analyst

4. As Produced By The Programmers

5. As Installed

6. What The User Wanted

- When modeling the organizational setting:
  - **Stakeholders** as, for example, engineers explain their understanding of the organization and other business processes;
  - **Software modelers** represent what they understand of the business processes using a modeling language containing its own limitations.
- When eliciting and modeling user requirements:
  - **End users** explain their expectations of what the system should do;
  - **Software modelers** represent what they understand of end user requirements using a modeling language containing its own limitations.

- When designing the software application, software designers build design models (using a modeling language containing its own limitations) on the basis of what they understand of the provided analysis models and other artifacts produced by analysts..
- When implementing the system, developers produce a software system (using programming languages containing their own limitations) on the basis of what they understand of the provided design models and other artifacts.

Each actor involved in the software development process has to deal with:

- His own rationality which is by essence bounded;
- The bounded rationality of the other actors he works with;
- The inherent limitations of the modeling languages he has to deal with (models are by essence limited and do not allow to capture the whole of the reality of the problem, see (Rumbaugh et al., 1999).

The bounded rationality principle is in accordance with the rationality used in social sciences. This concept has allowed the emergence of behavioral economics which tend to be more and more dominant[2]. Using such a vision implies to take into account that human beings cannot evaluate perfectly the moving contexts and that this misunderstanding of the situation leads them to seek a *satisfactory solution*. This satisfactory solution depends directly on each individual and the quest for a satisfactory solution allows people to meet their fundamental needs and to develop themselves. In this human reasoning model, no way exists to determine if this "satisfactory solution" maximizes a specific utility function or to know if another choice would have provided an higher level of satisfaction.

Actors Rationality and SE Methodologies

The bounded rationality principle is an interesting concept for the theoretical analysis of software development. It allows characterizing the complexity observed in software solutions to give an efficient response to organizational problems by nature hard to define. Organizational interactions allow project stakeholders to improve their knowledge in an iterative manner and to improve their requirements comprehension. That is why, facing such a context, one need an accurate modeling language as well as a development process designed to favor stakeholders' knowledge evolution and allowing to constantly adapt the software product with those new refinements. Iterative software development where requirements are collected and revised progressively on the basis of early testing to get the best adequacy between stakeholders' knowledge and the developed products is better in line with actors' bounded rationality. Through the use of a process better in line with human rationality as the iterative one, users' perceived quality and adequacy of the software solution can then be improved.

Macro-Level Approach: Lakatosian Lecture of an Artificial Science

In this section we will present the Popperian knowledge growth model applied to SE developments at macro-level (a micro-level application is also briefly done but is secondary to the demonstration) and nuance this application with the Lakatosian falsification principle. We will then emphasize that a Lakatosian epistemology is directly in line with the notion of bounded rationality evoked in the previous section.

The Knowledge Growth Theory: An Application to SE Methodologies

According to Popper (1972), scientific knowledge evolves thanks to a continuous and infinite problem resolution process. Knowledge increases by confronting theories with reality. This confrontation, called *falsification* by Popper himself, often generates new problems that theoreticians have to define, theorize and solve. The empirical refutation of a proposed theory induces the emergence of new theories subject to empirical refutation creating other problems and so on. The knowledge growth process is ad infinitum because, according to Popper, the resolution of new problems requires new knowledge (i.e. new theories and new conceptual tools). Popper calls "crucial experiment" (Popper, 1959) any theory refutation allowing the emergence of new problems. This refutation constitutes a source of inspiration for the development of new theories supposed to solve the new problems.

Strictly speaking Popperian epistemology has to be applied onto the macro level of the defined system. Indeed, SE methodologies, the theoretical frameworks envisaged into this article have, following Popper, to be subject to falsification through a crucial experiment. This vision is, following us, not really adapted to study the evolution towards the nowadays SE methodologies using advanced modeling languages and mature SDLCs since the process is more evolutionary and not subject to direct refutation. This is studied in details into the next section.

Before continuing the macro-level analysis, a parenthesis is done here and we apply the Popperian knowledge growth theory to the micro level to evaluate if this could have consequences on the theoretical frameworks at macro-level. In that perspective, according to (Toffolon & Dakhili, 1999), the Popperian knowledge growth model can be used to justify the better performance of iterative software development (in terms of matching with user requirements). Indeed, by disturbing the established relations in a particular organizational context, each software solution generates new problems which are specific to this organization. It is impossible to predict exactly how a new software solution will disturb the organizational context. This context is often very complex because a lot of interactions between its components exist and, moreover, an iterative process leads to a moving evolution of this context. Stakeholders, by using a software solution, modify their needs to solve the new problems created by this system and then improve their use of the system. Stakeholders' requirements cannot be fully described and specified before the implementation because they evolve when they approach the software system. Consequently their requirements evolve iteratively during the software development. Toffolon and Dakhili (1999) explain that this evolution can be characterized by a Popperian lecture. This consequently points, at macro-level, to the adoption of a SDLC envisaging the project knowledge evolution in an iterative manner.

Criticize of the Falsification Principle at the Light of SE Methodologies Evolution

In his work about the mathematical formalisms, Imré Lakatos proposes two categories of theories: *Euclidean* and *quasi-empirical* theories. Whereas the firsts are connected with an axiomatic approach (imposing a purely deductive logic from a priori axioms), the seconds are determined by the empiricism because they evolve through a continuous feed-back between the theory and its empirical results. Indeed, a quasi-empirical science can be tested empirically but remains specific to a particular context that explains the "quasi" diminutive. In relation to Simon's works, all artificial sciences[3] can be seen as quasi-empirical sciences but the inverse is not necessary true (Gianluigi, 2006). As we will show in this section, this point of view is different from the Popperian one because in his epistemology, theoreticians have to change the whole theory if it is falsified. We think that the Lakatosian epistemology about quasi empirical theories is useful for the study of knowledge evolution in the SE science (at macro-level) because the process of theories adjustment he proposed is directly in line with the quasi-empirical logic observed in this field. The aim of this section is to moderate the use of Popperian epistemology at macro-level. At first sight, the Popperian knowledge growth model is very close to what Lakatos calls the "quasi-empirical theories". The two visions are however different and, according to us, only the Lakatosian is adequate for a study of SE methodologies evolution.

Popper developed his epistemology for "hard sciences", especially physics. Science is mainly considered in terms of "representation of the world" rather than in terms of "efficient answers" as it would be in the field of applied ones. This detail is of primary importance since, at the opposite of hard sciences, a universal framework performing at best in every software development cannot exist. For showing this we will briefly refer to the micro level. Indeed, as it has been shown previously there is no universal and optimal software solution: no development is identical to one another since each organization is different. Contrary to hard sciences which describe the "reality" as it is, SE incorporates in its processes individuals' way of solving specific problems. The practical experiment supposed "to falsify" the developed solution appears to be extremely complex and multiple. In this context, it is impossible to dispose of what Popper calls a "crucial experiment". Indeed, each new project is a new experiment based on various theoretical concepts (modeling languages, development life cycles, programming languages, etc.) and trying to satisfy various requirements. Each software solution is developed for a particular organization employing various people pursuing various goals and it is very difficult to compare with one another so that the reasons of an empirical failure

are hard to determine. Moreover, in software development it is very hard to correctly identify the nature of the error (Priestley, 2005). The reason(s) of an empirical failure can be conceptual or result from a bad representation of the organizational logic but it could simply be the consequence of a programming mistake or to a technical problem at physical layer. The variety of errors strongly complicates the idea of a "crucial experiment". We can consequently not, in case of empirical failure, reject all the applied SE theoretical bases as for instance the methodology used within that project. Theoretical tools can be very powerful and particularly well indicated in the context of the "failed" development but the reason of failure could be exterior to them. On the basis of those overviewed characteristics of software development we categorize SE as a "quasi empirical applied discipline".

The falsification principle specific to the Popperian epistemology can consequently not be applied to the quasi-empirical (or artificial) discipline of software engineering as it would be to disciplines of hard sciences. This subscribes the fact that the nature of SE can also be found in social sciences rather than only in hard ones. For sure, the empirical failure of a software solution has to lead to calling into question the SE theoretical foundations but they cannot be directly and purely rejected. The Popperian model of knowledge (also called "dogmatic falsificationnism" in philosophy of science) appears to be too radical for an epistemological reading of SE theoretical frameworks evolution. This Popperian radicality has already been recognized and caused a plentiful literature in philosophy of science (see e.g., (Kuhn, 1996) or (Lakatos, 1977)). In line with the opposition to the radicalism of falsification, Lakatos developed its methodology of "research programme" (see (Lakatos 1977) for the theoretical basis and (Wautelet et al. 2008) for an application on object and agent orientation).

Software Engineering Research at the Light of Adaptive Rationality

The Lakatosian epistemology (often "called methodological falsificationnism") is less radical than the Popperian one. Indeed, Lakatos tries to explain why scientific theories continue to exist in spite of the existence of empirical refutations. Even if empiricism plays a very important role in the evolution of the knowledge, Lakatos recognizes that all the theories born, are refuted and die refuted. The Hungarian philosopher strongly criticizes the concept of "crucial experiment" and argues it is impossible to explain the evolution of science only in Popperian terms. Lakatos recognizes the importance of empiricism since it is precisely through the confrontation to the real world that sciences evolve, however, the philosopher explains why the "ad hoc"[4] characteristic often observed in empirical studies can be useful to improve the theory. In the Lakatosian vision of science, it is not necessary to change the whole theory in case of refutation. The empirical failure just represents a sign of a problem which must be solved by improving the tested theory. However, as long as the tested theory does not face a continuous empirical failure (which would mark the degenerative character of the research programme in which the theory has been developed), nothing obliges the theorists to modify their theoretical framework[5]. This vision is particularly well adapted to an epistemological reading of SE.

The Lakatosian epistemology is based on the notion of adaptive rationality which could be seen as the result of Simon's bounded rationality. Indeed, theoreticians do not reject a theory when it is falsified because they will try to improve it by developing some new solutions. Thanks to this process, the descriptive dimension of theory will be improved. No theory can claim describing directly and perfectly the "reality" because theoreticians (SE researchers) are governed by a bounded rationality leading them to a continuous knowledge acquisition process along all the software projects they are facing. Their knowledge grows progressively in an iterative manner as it is for the knowledge of the people involved onto a software project. A kind of parallel can here be drawn between the macro and micro levels even if the approach of those two types of actors is rather different and can therefore not be directly compared. In line with Lakatos, Simon is opposed to the Popperian falsificationnism because it implies to ask whether theoreticians are perfectly rational or not (Simon, 1991). According to Simon (1991), theoreticians have always good reasons to do what they do; once they are governed by bounded rationality and they are just unable to describe directly and totally the "reality" like the falsificationnism presupposes it. The bounded rationality developed by Simon can be seen as a justification of the Lakatosian epistemology (LeMoigne, 1994).

The adaptive character of the human mind results from a bounded rationality. This iterative vision of knowledge described by Lakatos is directly in line with the evolution of SE theoretical frameworks (for example from Merise to UML, from waterfall to iterative development, etc.). By solving specific organizational problems, SE can be considered as an "artificial science" that can better be analyzed using a Lakatosian perspective than a Popperian one.

IMPLICATIONS

Everyday work implications of the study of knowledge evolution into software projects and onto development life cycles gave several interesting conclusions important in the daily practice of researchers and other practitioners. Figure 3 summarizes the conclusions taken from our epistemological analysis.

Our epistemological approach of the **micro level** defined earlier in the article points out that:

Figure 3. Software engineering's systematic approach: main epistemological analysis conclusions

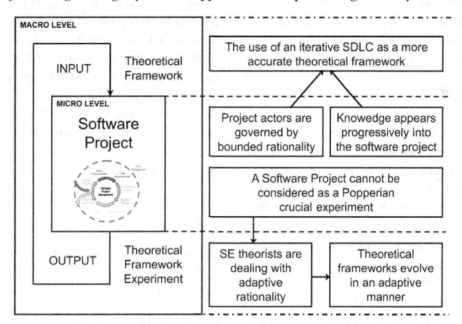

- The ability to express requirements and to understand their nature is by essence limited since actors are dealing with bounded rationality representing problems and designing software solutions with by essence models so that this process cannot be proceeded once for all into the software project but should rather be continuous;
- Knowledge grows within human organizations. When developing software solutions, knowledge about user requirements and further expectations grow during the project life cycle. Previously identified requirements should not be refuted but rather refined continuously at the light of users' feedbacks.

Iterative development allows to better deal with actors' bounded rationality and with the knowledge evolution into the software project thanks to the feedback loop on the produced solutions it offers (micro level feedback loop).

At macro-level, the most important aspect that can be deduced from our work is that SE does not belong to hard sciences but can rather be considered as a quasi-empirical discipline as defined by Lakatos. Theoretical frameworks produced by SE researchers are subject to evolutions and adaptations since they are dealing with adaptive rationality (macro level feedback loop). Evolution in SDLCs frameworks has nowadays led to iterative development life cycles as overviewed in section 2 for some of the reasons evoked above but the framework will evolve by adoption of further evolutions.

Some derived conclusions can also be pointed out for software engineering researchers. Indeed, due to the fact that with a Lakatosian reading of SE knowledge evolution no crucial experiment can reasonably be established, empirical testing of the developed SE theories should be realized on case studies but the quantitative burden of the proof of their better performance can hardly be established. This consequence is notably useful for researchers working on the elaboration of new SE methodologies. Their experimentation aimed to establish the better performance of their development models/processes/frameworks should be as most as possible quantified but since this cannot constitute an unambiguous proof, it must be complementary to a qualitative typology.

CONCLUSION

User requirements that have been poorly taken into account as well as modeling and development languages inspired by programming concepts as opposed to organization and enterprise ones has led to a software crisis. Solutions can be found at different levels, and among those conceptual modeling and iterative development have been noticeable evolutions. Indeed, proceeding iteratively allows, thanks to continuous feedback loops, to develop a software product having a perceived quality in better accordance to users expectations.

This article has presented an epistemological reading of knowledge evolution in SE at both the level of software projects (micro level) and at the level of SE frameworks (macro level). At micro level, we studied knowledge evolution into a software project involving tens of actors governed by bounded rationality. At macro level, the article concludes SE is a quasi-empirical discipline; indeed due to the impossibility of a crucial experiment, upcoming innovations can be based on refinements of existing theories and do not induce a complete refutation of existing techniques. SE theorists and researchers are governed by an adaptive rationality. The article concludes and advocates that on the basis of our epistemological lecture, the use of iterative development is better adapted to drive SE projects due to knowledge evolution and with bounded rational actors and SE theoretical frameworks evolve in an adaptable manner. SE can be considered as a quasi-empirical discipline rather than a hard science. Finally, the article constitutes a contribution to computer science philosophy.

More work should be carried out in SE fundamentals by studying other methodological frameworks and epistemological foundations to provide the computer science researcher a more accurate vision of the research field that he or she is working on. Other works showed that aspects such as object and agent-orientation are also strongly in line with Lakatosian theories. An interesting point would be to study agent software entities at the light of Simon's theories.

REFERENCES

Ambler, S. (2002). *Agile Modeling*. John Wiley & Sons.

Arlow, J., & Neustadt, I. (2002). *UML and the Unified Process*. The Object Technology Series. Addison Wesley.

Arthur, W. B. (1994). *Inductive Reasoning and Bounded Rationality*. American Economic Association Annual Meetings.

Basili, V. (1992). The experimental paradigm in software engineering. In D. Rombach, V. Basili, & R. Shel (Eds.), *Experimental Software Engineering Issues: Critical Assessment and Future Directives*. Springer-Verlag.

Beck, K. (2005). *Extreme Programming Explained: Embrace Change* (2nd ed.). Addison-Wesley.

Boehm, B. (2000). Spiral Development: Experience, Principles, and Refinements. In W. J. Hansen (Ed.), *Spiral Development Workshop*.

Booch, G., Rumbaugh, J., & Jacobson, I. (1999). *The Unified Modeling Language User Guide*. Object Technology Series, Addison-Wesley.

Gianluigi, O. (2006). Mathematics as a Quasi-Empirical Science. *Foundations of Science, 11*(2), 41–79. doi:10.1007/s10699-004-5912-3

IBM. (2003). *The Rational Unified Process. Version 2003.06.00.65*. Rational Software Corporation.

Kahneman, D. (2003). Maps of Bounded Rationality: a Perspective on Intuitive Judgment and Choice. *Nobel Prize Lecture*, 8 December 2002, also in *The American. Economic Review, 93*(5), 1449–1475. doi:10.1257/000282803322655392

Kaisler, S. H. (2005). *Software Paradigms*. John Wiley & Son.

Kaplan, S., & Kaplan, R. (1982). *Cognition and Environment: Functioning in an Uncertain World*. Praeger.

Kuhn, T. (1996). *The structure of scientific revolutions* (3rd ed). University of Chicago Press.

Lakatos, I. (1977). *The Methodology of Scientific Research Programmes: Philosophical Papers*. Volume 1, Cambridge University Press.

Latour, B., & Woolgar, S. (1988). *La vie de laboratoire: la production des faits scientifiques*. Editions La Découverte, Paris.

LeMoigne, J.-L. (1994). *Sur la capacité de la raison à discerner rationalité substantive et rationalité procédurale*. In Frydman (Ed.), Quelles hypotheses de rationalité pour la science économique? L'Harmattan, Paris.

Lyotard, J.-F. (1979). *La condition postmoderne*. Paris, Editions de Minuit.

OMG (2007). *OMG Unified Modeling Language Specification*. Version 2.1.2.

Popper, K. R. (1959). *The Logic of Scientific Discovery*. London: Hutchinson.

Popper, K. R. (1972). *Objective Knowledge, An Evolutionary Approach*. Oxford University Press.

Priestley, M. (2005). *The Logic of Correctness in Software Engineering*. CAiSE Workshops.

Rorty, R. (1979), *Philosophy and the Mirror of Nature*. Princeton: Princeton University Press.

Royce, W. (1970). Managing the Development of Large Software Systems. In *Proceedings of the IEEE WESCON* (pp. 1-9).

Royce, W. (1998). *Software Project Management. A Unified Framework*. Addison-Wesley.

Rumbaugh, J., Booch, G., & Jacobson, I. (1999). *The Unified Modeling Language Reference Manual*. Object Technology Series, Addison-Wesley.

Simon, H. A. (1983). Models of Bounded Rationality. Cambridge: MIT Press.

Simon, H. A. (1991). *Rationality in Political Behaviour*. Working paper of Carnegie Mellon University, 1991.

Toffolon, C., & Dakhili, S. (1999). Requirements Elicitation Process: An Iterative Approach based on the Spiral Model. In *Proceedings of the XVIth International Symposium on Information and Computer Sciences (ISCIS'99)*, Izmir, Turkey.

Wautelet, Y. (2008). *A Goal-Driven Project Management Framework for I-Tropos Multi-Agent Iterative Software Development*. PhD thesis, Louvain School of Management, Université catholique de Louvain, Louvain-la-Neuve, Belgium.

Wautelet, Y., Schinckus, C., & Kolp, M. (2008). A Modern Epistemological Reading of Agent Orientation. *International Journal of Intelligent Information Technologies, 4*(3), 46–57.

ENDNOTES

[1] In the context of this article, SE methodology and SE development process are considered as synonyms, when using these terms we refer to a modeling language and a software development life cycle.

2   Daniel Kahneman psychology professor at Princeton won, in 2002, the Nobel Prize in economics for having integrated insights from psychological research into economic science, especially concerning human judgment and decision-making under uncertainty (see (Kahneman, 2002)).

3   Herbert Simon's work is structured around three themes [Parthenay05]: bounded rationality, organizational processes and epistemology of artificial sciences. Bounded rationality and organizational processes were presented in section 3.2 as an accurate conceptual framework to describe project actors' rationality. Simon defines *Artificial Sciences* as disciplines constructed by human mind to solve specific problems at a specific time [Simon69]. The artificial character refers to the contingent nature of the solution.

4   *Ad hoc* is a latin expression which means *"for this purpose"*. In philosophy of science *ad hoc* often means the addition of corollary hypotheses to a scientific theory to prevent this theory from being falsified by anomalies not anticipated by its initial theory. Popper rejects this "ad hoc" character in science and, following him, this should be considered as a kind of intellectual dishonesty (see (Popper, 1959)).

5   (Lakatos 1977) reminds that science is a human practice and that it is sometimes very difficult for scientists to reject a theoretical framework when they have devoted several years of their life working on and developing it.

This work was previously published in the International Journal of Information Technologies and Systems Approach, Volume 3, Issue 1, edited by Frank Stowell and Manuel Mora, pp. 21-40, copyright 2010 by IGI Publishing (an imprint of IGI Global).

Chapter 3
A Holistic Approach for Understanding Project Management

Theresa A. Kraft
University of Michigan, USA

Annette L. Steenkamp
Lawrence Technological University, USA

ABSTRACT

Companies invest significant sums of money in major Information Technology (IT) projects, yet success remains limited. Despite an abundance of IT Project Management (ITPM) resources available to project teams, such as the Project Management Institute (PMI) Body of Knowledge, IT standards and IT governance, a large percentage of IT projects continue to fail and ultimately get scrapped. Recent studies have shown an average of 66% IT project failure rate, with 52% of the projects being cancelled, and 82% being delivered late. The purpose of this research was to provide a way for uncovering potential causes of IT project failures by utilizing a systemic and holistic approach to identify critical success factors for project management. The holistic approach has enabled the development of an ITPM conceptual model, which provides a method to evaluate the critical success factors of a given project, and their alignment with each other. The adoption of the systemic methodology and its implementation increase the potential for IT project success, and alert project leaders of potential problems throughout the life of the project.

INTRODUCTION

Companies invest large sums of money for major information technology projects yet achieve limited success. In efforts to reduce the risks associated with the failure of information technology projects, enterprises have opted to replace existing legacy systems with packaged solutions. Some use commercial-off-the-shelf (COTS) software,

rather than incurring the costs and risks involved in software development. Despite the availability to project teams of body of knowledge on IT project management, IT standards and governance, a large percentage of IT projects are scrapped, over budget, or delayed. A comparison of project management studies by Forrester Research Inc. has shown that there is a sixty-six percent project failure rate, with fifty two percent of the

DOI: 10.4018/978-1-4666-1562-5.ch003

projects being cancelled and eighty two percent being delivered late. Sixty seven percent of the companies surveyed feel their program or project management practices are "in need of repair" (Visitacion, 2006, p. 5). According to Charette (2005, p. 43) "five to fifteen percent of the IT projects initiated will be abandoned before, or shortly after, delivery as hopelessly inadequate and many others will arrive late and over budget or require massive reworking".

Typical project management articles have documented factors that contribute to project success or failure in terms of budget constraints, resource costs, ability to meet schedules, and satisfy objectives. Despite numerous methods and techniques that have been developed "project management remains a highly problematic endeavor" (White & Fortune, 2002, p. 1). The purpose of this research project was to provide a way for uncovering potential causes of IT project failures by utilizing a systemic and holistic approach to identify critical success factors for project management and thus to expand the body of knowledge related to IT Project Management of COTS software procurement and implementation.

The contribution of the paper is in the development of a systemic conceptual model illustrating the critical factors that impact project success. The conceptual model was developed based upon an extensive analysis of four case studies selected from industry. The conceptual model was refined utilizing interviews and surveys of industry experts who have experience with project management, and who are certified Project Management Professionals (PMPs). The paper proceeds with a review of the related literature, formulation of the conceptual model, discussion of the results from validation of the model by experts in the field and conclusion.

LITERATURE REVIEW AND FINDINGS

The purpose of the initial literature review was to understand the existing subject matter on system modeling approaches and factors related to project management. The literature review focused on the body of knowledge of the systems approach, factors contributing to the success and failure of IT PM, and IT systems delivery.

IT Project Management Issues

Project success factors found in the literature include measures such as on-time project delivery to the customer, adherence to the project schedule, project cost and budget control, quality of the project management process and customer satisfaction (Jugdev & Muller, 2005). "Measures of project success need to include the diversity of shareholder interests" (Milosevic & Patankul, 2005, p. 183). Additionally, standardized PM tools, processes, and skills, in connection with project team interpersonal relationships and organizational culture also affect project success.

Jugdev and Muller (2005) state that project management can have strategic value when the project's products and services provide business value. Literature on the tradeoffs between time, cost, quality and scope indicate that scope is one of the primary determinants of project success. The meta analysis of the literature indicated that project management publications are primarily focused on tools and techniques, and project management methodology at the tactical level. "Few publications discuss project management in the context of strategic planning, company mission, and the importance of corporate management performance" (Jugdev & Muller, 2005, p. 21).

IT has become so central to modern organizations that the implementation of IT projects must also take into consideration the comprehensive evaluation of change management within the organization. The IT project is usually part of a wider business strategy, which includes business process reforms of existing business systems, organizational structure and team efforts (Ives, 2005). "The alignment of IT with business goals has been a critical issue for organizations for as long as IT has been an important factor in the success of organizations. As organizations cope with rapid changes in their business and technological environments, alignment issues have been at or near the top of the list of critical issues in IT management for the past fifteen years" (Chen et al., 2006, p.6). Current IT PM literature and research topics are lacking application to real-life practical IT Software projects, and do not closely relate to everyday project issues and demands (Tesch et al., 2003). It appears that project management at the organizational level must shift attention away from performance and effectiveness metrics, and reflect a more systemic and holistic view of the value of project management as a core or strategic value to attain success.

Systems Approach to Project Management

Software project management is part of the Information Systems (IS) field and includes many disparate disciplines; hence, it is suitable to analysis using a systemic and holistic approach. A systems approach "to a problem requires recognition that it is capable of being dealt with in parts, which are strung together in a logical order" (Stainton, 1984, p. 146). Systemic or holistic means that the system must be evaluated in its entirety and that "the wholes must be taken at face value, understood by themselves" (Stainton, 1984, p.147).

Many different types of system approaches have been developed and proposed in the literature. Tsouvalis and Checkland (1996) have identified two alternative system paradigms as working with Hard Systems, which is most effective with well-structured problems, and Soft Systems thinking, which is best suited to ill-structured problems. Soft systems thinking can be applied to situations in which interconnections are cultural, and situations dominated by the meanings attributed to their perceptions by autonomous observers (Stainton, 1984). "The aim of the Soft System approach is to structure a systemic process of inquiry rather than to provide a means of optimizing" (Stainton, 1984, p. 149).

The Soft Systems Methodology was first published in 1972 (Tsouvalis & Checkland, 1996) based upon the principle that development of a methodology has to stem from neither theory nor practice, but from the interaction between the two. Soft Systems Methodology (SSM) addresses the reality that all real world problem situations are characterized by people trying to take purposeful action. A set of activities linked together so that the set is purposeful, was treated as a new kind of systems concept, a human activity system. Stages of the SSM include real world activities necessarily involving people in the problem situation and 'system thinking' activity, which may not involve those in the problem situation. SSM attempts to look at the real world problem situation in terms of social system analysis, cultural system analysis, or political systems analysis with the people involved in the problem situation and then attempts to apply systems thinking to the development of models and comparisons of the models to the real world (Tsouvalis & Checkland, 1996). The Soft Systems Model given in the text of Soft Systems Methodology in Action (Checkland & Scholes, 1990) has become the preferred version (Tsouvalis & Checkland, 1996) and is shown in Figure 1.

The dashed dividing line in Figure 1 is a separation of the everyday real world of the problem situation from the consciously organized system thinking about the real world situation. The dividing line separates the distinct kinds of activities, which are real world activities involv-

Figure 1. The current model of SSM[1]

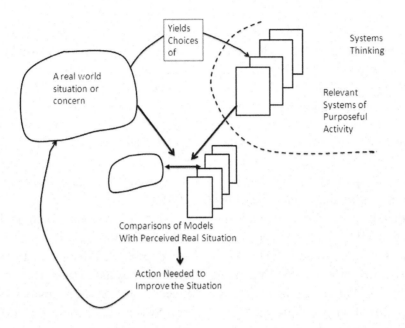

ing people in the problem situation and systems thinking activity, which may not involve people in the problem situation (Tsouvalis & Checkland, 1996). The real world situation is concerned with the unreflective engagement in and with the problem situation and the everyday language and concepts. Systems' thinking is the reflective engagement in and with the problem situation so that the conscious reflection can be carried out related to the real world situation. The Soft Systems Methodology (SSM) entails finding out about the problems situation in the real world, building relevant models of purposeful activity, using the models to question the real world in order to define purposeful actions, and then implementing the agreed action (Checkland & Winter, 2006).

Literature Research Synopsis

The review of the literature on systems approaches revealed that the SSM is a valid approach to adopt in this research. The utilization of the four case studies represents the real world situation (or concern) in the current model of SSM, while the research analysis and systems thinking corresponds to the development of the initial conceptual model. The comparison and refinement of the model based upon interviews and qualitative feedback from industry yielded the completed conceptual model. The research also utilized a multi-method research approach as supported by Mingers (2001), by means of interviews, surveys and case studies.

RESEARCH DESIGN PROCESS

The four main steps for the research process in this study are:

Step 1 Literature Review: An enhanced understanding of different systems approaches and factors contributing to IT PM success and failure were achieved based upon an extensive literature review. The analysis of the literature identified key variables and factors contributing to success and failure of IT projects and provided an in depth review of trends regarding the research topic of applied systems approaches.

Step 2 Conceptualization: The development of the conceptual model of the research problem was the first activity of this step. An analysis was performed on historical documentation of various case studies in order to identify key variables and to formulate a conceptual model in terms of critical success factors and the potential dependencies among them.

Step 3 Experimentation: The conceptual model was evaluated with certified project management professionals using structured interviews and a survey. Experimentation was accomplished utilizing mixed methods, with the quantitative data consisting of the survey results and the qualitative data of the critiques of the draft conceptual model during the interview process.

Step 4 Validation: The objective of this final research activity was the validation and refinement of the conceptual model. The results of the two additional case studies were examined to validate the conceptual model

Research Methodology

The research approach is case study based making use of four unique real-life IT COTS projects with applications in the automotive industry. The analyses of the four case studies were performed using mixed research methods (quantitative and qualitative). Qualitative modeling allows the researcher to view the organization's synergistic existence as a whole entity versus the sum of its parts, in supporting the overall organization's objectives and functions, and the alignment to IT systems (Chen et al., 2006). This examination of the IT PM synergistic existence of the whole system versus the sum of its parts, and the interdependencies of critical success factors, has been termed a systemic and holistic research approach.

According to Eisenhardt (1989), case study research is necessary "at times when little is known

about a phenomenon and current perspectives seem inadequate because there have little empirical substantiation." Thus, it was appropriate to use case studies in Step 2 to develop a strategic vision of project management critical success factors, since there is little documented about the dependencies between IT project success rates and the alignment of the business processes, IT standards and governance, and organizational dynamics to the proposed IT solution. The main goal of conducting case study research using several case studies is to enable the investigation of differences across the cases, and to determine if the data provides sufficient evidence to support the stated proposition. The case study approach allowed the researchers to understand the interactions among IT PM processes, IT governance and standards, and the impact on the organization in implementing IT projects to satisfy business requirements. By employing the grounded theory approach the draft conceptual model was developed and refined as each successive case study was analyzed, finally resulting in the refined conceptual model proposed in this paper.

To summarize, this research included a multi-method approach of performing case study analyses, surveys and interviews to develop a comprehensive understanding of the variety of factors contributing to project success. This research utilized the concepts of the Soft Systems methodology, in conjunction with a multi-method research approach and critical realism.

Data Collection Method

The data collection method encompassed several techniques, with data obtained from multiple historical sources and interviews with project participants as well as personal experiences on the projects. Historical data include archival records, archived interviews, documentation, direct observations, participant observation, and physical artifacts (Yin, 2003). Some of these sources of evidence were collected during the time the researcher actually participated as project manager for these real-world cases as summarized below. The advantage of multiple sources of evidence is that it provides a better understanding of the situation. Disadvantages include time, cost, and potentially lack of qualification of the person collecting the data. Data was collected for each case study from the following specific historical documents:

- Actual Business Requirements and System Requirements
- User Acceptance Testing
- Software Evaluations
- Business Process Models and Gap Analysis
- Project Management Historical Documentation
- Interviews with Project Team members

The quantitative historical data consist of business users completion of the user acceptance testing, the software evaluations, and other data collected from the business user community with surveys and questionnaires. Other data, such as the architecture designs and the compatibility of the IT architecture with IT governance policies and standards, are qualitative. The project management methods and practices used by each case study project team were also examined.

CONCEPTUAL MODEL DEVELOPMENT

Systemic and Holistic Approach

A systemic approach represents the ability to approach the problem with analytical skills and methods. This analysis breaks the problem down into many different aspects. The systems analysis of each aspect of the problem isolates the causative factors of the problem, and how they relate to each other and their interdependencies. In addition, a systemic approach views a system in a holistic manner. The systems analyst attempts to think about, and understand, the system by examining the linkages and interactions between the elements that comprise the entirety of the system. A systemic approach incorporates the following tenets:

- **Interdependence of objects and their attributes:** Independent elements can never constitute a system.
- **Holism:** Emergent properties, which are not possible to detect by analysis, should be possible to define by a holistic approach.
- **Goal seeking:** system interaction must result in some goal or final state.
- **Inputs and outputs:** In a closed system, inputs are determined once and remain constant. In an open system, additional inputs are admitted from the environment.
- **Transformation of inputs into outputs:** This is the process by which the goals are obtained.
- **Entropy:** The amount of disorder or randomness present in the system.
- **Regulation:** A method of feedback is necessary for the system to operate predictably.
- **Hierarchy:** Complex wholes, which are made up of smaller subsystems.
- **Differentiation:** Specialized units perform specialized functions.
- **Equifinality:** Alternative ways of attaining the same objectives (converge).
- **Multifinality:** Attaining alternative objectives from the same inputs (diverge) (Skyttner, L., 2006).

The systemic approach to project management allows the researcher to view all aspects of the project management activities. The examination of the project management methodology as a system of inputs, processes and outputs, allows the researchers to proceed in a logical sequential order. The entire project management process and the interactions with the organization may be considered a "system". The project management systemic approach envisions a PM system, which starts with the organizations strategy as input and results in the output of a successful implementation of an IT project, to satisfy the organizational requirements. Thus IT PM is viewed as a holistic system of corporate strategic goals as inputs, interdependent interacting parts, feedback and control of project management activities and outputs of IT project deliverables. The systems analyst attempts to think about and understand the IT PM system by examining the linkages and interactions between the elements that comprise the entirety of the system (Kraft, 2009).

In so examining a PM system, from the top down, it can be seen that it has a specific purpose. The goal is to satisfy company objectives and strategy with the successful utilization of IT projects. The systemic approach addresses the idea that all the properties of a given PM system cannot be determined or explained by the sum of its component parts alone. Instead, the system as a whole determines in an important way how the critical success factor components behave and

interact. A systemic PM Framework is illustrated in Figure 2.

The approach we have taken shows the interconnectedness of the factors affecting project management along the principle of systemicity defined by Mitroff and Linstone (1994), and the predominant levels of management, where it plays a role, namely Strategic Management, Tactical Management and Operational Management. The ovals on the Systemic PM Framework describe the PM activities performed at each management level. The PM activities for each managerial level must be in alignment with each other, as illustrated by the arrows. The systemic PM framework is based on the business process methodology (Harmon, 2007), which attempts to create a business process architecture for the organization by examining the enterprise level, the business process level and the implementation level. The premise is that the business processes must be analyzed at each of these levels to gain insight and distinguish between the different participants, different methodologies, and different types of

Figure 2. Systemic project management framework

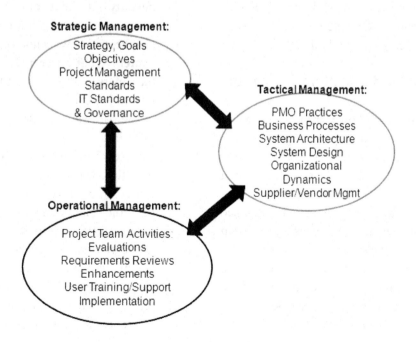

support and resources required at each level of concern.

Conceptual Model Flowcharts

The conceptual model proposed by this research addresses critical success factors that contribute to the success or failure of an IT Systems Project. The conceptual model is divided into two separate domains. In the first domain, the critical success areas for the business domain are examined, including the business processes, business goals and objectives, and the overall organizational dynamics. In the second domain, the critical success areas are examined for the IT domain, including IT governance, PM standards and practices, adaptability and flexibility of IT governance and the responsiveness and adaptability of the software vendors. The processes of implementation of the conceptual model for the business domain and the IT domain are shown in Figure 3 and Figure 4, respectively. As can be seen, there is a linkage from each domain such that when the analysis of the business domain is complete, the analysis must be performed on the IT domain. The proposition of this research was that IT projects will be successful if both the business goals and objectives are satisfied, and the delivered system complies with the IT governance standards.

Conceptual Model System Elements

Though the approach followed in the research was based on a hard systems approach after Jackson (2003), the system elements were not assumed to be in final form but rather they were refined using additional case studies. In this way the process may be seen as a form of learning that took place during the research and to a degree adds certain aspects relating somewhat to soft systems thinking due to the learning about the system (Jackson, 2003). The system elements incorporated in the conceptual model are summarized below.

- **Business Process Alignment:** Business process modeling is the activity to depict the current business activities and the desired future state in an attempt to improve the business by implementing a change to processes. The new business process model is utilized to drive the requirements for a new IT application. The business processes and activities must be compatible with the functionality and design intent of the IT application, and the application must be able to support the new business processes.
- **System Design and Functionality:** The features and functions supported by the new software application are developed based upon the system requirements, business requirements and the logical and physical design specifications.
- **Organizational Dynamics:** The organizational dynamics refers to the composition of the project team, the level of management support for the project, and the culture of the organization. Organizational dynamic factors that impact project management include the level of support and involvement from the end user community, quality and quantity of training, quality and quantity of user support, organization culture to embrace change, and new technology.
- **System Architecture:** The system architecture refers to the design and structure of the physical components, the implementation of the hardware, software and networking infrastructure.
- **Project Management Standards and Practice:** The techniques and methodology utilized to organize the resources assigned to the project, including time schedules, costs, labor resources, computer resources, etc. and the degree to which the project management techniques were utilized.
- **IT Governance Adaptability and Flexibility:** The ability of an enterprise to change and revise its corporate policies, procedures,

Figure 3. Conceptual model implementation for business domain

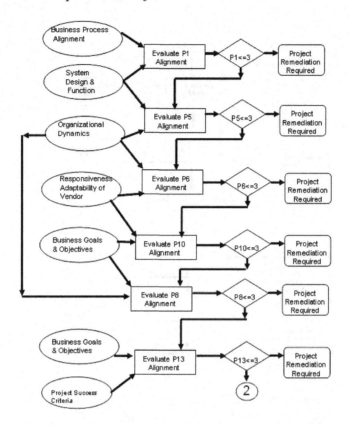

standards, and organizational processes for IT governance in a manner which provides competitive advantage and allows the firm to utilize next generation technology. Advances and changes to technology and external economic forces "requires agile and adaptable enterprises: enterprises that *sense* what is happening in the market; use knowledge assets to *learn* from that and *innovate* new products, services, channels and processes; then *mutate* rapidly to bring innovation to market" (IT Governance Institute, 2003).

- **IT Governance and Standards:** Corporate policies, standards, and procedures established by company leadership with "supporting organizational structures and processes that ensure the organization's IT utilization sustains and extend the or-

ganizations strategies and objectives" (IT Governance Institute, 2003).

- **Responsiveness and Adaptability of the Software Vendor:** The customer may have various degrees of influence on future software enhancements and software product direction. The responsiveness and ability to address and satisfy new customer requirements by the software vendor is ultimately driven by financial considerations of potential market demands for the new functionality or custom funded development.

- **Business Goals and Objectives:** The goals of the business unit or division could include faster response times, reduction of costs, improvements to quality etc. The business goals and objectives are the drivers to implement business process changes and utilize new IT systems.

Figure 4. Conceptual model implementation for IT domain

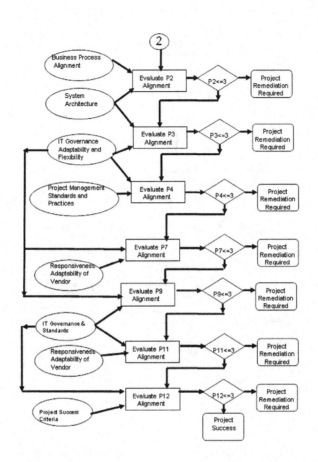

CONCEPTUAL MODEL VALIDATION

As stated earlier the primary purpose of this research was to expand the PM body of knowledge regarding factors that contribute to IT PM success, with the specific goal of expanding the traditional project management techniques of cost, schedule, resources, and scope to include business process alignment, IT governance and flexibility, and organizational dynamics. The conceptual model was further refined based upon the analysis by information obtained in interviews with IT project management subject matter experts. The interview results were analyzed to evaluate the rankings of the different critical success factors.

Survey Results

Data collection were accomplished using interviews and surveys with subject matter experts and project management professionals (PMP certified). Each project manager was asked to rank, on a Likert scale of one to five, the importance of the critical success factors organized into the following categories:

1. Project Management Practices
2. Business Process Alignment
3. System Design and Architecture Alignment
4. Organizational Dynamics
5. IT Governance and Standards
6. IT Governance and Project Management
7. Software Vendor/Supplier Responsiveness.

The results of the Likert rankings for each subject area were totaled since an advantage of the Likert scale is the ability to obtain a summated value, or total score. The total score represents an index of attitudes toward the major subject area as a whole (Alreck & Settle, 1985). The total values for each subject area is provided in Table 1.

The high number of total responses for each of the seven critical success areas of the survey confirms that the conceptual model does address those critical success factors considered important, or highly important, by the project manager experts. Common themes emerged from the interview process regarding weaknesses in project management. Evaluation and examination of these project management weaknesses was performed to identify which critical success factor would address each weakness. The result of this analysis led to classification and assignment of the identified project management weaknesses into one or more of the seven critical success factor categories, as follows:

1. Project Management Practices
   ◦ Lack of clear project definition
   ◦ Lack of communication
   ◦ Weak communication
   ◦ Poor scope control management
   ◦ Inaccurate project effort and schedule estimates
   ◦ Improper knowledge management for project management practices
   ◦ Inadequate Project Management Financial Data
   ◦ Lack of detailed risk management plan
2. Business Process Alignment
   ◦ Collection and clarification of requirements
   ◦ Poor scope control management
   ◦ Weak requirements gathering expertise
   ◦ Weak scope control and management
3. System Design and Architecture Alignment
   ◦ Acceptance testing
   ◦ No complete testing plans
4. Organizational Dynamics
   ◦ Poor Communication
   ◦ Lack of executive sponsorship
   ◦ Involvement of business user participants
   ◦ Weak project management leadership
   ◦ Lack of communication
   ◦ Weak communication
5. IT Governance and Standards
   ◦ Project managers not following a repeatable process
   ◦ Weak risk planning management
   ◦ Incomplete testing plans
   ◦ Lack of consistent standards and policies for IT and Business
6. IT Governance and Project Management
   ◦ Project managers not following a repeatable process
   ◦ Weak risk planning management
   ◦ Gross underestimation of resources, cost and time frames.
   ◦ Weak Project Management Office stipulation PM best practices
   ◦ Inadequate Project Management Training
   ◦ Ineffective project change controls
7. Software Vendor/Supplier Responsiveness
   ◦ Lack of focus on quality delivery

Table 1. Summarized survey results

Subject Area	1	2	3	4	5
Project Management Standards and Practices	1		5	25	29
Business Process Alignment		3	8	19	30
System Design and Architecture Alignment	7	3	10	30	34
Organizational Dynamics	4	5	12	32	54
IT Governance and Standards	6	4	12	22	16
IT Governance and Project Management	1	2	3	23	19
Software Vendor/Supplier Responsiveness	5	2	6	23	12

The Case Studies

Case studies, which were utilized for the development and validation of the conceptual model, are discussed below.

Case #1: Manufacturing Quality Desktop Application

The first case study was the original attempt to satisfy the business requirements for the manufacturing process failure mode effect analysis (PFMEA) using a vendor based software application for data entry and reporting. This software project had major problems, unresolved software quality issues and very dissatisfied end users after three years of effort.

A factor contributing to the failure of the Desktop PFMEA project included the change of scope from a desktop-based solution to a centralized web hosted server. The software vendor's lack of system administration expertise resulted in the server having to be reloaded numerous times because the software would crash and lock up. The overall failure to comply with corporate standards for the computer architecture requirements, namely utilizing a CITRIX™ server, was an additional contributing factor to this project failure. Additional factors included complexity of the software, since the user interface was not acceptable to the casual plant user, and there was an overall lack of a good implementation methodology. The training and user support from the software vendor were also not acceptable.

Case #2: Manufacturing Quality WEB Based Application

The second project was a manufacturing quality initiative to perform manufacturing process failure mode effect analysis (PFMEA) using a centralized web-based server for data entry and reporting. The project goal was to select a COTS application to satisfy all the PFMEA requirements of the global manufacturing plant sites, and to ensure compliance to the QS9000 quality standards. The project was started and successfully deployed within 18 months. Factors that contributed to the success are listed below:

- The project complied with IT standards for software project management and the system delivery company standards.
- Understanding of Business Requirements and the End User Requirements was very thorough.
- The software vendor was able to satisfy corporate IT standards for hardware, software technology and operating system infrastructure.
- Ability of the software vendor to satisfy new business requirements for enterprise wide reporting were not part of the base software application. Development was completed in approximately nine months. The new functionality was viewed as a major enhancement to the overall reporting module, which provided a competitive advantage to the software vendor.

Case #3: CAD Data Management

The third project was the data management of AutoCAD drawings files using Product Data Management (PDM). The project goal was to replace the legacy application developed internally using the relational database Ingress with a corporate COTS standard PDM application. The business organization had originally developed the customized data management system based upon Ingress for the document management of the machinery drawings and related bill of materials (stock lists). The management direction and vision was to replace the legacy system, which was costly to maintain and upgrade it with a commercially available package.

The AutoCAD Data Management project was overall a very unsuccessful project. The project was started but could not be deployed after six years of dedicated effort. Factors that contributed to this project failure are:

- The Organizational Dynamics were extremely resistant to change. There was a lack of management direction and support to encourage and foster an organizational climate, which would be acceptable to changes in the business practices.
- Lack of software vendor support since the product direction and marketing plans for the corporate standard PDM system did not support AutoCAD™.
- Business processes, which were not consistent and not supported by the design architecture of the Corporate Standard PDM system.
- Lack of management support to request changes to the IT standards committee to have the other commercially viable software product added to the approved vendor list.

Case #4: Advanced Invoice Management System

The fourth project, Advanced Invoice Management System (AIMS), was the implementation of an E-Commerce invoicing system for the Legal department that provides for electronic invoice delivery, management and workflow. It would allow for online review, adjustment and approval of invoices. The AIMS project was an overall successful project, which was completed and deployed within twelve months. Factors that contributed to the success of this project:

- Executive sponsorship and leadership was high and influenced both the legal suppliers submitting the invoices and the business user community.
- The business user community was very willing to participate in the project, iden-

tify their requirements, work with the software vendor to develop training materials, and devote time to the testing process.
- Compliance to IT standards for software project management and understanding of business requirements and the end user requirements was very thorough.
- Ability of the project management staff to obtain the Microsoft SQL server approval from Corporate IT standards for hardware and operating system infrastructure.

CONCLUSION

This research has culminated in the development of an ITPM conceptual model, which serves as a diagnostic method to predict those projects that are likely to become challenged, require immediate attention and potential project remediation. It is envisioned by the researchers that the application of the conceptual model, which addresses new critical success factors and alignment areas for the management of IT application projects, could improve the likelihood of project success rates.

The research findings discussed here clearly indicate that applying the ITPM model to the four case studies yields a significant business benefit in understanding those factors that contributed to the success or failure of each case study. It can be concluded that the holistic approach to the project management of IT applications using the ITPM model provides a useful diagnostic tool and beneficial project management method for estimating the likelihood of project success or failure. Another finding is that the adoption of a holistic approach in IT projects improves the potential for the successful implementation of IT solutions.

This research was based on the project management experiences of the primary author. Limiting the research to the experience of one project manager clearly presents a limitation. Additional studies from other industries and a wider representation of IT applications project activities should be analyzed to further validate the conceptual model and potentially modify it with the addition of newly identified critical success factors. Additional research should be performed for different industry sectors and various organizational sizes. Small to midsize companies were not targeted in this research. Additionally there is a need to identify if the scope of the company operations (a global industry player versus a small sized national company) has any impact on the research findings.

Further validation of this research may be achieved by implementing the proposed ITPM conceptual model in future IT projects. Furthermore, it is recommended that future projects in industry leverage the findings of this research with the expectation of improving overall project success rates. Improvement to project management performance should enable companies to successfully execute their strategy, and leverage IT investments to drive business growth. In conclusion, the research reported in this paper, although applied to several cases, shows that adoption of a systemic and holistic approach to IT projects improves the potential for the successful implementation of IT solutions.

REFERENCES

A Guide to the Project Management Body of Knowledge PMBoK Guide. (2000). Newtown Square, PA: Project Management Institute (PMI).

Alreck, P. A., & Settle, R. B. (1985). *The Survey Research Handbook*. Homewood, IL: Irwin Publishers.

Charette, R. N. (2005, September). Why Software Project Fails. *IEEE Spectrum*, 42-49. Retrieved October 2006 from www.spectrum.ieee.org

Checkland, P., & Scholes, J. (1990). *Soft Systems Methodology in Action*. Chichester, UK: John Wiley & Sons, Inc.

Checkland, P., & Winter, M. (2006). Process and Content: two ways of using SSM. *The Journal of the Operational Research Society, 57*, 1435–1441. doi:10.1057/palgrave.jors.2602118

Chen, H. M., Kazman, R., & Garg, A. (2006). BITAM: An Engineering Principled Method for managing misalignments between Business and IT architectures. *Science of Computer Programming, 56*, 5–26.

Eisenhardt, K. M. (1989). Building Theories from Case Study Research. *Academy of Management Review, 14*, 532–550. doi:doi:10.2307/258557

Harmon, P. (2007). *Business Process Change: A Guide for Business Managers and BPM and Six Sigma Professionals* (2nd ed.). San Francisco, CA: Morgan Kaufman Publishers.

IT Governance Institute. (2003). *Board Briefing on IT Governance* (2nd ed.). Retrieved January 18, 2006 from http://www.isaca.org/Content/ContentGroups/ITGI3/Resources1/Board_Briefing_on_IT Governance/26904_Board_Briefing_final.pdf

Ives, M. (2005). Identifying the Contextual Elements of Project Management within Organizations and their impact on Project Success. *Project Management Journal, 36*(1), 37–50.

Jackson, M. C. (2003). *Systems thinking: Creative holism for managers*. Chichester, UK: John Wiley & Sons, Inc.

Johnson, W. J., Leach, M. K., & Liu, A. H. (1999). Theory Testing Using Case Studies in Business to Business Research. *Industrial Marketing Management, 28*(3), 201–213. doi:10.1016/S0019-8501(98)00040-6

Jugdev, K., & Muller, R. (2005). A Retrospective Look at Our Evolving Understanding of Project Success. *Project Management Journal, 36*(4), 19–31.

Kraft, T. (2009). *Business Process Alignment for Successful IT Project Management*. Saarbrücken, Germany: VDB Publishing House Ltd.

Milosevic, D., & Patanakul, P. (2004). Standard Project Management may Increase Development Project Success. *International Journal of Project Management, 23*, 181–192. doi:10.1016/j.ijproman.2004.11.002

Mingers, J. (2001). Combining IS Research Methods: Towards a Pluralist Methodology: Towards a Pluralist Methodology. *Information Systems Research, 12*(3), 240–259. doi:10.1287/isre.12.3.240.9709

Mitroff, I., & Linstone, H. (1994). *The Unbounded mind: Breaking the chains of traditional business thinking*. Oxford, UK: Oxford University Press.

Skyttner, L. (2006). *General Systems Theory: Problems, Perspective, Practice*. Hackensack, NJ: World Scientific Publishing Company. doi:10.1142/9789812774750

Stainton, R. S. (1984). Applicable Systems Thinking. *European Journal of Operational Research, 18*, 145–154. doi:10.1016/0377-2217(84)90180-2

Tesch, D., Kloppenborg, T. J., & Stemmer, J. K. (2003). Project Management Learning What the Literature Has to Say. *Project Management Journal, 34*(4), 33–39.

Tsouvalis, C., & Checkland, P. (1996). Reflecting on SSM: The Dividing line Between 'Real World', and 'Systems Thinking World'. *Systems Research, 13*(1), 35–45. doi:10.1002/(SICI)1099-1735(199603)13:1<35::AID-SRES73>3.0.CO;2-O

Visitacion, M. (2006). *What Successful Organizations Know about Project Management*. Retrieved from www.forrester.com

White, D., & Fortune, J. (2002). Current Practice in Project Management – an Empirical Study. *International Journal of Project Management, 20*. Retrieved from www.ebsevier.com. doi:10.1016/S0263-7863(00)00029-6

Yin, R. K. (2003). *Case Study Research: Design and Methods* (3rd ed.). Thousand Oaks, CA: Sage Publications.

ENDNOTE

[1] Tsouvalis, C., Checkland, P., (1996), Reflecting on SSM: The Dividing line Between 'Real World', and 'Systems Thinking World', Systems Research, 13(1), 35-45.

This work was previously published in the International Journal of Information Technologies and Systems Approach, Volume 3, Issue 2, edited by Frank Stowell and Manuel Mora, pp. 17-31, copyright 2010 by IGI Publishing (an imprint of IGI Global).

Chapter 4

The Importance of Systems Methodologies for Industrial and Scientific National Wealthy and Development

Miroljub Kljajić
University of Maribor, Slovenia

ABSTRACT

The relationship between industrial and scientific knowledge and systems methodologies is discussed in this paper. As the measure of the former on the macro level, Gross Domestic Product (GDP) is assumed to be the consequence of systems' Research and Development (R&D), which is estimated indirectly by the number of articles published in academic journals in the last 40 years. It is assumed that Production, Management and Information Systems (IS) can be considered suitable main representatives of the quality of organizational processes and that GDP is their consequence. In turn, the Systems Approach (SA), Systems Engineering (SE), Operational Research (OR), Information Systems Development (ISD) and Simulation represent the methodology set for coping with organizational complex processes. We looked for the articles containing the aforementioned variables as topic keywords in core scientific databases. Results show a sufficient correlation between the number of publications and the GDP.

INTRODUCTION

The fact that "complex systems" is one of more frequently-used terms in scientific literature indicates its importance. Our goal is to analyze the proportion of methodology and process aspect devoted to this subject in scientific journals. This is library research based on WoS publications over the last 40 years. The aim is to clarify both the relevance of R&D as well as the methodologies that contributed to the development of complex systems. From the research point of view, human activity in order to gather new knowledge can be considered from two aspects: the subject of the research itself (process) and the methodology using different methods, tools and techniques for process analyses (Mingers, 2008).

DOI: 10.4018/978-1-4666-1562-5.ch004

With a conception of complex systems, we understood a system within which a complexity of interaction among system elements plays a main role. One of the most complex systems is human-made organizations. Organizational systems are complex because production, information, management as well as psychological, social, material, financial, and energetic relations interplay between subsystems and their surroundings. The goal and interests enforce characteristics and activities that condition systems behavior and its development. Decision making is the main force for the organization of harmonious development. It comprises different activities of R&D and management processes in order to control the desired behavior as well as anticipate future behavior. A decision-making problem is a complex one since we have to deal with complex information and "… the capacity of the human mind for formulating and solving complex problems is very small compared with the size of the problem" (Simone, 1957). For this reason, systems methodology and IS for decision assessment of complex problems should play a central role (Kljajić, 2000).

It is supposed that the quality of new goods is the consequence of market-driven R&D that, as a consequence, results in income as well as in published articles in relevant journals and conferences. We looked for articles that included topics such as: Production, Management, Information systems (IS), Simulation, Systems Approach (SA), Systems Engineering SE, Operational Research (OR), which sufficiently depict correlations with GDP and carrying information on sustainable development. It was supposed that Production, Management and Information Systems are the main representatives of quality of organizational process and that GDP is their consequence, while SA, SE, OR, ISD and Simulation represent well-established methodologies for coping with complex organizational process. The argument for this can, in part, be found in the paper (Hosman et al., 2008), in which the relations between investment in IS and its impact on GDP were

analyzed. More detail about the meaning and definition of the abovementioned variables can be found in the papers (Mora et al., 2008; Petkov et al., 2008; etc,). In (Kljajić & Farr, 2008) it was found that Simulation and SA are far more dominant than other methods. In the same paper, the deep relationship among different methodological disciplines for complex systems development and maintenance is also discussed in depth. For example, SE is understood as a composition of SA and engineering of solutions for systems problems independent of the type of process. However, a SA can be also considered as an enhanced SE for complex problem solving, taking into account not only stakeholders' requirements but also the environment's requirements. That means considering a complex system from all relevant points of view in its environment during developing, maintaining and functioning. The reason for similarities and differences of methodology titles were discussed in Lazanski and Kljajić (2006). The role of the simulation methodology in the understanding of systems is constantly evolving and increasing. Currently, in modern organizations two words are dominant: change and learning, from which are derived "change management" and "learning management." Human knowledge, the simulation model and decision methodology, combined in an integral information system, offer a new standard of quality in management problem solving (Simon, 1967). The simulation model is used as an explanatory tool for a better understanding of the decision process and/or for defining and understanding learning processes. An extensive study on using the simulation method in enterprises can be found in Gopinath and Sawyer (1999). Information systems and decision support is an important area in Management Information Systems (MIS), as a part of complex SE (Mora et al., 2008).

The main goal of this paper is studying the relationship between industrial and scientific national progress/development and systems methodologies. Others studies have researched the value of of them on particular projects (Baker &

Derman, 2003; Honour, 2004) but few (if any) have addressed macro-issues. For this research macro view, a library-oriented research based on the Web of Science database (WoS) has been conducted. The aim was to clarify, the relevance of R&D and systems methodologies to national development. As the measure of system development on the macro level, we consider GDP as a consequence of Research and Development (R&D), not only in process innovation and invention but also in methodology disciplines. While GDP can be found easily in IMF and WB statistics, R&D has been estimated indirectly by the number of published articles in last 40 years (although such data can be estimated directly by the fraction of GDP devoted to investment in R&D). This article is mainly based on the data analyzed including with 2006 and presented in the paper (Kljajić, 2008). In this paper, an updated analysis is reported. However, main findings from previous research remain the same. Although systems methodologies (Simulation and System Approach) are dominant in research we argue that they slowly migrate into organizational systems. Current global ecological and economy crisis call for more intensive use of simulation and SA methodologies in studying complex phenomena for sustainable development.

METHOD

Problem Definition and Hypothesis

For the purposes of this research, the relevance of articles is understood by the number of publications per year in (WoS, 2009). It is quite natural that the frequency of use of some variables over time indicates the importance of the process described by those variables and its impact on other research areas.

For research proposes, we looked in the database for the papers that contain characteristic keywords for certain variables, including: Production, Management, Information System, Simulation etc. Such a definition is rather broad but convenient for the supposition that keywords reflect the main content of the articles. For example, if someone does research in nanotechnology with reference to production or if somebody studies the production of honey, it will be detected as a paper devoted to the variable production. Similar reasoning can be applied to each variable. We think that such a definition is natural because gathering any new knowledge through research contributes to the welfare of society.

Now we can posit the Hypothesis HA1

HA1 (alternative hypothesis): Scientific and industrial knowledge on systems methodologies (number of publications) is positively associated to national wealthy (GDP measure)

H01 (null hypothesis): Scientific and industrial knowledge on systems methodologies (number of publications) is not associated to national wealthy (GDP measure)

In order to answer the posted problem and test the hypothesis **HA1,** we defined the following variables:

- **Independent:** (papers containing topic keywords) Production, Management and IS; synonyms for Process and Simulation, SA, SE, OR and ISD; synonyms for Method.
- **Dependent:** GDP

We can write the equation $GDP = f(P, M)$, where P represents a set of variables describing Process and M a set of variables signifies methodology.

Systems View on Management and Development

In order to clarify the previously-stated hypothesis and defined variables, we will consider our problem from a very general point of view, yet specific enough for further discussion.

In nature, three basic elements Energy, Matter and Information are supposed to be universal. In organizational systems, Production (process), Management and Information can also be considered to be universal. Production is defined as the transformation process (in space and time) from elementary to complex products with new added values. Management represents a way of controlling transformation processes according prescribed tasks and goals, by means of Information (feedback and feed forward), while Information Systems metaphorically represents the central nervous systems of any organization that provides information for management. A cybernetic view of organizational systems is shown in Figure 1.

Figure 1 is self-evident: the production process results in new goods with new added value; the information from output management represents feedback for the control of prescribed and achieved performance of the goods, while information from input requirements to management represents anticipation of the future behaviors of market. From the control point of view, organizational processes can be described by (1) and (2)

$$P : X \times U \rightarrow Y \qquad (1)$$

$$M : X \times Y \rightarrow U \qquad (2)$$

where process P is the mapping of Cartesian products of input X (Market Demands) and control U (Managerial Decision) into output Y new goods, and M (Managerial Decision) represents the mapping of Cartesian products based on information about Market requirements (anticipative information) X and achieved output Y (feedback).

There is no doubt that the innovation of one product and its advantage on market is proportional to R&D capacity and that holistic organization and invention as consequence of that. That is especially important if we wish to adjust classical production to a more sustainable one. In order to test dynamic hypothesis H about the functional dependence between R&D and the welfare of one society in Figure 2, a simplified causal loop diagram (CLD) among Gross Domestic Product (GDP), R&D and Education is shown. It is supposed that GDP is proportional to the successfully realized Production on a market.

From Figure 2, on the macro level it is supposed that investment in research and education directly influence new added value of production and so to GDP. This analogy can be deduced *mutatis mutandis* at lower levels on an actual company. The explanation is trivial: from govern-

Figure 1. Cybernetic view of organizational process

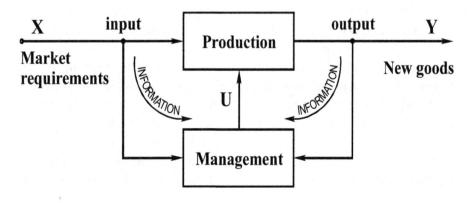

Figure 2. Model of growth: CLD diagram of relationship among production, R&D and education

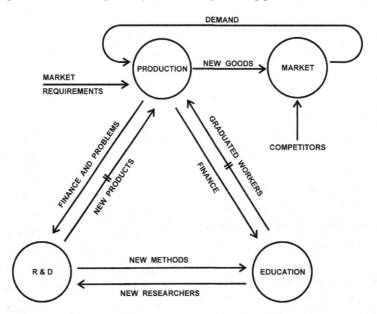

ment or firms' management, the R&D department gets money for the problem to be solved. However, R& D sends back, after a delay, new ideas and knowledge for new products. This means more money for the R&D department, allowing it to employ more new researchers, investigate new projects and equipment; consequently, innovations and new knowledge can be delivered to the corporation. Similarly, we can explain all other interactions on Figure 2, which mainly represents a positive loop characteristic for growth and development.

It is supposed that the quality of new goods as the consequence of market driven R&D had results in income as well as in publication. It is important that researchers publish their discoveries and inventions. According to Figures 1 and 2, it is supposed that articles covered by the topics of Production, Management and Information are the main representative of quality of organizational process and that GDP is their consequence, while SA, SE, OR, ISD and Simulation represent well-established methodologies for coping with complex organizational processes. In this way, we can logically establish Hypothesis H.

RESULTS

We analyzed the number of articles of the aforementioned variables published in the Web of Science database. WOS represents only articles from JCR and represents publications with strong international review. In fact, we used keywords in our research, meaning that the articles that used words "Production" in the topic are expected to deal with the context of production. We did not analyze for cross correlation among variables. This aspect was partly treated in by Kljajić and Farr (2008). Figure 3 shows the number of articles from 1970 to 2008: PROD=Production, MAN=Management and IS=Information Systems represent organization growth, while SIM=Simulation, SA, SE, OR and ISD variables represent methodology.

It is obvious that Production and Management have the largest number of articles/year and almost the same distribution while Information systems are considerable lower. It is clear that Simulation is close to the Production and Management and almost two times higher that SA, which is considerably higher than the remaining variables. A slow, almost linear growth of all variables can be

Figure 3. Number of articles over time: PROD=Production, MAN=Management, IS, SIM=Simulation, SA, SE, OR and ISD, Source WOS (2009)

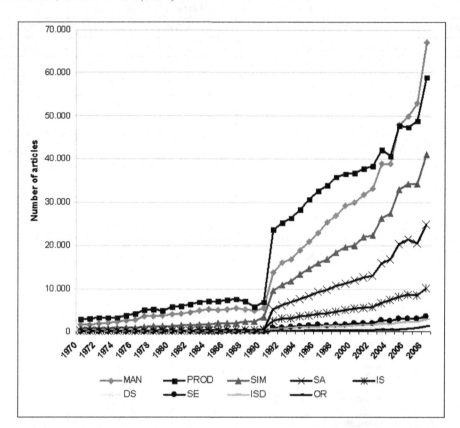

observed with a significant jump from 1990 to 1991 and then continues with growth but with a much higher gradient. Table 1 shows this dynamics of dynamics linear trends with the jump in the years 1990-91.

We suppose this change of gradient is the consequence of internet maturation and the emergence of e-business. It is obvious that Simulation and SA are far more dominant among other variables denoting methodology. This finding is in good agreement with the previous research (Kljajić & Farr, 2008). Now, Hypothesis H will be tested regarding correlation between GDP and number of published articles as defined in Section 2.

In Figure 4, the GDP of the top ten most developed countries, expressed in % of total world GDP and Simulation and SA for the same countries also expressed in % of total world publication. It

is an obvious constant relative value of all three variables. We found very high correlation between GDP and number of articles of Simulation and SA of these countries r=0.94 and r=0.95, respectively. With this, we have indirectly proved the dynamic hypothesis that the abovementioned variables are good representatives for R&D. These findings were explained by a model of growth expressed by causal loop diagram (CLD) among GDP, R&D and Education (Figure 2) as well as general control schemata of organizational systems (Figure 1). All this will be considered in light of sustainability growth. The correlation coefficient between GDP and the systems approach can explain Production as well as Simulation in 2008 by investigation into Research and Development. From Figure 4, a similar pattern can be observed among variables with the exception of China, which has a relatively

Table 1. Number of articles/year in the period from 1970 to 2008

Name of variable	Number of articles / year in the period		
	1970-1990	**1990-1991**	**1991-2008**
PROD	204	16768	2081
MAN	185	8399	3142
IS (Inf systems)	8	2172	448
SIM	102	6828	1848
SA(system or systems) appr	12	4873	1153
SE(systems or systems engineering)	1.6	2774	163
ISD information (systems or system) development	1	596	128

Figure 4. Relative value of GDP of the top ten most developed countries, for 2008 expressed in % of total word GDP and Simulation and SA for the same countries expressed in % of total world publication for 2008

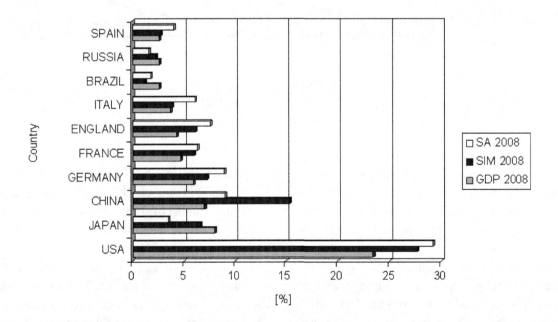

higher portion of Simulation in comparison to other countries. Such results can be interpreted as the Chinese effort to become a developed country. It is well known that using simulation for testing the performance of complex systems can reduce costs and foster development.

DISCUSSION

In order to explain the growth of the abovementioned variables from a broader aspect (from all articles in the database), we will analyze their relative changes defined as ratio of certain variables

Figure 5. Ratio of number of variable Xi and all variables per year

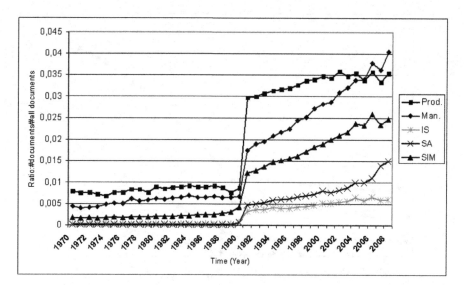

at time with all articles in data base, expressed by Equation 3.

$$r_j(k) = X_j(k) / \sum_{i=1}^{m} X_i(k), \ k = 1, 2, ...n \qquad (3)$$

The results are shown on Figure 5, where we select only most relevant variables. The shape of Figures 5 and 4 are similar, indicating that the high growth of the number of variables per year is also higher when comparing the whole database, especially after 1991. Another view of Figure 5 as the cumulative function defined by Equation 5 is shown in Figure 6.

$$R_j(k) = \sum_{1}^{k} X_j(k) / \sum_{1}^{k} \sum_{i=1}^{m} X_i(k), \ k = 1, 2, ...n$$
$$(4)$$

Equation 5 represents the ratio of cumulative value of variable X_j and the cumulative value of all variables from the database. This ratio of cumulative functions clearly shows that, in the period from 1970 to 1991, all considered variables have an almost constant value with dif-

ferent coefficients. This means that all variables in the nominator and denominator had the same proportion of growth. However, after a jump in 1991, all considered variables have positive linear increases in time with respect to all data, meaning that all considered variables became more active in comparison to the whole database.

Without intending to study the rapid growth of all considered variables in detail, we presume in the Results section that this change of gradient with jump is the consequence of internet maturation, the emergence of e-business and the importance of systems methodologies for complex systems development.

It is known that microprocessor-antecedent internet development and the internet itself is condition for radical change in IS, organization, society, ecology and also methodology development. The first two papers on the microprocessor were published in Journal from JCR in 1970 (Hornbuck & Ancona, 1970; Cook & Flynn, 1970); the next 14 articles came in the following four years. Eighteen years after first publication on microprocessors, two papers in Journal from JCR was published on the topic of the internet (Abdelwahab et al., 1988; Anon, 1988) and continue with next years

Figure 6. Cumulative ratio of number of variable Xi and all variables per year

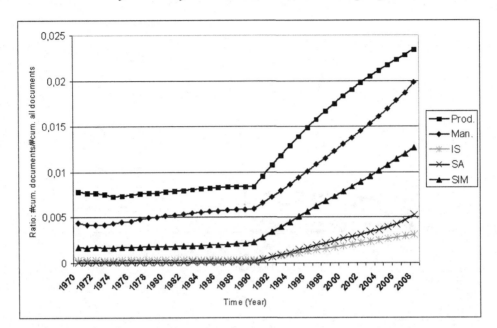

with seven articles. On Figure 7, we plotted the variables Microprocessor and Internet.

Next, Figure 8 shows the variables Simulation & Management, Simulation & Production, Internet & Simulation, Internet & Production and Internet & Management in order to show the impact of the internet in 1991 on the change of growth of our variables. It is obvious from Figure 7 and 8 that Simulation and Management, Simulation and Production as well as Microprocessor have characteristic Jump from 1990 to 1991 but first two continue to grow exponentially while Microprocessors remain constant. The first articles associated with the Internet (Internet & Management, Internet & Production and Internet & Simulation) were published in 1989 (Lu & Sundareshan, 1989; Tolcher, 1989), 1992 (Storm & Kalinoski, 1992) and 1993 (Schwartz, 1993; George & Schlecht, 1993; Mishra et al., 1993); papers on this subject continue to grow exponentially.

Again, papers on the internet starting in 1988 with Abdelwahab et al. (1988), and Anon (1988) had continuing exponential growth without a jump. Besides microprocessors, we also analyzed other well-established research topics where we found the cumulative function rather saturated. With this, we factually established that Simulation and the Systems Approach are in fact, according our definition of relevance, very important now in the research of complex systems. In order to clarify this fact on Figure 9 we show their fraction of SSCI over time. Comparing data from Figure 4 for the aforementioned variables, it is obvious that the majority of Simulation and SA articles were from the area of classical sciences (hard science) while publication of SIM an SA in social systems is relatively small (about 4%) over the last decade for Simulation and 10% for System Approach. Further analysis could find that both variables are almost uniformly distributed among Management, Economy and Operation Research & Managements. The current global ecological and economic crisis call for more intensive use of simulation and SA methodologies in studying complex phenomena for sustainable development.

The reason for importance of Simulation and SA was discussed in depth in the paper (Kljajić

Figure 7. Time course of variables/year of: Microprocessor and internet

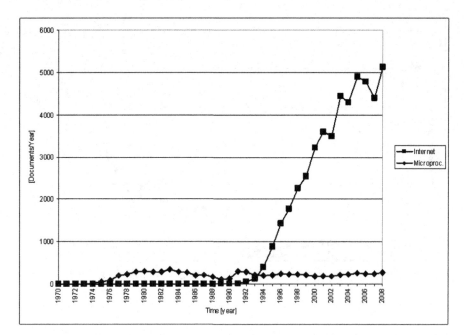

Figure 8. Variables/year over time of: Simulation and management, simulation and production, internet and simulation, internet and production and internet and management

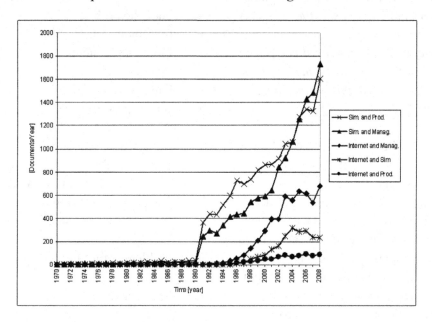

Figure 9. Variables/year over time of: Simulation and system approach in SSCI index

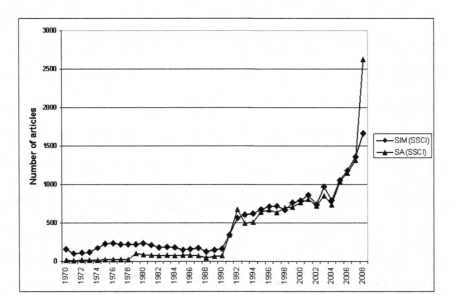

& Farr, 2008). Let us briefly repeat those findings in the light of present findings.

All classical methods initially developed for specific problems and processes converge with the development of IT and society into one holistic methodology colored with specific problems (context) and user preferences. A common name for SE or ISD can be SA or more precisely SA to SE and SE with SA as a holistic methodology for complex problem solving as we discussed in (Kljajić & Farr, 2008).

A backbone for the development of all these methods is IS based on the internet. One cannot imagine how to test reliability, stability, functioning and behavior of global (complex) systems, without SA methodology combined with systems simulation. Systems simulation is associated with two methodologies: Systems Approach and Simulation. Simulation always involves a computer for experimentation with kinds of systems methodologies, while the Systems Approach is a more abstract paradigm not necessarily dependant on a computer for simulation. To demonstrate

this statement, we will briefly compare their methodologies.

The Systems Approach paradigm can be defined as holistic methodology consisting of next interrelated steps:

- State the problem
- Investigate alternatives
- Model the system,
- Integrate,
- Launch the system,
- Assess performance,
- Re-evaluate

Which is in Bahill and Gissing (1998) was named with the acronym **SIMILAR.**

The Modeling paradigm in Computer Simulation can be stated (Forrester, 1994; Kljajić, 1994):

- Problem definition
- Goal
- Research design
- Mathematical model (block building)
- Computer program (any general or block-oriented language)

- Model validation
- Experiment set up (scenario preparation)
- Simulation and analysis

Obviously, the two paradigms are almost the same; a small difference could be observed only on the level of execution.

A more general Simulation Model SM can be defined on the set: $SM \subseteq (P, C, T, G, M)$, where P, C, G, M, T denote Problem, Context, Goal, Theory and Model; or functionally by Expression (5)

$$T : P \times C \times G \times M \rightarrow SM \qquad (5)$$

This means that SM is defined as the systems on the Cartesian product of the Problem, Goal, and Context within certain Theory. In other words, SM is the model implemented on a computer convenient for experimentation under different conditions and assumptions within a certain theory.

The advantage of the simulation model as a part of SA is in the fact that a problem defined in natural language can be easily transformed into a directed graph convenient for qualitative and quantitative analysis in computer program. In this case, the user can always check the validity of the stated problem within a certain theory and further its translation to computer programming. Furthermore, by simulation model one can, at the tentative set of assumptions, verify the model-based theory (Schwaninger & Grösser, 2008). This is important especially in cases of complex problems where feedback loops, stochastic relations and nonlinearity are present, regardless of the process being a continuous or discrete event. Big picture presentations and 3-D animation of simulated process make this technique flexible and transparent for testing systems performance of all phases of system design and deployment. With progress in ICT visual interactive modeling (VIM) and animation, modeling and simulation (M&S) have become ever more central to the development of modern systems. This has made it possible to examine the projected performance of systems over wide excursions of design and environmental assumptions very early in the development process when key resources are committed. Today's M&S tools make it possible to perform extensive enterprise and other process simulations and evaluate alternate architectures at reasonable cost and early enough to make a difference.

CONCLUSION

In this paper, the relevance of systems methodologies on the development of complex systems, which become (a part) in innovations for goods and services, which lead to nation wealthy measures (like GDP) was studied. It was investigated the number of publications per year for a set of specific topics as a measure of the utilization of systems methodologies. A library-based search was conducted on WoS database over the last 40 years for the papers containing topics characteristic for certain variables in their keywords. The relationship between GDP and R&D expressed indirectly with the number of articles published in JCR such as: Production, Management and Information systems representing organizational processes as well as Simulation, SA, SE, OR, and ISD as methodologies was discussed. It was found that Production and Management have the largest numbers of articles /year and almost the same levels. Simulation is close to the Production and Management and more than two times greater than SA, which is considerably higher than remaining considered variables. A slow, almost linear growth of all variables can be observed with a significant jump from 1990 to 1991 and then a continual rise but with a much higher gradient. This impact was attributed to the information systems based on the internet.

It was found that Simulation and SA are greatly dominant among methodologies, which is in good agreement with previous research (Kljajić & Farr, 2008). A very high correlation was found between GDP of the top ten most developed countries, and the number of articles of Simulation and SA of these countries was r= 0.94 and 0.95, respectively. With this, we indirectly prove the dynamic hypothesis that the abovementioned variables are good representatives for investigation in R&D and Education. These findings were explained by the CLD model of growth among GDP, R&D and Education and, consequently, publication of these findings. In the discussion, we have highlighted such findings, which mainly were anticipated in previous paper (Kljajić & Farr, 2008).

The advantage of the simulation model as a part of SA is in the fact that a problem defined in natural language can be easily transformed into a directed graph convenient for qualitative and quantitative analysis in computer program. In this case, the user can always check the validity of the stated problem within a certain theory and further its translation to computer programming. This is important especially in cases of complex problems where feedback loops and stochastic relations are present, regardless of the process being a continuous or discrete event. Big picture presentations and 3-D animation of simulated process make this technique flexible and transparent for testing systems performance of all phases of system design and deployment.

This has made it possible to examine the projected performance of systems over wide excursions of design and environmental assumptions very early in the development process when key resources are committed. Simulation together with the Systems Approach has become ever more central to the development of complex systems. Human knowledge and the simulation methodology combined in decision a support system offers new quality in decision making and research. In the near future, we expect that the methodologies of Simulation and System Approach should be more intensively fused into one holistic methodology: the Systems Simulation methodology and also more intensively applied on the social and ecological systems.

ACKNOWLEDGMENT

This research was supported by the Ministry of Science and Technology of the Republic of Slovenia. The author would like to express his gratitude to members of the Laboratory for Cybernetics at the Faculty of Organizational Sciences, University of Maribor for their help.

REFERENCES

Abdelwahab, H. M., Guan, S. U., & Nievergelt, J. (1988, November). Shared workspaces for group collaboration - an experiment using internet and unix interprocess communications. *IEEE Communications Magazine, 26*(11), 10–16. doi:10.1109/35.9125

Anon., (1988, August 1). A close-up of transmission control protocol internet protocol (TCP/IP). *Datamation, 34*(15), 72–72.

Bahill, A. T., & Gissing, B. (1998, November). Re-evaluating systems engineering concepts using systems thinking. *IEEE TSMC Part C-Applications and Reviews, 28*(4), 516–527.

Baker, B., & Verma, D. (2003). Systems Engineering Effectiveness: a Complexity Point Paradigm for Software Intensive Systems in the Information Technology Sector. *Engineering Management Journal, 15*(3), 29–25.

Cook, R. W., & Flynn, M. J. (1970). System design of a dynamic microprocessor. *IEEE T Comput C, 19*(3), 213. doi:10.1109/T-C.1970.222899

Forrester, J. W. (1994). System Dynamics, Systems Thinking, and Soft OR. *System Dynamics Review, 10*(2-3), 245–256. doi:10.1002/sdr.4260100211

George, J. A., & Schlecht, L. E. (1993). The NAS hierarchical network management-system. *IFIP Trans C*, *12*, 301–312.

Gopinath, C., & Sawyer, J. E. (1999). Exploring the Learning from an Enterprise Simulation. *Journal of Management Development*, *18*(5), 477–489. doi:10.1108/02621719910273596

Honour, E. (2004).Understanding the Value of Systems Engineering. In *Proceedings of the 14th International INCOSE Symposium*, Toulouse, France (pp. 1-16).

Hornbuck, G. D., & Ancona, E. I. (1970). lx-1 microprocessor and its application to real-time signal processing. *IEEE T Comput C*, *19*(8), 710. doi:10.1109/T-C.1970.223021

Hosman, L., Fife, E., & Armey, L. E. (2008). The case for a multi-methodological, cross-disciplinary approach to the analysis of ICT investment and projects in the developing world. *Information Technology for Development*, *14*(4), 308–327. doi:10.1002/itdj.20109

Kljajić, M. (1994). *Theory of system*. Kranj, Slovenia: Moderna organizacija.

Kljajić, M. (2000). Simulation Approach to Decision Support in Complex Systems. In M. Daniel (Ed.), *Proceedings of the Third International Conference on Computing Anticipatory Systems (CASYS '99) International Journal of Computing Anticipatory Systems*, Hec Liege, Belgium. Liege, Belgium: CHAOS.

Kljajić, M. (2008). Significance of simulation and systems approach methodology in development of complex systems. Lasker, G., Kljajić, M., Mora, M., Gelman, O. and Paradice, D. (eds.). Symposium on Engineering and Management of IT-based organizational systems, Baden-Baden, Germany, *Engineering and management of IT-based organizational systems: a systems approach*. Tecumseh, Ontario: The international institute for advances studies in system research and cybernetics, 34-38.

Lazanski, T. J., & Kljajić, M. (2006). Systems approach to complex systems modeling with special regards to tourism. *Kybernetes*, *35*(7-8), 1048–1058.

Kljajić, M., & Farr, J. (2008). The role of systems engineering in the development of information systems. *International Journal of Information Technologies and Systems Approach*, *1*(1), 49–61.

Lu, W. P., & nd Sundareshan, M. K. (1989, October). Secure communication in internet environments - a hierarchical key management scheme for end-to-end encryption. *IEEE T Commun*, *37*(10), 1014-1023.

Luthi, H. P., Almlof, J., Storm, W., & Kalinoski, R. (1992). TIMS/DADS - a project to develop a system of linking national and international repositories of multimedia information. *Ifla J-Int Fed Libr*, *18*(3), 223–227.

Mingers, J. (2008). Pluralism, Realism, and Truth: The keys to knowledge in information systems research. *International Journal of Information Technologies and Systems Approach*, *1*(1), 79–90.

Mishra, P. P., Sanghi, D., & Tripathi, S. K. (1993). TCP flow-control in lossy networks - analysis and enhancement. *IFIP Trans C*, *13*, 181–192.

Mora, M., Gelman, O., Moti, F., Paradice, D. B., Cervantes, F., & Forginonne, G. A. (2008). Toward an interdisciplinary engineering and management of complex IT-intensive organizational systems: A systems view. *International Journal of Information Technologies and Systems Approach*, *1*(1), 1–24.

Petkov, D., Edgar-Nevill, D., & O'Connor, R. (2008). Information systems, software engineering, and systems thinking: Challenges and opportunities. *International Journal of Information Technologies and Systems Approach*, *1*(1), 62–78.

Schwaninger, M., & Grösser, S. (2008). System Dynamics as Model-Based Theory Building. *Systems Research and Behavioral Science, 25*, 447–465. doi:10.1002/sres.914

Schwartz, M. F. (1993). Internet resource discovery at the University of Colorado. *Computer, 26*(9), 25–35. doi:10.1109/2.231273

Simon, H. (1957). *Administrative Behavior; a Study of Decision-Making Processes in Administrative Organisation*. New York: Macmillan.

Simon, H. (1967). *Model of Man* (5th ed.). John Wiley and Sons, Inc.

Tolcher, D. J. (1989). Project admiral - the management of services on an internet. *Brit Telecom Technol, 7*(1), 20–24.

WoS Expanded. (2009). *Tecumseh, Ontario: The international institute for advances studies in system research and cybernetics, 2008* (pp. 34-38). Retrieved October 28, 2009 from the world wide web.

This work was previously published in the International Journal of Information Technologies and Systems Approach, Volume 3, Issue 2, edited by Frank Stowell and Manuel Mora, pp. 32-45, copyright 2010 by IGI Publishing (an imprint of IGI Global).

Chapter 5
An Integrated Systems Approach for Early Warning and Risk Management Systems

Walter Hürster
Private Researcher and Independent Consultant, Germany

Thomas Wilbois
T-Systems, Germany

Fernando Chaves
Fraunhofer IITB, Germany

ABSTRACT

An integrated and interdisciplinary approach to Early Warning and Risk Management is described in this paper as well as the general technical implementation of Early Warning and Risk Management Systems. Based on this systems approach, a concept has been developed for the design of an Integrated System for Coastal Protection. In addition to this, as a prototype implementation of a modern environmental monitoring and surveillance system, a system for the Remote Monitoring of Nuclear Power Plants is presented here in more detail, including a Web Portal to allow for public access. The concept, the architectural design and the user interface of Early Warning and Risk Management Systems have to meet high demands. It is shown that only a close cooperation of all related disciplines and an integrated systems approach is able to fulfil the catalogue of requirements and to provide a suitable solution for environmental monitoring and surveillance, for early warning and for emergency management.

INTRODUCTION

With the upcoming global warming and resulting climate changes, it can be observed that the frequency and the severity of environmental disasters are increasing continuously, although not all of them are due to global warming. Hurricanes, heavy thunderstorms, floods and landslides, earthquakes, tsunamis, volcanic eruptions and wildfires alternate with tanker collisions, oil spills, coastal pollution and accidents in chemical or nuclear plants (accompanied by the emission of toxic

DOI: 10.4018/978-1-4666-1562-5.ch005

gases or radioactive nuclides). Independent of the originating causes, natural or anthropogenic, the latter ones ranging from careless passivity over targeted misuse up to terrorist attacks, these disasters affect human and animal populations, surface infrastructures, atmosphere and oceans in a harmful way.

The loss of human life and the tremendous damages caused by those catastrophes as well as the increasing sensitivity of the general public make it reasonable to protect the population and the environment by means of a new generation of intelligent surveillance, information, early warning and emergency management systems. This includes a highly sensitive monitoring, fast and reliable prognostic calculations, but also a timely dissemination of the relevant information to the general public within the endangered area and in adjacent regions. This challenge calls for a cooperation of academia, industry and public administration, for interdisciplinary approaches involving physicists, chemists, biologists, computer scientists, application engineers and medical staff.

INTERDISCIPLINARY COOPERATION AND INTEGRATED APPROACH

In a first step, the relevant stakeholders and experts from all related disciplines and organizations will have to meet and to produce a catalogue of requirements, as a prerequisite for a more detailed functional specification and for the technical design of the solution, including the specification of the communication links with the corresponding interfaces. Not only the technical problems but also the amalgamation of informational and communicational aspects with the organizational ones will add to the complexity of such a system. Organizational implications tend to have a serious impact on the design of the system.

Facing the complexity of the challenge, it is obvious that only a network of computers with

dedicated individual tasks and appropriate communication structures can provide a promising approach to solve the problem of monitoring, surveillance, threat prediction, decision support, early warning and emergency management. However, defining an adequate logical structure for those networks, a variety of subtasks and prerequisites have to be fulfilled in each case in order to include intelligence in various ways and to reach the goal of an integrated operational system:

- Development/integration of adequate sensor systems and sensor networks (autonomous or remotely controlled) providing data and background information. This may include mobile sensory platforms and remote sensing systems (air space surveillance and satellite systems). Figure 1 shows an example for the integration of remote sensing systems (radiological surveillance / area scan by helicopter). The variety of sensor types to be used clearly depends on the disaster type and the involved scientific disciplines. Synergy effects can be obtained by interdisciplinary cooperation, e.g. by upgrading radiological measuring stations with meteorological equipment or by using already existing meteorological stations and installing additional sensors for pollution, air quality and so on.

The subsequent tasks are:

- Advanced modelling, i.e., development/ improvement of scientific prediction models for prognostic calculations of each disaster type supporting interpretation and extrapolation of data, e.g. calculation of the atmospheric dispersion in case of NBC releases, taking into account the current meteorological situation and the expected forecast values. Similar examples are the prognostic calculation of tsunami waves based on seismological data, on hydrody-

Figure 1. Radiological surveillance, helicopter flight path

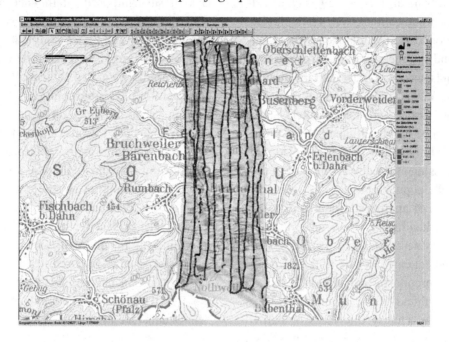

namics and 3D models of the seaground and of the coastal environment, or the formation and propagation of a flood wave in a river basin, using the actual cross section of the river, the precipitation forecast for its catchment area and the saturation of the soil, the latter depending on the precipitation in the recent past and other parameters.

- Integration of these scientific prediction modules into operational systems and definition of adequate interfaces to allow for fast response actions even under critical conditions. This implies the online availability of all relevant data and reasonable processing times for the scientific models and modules to be used. Under certain circumstances, a fast response time can be more important than an accuracy of seven digits following the decimal point.

- Integration of the functionalities provided by Geographical Information Systems (GIS) for an online situation display, using various types of geographical maps to facilitate the recognition of affected areas. A sophisticated overlay technique using semi-transparent maps may be required to generate and to combine different views.

- Development and implementation of risk analysis and decision support systems. Based on sensor data, prognostic calculations and disaster specific experience, an "intelligent" system may provide a number of alternatives for actions to be taken – in each case depicting the consequences of the corresponding action.

- Development/improvement and inclusion of knowledge management components (in general and disaster specific) to integrate the long-term experience of experts and observations made in the past – a challenging task for computer scientists and artificial intelligence, but hopefully providing the "golden" recommendation for the measures to be taken.

- Definition of adequate information, alarm and warning strategies, using the full range of state-of-the-art technology, such as satellite communications, web technologies, radio broadcast, TV, telephone (fixed network and mobile systems), siren systems and loudspeakers. Under certain circumstances, even "old fashioned" devices, such as sirens and loudspeakers, have proven to be highly efficient - by combining a minimum delay time of the alert with an addressing efficiency of almost 100 percent of the population.

- Definition of appropriate interfaces to catastrophe handling and resource management subsystems (transport facilities, shelters, medical care....). The fastest alert and the best prognostic calculation is bound to be worthless, if the communication is impeded by clumsy interfaces or baffled by incompatible or non existing links. Therefore, highest attention has to be paid to the interoperability of the connected subsystems.

- Definition of the operational environment and of the organizational background. It is essential to clarify the operational responsibilities in the very early phase of the project. The same holds for the provision of the necessary data, for access privileges and related topics. The interdisciplinary approach on the scientific side will have to be met by its organizational counterpart, i.e. cooperation across the involved organizations and interoperability of the connected (sub)systems.

APPLICATION OF THE HOLISTIC SYSTEMS APPROACH: THE CONCEPT FOR AN INTEGRATED SYSTEM FOR COASTAL PROTECTION

The present situation with respect to coastal protection is (in many countries) characterized by a lack of superimposed intelligence, recognition of the situation, co-ordination, communication and integration of the existing subsystems and sources of information. Therefore, it is indicated to choose an integrated, essentially centralized approach for a possible solution.

One essential component of such an integrated system for coastal protection will be a central data and communication platform where all relevant data streams converge and which can act as an information turntable and distributor for the connected subsystems. It can also serve as a knowledge base for spread information thus providing the metadata of external sources that can be accessed, if required.

Then, connected with this platform, there are the following main functional components or subsystems (see Figure 2):

- Surveillance
- Threat analysis and situation display
- Alarm function (early warning and alarm raising)
- Emergency management

Surveillance here primarily means surveillance of vessel traffic, but also surveillance of the air space and of maritime pollution (e.g., oil slicks). Various types of sensor systems, including mobile sensor platforms, are to be used for this purpose (helicopters, marine patrol aircraft, satellites).

In addition to online representation of the current situation, a threat analysis has to be accomplished if indicated by the danger situation at hand. This could, e.g., require collision calculations and collision warnings for vessel traffic, as well as calculations for the dispersion of harmful substances in the water, on the surface and in the atmosphere. In doing so, the current meteorological and hydrographical data will have to be taken into account as well as their forecast values. Contributions from biology, chemistry and medicine are very essential at this step.

Figure 2. Integrated system for coastal protection

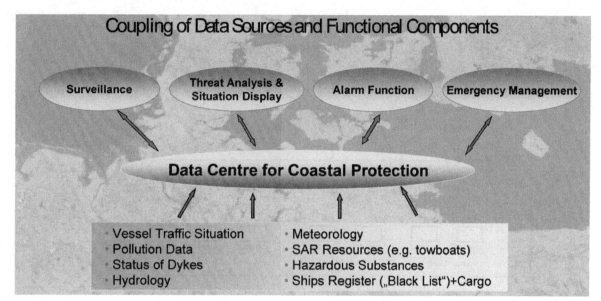

With respect to early warning, alarm raising and information of the public, all usable and widespread systems of telecommunication and media technology have to be applied.

Computer supported emergency management means in particular digitized emergency protocols with a suitable representation on geographical maps as well as numerous status overviews (dykes, embankments, evacuation areas, emergency sheltering capabilities, traffic routes, means of transportation, hospitals, ambulances, mission and SAR vehicles, etc.)

An additional and essential feature of computer support is simulation, i.e. the possibility to prepare mission scenarios, to modify them and to run them as a training exercise for emergency management.

Finally, there remains to be mentioned the fact that effective coastal protection is only possible if international data exchange takes place among the different systems of neighboring coastal countries, fulfilling the requirements of early recognition of danger situations and mission co-ordination across national boundaries.

THE UNIVERSAL STRUCTURE OF THE SYSTEM

After having applied the holistic systems approach to the concept for an integrated system for coastal protection, it was straightforward to generalize the structure that has been found to the basic structure of a combined system for various types of threats.

The proposed logical structure of such a combined system is shown in Figure 3 in the form of a Local Area Network (LAN), although some components may be linked together physically by means of a Wide Area Network (WAN), depending on the actual needs of the system under construction.

It is strongly recommended to use a communication server to handle the input data streams from various sensor systems and sensor networks and to convert different data formats, if necessary. This server may also handle the connection to external information networks. In case of higher system loads or larger systems, a specific server computer may be used for this purpose, e.g., a dedicated web server.

Figure 3. Structure of the system

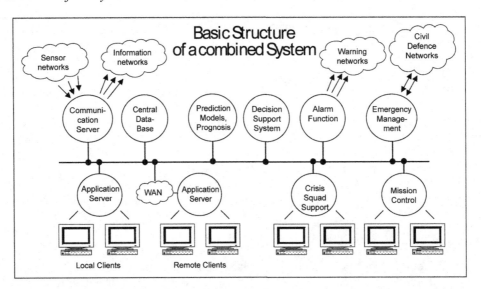

Since most of the data are usually needed for central access, the concept of a central database has been confirmed by practical experience. The distribution of specific subsets of the data for decentralized use (e.g., remote application servers) can be achieved by means of dedicated replication functions.

Prediction models and prognostic calculations, such as those for the atmospheric dispersion of toxic gases or radionuclides, tend to need large sets of data and therefore are also best served by a central access. However, since they also tend to require high computing power, it is only advantageous to run them on a dedicated server. Agent technologies and service access layer ontologies have proven to be most suitable for the integration of the various scientific components into an operational system.

Decision support systems, based on data describing the actual situation as well as the prognostic development, will reflect the implications for the population in the affected areas and thus help the crisis squad to make their decisions. These systems will have to include advanced knowledge management components and sets of metadata providing access to the long-term disaster specific experience of experts and to observations made in the past.

The increasing sensitivity of the general public and the enhanced public awareness of environmental threats call for Web-based information systems. Therefore, and in order to allow for public access to the system, it is recommended to provide a Web Portal. This portal function may be collocated with the communication server. However, based on fail safe considerations and for security reasons, it is most recommendable to run it on a separate server, too.

THE WEB PORTAL

There is no doubt that the elementary backbone of an early warning and risk management system is represented by the operational kernel. However, due to the increasing importance of web services, the portal function deserves some brief but special consideration. More detailed technical descriptions are given by Hürster et al. (2006, 2007).

Different user groups and stakeholders have different specific needs and therefore emphasize different aspects of the system. The following user groups can be identified and categorized (see Figure 4):

- Administrative Sector
- Operational Sector
- Restricted Public Sector
- Public Sector

The administrative sector covers the system administration, maintenance of configuration lists, adaptation and optimization of the system itself and of the related workflows.

The operational sector deals with the main task of the system, i.e., surveillance and monitoring functions, display of the current and prognostic situation, risk assessment and decision support.

The restricted public sector will provide the necessary information for the crisis squad, for public services (the staff of rescue forces, fire brigades etc.) and all other authorities responsible for civil protection. This may contain confidential information or security related orders which are not foreseen for public disclosure, e.g., in order to avoid panic reactions and pillage.

Finally, the public sector will serve as an information platform for the general public, giving an overview about the current threat situation, exposure risks and the development of these risks. The public sector will also provide general and specific recommendations in case of an imminent dangerous situation.

The large extent and the complexity of the available information combined with various views of diverse user groups call for specific selection and preparation of the data for display in graphical and/or tabular form (depending on the user group). This is the core point for the design and implementation of the Web Portal: to provide for each user group a specific set of web pages which contains the information needed to achieve the assigned tasks in the best way possible.

By analyzing the required functionalities and the customer needs, a more detailed set of requirements can be derived, as described and listed by Hürster et al. (2007).

Further requirements can be deduced from the demand for reliability and high performance of

Figure 4. Basic concept, overview and structure

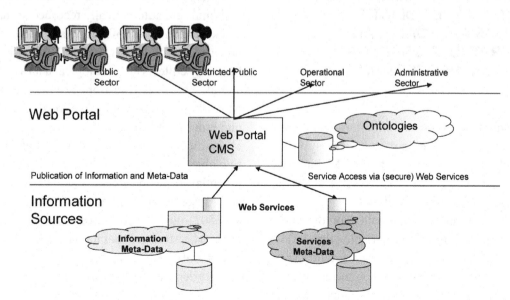

the portal. In any case, a highly reliable network infrastructure with good performance will have to be provided.

A typical publication of web reports may a.o. include the following information:

- Protective measures, including their representation on geographical maps
- Evacuation areas/safe areas and their current availability status
- Overview of arterial roads, traffic flow and means of transportation (incl. status information)
- Layout plans for assembly and collecting points in case of collective transports
- Emergency stations for medical care, including hospital trains and hospital ships
- Overview of regular hospitals and medical centres (incl. status and capacity information)
- Layout plans of schools, kindergartens and retirement homes
- Layout plans of emergency sheltering capabilities, such as gymnasiums, roof covered stadiums

REFERENCE IMPLEMENTATION BASED ON THE HOLISTIC SYSTEMS APPROACH: AN INTEGRATED SYSTEM FOR RADIATION PROTECTION

As a prototype example for the implementation of a modern environmental monitoring and surveillance system, based on the holistic systems approach, a system for the Remote Monitoring of Nuclear Power Plants (RM/NPP) shall be presented here in more detail.

This system includes the collection of radiological and meteorological variables that influence the diffusion and deposition of radioactive nuclides. A central role of the monitoring system is the use of these variables in the calculation of radiation exposure values and areas. These results are used for decision support, dissemination of information and the issuing of public warnings.

In the event of an imminent, occurring or already terminated release of radioactive nuclides, safety measures pertaining to disaster control and the provision of radiation protection could be required. For instance, the distribution of iodine tablets or a precautionary evacuation are included among these measures.

In its role as a supervisory authority for the nuclear facilities (Obrigheim, Philippsburg and Neckarwestheim) in the Federal State of Baden-Württemberg, Germany, and for foreign facilities close to the German border (Fessenheim/France and Leibstadt/Switzerland), the Ministry of Environment in Baden-Württemberg has been operating such a remote monitoring system for nuclear power plants for almost 20 years. Recently, the system has been completely renewed using modern hardware platforms and software technologies (Obrecht et al., 2002; Hürster et al., 2005).

As described by Hürster et al. (2005), the RM/NPP is a complex measuring and information system which records and monitors approximately 20 million data sets per day. The actual operational state of the nuclear facilities including their radioactive and non-radioactive emissions are automatically recorded around the clock, independently of the operator of the nuclear power plant. In addition, the RM/NPP system continuously collects meteorological data at the sites and also receives data from external measuring networks (national and international). It provides numerous possibilities to visualize the data and to check them against threshold values and protection objectives. In the case of a radioactive leak, potentially affected areas can be determined at an early stage by a transport calculation (Schmidt et al., 2002) and protective measures can be adopted by the Ministry in cooperation with the authorities responsible for civil protection.

In order to allow for a broader but selective access to the information kept within the Operational

System, the decision was taken by the Ministry to establish a web access function by means of a dedicated Web Portal (Hürster et al., 2006). Similar applications are envisaged by the Federal States Baden-Württemberg and Saxony-Anhalt in order to open the access to general environmental information, as imposed by legislation (Schlachter et al., 2006).

Both, the operational system and the web portal have been designed and developed in accordance with the logical structures described above (see Land Baden-Württemberg, 2004; Wilbois & Chaves, 2005). The client software offers numerous possibilities to visualize the data by means of a modern graphical user interface with GIS functions. It also provides standardized export interfaces to office and graphical applications.

For demonstration purposes, a first prototype version of the Web Portal has been implemented which is being intensively used and is therefore considered to be highly accepted by the user groups. Actually, an animated presentation of a propagation cloud has been selected thus illustrating the results of a Dispersion Modelled Transport Calculation (DMTC) for radio nuclides (Figure 5). This type of calculation has to be carried out in case of a radioactive incident or accident and the result is of greatest importance for radiological protection and emergency management.

THE IMPORTANCE OF THE HOLISTIC, INTERDISCIPLINARY SYSTEMS APPROACH IN THE REMOTE MONITORING OF NUCLEAR POWER PLANTS

Nuclear physics, thermodynamics, electrical engineering and radiology though are not sufficient, when dealing with the operation of nuclear power plants. In addition, the collection of the significant meteorological variables (with influence on diffusion and deposition of radioactive nuclides) and the calculation of radiation exposure in the vicinity of nuclear power plants constitutes a central responsibility of a remote monitoring system for nuclear power plants, especially regarding the determination of the affected area and decision support.

For instance, the as-precise-as possible determination of precipitation patterns is an essential factor in the wet deposition of radioactive nuclides, which (as a logical consequence) has a considerable influence on radiation exposure ("hot spots"). The precipitation events in the southern part of Germany during the Tchernobyl nuclear accident are a prominent example of this. By precipitant washout, these rainfalls contributed to a considerably stronger deposition of radioactive nuclides south of the Danube River in Bavaria and Upper Swabia than in the rest of Germany. Therefore taking into account an inhomogeneous distribution of precipitation considerably increases the quality of dispersal calculation results.

In order to be able to carry out a reliable risk assessment it is even necessary to expand the meteorological basis — in terms of space (supraregional data) and time (prognostic data). Adding the biological and medical considerations (which are not described here), this emphasizes once more the importance of an interdisciplinary cooperation as suggested by the holistic systems approach.

CONCLUSION

Due to the increasing importance of early warning and emergency management systems and recognizing the great attention paid to the subject by a sensitive general public, a large number of initiatives and projects on a national, international and even global scale are searching for adequate solutions. It has been shown that, based on an interdisciplinary and holistic systems approach and on a detailed requirements analysis, an integrated concept for Early Warning and Risk Management Systems can been derived. In a logical sequence, an IT concept has been produced in accordance

Figure 5. Propagation cloud on the background of a topographical map

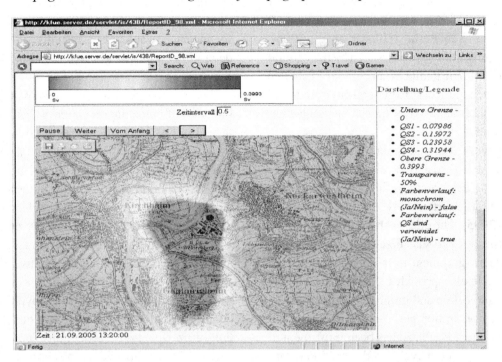

with the integrated concept and with the aim to fulfil the identified requirements to the largest possible extent. The feasibility of the concepts has been proven by the application to an Integrated System for Coastal Protection and by the prototype implementation for the Remote Monitoring of Nuclear Power Plants.

The reference implementation of the operational system and the pilot installation of a Web Portal received a great deal of interest from the user groups. The actual value received by the stakeholders was confirmed to be high and the good cooperation with the representatives from all involved disciplines gives rise to an optimistic view for further developments and implementations.

Having started with coastal protection and with radiation protection (including the related emergency management), we are confident that the system structure presented here can significantly contribute to a general solution for the indicated problems. The proof will be left to international multi risk scenarios and corresponding across border exercises, based on extended ITC networks on a large scale.

ACKNOWLEDGMENT

The system "Remote Monitoring of Nuclear Power Plants" was contracted to T-Systems by the Federal State of Baden-Württemberg, Ministry of Environment, as a turnkey system, with the integrated service "DMTC" provided by the Institut für Kernergetik und Energiesysteme (Institute for Nuclear Energetics and Energy Systems) of the University of Stuttgart (IKE). The research work related to the development and integration of the DMTC was supported by the Ministry of Environment within the framework "Environmental Information System" Baden-Württemberg. The underlying program modules of the DMTC were taken from the library of the OECD Nuclear Energy Agency.

REFERENCES

W3C. (2002). *Web Services Description Language (WSDL), World Wide Web Consortium (W3C), Web Services Description Working Group*. Retrieved November 19, 2009 from http://www.w3.org/2002/ws/desc/

W3C (2005, January 7). The Synchronized Multimedia Integration Language (SMIL 2.0) (2nd ed.). Presented at the *World Wide Web Consortium (W3C)*. Retrieved November 19, 2009 from http://www.w3.org/AudioVideo/

Chaves, F., Wilbois, T., & Grinberg, E. (2005). *IT-Konzept für die Erstellung eines KFÜ-Portals.* Karlsruhe, Germany: Fraunhofer IITB.

Hürster, W. (2005). Remote Monitoring of Nuclear Power Plants in Baden-Württemberg, Germany. In Hilty, L., Seifert, E., & Treibert, R. (Eds.), *Information Systems for Sustainable Development* (pp. 333–341). Hershey, PA: IGI Global.

Hürster, W. (2006). A Web Portal for the Remote Monitoring of Nuclear Power Plants. In Tatnall, A. (Ed.), *Encyclopaedia of Portal Technology and Applications* (pp. 1151–1156). Hershey, PA: IGI Global.

Hürster, W., et al. (2007). A Web Portal for Early Warning and Risk Management. In M. Khosrow-Pour (Ed.), *Managing Worldwide Operations and Communications with Information Technology, Proceedings of the 2007 IRMA International Conference,* Vancouver, BC, Canada (pp. 497-501). Hershey, PA: IGI Global.

Land Baden-Württemberg. (2004). *Das Corporate Design im Internet, Styleguide für das Landesportal und die Ministerien-Websites, mit allgemeinen Regelungen zur Gestaltung weiterer Auftritte (Stand 07/2004).* Stuttgart, Germany: Land Baden-Württemberg.

Moßgraber, J. (2005). *Entwicklungshandbuch für WebGenesis (Version 7.10).* Karlsruhe, Germany: Fraunhofer IITB.

Obrecht, R. (2002). KFÜ BW - Erneuerte Kernreaktorfernüberwachung in Baden-Württemberg. In Mayer-Föll, R., Keitel, A., & Geiger, W. (Eds.), *Projekt AJA, Anwendung JAVA-basierter Lösungen und anderer leistungsfähiger Lösungen in den Bereichen Umwelt, Verkehr und Verwaltung – Phase III 2002 (Wissenschaftliche Berichte FZKA-6777).* Karlsruhe, Germany: Forschungszentrum Karlsruhe.

Schlachter, T. (2006). Environmental Portals of the federal states of Baden-Wuerttemberg and Saxony-Anhalt with access to the administrative environmental information. In Tatnall, A. (Ed.), *Encyclopaedia of Portal Technology and Applications.* Hershey, PA: IGI Global.

Schmidt, F. (2002). KFÜ-ABR – Weiterentwicklung des Dienstes Ausbreitungsrechnung in der Kernreaktor-Fernüberwachung Baden-Württemberg. In Mayer-Föll, R., Keitel, A., & Geiger, W. (Eds.), *Projekt AJA, Anwendung JAVA-basierter Lösungen und anderer leistungsfähiger Lösungen in den Bereichen Umwelt, Verkehr und Verwaltung – Phase III 2002 (Wissenschaftliche Berichte FZKA-6777).* Karlsruhe, Germany: Forschungszentrum Karlsruhe.

Wilbois, T., & Chaves, F. (2005). *Fachkonzept für die Erstellung eines KFÜ-Portals.* Karlsruhe, Germany: Fraunhofer IITB.

This work was previously published in the International Journal of Information Technologies and Systems Approach, Volume 3, Issue 2, edited by Frank Stowell and Manuel Mora, pp. 46-56, copyright 2010 by IGI Publishing (an imprint of IGI Global).

Chapter 6
Software Development Life Cycles and Methodologies:
Fixing the Old and Adopting the New

Sue Conger
University of Dallas, USA

ABSTRACT

Information Systems as a discipline has generated thousands of research papers, yet the practice still suffers from poor-quality applications. This paper evaluates the current state of application development, finding practice wanting in a number of areas. Changes recommended to fix historical shortcomings include improved management attention to risk management, testing, and detailed work practices. In addition, for industry's move to services orientation, recommended changes include development of usable interfaces and a view of applications as embedded in the larger business services in which they function. These business services relate to both services provided to parent-organization customers as well as services provided by the information technology organization to its constituents. Because of this shift toward service orientation, more emphasis on usability, applications, testing, and improvement of underlying process quality are needed. The shift to services can be facilitated by adopting tenets of IT service management and user-centered design and by attending to service delivery during application development.

INTRODUCTION

Information Systems as a discipline is over 60 years old. Over that time, practices have been created and forgotten almost as fast as the technology has changed. An enormous amount of research has produced thousands of research papers relating to information systems development, with many seminal breakthroughs by luminaries such as Avison, Bjorn-Anderson, Boehm, Booch, Brooks, Checkland, Codd, Date, De Marco, Dijkstra, Fitzgerald, Gregor, Hoare, Jackson, Lyytinen, Martin, Mumford, Osterweil, Parnas, Rumbaugh, Schneiderman, Weber, Yourdon and many others.

DOI: 10.4018/978-1-4666-1562-5.ch006

Even with the thousands of research projects, the track record of information technology (IT) in organizations is dismal. The "IT Department is a source of tremendous frustration, missed opportunity, and inefficiency in companies" (Baschob & Piott, 2007, p. 11). By one report in 1994, 53% of projects overran original schedules by an average of 222% (Baschob & Piott, 2007). In addition, 31% of projects were cancelled. Completion of projects on time and within budget in large companies was 9% and only 42% of all projects delivered planned benefits (Baschob & Piott, 2007). The situation is such that the IT-business relationship is characterized as hostile in many situations (Agar, et al., 2007; Avison & Gregor, 2009).

Even with the huge body of research, some IT failures are due to goals that outstrip the techniques and technology of the time. The desire for greater software integration across enterprises, use of leading-edge technologies, and increasing complexity of IT operations technology all have contributed to project failures (Boehm, 2006).

Accompanying the technological aspects of applications that continuously change and get more complex, business too is changing. The current changes business is undergoing are to servitize business operations such that physical products are accompanied by, or embedded in, revenue-generating services. The move to services in the U.S. economy alone is such that over 85% of the economy is involved in service delivery of some type (Gallagher et al., 2005). As a result, IT that supports business service delivery has become desirable.

At the same time that service orientation is becoming important in business, IT Departments are under pressure to demonstrate their value to their organizations. Statements like, 'do more with less,' 'learn to run IT like a business,' and 'join the rest of the company' demonstrate the pressures on IT organizations (Conger & Schultze, 2008; Cuyler & Schatzberg, 2003). This confluence of pressures, change of emphasis, and history of failures is useful to force self-reflection on the profession to determine its next steps to develop a better rapport with its customers, improve the quality of its offerings, and demonstrate its value to its parent organization.

This paper reflects on the history of software development and its role in the present state of IT in organizations. The discussion focuses on software development life cycles (SDLC) and methodologies and their roles and outcomes as contributing to the pervasive failing state of IT. Key successes and failings are identified to establish a baseline for discussion of how to remedy past weaknesses and improve to address current needs. Then, tenets of design science are adapted to application development issues to discuss needs for changes in practice to adapt to the business shift to services. The outcome is a series of recommendations for academics and professionals to reinvent IT to develop holistic IT services to align more closely to the business services they support.

SDLCS AND METHODOLOGIES

The most common way of thinking of the SDLC is the waterfall model within which phases of activity are defined based on the thought processes required to conduct the activities (see Figure 1) (Royce, 1972). Output of each phase is input to the next phase. Phases historically included the following with the key focus in parentheses: feasibility (readiness), analysis (what), design (how), detailed design (how), coding and unit testing (technology), testing (correctness), and implementation (transition to operation). Ongoing maintenance accounts for about 80% of an application's life cycle cost and follows each phase but with a narrower scope than the whole application. In this model, application development ceases at implementation with little attention to use of the application in its various contexts.

The traditional waterfall outcome is an entire application. Waterfall alternatives are iterative,

Figure 1. Waterfall software development phases (Adapted from Royce, 1970)

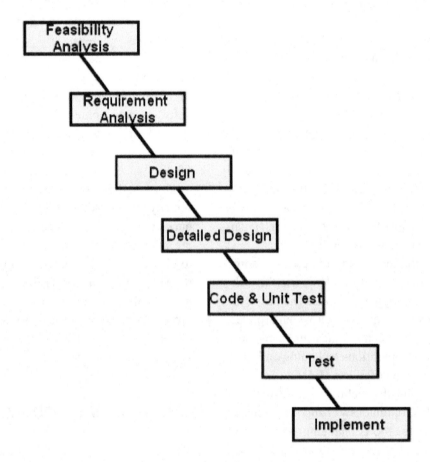

non-sequential ways of performing the work such as spiral, prototype, and agile (Boehm, 1998; Beck et al., 2001). Waterfall alternatives are non-sequential development sequences, by which waterfall steps are done on partial functionality with iterations until all functionality is automated. Both of these views of application development focus on application functionality, as opposed to other aspects of the application such as its operational environment, its usability, or its social context. Some authors consider SDLC and prototyping as methodologies (e.g., Avison & Fitzgerald, 2006), while others view them as skeletal guidelines within which methodologies operate (Conger, 1994). The latter view is taken by this research.

A methodology is the tenets, tools, philosophy, and so on about how to approach problem analysis and design. Within a life cycle stage, a methodology guides the work via tools and techniques, focusing analysis on a specific aspect of the work (see Figure 2). Commonly used methodologies foci include process (DeMarco, 1978; Yourdon & Constantine, 1975), data (Jackson, 1975; Martin, 1991), objects (Jacobson et al., 1999), or stakeholders and the social context (Checkland, 1981).

Criticisms of all of these life cycles and methodologies abound. The most condemning statement is that they appear to make no difference to the resulting quality of an application (Avison & Fitzgerald, 2006). Another is that every focus on

Figure 2. Perspectives from life cycles and methodologies

Charact-eristic	Life Cycles		Methodologies	
	Sequential SDLC	Iterative SDLC-- -Prototype, Agile	Soft Systems Methods –	Process, Data, Object Method –
Purpose	Design and implementation of work support systems	Focus on functionality and/or timing of delivery	Focus on contexts and stakeholder rights	Focus on area of interest
Goal	Complete functionality	On time, short-term delivery of partial functionality	Contextualized design	Focus on area of complexity to ensure its correctness
Perspective	Design thought processes	This period's functionality	Organization, information, technology, and socio-technical aspects of the problem	Functional quality of the most complex aspect

one aspect of an application results in ignoring, constraining, or assuming other aspects of the application (Boehm, 2006; Suchman, 1983).

Research on application and software development, methodologies, and SDLC, has led to many discussions of what is wrong with life cycles and methods and invariably, what is next (Avison & Fitzgerald, 2003; Fitzgerald & Fitzgerald, 1999). One answer to that issue is the addition of service perspective to parallel the economic changes to service orientation. Yet, to add new requirements on top of failing work is illogical. Therefore, further assessment of the successes and failures of SDLCs and methodologies is needed to determine what is needed to improve application quality.

Figure 2 summarizes the SDLCs and methodologies to identify their focus and perspective as these constrain how the problem is perceived and, therefore, how the problem is automated. Followers of the waterfall life cycle develop whole applications, decomposing the problem into phases that reflect the thinking for each phase. In contrast, iterative SDLCs focus on chunks of an application and the current period's functionality. By taking a piecemeal view of applications, the

iterative SDLCs often result in partially built software that experiences difficulty with integration of later-developed functionality (Abrahamsson et al., 2002; Boehm, 2006).

Soft Systems methods originate from Checkland (1981) and are expanded by Wood-Harper and others (Doyle et al., 1993). The focus of Soft Systems is the social system as a basis for change that results in an application. The Soft Systems approach views application development as a cultural activity inclusive of as many stakeholders as can be accommodated, and therefore, can drag on without progress for long periods. Contradictions arise when different groups air their priorities and the contradictions can be difficult to resolve (Mathiassen & Nielsen. 1989). Once complete, Soft Systems applications result in high levels of user satisfaction (Checkland, 1981). Soft Systems highlights the importance of situated work that requires attention by IT of both the automated and non-automated aspects of the work (Suchman, 1983).

Process, data and object methods are grouped because they all focus attention on a key area of complexity in the application as functionality, data, or objects, respectively. Object methods have matured somewhat and morphed into service oriented architectures (SOA) but object concepts and focus do not change in SOA. As a focusing mechanism, these methodologies function as intended. However, these methodologies constrain thinking in the same way as the SDLCs and other methods through the very focus they seek. By focusing on functionality, the social system, interface design, or other aspects of an application may be ignored.

All of the SDLCs and methodologies have shortcomings as a group in that they provide tools and techniques without providing an overall checklist of what should be evaluated and considered within the context of applications development. Moreover, the SDLCs and methodologies alone do not give clues about how to fix the failures of application development let alone how to improve it to deal with today's application needs. The next section looks at successes and failures in application development practice to determine the characteristics most needed in successful applications.

APPLICATION DEVELOPMENT

With all of the failures of information systems, we sometimes forget that there are also impressive successes. The aerospace and defense industries have sent and returned people to the moon and kept bombs from exploding before their time. Virtually every home device has imbedded computer chips, which run appliances and simplify our lives. These successes have many characteristics in common. These characteristics may vary by type of application but some characteristics cross application types.

Successes in Application Development

Systems success is best summarized by the De-Lone and McLean success model (1992, 2003; Petter et al., 2008), which found the constructs of importance in Figure 3.

DeLone and McLean built on hundreds of other research projects to develop both a parsimonious list of critical factors that generally fits all applications. The details of each characteristic is beyond the scope of this paper, but the key drivers are of interest because they span applications types in some form with many sub-factors seeming to be universal, as well. Three types of quality are expected of successful applications: System, information and service. Systems quality refers to the application in its operational environment and the extent to which it performs at the time needed and in the manner expected. System quality is important because inattention to system quality early in the development cycle can easily result in poor quality upon implementation.

Information quality refers to the suitability and usefulness of the data provided to the user. Information quality in any transactional system needs to be complete and accurate. Similarly, relevant, secure data seem to be universally appropriate across application types.

Service quality also may be appropriate for all applications but in a different sense than expressed by the sub-factors provided here. The sub-factors in the De Lone and McLean list are from SERVQUAL, a well researched model of service quality in an online environment (Parasuraman et al., 1988). SERQUAL needs additional research to determine characteristics that fit other arenas of IT support. For instance, extensions to SERVQUAL to adapt measures of quality from the total quality movement might be appropriate.

Figure 3. Key drivers of successful information systems (adapted from DeLone & McLean, 2003, p. 26)

Key Driver	Sub-Characteristics
Systems quality	Adaptability Availability Reliability Response time Usability
Information quality	Completeness Ease of understanding Personalization Relevance Security
Service quality	Assurance Empathy Responsiveness
Use	Nature of use Navigation patterns Number of site visits Number of transactions executed
User satisfaction	Repeat purchases Repeat visits User surveys
Net benefits	Cost savings Expanded markets Incremental additional sales Reduced search costs Time savings

In a broad services context, service quality refers to overall quality provided by the 'system' and can include the application, help desk, maintenance staff, and others in the IT Department who might interact with users for some reason. Specifics of services are not yet incorporated into service quality research or measures. Thus, a more general view of services, which is consistent with servitizing tenets (Van Bon, 2007) indicates a need for expansion of SERVQUAL for IT services management quality. Gap analysis to evaluate expectations versus attributes of objective product, specific characteristics of service quality (e.g., help desk resolves problem during first contact), definition of customer benefits, and usefulness are other potential additions to SERVQUAL that may improve its applicability to information systems (Chen & Sorenson, 2007). Further, contextual-

izing service concepts may lead to more accurate measures of service. For instance, in e-commerce, service and system quality are interwoven and no known research has teased out the nuances of their differences.

User satisfaction also is a well-researched area but it has little research relating user satisfaction across application types. The complexity of attitudes and the nature of the application types, designs, and possibly other factors may impact user satisfaction (Melone, 1990). Therefore, while the concept seems relevant across all applications, the details of its measurement as presently operationalized need further contextualization.

The final component of applications success, net benefits, also seems to apply across the board to all applications. The concept of net benefits in terms of evaluating business outcomes is not new but has been elusive and difficult to quantify (Brynolffson & Hitt, 2003). Research on how individual IT efforts relate to, support, and ultimately contribute to business outcomes is critical as IT struggles to remain relevant to its parent organization (c.f., Cuyler & Schatzberg, 2003).

Thus, even though De Lone and McLean's success model and SERVQUAL measures appear to have significant carryover across application types, more research is needed to contextualize their constructs (Petter et al., 2008).

Failures in Application Development

By examining SDLC and methodological failures, we can back into a definition of what leads to successful implementations. The shortcomings are not simple however, as SDLCs and methodologies are not the only issues. This section examines failings of IT development and acquisition organizations, and thereby, determine what aspects, if done some other way, could contribute to success. In addi-

tion, research on information systems risks also is relevant to failure discussions because risks not attended to are likely to lead to failures of the resulting information systems.

Confusion about SDLCs and Methodologies

From a standards perspective, there are simply too many standards relating to SDLCs and methodologies. By one count, there are over 1,000 methodologies alone (Avison & Fitzgerald, 2006). This quagmire of differing descriptions of essentially the same things, all with different breadth, depth, and focus, is a source of significant confusion. Figure 4 shows just standards of the International Standards Organization (ISO), the Institute of Electrical and Electronics Engineers (IEEE), and U.S. Department of Defense and their intellectual linkages.

Figure 5 shows one description of the full extent to which whole bodies of knowledge relat-

Figure 4. Software development frameworks c. 2000 (Doran, 2000, p. 3)

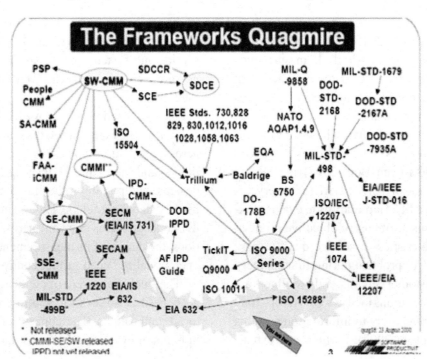

ing to many hundreds of methodologies and life cycles proliferate (Boehm, 2006). It also shows the development of information systems as a profession that has adapted and changed to deal with the overriding complexity of each decade. For instance, the craft of programming gave way to structured methods, which morphed into productivity-oriented frameworks, that then needed to deal with concurrency, increased pressures for productivity, and eventually, global connectivity.

As these figures depict, the linkages and profusion of frameworks foster confusion more than understanding. Companies trying to determine which, if any, method or SDLC is right for a single project often abandon the search when faced with the variety of available choices. Some authors recommend evaluating the suite of alternatives to develop the set of techniques, tools, life cycle, and methods that best fit the problem (Brinkkemper, 1996). But, as a result of confusion relating to the plethora of tools, techniques, methods, and so on, companies that do use methodologies often select one, using it as the guiding outline for all project work. This practice leads to the second major shortcoming: Practice failings.

Practice Failings

Several practice failings are discussed in this section. First, the use of a single methodology to guide all project work is a failing because there is 'no silver bullet' and no one SDLC or methodology can usefully guide the variety of work done in a typical IT development department (Brooks, 1975, 1987).

Second, practitioners do not do a good job of practicing what is taught or researched. As many as 50% of programmers have less than four years of college, are overwhelmed by their work, and do not use good software or design practices (Boehm, 2006). The same applies to newer disciplines, such as user-centered design (Høegh, 2006; Mao, 2005)

Third, many risks attendant on development projects are ignored. Major project practice risks relate to realism of schedule and budgets (Boehm, 1981); insufficient user involvement (Dodd & Carr, 1994); insufficient attention to functional complexity (Boehm, 2006; Ewusi-Mensah, 2003); inability to learn from past failures (Lyytinen & Robey, 1999); insufficient attention to user interface (Keil & Carmel, 1995); problem avoidance (Keil, 1995; Sherman et al., 2006);

Figure 5. Progressive development of methodologies and life cycles (Adapted from Boehm, 2006, p. 16)

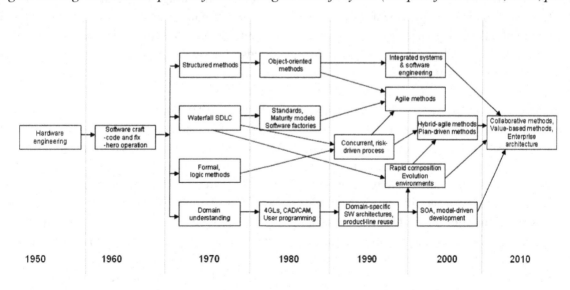

inability to control project scope (Boehm, 1991; Ewusi-Mensah, 2003; Markus & Keil, 1994); and lack of adequate technical skills (Boehm, 2006; Ewusi-Mensah, 2003; Sumner, 2000).

Development practices and failure to manage risks are not the only failing. Most companies do not follow any methodology or life cycle. They simply use the same tools and practices they have used in the past, much like using a hammer to fit a screw because it is the tool that is known. Such uses of methods that do not fit the problem are known to contribute to project failures (Boehm, 2006; Brinkkemper, 1996; Mao, et al., 2005).

Agile has recently been touted as a life cycle that provides productivity with less formality than past methods and life cycles. It provides a useful example of the shortcomings that are present to greater or lesser degrees in other methods and life cycles. Many practitioners of the current fad, Agile do little or no requirements definition before beginning to code (Abrahamsson et al., 2002). In addition, there are several different methods within the 'agile' life cycle and each is limited in some way. For instance, agile spreadsheet development (ASD) focuses on concepts and culture rather than on functionality and correctness; extreme programming (XP) develops no overall view, making integration of final products difficult; rational unified process (RUP) does not provide details on how to obtain requirements or how to tailor its methods for a given project type; and Scrum details 30-day release cycles but provides no integration or acceptance testing in its methodology descriptions (Abrahamsson et al., 2002). In addition, many practitioners of agile methods select simple, easily implemented functionality as the early project work to provide fast turnaround and build rapport with their clients (Boehm, 2006). However, they then miss the complexity of later functionality and experience difficulty integrating complex functions after-the-fact (Boehm, 2006). When this functionality affects the user interface, projects are more likely to be cancelled (Markus & Keil, 1994).

Application Development Management Issues

Developers are not alone in their application development failings. Managers also are less attentive to application development than needed to ensure their success (Sumner, 2000). The role of a project manager traditionally has been as the most senior technical person who also has managerial duties for the project (Conger, 1994). For instance, the project manager and key technical staff decide the methodology, the life cycle, the tools, and the resources needed for the project. In addition, the project manager, with key staff, develops the work breakdown, project plan, and skills desired for each task. The project manager is the main client liaison. In this role, the project manager attends the requirements elicitation meetings, sometimes as the analyst, gaining the understanding of the required functionality. In addition, the project manager is the official communicator of project status, problems, and work. Thus, the role has many gate-keeping functions that provide for filtering information (Keil, 1995), gaining commitment of other managers and user management (Sumner, 2000), and hiring or firing employees from a project (Conger, 1994; Sumner, 2000).

Risks associated with the managerial roles include scheduling, budgeting, assignment of personnel, management of personnel, acquisition of sufficient IT resources, dealing with training needs of assigned staff, ensuring sufficient user involvement dealing with problems as they arise, and controlling scope creep (Boehm, 2006; Ewusi-Mensah, 2003; Markus & Keil, 1994; Sherman et al., 2006; Sumner, 2000). To the extent that these risks are not attended to, project success becomes less likely.

Thus, from analysis of failures, if the wrong people do the wrong things, use the wrong methods and techniques, and do not attend to the necessary variety of complexity, application success is unlikely. Fixing these problems sounds like a simple matter of attention to details but there is an elusive 'sweet spot' of project contextualizing that needs further research to become fully articulated (Conger, 2011b).

KEY ISSUES IN FUTURE APPLICATION DEVELOPMENT

This section takes a design science perspective of the future needs in IT systems design to address the shortcomings and incorporate the positive aspects of application development from the previous section (Hevner et al., 2004). By adapting the seven guidelines from Hevner et al. (2004) all aspects of future systems design are evaluated to identify repetitive themes of application development. The themes are used to develop the key issues for future systems design.

Systems Artifacts

Application systems are the key artifacts that derive from the development process (Guideline #1, Hevner et al., 2004). However, contrary to what is taught in most systems analysis and design (SAD) texts, the system should not be the sole focus of development.

The perspective needs to shift from application-as-end to application-as-imbedded component within work service systems (see Alter, 2010). The two work systems of interest are the one that serves the main business purpose and the one that supports the operational application within IT. One way of altering the SDLC is to review each area of operational support needs during each phase of the chosen life cycle to determine the applicability of the various services activities (Gupta, 2008). In particular, during requirements elicitation, the non-functional requirements should be defined for security, reliability, accessibility, application support, and capacity, to name a few. The purpose of application development then shifts to become the delivery of IT-based work support capabilities

that provide measurable business value within a services delivery context.

ISO/IEC 15288:2002 for application development is appropriate to initiate this shift (ISO/IEC, 2002). The standard identifies not only the functional application requirements for its focus but also advocates consideration of key operational aspects of applications during development. For instance, the phases in the standard include concept, development, production, utilization, and support (ISO/IEC, 2002). Each phase contains activities that look forward to the ability to operate the application as shown in Figure 6.

The ISO/IEC 15288 standard is too generic to guide all activities but it does provide a checklist of major items for consideration during each phase of development. If coupled with ISO/IEC 20000-1, the standard for IT service management, anticipating the needs of the operational environment at each stage makes application compatibility with the service in which it is imbedded more likely (ISO/IEC, 2005).

Problem Relevance

In this discussion, relevance (Guideline #2, Hevner et al., 2004) relates to the business need for the application and the extent to which the need is met. This broad definition moves focus from the application artifact to its situated operational context and includes all aspects of support for applications use in addition to its development quality.

Financial Relevance

A cost-benefit analysis of the application that includes risk assessment and mitigation strategies, work breakdown and project plan, and an analysis of the expected financial payback are assumed. As many as 80% of projects are conceived and begun without any planning beyond what is due in a given time frame (Eberlein & Sampaio do Prado Leite, 2002). Without expected benefits, application relevance can easily be sidetracked.

Figure 6. Application and operations activities (ISO/IEC, 2002)

Phase	Application Activities	Operational Activities
Concept	"The preparation and baselining of stakeholder requirements and preliminary systems requirements (technical specifications for the selected system concept and usability specifications for the envisaged human-system interactions)" (p. 44)	Initial specification of infrastructure (p. 44)
Development	Technical data package, including as appropriate: 1) hardware diagrams, simulations; 2) software design documentation; 3) production plans training manuals for operators; and 6) maintenance procedures (p. 45)	Refined objectives for the production, utilization, support, and retirement (p. 45)
Production	It is presumed that the organization has available the production infrastructure, consisting of production equipment, tools, procedures and competent human resource (p. 45) to operate the application	Outcome packaged product transfer to distribution channels or customers (p. 46)
Utilization	The application is "installed and used at the intended operational sites" (p.46).	The application is "installed and used at the intended operational sites" (p. 46).
Support	"The Support Stage begins with providing maintenance, logistics and other support for the system operations and use" (p. 47)	Support includes " Maintained system product and services and the provision of all related support services " and " logistics, to the operational sites" (p. 47)

In addition to developing application expectations, post-implementation audits and performance measures should be conducted to determine that the payback is, in fact, gained. However, 80% of U.S. companies have no post-implementation audit (Levinson, 2003) and 84% of U.S. companies do not report metrics on financial performance. One study of seven countries found that at least 67% of companies did not measure IT value of any kind (Infosecurity.com, 2009).

Business Process Relevance

The relationship between business processes and automation that supports them is not a well researched area. By focusing on application artifact development and ignoring its operational context, the solution is likely sub-optimal (Conger, 2011a; Checkland, 1981). In addition, automation without process management is likely to yield no payback to the parent organization while process design preceding automation can yield a 20% return (Dorgan & Dowdy, 2004).

Processes are the heart of services; they are the "interface between the strategy and its execution" (Goldenstern, 2010, p. 6). With this crucial role, Goldenstern recommends that software should conform to an optimized process, interfaces should be simple and managed, reliance on time and resolution in support actions, task training, and service training all should be developed. Outcomes of these efforts are rewarded with an average 18% reduction in incident resolution times and a focus on providing customers the 'best' service (Reichheld, 2003), improved customer satisfaction and loyalty, and sales (Goldenstern, 2010). In addition, process "standardization truly enables leverage," leading to reduced cost of creating applications by 50% to 80% while boosting companies' ability to bring new products to market faster (King, 2009, p. 1). Process standardization can generate repeatable outcomes at a defined level of quality. Processes need to be viewed, not as stand-alone any more than an application is stand-alone, but as embedded within a service context that delivers value to the organization's customers. The notion of process as embedded in a service is discussed in the section on contribution.

A focus only on the business process of an application means ignoring the support processes needed by IT staff. Some authors argue for addition of user interaction analysis, non-functional requirements, and change management to improve software quality (Conger, 2011a; Eberlein & Sampaio do Prado Leite, 2002; Gupta, 2008; Pollard & Cater-Steel, 2009). For example, standardized messages that identify failings in an application should be designed and used across applications to simplify help desk outage resolution (Gupta, 2008). This implies design of two types of error messages -- those for business users and those for IT users. In addition to these simple changes, definition of standard processes for the IT function that incorporate services perspectives should lead to improved application quality both for the business function and for IT operations support functions.

Development Rigor

Rigor in Hevner, et al. (Guideline #5, 2004) refers to research rigor while herein the rigor is directed at application development and its operational instantiation. System quality is the focus of this discussion.

System quality has been viewed from several perspectives relating to the overall system, application, and its information. System quality in terms of operations refers to reliability, availability, accessibility, security, and compliance (Gorla & Lin, 2010; Van Bon, 2007). Application quality relates to effective development and deployment

of applications (Arnott & Pervan, 2008); reliability, ease of use, and usefulness (Gorla & Lin, 2010); and completeness, consistency, simplicity of learning, flexibility, sophistication, reliability, customizability, and functionality (Guimaraes et al., 2009; Petter et al., 2008). Information quality characteristics relate to accuracy, completeness, currency and format (Nelson et al., 2005).

System quality research is an expansion of application quality that includes characteristics of operational, information, and service quality as contributing to overall quality perceptions (Arnott & Pervan, 2008; Gorla & Lin, 2010; Petter et al., 2008). Key facets of application context are omitted by failing to evaluate the human-computer interface or the variety of users from business users to IT operations users and Help Desk staff (cf., Guimaraes et al., 2009). Yet, no comprehensive definition of system quality in all of its contexts has emerged. Operational quality present in, for instance, the IT Infrastructure Library (ITIL) (Van Bon, 2007), is not discussed in texts on systems analysis and design. Nor do the frameworks and standards that include operational quality describe how best to design applications for operational or service quality. These are areas for future research. As a result, system quality needs careful definition for each application context to ensure that the development activities address all requirements.

Systems as Search Process

Thinking of a system as a search process (Guideline #6, Hevner et al., 2004) leads to discussion of innovation and improvisation in the application development activity.

Innovation

Innovation relates to the introduction of processes, artifacts, tools, techniques, or technology that is new to an organizational setting (Prescott & Conger, 1995). Innovation is a key CIO priority (CIO, 2009). Innovation is viewed as integral to information systems since the IT function is generally tasked with bringing new technologies into the organization. Innovation research relating to IT usually refers to the adoption of technology. Most studies relate to organizational adoption that omits or minimizes the role of IT organizations in the adoption process (Prescott & Conger, 1995).

Innovations in IT units can be either technology or process related. Of six such studies, five relate to individual adoption of a technology and one relates to general database machine innovation (Prescott & Conger, 1995). One shortcoming of research on IT innovation is that research on adoption and use of new techniques, methods, design ideas, frameworks and other process-related innovations is lacking. As a result, innovation impacts on the IT organization remain largely unknown.

Changes to life cycles for innovation are also mostly missing with the exception of environmental innovations. Environmentally sustainable innovations are the "IS-enabled organizational practices and processes that improve environmental and economic performance" (Melville, 2010, p. 1). Evaluation of outsourcing, co-production, and environmentally improved technology for any new application can reduce its environmental impacts (Conger, 2011a). Altering application development to include a life cycle analysis of the application's environmental impacts and mitigating or negating the impacts to the extent possible is also suggested (Melville, 2010). Such altering of the life cycle might be done for any innovation, but the environmental innovation recommendations demonstrate opportunities to develop innovation adoption research and practice for IT applications beyond its present state.

Improvisation

Improvisation is comprised of extemporaneous processes based on expertise that serve as coping mechanisms (Ciborra, 1996, 1998). Improvisation is important in information systems development because regardless of how standardized a process

is, unexpected events, outcomes from prior decisions, and actions by project members require constant evaluation of impacts and adjustment of schedule, outcome definition, or budget, as needed.

While improvisation is needed, the result still needs the requisite discipline of any planned activity (Ciborra, 1998). The balance between improvisation and standardization is precarious but the outcomes of both require knowledge and discipline to develop purposefully designed artifacts (Hevner et al., 2004). More research on the nature, idiosyncrasy, and manageability of improvisation is needed to understand how it works in IT applications sourcing.

Design Evaluation

This section discusses design evaluation for application systems in terms testing and walkthroughs (Guideline #3, Hevner et al., 2004)

Walkthroughs are structured meetings for finding errors in requirements, designs, code, test plans, or other system artifacts (Conger, 1994). Walkthroughs are successful at finding significant errors and, by having the errors corrected during the development process, walkthroughs significantly reduce the cost of the application. The estimated annual cost of software defects is $59 billion, of which $22 billion could be avoided through walkthroughs (Rombach et al., 2008). Only about 35% of companies practice any type of walkthrough, providing a significant opportunity for its adoption (Rombach et al., 2008).

Testing is the art of finding problems in code (Myers, 1979). Testing as an area of application activity can focus on everything from individual code modules to stress testing to find limits of an application's use. Problems can relate to functionality, formatting, lack of relationship to requirements, limits or constraints, security, usability, and performance, to name a few (Myers, 1979; Kaner, 2001, 2003). Many organizations have a quality assurance function that develops acceptance tests as a gate keeping function for the client organizations.

Testing failures are well known and some of those failures lead to tragedy. Between 2008 and 2010, "system vendors reported 260 system malfunctions that caused 44 injuries and six deaths" in a single application (Brewin, 2010, p. 1). Most applications enter their production state with known errors and many applications experience errors throughout their productive lives (Baschob & Piott, 2007).

There is little agreement on many issues in testing, including the following. What constitutes testing? Are there testing 'best practices'? Is all testing contextual and unique? Should waterfall or agile be used as the overall model for when testing should be done? Should testing focus on functionality or usability or something else? Are scripts the best method for testing (Kaner, 2001, 2003)? The ultimate goal of testing research is fully automated testing but that remains an elusive dream at present (Bertolino, 2007). In addition to needing more research, testing is a subject often left out of programming classes beyond getting syntax and logic of simple programs to work. As a result, while testing sophistication has increased measurably in the last ten years, most practitioners do not know about that progress (Bertolino, 2007).

Organizational Contribution

While Hevner et al. (Guideline #4, 2004) address research contribution, in the context of application quality, thinking of organizational contribution is more appropriate. Completing an application is insufficient to develop a contribution. Rather, the application in use, must comply with all of its needs. The irony of the prior statement is that application developers tend to think of 'needs' as only functional requirements. Rather functional and non-functional requirements are necessary, as are requirements for more ephemeral aspects of contribution such as simplicity, learnability, and so on (Nielsen, 2000). To determine value added

to an organization, IT must measure and manage its activities, particularly those that determine organizational success. Current thinking on these operational activities is that taking a services orientation that mirrors the services orientation the organization seeks to perfect, will lead to value-adding outcomes for IT. This section develops the concepts of service orientation and discusses it in the context of the IT operations environment.

A 'service orientation' is one in which the organization provides intangible service thus, generating value to its customers. Value includes many characteristics for instance, need satisfaction, prompt and friendly interactions, and minimal clicks on a web site (Conger, 2011b; Deloitte, 2002). A service design takes a defined process and situates it in a governance and management structure, defines number and nature of work for multiple locations, defines software, data, and IT resource support for the functions and roles, and defines service levels for customer delivery including response time, service desk response time, and so on (Conger, 2010). This differs from typical application design by defining the application plus its customer context, plus its IT contexts for on-going operation. Services are composed of key components for utility and warranty. Utility addresses the traditional functional aspects of applications and conduct of work (Conger, 2010). Warranty addresses the non-functional, but increasingly important aspects of IT work. Examples of warranty include computing availability and reliability, response time for a service request, response time for simple outages, etc. Services have a life cycle that parallels the business product life cycle, beginning with business strategy, progressing to initiatives, tactics, processes and products, and production. ITSM life cycle mirrors this business life cycle and should be fully integrated and part of each step of the business service life cycle, from strategy formulation through retirement (Conger, 2010).

Moving to a service orientation is not without cost. Some of the key costs relate to training, travel, and communications for project team members involved in design and implementation of the services efforts. Understanding and communicating semantic nuances of terminology and getting to an understanding of what it means to deliver a service is an early challenge (Winniford et al., 2009). Training and communications costs extend to anyone touched by or managing services changes. Changing culture to a service-orientation is a difficult aspect of services adoption and also adds to service adoption costs (Conger & Picus, 2009).

ITSM innovation requires management of tradeoffs – development of an ITIL bureaucracy versus standardizing but remaining Spartan, blind adoption of all of ITIL or ISO/IEC 20000 versus adoption of selected processes and services based on need and value-adding potential, and rote versus contextualized adoption of processes and service (Cater-Steel et al., 2008; Conger & Schultze, 2008; Marrone & Kolbe, 2010a, 2010b).

Many benefits have accrued to companies that successfully implement services. Examples of benefits include missed service level agreement target penalty reductions of as much as 80% in two years (Conger & Picus, 2009), increases in service quality, global process standardization and resulting reduced expenses and increased customer satisfaction, reduced outages and related downtime of operations, improved staff mobility, improved financial control, and improved IT morale (Cater-Steel et al., 2008; Conger & Picus, 2009; Conger & Schultze, 2008; Dubie, 2002; Hochstein et al., 2005; Lynch, 2006; Marrone & Kolbe, 2010a, 2010b; Pollard & Cater-Steel, 2009; Potgeiter et al., 2005).

Though services provide significant benefits upon adoption and maturation of practice, issues with ITSM adoption exist. Challenges of adopting ITIL include the need for executive sponsorship, the need for business understanding of ITIL objectives, adequate resources, time, people with ITIL and change management knowledge and skills, funding for training, travel, certification if needed,

and implementation activities, and maintenance of momentum toward changes (Marrone & Kolbe, 2010). The demonstration of results after a short period of ITIL use is important to silencing change critics (Hochstein et al., 2005). Yet, virtually every project reports resistance even with quick results that must be successfully countered to ensure project success (Cater-Steel et al., 2008; Conger & Schultze, 2008; Conger &Picus, 2009; Marrone& Kolbe, 2010).

The risk-reward payoff is significantly weighed in favor of rewards for successful ITSM projects (Cater-Steel et al., 2008; Conger & Picus, 2009; Conger & Schultze, 2008; Potgeiter et al., 2005). However, two aspects of services are important to consider for organizational contribution. First, is the application as imbedded in its business service function and the value that accrues to the organization as a result of the application. There is little research on this area but it is a crucial aspect of an application that determines its importance to the business. Second, is the application's operational environment and how process-driven and smoothly it operates in both normal and outage situations. There is also little research on this area beyond case studies. Thus, both areas need further research to describe how best to accomplish service embeddedness and its contribution to the business.

Systems as Communication

The concept of systems as communication, adapting from Hevner, et al. Guideline #7 (2004), is not well articulated. One conception is that of how information accessibility is a form of communication between the application and the user (Culnan, 2007). From this perspective, communication occurs from physical access to the source, the interface to the source, and the ability to physically retrieve potentially relevant information (Culnan, 2007).

A different perspective is that the human interface is a form of communication between the developers (and management) to the application users (Nielsen, 2000). From this perspective, application usability and user experience are key outcomes of the communication.

In both senses of the term communication, application usability refers to incorporation of both needed functionality to accomplish a goal and characteristics such as effortless learning and remembering, usage efficiency, eliciting few errors, and subjectively pleasing use (Nielsen, 2000). Usability is an application feature that has a long history in terms of human-computer interaction (HCI) research with seminal works by, for instance, Ben Shneiderman (1997). Low usability relates to non-use of applications (Markus & Keil, 1994). However, usability is measured as a component of information quality, implying that the only usability is for data generated by an application (Petter et al., 2008). Usability should also be a feature of application quality to develop measures of the extent to which the interface engages and is useful to its users (Nielsen, 2000, 2005).

User experience refers to the feelings and attitudes developed by users of an application and embodied in the application characteristic usability. The term user experience is more general than many related, constituent predecessor terms such as user satisfaction, information system effectiveness, performance, and so on (Melone, 1990).

Product usability and user experience are related because they evaluate different aspects of the same phenomena. The phenomenon under study ultimately is the user experience. The assumption is that the more enjoyable and satisfying the experience, the more likely the user is to use a system. Melone (1990) analyzes outcomes while the research conducted by Nielsen (2000) analyzes characteristics that lead to the outcomes. Nielsen articulates characteristics to be designed into an IT artifact, which ultimately is the goal of application development and the approach that will be discussed here.

Key components of usability are ease of learning, ease of remembering, usage efficiency, mini-mal error elicitation, and usage esthetics (Nielsen, 2000). Note that functionality is still important in terms of practical acceptability but that usability focuses on user perceptions and ability to actually use the application. Learnability and memorability both have aspects of design for experts and novices in either the knowledge domain or in use of computer interfaces. Learnability refers to the length of time and amount of effort required to learn the software. Memorability refers to the extent to which the software is easily memorized. At best, a usable interface is intuitive, requiring little or no learning and little effort. One problem with usability is that the user is defined as the end user, who will be the daily user of the interface. However, little attention is given to the Help Desk staff that must also interface with the application whenever it exhibits problems. Similarly, there is little thought given to error messages. For instance, "Bad data" often seen as an error message, however, the name of the data field, its location in the program, the exact error, and guidelines on how to fix the error all are missing. If provided, the time to locate and remedy bugs can be cut by orders of magnitude (Gupta, 2008).

Efficiency relates to user development of a consistent, steady-state of performance over time that does not require extraneous, non-value adding activities. Efficiency, too, is viewed from the perspective of the business end user. If Help Desk efficiency were also considered during design, resolution time for user and system problems would be reduced (Gupta, 2008). With poor error messages, no learning can take place beyond how to locate a problem in this program, and therefore, no efficiencies can be gained.

Satisfaction relates to game-like qualities that allow a user to develop a state of flow such that they become engaged in the application and derive satisfaction from its use. Most applications ignore this aspect of design for all users, not just IT support. While there is high quality research on interface design and usability, there is no known research that links all of the characteristics to user experience (e.g., Norman, 2002; Shneiderman, 2004). Most application research links usability characteristics to application usage or generic user satisfaction. There are few best practices that identify all aspects of all of the components in a single publication or that are universally applicable across application areas, cultural contexts, or user types (Nielsen, 2000). As a result the application developer must read a significant body of work (c.f., Jokela et al., 2003; Jones, 1992; Kaikkonen et al., 2005; Lewis, 1995; Nielsen, 2000, 2005; Norman, 1998; Park, 1997; Shneiderman, 2000, 2004) to develop even an inkling of the global thought on usability and the parent field of research on human computer interaction (HCI) (Zhang et al., 2007).

Early ISO standards relate to usability – ISO/IEC 13407 and ISO/IEC 9241-11 (ISO/IEC, 1999; Jokela et al., 2003). ISO 13407 defines user-centered design as the "level of principles, planning, and activities" while ISO 9241-11 approaches usability from a goal-oriented perspective to achieve "effectiveness, efficiency, and satisfaction" (Jokela et al., 2003, p. 54). Both are replaced by ISO 9241-210:2010, part of a comprehensive standard that includes 28 sub-standards relating to every area of human interaction (ISO 9241-210:2010, 2010). However, all of the standards are generic, non-specific, and oriented toward a process for involving users in the development of interfaces. This approach, while useful, ignores the characteristics of usability and, as a result, is too abstract to guarantee any usability outcomes.

User-centered design methods, based on the ISO standards developed to deal with usability issues and ensure that user needs are included in interface design (Mao et al., 2005; Thayer & Dugan, 2009). User-centered design has grown in practice but its practice has no standard method for its conduct (Alonso-Rios et al., 2010; Mao, et al., 2005; Thayer & Dugan, 2009). Even with all of the standards and methods, user-centered design has not found its way into mainstream industry

practice and is used by under 40% of projects (Mao, et al., 2005; Thayer & Dugan, 2009).

Finally, much usability research is nonspecific, fragmented, not linked to user experience and not universally applicable. Usability has no agreed on definition and is studied with many interpretations (Alonso-Rios et al., 2010). In addition, systems analysis and design texts generally cover interface design in chapters that provide information at the level of the ISO standards (cf. Valacich et al., 2009). Few programmers learn anything beyond rudimentary rules of thumb for interface design and, as a result, user satisfaction with custom-developed software because of poor interface design tends to be very low (Norman, 2002).

To summarize, this section has evaluated the state of application development from the perspective of design research. Practice has narrowed over the years to focus on only the aspects of applications that are articulated in SDLCs and methodologies. As a result, key aspects of applications are missing or insufficient for their purpose. These aspects include usability, quality, operatability, and attention to all user communities. Each area discussed in this section provides many opportunities for future research and improved integration in pedagogy and practice.

LIMITATIONS AND FUTURE RESEARCH

This paper provides a necessarily abbreviated discussion of the history, state, and issues with SDLC and software analysis and design methodologies to determine future needs to improve quality and usefulness throughout the organization.

Future research was identified and discussed in the following areas: A need to define the relative importance of key drivers of successful applications, specific techniques and processes for developing usable interfaces, best practices in servitizing applications development, SERVQUAL modifications to include IT services evaluation and to tease out the nuances between system and service in web sites, application use and satisfaction relationship elaboration, common methodological checklists of items for application development consideration, methods to move new techniques into industry practice, checklists for managerial roles in applications development, usability and user experience, testing and system characteristics such as ease of use, the role of process in application development, the extent to which process standardization can contribute to a higher quality IT product, innovation driven by IT, innovation within IT, the extent to which improvisation can be institutionalized, uses of improvisation, measurement of application business value, and communication aspects of applications.

CONCLUSION

This paper evaluates application of methodologies to design systems artifacts and the challenges of the process. Through this analysis a series of changes to current practice and needs for future research and practical adaptation are identified. When these changes, additions, and future needs are examined, they do not differ substantively from recommendations of many research projects in the related areas. As a profession, we seem to forget our roots by omitting traditional activities that have led to past successes. Some of these activities include interface usability design, testing, product quality, and risk management. If collective forgetting continues, we are forever doomed to repeat past failings in a never-ending redevelopment of basic tenets. However, if we return to our roots and begin to identify and hone enduring practices, we improve the probability of future success in application design and development processes and as a result we also improve the potential for organizational contribution and relevance. More complex life cycles or methodologies do not necessarily result. Rather, checklists of issues to be considered and factored into application development, as needed, are required.

A move toward development of usable applications embedded within organizational services requires some changes. A services orientation requires understanding that no application is an end of itself. Rather the application is embedded in an organizational setting, is used by humans in the course of their work, and should add value to that work. The 'application user' includes all users, not just those in the non-IT community. The value adding aspects of applications include their ability to decrease cycle times, increase quality of services supported, and improve the work life of the application user. Remedying problems of application development and attending more to needs for usable services and should reduce costs of in-house development, increase user satisfaction, and provide clearer value contribution to business success.

REFERENCES

Abrahamsson, P., Salo, O., Ronkainen, J., & Wartsa, J. (2002). *Agile Software Development Methods: Review and analysis*. Oulu, Finland: VTT Electronics.

Agar, M., Ali, F., Bhasin, S., Kota, N., Landa, R., & Linares, G. L. (2007). *IT Assessment: Final Report*. Dallas, TX: University of Dallas.

Alonso-Ríos, D., Vázquez-García, A., Mosqueira-Rey, E., & Moret-Bonillo, V. (2010). Usability: A Critical Analysis and a Taxonomy. *International Journal of Human-Computer Interaction, 26*(1), 53–63. doi:10.1080/10447310903025552

Alter, S. (2010). Viewing Systems as Services: A Fresh Approach in the IS Field. *Communications of the Association for Information Systems, 26*(1). Retrieved June 23, 2010, from http://aisel.aisnet.org/cais/vol26/iss1/11

Arnott, D., & Pervan, G. (2008). Eight key issues for the decision support system discipline. *Decision Support Systems*, *44*(3), 657–672. doi:10.1016/j.dss.2007.09.003

Avison, D. E., & Fitzgerald, G. (1988). Information systems development: Current themes and future directions. *Information and Software Technology*, *30*(8), 458–466. doi:10.1016/0950-5849(88)90142-5

Avison, D. E., & Fitzgerald, G. (2003). Where now for Development Methodologies? *Communications of the ACM*, *46*(1), 79–82. doi:10.1145/602421.602423

Avison, D. E., & Fitzgerald, G. (2006). Developing and Implementing Systems. In Currie, W., & Galliers, R. (Eds.), *Rethinking MIS* (pp. 250–278). Oxford, UK: Oxford University Press.

Avison, D. E., & Gregor, S. (2009). An exploration of the real or imagined consequences of information systems research for practice. In S. Newell, E. Whitley, N. Pouloudi, J. Wareham, & L. Mathiassen (Eds.), *Proceedings of the 17th European Conference on Information Systems*, Verona, Italy (pp. 1780-1792).

Baschab, J., & Piott, J. (2007). *The Executive's Guide to Information Technology* (2nd ed.). New York: Wiley.

Beck, K., Beedle, M., van Bennekum, A., Cockburn, A., Cunningham, W., Fowler, M., et al. (2001). *The Agile Manifesto*. Retrieved May 1, 2010, from http://agilemanifesto.org/

Bertolino, A. (2007, May 23-25). Software Testing Research: Achievements, Challenges, Dreams. In *Proceedings of the 2007 Future of Software Engineering -- International Conference on Software Engineering* (pp. 85-103). Washington, DC: IEEE Computer Society.

Boehm, B. (1981). *Software Engineering Economics*. Upper Saddle River, NJ: Prentice Hall.

Boehm, B. (1998). A Spiral Model for Software Development and Enhancement. *Computer*, *21*(5), 61–72. doi:10.1109/2.59

Boehm, B. (2006, May, 20-28). A View of 20th and 21st Century Software Engineering. In *Proceedings of the International Conferences on Software Engineering '06,* Shanghai, China (pp. 12-30). New York: ACM.

Booch, G., Rumbaugh, J., & Jacobson, L. (1999). *The Unified Modeling Language User Guide*. Reading, MA: Addison-Wesley Longman.

Brewin, B. (2010). *Glitch prompts VA to Shut Down e-health data exchange with Defense*. Retrieved April 27, 2010, from http://www.nextgov.com/site_services/print_article.php?StoryID=ng_20100304_9977

Brinkkemper, S. (1996). Method Engineering: Engineering of information systems development methods and tools. *Information and Software Technology*, *38*, 275–280. doi:10.1016/0950-5849(95)01059-9

Brooks, F. P. (1975). *The Mythical Man-Month*. Reading, MA: Addison-Wesley.

Brooks, F. P. (1987). No silver bullet: Essence and accidents of software engineering. *IEEE Computer*, *20*(4), 10–19.

Brynjolfsson, E., & Hitt, L. (2003). Computing Productivity: Firm-level Evidence. *The Review of Economics and Statistics*, *84*(4),

Cater-Steel, A., & Toleman, M. (2007). Education for IT service management standards. *International Journal of IT Standards and Standardization Research*, *5*, 27–41.

Checkland, P. (1981). *Systems Thinking, Systems Practice*. London: Wiley.

Chen, X., & Sorenson, P. (2007, November). Toward TQM in IT Services. In *Proceedings of the ASE Workshop on Automating Service Quality*, Atlanta, GA (pp. 42-48).

Ciborra, C. (1996). The Platform Organization: Recombining Strategies, Structures, and Surprises. *Organization Science, 7*(2), 103–118. doi:10.1287/orsc.7.2.103

Ciborra, C. (1998). Notes on Improvization and time in Organizations. *Journal of Accounting. Management and Information Technology, 9*, 77–94. doi:10.1016/S0959-8022(99)00002-8

Conger, S. (1994). *The New Software Engineering*. New York: Thomson Publishing.

Conger, S. (2009). Information Technology Service Management and Opportunities for Information Systems Curricula. *International Journal of Information Systems in the Service Sector, 1*(2), 58–68.

Conger, S. (2010). IT Infrastructure Library ITIL v3. In Bigdoli, H. (Ed.), *The Handbook of Technology Management* (*Vol. 1*, pp. 244–256). New York: John Wiley & Sons.

Conger, S. (2011a). *Process Mapping and Management*. New York: Business Expert Press.

Conger, S. (2011b). *Finding the Sweet Spot in ITIL Implementation*. Paper presented at the Pink Elephant IT Management Conference, Las Vegas, NV.

Conger, S., & Landry, B. L. J. (2009, May 19-24). Problem Analysis: When established techniques don't work. In *Proceedings of the 2nd Annual Conf-IRM Conference*, Al-Ain, UAE.

Conger, S., & Picus, B. (2009). Sustainable Certification using ISO/IEC 20000. In *Proceedings of the American Society for Quality's Quality Management Forum* (pp. 14-19).

Conger, S., & Pollard, C. (2009, December 14). Servitizing the Introductory MIS Course. In *Proceedings of the AIS Special Interest Group on Services (SIG SVC) Workshop*, Phoenix, AZ.

Conger, S., & Schultze, U. (2008). *IT Governance and Control: Making sense of Standards, Guidelines, and Frameworks*. Chicago: The Society for Information Management International, Advanced Practices Council.

Conger, S., Venkataraman, R., Hernandez, A., & Probst, J. (2009). Market Potential for ITSM Students: A Survey. *Information Systems Management, 26*(2), 176–181. doi:10.1080/10580530902797573

Culnan, M. J. (2007). The dimensions of perceived accessibility to information: Implications for the delivery of information systems and services. *Journal of the American Society for Information Science American Society for Information Science, 36*(5), 302–308. doi:10.1002/asi.4630360504

Cuyler, T., & Schatzberg, L. (2003). Customer service at SWU's Occupational Health Clinic. *Journal of Information Systems Education, 14*(3), 241–246.

Deloitte. (2002). Achieving, Measuring, and Communicating IT Value. *CIO Magazine*. Retrieved from http://www.cio.com/sponsors/041503dt/complete.pdf

DeLone, W. H., & McLean, E. R. (1992). Information Systems Success: The Quest for the Dependent Variable. *Information Systems Research, 3*(1), 60–95. doi:10.1287/isre.3.1.60

DeLone, W. H., & McLean, E. R. (2003). The DeLone and McLean Model of Information Systems Success: A Ten-Year Update. *Journal of Management Information Systems, 19*(4), 9–30.

DeMarco, T. (1978). *Structured analysis and system specification*. Upper Saddle River, NJ: Prentice Hall.

DeMarco, T., & Plauger, P. J. (1979). *Structured Analysis and System Specification.* Upper Saddle River, NJ: Prentice Hall.

Dodd, J. L., & Carr, H. H. (1994). Systems development led by end-users. *Journal of Systems Management, 45*(8), 34.

Doran, T. (2000, October 25). Compliance Frameworks: Software Engineering Standards. In *Proceedings of the NDIA Systems Engineering & Supportability Conference,* Washington, DC. Retrieved from http://sce.uhcl.edu/helm/ SENG_DOCS/compliance_framework.pdf

Dorgan, S. J., & Dowdy, J. J. (2004). When IT lifts productivity. *The McKinsey Quarterly, 4,* 13–15.

Doyle, K. G., Wood, J. R. G., & Wood-Harper, A. T. (1993). Soft systems and systems engineering: on the use of conceptual models in information system development. *Information Systems Journal, 3*(3), 187–198. doi:10.1111/j.1365-2575.1993. tb00124.x

Dubie, D. (2002). *Procter and Gamble touts IT services model, saves $500 million.* Computer-World Management.

Eberlein, A., & Sampaio do Prodo Leite, J. C. (2002, September). Agile requirements definition: A view from requirements engineering. In *Proceedings of the International Workshop on Time-Constrained Requirements Engineering (TCRE'02).*

Ewusi-Mensah, K. (2003). *Software development failures: anatomy of abandoned projects.* Boston: MIT Press.

Fitzgerald, B., & Fitzgerald, G. (1999, June 23-25). Categories and Contexts of Information Systems Development: Making Sense of the Mess. In J. Pries-Heje, C. U. Ciborra, K. Kautz, J. Valor, E. Christiaanse, D. Avison, et al. (Eds.), *Proceedings of the Seventh European Conference on Information Systems,* Copenhagen, Denmark (pp. 194-211).

Gallagher, M., Link, A., & Petrusa, J. (2005). *Measuring Service Sector Research and Development.* Washington, DC: National Institute for Science and Technology. Retrieved May 1, 2010, from http://www.nist.gov/director/prog-ofc/ report05-1.pdf

Galup, S., Dattero, R., Quan, J., & Conger, S. (2009). An Overview of IT Service Management. *Communications of the ACM, 52*(5), 124–128. doi:10.1145/1506409.1506439

Goldenstern, C. (2010). *Closing the 21st Century Service Capability Gap.* Retrieved April 28, 2010, from http://www.tsia.com/secure/whitepapers/ Closing_the_21st_Century_Service_Capability_Gap.pdf

Gorla, N., & Lin, S.-C. (2010). Determinants of software quality: A survey of information systems project managers. *Information and Software Technology, 52*(6), 602. doi:10.1016/j. infsof.2009.11.012

Guimaraes, T., Armstrong, C. P., & Jones, B. M. (2009). A New Approach to Measuring Information Systems Quality. *The Quality Management Journal, 16*(1), 42–55.

Gupta, D. (2008, September 14-16). *Servitizing Applications.* Paper presented at the 3rd Academic Forum at the itSMF-USA Conference, San Francisco.

Hevner, A. R., March, S. T., Park, J., & Ram, S. (2004). Design Science in Information Systems Research. *Management Information Systems Quarterly, 28*(1), 75–105.

Hochstein, A., Tamm, G., & Brenner, W. (2005, May 26-28). Service-Oriented IT Management: Benefit, Cost and Success Factors. In D. Bartmann, F. Rajola, J. Kallinikos, D. Avison, R. Winter, P. Ein-Dor, et al. (Eds.), *Proceedings of the Thirteenth European Conference on Information Systems,* Regensburg, Germany (pp. 911-921).

Høegh, R. T. (2006, November 20-24). Usability problems: do software developers already know? In J. Kjeldskov & J. Paay (Eds.), *Proceedings of the 18th Australia Conference on Computer-Human interaction: Design: Activities, Artifacts and Environments (OZCHI '06),* Sydney, Australia (pp. 425-428).

InfoSecurity.com. (2009). *Companies Invest in IT but Do Not Measure It.* Retrieved May 1, 2010, from http://www.infosecurity-us.com/view/3046/companies-invest-in-it-but-do-not-measure-it-value/ ISO/IEC. (1995). *ISO/IEC 12207:1995 Standard for Information Systems Life Cycle Processes.* Washington, DC: International Organization for Standardization and International Electrotechnical Commission (ISO/IEC).

ISO/IEC. (2002). *ISO/IEC 15288:2002. Standard for Systems Engineering.* Washington, DC: International Organization for Standardization and International Electrotechnical Commission (ISO/IEC).

ISO/IEC. (2005). *ISO/IEC 20000-1: 2005 Standard for Information Technology – Service Management, Part 1: Specification.* Washington, DC: International Organization for Standardization and International Electrotechnical Commission. (ISO/IEC).

ISO/IEC. (2008). *ISO/IEC 12207:2008 Systems and software engineering -- Software life cycle processes.* Washington, DC: International Organization for Standardization and International Electrotechnical Commission (ISO/IEC).

ISO/IEC. (2010). *ISO/CD 9241-210:2010: Ergonomics of human- Part 210: Human-centred interactive systems.* Washington, DC: International Organization for Standardization and International Electrotechnical Commission (ISO/IEC).

Jackson, M. A. (1975). *Principle of Program Design.* New York: Academic Press.

Jacobson, I., Booch, G., & Rumbaugh, J. (1999). *Unified Software Development Process.* Reading, MA: Addison-Wesley.

Jokela, T., Iivari, N., Matero, J., & Karukka, M. (2003, August 17-20). The standard of user-centered design and the standard definition of usability: analyzing ISO 13407 against ISO 9241-11. In *Proceedings of the Latin American Conference on Human-Computer interaction*, Rio de Janeiro, Brazil (Vol. 46, pp. 53-60). New York: ACM.

Jones, J. C. (1992). *Design Methods* (2nd ed.). New York: John Wiley & Sons.

Kaikkonen, A., Kallio, T., Kekäläinen, A., Kankainen, A., & Cankar, A. (2005). Usability Testing of Mobile Applications: A Comparison between Laboratory and Field Testing. *Journal of Usability Studies, 1*(1), 4–16.

Kaner, C. (2001). *NSF grant proposal to lay a foundation for significant improvements in the quality of academic and commercial courses in software testing.* Retrieved April 27, 2010, from http://www.testingeducation.org/general/nsf_grant.pdf

Kaner, C. (2003). *Measuring the Effectiveness of Software Testers.* Retrieved April 27, 2010, from http://www.testingeducation.org/a/mest.pdf

Keil, M. (1995). Pulling the Plug: Software Project Management and the Problem of Project Escalation. *Management Information Systems Quarterly, 19*(4). doi:10.2307/249627

Keil, M., & Carmel, E. (1995). Customer-developer links in software development. *Communications of the ACM, 38*(5), 33–44. doi:10.1145/203356.203363

King, J. (2009). *IT's top tier: Strong and steady leadership.* Retrieved June 23, 2010, from https://www.computerworld.com/s/article/print/344381/IT_s_top_tier_Strong_and_steady_leadership?taxonomyName=Management&taxonomyId=14

Levinson, M. (2003, October 1). How to Conduct Post-Implementation Audits. *CIO Magazine.* Retrieved March 10, 2010, from http://www.cio.com/article/29817/How_to_Conduct_Post_Implementation_Audits

Lewis, J. R. (1995). IBM Computer Usability Satisfaction Questionnaires: Psychometric Evaluation and Instructions for Use. *International Journal of Human-Computer Interaction, 7*(1), 57–78. doi:10.1080/10447319509526110

Lynch, C. G. (2006, March 6). Most Companies Adopting ITIL® Practices. *CIO Magazine.*

Lyytinen, K., & Robey, D. (1999). Learning Failure in Information Systems Development. *Information Systems Journal, 9*, 85–101. doi:10.1046/j.1365-2575.1999.00051.x

Mao, J.-Y., Vredenburg, K., Smith, P. W., & Carey, T. (2005). The state of user-centered design practice. *Communications of the ACM, 48*(3), 105–109. doi:10.1145/1047671.1047677

Markus, M. L., & Keil, M. (1994). If We Built It, They Will Come: Designing Information Systems that People Want to Use. *Sloan Management Review, 35*(4), 11–25.

Marrone, M., & Kolbe, L. M. (2010a, February 23-25). Providing more than just operational benefits: An empirical research. In M. Schumann (Ed.), Proceedings of Multikonferenz Wirtschaftsinformatik 2010 (pp. 61–63). Göttingen, Germany.

Marrone, M., & Kolbe, L. M. (2010b, June 6-9). ITIL and the creation of benefits: An empirical study on benefits, challenges and processes. In *Proceedings of the European Conference on Information Systems (ECIS),* Pretoria, South Africa.

Martin, J. (1991). *Rapid Applications Development.* New York: Macmillan.

Mathiassen, L., & Nielsen, P. A. (1989). Soft Systems and Hard Contradictions - Approaching the Reality of Information Systems in Organizations. *Journal of Applied Systems Analysis, 16.*

Melone, N. P. (1990). A Theoretical Assessment of the User Satisfaction Construct in Information Systems Research. *Management Science, 36*(1), 76–86. doi:10.1287/mnsc.36.1.76

Melville, N. P. (2010). Information Systems Innovation for Environmental Sustainability. *Management Information Systems Quarterly, 34*(1), 1–21.

Myers, G. J. (1979). *The Art of Software Testing.* New York: John Wiley & Sons.

Nelson, R. R., Todd, P. A., & Wixom, B. H. (2005). Antecedents of information and system quality: an empirical examination within the context of data warehousing. *Journal of Management Information Systems, 21*(4), 199–235.

Nielsen, J. (1994). *Using discount usability engineering to penetrate the intimidation barrier.* Retrieved June 8, 2010, from http://www.useit.com/papers/guerrilla_hci.html

Nielsen, J. (2000). *Usability Engineering.* San Diego, CA: Kaufmann.

Nielsen, J. (2005). *Ten Usability Heuristics*. Retrieved April 27, 2010, from http://www.useit.com/paper s/ heuristic/heuristic_list.html

Norman, D. A. (1998). *The Design of Everyday Things*. New York: Basic Books.

Parasuraman, A., Zeithaml, V., & Berry, L. L. (1988). SERVQUAL: A Multiple-item Scale for Measuring Consumer Perceptions of Service Quality. *Journal of Retailing, 64*(1), 12–37.

Parasuraman, A., Zeithaml, V., & Berry, L. L. (1994). Reassessment of Expectations as a Comparison Standard in Measuring Service Quality: Implications for Further Research. *Journal of Marketing, 58*(1), 111–125. doi:10.2307/1252255

Park, K. S. (1997). Human Error. In Salvendy, G. (Ed.), *The Handbook of Human Factors and Ergonomics* (2nd ed.). New York: John Wiley & Sons.

Petter, S., Delone, W., & Mclean, E. (2008). Measuring information systems success: models, dimensions, measures, and interrelationships. *European Journal of Information Systems, 17*(3), 236–263. doi:10.1057/ejis.2008.15

Pollard, C., & Cater-Steel, A. (2009). Justifications, Strategies, and Critical Success Factors in Successful ITIL Implementations in U.S. and Australian Companies: An Exploratory Study. *Information Systems Management, 26*(2), 164–172. doi:10.1080/10580530902797540

Potgieter, B. C., Botha, J. H., & Lew, C. (2005, July 10-13). Evidence that use of the ITIL framework is effective. In *Proceedings of the 18th Annual Conference of the National Advisory Committee on Computing Qualifications*, Tauranga, New Zealand.

Prescott, M., & Conger, S. (1994). Information technology innovations: A Classification by IT locus of impact and research approach. *Database, 26*(2-3), 20–42.

Reichheld, F. F. (2003, December 1). The One Number You Need to Grow. *Harvard Business Review*. Retrieved April 28, 2010, from http://harvardbusinessonline.hbsp.harvard.edu/b02/en/common/item_detail.jhtml?id=R0312C&referral=2340

Rombach, D., Ciolkowski, M., Jeffery, R., Laitenberger, O., McGarry, F., & Shull, F. (2008). Impact of research on practice in the field of inspections, reviews and walkthroughs: learning from successful industrial uses. *SIGSOFT Software Engineering Notes, 33*(6), 26–35. doi:10.1145/1449603.1449609

Royce, W. W. (1970). Managing the Development of Large Software Systems: Concepts and Techniques. *Proceedings of Western Electronic Show and Convention* (WesCon) August 25-28, 1970, Los Angeles

Sherman, D. K., Mann, T., & Updegraff, J. A. (2006). Approach/Avoidance Motivation, Message Framing, and Health Behavior: Understanding the Congruency Effect. *Motivation and Emotion, 30*(2), 165–169. doi:10.1007/s11031-006-9001-5

Shneiderman, B. (2000). Universal Usability. *Communications of the ACM, 43*(5), 84–91. doi:10.1145/332833.332843

Shneiderman, B. (2004). *Designing the User interface: Strategies for Effective Human-Computer Interaction* (4th ed.). Reading, MA: Addison-Wesley.

Suchman, L. A. (1983). Office procedure as practical action: models of work and system design. *ACM Transactions on Information Systems, 1*(4), 320–328. doi:10.1145/357442.357445

Sumner, M. (2000). Risk factors in Enterprise Wide Information Management Systems. In *Proceedings of the AMC SIG CPR Conference*, Evanston, IL (pp. 180-188).

Thayer, A., & Dugan, T. E. (2009, July 19-22). Achieving design enlightenment: Defining a new user experience measurement framework. In *Proceedings of the 2009 IEEE International Professional Communication Conference*, Waikiki, HI (pp. 1-10).

Valecich, J., George, J., & Hoffer, J. (2009). *Essentials of Systems Analysis and Design* (3rd ed.). Upper Saddle River, NJ: Prentice-Hall.

Van Bon, J. (2007). *IT Service Management: An Introduction*. London: itSMF International.

Winniford, M. A., Conger, S., & Erickson-Harris, L. (2009). Confusion in the Ranks: IT Service Management Practice and Terminology. *Information Systems Management, 26*(2), 153–163. doi:10.1080/10580530902797532

Yourdon, E., & Constantine, L. L. (1975). *Structured Design*. New York: Yourdon Press.

Zhang, P., Galletta, D., Li, N., & Sun, H. (2007). Human-Computer Interaction. In Huang, W. (Ed.), *Management Information Systems*. Beijing, China: Tsinghua University Press.

This work was previously published in the International Journal of Information Technologies and Systems Approach, Volume 4, Issue 1, edited by Frank Stowell and Manuel Mora, pp. 1-22, copyright 2011 by IGI Publishing (an imprint of IGI Global).

Chapter 7
Model–Driven Engineering of Composite Service Oriented Applications

Bill Karakostas
City University London, UK

Yannis Zorgios
CLMS Ltd., UK

ABSTRACT

Composite applications integrate web services with other business applications and components to implement business processes. Model-driven approaches tackle the complexity of composite applications caused by domain and technology heterogeneity and integration requirements. The method and framework described in this paper generate all artefacts (workflow, data, user interfaces, etc.), required for a composite application from high level service oriented descriptions of the composite application, using model transformation and code generation techniques.

INTRODUCTION

Contemporary application development is faced with multiple challenges, caused mainly by the new turbulent business environment in which organisations (and consequently their IT systems) operate. Agility, flexibility, resilience, adaptability and Web enablement, are no longer options but mandatory requirements that need to be engineered in today's applications and systems.

For almost a decade now, Model Driven Engineering (MDE) under various initiatives such as MDA (Miller & Mukerji, 2001), has promised to transform the speed at which applications are developed. By advocating model-based system specification and code generation via model transformations techniques, to replace traditional specify-design-code system lifecycles, MDE promises enhanced quality resulting from less manual coding and thus less scope for programming errors.

Service Oriented Architecture (SOA) plays an orthogonal role to MDE, by unifying concepts and approaches to software development under the single paradigm of a *service*. The natural synergy and complimentarity of MDE and SOA, has resulted in the new paradigm of *model-driven service engineering* (Marcos et al., 2009). This

DOI: 10.4018/978-1-4666-1562-5.ch007

new paradigm advocates the use of service models across all phases of software development, with service modelling techniques replacing the manual crafting of software (web) services. SOA helps to align IT capabilities to achieve business goals in offering value propositions, for instance to "orchestrate" lower level IT infrastructure services (Chen et al., 2009).

To date, model driven service engineering has been primarily applied to the development of systems composed purely of services, e.g. to automate tasks of service composition (Orriens et al., 2003) or orchestration (Mayer et al., 2008). Typical business applications, however, are a combination of automated tasks that can be performed by service or other application components, and of manual (user driven activities), all underpinned by technologies such as middleware, DBMS, Web, etc. Thus, significant productivity improvements can apply only by tackling the whole spectrum of application development, not only the service part.

The aim of *Model-Driven SOA* is to create Service-Oriented Business Applications (SOBA) that truly support an organization (den Haan, 2009). Composite service oriented applications therefore, simplify integration by allowing access and integration of heterogeneous information resources and automation of business processes, using SOA principles and architectures.

Service oriented business applications will need to integrate underlying technologies for process and data management, workflow, user interface etc. Service oriented models of business processes need to directly lead to executable code, either by direct execution (e.g. using a workflow engine, rule engine etc), or by transformations to executable models. Thus, as we argue in this paper, model driven service oriented application development is well suited to the complex business and integration requirements of contemporary composite applications. This paper proposes a method and framework for achieving model driven engineering of composite service oriented applications.

The following section of the paper explains the features of composite applications. Then, the paper reviews existing composite application frameworks and introduces a model driven service oriented composite application development methodology. It explains the steps of the method as well as the underlying foundations (meta-models), using the issue management business process as a case study. Finally, the paper compared the discussed approach with related service oriented engineering methodologies and techniques, and identifies directions for further research.

FEATURES OF COMPOSITE SERVICE ORIENTED APPLICATIONS

A composite application integrates functionality provided by different sources such as conventional applications, systems such as middleware, DBMS, or web services.

Composite applications need therefore to introduce an orchestrating framework to coordinate the interactions between their constituting components, to produce the new, derived, functionality.

Multiple web services combined in composite applications require interoperable mechanisms to control business process activities start, end, success, failure etc, to create, access and manage process context information, and to inform participants of changes to an activity. Composite applications might also need to work with several transactional models such as one and two phase transactions, long running transactions and so on (OASIS, 2003).

Environments for building service oriented composite applications need to facilitate easy and visually composition of the business services in a way that makes sense to IT or business analysts (SAP, 2005). Ensuring such business services are reusable across the enterprise via some form of repository such as UDDI is also critical. Finally, providing the ability to assemble these different business services together to form the actual composite application, without coding, is also critical (Frye, 2005).

COMPOSITE APPLICATION FRAMEWORKS

Various research and commercial frameworks for composite application development have been proposed, with the most prominent ones reviewed below.

OASIS Web Services Composite Application Framework (WS-CAF), is an open framework developed by the standards organisation OASIS. Its purpose is to define a generic and open framework for applications that contain multiple services used together, i.e. composite applications (OASIS, 2003).

SAP Composite Application Frameworks (SAP, 2005), is a application framework that runs on SAP's Netweaver platform and uses services and data from existing applications and components to provide an integrated view of processes, data, and information, and to facilitate user interaction and collaboration. According to SAP (2005), CAF applications act as mediators between users and user-centric processes, and data and business processes. CAF employs a service-oriented architecture that combined with business object access, allows all business processes to be treated as services and business objects, independent of the underlying system.

A MODEL-DRIVEN COMPOSITE APPLICATION ENGINEERING METHODOLOGY

As explained above, a service oriented composite application framework needs to integrate seamlessly the service execution layers with the business process and UI layers that use the services. In other words, composite application frameworks need to support cross-component and cross domain collaboration, where a *component* is an external application or data service, and a *domain* is an application area or technology such as an infrastructure for data or workflow management. Composite applications have a user interface, although they might also contain automated process activities that do not involve user interaction. Composite applications are driven by the underlying business process/workflow management system. Services and other non service components are used to realize the process activities.

Model driven engineering of composite applications needs therefore to begin with a process oriented view of the application, that shows how user and automated activities collaborate to realize the process.

It is important that this view is technology independent, to allow different underlying technologies and platforms to be used to realize the business process, and to allow easy adaptation of the process for different business and technical environments.

It is also necessary to coordinate the development of the different components under this shared process view. Ideally, components for user interaction, workflow and other domains should be derived from the common business process model.

In our approach, integration of composite applications components is achieved through metamodel driven model transformations that connect the different domains, and allow the generation of artefacts. To use MDA terminology, in our approach the business process model (CIM) is transformed to implementation independent models (PIMs) which in turn are transformed into platform specific models (PSM), depending on the chosen architectural style and implementation platforms. This is illustrated in Figure 1.

A composite application development project according to our approach, will result in a number of implementation specific artefacts (PSMs) that realize a composite application using collaborating components (i.e. web services and possibly other user driven or automated ones). We can say

Figure 1. Meta-models and transformations

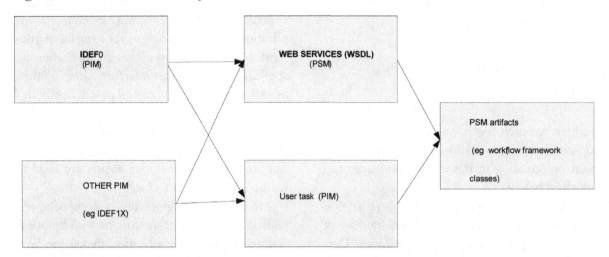

therefore that a composite application starts with (one or several) CIMs that are gradually transformed to PIMs. Thus, this approach creates multiple CIM and PIM models that enable the description of the composite application at different levels. A PIM model describes the business process realised by the application, while a set of PIM/PSM might describe the process realisation.

Our approach, described more extensively in (Karakostas & Zorgios, 2008), has been influenced by the system modeling method IDEF0 (Integration Definition for Function Modeling). IDEF0 activities are the building blocks used to realize a composite application. An IDEF0 activity can be automated (e.g. by a web service) or manually performed (human activity).

An activity is characterized by:

- **Inputs** which are the conditions required for an (instance of) an activity to be performed. Typically inputs are data that must be made available to the activity as inputs from other activities.
- **Outputs** which are the outcomes of performing an activity. In our approach these are specified in an implementation neutral way, using conceptual data modeling notations such as IDEF1X, or business object

models. These can be subsequently transformed to computer specific models such as WSDL descriptions.

- **Control rules** which specify declaratively the business rules or constraints imposed on an activity. Business rules are also described in a technology independent language that allows subsequent generation of the appropriate code such as SQL statements, C#, or Java code.
- **Mechanism** that implements the activity. This can refer to an external system or service, a business object, a human actor, and so on. In the case of service activities, mechanisms are used for example to specify how the service specification will be bound to a concrete service.

Using model transformations, the IDEF0 model is used to derive models of all required artefacts of the composite application such as web service descriptions, user interface models etc as illustrated in Table 1.

We argue that this approach offers several advantages for both analysts and developers, by providing a uniform treatment of composite application components as IDEF0 activities and abstract descriptions of the business process, and allowing these to be refined into computer specific implementations through hierarchical decomposition of the IDEF0 model and through model transformations. An IDEF0 activity, at a sufficiently abstract level, can be manual, automated, or a mixture of both (i.e. a sub-process). It is only when the activity is decomposed sufficiently that we decide whether this activity is a web service or a (manual or computer based) task. Once we describe activity (IDEF0) models at a sufficiently detailed level, we are able to generate the computer specific (but implementation independent) artefacts such as service description documents (WSDL), business object calls or user interface constructs. Ultimately, based on our architectural choices and underlying software technologies, we can employ code generation techniques to generate software components i.e. Java or .NET classes that realize the composite application.

Meta Models

Figure 2 shows a graphical view of one of several metamodels used by our approach. This metamodel describes the constituting parts of an activity. Such metamodels guide the behaviour of our modelling tools and editors, and the structure of the composite application artefact repository. Meta models also support completeness and consistency checking of the generated artefacts.

Finally, a metamodel also captures dependencies to other metamodels.

CASE STUDY: DEVELOPING A COMPOSITE ISSUE MANAGEMENT APPLICATION USING SERVICES

We illustrate the steps of our approach by using a case study from the application domain of issue tracking systems. An issue tracking system (also known as *support ticket, incident ticket system,* etc) is an application that manages and maintains lists of issues, for example in a customer support centre.

The most common architecture of issue tracking systems today is a three tiered, client server one. A database management system is used as the main storage repository for all data. A business logic, application workflow or similar layer, interprets the data describing issues and acts according to the defined rules for processing issues, e.g. by categorising them, prioritising them, and forwarding them to suitable issue handlers. Issue data can include the name of the customer/user experiencing the issue (whether external or internal), date of submission, detailed descriptions of the problem being experienced, existing attempted solutions or workarounds, and other relevant information.

Table 1. Moving From Computer independent to computer specific application models

Composite Application Domains	Business Process	Business Logic	Information models	User Interaction models
Business models (CIM)	IDEF0	Business rules (part of IDEF model)	IDEF1X information models	IDEF0
Computer Specific but Platform independent models (PIM)	BPEL	**Business rules in a high level rule language**	UML classes	XAML
PSM Implementation (Platform) Specific models	BPEL code, or other middleware platform specific	Code in java, C# SQL etc.	Relational (DBMS) schema	Depending on the execution environment, e.g. ASP. NET or JSP pages

Figure 2. Metamodel for linking service engineering domains

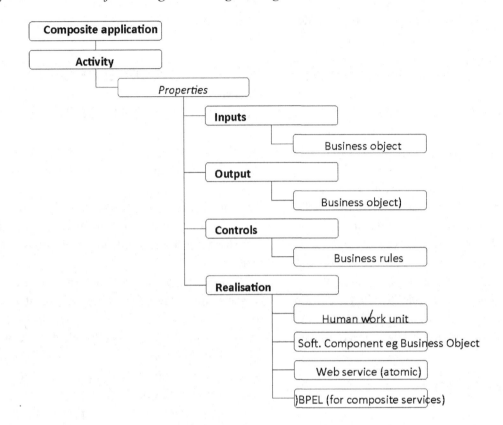

The suitably formatted data about an issue are then presented to the issue handler (e.g. a support technician) by another application with a front end such as a web page. Based on defined authorizations, issue handlers can create entirely new issues, read existing issues, modify existing ones, resolve issues and so on. Anytime an issue handler makes a change, the issue tracking system will record the action and its creator, so as to maintain a history of the actions taken.

Issues can have several facets. Each issue in the system may have an urgency value assigned to it, based on the overall importance of that issue. Severe (critical) issues take precedence over all other issues and must be handled immediately. Lower priority issues need to be logged to be resolved as time permits.

The issue handling workflow varies with different organizations and environments. A typical workflow scenario for issue tracking could be as follows.

- Issues are received from issue reporting services which are services that expose other applications automatic error reporting facilities (e.g. exception handling).
- Issues are filtered by the incoming issue handling (an automated activity) according to their severity. Issues that are marked as severe are assigned to a (human) issue handler. Issues that are less severe are dispatched to an issue queuing service where they are handled by as resources permit.
- The task of the issue handler is to verify that the problem is real, and not just perceived. The issue handler needs to ensure that enough information about the problem is obtained from the customer/user. This

information generally includes the environment of the customer/user, when and how the issue occurs, and all other relevant circumstances.

- The issue handler creates the issue in the system, entering all relevant data, as provided by the customer.
- As work is done on that issue, the system is updated with new data by the issue handler. Any attempt at fixing the problem is recorded in the issue system.
- After the issue has been fully addressed, it is marked as resolved in the issue tracking system.

The rationale for developing issue management using a CAF framework, is that service orientation allows better flexibility in terms of business process alignment, flexibility and speed of response. Heterogeneous systems (both of customers and internal ones, for example customer relationship management systems) can be easier integrated. Issue handling tasks can be supported on diverse environments (including mobile ones) without having to tie down the users to specific applications and interfaces. New services can be added that build on top of and add value to existing ones, for example services to build an organisation wide knowledge base and learning (knowledge management) capability.

Below we describe the steps for developing a composite application for issue management according to our approach. We use screenshots from a prototype implementation of the issue management application, done using a model driven application development environment called AppDev2.0, originally introduced in (Karakostas & Zorgios, 2008).

Step 1: Analyse the Requirements of the Issues Management Application

Types and areas of requirements that need to be collected and analysed are:

- **Handling Multiple sources of data:** Track the issues coming out of multiple systems supporting different interfaces.
- **Reporting Requirements:** Make the current status of all issues known to project managers.
- **Authorisation Requirements:** Define a single owner who must resolve the issue
- **Workflow Requirements:** Flexible workflow to fit unique processes of the organisation, easily configurable and customizable per project.
- **Architectural Requirements:** Scaleable, distributed architecture, to cater for increases in number of issues, as well as number of issue handlers, working in a distributed environment.
- **Usability Requirements:** intuitive, simple, and straight-forward user interface suited to the tasks of issue management.

Step 2: Define the Context of the Composite Application and its Architectural Style

Context is defined in terms of the application domain model(s), that includes user domain concepts (perhaps modelled as business objects or other conceptual structures), input/output dependencies with other business processes and systems, controlling parameters in terms of policies and governance that the application and roles of the users of the application.

In our case study, the issue handling composite application operates within the context of the issue management process. The process includes several types of actors, such as customer/end users, issue handlers and issue handling managers. The application will need to interoperate with other systems involved in issue handling. Based on the collected requirements, it is decided that the application will be developed on a three tier web architecture.

Step 3: Identify the Core Services, Activities and Data that will Realise the Composite Application.

The reason for building composite applications is to reuse existing services and avoid duplication of effort in developing service functionality. In addition to services that can be reused, other services will need to be built from scratch. Finally, some services will need to be composed from simpler (atomic) services.

For example, in our case study the *issue filtering service* can pre-exist, while the *issue queuing service* may need to be implemented from scratch.

Assessing existing services for reuse potential is both a business as well as technical task that goes beyond the realm of the current project and into the business and IT SOA governance framework that is employed.

For example, a candidate for reuse service needs to be assessed with regards to its technical suitability, architectural conformance, but also with its long term viability and plans for future evolution. Thus, Step 3 ideally needs to be carried out within a defined SOA governance framework.

Data sources required for the issue management application will also need to be identified and accessed at this stage. Such data sources could include pre-existing business object models for the issue management application domain, XML descriptions of the various data and documents used in issue management, etc.

At the earlier stages of application specification such data sources need to be abstracted as business objects or abstract data services.

Figure 3 shows as an example a UML class diagram for the *Issue* business object and its supporting object classes, that can be used to provide the business logic and data required to support services.

Step 4: Model the Collaborations of the Activities that Realise the Complex Application

This step essentially entails creating a service oriented process model of the composite application.

A service interaction model consists of interconnected services and human work activities. Services are assumed to be automated units of activity that do not require human participation. Human work activities are units of work that involve a human actor and a computer interface such as a web browser.

In our approach the logical interaction model is based on the IDEF0 notation which allows modelling of input output and control dependencies. The implementation independent nature of this model allows implementation decisions to be deferred and become automated, based on the choice of architecture as described above.

Figure 4 shows the IDEF0 composition of activities that realise the issue handling process. The diagram indicates which of the activities are automated (e.g. web services) and which are human activities.

Logical relationships between services and other components in terms of context and mode of interaction (transactional behaviour) are also described in this step. If a subset of interactions must be carried out within the same context, i.e. as a single transaction, this is specified by annotating the model (see Figure 5). Note that the actual mechanism for the implementation of the transactional context, rollback or compensation mechanisms, etc., is deferred until the construction phase.

Figure 5 shows how the activation and execution context of activity *ReportIssueStatus* can be defined. Such definitions will be used in subsequent steps to generate correct context (transactional) models.

Figure 3. Business object Issue (and associated value classes)

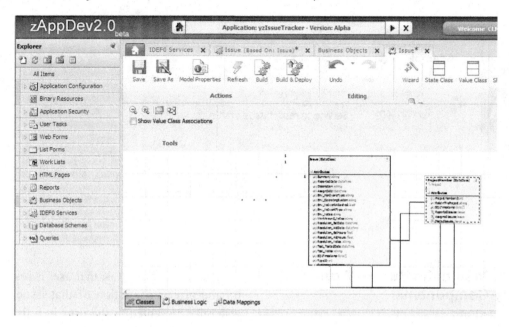

Step 5: Design the New Services

New services can be either atomic or a composition of other existing services. Atomic services are defined in terms of business logic and data services. The service output is described in terms of business object properties so that a WSDL, SOAP message, and other SOA infrastructure can be automatically generated. Composite services can be described in terms of a BPEL composition. Newly defined services can be deployed to the company's service registry.

The business logic of the service can be described in this step, using a business rule editor such as the one shown in Figure 6.

Figure 4. Defining a composition of activities

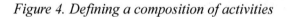

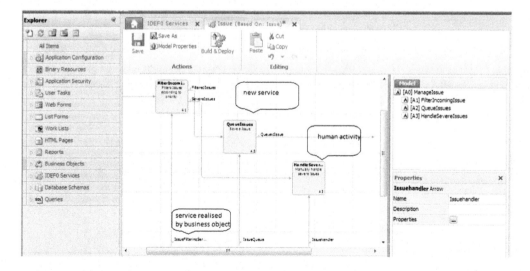

Figure 5. Behavioural properties of an activity

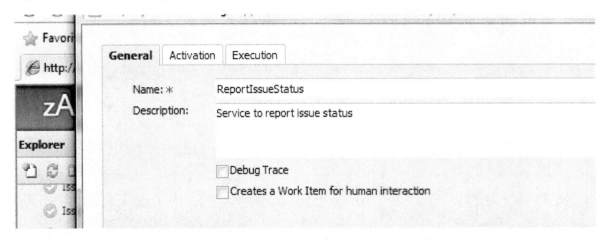

Step 6: Design the Human Work Activity Components

Each human work activity identified in Step 4 must now be designed. Based on the input output dependencies of the activity, as captured in the IDEF0 composition diagram, a template of user tasks can be automatically generated in this stage. Each user of the system may have issues assigned to them, that is, that user is responsible for the proper resolution of that issue. This is generally presented to the user in a list format. The user may have the option of re-assigning an issue to another user, if needed. For security, an issue tracking system will authenticate its users before allowing access to the systems.

Figure 7 shows typical user tasks for the *create new issue* activity. Authorisations can also be

Figure 6. Defining business logic for Issue business object

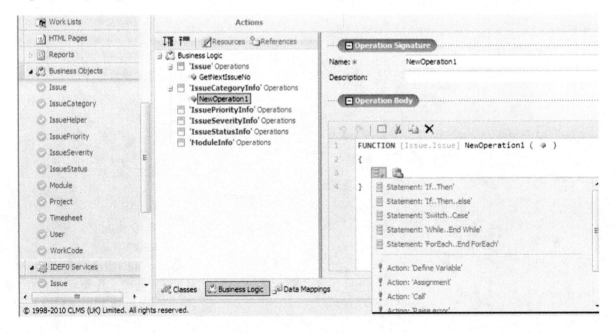

described here, based on the mechanism descriptions attached to the human work activity, in Step 4 (see Figure 8)

In this step, implementation independent task descriptions (e.g. in XAML) are employed, to minimise dependencies on specific technologies for user interfaces. This is important in order to be able to reuse the composite application description, and redeploy it in different user environments such as mobile devices.

Step 7: Generate the Composite Application Artefacts

This includes generating code such as calls to business objects (DLLs or JARs), WSDL, forms, workflow code, transaction handling code and so on. Whole subsets of IDEF0 compositions can be

automatically translated to BPEL code, as reported in (Karakostas et al., 2006)

Based on models created and architectural decisions made in the previous steps, all required artefacts can now be auto-generated. Dependencies on libraries and other underlying execution infrastructure (e.g. calls to transaction or workflow services in .NET or EJB) are taken into account in order to generate the correct executables.

To generate the software modules that realize the business logic, we employ code templates. A template can share variables and trigger the processing of other templates, therefore allowing the user to define the workflows of the code generation process. Templates consist of two types of content: static and dynamic. Dynamic content is expressed in a scripting language and is enclosed between the [% and %] delimiters. Everything that exists outside those delimiters is considered

Figure 7. User tasks for create new issue activity

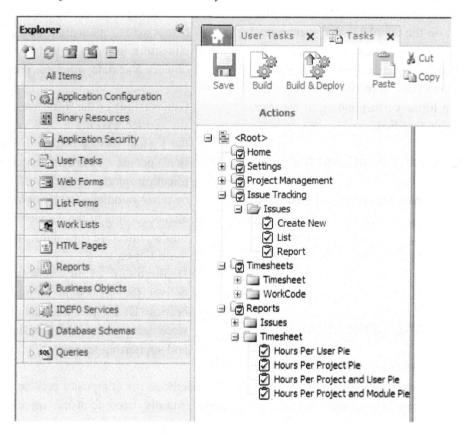

Figure 8. User authorizations

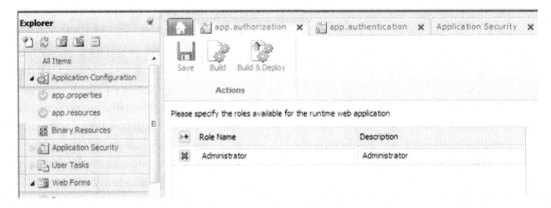

to be static content. Dynamic content populates the static content with data from the models.

For example, consider the template of Figure 9. This template is used to generate a Java class definition. When the script inside the template is executed the names within the delimiters will be substituted for the actual names of the Java class and of its attributes.

Graphical user interface artefacts can be fully defined based on the templates that were auto-generated in the previous step. Business objects modelled in previous steps are used as sources of data for the web forms. Figure 10 shows the design editor for Web forms corresponding to the user tasks previously identified.

Step 8: Deploy the Application

Generated composite applications can be executed from inside the AppDev development environment or packaged together with runtime artefacts as installable packages for deployment on other computers.

DISCUSSION AND CONCLUSION

As organisations move to dynamic and virtual collaborative business models, their IT infrastructures need to follow suit. Composite applications represent the future of applications development. Composite service oriented applications connect front, middle, and backend systems, and are vital for forming an agile business.

The approach to model driven engineering of service oriented composite applications, described in this paper can be summarized as:

- **Modelling:** of services and non service components' conceptual and physical architecture in terms of underlying business objects and data services, user interfaces etc.
- **Generation:** of the infrastructure required for service execution. Artefacts that map the logical service design to implementation specific constructs based on the application platform (or workflow engine or other middleware(s) employed. This is also according to the decided implementation architecture (i.e. single, two tier-web, multi tier etc)
- **Deployment:** of all artefacts required to deliver the service including runtime libraries (DLLs, jars etc), database/middleware connections, web interfaces (HTML) and supporting scripts.

Methods for composite service applications have mainly been focusing on the automatic

Figure 9. Example of a template for code generation

```
public class [%=class.name%] {

[%for each attribute in class.attribute%]

private [%= attribute.type] [%= attribute.name %];

[%next%]

}
```

generation of service compositions. The high level descriptions of the composite application are defined in UML, arguably not an end user oriented specification language. For example, in an approach described in (Grønmo et al., 2004), web service descriptions (in WDSL) are converted to UML, their UML models are integrated to form composite web services, and then the new web service descriptions are exported.

Another published approach to composite applications is based on the construction of Web applications that compose Web services in order

to support arbitrarily complex processes (Brambilla, et al., 2006).

Finally, Yu et al. (2007) propose a composite application development framework that capitalizes on the UML profile for enterprise distributed object computing (EDOC), MDA, and Web services. Within their framework, firstly, a general PIM is created using the EDOC CCA structural and choreography specifications. The general PIM is broken down into sub-PIMs, each of which is implemented in a Web service. All of the PIMs are transformed to WSDLs. Finally, each PIM

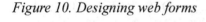

Figure 10. Designing web forms

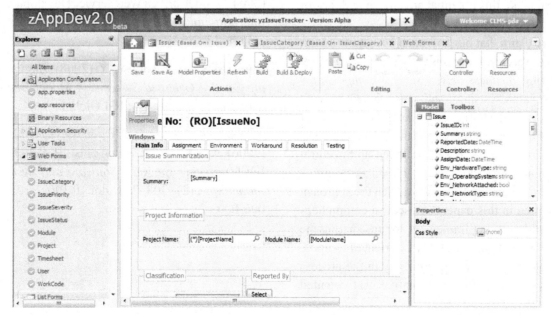

is transformed to a BPEL specified Web service orchestration model.

Approaches such as the above, while improving the speed of composite application development, do not address all domains of composite applications (e.g. middleware and user task models) as proposed in this paper.

As reported in van den Heuvel et al. (2009) two main research challenges in software service engineering are:

1. The mapping from requirements to services fulfilling them.
2. Bridging the modelling chasm between design/develop and delivery/execution.

We believe that our approach tackles both challenges as it models requirements (i.e. business process models) as well as the services that realize them in a uniform way (IDEF0).

Papazoglou et al. (2006) also argue that one of the main ideas of service oriented applications is to abstract away the logic at the business level from its non-business related aspects, such as the implementation of transaction, security, and reliability policies. The authors continue that provision of automated composition techniques, which make this potential advantage real, is still an open problem.

We claim that our approach goes quite a long way towards solving this research challenge, by allowing *business-driven service compositions* that separates business and system level concerns and allows generation of the complete and correct set of artefacts required to implement the business composition, based on taken architectural decisions and underlying execution platforms.

Thus, to conclude, we argue that the approach presented in this paper represents a comprehensive and unifying framework for automating the development process of service oriented composite applications. We are currently in the process of trying to integrate alternative user oriented process descriptions such as BPMN in the above described framework.

REFERENCES

Brambilla, M., Ceri, S., Fraternali, P., & Manolescu, I. (2006). Process modeling in Web applications. *ACM Transactions on Software Engineering and Methodology*, *15*(4), 360–409. doi:10.1145/1178625.1178627

Chen, H. M., Perry, O., & Kazman, R. (2009, August 12-15). An Integrated Framework for Service Engineering: A Case Study in the Financial Services Industry. Paper presented at ICEC '09, Taipei, Taiwan.

den Haan, J. (2009). *The Science of Model-Driven SOA*. Retrieved from http://www.theenterprisearchitect.eu/archive/2009/04/14/the-science-of-model-driven-soa

Frye, C. (2005). *QUESTION & ANSWER The role of composite applications in an SOA*. Retrieved from http://searchsoa.techtarget.com/news/interview/0,289202,sid26_gci1109080,00.html

Grønmo, R., Skogan, D., Solheim, I., & Oldevik, J. (2004). Model-driven Web Service Development. *International Journal of Web Services Research*, *1*(4), 1–13.

Karakostas, B., & Zorgios, Y. (2008). *Engineering Service Oriented Systems: A Model Driven Approach*. Hershey, PA: IGI Global.

Karakostas, B., Zorgios, Y., & Alevizos, C. C. (2006). Automatic derivation of BPEL4WS from IDEF0 process models. *Software and Systems Modeling*, *5*(2), 208–218. doi:10.1007/s10270-006-0003-2

Marcos, E., Papazoglou, M. P., Piattini, M., de Castro, M. V., Vela, B., Caballero, I., et al. (2009, November 6). Forward. In *Proceedings of the First International Workshop on Model Driven Service Engineering and Data Quality and Security (MoSE+DQS 2009),* Hong Kong.

Mayer, F., Schroeder, A., & Koch, N. (2008). MDD4SOA: Model-Driven Service Orchestration. In *Proceedings of the 12th International IEEE Enterprise Distributed Object Computing Conference.*

Miller, J., & Mukerji, J. (Eds.). (2001). *OMG Model Driven Architecture.* Retrieved from http://www.omg.com/mda

OASIS. *Web Services Composite Application Framework (WS-CAF).* Retrieved from http://www.oasis-open.org/committees/ws-caf/charter.php

Orriens, B., Yang, J., & Papazoglou, M. P. (2003). *Model Driven Service Composition Service-Oriented Computing.* Paper presented at ICSOC 2003.

Papazoglou, M. P., Traverso, P., & Dagstuhl, S. (2006). Service-Oriented Computing Research Roadmap Seminar. In *Proceedings of the Service Oriented Computing (SOC) Conference.* Retrieved from http://drops.dagstuhl.de/opus/volltexte/2006/524 April 2006

SAP. (2005). *Developing composite applications with SAP composite application framework.* Retrieved from http://sdn.sap.com

van den Heuvel, W.-J., Zimmermann, O., Leymann, F., Lago, P., Schieferdecker, I., Zdun, U., et al. (2009, May 18-19). Software Service Engineering: Tenets and Challenges. In *Proceedings of PESOS'09* Vancouver, BC, Canada.

Yu, X., Zhang, T., Wang, L., Hu, J., Zhao, J., & Li, X. (2007). A model-driven development framework for enterprise Web services. *Information Systems Frontiers, 9,* 391–409. doi:10.1007/s10796-007-9042-7

This work was previously published in the International Journal of Information Technologies and Systems Approach, Volume 4, Issue 1, edited by Frank Stowell and Manuel Mora, pp. 23-37, copyright 2011 by IGI Publishing (an imprint of IGI Global).

Chapter 8
A Service Oriented Architecture for Coordination in Collaborative Environments

Beatriz Jiménez Valverde
University of Granada, Spain

Miguel Sánchez Román
University of Granada, Spain

Francisco L. Gutiérrez Vela
University of Granada, Spain

Patricia Paderewski Rodríguez
University of Granada, Spain

ABSTRACT

An important feature in collaborative environment is coordination, defined as the act of managing interdependencies between activities performed to achieve a goal. These interdependencies can be the result of loosely integrated collaborative activities (the use of coordination processes within the collaboration activities is not required) or tightly integrated collaborative activities (sophisticated coordination mechanisms are necessary). The existence of both activities along with the dynamic nature of these environments adds a greater complexity to the coordination that has not been taken into account in traditional collaborative systems. In this work, the authors present a partially Services Oriented Architecture (SOA) that defines and maintains dynamic coordination polities in collaborative systems based on coordination models.

INTRODUCTION

The development of groupware systems is a complex task. As these types of systems support collaborative activities, it is therefore necessary to manage dynamic elements such as the orga-nizational structure of a work group, the set of responsibilities and activities involved during the work, or the assignment of resources and tools that of resources and tools that may be required.

At architectural level, it is appropriate that these systems be built on an architecture that facilitates

DOI: 10.4018/978-1-4666-1562-5.ch008

changes, as they should be able to adapt easily to changes in the organization and to any new requirements that may arise in the future.

The incorporation of collaborative activities into the work groups of current companies generates an increase in the performance of their business processes as much at an individual level as a group one. In order to support collaborative activities, the information systems of a company must possess a specific infrastructure. Activities such as communication, coordination and collaboration are essential to ensure that group work is successful and resources used in an efficient way.

The diversity of business process categories to be implemented within these systems is as great as the variety collaboration types between business organizations. For each organization in the system, the basic problem is to be able to establish fruitful connections with other organizations as cost-effectively and as quickly as possible.

There are different levels of collaborative maturity that can be used to characterize a collaborative system:

- **Communicating:** capable of exchanging and sharing information.
- **Open:** capable of sharing business services and functionalities with others.
- **Federated**: capable of working with others according to a set of collaborative processes that have a common objective and to assure its own objectives.
- **Interoperable:** capable of working with others so that the set appears as a homogeneous and seamless system.

The level of interoperability, or the ability to exchange and work at the highest level of collaboration, can only be achieved efficiently if an effective coordination is established.

One of the biggest problems identified in current enterprise systems relates to how coordination can be established in a correct and efficient manner. The technological solutions offered for this problem use a group of heterogeneous devices and software elements that require coordination with one another. For example, in a bank system the study and approval of a bank loan will involve a diverse group of actors (employee in charge of the loan, bank director, etc.) that will use different applications (loan request, consultation of clients, consultation of debts, risk calculation, etc.) and that must be coordinated in order to execute a complex group activity.

Coordination is usually defined as "the act of managing interdependencies between activities that are carried out to achieve an objective".

We can determine two coordination types depending on the kind of collaboration that is carried out:

- **Loosely integrated collaborative activities.** Here, the use of coordination processes within the collaboration activities is not required, for example, when a "Chat" is being used to carry out a decision activity. The coordination process is not explicitly described, despite the existence of implicit social protocols. The coordination can be described as culturally established and strongly dependent on mutual awareness.
- **Tightly integrated collaborative activities.** Here, the existence of sophisticated coordination processes, and consequently associate coordination mechanisms, are necessary. Dependencies exist between the activities and the actors that carry them out, requiring that everything be controlled. Examples of tightly integrated activities may be found in workflow procedures, e-learning, collaborative authoring, multi-user computer games, amongst others. As a special case of e-learning, it is worth mentioning JIGSAW (Aronson & Patnoe, 1997) in which it is necessary to define coordination policies between members of a group of experts, between the groups

themselves, or to present the knowledge gained from one group to another.

In most cases, traditional coordination systems have focused on the second coordination type, ignoring the activities of the first, as they do not require strict coordination. However, the problem with this approach is that a narrow relationship between the two types of activities exists and must be mutually coordinated. Although the activities carried out within an unstructured process cannot be strictly coordinated, this process must still be integrated with others.

Another important issue concerning coordination processes is the necessity to incorporate a dynamic nature into the activities. For example, in the case of the management of a bank loan, it is essential to bear in mind such factors as: what happens if the bank director is absent? Who takes responsibility for approving the loan? If the loans assignment policy changes, how can these changes be incorporated? If changes affect the organizational structure of the bank, how do we include them in the applications that are currently operating within our system?

We find the answer to all these issues through the incorporation of the internal representation of a set of models created during the requirements elicitation and analysis in a web service architecture. These conceptual models can model associations of a different nature, such as: the ability of users to change from one role to another allowing us to adapt to changes in the environment or the goal associated with a task allowing us to represent unstructured tasks.

This paper is organized as follows: First, we discuss related works found in the literature on coordination mechanisms for collaborative systems. Second our approach, based on service oriented architecture to support collaborative systems, is highlighted. Next, we detail a set of web services to support coordination in collaborative systems and we explain the specific web service for managing coordination, the Web Service Coordination.

Finally, we outline our conclusions and future lines of research.

RELATED WORKS

The development of collaborative systems has been approached from different perspectives. Works such as, i* (Yu, 1995), AMENITIES (Garrido, 2003), CIAM (Molina, 2006) or TOUCHE (Penichet, 2007) present methodologies for modeling cooperative environments that facilitate the detection of the most relevant aspects of these systems.

Our works is related with three important topics: interoperability, coordination in collaborative process and collaborative systems which are supported by Service-Oriented Architectures.

From the point of view of interoperability, which is the ultimate rung of the collaborative maturity ladder, different research works have been developed: European Interoperability Framework (EIF) (IDABC, 2004), ATHENA Interoperability Framework (AIF) (Athena, 2007), Interoperability Development for Enterprise Applications and Software (IDEAS) (IDEAS, 2002) and e-Government Interoperability Framework (e-GIF) (E-gif, 2005).

EIF and e-GIF focus on interoperability within the eGovernment and eAdministration projects of the eEurope Action Plan (2005) by defining a set of recommendations in several dimensions: technical (use of XML Schema, Web Services, etc.), semantic (metadata definition, taxonomies, ontologies, etc.) and organizational (establishing business process models, categorization of services, etc.).

The AIF provides a compound framework, associated with a reference architecture, as much for the capture of research elements as solutions to interoperability problems.

The IDEAS project provides four different areas for structuring the interoperability issues in enterprise applications: *Business layer,* focusing on business environment and processes; *Knowledge layer,* focusing on organizational roles, skills and competencies of employees, and knowledge assets; *ICT systems layer,* focusing on applications, data and communication components; *Semantic dimension,* which cuts across and provides support for the previous three layers.

The Mediation information System (MIS) (Bénaben et al., 2008) addresses the interoperability elements previously identified, and is dedicated to dealing with exchanged data, shared services and collaborative processes. The MIS design combines the different abstraction layers (business, logic and technological) according to Model-Driven Architecture (MDA) principles, and at each level makes use of the associated models in order to construct models for the next level. The principal limitation of this approach is the difficulty of proving semantically the accuracy of the specification and the rules generated.

In the work of (Bénaben et al., 2008) a design patterns system is proposed to help software designers model the coordination services required to support mobile collaboration. This conceptual framework allows developers to analyze the interactions between several mobile workers, considering time and space dependence when performing an interaction. Likewise, other researchers have proposed similar solutions to support coordination on fixed networks (Arvola, 2006; Avgeriou, 2006).

In (Lukosch & Schümmer, 2008) the explicit notion of how roles influence social interaction in a computer-mediated context is demonstrated. Patterns are presented that help the designer of collaborative systems to represent roles in the system design and thereby steer group interaction.

In recent years SOC (Service Oriented Computing) has emerged as a computing paradigm that supports interoperability for facilitating the development of applications.

SOC utilizes services as fundamental elements to support rapid, low-cost development of distributed applications in heterogeneous environments. The services are loosely coupled in order to flexibly create dynamic business processes and agile applications with the ability to span organizations and computing platforms, and adapt quickly and autonomously to changing mission requirements.

Developing the SOC involves developing Service-Oriented Architectures (SOAs) (Booth et al., 2004; Burbeck, 2000) and corresponding middleware that enables the discovery, utilization, and combination of interoperable services to support any business process in any organizational structure. SOAs allow application developers to overcome many distributed enterprise computing challenges, including designing and modelling complex distributed services, performing enterprise application integration, managing business processes, ensuring transactional integrity and QoS, and complying with agreements, while leveraging various computing devices and allowing reuse of legacy systems (Alonso et al, 2004).

The design principles of SOA (Anagol, 2004; Burbeck, 2000) are independent of any specific technology. In particular, SOA prescribes that all functions of SOA-based application are provided as services (Levi, 2002). Each service in a SOA based application may implement a brand-new function, it may use parts of old applications that were adapted and wrapped by the service implementation, or it may combine new code and legacy parts.

Jørstad et al. (2005) proposes and describes a set of generic coordination services for distributed work scenarios. These services include locking, presentation control, user presence management and communication control.

Web Services have become the preferred implementation technology for creating SOAs (Heather, 2003). Web Services are designed to provide interoperability between diverse applications. The platform and language-independent interfaces of Web Services allow the easy integration of heterogeneous systems. Web specifications such as universal description, discovery, and integration (UDDI), web services description language (WSDL) and simple object access protocol

(SOAP) define standards for service discovery, description and messaging protocols.

A SERVICE ORIENTED ARCHITECTURE

One feature that software systems currently require is the ability to interoperate or to integrate with existing systems.

At an architectural level, this means using a flexible and standards-based architecture in order to satisfy current demands and plan ahead. In other words, the architecture should be able to integrate new applications into the system. An architecture that is effective and easily adapts to changes must permit:

- The provision of tools to simplify the design, implementation, and changes of the system processes.

  ○ The design of applications as services so that they will be part of a process. A process can be divided into services, and set of services can be combined into a process.

Therefore, the SOA provides a methodology and a framework to support integration and consolidation activities.

Our approach is based on the use of service oriented architecture to support collaborative systems (Gutierrez et al., 2007).These systems include an additional dynamism because they require the coordination information to adapt to changes in the environment. SOA is a perfect solution given these conditions.

This problem can be solved by creating an internal representation of the models created during the requirements elicitation and analysis in our web services. These models depend on the methodology used. We chose to use the models described in Gutierrez et al. (2006) and the de-

Figure 1. Organizational model

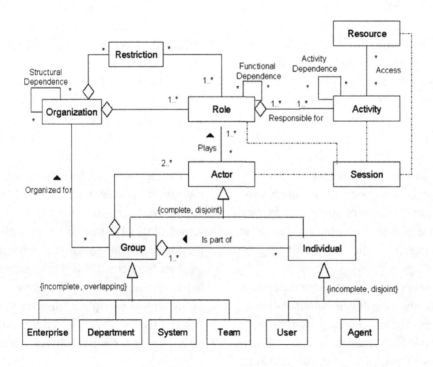

velopment methodology TOUCHET (Penichet, 2007). Figure 1 shows a partial organizational model resulting from the application of the methodology TOUCHET.

This conceptual model defines an organization as a set of roles and functional dependencies between them. As a result we can model associations of a different nature, such as the ability of users to change from one role to another. In addition, introducing restrictions on the roles within the organization (cardinality of roles, separation of duties, etc.), as well as the functional dependencies, allows a dynamic character to be given to the allocation of roles, providing sensitivity and flexibility for whichever environment they are used in.

An "actor" refers to individual actors (a user, a software agent, a robot, etc.) as well as groups. By including the groups in the concept of actor we can assign common user group abilities to actors. An actor (organizational or individual) plays at least one role in the organization. Playing a role implies that the actor is responsible for conducting activities associated with that role. Implicitly we assume that an actor must have the permissions and capabilities required to carry out the relevant activities and associated resources.

Through the session concept, the model indicates roles that are active for a particular actor and the current state of the workflow process of the organization,(for example: which actor is performing a task, with which role an actor is undertaking a task and which resources are used).

In our proposal, the coordination management is centralized in the Web Service Coordination, which interacts with other web services in our architecture, such as: Web Service Authorization, Web Service Tasks, Web Service Session and Web Service Resources and Tools. Our architecture is shown in Figure 2. In addition to the web services mentioned above, we have included various collaborative tools (for example. Chat and Blackboard, Voting System, Collaborative Editor, etc) that can be accessed using web service.

Each of these services is discussed in more detail in the following sections.

WEB SERVICES TO SUPPORT COORDINATION

An important part of a collaborative system is the "coordination process", which involves activities such as the identification of aims or synchronization between activities.

In our architecture, the Web Service Coordination is a complex service that interacts with other web services to determinate a set of appropriate coordination actions in each case. To achieve this the Web Service Coordination considers the information provided by the other services such as users who are connected, a role that a user plays, the next task to be carried out and which users have permissions to perform the task. The most important web services that interact with the Web Service Coordination are subsequently discussed.

Web Service Authorization

The Web Service Authorization stores and manages information according to the authorization policies implemented in the system. These policies are constructed in compliance with an access authorization model based on Role Based Access Control (RBAC) (Ferraiolo et al., 2007; Sandhu et al., 2006), which is defined according to the organization model presented in Figure 1. The information used to implement the coordination between different actors is related to: roles that a user can play, user/role's access permissions to resources, tasks that a user/role can perform, etc.). Some methods that provide this web service are:

- **Register users and roles:** This operation stores information about the users belonging to the system and the responsibilities that can be carried out by these users (roles).

Figure 2. Service oriented architecture

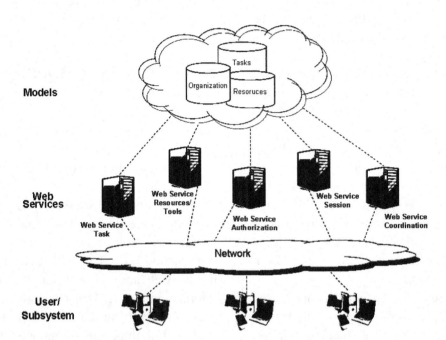

• **Link users and permissions to roles:** This is used to model part of the organizational system structure and associate users with their responsibilities (roles). The operation is also used to indicate resource and task access permissions for each role.

• **Verify the access to resources according to the user's active permissions:** This is used to indicate whether a user who carries out responsibilities (roles) within the system has permission to access a specific resource.

• **Check the access to activities according to the user's active permissions:** This is used to indicate whether a user playing a specific role has permission to perform a task or activity.

• **Modify roles currently played by a user:** This allows the structure of responsibilities in the organization to be modified, to establish or remove a user/role assignment.

Two types of access are used to facilitate service management: "user mode access" used by applications to control access to shared resources, and "administrator mode access" with which modifications in the authorization models can be performed.

Web Service Task

The information that describes the tasks/activities which can be carried out in the system is managed and stored by the Web Service Task. This service is based on the tasks model shown in Figure 3 which uses the multilevel hypermedia network developed by us Jiménez et al. (2007) and follows Paterno's CONCURTASKTREE approach (Paterno, 1999) for modelling collaborative tasks. An important difference from the Paterno approach is the inclusion of goals in the net in order to represent and manage unstructured process.

In this model tasks are classified into abstract, individual, and team tasks. While abstract tasks are tasks that gather others, team tasks can be

Figure 3. Tasks model

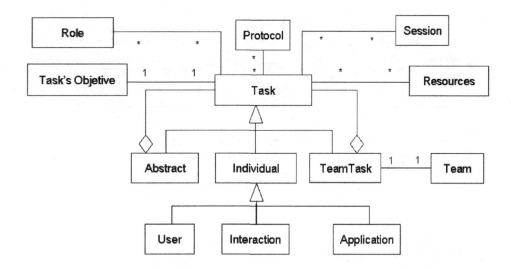

defined as one or more tasks carried out by user groups sharing common aims.

Both abstract tasks and team tasks occasionally consist of individual tasks. In team tasks, the individual tasks are performed by different team members (under the influence and dynamics of teamwork) with a shared, but not clearly assigned, responsibility. Individual tasks are considered application tasks, interaction tasks, or user tasks.

Figure 4 shows an example of a hypermedia network, which represents the Diagnostic process involved in the Management Incidents department of a business organization (Jiménez et al., 2007)

The Web Service Task covers all aspects related to the workflow of a system. In this way, an application, which interoperates in the system, can steer part of their internal application logic towards the web service. Some methods that provide this web service are:

- **Register a task:** This is used to incorporate a new functionality into the system.
- **Link activities to tasks and roles:** This is used to associate activities with a task and the set of permissions necessary for their execution.

- **Link resources to a task:** This is used to associate the resources that are needed to execute an activity, resources which must be available at the beginning of an activity.
- **Register the aim associated with a task:** This is used to associate the necessary aims with the task in order for the task to be completed.
- **Register interruption events:** This operation registers the tasks and/or roles that can be interrupted by other tasks. A task can be interrupted during its execution by means of a condition related to the task.
- **Register final states for activities:** This is used to obtain final states for an activity which will determine the activity sequence and therefore the associated work flow.
- **Register initial states for activities:** This is used to obtain possible initial states for an activity.
- **Register an aim:** This is used to obtain the specification of an aim as a series of individual sub-aims.
- **Register transaction rules:** This is used to register the rules which determine navigation between activities based on tempo-

Figure 4. Hypermedia network for diagnostic process

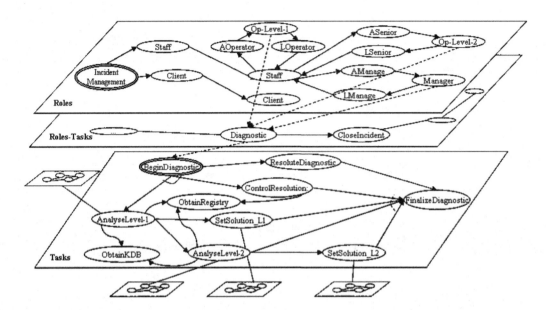

rary expressions. In a first approximation, we have used the temporary operators defined in the CONCURTASKTREE model (Paterno, 1999).

- **Operations which can be used to modify and delete the model information**. One of the most important requirements of these operations is to leave the system workflow, which is modeled by our hypermedia network, in a consistent state at all times. Changes that are made in the context of the system can quickly be applied to the model and indirectly to the web service task, thus allowing the system to rapidly adapt to the new changes.

Web Service Session

In collaborative systems it is very important to know the current state of the system context (roles, active users, tasks or activities in execution etc) even more so when dealing with collaborative processes, whose coordination processes depend heavily on what actors are doing and the state of shared resources. The inclusion of context is crucial for functions as the awareness or access control to resources, both elements often determinate which architecture should be implemented.

This information is necessary for managing user and task access control. Our architecture includes a Web Service Session in order to do is. The Web Service Session maintains a representation of the dynamic use of the system (current context and record of the finished process). Its main objectives are to register the finished and active tasks performed by each user playing a specific role in the system. The services register a set of elements related to the context in which the activities are carried out. We can therefore control the state of each user/subsystem using the information stored during a session. Some methods that provide this web service are:

- **Register the finish of an activity within a task:** To register the final state of an activity. This information allows us to include the workflow and make organizational changes to the roles.

- **Register active activities in a task:** This operation is used to register the activation of one activity in a task.
- **Register roles linked to users:** Registering these links allows us to monitor and control activities in the system.
- **Register connected users in the system showing their active roles in the current session:** To register connected users and their linking roles enabling us to control the interaction between users and activities in the system.
- **Query finishing activities in a task:** This is used to obtain the point reached in the work flow sequence of a given a task.
- **Query partial aims reached up to a link to a global aim:** to obtain the partial aims reached and the link with the global aim of a given task.
- **Query active activities in a task:** These operations can be used to obtain how many activities are active in a task.
- **Query resources which are being accessed for an active activity:** to obtain resources which are being used by an active activity enabling us to control and monitor the relation of other activities in the system.
- **Query the active role or roles for a user performing an activity:** to obtain user roles in an activity. This information allows us to make decisions that will determine whether activities are performed by one role or another.
- **Query final state of an activity in a task:** in order to obtain the final state of an activity, it is necessary to determine the work flow which will be followed. In many situations this is determined by the result of each activity.
- **Query active activities in a task, users executing the task and the group to which the users belong**: This enables us

to determine the access control for a user on a task, if a series of activities has been completed.

- **Query active roles for group users:** Obtaining this relation determines the functional dynamism with respect to making decisions about changes in roles in the organization.
- Query resources which are being used by a user, user role and user group – Obtaining this relation will determine both decision-making about role changes and the availability of shared resources.

Web Service Tools and Resources

The Web Service Tools and Resources storages and manages information relating to resources and tools that are used by the system, such as resource type (synchronous or asynchronous), and the association between resources and tasks or actors who are responsible for resources. This information is structured following the resources models shown in Figure 5. The management of this information is important for coordination of collaborative systems, which include informal tasks (for example, evaluation of a collaborative exercise carried out by several students). The use of one tool or another will influence the choice of coordination policy to be used in the resolution of a collaborative task.

Some methods that this web service provides are:

- **Register resources or tools:** This operation is used to register the resources or the tools used by a structured or unstructured task.
- **Link resources or tools to a task:** This is used to associate resources or tools needed to execute an activity which must be available at the beginning of an activity.

Figure 5. Resources and tools model

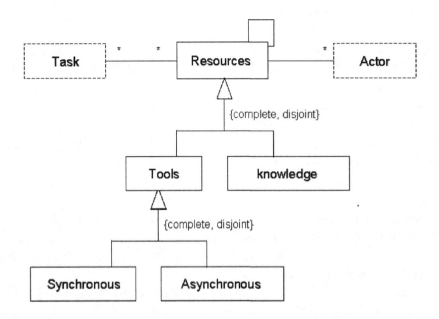

Web Service Coordination

In our architecture, overall control of the system is centralized under requests to a service for managing coordination, the Web Service Coordination. To reduce dependency on the coordination system, the subsystems that carry out activities send requests to coordinate with the coordination service. The Web Service Coordination implements a centralized and shared management environment for all elements/applications of the system.

Here we propose a global metamodel for coordination. We pay special attention to the processes of unstructured or informal nature. Such processes are very important because in collaborative activities many of the actions undertaken are of this type. Unstructured processes are processes whereby the sequence of activities is not always clear and in most cases we can only set the proposed aims, the amount of resources we have available and how we can use/share them.

We believe the models necessary to describe a system for coordinating tasks are: an actor model, an organizational model, a session model, a task-goal model and a resource-tool model. We add a fifth model, a coordination model to represent coordination policies. These policies allow us to coordinate the interaction between users and users with shared resources, avoiding conflicts that lead to inconsistency in the information.

Coordinating policies ranking from levels that include unstructured information (such as those required in a Chat, where coordination is not explicitly defined but implicit social protocols of conduct are associated with the tool), to levels which focus on interactive work towards a common goal ("Brainstorming" or Voting systems are tools that need to define such policies).

All these models form a unique metamodel containing the information necessary be reflected in the Web Service Coordination.

Some methods that this service provides are:

- **Register a policy:** This is used to incorporate a new policy into the system.
- **Begin/End coordination session:** Begin a coordination session for a collaborative

application and register the end of this session.

- **Modify/Query coordination policies:** This method is used to query and modify policies previously defined.

Next, we describe an example to show the interaction between the different web services within the Web Service Coordination to support an application for management brainstorming (Figure 6).

In brainstorming, users contribute ideas on a particular topic and are able to decide for or against the ideas of others. In this application, as in most collaborative applications, internal processes of users are involved. User processes are those that run an explicit order, while internal processes only respond to internal system applications, such as the distribution of updates on a shared object. In brainstorming, users can send messages (with ideas and arguments for or against) that are viewed by other users. It may also happen that a new user joins the working session, or that any user leaves the meeting. In this case, the user simply enters the session or leaves. However, the group should be notified of the input or output of a user. In this case an event is automatically communicated to all users in the group, via the message generated by an internal process. It may also be the case that a user who has just entered the system whises to see what has happened during the session (the history). In this instance, the user asks to see step by step ideas that have been generated and the accept or reject process of others' arguments.. The decision may also be made to rethink new arguments about an idea previously rejected. The system must keep a track of the history of the session.

When a brainstorming instance is initiated into a group (*GroupId*), a connection is established with the Web Service Coordination in order to generate a coordination session, which is identified by a session identifier (*SessionId*). Once a user

(*UserId*) decides to participate in brainstorming, the Web Service Authorization notifies whether the user is authorized or not. Then, the instance asks the Web Service Task what is the next task to be performed by the user.

The Web Service Task makes a request to the stored task model for the next task (*TaskId*) to be carried out by the user. In order to find out which is the next task the Web Service Task uses information provided by the Web Service Authorization (to know if the user has permission to perform the task) and to the Web Service Session (to identify the current context, such as tasks performed, connected users, etc.). Finally, the Web Service Task asks the coordination service to check that the initial coordination policy was followed while the task was performed.

CONCLUSION AND FUTURE WORK

In this paper, we have analyzed the necessity of software systems to interoperate and integrate with existing systems, in addition to the fact that SOA (Service Oriented Architecture) provides a methodology and a framework to support this integration and the consolidation of activities. Consequently, we have presented a service oriented architecture that provides the necessary services to represent aspects of coordination within a collaborative system. Thanks to this architecture we are able to manage interdependencies between the activities that are carried out in collaborative systems in order to achieve a common objective.

Due to the dynamic nature of collaborative systems it is necessary to establish mechanisms to adapt the coordination information to the changes on the environment. As a consequence, we maintain an internal representation of a set of models (actor model, organizational model, session model, task-goal model, resource-tool model and coordination model) that are created during the requirements elicitation and analysis. These mod-

Figure 6. Brainstorming sequence diagram

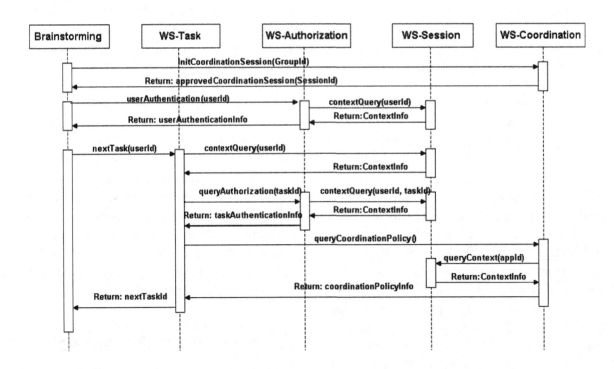

els permit constancy in the active session concept and the current workflow state of an organization process. These models are represented in our web services so that any change in the environment can be easily reflected in our architecture.

The management of this coordination is centralized in the Web Service Coordination, which interacts with other services of our architecture including: the Web Service Authorization, the Web Service Tasks, the Web Service Session and the Web Service Resources and Tools. We have described an example showing the interaction between the different web services within the Web Service Coordination to support an application for the management brainstorming.

Our future work will concentrate on the use of conceptual patterns (Gutierrez et.al, 2007) during development phase. This will minimize the shaped efforts and enable us to generate more optimized design solutions. Hence we are currently working to find conceptual patterns which allow us to model policies of coordination and security.

REFERENCES

Alonso, G., Casati, F., Kuno, H., & Machiraju, V. (2004). *Web Services: Concepts, Architectures and Applications*. New York: Springer.

Anagol, A. (2004). *J2EE Web Services on BEA WebLogic*. Upper Saddle River, NJ: Prentice Hall.

Aronson, E., & Patnoe, S. (1997). *The jigsaw classroom: Building cooperation in the classroom* (2nd ed.). New York: Addison Wesley Longman.

Arvola, M. (2006). Interaction design patterns for computers in sociable use. *International Journal of Computer Applications in Technology, 25*(2-3), 128–139. doi:10.1504/IJCAT.2006.009063

ATHENA. (2007). *ATHENA Integrated Project.* Retrieved from http://www.athena-ip.org/

Avgeriou, P., & Tandler, P. (2006). Architectural patterns for collaborative applications. *International Journal of Computer Applications in Technology, 25*(2-3), 86–101. doi:10.1504/IJ-CAT.2006.009062

Bénaben, F., Touzi, J., Rajsiri, V., Trupril, S., Lorré, J. P., & Pingaud, H. (2008). Mediation Information System Design in a Collaborative SOA Context through a MDD Approach. In *Proceedings of the First International Workshop on Model Driven Interoperability for Sustainable Information Systems* (pp. 89-103).

Booth, D., Hass, H., McCabe, F., Newcomer, E., Champion, I. M., Ferris, C., et al. (2004). *Web Services Architecture.* Retrieved from http://www.w3.org/TR/2004/NOTE-ws-arch-20040211/

Burbeck, S. (2000). *The tao of e-business services: The evolution of Web applications into service-oriented components with Web services.* Retrieved from http://www.ibm.com/developer-works/library/ws-tao/

E-gif. (2005). *E-government Interoperability Framework.* Retrieved from http://www.e.govt.nz/standards/e-gif/e-gif-v-3-3/

Ferraiolo, D. F., Kuhn, D. R., & Chandramouli, R. (Eds.). (2007). *Role Based Access Control* (2nd ed.). Boston: Artech House.

Garrido, J. L. (2003). *AMENITIES: Una metodología para el desarrollo de sistemas cooperativos basada en modelos de comportamiento y tareas.* Unpublished doctoral dissertation, University of Granada, Granada.

Gutiérrez, F. L., Isla, J. L., Paderewski, P., Sánchez, M., & Jiménez, B. (2007). An Architecture for Access Control Management in Collaborative Enterprise Systems Based on Organization Models. *International Journal of Science of Computer Programming, 66*(1), 44–59. doi:10.1016/j.scico.2006.10.005

Gutiérrez, F. L., Penichet, V., Isla, J. L., Montero, F., Lozano, M. D., Gallud, J. A., et al. (2006). Un marco Conceptual para el Modelado de Sistemas Colaborativos Empresariales. In *Proceedings of the VII Congreso de Interacción Persona Ordenador* (pp. 269-278).

IDABC. (2004). *European interoperability framework for pan-European egovernment services, version 1.0.* Brussels, Belgium: Author.

IDEAS. (2002). European IST-2001-37368 project IDEAS: Interoperability Developments for Enterprise Application and Software - Roadmaps.

Jiménez, B., Sánchez, M., Gutiérrez, F. L., & Medina, N. (2007). Task Models Representation of a Collaborative System Using Hypermedia Networks. In *Proceedings of the 3rd International Conference on WEBIST* (pp. 113-120).

Jørstad, I., Dustdar, S., & Van Thanh, D. (2005). Service Oriented Architecture Framework for collaborative services. In *Proceedings of the 14th IEEE International Workshops on Enabling Technologies: Infrastructure for Collaborative Enterprise* (pp. 121-125).

Kreger, H. (2003). Fulfilling the Web services promise. *Communications of the ACM, 46*(6), 29. doi:10.1145/777313.777334

Levi, K., & Arsanjani, A. (2002). A goal-driven approach to enterprise component identification and specification. *Communications of the ACM, 45*(10), 45–52. doi:10.1145/570907.570930

Lukosch, S., & Schümmer, T. (2008). The role of roles in collaborative interaction. In *Proceedings of the 13th European Conference on Pattern Languages and Programs, EuroPLoP.*

Molina, A. I. (2006). *A methodology for the development of groupware user interfaces.* Unpublished doctoral dissertation, Universidad de Castilla-la Mancha (UCLM).

Paterno, F. (1999). *Model-based Design and Evaluation of Interactive Applications.* Berlin: Springer Verlag.

Penichet, V. (2007). *TOUCHE (Task-Oriented and User-Centred Process Model for Developing Interfaces for Human-Computer-Human Environments): A process model and a methodology for the development of groupware applications from the requirements gathering up to the implementation stage.* Unpublished doctoral dissertation, Universidad de Castilla-La Mancha (UCLM).

Sandhu, R. S., Coyne, E. J., Feinstein, H. L., & Youman, C. E. (2006). Role-based access control models. *IEEE Computer, 29,* 38–47.

Yu, E. (1995). *Modeling Strategic Actor Relationships for Business Process Reengineering.* Unpublished doctoral dissertation, University of Toronto, Department Computer Science.

This work was previously published in the International Journal of Information Technologies and Systems Approach, Volume 4, Issue 1, edited by Frank Stowell and Manuel Mora, pp. 79-92, copyright 2011 by IGI Publishing (an imprint of IGI Global).

Chapter 9
Mobile Enterprise Architecture Framework

Zongjun Li
Government of Ontario, Canada

Annette Lerine Steenkamp
Lawrence Technological University, USA

ABSTRACT

The Mobile Enterprise is a new form of enterprise in the contemporary mobile era. Although several well-known enterprise architecture frameworks are used by enterprises, it is apparent that there is no industry standard available to enable an enterprise to transform its business processes to incorporate mobile technologies to advantage. This paper presents a conceptual Mobile Enterprise Architecture Framework and supporting methodology and process model which can aid enterprise decision makers to evaluate the business values, and analyze the risks and other critical business and technical factors for enterprise mobile initiatives and mobile transitions. The framework covers both the enterprise and mobile enterprise architecture domains that represent the Enterprise, Business, and Mobile Adoption levels. The goal at the Enterprise Level is to obtain a mobile enterprise and the technologies adopted at the Mobile Adoption Level are the different mobile technologies to be incorporated. Each level contains some important components impacting the mobile enterprise transformation. The methodology and process model cover the Strategy, Analysis, Design, Implementation, and Maintenance stages for each mobile initiative, and were validated in a research project against some Ontario Government mobile initiatives.

INTRODUCTION

With a myriad of mobile technologies emerging in what is called the mobile era enterprises have interesting opportunities for innovation, but at the same time are facing huge challenges similar to those experienced at the beginning of the Internet era. The Mobile Enterprise (ME), a new form of enterprise, is any enterprise whose employees are integrated with business processes on a continuous basis from any location inside or outside the enterprise facilities (Dulaney, 2003). The adoption and implementation of emerging mobile technologies is a more recent enterprise trend (Fenn and Linden, 2004; Kalakota and Robinson, 2002). There is limited research on the

DOI: 10.4018/978-1-4666-1562-5.ch009

impacts, values, and best practices of MEs. Most research has focused on the enablers and drivers of mobile technologies in enterprises (Dulaney 2003; Ferguson and Pike 2001; Steenkamp and Li, 2006). Others have examined potential mobile application areas (Varshney and Vetter, 2001; Chen and Skelton, 2005). Mobile Enterprise Architecture (MEA) research is limited to separate aspects, such as the mobile application architecture (Lee et al., 2004; Wireless Center, 2008), the mobile data architecture, the mobile infrastructure, and the mobile security architecture (Chen et al., 2006).

The use of a conceptual Enterprise Architecture (EA) and EA framework at the Enterprise Level is a recent trend. The EA is a comprehensive framework used to manage and align an enterprise's business and management processes, information technology (IT) software and hardware, local and wide area networks, people, operations and projects with the enterprise's overall strategy. Based on a survey from the Institute for Enterprise Architecture Developments (Schekkerman, 2005), the responsibility of the EA is shifting from that of IT management to business management. Current enterprises use different architecture(s) within enterprise architecture practices revealed by the survey results:

- Enterprise Architecture (15%);
- Business Architecture (10%);
- Information Architecture (13%);
- Information-Systems Architecture (14%);
- Technology Infrastructure Architecture (15%);
- Security Architecture (15%);
- Governance Architecture (7%);
- Software Architecture (11%);

The complexity inherent in the functioning of the contemporary enterprise has impacted the way the enterprise system and its architectures are conceptualized (Feurer et al., 2001). The findings above indicate that enterprises are using different architectures for their specific business needs. The different types of architectures used in the enterprises represent different points in the continuum of architectures (The Open Group, 2009) and are not fixed stages in a process. The continuum of architectures illustrates how architectures are developed across a continuum ranging from foundational architectures, through common systems architectures, and industry-specific architectures, to an enterprise's own individual architectures, and represents a progression, which occurs at several levels:

- Logical to physical;
- Horizontal (IT technology focused) to vertical (business focused);
- Generalization to specialization;
- Taxonomy to complete and specific architecture specification;

An EA is very relevant to the IT customer community, since it describes and guides the final deployment of user-written or third-party components. Such systems constitute effective solutions for a particular enterprise, or enterprises that have a need to share information. The EA guides the final customization of the solution, and has the following characteristics:

- Provides a means to communicate and manage the IT environment;
- Reflects requirements specific to a particular enterprise;
- Defines building blocks specific to a particular enterprise;
- Contains organization-specific physical data, applications, and process models, as well as business rules;
- Provides a means to encourage implementation of appropriate IT systems to meet business needs;
- Provides the criteria to measure and select appropriate products, solutions, and services;

- Provides an evolutionary path to support growth and new business needs;

The complexity within the enterprise mandates that IT systems must not be viewed in isolation, and that all relevant factors should be taken into consideration, such as principles, stakeholders, content, layers, aspects, standards and tools (Boar, 1999; Andrade et al., 2004; Steenkamp and Kakish, 2004; Steen et al., 2004). An architecture framework provides a conceptual frame of reference when thinking about EA.

The survey report by Schekkerman (2005) shows that many well-known EA frameworks are used by enterprises. The top four EA frameworks were found to be the Zachman Framework, the Federal Enterprise Architecture Framework (FEAF), the Open Group Architecture Framework (TOGAF) and the Gartner Framework (Sessions, 2007). Still, many enterprises own their EA frameworks (22%), or define their own framework, often based on existing ones. None of them includes consideration of the mobile enterprise, MEA or Mobile Enterprise Architecture Framework (MEAF). While these EA frameworks do not share consistent terminology, they do share a common concern for the various components of the enterprise that must be captured and analyzed (Boar, 1999; McDavid, 1999; Sessions, 2007). This paper argues that adopting the marketed EA frameworks to describe a MEA is not a good option. A generic MEAF, based on common EA elements and informed by current EA frameworks, is needed.

In response to this need a research project was undertaken to investigate the theoretical and practical aspects of enterprise stakeholder concerns about how to adopt emerging mobile technologies in the enterprise in support of the business processes. The next section outlines the research design of this research project. Following this a new conceptual MEAF is presented, and an MEA process model and methodology that may be used directly by enterprises to aid decision-makers when considering a transformation from a non-mobile to a mobile enterprise. The MEA methodology prescribes how to perform analysis, design, implementation, and maintenance of enterprise mobile initiatives that will add value to the enterprise.

RESEARCH DESIGN

A framework and methodology for creating a ME is a rather new research area, with limited theoretical or methodological support. To identify the main issues and to generate a solution for designing a generic framework for an enterprise in a purely deductive way seems difficult. First, one has to achieve an understanding of the problems and then determine how to investigate and solve these problems in order to develop an approach for building an ME from a non-ME, as depicted in Figure 1.

With respect to the nature of the research problems and hypotheses, Sol (1988) argues that the research problem typically represents an ill-structured problem. In the heuristic process to gain insight into the problems the researcher creates an image of reality, and raises questions and imposes requirements on the research approach.

A systematic research approach based on the inductive-hypothetic research strategy depicted in Figure 2 was well suited to the characteristics of this research. The strategy consists of five activities (Sol, 1982; Van Meel, 1994; de Vreede, 1995), as summarized below. The strategy is organized in terms of the execution of five steps and four model types.

In Step 1, one or more descriptive empirical models are constructed each describing a perceived situation in the specific field of interest, i.e. designing mobile services. Analyzing these perceived situations should provide a better understanding of the research area. The empirical models may contain elements from practice and from theory.

Figure 1. Roadmap from non-mobile to mobile enterprise

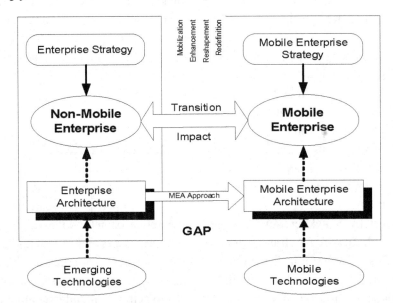

During Step 2 an abstraction is made from the empirical models, which results in a single descriptive conceptual model. This model describes the problems found in the perceived situation at a generic level, and gives indications of possible solutions.

During Step 3 the solutions are combined into a general theory, or grounded theory for solving the problems identified. "Note that in the context of the inductive-hypothetic strategy, the term 'theory' is used in a broad sense. A theory constitutes a proposed solution for a problem situation, for example, in terms of (a combination of) a set of problem handling guidelines and modeling concepts, modeling support, or an inquiry system" (de Vreede, 1995).

Step 4 elaborates the prescriptive conceptual model into one or more prescriptive empirical models. This implies that the proposed approach is applied in practice, i.e. in the specific area of designing mobile information services in an inter-organizational setting.

Figure 2. Inductive-hypothetic research strategy (Sol, 1982)

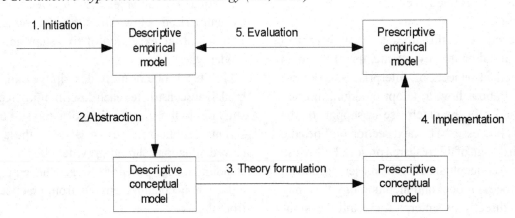

Step 5 compares the prescriptive empirical and prescriptive conceptual models allowing us to evaluate the effectiveness of the proposed theory. The models are evaluated in this way and may result in additional requirements for improving the prescriptive conceptual models and an iteration of the cycle.

In this research the proposed MEAF was applied in a local government context by means of the Action Research Case Method (Avison et al., 1999) to demonstrate how the framework, the MEA process model, and methodology could be used to create an m-Government environment. In order to constrain the scope of the demonstration of concept the case study focused on the first three process model stages (refer Figure 5), namely the Feasibility Stage, MEA Stage, and Alternatives Analysis Stage. The Deployment and Maintenance Stages only illustrate the possible activities for the Virtual Mobile Government (VMG) Blackberry initiative.

The literature review included determining background and focal theories and applications for both non-ME and ME, from the points of view of the enterprise business model, enterprise strategy, EA and emerging technologies for ME related business models, ME strategies, MEA, and emerging mobile technologies, as shown in Figure 1. The reviewed literature and business cases studied show that there is no existing MEA approach available for creating the ME. A number of ME studies were found, with most of them focused on the enterprises of mobile technology players. Very little research is related to the enterprise behaviors, such as enterprise mobility which impacts the enterprise business processes and organization structures.

A huge number of mobile solutions provided by the mobile industry solution vendors, such as IT consulting firms, mobile service providers and individuals, focus on special business needs. Those solutions could so far not convince the enterprise decision makers to make the appropriate level of investment in mobile initiatives to obtain maximum benefits from the emerging mobile technologies. While enterprises have invested in some mobility practices, they have not received the anticipated returns from their mobile investments. Enterprises may not be aware that more returns may be obtained by expending a little extra effort. Many enterprises are still waiting for maturity of mobile technologies and hence lose the window of opportunity that may have provided them with a competitive edge. Based on these findings the research turned to developing a generic approach, framework and methodology for creating an ME to help decision makers to make the proper mobile investment decisions, and finally transition the enterprise to a mobile one.

Figure 5. Five stage mobile enterprise architecture process model

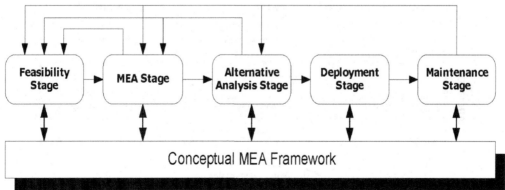

125

CONCEPTUAL FRAMEWORK

The comprehensive and integrative requirements of an MEA indicate the need for a holistic perspective, with architectural decisions driven by the enterprise, business and mobile strategies. The challenge is to integrate the enterprise, business and mobile adoption levels in terms of goals and measures, design and implementation and management, and related components of each domain.

A new conceptual MEAF is proposed, as depicted in abstract form in Figure 3, and elaborated in the following aspects:

- MEAF components;
- Three-level enterprise structure;
- MEA Approach;
- Top-down flow and the bottom-up flow.

Key Components of the Framework

An ME at the top of the conceptual framework is the key component representing the vision of the enterprise and the long term goals of its mobile initiatives. At the Enterprise Level there are five key components: Enterprise Strategy, Mission, Regulation, Legislation, and Outcomes. The Enterprise Strategy is the control center for all the ME activities. The Mission includes the enterprise goals and objectives for an enterprise transforming to a mobile one. The Regulation and Legislation components are for the governance of mobile initiatives. The Outcomes are the results of the analysis of the values, risks and costs for the mobile initiative(s). At the Business Level key components include: Business Strategy, the business system related Environment, Processes, Workflows, Finance, People and Quality; and the mobile system related Quality, m-Communication,

Figure 3 Conceptual mobile enterprise architecture framework

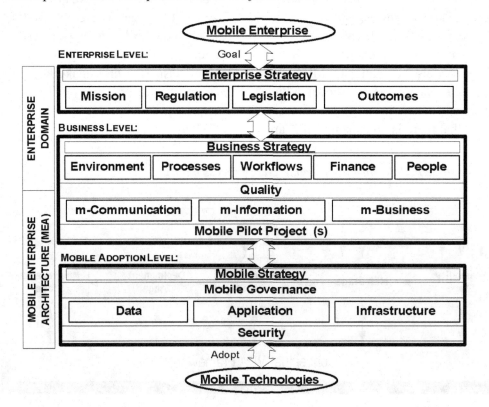

m-Information, m-Business, and Mobile Pilot Project(s). At the Mobile Adoption Level, key components include Mobile Strategy, Mobile Governance, and mobile initiative related Data, Application, Infrastructure, and Security. The Mobile Technologies component at the bottom of the conceptual framework is a key component, embodying the mobile technologies that drive the mobile initiatives and in which the enterprise invests.

Three-Level Mobile Initiative Structure

Besides ME and mobile technologies, all the key components are located in the three-level mobile initiative structure: Enterprise Level, Business Level and Mobile Adoption Level.

At the Enterprise Level the activities focus on enterprise strategy development, regulation and legislation, and outcome measurement; designing business and information architectures; and planning, monitoring, reviewing, and controlling of all mobile initiatives. This should be treated differently from other IT initiatives, since all mobile initiatives must be under the direction of enterprise regulation and rules. Many of the resources, products, services, and especially the lessons learned can be shared at the enterprise level. Large utilization of third parties' mobile products and services can bring more benefits as well, such as bulk discounts from mobile operators and service providers. Business Level activities focus on the business strategy, which supports the enterprise strategy; the improvement of the environment of the business units; business processes, workflow, finance, people, quality of products and services from the facilities provided by mobile initiatives: m-Communication, m-Information, m-Business; and Business Level planning, monitoring, reviewing and controlling of mobile initiatives.

Mobile Adoption Level activities focus on mobile enablement based on the enterprise strategy and business strategy, the pilot project plan, design, governance related to mobile data, application, infrastructure, and security.

Architecture Approach

The complexity of developing system architectures has motivated the adoption of a systems approach, starting with the MEAF, supported by a process model and methodology. The MEA approach provides a systemic way to realize an enterprise mobile initiative, drawing on the ideas of systems thinking expressed by Petkov et al. (2008). The MEA approach integrates the notions of a generic conceptual framework, architecture process model, and methodology. The EA approach, applicable for all enterprises, can also be adopted to model the dynamic processes for transformation from a non-mobile enterprise to ME in a systemic way. Because there is no uniform EA or MEA standard available in industry, using specific industry EA models would not meet the needs of all enterprises.

The conceptual architecture model in the recommended practice for developing an architecture description for software-intensive systems, proposed by the IEEE Architecture Planning Group (IEEE, 2000), was used as a foundation for the proposed conceptual MEA shown in Figure 4. In this UML diagram the Mobile Enterprise (ME) is a system which fulfils the ME Strategy Plan(s) and Vision (Steenkamp and Li, 2006; Steenkamp et al., 2004). An ME inhabits an ME environment, and an ME environment influences that ME. The ME environment (or context) determines the setting and circumstances of developmental, operational, political, and other influences upon that ME. The ME environment can include other enterprises (third party enterprises) that interact with the ME of interest, either directly via interfaces, or indirectly in other ways. The ME environment establishes the boundaries that define the scope of the ME of interest relative to other enterprises. An ME has one or more stakeholders. The ME stakeholders are those individuals, teams, and enterprises with interests in, or concerns relative to, that ME. Concerns are those issues that pertain to the development, deployment, operation, or other aspects of the ME that are critical (or otherwise important) to one or more ME stakeholders. Concerns include ME attributes such as performance, security, effectiveness, efficiency, reliability, availability, compliance, integrity, quality, and the like. An ME exists to realize one or more ME Strategy Plan and Vision in its ME environment. An ME Strategy Plan and Vision is drawn up for initiatives concerned with processes for which an ME is intended, as required by one or more ME stakeholders to meet some set of enterprise objectives.

The MEA is the highest-level conception of an ME in its environment. Every ME provides the rationale for the definition in the context of MEA practice. An MEA should conform to ISO 9126 Quality Attributes (Sowa and Zachman, 1992) that realize the quality concerns. An MEA

can be recorded by an MEA description. The MEA Description (MEAD) is a collection of products (the key components proposed in the conceptual framework) to document an MEA. The complexity and scope of the MEAD influenced the decision to consider the architecture in terms of a number MEA views.

An MEA view addresses one or more concerns of the ME stakeholders, such as m-Business, m-Data, and m-Infrastructure as listed in Table 1. A Viewpoint establishes the conventions by which the MEA views are depicted and the particular architectural techniques or methods employed to create and document those views. In this way an MEA view conforms to a viewpoint. The MEAD represents one or more viewpoints for the expression of the MEA views contained in it. The selection of viewpoints is typically based on consideration of the ME stakeholders to whom the MEAD is addressed, and their concerns. A viewpoint may originate with the MEAD, or it

Figure 4. Conceptual mobile enterprise architecture model

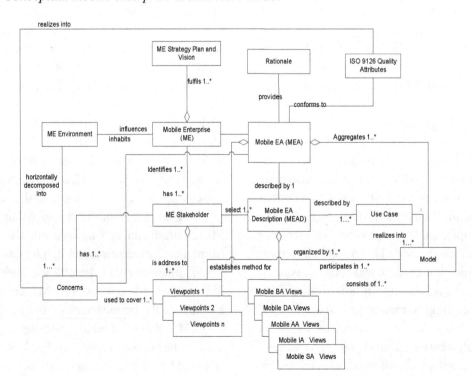

may have been previously defined. Enterprise Mobility, Security, and Quality of Service may be three important viewpoints in the MEA (Skelton, 2003). An MEA view consists of one or more MEA models. Each such MEA model is developed using the methods established by its associated ME view and viewpoint. An MEA model may participate in more than one MEA view. The MEAD may be described by one or more Use Cases and realized into one or more MEA models.

Top-Down and Bottom-Up Flow

The top-down flow in the MEA Framework indicates that enterprise mobile initiatives start from the enterprise strategy. The vision of the ME results

in regulations and legislations for Enterprise Level mobile activities. This is followed by the business strategy of the business units that identifies how to use mobile technologies to meet their business requirements. The focus here is especially on how to improve the business environment, processes, workflows, and quality of products and/or services utilizing mobile communication, information and business platforms. In order to obtain benefits from the financial and human perspectives, mobile platforms are implemented by many individual mobile pilot projects.

The enterprise should formulate a mobile strategy that guides the adoption of proper technologies to meet the enterprise's data, application, infrastructure, and security requirements. This will

Table 1. Example taxonomy of mobile enterprise architecture views (Modified from TOGAF 2007)

The ME Stakeholders			
m-Business Users	m-Data Designers and Administrators	m-Application Engineers	m-Infrastructure Acquirers, Operators
Views			
m-Business	**m-Data**	**m-Application**	**m-Infrastructure**
Function	Entity	Software Engineering	Mobile Computing/ Hardware View
Services	Data Flow	Interoperability	m-Communications
Process	Logical Data View	Software Distribution	Processing
m-Information			Cost
Locations			Standards
Logistics			
People			
Workflow			
Usability			
Strategy and Goals			
Objectives			
Rules			
Events			
Performance			
	System Engineering Viewpoint		
ME Security Viewpoint			
ME Manageability (Governance) Viewpoint			
ME Quality of Service Viewpoint			

provide input when building mobile platforms with sound emerging mobile technologies selected from many vendors. The bottom-up flow in the framework indicates that the enterprise starts from investing in mobile technologies, prototyping within the business units, and populating the results to the rest of the enterprise, and ends with achieving the goal by finally transforming the enterprise into a mobile enterprise.

ARCHITECTURE PROCESS MODEL AND METHODOLOGY

Architecture practices use a four stage architecture process model for IT adoption (Steenkamp and Li, 2006). In this paper an updated MEA process model is proposed, as in Figure 5. The methodology draws on the MEAF and supports the processes in the five stages. The methodology provides steps to define, capture, and measure values associated with enterprise mobile initiatives, to fully account for costs, and to identify and consider the risks and values from the mobile adoption lifecycle.

Feasibility Stage

The Feasibility Stage follows on the Enterprise Strategy during which mobile initiatives that directly address the strategic enterprise mobile objectives are analyzed. The steps that execute the processes of the Feasibility Stage may vary from one enterprise to another. The common tasks and the deliverables for this stage are as illustrated in Table 2.

Mobile Enterprise Architecture Stage

The MEA Stage is the key architecture stage and impacts the entire enterprise mobilizing process. Frequently iteration to the Feasibility Stage may be needed. The strategic planning and EA process hierarchy, and the Architecture Stage (Steenkamp and Li, 2006) may be modified for the MEA context

in the MEA Stage, as shown in Figure 6, which only shows the processes of MEA Analysis and Design Phases for the business architecture and IT/Mobile architecture aspects. The processes start from the analysis of business needs of mobile communication, information and business, and end in the physical modeling of the viewpoints, the mobile infrastructure, m-application architecture, m-data integration, and m-security, and finally the synthesis of the viewpoints. The common tasks and the deliverables for this stage are as illustrated in Table 3.

Alternative Analysis Stage

The Alternatives Analysis Stage involves estimation and evaluation of all value, cost, and risk factors leading to the selection of the most effective mobile solution that addresses a specific business need (e.g., service, policy, regulation, business process or system). In general, three to five alternatives for each mobile initiative are recommended, that may be provided by several mobile solution providers.

A "base case" is the alternative where no change is made to current practices or systems. All other alternatives are compared against the base case,

Table 2. Feasibility stage tasks and deliverables

Feasibility Stage	
Tasks	**Deliverables**
Identify Enterprise Current Status	Management checklist and results analysis
Develop the ME Strategic Plan	ME strategy process model and Strategic Plan
Define the ME Value Web	ME value web model
Identify the Value Factors	Value factor model
Identify the Risks	Risks inventory (initial), risk tolerance boundary model
Identify the Costs	Tailored cost model
Document Conceptual Framework Key Components	All level key components

Figure 6. Processes in the mobile enterprise architecture stage

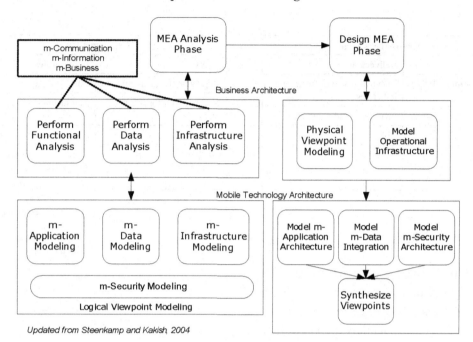

Updated from Steenkamp and Kakish, 2004

as well as to each other. An alternatives analysis requires a disciplined process to consider the range of possible actions to achieve the desired benefits. This analysis involves re-iterating the phases of the other two stages: Feasibility Stage and MEA Stage to determine the optimal mobile initiative (or alternative). If the alternative does not meet the business requirements, or the MEA

is not fit for the specific enterprise environment, the process needs to return to the Feasibility Stage and the MEA Stage respectively. The common tasks and the deliverables for this stage are as illustrated in Table 4.

Deployment Stage

The Deployment Stage starts with analyses that are necessary to build confidence in value projections and cost estimates. Results of these analyses are adjusted to account for uncertainty, and are further analyzed to define the probability and impact of identified risks. In this stage these elements are integrated in order to understand how they relate to one another. Several managerial tasks are performed before proceeding with the deployment of the selected alterative. The common tasks and the deliverables for this stage are as illustrated in Table 5.

Table 3. Tasks and deliverables in the mobile enterprise architecture stage

MEA Stage	
Tasks	**Deliverables**
Determine/Revise MEA Principles	MEA principles
Identify Business Need(s)	Concerns, Viewpoints
Determine Mobile Technological Direction	Mobile technology profile
Pilot Mobile Initiatives	Project requirements
Design MEA	MEAD
Document Conceptual Framework Key Components	All level key components

Table 4. Tasks and deliverables in the alternatives analysis stage

Alternatives Analysis Stage	
Tasks	**Deliverables**
Identify and Define MEA alternatives	Viable alternatives for mobile initiatives
Estimate Values and Costs	Investment and return analysis
Conduct Risk Analysis	Risk analysis
Document Conceptual Framework Key Components	All level key components

Maintenance Stage

All mobile initiative processes need to be assessed over time for their quality and compliance with control requirements. This stage may involve re-iterating the other stages, namely the Feasibility Stage, MEA Stage, and Alternatives Analysis Stage to adapt or enhance the implemented mobile initiative(s). For example, it might mean that the Feasibility Report needs to be reviewed and updated with new recommendations; the MEA revised in light of an architecture change request; or the mobile initiative needs to adopt another alternative. The common tasks and the deliverables for this stage are as illustrated in Table 6.

DEMONSTRATION OF CONCEPT

As stated in the Research Design section the demonstration of the conceptual MEAF, with its methodology and process model, was performed by means of the Action Research Case Method in the VMG environment, a subset of the Ontario Provincial Government (Li, 2006).

VMG has more than 40,000 public service employees, with considerable interest in opportunities offered by new mobile technologies. Facing the challenge of mobile innovation, VMG began the development of a mobile strategy in fiscal year 2002 – 2003. In response to the interest

Table 5. Tasks and deliverables in the deployment stage

Deployment Stage	
Tasks	**Deliverables**
Aggregate the Cost Estimate	Cost estimate
Simulate ROI for Alternatives	ROI metrics, Values
Evaluate the Risk	Risks on value and cost
Compare Value, Cost, and Risk	Comparison of ROIs for alternatives
Communicate Value to Customers and Stakeholders	Documentation, insight, and support such as: • results-based management controls • enterprise financial data • communicating initiative values • improving decision making and performance measurement through "Lessons Learned"
Prepare Budget Justification Document	
Use Lessons Learned to Improve Processes	
Satisfy ad hoc Reporting Requirements	Change and ad hoc reporting requirements
Deploy the Optimized Mobile Initiative Alternative	Acquire and implement selected mobile initiative(s)
Document Conceptual Framework Key Components	All level key components

from all business units in VMG, such as Health, Transportation, and Police that provide public services a major research institution was selected to evaluate mobile interests, priorities and issues arising from the mobile front. In the last few years a number of priority mobile initiatives were undertaken. The early mobile practices across the VMG showed success to a certain degree in some business units. A number of issues related to broader mobile adoption have been identified from lessons learnt in previous and current mobile initiatives. Covering all the mobile initiatives is beyond the scope of this paper. A summary of the VMG Blackberry initiative case study is provided here for demonstration of the stages: Feasibility

Table 6. Tasks and deliverables in the maintenance stage

Maintenance Stage	
Tasks	**Deliverables**
Deliver and Support Mobile Products and Services	
Monitor and Evaluate Mobile Initiative Performance	The comparison of real outcomes and expected results
Monitor and Evaluate Internal Control	
Ensure Regulatory Compliance	
Provide Mobile Governance	Reengineering MEA mobile initiatives.
Evaluate the Mobile Initiative Maturity Status and Explore Next Mobile Solutions	New MEA mobile initiative(s)
Document Conceptual Framework Key Components	All level key components

Stage, MEA Stage, Alternatives Analysis Stage, Development Stage, and Maintenance Stage.

Feasibility Stage

The Feasibility Stage is an important stage for all VMG mobile initiatives that directly address enterprise mobile objectives. In this stage there are several tasks:

1. Identify VMG's current status using Blackberry mobile devices from the Strategy, Governance, Integration, Quality, Procurement, and Security perspectives. All of them are directly linked to the MEAF as defined in Section 3.
2. Develop the VMG Blackberry initiative strategic plan. The Blackberry initiative is an enterprise-level and ongoing multiphase project. The VMG strategy team chose to develop a relatively simple strategy structure focusing on the enterprise Mission and Outcomes.

3. Define a VMG Blackberry value model. In general, the value creators in VMG are employees, citizens, government partners, and suppliers. Because VMG has a strong IT team, tasks related to the mobile portal, mobile content creation, and application development can utilize internal IT resources. VMG cooperated with specific mobile networks and service providers such as Bell Mobility, who provided the dedicated mobile networks and services for the government mobile projects. Mobile devices, hardware and software platforms, and infrastructure equipment are project relevant, and are selected by VOR (Vendor of Records) or the VMG Bidding System. Based on this value model, the relationships of values, costs, and risks between VMG and the third parties can be identified as the next three tasks.
4. Identify the value factors.
5. Identify the risks.
6. Generate the value factors model, risk model and cost model. Some tools such as MetaStorm's ProVision and Microsoft Excel were used to manage the deliverables and documents.

Mobile Enterprise Architecture Stage

For the Blackberry initiative VMG did not have clear architecture requirements in its first pilot project and subsequent extensions. As stated earlier the MEA Approach was applied to the Blackberry initiative. There are a number of tasks in this stage:

1. Determine/revise MEA principles;
2. Identify the business needs: m-Communication, m-Information access, and m-Business;
3. Determine the mobile technology direction. Research in Motion (RIM) has several mobile products ranging from client-side Blackberry mobile devices to back-end middleware and servers for VMG. In the

VMG case study, the intent of adopting RIM mobile technologies was not to replace the existing technologies but rather to extend them;

4. Pilot some mobile initiatives. Based on the business needs for mobile communication, information and business, VMG had selected several mobile initiatives as pilot projects in the last few years;

5. Analyze and design the MEA. Figure 6 shows the steps for analyzing and designing the MEA for Blackberry initiatives.

At the end of this stage the MEA for the Blackberry initiative was delivered as shown in Figure 7. In this MEA, the Blackberry initiative is only one of VMG mobile solutions.

Alternatives Analysis Stage

For each of the VMG mobile initiatives, the VMG regulation requires at least three alternatives. In this stage, the first task is to identify and define MEA alternatives. In the Blackberry initiative, several alternatives were created. For each alterative the return-on-investment models were developed based on the MEA and mobile value web (Li, 2006); the cost/benefit analyses were performed using Microsoft Excel. Then the simulation method was used to analyze the outcomes of the alternatives with different value, cost and risk factors based on the models created in the first stage.

Deployment Stage

The alternatives were analyzed to build confidence in value projections, and cost estimations were conducted. Results of the analyses were adjusted to account for uncertainty and further analyzed to define the probability and impact of the identified risks.

Tasks in this stage are:

1. Aggregate the cost estimation. Understanding the relationship among cost, value, and risk is the key to determine the Blackberry initiative investment. The cost estimate is calculated by aggregating the expected value of each cost element in the value model defined in the Feasibility Stage;

2. Simulate ROI for alternatives. The ROI can be simulated in different ways such as the Monte Carlo simulation method;

3. Evaluate the risk. The probability of occurrence and impact of each identified risk factor is applied to areas of cost and value;

4. Compare values, costs and risks;

5. Communicate value to stakeholders. To move the Blackberry initiative toward implementation, VMG leadership had the information and supporting documentation to justify a course of action to the supporters and skeptics;

6. Prepare budget justification document. VMG withholds funding of mobile initiatives that are not justified by a sound business case. VMG has the business rules for comprehensive and rigorous analysis and justification to support funding requests;

7. Use the lessons learned to improve processes;

8. Satisfy ad hoc reporting requirements. As analyzed in the Alternatives Analysis Stage, changes in the business units have a significant impact on the comparison of value to cost, as well as on the decisions that affect the Blackberry initiative. Project management expects prompt response for questions concerning the justification of the Blackberry initiative, or inquiries regarding the impact of additional information, fluctuations in funding, or priorities. Using the framework and tools to make adjustments, e.g., adjustments of weighting factors, risks, and alternatives, to form better responses are necessary;

9. Deploy the optimized mobile initiative alternative. After the systematic analysis of

Figure 7. Virtual mobile government blackberry initiative mobile enterprise architecture

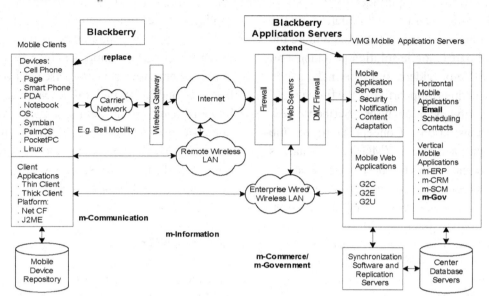

several alternatives and the VMG annual budget for mobile initiatives, select the optimized alternative. This alternative covers most of the Blackberry users, executives, managers, professionals, and especially the mobile workers.

Maintenance Stage

All Blackberry initiative processes should be regularly assessed over time for their quality and compliance with control requirements. This stage involves re-iterating the other three stages: Feasibility Stage, MEA Stage, and Alternatives Analysis Stage to adapt or enhance the initiative.

There are several tasks in this stage:

1. Deliver and support mobile products and services. The deliverables of the Blackberry initiative are the mobile services for internal employee communication and interaction, information access and businesses process improvement, employee productivity and immediacy improvements, and cost deduction from other investments;

2. Monitor and evaluate the mobile initiative performance. This process includes defining performance indicators, systematic and timely reporting of performance and prompt action on deviations from the alternatives analysis;

3. Monitor and evaluate internal control and ensure regulatory compliance. The Blackberry initiative requires the establishment of an independent review process to ensure compliance with laws and regulations defined in the conceptual framework;

4. Provide mobile governance;

5. The final task is to evaluate the mobile initiative maturity status, and explore other mobile solutions.

After four years, all the VMG managers, on site employees and most office employees are using the BlackBerry. Ongoing research on more than 20 real world mobile initiatives in VMG shows that the MEAF and its methodology and process model may be applied to other VMG mobile initiatives, thereby making it a systemic solution for the whole enterprise. The findings of this research confirm the importance of the mobile value web, which can be used to determine the business value, cost, and risk factors among the VMG third party mobile solution providers and mobile service providers, and then make sound strategic decisions. Supportive of the findings are a number of models and analyses described in Section 5 Demonstration of Concept. Moreover, the proposed approach enables VMG decision-makers to recognize the potential benefits in a systematic way and make sound decisions from the analyses, simulation, proof of concepts, and multiple real mobile initiative practices. More information about this is available from Li (2006) on request.

CONCLUSION

The paper presents a Mobile Enterprise Architecture Approach for creating a Mobile Enterprise based on a research project reported in Li (2006). This is a new systematic approach for aiding enterprise decision makers and enterprise architects to perform analysis, design, implementation, and maintenance of enterprise mobile initiatives when implementing a strategy to transform the enterprise from a non-ME to an ME. The MEA Framework entails four tenets, namely: 1) the key components for the ME, 2) a three-level structure corresponding to the enterprise structure, 3) the MEA approach, and 4) the top-down and bottom-up flow. To use the MEAF, a five stage MEA process model is proposed, along with the processes, tasks and deliverables for each stage. Other viewpoints, such as ME Security and ME Quality of Service are described by Li (2006) and Steenkamp and Li (2006). The proposed MEAF and its methodology and process model have been demonstrated by means of a case study in a real world context, and the findings support the utility and anticipated benefits for mobile initiatives in practice.

This research is the first step toward developing the complex framework and methodology for an enterprise adopting mobile technologies using the MEA Approach, and the reference theories and applications are limited. This is because the history of ME is short, and the ability to fully evaluate the approach lacks comprehensive experimentation in other real world enterprise environments. Both ME and MEA are large research areas with limited theoretical and methodological grounding in the fields of framework and methodology for creating an ME. Despite the mentioned constraints this research has made some significant initial contributions in these areas.

REFERENCES

Andrade, J., Ares, J., Garcia, R., & Pazos, J. (2004). A Methodological Framework for Viewpoint-oriented Conceptual Modeling. *IEEE Transactions on Software Engineering, 30*(5), 282–294. doi:10.1109/TSE.2004.1

Avison, D. E., Lau, F., Myers, M., & Nielsen, P. A. (1999, January). Action Research. *Communications of the ACM.*

Boar, B. H. (1999). *Constructing Blueprints for Enterprise IT Architectures.* Wiley.

Chen, L. D., & Skelton, G. W. (2005). *Mobile Commerce Application Development.* Cyber Tech Publishing.

Chen, T., Yu, H., Feng, C., & Wei, H. (2006). A New Security Architecture for Mobile Communication, In R. Wamkeue (Ed.), *Proceedings of the 17th IASTED International Conference on Modeling and Simulation: International Association of Science and Technology for Development* (pp. 424-429). Anaheim, CA: ACTA Press.

de Vreede, G. J. (1995). *Facilitating Organisational Change; The participative application of dynamic modeling.* Doctoral Dissertation, Delft University of Technology, Delft.

Dulaney, K. (2003, December). *Predictions 2004: Mobile and Wireless* (ID: AV-21-5094). Gartner Inc.

Fenn, J., & Linden, A. (2004). *Gartner's Hype Cycle Special Report* (ID: AV-23-0877). Gartner Research.

Ferguson, G. T., & Pike, T. H. (2001). Mobile Commerce – Cutting Loose. *Accenture Outlook, 1*, 64–69.

Feurer, R. C. K., Weber, M., & Wargin, J. (2001). *Aligning Strategies, Processes, and Information Technology: A Case Study.* In J.M. Myerson, (Ed.), *Enterprise Systems Integration* (pp. 11-28).

Kalakota, R., & Robinson, M. (2002). *M-business: the race to mobility.* McGraw Hill.

Lee, V., Schneider, H., & Schell, R. (2004). *Mobile Applications: architecture, design, and development.* Upper Saddle River NJ: Prentice Hall PTR.

Li, Z. (2006). *Enterprise Goes Mobile: A Framework and Methodology for Creating a Mobile Enterprise.* Doctoral Dissertation, Lawrence Technological University, Michigan, USA.

McDavid, D. W. (1999). A standard for business architecture description. *IBM Systems Journal, Enterprise Solutions Structure, 38*(1).

Petkov, D., Edgar-Nevill, D., Madachy, R., & O'Connor, R. (2008, January-June). Information Systems, Software Engineering, and Systems Thinking: Challenges and Opportunities. *International Journal of Information Technologies and Systems Approach, 1*, 17–19.

Schekkerman, J. (2005). *Trends in Enterprise Architecture.* Institute For Enterprise Architecture Developments.

Sessions, R. (2007). *A comparison of the top four enterprise architecture methodologies.* Microsoft Developer Network Architecture Center.

Skelton, G. W. (2003). *Wireless Application Development,* Boston, MA: Course Technology.

Sol, H. G. (1982). *Simulation in information systems development.* Doctoral dissertation, University of Groningen, Groningen.

Sol, H. G. (1988). Information systems development: a problem solving approach. *Proceedings of the Symposium and Systems Analysis and Design,* Atlanta, USA.

Sowa, J. F., & Zachman, J. A. (1992). Extending and Formalizing the Framework for Information Systems Architecture. *IBM Systems Journal, 31*(3).

IEEE Std. 1471-2000 (2000). *IEEE Recommended Practice for Architectural Description.*

Steen, M. W. A., Akehurst, D. H., ter Doest, H. W. L., & Lankhorst, M. M. (2004). Supporting Viewpoint-Oriented Enterprise Architecture. *Proc. of 8th IEEE Intl Enterprise Distributed Object Computing Conf. (EDOC 2004).* IEEE.

Steenkamp, A. L., & Kakish, K. (2004). An Approach to Developing Information Technology Architectures. *Proceedings of ICIER2004,* Washington DC, USA.

Steenkamp, A. L., & Li, Z. (2006). An Approach to Developing IT Architectures – Enterprise Mobility Viewpoint. *Open Group IT Architecture Practitioners Conference,* Lisbon, Portugal.

Steenkamp, A. L., Li, Z., & du Plessis, E. (2004). Strategic Planning for Small IT Business. *Proceedings of AMCIS2004 Conference,* New York.

Tarasewich, P., Nickerson, R.C., & Warkentin, M. (2002). Issues in Mobile E-Commerce, *Communication of the AIS, 8*(41).

The Open Group. (2009). *TOGAF (The Open Group Architecture Framework) Version 9 "Enterprise Edition".* Available from http://www.opengroup.org

van Meel, J. W. (1994). *The Dynamics of Business Engineering. Reflections on Two Case Studies within the Amsterdam Municipal Police Force.* Doctoral Dissertation, Delft University of Technology, Delft, The Netherlands.

Varshney, U., & Vetter, R. (2001). Mobile Commerce: Framework, Applications, and Networking Support. *Mobile Networks and Applications*, 7(3), 185–198. doi:10.1023/A:1014570512129

Wireless Center. (2008), Mobile Application Architectures. Available from http://www.wireless-center.net/Mobile-and-Wireless/Mobile-Application-Architectures.html

Wu, M. C., & Unhelkar (2008). Extending enterprise architecture with mobility. *IEEE Vehicular Technology Conference.* VTC. Available from http://ieeexplore.ieee.org

This work was previously published in the International Journal of Information Technologies and Systems Approach, Volume 3, Issue 1, edited by Frank Stowell and Manuel Mora, pp. 1-20, copyright 2010 by IGI Publishing (an imprint of IGI Global).

Chapter 10
Testable Theory Development for Small-N Studies:
Critical Realism and Middle-Range Theory

Matthew L. Smith
International Development Research Centre, Canada

ABSTRACT

Theory testing within small-N research designs is problematic. Developments in the philosophy of social science have opened up new methodological possibilities through, among other things, a novel notion of contingent causality that allows for contextualized hypothesis generation, hypothesis testing and refinement, and generalization. This article contributes to the literature by providing an example of critical realist (one such new development in the philosophy of social science) theory development for a small-N comparative case study that includes hypothesis testing. The article begins with the key ontological assumptions of critical realism and its relation to theory and explanation. Then, the article presents an illustrative example of an e-government comparative case study, focusing on the concept of trust, which follows these ontological assumptions. The focus of the example is on the nature and process of theory and hypothesis development, rather than the actual testing that occurred. Essential to developing testable hypotheses is the generation of tightly linked middle-range and case-specific theories that provide propositions that can be tested and refined. The link provides a pathway to feed back the concrete empirical data to the higher level (more abstract) and generalizable middle-range theories.

INTRODUCTION

Theory-testing in small-N studies is problematic. Small-N studies refer to studies with a small number of observations where the goal is not to represent a relevant population, but rather to conduct a more intensive study of a small number of phenomena (Gerring, 2007). From the positivist perspective, the small number of observations means that it is difficult to attain statistical significance. Consequently, researchers, especially qualitative researchers, have been advised in the past to increase the size of N as the best way to "enhance the inferential leverage of empirical

DOI: 10.4018/978-1-4666-1562-5.ch010

tests" (Collier, Seawright, & Munch, 2004, p. 27). From the interpretivist epistemological perspective, research is not thought to be subject to the same evaluation criteria as positivist work (Klein & Myers, 1999; Weber, 2004) as the goal of research is to understand, not to discover (Orlikowski & Baroudi, 1991, p. 14) or test (Avgerou, Ciborra, & Land, 2004).

There is a third perspective, underpinned by new developments in the philosophy of social science, known as critical realism. This article provides an example of how contextualized hypothesis (theory) generation and hypothesis testing and refinement are possible based upon the critical realist notion of contingent causality. It is this form of theory building that makes possible a qualified form of theory-testing in small-N studies. Perhaps not coincidentally, there are many other *scientific* realists and methodologists who, while not explicitly critical realists, have similar positions regarding causality (e.g., Bunge, 2004a; Bunge, 2004b; Cartwright, 2004; Shadish, Cook, & Campbell, 2002).

The goal of this article is not to argue for the relevance or superiority of critical realism; rather, it is to demonstrate how the critical realist notion of a contextualized causality can be used to develop testable theory that is appropriate for small-N studies. This article uses a comparative case study example to show the thought process behind the development of testable hypothesis following critical realist assumptions. In particular, it presents an approach to multi-level theorizing (including middle-range and case-specific hypotheses) that makes it possible for empirical evidence to feed back to more abstract theories. The contextually dependent causality and the different levels of theory are particularly useful for researchers who wish to explore empirical sites more in-depth, but also would like the potential to build on, test, and refine already existing theory. In doing so, this article looks to contribute to the broader discussion on how critical realism can contribute to information systems research.

The article proceeds as follows. First, there is a consideration of the key ontological assumptions of critical realism and its relation to theory and explanation. Second, the article presents an illustrative example of a comparative case study following a critical realist philosophy. In order to show how critical realist assumptions influenced the research process, the illustration delves into the reasoning behind the process of middle-range and case-specific theory and hypothesis generation, and the method of theory integration. Finally, the article concludes with a summary and some thoughts on the difficulties stemming from the approach to theorization taken here.

HOW DOES CRITICAL REALISM INFLUENCE RESEARCH?

Critical realism is a relatively new philosophy of the natural and social sciences developed in the late 70s and early eighties (Bhaskar, 1978, 1998b). Since then it has provided the basis for a range of social science research (Carter & New, 2004; Danermark, Ekstrom, Jokobsen, & Karlsson, 2003; Mingers, 2000, 2004d; Pawson & Tilley, 1997). In the information systems literature, the potential benefits of critical realism have already been touted (Carlsson, 2004; Dobson, 2002; Houston, 2001; Mingers, 2004a, 2004c, 2004d; Smith, 2006). Recently, more examples of critical realism actively applied in information systems research are emerging (Bygstad, 2008; Dobson, Myles, & Jackson, 2007; Morton, 2006; Reimers & Johnson, 2008; Volkoff, Strong, & Elmes, 2007).

Part of its broadening appeal is that critical realism arguably "subsumes" positivism and interpretivism, effectively ending the paradigm wars (Mingers, 2004b, 2004d). This statement can be understood when one views critical realism as an ontology. The core of critical realism is a series of metaphysical ontological assumptions that emerged from an examination of scientific activity of what must be common to all things for research to be possible. It is through this new metaphysical framework that critical realism provides the common denominator upon which to integrate (and thereby subsume) research from within other research paradigms.

Integrating research effectively equates to a process of reinterpreting research in light of these critical realist ontological assumptions (Befani, 2005; Fleetwood, 2001; Pratschke, 2003; Ron, 2002). However, reinterpreting research *ex post* does not necessarily imply a change in the activity of research itself. If this is the case, then arguably critical realism does not appear to offer anything new to research practice, other than some new metaphysical concepts and jargon. To come to this conclusion, however, would be to underplay the critical realist contribution; a contribution that flows from its strong ontological assumptions, and in particular its notion of causality.

The Generative Mechanism

If one accepts the critical realist set of ontological assumptions, the logical consequence is a particular relationship between the research object and the practice of research. Critical realism works at the level of metaphysics, and thus does not comment directly on the content of scientific level concepts or on what research strategies or methods to use (Bhaskar, 1978; Lawson, 2004; Martins, 2006). Rather, these assumptions provide a framework that underwrites causal-explanatory research and an emphasis on causal theory (Danermark et al., 2003, pp. 108-112). Thus, critical realism justifies research that is tilted for theory confirmation or refutation (Dobson et al., 2007).

To truly appreciate the contribution and influence of critical realism as a philosophy of science requires a much longer and more detailed explanation that is offered here. As mentioned, there are a series of ontological assumptions at the core of critical realism, including a novel notion of causality and a theory of the nature of social structure. For the purposes here, it suffices to focus on what

is considered the "lynchpin" of critical realism: the generative mechanism (Bhaskar, 2002; Groff, 2004, p. 138; Sayer, 2000).

This notion of causality as a generative mechanism is based upon a stratified reality that is broken up into three ontological domains: the real, the actual, and the empirical (Bhaskar, 1978, p. 13). The real consists of the "realm of objects, their structures and powers" (Kazi, 2003, p. 23). A structure consists of a set of relations that is held together by bonds of some sort (Bunge, 2004b, p. 188). Emerging from these relations are the particular capacities to behave (causal powers) that are "nothing other than the way of acting of a thing" (Bhaskar, 1998a, p. 38). Thus, the internal relations that constitute the structure of a thing give it both its qualitative properties as well as its causal powers. For example, water has a structure of two hydrogen molecules and one oxygen molecule. The emergent properties of water properties consist of causal powers such as the capacity to flow and to make wet. These generative mechanisms are radically different than those of the parts taken separately (Sayer, 2000, pp.12-13).

What makes this notion of causality especially powerful is that its abstract conceptualization provides the base commonality for a wide variety of different types of causes, both social and natural. For example, beliefs and desires can be causal (Archer, 1995; Meckler & Baillie, 2003, p. 275) as they emerge from the internal biological and cognitive structure (Archer, 2000). Generative mechanisms are also formed through social combination. Social structures like a church, legislature, market, nation state, or culture all have generative mechanisms that causally impact on people by virtue of the individual's position relative in these social relationships (Archer, 1998, p. 192).

Despite the mechanistic terminology, this notion of causality is highly context dependent. Social and natural objects are always embedded in a context of other mechanisms (social and technical) and thus may or may not be active depending upon their circumstances (Bhaskar, 1978, p. 173). Only when mechanisms are activated in a particular context do they exercise their causal power to generate events in the world. In contrast to an "if *a* then *b*" notion of causality, a simplified formulation of a generative mechanism includes three components: "*x* causes *y* (in circumstances *c*)" (Cartwright, 2003).

This contextually dependent nature of the generative mechanism also ultimately implies that causality is non-deterministic. The nature of real objects at a given time does not pre-determine what they will do or what events they may generate (Sayer, 2000, p. 95). A generative mechanism is never in the same place twice. Events that happen in the world are always co-determined by a variety of concurrently active and interacting mechanisms. A mechanism may be active but, due to the presence of other active mechanisms, the events they produce will be modified or, perhaps, might not even produce an empirical event at all. Such an appreciation of the complexity and co-determined nature of the world makes notions of determinism irrelevant, especially in the social domain.

While mechanisms are always embedded in a world of other mechanisms, they still are characterized by a particular structure and causal power. While the activation of two of the same generative mechanisms may never be exactly the same given the different contexts, their fundamental causal "tendency" is the same. For example, an increased tax on luxury items has the tendency of a disincentive to buy luxury items. However, the impact of this incentive will, of course, be differential depending upon their particular social position in relation to economic resources, the government, etc. For this reason, generative mechanisms are commonly referred to as *tendencies* (Bhaskar, 2002).

Theory and Explanation

This notion of causality influences research as causality and explanation are intimately related

(Gregor, 2006, p. 618). Recently, philosophers of science have begun to substitute talk about causality for scientific explanation (Cartwright, 2004). In the case of critical realism, a simple definition of explanation would be uncovering the influential generative mechanisms that brought about any particular outcome of interest. Note that the inclusion of generative mechanisms at the psychological level makes it possible for researchers who are interested in *understanding* to engage in hypothesis testing and refinement.

This particular philosophical position creates a distinctive set of goals for theorization and explanation. First, one attempts to identify the distinctive core properties of the generative mechanism at work. These core properties are the essential components and their interrelationships from which the causal tendency emerges. Thus, a causal theory of a generative mechanism includes both the structural components and the outcome tendency. In this way, it is also possible to think about it in terms of a causal process. Central to this endeavor is that this is an ideal typical abstraction which means that a) it separates the necessary causally efficacious features from the nonessential ones (Shadish et al., 2002, p. 9), and b) the actual manifestations of these theories in the world will always diverge by some degree from the ideal.

Explanation, however, can move beyond simply revealing causal powers – it should also include in what circumstances they are active (Fay, 1994, p. 95). If this is the case, then explanation requires a contextual notion of causality. Thus, explanation includes the structure that underlies the generative mechanisms (structure of *x*), the outcome that these mechanisms tend to produce (*y*), and finally the elements of context that trigger or inhibit the firing of these generative mechanisms (*c*). Any explanation must include all three of these elements. The end result is that we are interested in, to paraphrase Carlsson (2003) and Pawson & Tilley (1997, p. 210), *how, for whom, and in what circumstances* particular mechanisms generate particular outcomes.

This approach to explanation allows for an analytical approach to deal with the complexity of an embedded and non-deterministic notion of causal mechanisms. Complexity does not preclude some form of necessarily simplified, explanation of events. The following section presents one approach to building up theory based upon this particular approach to explanation. This approach requires a direct confrontation with the complexity of the situation by focusing theory on the potentially active causal mechanisms.

BUILDING THEORY FOR A COMPARATIVE CASE STUDY

This section demonstrates how multi-level testable theory was constructed following critical realist assumptions for a small-N comparative case study of the impacts of e-government on trust in Chile. This study began with a relatively simple assumption and research question. The assumption is that there is a causal link between e-government services and citizens' trust in government institutions. The research question explores that link: *how, for whom, and in what circumstances do e-services impact on citizens' trust in government?* Another way of framing the question is: *what are the generative mechanisms that connect e-services to changes in citizens' trust perceptions of government?*

The following discussion presents a picture of theorization that appears as if it were completed before the first foray into the field began. The reality is, of course, more complex. However, for considerations of space and simplicity, it is presented in linear order. Theorization as performed for this research was done in layers, from abstract ideal-typical theories to concrete. There are two levels of theory that were used: middle-range theories and case-specific testable hypotheses.

Developing Middle-Range Hypotheses

Building up the conceptual framework for e-government and trust requires three levels of theory integration where each level provides the structure upon which the subsequent level is constructed (see Figure 1). The first layer establishes a core theory of trust. This phase of the study identified several components of trust that were arguably

Figure 1. Levels of theory. The starting point for building theory is the general understandings of trust from sociology and psychology. This is followed by theories of institutional trust, generally drawn from political science. The final layer includes theories of building institutional trust through e-government, a very specific instantiation of institutional trust. The final stage of theory requires a detailed understanding of the interaction of ICT in the public sector. This is a movement from a core theory of trust to a specific instance of trust.

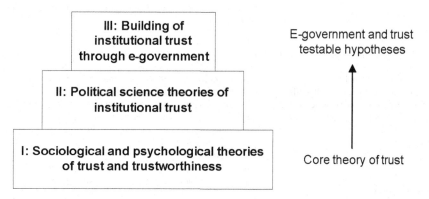

essential for the concept: a distinction between trust and trustworthiness, the two dimensions of trustworthiness of motivation and competence, the notion of trustworthiness cues that communicate these dimensions, and finally that placing trust requires a cognitive and emotional component for the truster. The conceptualization directs the researcher to understand the components of institutional trust interaction: a) the objective characteristics of institutional trustworthiness, b) how trustworthy cues emanating from these characteristics are communicated through action (or non-action), and c) the perception and interpretation of these characteristics.

Building upon this trust foundation, the second level integrates political science theories of trust in government, and specifically, institutional trust. This level provides the framework of how this research will approach the question of what it means to trust in government (institutional trust), and if such trust is even possible. The third level is broken up into two parts. The first part provides a theoretical understanding of the dynamics of

ICT in the public sector providing insight into the types of changes that can be expected with the introduction of e-government. Here is where the technological artifact enters into the causal equation. The second part of level three then integrates all of the theory and draws from empirical work to form the final sets of testable hypotheses that connect e-government to institutional trust.

The end result of this process in this study was a series of fifteen ideal-typical middle-range theories (see Table 1). Middle-range theories fall between high-level, non-testable theory and concrete descriptions (Merton, 1967). For critical realists, it is working at this middle-range level of theory where theory building can happen in a cumulative and more rigorous way (Danermark et al., 2003; Pawson & Tilley, 1997). The reason for this is because these theories are concrete enough that they can be tested and refined through empirical engagement with specific cases, and abstract enough to generalize from the case-specific theories.

Table 1. Examples of the ideal-type, middle-range hypotheses developed from the theory. Only 7 of the 15 testable middle-range hypotheses that were developed and tested are shown here.

Institutional trust theory	Examples of "Building institutional trust through e-services" hypotheses
COMPETENCE **Good institutional performance** that can be communicated, understood, and that is perceived to meet or exceed citizens' expectations of performance tends to build trust.	**Efficiency/effectiveness** E-services perceived to be more effective and efficient (faster, more accurate, cost saving) tend to build trust. E-government services that improve the efficiency and effectiveness of service at the institution's physical office tend to build trust. **Performance transparency** Performance transparency that meets citizens' expectations tends to build trust.
MOTIVATION **If the institution's policies encompass the interests of the citizen, trust tends to be built.** (1) Mechanisms that work to align (such as voice and exit) the interests of the institution and citizen tend to build trust. (2) Establishing credible institutional commitments through credible and effective institutional checks and balances that keep the public sector's interests in line with citizens' interests tends to build trust.	**Considering users interests** User benefits: E-services that bring user benefits tend to increase trust. E-service quality: Good e-services quality indicates that the institution considers citizens' interests and therefore tends to build trust. **Transparency and accountability** Institutional transparency and accountability: Increased transparency made possible through the increased visibility of internal processes and service outcomes accompanied by perceived effective accountability mechanisms tend to build trust. **Corruption** Reduced corruption: A reduction of corruption due to the computerization and rationalization of government processes tends to build trust.

A quick note helps to explain the nature of the resultant hypotheses. The institutional trust theories elaborate the main categories of causal pathways through which the structure and activities of institutions might communicate trustworthiness to citizens. It is this communication that has the potential to build citizens' trust. This general theory is then decomposed into a variety of causal mechanism hypotheses that may or may not be active for any one e-service. Ideally, this decomposition also includes the relationship between these components that shows how they interact to generate particular institutional trust outcomes. For example, good governmental performance has been linked to positive trust responses in survey work (Espinal, Hartlyn, & Kelley, 2006; Miller & Listhaug, 1999). Each individual component is then made more contextually applicable through a consideration of how the particular e-service (although still generally speaking) might impact institutional trust along the already identified dimensions. This requires the integration of institutional trust theory and an understanding of the interaction of ICT in the public sector. The ICT in the public sector theory provides the more specific hypothetical outcomes that fit within the more general institutional trust theory. Extending the performance example, we can then hypothesize that a more efficient service vis-à-vis computer automation is a specific example of institutional performance that will tend to build trust. It is important to note that, given the relational nature of trust, these hypotheses are always relative to the truster. For example, good performance must be perceived by the truster in order for it to build trust.

Integrating Theory: Not One but Many Middle-Range Theories

The theorization so far was based on the assumption that (at least *a priori*) there is no single theory that will be sufficient to explain what may be happening in Chile with citizens, e-government services, and trust. Perhaps after engaging in research one theory will provide sufficient explanatory power through identification of a big effect; that is, a large causal influence that overrides most of the other contextual causal mechanisms. Beforehand, however, it was not possible to know what the most influential causes might be. This means that theory was drawn from relevant sources that provide insight into the potential causal activities in particular aspects of the research object domain. For example, theories of ICT in public sector administration are helpful to understand how these implementations might alter the trustworthiness of the public sector institutions. However, these social psychological or psychological theories are helpful when trying to understand citizens' interpretations and resulting trust judgments of their interaction with the e-services. Furthermore, they need to be linked with the political theory that leads to an understanding of democracy and how citizens form judgments about the state. This integration of theory from across disciplines is made possible by working at the middle-range level and viewing each theory as contributing interesting causal components (George & Bennett, 2005).

The benefit of a focus on causality for theoretical integration is easily seen when considering trust theory. There is a vast literature on trust from a variety of disciplines that says a lot about the types of causal mechanisms that might connect e-services to citizens' perceptions, including theory from political science, sociology, psychology, information systems, and public administration. The research here exploits the current state of knowledge as a theoretical starting point and a means to generate an initial set of research orienting theories (for an overview of the objective of the research, areas of discipline, and theory used in this research, see Table 2). Integration is made possible through a reinterpretation of individual theories as generative mechanisms. For example, one area of contention in the trust literature is whether trust should be seen as a fundamentally

Table 2. Social objects, research areas, and major theorists referred to in the development of the conceptual framework for thinking about the relationship between e-government and trust

Social object	Description of research area	Sources of theories
Trust	• What is trust? What does it consist of? What are the outcomes of trust? How is trust built/ destroyed? • How do people interpret trustworthy cues? Which cues do they pay attention to? How/why do people turn particular interpretations into trust judgments?	**Sociology** Barber (1983), Seligman (1997), Luhmann (1979, 1988), Giddens (1990), Gambetta(1988; 2005), Fukuyama (1995) **Social psychology, psychology** Hardin (1993), Blackburn (1998), Braithwaite (1998), Harré (1999)
Trust in the state, institutional trust	• What constitutes a trustworthy public sector? • What types of experiences are important for a trustworthy state?	**Political science** M. Levi (1998), Harding (1996, 2002, 2004), Cook (Cook, Hardin, & Levi, 2005), Warren (2004, 1999), Norris (1999)
E-government (ICT in public administration, bureaucracy)	• Changes in public sector agency administration and services due to introduction of ICT	**Info. systems, organizational theory, public administration** Fountain (2001), Kallinikos (2004), Dunleavy (2006), Heeks (1999), Bhatnagar (2004), Zucker (1986)
E-services and building trust in the state	• How do e-services influence institutional trust? What factors influence the perception and use of e-services?	**Empirical work** Moon (2003), West (2005), Tolbert & Mossberger (2006), Avgerou *et al.* (2005)

rational concept, or one that is moral in nature. From the critical realist perspective, these conceptions are not competing. Rather, they represent theories that point to different causal components that may lead to trustworthy behavior ('it is in my interest to do so *and* I think it is the honorable thing to do') and to trusting behavior ('I think she will do it because it is in her interest *and* I think she is a virtuous person'). If this is the case, the question becomes when and why these different motivators come into play. This approach is deeply rooted in the notion of a non-deterministic causality that provides only a partial explanation as other co-active mechanisms are always active in a particular context.

Case-Specific Hypotheses

The final stage of theory/hypothesis generation is the development of case-specific testable hypotheses (see Table 3). This movement from abstract to concrete requires some knowledge of the actual case site. The specificity of the theory is analytically crucial as it allows the location of

variation across cases. For example, consider a statistical analysis of survey results of people's trust in government after interacting with e-government web pages, a common approach to studying e-government and trust. Such a study smoothes over the variations of the independent variables: the differences between the web pages and individuals. It is these variations that are included in the context specific theories. It is at this level that we really get at the core of explanation: the how, for whom, and in what circumstances e-government services will build institutional trust. The specificity of the theories also allows them to be subjected to within-case empirical testing.

The concern with variation is essential because the case specific hypotheses will necessarily vary from the ideal-typical theory of which it is an instantiation. Understanding this deviation is necessary for judging the validity of the test for any one hypothesis. In other words, if we are going to test, say, if institutional transparency builds trust, it is necessary to establish the quality of the transparency in the case; we must first sufficiently establish the antecedents to know if it is

Table 3. Some examples of case-specific hypotheses developed from the e-tax system run by the SII (the Chilean tax authority). Each case-specific hypothesis is a contextually specific manifestation of a middle-range theory developed earlier.

	Middle-range institutional trust and e-services hypotheses	Case-specific e-tax trustworthiness-to-trust hypotheses
Considering users interests		
I1	User benefits: E-services that bring user benefits will tend to increase trust.	Increased user benefits in terms of time and cost savings for those who use the e-service will tend to build trust.
I2	E-service quality: Good e-service quality indicates that the institution considers citizens' interests and therefore tends to build trust.	High ease of use (completed tax proposal) and the usefulness of the e-service (a necessary obligation for taxpayers) indicates that the SII takes the citizen's interests into account and will tend to build trust.
Transparency and accountability		
I3	Institutional transparency and accountability: Increased transparency of internal processes and service outcomes accompanied by perceived effective accountability mechanisms will tend to build trust.	While the website presents the rules and regulations of tax processes as well as increases the transparency of the activities of the SII vis-à-vis the citizen, the lack of effective accountability mechanisms will tend to have no impact on trust.
Corruption		
I4	Reduced corruption: A perceived reduction of corruption due to the computerization and rationalization of government processes will tend to build trust.	Moderately decreased opportunities for SII employee corruption through the computerization of many tax processes will tend to have a moderate impact on building trust.

a true test of the higher-level theory. In other words: If we want to test or refine the theory "if a then b (in circumstances c)" we have to first establish a and c. Understanding how the case specific instantiation (say, a_1) varies from the ideal typical theory of transparency and trust building is crucial for making plausible inferences to deal with the inability to ever truly falsify theories. In other words, if transparency does not build trust in this specific case, is the higher level theory wrong or does the case itself deviate from the ideal-type theory? And how and why might the deviation (i.e., the difference of structure between a and a_1) alter the outcome? For example, imagine a web site that provides information of poor quality and timeliness. It would be a mistake to hypothesize that this web site would be trusted due to transparency if our theory of transparency includes good quality timely information. However, if it the website does indeed increase trust, and we can explain how and why, then we would have an interesting addition to the understanding

of the relationship between web site transparency (information and quality) and trust.

In this study, each theory was first tested on a within-case basis. Each subject (e-service user) was considered an individual test of each theory. Do they trust? Why? What is it about this person that makes them trust (past experience, disposition, socio-economic position, positive interaction, something else)? Given the partial explanatory nature of each theory, during the analysis a concern is always maintained with the potential interactions between the causal components of the theory. After within case testing, theories were compared across cases, taking analytical advantage of the cases specific variations.

It should be noted that, as it was employed in this study, case studies have the advantage especially in the exploratory stage of research to "allow one to test a multitude of hypotheses in a rough and ready way" (Gerring, 2007, p. 41). While such testing is potentially subject to errors of inference, if the focus is on the testing and refinement of the casual mechanisms and their contingent activation we have increased faith in their internal validity (Gerring, 2007; Tsoukas, 1989). The viability of a within-case analysis is enhanced by the use of within-case comparisons (George & Bennett, 2005), which in this case was between the e-service users. Finally, the use of the cross-case comparison adds extra analytical power to the testing and refinement of the theories (Eisenhardt, 1989).

CONCLUSION

This article provides one example of how critical realism influenced the process of research, and in particular, the process of theory development. One might remark that the form of theory development presented above does not appear radically different, or is a mish-mash of activities, that researchers already do. It is thus important to understand the contribution of critical realism. Critical realism is not re-inventing the research wheel. Rather, this article argues that critical realism, in particular through its notion of generative mechanisms, provides a way of thinking about the link between theory and research practice that informs research design and theory development. The practicalities of theorization and research then draw from the various methodological and theoretical tools and processes that are appropriate for the given research.

This article argues that the perspective described here is particularly useful for a researcher who wishes to engage in a small-N study *and* theory testing. The key to the critical realist perspective comes from its view of theory itself. Theory is causal-explanatory and highly contextualized. It is this combination that makes this type of theory so powerful for small-N studies. This provides an alternative approach to small-N case studies in place of either overly descriptive approaches that lack generalizability, or a study that applies abstract theories (e.g., structuration theory, actor-network theory) that act as a lens, but lack testable propositions.

Central to the ability to test and refine theory in a small-N study is the tight link between different levels of theory. This provides a direct mechanism of feedback between the levels of theory. This link allows for the movement from case-specific empirical data to more generalizable statements. Thus, a within-case analysis can test and refine each of the different case-specific hypotheses separately. These refined theories can then provide feedback for the more abstract middle-range theories which are more portable than case-specific theories. The middle-range theories can be tested and refined in other research situations by creating other case-specific instantiations that correspond to the new empirical site. This allows for the flexible deployment of these theories in a variety of contexts, which also leads to the improved generalizability of these theories as they are made increasingly nuanced through the understanding of how they interact with different contextual mechanisms.

Of course, theory building does not always have to be done prior to research. The research approach taken here was heavy on front-end theorizing and used research cycles and comparative analysis to generate case-specific theories and then test and refine them. However, it would be perfectly consistent with the critical realist approach to generate theory inductively if it was appropriate for the given research goals and subject. For example, Volkoff *et al*. (2007) conducted a longitudinal study of technology and organizational change using grounded theory underpinned by critical realism. The key is that the emerging theory should be of the causal-explanatory type discussed above.

All research has its problems as well. In particular, the approach proposed here is heavy on front-end theorizing and theory-integration. It demands extensive multi-disciplinary exposure. Undoubtedly, this adds significant richness to the theoretical propositions, and potential understanding when confronting the empirical site. It also helps to prevent social scientists from reinventing the wheel. However, there is a significant risk that a jack-of-all-trades is really a master of none. Furthermore, the result of theorization for the case presented here was a very broad set of potential causes (social systems are complex!) on which the author tried to gather data. The end result was breadth rather than depth, and plenty of time was spent on particular causes that, in the end, were not of any importance.

REFERENCES

Archer, M. (1995). *Realist social theory: the morphogenetic approach.* Cambridge: Cambridge University Press.

Archer, M. (1998). Introduction: realism in the social sciences. In M. Archer, R. Bhaskar, A. Collier, T. Lawson, & A. Norrie (Eds.), *Critical realism: essential readings* (pp. 189-205). London: Routledge.

Archer, M. (2000). *Being human: the problem of agency.* Cambridge: Cambridge University Press.

Avgerou, C., Ciborra, C., Cordella, A., Kallinikos, J., & Smith, M. L. (2005). *The role of information and communication technology in building trust in governance: toward effectiveness and results.* Washington, D.C.: Inter-American Development Bank.

Avgerou, C., Ciborra, C., & Land, F. (2004). Introduction. In C. Avgerou, C. Ciborra & F. Land (Eds.), *The Social Study of Information and Communication Technology: Innovation, Actors, and Contexts* (pp. 1-14). Oxford: Oxford University Press.

Barber, B. (1983). *The logic and limits of trust.* New Brunswick: Rutgers University Press.

Befani, B. (2005). The mechanisms of suicide: a realist approach. *International Review of Sociology, 15*(1), 51–75. doi:10.1080/03906700500038504

Bhaskar, R. (1978). *A realist theory of science* (Second ed.). Sussex: The Harvester Press Limited.

Bhaskar, R. (1998a). Philosophy and scientific realism. In M. Archer, R. Bhaskar, A. Collier, T. Lawson & A. Norrie (Eds.), *Critical realism: Essential readings* (pp. 16-47). London: Routledge.

Bhaskar, R. (1998b). *The possibility of naturalism: a philosophical critique of the contemporary human sciences* (Third ed.). London: Routledge.

Bhaskar, R. (2002). *From science to emancipation: alienation and the actuality of enlightenment.* Delhi: Sage Publications India Pvt Ltd.

Bhatnagar, S. (2004). *E-government: from vision to implementation.* London: Sage Publications Ltd.

Blackburn, S. (1998). Trust, cooperation, and human psychology. In V. Braithwaite & M. Levi (Eds.), *Trust and Governance* (pp. 28-45). New York: Russell Sage Foundation.

Braithwaite, V. (1998). Communal and exchange trust norms: their value base and relevance to institutional trust. In V. Braithwaite & M. Levi (Eds.), *Trust and Governance* (pp. 46-74). New York: Russell Sage Foundation.

Bunge, M. (2004a). Clarifying some misunderstandings about social systems and their mechanisms. *Philosophy of the Social Sciences, 34*(3), 371–381. doi:10.1177/0048393104266860

Bunge, M. (2004b). How does it work? The search for explanatory mechanisms. *Philosophy of the Social Sciences, 34*(2), 182–210. doi:10.1177/0048393103262550

Bygstad, B. (2008, December 14-17). *Information infrastructure as organization: a critical realist view.* Paper presented at the International Conference on Information Systems, Paris.

Carlsson, S. A. (2003). Advancing information systems evaluation (research): a critical realist approach. *Electronic Journal of Information Systems Evaluation, 6*(2), 11–20.

Carlsson, S. A. (2004). Using critical realism in IS research. In M. E. Whitman & A. B. Woszczynski (Eds.), *The hanbook of information systems research* (pp. 323-338). Hershey: Idea Group Inc (IGI).

Carter, B., & New, C. (Eds.). (2004). *Making realism work: realist social theory and empirical research*. Oxfordshire: Routledge.

Cartwright, N. (2003). *Causation one word many things*. London: Centre for Philosophy of Natural and Social Science.

Cartwright, N. (2004). From causation to explanation and back. In B. Leiter (Ed.), *The Future for Philosophy* (pp. 230-245). Oxford: Oxford University Press.

Collier, D., Seawright, J., & Munch, G. L. (2004). The quest for standards: King, Keohane, and Verba's designing social inquiry. In H. E. Brady & D. Collier (Eds.), *Rethinking social inquiry: diverse tools, shared standards* (pp. 21-50). Lanham: Rowman & Littlefield Publishers, Inc.

Cook, K. S., Hardin, R., & Levi, M. (2005). *Cooperation without trust?* New York: Russell Sage Foundation.

Danermark, B., Ekstrom, M., Jokobsen, L., & Karlsson, J. C. (2003). *Explaining society: critical realism in the social sciences*. London: Routledge.

Dobson, P. J. (2002). Critical realism and information systems research: why bother with philosophy? *Information Research, 7*(2).

Dobson, P. J., Myles, J., & Jackson, P. (2007). Making the case for critical realism: examining the implementation of automated performance management systems. *Information Resources Management Journal, 20*(2), 138–152.

Dunleavy, P., Margetts, H., Bastow, S., & Tinkler, J. (2006). *Digital era governance: IT corporations, the state, and e-government*. Oxford: Oxford University Press.

Eisenhardt, K. M. (1989). Building theories from case study research. *Academy of Management Review, 14*(4), 532–550. doi:10.2307/258557

Espinal, R., Hartlyn, J., & Kelley, J. M. (2006). Performance still matters: explaining trust in government in the Dominican Republic. *Comparative Political Studies, 39*(2), 200–223. doi:10.1177/0010414005281933

Fay, B. (1994). General laws and explaining human behaviour. In M. Martin & L. C. McIntyre (Eds.), *Readings in the Philosophy of Social Science* (pp. 91-110). Cambridge, Massachusetts: The MIT Press.

Fleetwood, S. (2001). Causal laws, functional relations and tendencies. *Review of Political Economy, 13*, 201–220. doi:10.1080/09538250120036646

Fountain, J. E. (2001). *Building the virtual state: information technology and institutional change*. Washington, D.C.: Brookings Institution Press.

Fukuyama, F. (1995). *Trust: the social virtues and the creation of prosperity*. London: Penguin Books Ltd.

Gambetta, D. (1988). Can we trust trust? In D. Gambetta (Ed.), *Trust: making and breaking cooperative relations* (pp. xi-xiv). New York: Basil Blackwell, Inc.

Gambetta, D., & Hamill, H. (2005). *Streetwise: how taxi drivers establish their customers' trustworthiness*. New York: Russell Sage Foundation.

George, A. L., & Bennett, A. (2005). *Case studies and theory development in the social sciences*. Cambridge, Massachusetts: MIT Press.

Gerring, J. (2007). *Case study research: principles and practices*. New York: Cambridge University Press.

Giddens, A. (1990). *The consequences of modernity*. Stanford: Stanford University Press.

Gregor, S. D. (2006). The nature of theory in information systems. *MIS Quarterly, 30*(3), 611–642.

Groff, R. (2004). *Critical realism, post-positivism and the possibility of knowledge*. London: Routledge.

Hardin, R. (1993). The street-level epistemology of trust. *Politics & Society, 21*(4), 505–529. doi:10.1177/0032329293021004006

Hardin, R. (1996). Trustworthiness. *Ethics, 107*(1), 26–42. doi:10.1086/233695

Hardin, R. (2002). *Trust & trustworthiness*. New York: Russell Sage Foundation.

Hardin, R. (2004). Distrust: manifestations and management. In R. Hardin (Ed.), *Distrust* (pp. 3-33). New York: Russell Sage Foundation.

Harré, R. (1999). Trust and its surrogates: psychological foundations of political process. In M. E. Warren (Ed.), *Democracy and Trust* (pp. 249-272). Cambridge: Cambridge University Press.

Heeks, R. (1999). Reinventing government in the information age. In R. Heeks (Ed.), *Reinventing government in the information age: international practice in IT-enabled public sector reform* (pp. 9-21). London: Routledge.

Houston, S. (2001). Beyond social constructionism: critical realism and social work. *British Journal of Social Work, 31*(6), 845–861. doi:10.1093/bjsw/31.6.845

Kallinikos, J. (2004). The social foundations of the bureaucratic order. *Organization, 11*(1), 13–36. doi:10.1177/1350508404039657

Kazi, M. A. F. (2003). *Realist evaluation in practice: health and social work*. London: Sage Publications.

Klein, H. K., & Myers, M. D. (1999). A set of principles for conducting and evaluating interpretive field studies in information systems. *MIS Quarterly, 23*(1), 67–94. doi:10.2307/249410

Lawson, T. (2004). A conception of ontology. University of Cambridge: Faculty of Economics.

Levi, M. (1998). A state of trust. In V. Braithwaite & M. Levi (Eds.), *Trust and Governance* (pp. 77-101). New York: Russell Sage Foundation.

Luhmann, N. (1979). *Trust and power: two works by Niklas Luhmann*. Avon: John Wiley & Sons Ltd.

Luhmann, N. (1988). Familiarity, confidence, trust: problems and alternatives. In D. Gambetta (Ed.), *Trust: making and breaking cooperative relations* (pp. 94-108). Oxford: Basil Blackwell, Ltd.

Martins, N. (2006). Capabilities as causal powers. *Cambridge Journal of Economics* (Advance Access).

Meckler, M., & Baillie, J. (2003). The truth about social construction in administrative science. *Journal of Management Inquiry, 12*(3), 273–284. doi:10.1177/1056492603257724

Merton, R. K. (1967). *On theoretical sociology: five essays, old and new*. New York: The Free Press.

Miller, A., & Listhaug, O. (1999). Political performance and institutional trust. In P. Norris (Ed.), *Critical citizens: global support for democratic government* (pp. 204-216). Oxford: Oxford University Press.

Mingers, J. (2000). The contribution of critical realism as an underpinning philosophy for OR/MS and systems. *The Journal of the Operational Research Society, 51*(111), 1256–1270.

Mingers, J. (2004a). Critical realism and information systems: brief responses to Monod and Klein. *Information and Organization, 14*(2), 145–153. doi:10.1016/j.infoandorg.2004.02.003

Mingers, J. (2004b). Paradigm wars: ceasefire announced who will set up the new administration? *Journal of Information Technology, 19*(3), 165–171. doi:10.1057/palgrave.jit.2000021

Mingers, J. (2004c). Re-establishing the real: critical realism and information systems. In J. Mingers & L. P. Willcocks (Eds.), *Social Theory and Philosophy for Information Systems* (Vol. 372-406). Sussex: John Wiley & Sons Ltd.

Mingers, J. (2004d). Real-izing information systems: critical realism as an underpinning philosophy for information systems. *Information and Organization, 14*(2), 87–103. doi:10.1016/j.infoandorg.2003.06.001

Moon, M. J. (2003). *Can IT help government to restore public trust? Declining public trust and potential prospects of IT in the public sector.* Paper presented at the 36th Hawaii International Conference on System Sciences, Hawaii.

Morton, P. (2006). Using critical realism to explain strategic information systems planning. *Journal of Information Technology Theory and Application, 8*(1), 1–20.

Norris, P. (Ed.). (1999). *Critical citizens: global support for democratic government.* Oxford: Oxford University Press.

Orlikowski, W. J., & Baroudi, J. J. (1991). Studying information technology in organizations: research approaches and assumptions. *Information Systems Research, 2*(1), 1–28. doi:10.1287/isre.2.1.1

Pawson, R., & Tilley, N. (1997). *Realistic evaluation.* London: SAGE publications Ltd.

Pratschke, J. (2003). Realistic models? Critical realism and statistical models in the social sciences. *Philosophica, 71*(1), 13–38.

Reimers, K., & Johnson, R. B. (2008, December 14-17). *The use of an explicitly theory-driven data coding method for high-level theory testing in IOIS.* Paper presented at the International Conference for Information Systems, Paris.

Ron, A. (2002). Regression analysis and the philosophy of social science. *Journal of Critical Realism, 1*(1), 119–142.

Sayer, A. (2000). *Realism and social science.* London: SAGE Publications Ltd.

Seligman, A. B. (1997). *The problem of trust.* Princeton: Princeton University Press.

Shadish, W. R., Cook, T. D., & Campbell, D. T. (2002). *Experimental and quasi-experimental designs for generalized causal inference.* Boston: Houghton Mifflin Company.

Smith, M. L. (2006). Overcoming theory-practice inconsistencies: critical realism and information systems research. *Information and Organization, 16*(13), 191–211. doi:10.1016/j.infoandorg.2005.10.003

Tolbert, C., & Mossberger, K. (2006). The effects of e-government on trust and confidence in government. *Public Administration Review, 66*(3), 354–369. doi:10.1111/j.1540-6210.2006.00594.x

Tsoukas, H. (1989). The validity of idiographic research explanations. *Academy of Management Review, 14*(4), 551–561. doi:10.2307/258558

Volkoff, O., Strong, D. M., & Elmes, M. B. (2007). Technological embeddedness and organizational change. *Organization Science*, *18*(5), 832–848. doi:10.1287/orsc.1070.0288

Warren, M. E. (Ed.). (1999). *Democracy and trust*. Cambridge: Cambridge University Press.

Warren, M. E. (2004). Trust in democratic institutions. In F. Ankersmit & H. te Velde (Eds.), *Trust: Cement of Democracy* (Vol. 49-69). Leuven: Peeters.

Weber, R. (2004). Editor's comments: the rhetoric of positivism versus interpretivism: a personal view. *MIS Quarterly*, *28*(1), iii–xiii.

West, D. M. (2005). *Digital government: technology and public sector performance*. Princeton: Princeton University Press.

Zucker, L. G. (1986). Production of trust: institutional sources of economic structure, 1840-1920. *Organizational Behavior*, *8*, 53–111.

This work was previously published in the International Journal of Information Technologies and Systems Approach, Volume 3, Issue 1, edited by Frank Stowell and Manuel Mora, pp. 41-56, copyright 2010 by IGI Publishing (an imprint of IGI Global).

Chapter 11
Multi–Level Service Infrastructure for Geovisual Analytics in the Context of Territorial Management

Giuseppe Conti
Fondazione Graphitech, Italy

Stefano Piffer
Fondazione Graphitech, Italy

Raffaele De Amicis
Fondazione Graphitech, Italy

Bruno Simões
Fondazione Graphitech, Italy

ABSTRACT

The management of a territory is a complex process, involving a number of different operators, administrators and decision makers. Territory management requires accessing and processing a wide range of heterogeneous and multi-dimensional GI (GI). Within a typical scenario, the process involves departments at public administrations responsible for urban planning, environmental control, infrastructure planning and maintenance. Additionally units such as civil protection, fire brigades also play a vital role when dealing with emergencies. Data to be managed range from alphanumerical information, stored within enterprise-level databases, to satellite imagery, vector data and information coming from on-site sensors. It is acknowledged that creating an infrastructure capable to provide access to such a range of information requires, an integrated system approach, both from a technological and from a procedural point of view. This article illustrates the benefit of adopting a system approach which makes use of Service-Oriented Architectures (SOA) and 3D geobrowsers to provide an answer to the aforementioned shortcomings. To do so the article presents the client-server platform designed to support decision makers and experts from local or regional administrations in the process of managing their territory. The infrastructure developed allows a large number of concurrent applications to access geographical data in a fully interactive way, within a 3D environment, thus providing support to territorial and environmental management tasks. The work illustrates also the results of the application of the infrastructure within a real-life scenario, thus providing the chance to discuss of implications of adopting such an approach.

DOI: 10.4018/978-1-4666-1562-5.ch011

THE IMPORTANCE OF GI FOR ENVIRONMENTAL MANAGEMENT

Environmental management is an articulated process, involving a number of public departments engaged in a variety of activities ranging from planning and maintenance of public infrastructures, to managing of natural and economical resources, as well as in the assessment of environmental risks. The complexity typical of the environmental management process poses a challenge to the development of a cross-department IT infrastructure. A wide range of different professional competences are involved with each operator having their technical background. In order to ensure the widest acceptance of a common platform this must then be characterised by a simple yet effective interface, characterised by high usability, whose use should not require specific technical background or training.

The implications of such complexity amplify the limits imposed by the adoption of most IT infrastructures deployed among public administrations. These are often composed of isolated subsystems run and managed by different departments and units for their specific tasks.

This scenario, from a purely technological perspective, involves the management of a wide range of information, all characterised by a geographical dimension, which need to be collected, made accessible and processed. This can be both data referring to spatial features stored in databases as well as real-time information coming from onsite sensors on weather, traffic or pollution conditions. Data are very heterogeneous, stored or transmitted in different data formats and the information exchange between different information systems in use among different departments is limited or based on a variety of different protocols. Each unit has independent responsibilities over the creation and maintenance of a specific data set. As a consequence interoperability is limited and data duplication is frequent. This has consequence in that data is not always updated and often different

units are not provided with real-time access to the information available.

It is well acknowledge that this complex technological as well as organizational scenario, together with the lack of interoperable tools, has very serious implications over the governance efficacy. A system approach is essential during management or planning tasks and, most crucially, it may be vital during when an emergency or crisis occurs. Interoperability becomes a critical issue also in the aftermath of crisis as demonstrated in a number of recent crises caused by natural disasters including the Ocean Tsunami on 2004, hurricanes and major earthquakes (Nourbakhsh et al, 2006). The operations following these events have demonstrated the importance of accessing GI in an interoperable way which can be critical to governments, relief aid and agency, local and international search and rescue teams.

Lack of interoperability is one of the causes for slow response times and it produces, within a number of government-related tasks, high social and economical costs. The extent and relevance of this issue is underlined within a report commissioned by the EU to assess the adoption of IT technologies at the regional level. The study highlights that 52% of public sector information in Europe is made of Geospatial Information (FTK, 2008) often characterised by data duplication (Ordnance Survey, 2006). These figures indicate that any technological development facilitating re-use of GI can bring significant social as well as economical benefits at local, national and international level. This is proved by a report from JRC (JRC, 2006) which highlights that the creation of harmonised geographical infrastructures yields fast Return of Investments (RoI).

This scenario underlines the importance of ensuring fast and interoperable access to public GI of environmental interest in the most efficient and technologically transparent form. It is acknowledged (Rajabifard & Williamson, 2004) (Mansourian et al., 2005) that this requirement can be satisfied through the development of integrated web-based IT system based on common standards. From the technological point of view this requirement is the main driving force of a shift from monolithic data-centric systems, custom-tailored to the specific requirements of different administrations, to interoperable service-centric infrastructures deployed according to common standards. Such infrastructures are designed as SOAs following a trend emerging from the domain of web-based enterprise applications. In the specific context of GI and environmental management, the adoption of SOA-based infrastructures has brought to the creation of federated systems referred to as Spatial Data Infrastructures or SDIs.

At the international level this trend has produced a number of initiatives to promote the definition of shared infrastructures based on common standards. Among the most relevant there are Global Monitoring for Environment and Security (GMES, 2008), Global Earth Observation System of Systems (GEOSS, 2008) as well as the European Spatial Data Infrastructure (ESDI). This is one of the major results of the EU directive INSPIRE (INfrastructure for SPatial InfoRmation in Europe) (INSPIRE, 2008), entered in force on March 2007. INSPIRE sets the foundation of a legal and technical framework with the intent to provide harmonised access to data of environmental interest. The directive represents a major milestone at the EU level and it is having profound effects, in technological, operational and political terms within national, regional and local administrations. From the technical standpoint, INSPIRE is promoting the definition of a European Spatial Data Infrastructure (ESDI) based on a multi-level federated architecture. The ESDI routes requests to National Spatial Data Infrastructure which in turn refer to Regional and Local SDIs when dealing with data or services of their relevance. This multi-level approach is based upon the concept that each administrative level becomes responsible for creating, publishing and maintaining GI at its own level through interoperable geographical web services.

The effort by international institutions has been backed by an equally significant standardisation attempt promoted by bodies such as The Open Geospatial Consortium (OGC, 2008a), International Organization for Standardization and the European Committee for Standardization.

THE ROLE OF 3D GI

As illustrated by (Zipf, 2008) the wide range of new specifications and protocols defined by OGC pave today the way to the adoption of 3D Geoservices, essential for advanced environmental management. Some of the first examples of this trend are publicly available such as Heidelberg 3D (GDI3D, 2008) and (Berlin 3D, 2008).

3D Geographic Information System (GIS) can provide higher usability and interactivity that can facilitate exchange of spatial information among stakeholders and government agencies (Grasso et al., 2006) (Grasso et al., 2008). As noted by (Sliuzas, 2003) the complexity of most standard GIS would be too great for decision makers who are not GIS experts. 3D visualization can instead provide a key aid to effectively understand 3D spatial relationships.

Since the early nineties, several authors (Koller et al, 1995) have developed real time 3D environments designed to handle GI. Several works have presented different ways to manipulate data within 3D environments using terrain textures to map additional information (Kersting & Doellner, 2002). The work in (Shumilov et al., 2002) presented a prototype GIS which allowed the construction of 3D and 4D models through the use of Time-dependent VRML (Virtual Reality Mark-up Language) geometries. More recently (Clark & Maurer, 2006) have presented an integrated interactive GIS proving that 3D GIS can be extended to provide features such as the direct manipulation of terrain features and creation of dynamic content. The system, developed as standalone application, requires an external tool to author the content. In a similar effort (Ohigashi et al., 2006) present a 3D application closely bound to a standard 2D legacy GIS through so-called "shadow copies". Other authors (Brooks & Whalley, 2005) have developed systems capable to integrate data layers, traditionally the data structure adopted within GIS systems, within a 3D view. However none of the previous works can support exchange of data between multiple instances in order to provide support for collaboration and cooperation.

However support for CSCW (Computer Supported Collaborative Work) within different operators involved in Environmental Management has become increasingly important and, as a consequence, several authors have developed different techniques to support collaboration within a 3D GIS. First efforts towards collaborative analysis of spatial data in a 3D environment was presented in (Manoharan et al., 2002), which presents a collaborative, interactive and location-independent working environment. The authors in (Ganesan et al., 2003) showed the importance of a scalable integration of sensor data and wireless sensor networks within a distributed system whilst maintaining their temporal relationship and thus achieving a distributed, 4D-enabled system. Further works of (MacEachren, 2005) extended the concept of geovisualization to support collaborative activities within a networked system. Recent research efforts on the same issue such as that reported in (Haist & Korte, 2006) propose a client-server system capable to ensure exchange of 3D content over a public network.

Today a large range of commercial applications widely in use among technical community provide 3D functionalities (ESRI, 2008) most of them provide 3D visualisation with few processing functionalities and are bound to commercial packages. However the last few years have seen the success of 3D consumer applications such as Google Earth, Microsoft Virtual Earth or World Wind (NASA, 2008). These applications, often referred to as 3D Geobrowsers, have been designed to provide high usability and this has contributed

to their pervasive use across the public. Their widespread adoption has opened up the geospatial field, traditionally limited to domain experts, to the wider public yielding a social-technological trend known as "Neogeography" (Turner, 2006). As a result an increasing number of web-based applications are being developed through the integration of technologies for mapping, indexing and processing, for diverse application domains, from traffic data visualization, to public sector service availability. Several experiences (Coughlin et al., 2008) have shown that 3D Geobrowsers can also provide a significant contribution to experts and operators in the field of environmental management. Natural disasters such as Hurricane Katrina and the 2005 earthquake in Pakistan have demonstrated the role that 3D Geobrowsers can play to support aid agency and rescue teams during large environmental crisis (Nourbakhsh et al., 2006).

Development in the field of 3D geobrowsers is being challenged by the exponential growth of data made available, coming from public administrations (e.g. regional plans), sensors and Earth Observation technologies. Rapid evolution of Earth Observation, satellite and sensor technologies is generating a constantly enlarging amount of data that needs new methods for processing, analysis and complexity reduction. A clear example of this is NASA Earth Science Data and Information System (ESDIS, 2008) that gathers several Petabytes (1 Mil Gigabytes) of data with a growth that, on 2005, was reported to be increasing at a rate of 3.5 Terabytes per day. Another example is ESA Envisat satellite mission that is producing 160 Gigabytes of data per Earth's orbit, for up to 14 orbits a day. That is 1 Petabyte every 5 years. This fast growing need to access large scale GI is also critical at consumer-level applications, an example of this being the announcement made by Microsoft on April 2008 unveiling its data centre at Boulder (USA), capable to store data up to 15 Petabyte for its Virtual Earth solution.

Such a wide range of multidimensional environmental information pose a great challenge to technologists and scientists to find effective ways to provide access to relevant data patterns within a vast and highly dynamic information flow. For this research has brought to an effective combination of data mining and information visualization, often referred to as Visual Analytics (VA). VA has emerged to promote effective forms of access to very large amount of multidimensional data related to the environment and its security. VA allows fast filtering of complex information and identification of key data patterns emerging from the simulated crisis scenario. A major role is being played by the National Visualization and Analytics Center (NVAC, 2008) in the U.S. which actively research the use of VA in contexts such as environmental and homeland security. As stated by (Hetzler & Turner, 2004) many existing VA systems are data-centric. They focus on a particular type of data and provide separate but linked environments for analysis of different types of information. This is the reason why several authors (Andrienko & Andrienko, 2004) explored how information synthesis can enable the analyst to handle dynamic information of all types in a seamless environment.

THE SYSTEM DEVELOPED

This article illustrates the results of an ongoing research effort to create a modular client-server infrastructure for Geographical Visual Analytics (GVA) to provide interactive access, distribution and processing of GI to support analysis of geographical data for territorial management.

The system builds on previous works by the authors (Conti & De Amicis, 2008) (Conti et al., 2008) (De Amicis et al., 2007). The first prototype, already tested within a real life context, has brought to promising results. The system in fact is in use at a local public administration department office as planning and control tool. The system is designed to provide operators with a user friendly 3D interface capable to ensure interactive access

to geospatial information present within the infrastructure through a number of OGC-compliant services (Conti & De Amicis, 2008) (Conti et al., 2008) (De Amicis et al., 2007). As visible in Figure 4, the user can navigate over the territory interacting with a very large dataset (Conti et al., 2008) made available through a number of web services specifically developed to deliver high-speed imaging through via Web Map Service (WMS) (OGC, 2008a). Points of Interest (POI) are made available in overlay; whenever the user selects a POI additional information is rendered in overlay to the environment. Information exchange is also provided through support of GeoRSS (Conti et al., 2008). This approach ensures fast update and exchange of information on events related to specific positions such as accidents, alerts etc. Each geo-referenced piece of information can be enriched with images and other multimedia information which is then distributed to all users registered to that specific topic (Conti et al., 2008).

The architecture developed is based on a multi-tier approach where the 3D client stands at the application level and a number of middleware component access a variety of repositories within file systems and spatial databases (PostgreSQL with PostGIS extension). Specifically, as illustrated in Figure 1, the infrastructure developed is based on a three-tier architecture where a number of 3D Geobrowsers, operating as clients, exchange information through a server infrastructure exposing a number of web services.

A Java-based 3D client, deployed as Java™ WebStart, JOGL-enabled (JOGL, 2008) application, has been developed on top of World Wind (NASA, 2008) libraries and it has been developed to interact with the service infrastructure. This choice makes it very lightweight and portable as it can run on a variety of operating systems. This can be started from a webpage accessible either from the Internet or within the intranet of a public administration. This way the client allows real-time 3D interaction with the GI that is processed and made available by a SOA infrastructure.

The middleware level is created as JEE (Java™ Enterprise Edition) infrastructure (Stearns et al., 2006) where a number of EJB (Enterprise Java™ Beans) deployed on a JBoss (JBoss, 2008) application server provide the geographical processing features. As illustrated in Figure 2, the functions necessary to access and process the geographical data are either accessed via RMI (Remote Method Invocation) or via Web Service deployed within a Tomcat (The Apache Software Foundation, 2008) servlet container. This approach allows maximising performance or interoperability depending on the requirements of the client application.

As illustrated in Figure 3, from the architectural point of view the middleware level is composed of two sub-levels providing base services, such as those necessary for mapping and providing raw access to the data level, and higher-level services, delivering complex functionalities to the final client application. Among the latter there is the component responsible for the authoring service which exposes all necessary functionalities to let operators define additional content within the system. This way authorised operator can,

from within the 3D client application, create new content and upload information such as vector or raster data. The information made available within the system is then made accessible to the whole set of users. This can be other operators as well as final citizens which can access GI in a very interactive way.

This approach allows a clear definition of access policies and can properly support complex decision making processes, typical of environmental managing, where different competences are delegated to different agencies or departments. The system thus becomes an important support to strategic decision making process as decision makers can access in a seamless way a wide set of data and services made available from different departments and units. This is done via a web-application in an interactive and very user-friendly environment.

Such a technological shift allows a profound re-organization both from a purely technological perspective as well as from the operational point of view as it predicates a novel vision whereby each unit or department is responsible of the creation and maintenance of a specific set service.

Figure 1. The multi-tier architecture

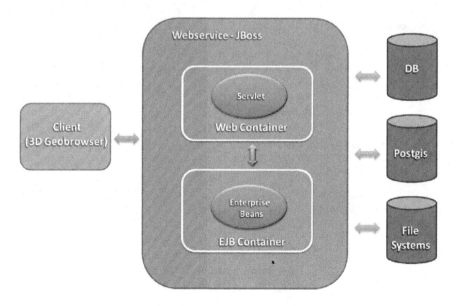

Figure 2. The architecture of each component deployed as EJB

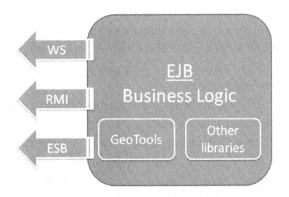

As visible from Figure 5, each unit or department is able to publish their own data within the infrastructure through a user-friendly authoring interface (Encarnação et al, 2008) integrated within the 3D client. Information present within the central repository can be modified, deleted or updated in a very intuitive manner, through an interaction process that benefits from the user friendliness of the interface to hide to the user all technical issues. In fact through an easy-to-use interface the operator can define the graphical representation of each geographical features present within the main repository. This information is then stored at the central level, as OCG-compliant SLD (Styled Layer Descriptor) (OGC, 2008), and made available to all users. SLD is an XML-based description of graphical layouts associated to geographical features.

However, to ensure the highest usability, this process is completely transparent to the user as the system automatically codes the XML while the operator graphically defines all the features required. As detailed in (Conti et al., 2008) the first prototype is being used by the public office responsible for urban planning, to access a vast amount of data related to a provincial urban plan, providing real-time access high resolution data of more than 6.200 Km^2 classified within 180 content layers. Providing functionalities to access and manage GI has brought to the advantage that data can be managed in an interoperable way through a common open architecture. This approach has helped solving de facto the issue of data interoperability and data duplication.

Figure 3. Details of the architecture

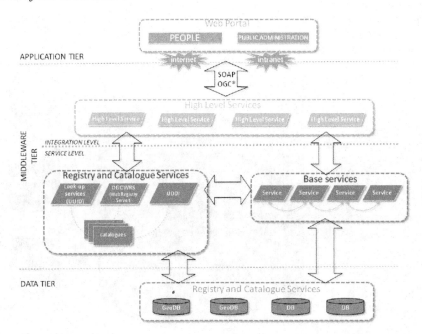

Figure 4. An image of the first version of the system

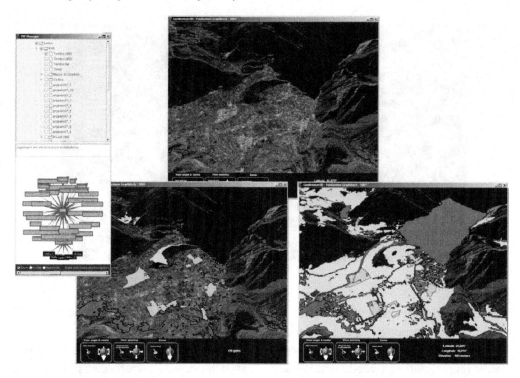

PROCESSING SERVICES AND INTERACTIVE SERVICE ORCHESTRATION

The assessment phase of the first prototype has provided essential requirements for tasks necessary for environmental management. To do so operators need to be provided with more advanced processing features, indispensable for analysis and planning. Thus the framework has been extended to support access to Web Processing Services (WPS) in the most user-friendly way, directly from within 3D client. Processes include algorithms, calculation or model that operates on spatially referenced data. This allows for publishing not machine-readable binding information and human-readable metadata that allows service discovery and use.

Within a typical scenario users can connect to the server exposing WPS over the infrastructure and retrieve the list of the available processing capabilities. Each processing services can be used

as a processing component of a more complex process chain. This approach can be used to create very complex procedures. Each processing unit is represented by an icon, briefly describing its functions, connected to several inbound and outbound slots. Each slot represents a data type which is required as input or resulting, as output, from the processing capability.

In a very user-friendly way the user can create complex processing structures by connecting in- and outbound connectors. As each block of the chain represents a processing service, this way the operators can perform very articulated service orchestration tasks in a completely transparent way, by just interacting with the relevant icons directly within the 3D representation of the territory. This approach has proved to be extremely user-friendly and it allows performing complex processing tasks with little training. Processing functionalities can be constrained to areas of the territory, for localised calculations. The user can interactively select, directly within the 3D scene,

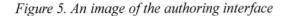

Figure 5. An image of the authoring interface

a specific area defining the area of interest. As visible from 7 once the process chain is created, this can be activated by pressing the relevant icon on the process representation, directly within the 3D scene. Each processing unit invokes a specific WPS which is executed by the remote server with the relevant input as defined through the process chain.

This approach has the advantage in that processing functionalities are off-loaded from the client and are centralised at the infrastructural level. From a system engineering perspective this allows for better scalability and consistency. Updates of existing processing features, as well as availability of new ones become immediately available to all users without them being required to install new piece of software. Finally it must be noticed that processing tasks are performed asynchronously therefore ensuring, at the client side, the maximum interactivity, as the client application does need to get to an halt waiting for the result of the processing task. As soon as the result of a processing unit is available this is passed from one WPS to the input of the relevant WPS component(s) according to the service chain defined by the user. The result becomes finally available to the user and visible on the screen as image, as 3D geometry resulting from the simulation, or as geographical features resulting from the processing tasks.

Figure 6. Representation of a processing unit

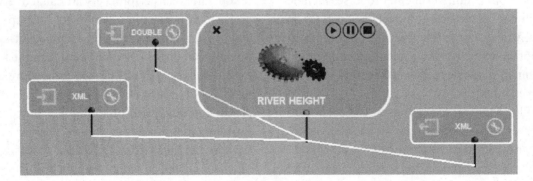

Figure 7. An example of processing chain directly created within the 3D scene

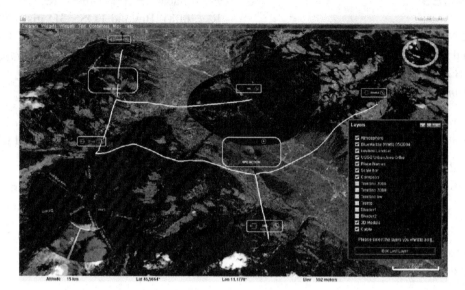

CONCLUSION AND FUTURE WORKS

Today interoperability is starting to become a reality thanks to the several international harmonization efforts, trying to solve the problem by offering open computing standards for management of GI. The research work presented shows how interoperability is key to connect many systems with large amounts of complex data sets. Visualizing this information in a way that maximizes usability and provides a profound understanding of the respective information space, is one of the big information visualization research challenges as traditional tools seem no longer adequate to cope with the enormous data being made available today.

The article has illustrated an ongoing research effort which aims at delivering a full infrastructure to access and process GI within a 3D environment. This approach, which has been applied in the context of environmental management, is targeted to public administrations and governmental agencies. The infrastructure has been founded upon the principle of federated architectures and therefore it well supports definition of domain competence and responsibilities. Its first use demonstrates its usability and it is providing key insights for future developments.

Furthermore the insights and feedback from operators using the system are being used as basis to define the requirements of further developments. It has emerged that providing real time access to concurrent engineering features is essential for daily workflow as collaboration among different operators is essential requirement of their working activities. A further clear need, that will be subject of future development, is the possibility of using the system within the context of a control station scenario, within a high-resolution visualisation environment capable of providing advanced visualisation, data processing and visual analytics capability.

ACKNOWLEDGMENT

Part of the achievements discussed in this article as well as the data shown in the images is the result of a project "Sviluppo di una Infrastruttura Dati Territoriali secondo una Architettura Orientata ai Servizi" commissioned by the Autonomous Provincia of Trento, Italy.

REFERENCES

Andrienko, N., & Andrienko, G. (2004). Interactive visual tools to explore spatio-temporal variation. *AVI'04: Proceedings of the working conference on Advanced visual interfaces.*

3DBerlin, S. (2008). Retrieved from http://www.3d-stadtmodell-berlin.de

Berlin 3D. (2008). Retrieved August 27, 2008, from 3D RealityMaps: http://www.realitymaps.de

Brooks, S., & Whalley, L. (2005). A 2D/3D hybrid GI system. In *Proc. of the 3rd intern. conf. on Computer graphics and interactive techniques in Australasia and South East Asia.* ACM.

Clark, R. W., & Maurer, R. (2006). Visual terrain editor: an interactive editor for real terrains. *J. Comput. Small Coll., 22*(2).

Conti, G., Andreolli, M., Piffer, S., & De Amicis, R. (2008). A 3D web based GI system for regional planning. In *proceedings of Webist,* Madeira, Portugal.

Conti, G., & De Amicis, R. (2008). New generation 3d web-based GI systems - The importance of integrated infrastructures for territory management. In *proceedings of Webist,* Madeira, Portugal.

Coughlin, J., Cuff, S., & Krause, N. (2008). SERVIR Viz: A 3D data access and visualization system for mesoamerica. *Directions Magazione Worldwide Source for Geospatial Technology.*

De Amicis, R., Witzel, M., & Conti, G. (2007). Interoperable networked service-based infrastructure for interactive. In *Proceedings of Proceedings of the NATO-OTAN Workshop on Development of a Prototype System for Sharing Information related to Acts of Terrorism to the Environment, Agriculture and Water systems,* Venice.

Encarnação, J., De Amicis, R., Conti, G., & J., R. (2008). Beyond FOSS 3D gis technologies: a chance for developing countries. In *proceedings of FOSS4G 2008 - Free and Open Source Software for Geospatial Conference,* Cape Town, South Africa.

ESDIS. (2008). *The earth science data and information system project.* Retrieved from http://esdis.eosdis.nasa.gov

ESRI - Environment System Research Institute. (2008). Retrieved from http://www.esri.com

FTK - Research Institute for Telecommunication. (2008, May 30). European ICT manifesto for the regions. Dortmund.

Ganesan, D., Estrin, D., & Heidemann, J. (2003). Dimensions: Why do we need a new data handling architecture for sensor networks? *SIGCOMM Comput. Commun.* (pp. 143–148).

GDI3D. (2008). *Spatial data infrastructure for 3d-geodata.* Retrieved from http://www.geographie.uni-bonn.de/karto/hd3d/webstart.en.htm

GEOSS - Global Earth Observation System of Systems. (2008). Retrieved from http://www.epa.gov/geoss

Gershon, N., & Eick, S. (1997). *Information visualization applications in the real world.* IEEE.

GMES - Global Monitoring for Environment and Security. (2008). Retrieved from http://www.gmes.info

Google Earth. (2008). Retrieved from http://earth.google.com

Grasso, V., Cervone, G., Singh, A., & Kafatos, M. (2006). Global environmental alert service. *American Geophysical Union, Fall Meeting.*

Grasso, V., & Singh, A. (2008). *Advances in space research.* Elsevier.

Haist, J., & Korte, P. (2006). Adaptive streaming of 3d gis geometries and textures for interactive visualisation of 3d city models. *9th AGILE Intern. conf. on Geographic Information Science.*

Hetzler, E. G., & Turner, A. (2004). Analysis experiences using information visualization. *IEEE Computer Graphics and Applications*, *24*(5), 22–26. doi:10.1109/MCG.2004.22

INSPIRE. (2008). Retrieved from http://inspire.jrc.ec.europa.eu

Intergraph SG&I - Geospatially Powered Solution. (2008). Retrieved from http://www.intergraph.com/sgi/default.aspx

JBoss. (2008). *jboss.org: community driven.* Retrieved from www.jboss.org

JOGL. (2008). Retrieved from Java binding for the opengl api: https://jogl.dev.java.net

JRC - Joint Research Centre. European Commission. (2006). *Report of international workshop on spatial data infrastructures, cost-benefit / return on investment*, Italy: Ispra.

Kersting, O., & Doellner, J. (2002). Interactive 3d visualization of vector data in gis. *Proc. of the 10th ACM intern. symp. on Advances in geographic information systems* (pp. 107–112). ACM.

Koller, D., et al. (1995). Virtual gis: A real-time 3d geographic information system. *Proc. of the 6th conf. on Visualization* (pp. 94–9).

MacEachren, M. (2005). *Moving geovisualization toward support for group work. Exploring geovisualization.* Elsevier.

Manoharan, T., Taylor, H., & Gardiner, P. (2002). A collaborative analysis tool for visualisation and interaction with spatial data. *Proc. of the 7th Int. Conf. on 3D Web technology* (pp. 75–83).

Mansourian, A., Rajabifard, A., & Zoej, J. (2005). *Development of a web-based gis using sdi for disaster management.* Springer.

NASA. (2008). *World Wind.* Retrieved from http://worldwind.arc.nasa.gov

Nourbakhsh, I., Sargent, R., Wright, A., Cramer, K., McClendon, B., & Jones, M. (2006). *Mapping disaster zones* (Vol. 439). Nature.

NVAC. (2008). *National visualization and analytics center.* Retrieved from http://nvac.pnl.gov

OGC - Open Geospatial Consortium. (2008). Retrieved from www.opengeospatial.org

OGC - Open Geospatial Consortium. (2008a). *Web map service.* Retrieved from Open geospatial consortium: http://www.opengeospatial.org/standards/wms

Ohigashi, M., Guo, Z. S., & Tanaka, Y. (2006). Integration of a 2d legacy gis, legacy simulations, and legacy databases into a 3d geographic simulation. In *Proc. of the 24th annual conf. on Design of communication* (pp. 149–156). ACM.

Open Geospatial Consortium. (2008). *Web processing service.* Retrieved from Open geospatial consortium: http://www.opengeospatial.org/standards/wps

Ordnance Survey. (2006, September). *Geographic information strategy.* Retrieved from http://www.ordnancesurvey.co.uk/oswebsite/aboutus/reports/gistrategy/gistrategy.pdf

Rajabifard, A., & Williamson, I. (2004). *SDI development and capacity building.* Retrieved from http://www.geom.unimelb.edu.au/research/SDI_research/

Shumilov, S., Thomsen, A., Cremers, A. B., & Koos, B. (2002). Managment and visualization of large, complex and time-dependent 3D objects in distributed gis. *Proc. of the 10th ACM international symposium on Advances in geographic information systems* (pp. 113–118). ACM.

Sliuzas, R. (2003). Governance and the use of gis in developing countries. *Habitat International*, *27*(4), 495–499. doi:10.1016/S0197-3975(03)00002-X

Stearns, J., Chinnici, R., & Sahoo. (2006, May). *Update: An introduction to the java ee 5 platform.* Retrieved from Java ee at a glance: http://java.sun.com/developer/technicalArticles/J2EE/intro_ee5/

Steed, A. (2004). Data visualization within urban models. In *Proc. of the Theory and Practice of Computer Graphics* (pp. 9–16). IEEE.

The Apache Software Foundation. (2008). *Tomcat.* Retrieved from http://tomcat.apache.org

Turner, A. (2006). *Introduction to Neogeography.* O'Reilly Media.

University of Bonn. (2008). *Heidelberg 3D.* Retrieved August 27, 2008, from 3D GDI Heidelberg: http://www.gdi-3d.de

Zipf, A. (2008). Small island perspectives on global challenges: The role of spatial data in supporting a sustainable future. *GSDI 10 Conference Proceedings.*

This work was previously published in the International Journal of Information Technologies and Systems Approach, Volume 3, Issue 1, edited by Frank Stowell and Manuel Mora, pp. 57-71, copyright 2010 by IGI Publishing (an imprint of IGI Global).

Chapter 12
Tracking Values in Web Based Student Teacher Exchanges

Thomas Hansson
Blekinge Institute of Technology, Sweden

ABSTRACT

When vocational student teachers communicate on a virtual platform in a combined campus and web based university course they focus on the contents of teaching and learning. However, in communicating professional teacher knowledge they implicitly express their personal values too. Without giving it much thought, they embed values in their verbal entries and they assess embedded values in their peers' texts. This article introduces a soft systems model for categorizing the influence of values on web based interactions.

INTRODUCTION

Reflective thinking, introspection and contemplation seem to activate people's consciousness and act as a catalyst for ethical behavior. People's moral conscience suggests what, when or how things should be done for whatever instrumental, economical or personal reasons. People's conscience is called upon in times of trouble, dilemmas and misfortune; for example when a certain activity, decision or process is instrumentally distant, economically damaging or morally harmful. This is when an individual process of ethical reflection (Brusling & Strömqvist, 1996) begins. So, values materialize when people put

rational thoughts into action and explore social interaction as dialogical relations, empathic feelings and ethical standpoints.

Western ambitions on democratic education aim at promotion of spiritual and moral growth. Typical fostering themes cover values clarification (Kirschenbaum, 1977), character education (Lickona, 1993), moral development (Kohlberg, 1981) and ethical literacy (Lovat et al., 2002). The Swedish upper secondary school curriculum (Department of Education, 1998, p. 10) explores social and cultural growth, saying (transl. by this author): "schooling should establish abilities in the students to understand and/or perform ethical commitment; respect for other people; protest

DOI: 10.4018/978-1-4666-1562-5.ch012

against oppression and abuse; help the suffering; develop empathy for others; protect the local and global environment." The national wide ranging objectives are however often referred to as "curricular poetry" and it is far from clear if the general objectives help transform people's attitudes into motivating operations and moral practices.

Ethical problems in education like lying, plagiarism or bullying seem to attract the teachers' attention. On a global scale people consider both factual knowledge and publicly acknowledged values as they deal with starvation, pollution and global warming. But believing that textual knowledge alone (Hansson, 2006) could provide a solution to ethical issues is an illusion. Teachers need to complement informative data, facts and truths with an awareness based on justice, integrity and self-control. According to Munro (1999, p. 527) this is an accepted contemporary paradigm, sometimes described as "technologies of the self". It covers compassionate holism, i.e. the idea of a personal dedication to help people cooperate, balance rationality with intuition and connect with the world. The purpose of learning about technologies of the self is that people are ready, willing and able to appreciate and act on moral themes, provided they experience a sense of social control along the way.

It makes sense that we should learn to establish a relational dialogue (Dysthe, 2003) regardless of contexts, power relations or values. It is also a fair assumption that people make collectively just decisions when hidden values, normative assumptions and judgmental manipulation are brought to the surface. Therefore educators must exercise pedagogical leadership and learn to establish – through ethical reflection – an actionable dialogue in which each step of the exchange is illustrated, motivated and negotiated. Some mediators have fine-tuned their skills and turned this process into inter- and intrapersonal work of art.

Development of modern ICT-software enables for qualified interactions. Focus on the mediating technology is relevant for the study of virtual communities of practice. However, many communicative qualities found in old post exchanges and modern (*Blackboard*) learning management systems interactions remain. Ngwenyama and Lee (1997, p. 149) mention: "The filtering out of social cues" and the "lack of personalization". They make up relevant foci whereas "feedback, channel and language" are left aside.

It would be an achievement if educators provided a practical perspective on Internet ethics or socially attractive netiquette (Shea, 2007) about an optimal input for practicing values in education. However, generous and ethically valid communication makes up a complex dimension of higher human cognition. It is also reasonable to assume that a collective of student teachers interacting on a LMS would generate "productive" verbal exchanges and increased performance for all. On the impact of LMS-exchanges, Ngwenyama and Lee (1997, p. 152) say that actors share every aspect of the organizational context and: "The context also defines the power, authority and status relationships of the individuals within it." Both young "native" and adult "immigrant" internet users look for, find out about and act on ethically secure communications as they practice in virtual contexts (Coutaz, et al., 2005), developing their personality, team roles and relations (Buber, 1988). In such situations their behavior is compatible with their expectations on personal, workplace and democratic values. Finally, the student teachers assess educational norms, the situation related to the task and the orientation of the peer whose written text they are expected to critically evaluate and respond to.

PREVIOUS RESEARCH

In an attempt at clarifying implicitly expressed intentions between US-university students, Pesendorfer and Koszegi (2006) confuse *values* with *behavior* in a study of synchronous and asynchronous negotiations. The authors' approach is too simplistic to form a basis for further analysis. Rather than clarifying values, they combine (ibid, p. 144) loosely defined characterizations like "spontaneous and unreflective emotional behaviour", "emerging emotions", "flaming", "impoliteness" and "constrained self-awareness". As could be expected from the design, the authors (ibid., p. 149) conclude that the interlocutors stick to protocol and produce text-specific contents during asynchronous communication.

It is difficult to extract hidden, implicitly understood and intuitive values from textual LMS-entries. But it is equally hard to measure values with the help of questionnaires. Yet, Malle and Edmonson (2007) mention survey values like *tradition, honesty, helpfulness, forgiveness, generosity, family relations, loyalty, relation with God, self-respect and politeness*. Unfortunately, they also include goals like "peace" and attitudes like "racism" on their list, concepts that people find hard to separate from values. At other times values are mixed up with qualities we would like to see in ourselves rather than the values we actually host.

Hofstede's (1984) classification of national cultures needs to be mentioned in the context of failing questionnaire-based value analyses. His study among IBM-employees separates between geographical spread in cultures by *power-distance, individualism, masculinity* and *uncertainty avoidance*. Scandinavian cultures score low on power distance, high on femininity and low on uncertainty avoidance. It is tempting to translate Hofstede's cultural dimensions into values. If the analyzed sample were typical Swedish student teachers, they would score high in the north-eastern corner of Figure 1 because according to Hofstede, "universalism" and "benevolence" make up (high) feminine values of the Swedish culture.

A Hindu-inspired religious movement materializes as a non-curricular program called *Living Values: An Education Program* for UK-education. The initiative (BKWSU, 1995, pp. 1-50) comprises of *peace, respect, love, tolerance, honesty, humility, co-operation responsibility, happiness,*

freedom, simplicity and *unity*. However, the collection of flower-power values are less valid than the proper values of a global study (Schwartz, 1992), exploring values that people attach to their impressions, perceptions and experiences.

Gilligan (1983) and Gilligan and Attanucci (1988) identify major moral voices based on gender differences. The male voice is characterized as "justice" and the female voice as "care". The authors' rather crude characterization has influenced the parallelism between feminine values like "care" and "self transcendence" plus masculine values like "justice" combined with "self enhancement" in Schwartz (1992). On the other hand Hansson (2000) refutes the implied parallelism between female "care" and "openness to change" plus masculine "justice" and "conservatism". So it would be a mistake to assume that an entry by a female student teacher would automatically contain self transcendent values.

BACKGROUND AND RATIONALE

A majority of the studied student and teachers are typical Swedes holding on to their national values. According to Gaunt and Löfgren (1984), traditional Swedish myths are orderliness in time and place (ibid., p. 50), rationality (ibid., p. 59), collectivism and envy (ibid., p. 102). This study presents the interlocutors' values as an integral part of their personality, identity and awareness. In order to be able to separate between the multitude of approaches to values, e.g. Gardner's (2000, p. 125) for investigating the impact of values on student teachers' web-based communications, it is, according to Goffman (1959), necessary to stay clear of poorly defined myths, cultural traits theory or dramaturgical 'fronts'.

One aim is to provide an analysis based on contexts, roles and relations in a social system operating on the Internet. Another aim is to establish a theory for describing how hidden, implicit and underlying values affect the quantity and quality

Figure 1. Proper values, ordering of values and value directions

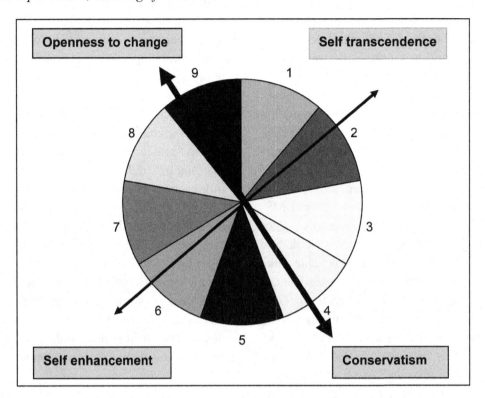

of vocational student teachers' interactions. There is a need to explore exactly what the concept *value* signifies. When people talk about proper values they think about *security, independence, success, friendliness, conservatism* and *freedom*. But these values are often confused with attitudes like *rationality, integrity* and *individualism*. They are also misinterpreted as goals like *pluralism, democracy* and *salvation*.

Value arguments and decisions have a natural position in educational discourse. For example, after the war a majority of Swedish politicians agreed on a democratic school system. Isling (1974, p. 12) defined systemic macro-level education that "safeguards democracy and by concrete democratic procedures helps develop democracy." One likely outcome of a reformed education system would be, says the author (ibid., p. 13), "Increased emphasis on social fostering to provide an increased ability to cooperate and

influence other people." (transl. by this author). However, even though the author defines democracy at length and in detail, the concept remains a political *objective* rather than a human *value*. From a normative point of view, however, Isling's approach to a whole school pastoral ethos is a valid aim. But the approach is an insufficient measure for fostering the students' personality and making them morally accountable citizens of a democratic society.

Balancing of Values

The structuring of professional teacher values has an impact on the succeeding analysis of verbal exchanges between web based interlocutors. The purpose of focusing on such values is to describe how collective interaction develops through relation building in a virtual context.

ESS Edunet (2007) introduces a globally relevant set of allegedly proper values that characterize human beings. The authors say (a) values are motivational and represent goals that people aspire to achieve. They are (b) implicitly understood and desirable guidelines that refer to specific objects, acts, events or situations. They function as (c) criteria for how/when/where/what to act, think or say. Finally they make up (d) a hierarchical system of ordered priorities functioning as guiding principles in people's lives. It seems likely that the single most important aspect of individual values lies in the motivating goals they express. For example, in order to be able to coordinate between a personal goal like self realization and a public objective like democracy, people need to *negotiate* their values. A multi-disciplinary philosophical, sociological, anthropological and psychological field of research identifies values that according to Schwartz (1992) are based on our *needs* as biological organisms, but also on our *ability* to coordinate social interaction by personal motive and our *drive* to lead good lives.

It is easy to see why values relate to an individual and a collective domain of attitudes and behaviors equally. Decision making is usually difficult in morally challenging contexts where issues of e.g. justice versus care surface. Sustainable society, pollution and ecology crave for difficult decision making. Either way we choose there are positives and negatives attached to the decision. On a daily basis people experience such naturally occurring issues, contradictions and dissonances. Insoluble moral dilemmas initiate a process of dissonance resolution (Festinger, 1957). Hence, a degree of collective social sensibility combined with generous individual reasoning is needed. This is true regardless if the issues are politically fortunate like immigration, economically profitable like interest rates or socially justified like white lies.

The student teachers' have an intuitive way of dealing with technologies of the self so as to present themselves, their ideas and their values generously and truthfully. Expressed differently, values are an indicator of a person's identity. How s/he succeeds in balancing opposing, contradictory, complementary or competing values suggests who that person is. A personal ability to deal with dissonance resolution explains how an individual's identity changes as a result of how s/he controls contradictory values. Mills (1958) in Byrne (1966, p. 215) says: "whenever a person is presented to a temptation to violate moral standards and then makes the decision not to do so, dissonance is created." The way which cognitive dissonance is reflected on, acted on and adjusted to is the origin of a process from which a person's identity and verbal behavior emerges.

Furthermore, values surface during natural contradictions as inter-personal conflicts or intra-personal dissonances. When value issues are activated, they are elicited from within the subject as an intra-personal quality. Whenever conflicting values appear, the rival opponents' inter- and intra-personal relations need to be managed by the individual's potential to activate, steer, process and control values in Self and in Other. Morally responsible behavior is a personal thing, beginning and ending with a virtuous ability to balance values. Alderman (1996, p. 34) says we must do away with intra-personal imbalances and make peace with ourselves by reviewing and bringing our behavior in line with collective inter-personal morals.

On the issue of self management and self consciousness Herrscher (2006, p. 411) says: "The responsibility for ultimate consequences (*of what we do*, author's comment) extends the limits to incorporate ethical, social, and ecological effects." Hence, this study explores a range of verbal behaviors from a perspective of human relations, interactions and outcomes, all of which are informed by the contention that human beings portray themselves as legitimate, valid and just communicators.

Relations

Long before social systems methodology (SSM) was the flower of the day, Russell (1952) identified social groupings, arguing that man is defined by actions within and between social systems. Buber's (1988, p. 67) theory complements Russell's global approach, suggesting an *I-It/I-Thou* account of internal double relations within *Self*, portraying how *I* wish to appear to *Thou,* how *I* really appear to *Thou* and how *I* reflectively appear to *I*. According to Buber (1988, p. 50), relation building contains a twofold principle of human life. This principle applies for identifying another human being in *Self* by acknowledging a primal setting at a distance that enables for establishing an independent opposite 'object'; and for contact-making by tacit, verbal, visual, audio or symbolic means between *Self* and *Other.* Thus people learn to enter a personal relation and making somebody present by imagining the *Other's* reality. Buber's (1988, p. 61) contention about the functioning of human relations suggests that: "the inmost growth of the self is […] accomplished in the relation between one and the other, between men, that is pre-eminently in the mutuality of the making present, in the making present of another self and in the knowledge that one is made present in his own self by the other." For the purpose of this study the scope of relations signifies a communicative space for mutual acceptance, affirmation and confirmation in a web-based community of practices. In further defining the context of systemic verbal relation building, Buber (1988, p. 50) says that *I-Thou* relations are future oriented acts made up of acceptance, confirming speech, genuine meetings and living processes. *I-It* relations, on the other hand, are one sided individual (memory-archive) connections with the past, containing little experiential access to knowledge. Such an instrumental *I-It* orientation is demonstrated for this study in some non-communicative short and detached entries that prove hard to respond to for the student teachers.

The impact of inter-human relation building theory for social systems is substantial because people prefer to think of themselves as self-controlled agents. But in spite of traditional conceptions of instrumental agency, it would be a mistake to assume that the world is *in* man or that man is *in* the world. On the contrary, *I* and *It* are encapsulated in each other as a holistic "whole". Also, there is no *I* by itself, but a conception of *I* which belongs to the *I-Thou* relation and (the same) *I* that belongs to the *I-It* relation.

As to the value-laden side of inter-human relation building by internalizing input, i.e. understanding of textual contents and externalizing output in individual texts, Buber (1988, p. 49) says the only way to expose the ethical principle of becoming human runs through dialogue with a purpose "to contrast its (*the Subject's*, author's comment) reading with that of other beings." Emphasis on dialogue indicates the complexity of web-based relations in social systems between *I, Thou* and the mediating tool, *It*.

Some interactions are ethically good because they appear to the interlocutors as being honest, comprehensive and generous. Other interactions are counterproductive to systemic growth, i.e. generation of long threads, because they fail to separate between a person's knowledge, conscience, consciousness and values. Unfortunately, digital information technologies are much too often managed and experienced as a mediating tool for distant-instrumental publication, rather than a social system for dialogical communication. If properly introduced, controlled and administered the LMS-software enables for the interlocutors to adjust their personified perceptions, reflections and cognitions to an inspiring input which influences positively a trajectory of motivating and informative threads.

THEORETICAL FRAMEWORK

In this article I study "the causal interdependencies, multiple influences, and evolving patterns of human communication" (Hansson, 2008, p. 371) related to web-based interactions among vocational student teachers. Such exchanges constitute a messy non-linear situation for which the exact outcomes are hard to predict. Put differently, the article focuses on the first step in a handful of procedures (Checkland, 2000) of a soft systems methodology (SSM), i.e., model building of purposeful activities for learning about the social norms and values of web-based relation-building between peers. Hirschheim et al. (1995, p. 242) says SSM should lead the researcher to an understanding of the studied phenomenon rather than facilitate a particular problem-solving process. According to Checkland and Scholes (1990) the object of study should cover CATWOE, i.e. **C**ustomers (students) who benefit; **A**ctors (students again) who perform; **T**ransformations (curricular knowledge and values); **W**eltanschauung (a common viewpoint or a model that makes the workings of the system intelligible); **O**wners (students) committed to team building, working and learning; **E**nvironmental limitations (located outside the actual context of the software). The first difficulty is to define the problem by identifying values that generate long threads at a proper level for representing all the data. Another problem is to accept that there will be only effective or ineffective entries rather than right or wrong solutions. The third challenge is to find alternative solutions on how to design research with the help of analytical concepts. Succeeding operations cover descriptive definitions rather than action-oriented transformations of structural, process or attitudinal qualities in communications between vocational student teachers. Operational action research ambitions (Munro, 1999) for facilitating learning through organizational or individual management of change are left aside.

Value Directions

Regardless of nationality, culture, gender, social status or other, Schwartz (1992) argues that people build their understanding of the world on comprehensive value categories. One diagonal opposition (see Figure 1) where moral dilemmas seem to appear is entrepreneurial *Openness to change* versus administrative *Conservatism*. Another opposition which causes a similar kind of cognitive dissonance appears between benevolent *Self transcendence* and egoistic *Self enhancement*. Figure 1 outlines proper values and their relations: 1. *Universalism;* 2. *Benevolence;* 3. *Conformity;* 4. *Security;* 5. *Power;* 6. *Achievement;* 7. *Hedonism;* 8. *Stimulation;* 9. *Self-direction*.

One dimension in Figure 1 (thin arrow) covers a focus on Self versus Other. Self transcendence in the North-Eastern corner includes *universalism, i.e.* understanding, appreciation and tolerance. The core value is *benevolence* for preserving and enhancing the welfare of those with whom one is interacting. An opposing Self enhancement direction resides in the South-Western corner. Here *power* equals social status and prestige, control and dominance over people. The core value is *achievement,* including personal success acquired through egoistic demonstration of competence. Another opposition (thick arrow) appears between values related to accommodating change and assimilative stability. Openness to change in the North-Western corner covers *stimulation,* i.e. appreciation of excitement, novelty and challenges. The core value, *self direction* is safeguarded through independent action by freedom to choose, create and explore given resources. An opposing Conservatism direction of values in the South-Eastern corner includes restraint of actions, outburst of emotions and spontaneous impulses. Core values of *security* and *social order* signify harmony and stability in relations, in Self and in Other.

However, the value directions also cover up some difficulties, e.g. the fact that value operations emerge as half-intuitive principles rather than reflected rules of conduct. Also, value formation processes usually hold true for many situations, but their validity is conditional for the researched context. As remedy to the way value directions have been analyzed historically, I study how an ethical dialogue is constituted by cases where the directions were given deductively before data collection and analysis, i.e. distributions between Openness to change-Benevolence versus Conservatism-Justice on the one hand and Self transcendence-Non-Maleficence versus Self enhancement-Autonomy on the other hand.

The student teachers' entries contain individual voices reflecting their combined personal and professional priorities. The suggested model for analyzing values aims at classifying if the student teachers colonize the discourse through a controlling push approach by related values. Alternatively, do the student teachers create an inviting pull for learning through a set of complementary values? Put differently, the student teachers act out either a distancing journalist writing-as-publication role for an anonymous audience, or they seek personal/professional dialogism by engaging in team interaction. Focus is on identifying what values a sample of entries harbors and how those texts signal specific values, the ordering of values and emerging value orientations.

Research Objective

Let us assume that the balancing of values affects the length of threads in an LMS-forum. It seems like a good idea to position the student teachers' values in an analytical framework of value orientations. Visschers-Pleijers et al. (2005, p. 28) define a similar starting point, saying university students prefer cumulative reasoning during verbal interactions. This bodes for a close-personal communication between the studied subjects as they are preoccupied with a professional teacher focus on general didactics. I investigate the influence of values on the length of communications in an

asynchronous e-mail discourse between a group of vocational student teachers. Neither formal logic, nor empiricism or introspection guarantees the appropriateness of analysis into human values. However, this study clarifies an axiomatic truth about how people integrate, evaluate, carry out and express values. Find hypotheses related to the research objective:

- $H_{(1)}$ Some vocational student teachers will exchange positive, i.e. benevolent, self direction and stimulation values, generating long threads.
- $H_{(2)}$ At least one of the studied texts will portray egoistic, i.e., achievement and power values, influencing negatively the contents and the length of threads.
- $H_{(3)}$ Swedish values like security, conformity and universalism will influence the frequency of responses positively.

DESCRIBING THE DATA

I asked another pre-study group of student teachers what inspired them to choose the teaching profession. Their motivating ambitions relate to a genuine interest in people: Meeting students; Apply knowledge; Like to learn; Fun to teach; Inspiring the students; Knowledge sharing. The majority of the student teachers' ambitions include a *drive to build relations with others*. Their objectives also cover *didactic classroom measures* rather than moral disciplinary measures, upbringing or fostering. The student teachers' strengths indicate a mix of *instrumental teacher professional* competence like structuring, assessing and analyzing contents plus *close personal* aspirations like patience, listening and negotiating with peers. The studied student teachers appreciated their roles as contributors to a shared team spirit in a virtual forum. The assignment states that they should structure, assess and analyze several titles in the course literature, post their entries at a certain data and respond to peer entries.

The studied texts (A-D) cover reflected first entries and comments among peers. The studied, described and model exchanges contain pedagogical, moral, and curricular contents. As could be expected, a shared curricular topic, theme or subject would attract many responses. Such threads express either push through negative cognitive dissonance or positive interpersonal pull, both of which seem to inspire the interlocutors and generate long threads. The students perform and benefit from creating (co-constructing, in Levin & Wadsmanly, 2008) transformations of curricular knowledge and values between themselves by identifying Self and Other, by significant expressions and by sharing a social LMS. The purpose of deploying the suggested model for collecting and analyzing data is to make the workings of the social system intelligible.

In-Depth Interview

An inspiration for the study emanated from a student teacher's spontaneous comment on the low frequency of responses to a peer's entry (2007-12-15) in a forum.

Dear T! Very few people have commented on your entry. Could the reason be that the text is short. Sometimes there is no explanation why people choose not to make any comments. At other times there are long entries that still do not attract any comments. Personally, if I receive a comment from a peer I tend to respond to that same person. A merry Christmas and a happy new year! A!

As a consequence of this generous social act by one female student teacher, I organized a one hour qualitative research interview (Kvale, 1997) six months later with a male student teacher (in the same group). The purpose of the interview was to acquire a "thick description" of how the student(s) experienced the assignment, i.e. how

they felt, acted and reacted to the entries. The interviewee indicated several reasons, saying it is a haphazard thing if he responded to an entry; the choice differs from person to person; he would respond to any entry he finds interesting; he would respond to a contents which lies close to his personal priorities; he prefers to respond to long entries; he believes people respond to peers they feel at ease with; finally he would respond to an entry which inspires discussion. He criticized many entries for quoting contents from the course literature. He also said he was pleased to receive a response to his own entry. Short first entries tend to generate short threads and boring responses. As the interview continued he said there must be an "opening" in an entry before he would respond. If the first entry "colonizes" the curricular contents he would feel awkward to respond because the opportunity to learn something new has been lost. He said some people would respond to an entry just to confirm a friendship relation. He argued that some peers would compose entries just to please the mentor/course administrator. He found such behavior immoral as those students would make a career at the expense of their peers. Finally he mentioned a laconic quote from the studied literature: "Direct your writing to the audience you seek and prefer."

The Assignment

The students were asked to discuss "Power at school", a typical theme in teacher education. This is a complex curricular issue for the students to explore by means of verbal interaction with relative strangers. It could well be that the chosen initial postings attracted a varying degree of interlocutor interest, as indicated in the qualitative interview, because of the length of the entry, the theme, peer sympathies, personal motivation or other. Although the reason could be chance, clarity, friendship, interest in the topic or other, the assumption is that individual submissions would attract peer interest because of the writer's embedded, i.e. implicitly transmitted values. All students' texts somehow mirror their attitudes to team building, working and learning. All of them also contain comparatively long entries. Text A (male) and Text B (female) attracted over three entries. Texts C (male) and D (female) failed to attract any responses.

Text A. (20070929) That is my experience of rules. / There are clear themes to follow. If you look at a manufacturer of bicycles, there are no clear themes. Then you must invent the wheel all by yourself. / Here there are no clear themes, / I am certain we carry many opinions about these things, otherwise we would not have chosen the profession. We must define objectives for the pupils. All of this must be accomplished according to the curriculum (LPf94) and together with the pupils. They must have a channel for influencing teaching and learning. Wouldn't it have been much easier if someone had just said, this is the way to do it? Imagine the hard work once you have grasped the contents and methodology of your job. Get to know the students, the course material, your colleagues and the premises. And your ideas start flying if somebody says to you: This is the way you should do it. The advantage of having a school operated through management by objectives is that once you have acquired the means for managing the process, you know what to do, and you will keep on doing it only if you are certain to reach the objectives. / You can achieve all this, provided you remember to reflect on what you do and motivate your thoughts.

- **Key words:** Creative images, concrete details, comparison between contexts.
- **Context, team role, relations:** Focus is equally on Self and Other. The text contains a comprehensive theme based on rules related to creativity. The student deals with course literature by objective reference rather than by dealing with the procedure for conducting exchanges between the student teachers. The text em-

phasizes security and stability. There is some concern for peers. The text also contains some relevant comparative examples. At times there is a focus on a collective 'us'. The student teacher emphasizes leadership through subjective argumentation and mentions a positive role model. Lone ranger self-control is a sought ideal. There is an implicit ends-justifying-the-means reasoning towards the end. There is also an inclusive use of 'we' combined with a strong 'I' perspective.

- **Values:** All (four) value directions in a balanced profile.

Text B. (20071004) This fact has inspired the politicians in the Local Board of Education to demand that the students register in their home municipality. / "Kronos till Kairos" p.70 says that the curriculum creates structure, stability and safety. But how is it possible to account for the price we have to pay for allowing this hunt for time! / Without doubt, it is important to coordinate between school subjects, but when demands are spelled out from above and the idea is that things should look OK to the citizens, the whole process becomes unnatural. / It is much better to have a school made up of functioning teams of teachers, where every individual team member is successful, complementing each other in a shared unit on the schedule and where every teacher is available so that the team can complete a project where core and characterizing subjects are given for the students' benefit. / Why making education a circus event by introducing a theme week? / Of course, I understand that the local schools will run into problems when there are so few students, but they must improve the quality of teaching and learning.

- **Key words:** Criticism against politicians, focus on functionality, dissatisfaction with management, idealism, openness to quality measurement and a dubious stand on publicity.

- **Context, team role, relations:** This text is concerned with the procedure for conducting exchanges between the vocational student teachers and the studied course literature contents. This is a comprehensive text about "quality of teaching and learning" rather than "power at school". The text focuses on adaptability in/by student teachers. There is a lot of concern for peers' wellbeing. The text contains an argumentative example, i.e., theme week. Emphasis is on collaboration in teacher teams rather than individual pedagogical leadership. The student teacher mentions a positive model of working. Professional, social and political awareness in teachers is a sought ideal. The writer identifies himself as an experienced idealist in a group of peers, i.e. seeing Other and covering an I/Thou perspective.
- **Values:** Conservatism and security balancing self-transcendence related to Other

Text C. (20071004) Lpo 94 says that the teacher must accommodate for each pupil's needs, abilities and experiences. Such teacher commitment is a pre-condition for managing motivational education. But the question is: Are our students mature to take responsibility for their own studies, for reaching national targets? Well, some of them will manage all right! But far from everybody will do so. An open dialogue with the teacher who analyses the student's level of knowledge and helps the student reach his/her targets must always be offered. Management of education today is often handled by municipal politicians. This is probably a poor solution. Education should be managed without political influencing, thus supporting a comprehensive structure, and avoid changes between periods in office for various political parties. / The students benefit from high degrees of self-control and acquire knowledge. / Students as well as educators need support from school management, psychologists and parents. In order

to be able to pick up on the good opportunities, teachers need to cooperate. As a response to the question as to who has got the power at school, I conclude that the national parliament sets the law. But according to my personal view, teachers and students are in power. Without their cooperation, we would not have a good school.

- **Key words:** A blend of neutral and agitated opinions, carefully balanced reasoning, politically correct opinions, reflective character.
- **Context, team role, relations:** This text covers a comprehensive theme but also displays a simplistic view on teaching and learning. It focuses on personal experience of a procedure for conducting exchanges between the student teachers and on the course literature. There are several normative should-expressions, questions, answers and an argumentative style. The text emphasizes a somewhat critical stand against politicians. There is some concern for the pupils, but the main focus is on student motivation and a compassionate student teacher identity. The student teacher emphasizes collaboration with the pupils. Being a teacher is a calling more than an intellectual challenge. Commitment seems to be a sought ideal. If teachers and pupils joined forces against the politicians everything would be fine.
- **Values:** Self transcendent and accommodating benevolence for the benefit of the students.

Text D. (20071011) Lpf94 clarifies how teachers should relate to the students and to teaching and learning. / The only thing for me to do is to follow my personal ethics and share my knowledge with the students in the best possible way. From this perspective it is a reasonable to claim that I should have the power to control education. In my role as a small dictator I make decisions based on my values about what the students should learn but how should I design teaching and learning? / This is where I get surprised. At least in the upper secondary school program where I am currently working, Industry [sic!], I see no other way to teach than to follow the principle of transmission of knowledge. / As teachers we should eagerly encourage and push our students so they learn to work in a self-controlled way and reach their targets. When we have reached this type of learning we have come close to how teaching and learning should be managed according to Lpf94. But my message is that my professional teacher skills must account for these ways of teaching and learning.

- **Key words:** Self centered, structural (first-then) clarity, instrumental pedagogy, obedient, individualist.
- **Context, team role, relations:** This text failed to attract responses because focus is more on Self defined as a strict (foreign) teacher personality than on relations with Other. The text explores the studied course literature and neglects a procedure for relating to peers. It is a comprehensive text in the sense that it expresses a conservative attitude to teaching and learning. The text emphasizes the 'moment of truth' when teachers meet the students. Authoritarian leadership, rules and stability seem to be prioritized values. There are some minor concerns for peers and students. The text contains an extreme comparison with reference to experience and to the literature. The student teacher emphasizes judgmental leadership, safety and security. Structuring of a pedagogical approach is the sought ideal. There is a means-end argument on security for the pupils too.
- **Values:** Self enhancement, power and stability.

ANALYZING THE DATA

The LMS discussion board is less effective in transforming curricular knowledge than in supporting the students' overall communicative competence. The objective of the succeeding analysis is to understand embedded ethical meanings of truthfulness, completeness, sincerity and contextual relevance (Ngwenyama & Lee, 1997, p. 151) in the students' textual messages. Habermas (1978, 1987) defines the essential objectives of such research as critical social theory (CST) with a focus on participation, observation and analysis of contextualized data. But neither a positivist approach for controlling an objective reality nor a CST-approach for liberating alienated relations between student teachers is a relevant focus for this study. On the contrary, I employ an interpretative SSM-approach for accommodating intra-subjective realities between virtual interlocutors. Hence, focus is on the student teachers' portrayal of their intuitive and implicit purpose to first identify and then build relations to Other by means of explicit curricular contents *and* implicitly transmitted values.

Hence, the studied context involves student teachers who take purposeful action. They have an explicit goal in mind and they form a social activity system. In order to explore both context and people, I deploy a SSM for modeling the interlocutors' verbal behavior. Checkland (2000, p. 14) says that in order to learn from a SSM (see Munro, 1998, p. 520) the researcher needs to decide what is the system under investigation, in this case a closed LMS-session, and what is the objective of the studied subjects, which is to pass a future exam. Checkland (2000, p. 30) suggests that the study of social systems should be guided by transparent criteria like *efficacy* – asking if the transformation of curricular knowledge works; *efficiency* – asking if the transformation process between the student teachers is socially appropriate; *effectiveness* – asking if the transformation meets long term objectives of becoming a professional teacher; ethics – asking if the transformation is morally correct; and finally *elegance* – asking if there is an aesthetically attractive transformation of a shared learning object and good teacher personality.

Before taking social action (Habermas, 1987), however, the students have a choice to make. They seem to discard of a discursive approach and focus on an *instrumental* and a *strategic* efficiency-effectiveness understanding of the social setting. And well aware of the priorities of the training program, they opt for *communicative* action. Ngwenyama and Lee (1997, p. 154) say people involved in such behavior: "depend on a common language and a shared understanding of the organizational context." As active processors and interpreters the students "enact meaning from each other's communicative actions" (ibid., p. 154). Thus, they acknowledge that the LMS-context contains an invitation to inspire, submit and receive responses that make up "rounded", i.e. completeness, truthfulness and appropriateness, text contributions.

The deployed approach yielded some valuable insights. As to *efficacy* (Checkland, 2000) flamboyant, agitated and argumentative entries are outnumbered by emotionally neutral entries. The former create a sense of pressure for change and hasty exploration. At this early stage of the teacher training program it is probably too much of a challenge for the student teachers to accommodate their minds to school politics, functionality of head teacher measures etc. As far as *efficiency* is concerned, it is a delicate situation for the student teachers to respond to their peers' entries. Being novice writers and quite often immigrant Internet users, the student teachers seem to prefer to respond to familiar values, typically transmitted in the kind of vivid examples which they recognize from working life experiences in home schools. A probable explanation to this reaction may be that in times of change, e.g. at the beginning of a program, people tend to prefer more of the same national values. In analyzing *effectiveness* it is obvious that by relying on conservative rather than dynamic values in their processing of initial entries, the student teachers assimilate the traditional values of their national culture into old conceptions about e.g. theme weeks, collective teacher teams or transmission pedagogy. They stick to activities, roles and relations that would seem familiar to them. Finally, there are a few quality criteria of *ethics and elegance*, i.e. polite language and display of a professional teacher personality. The hypothesized set of hosted and preferred values is portrayed (Figure 2) as polite, rather respectful and professional entries.

DISCUSSION

The chosen design for successful long-thread-generating-entries is made up of a mix of professional, factual and personal values, all resting on security and conformity. The studied texts are void of contradictory influences on Openness to change versus Conservatism. Contradictory influences seem to appear between Self transcendence and Self enhancement values. More specifically, values related to contradictory influences are given as Universalism & Benevolence versus Power & Achievement. Successful Text A (Figure 2) contains neutral and non-committed values and equally successful Text B expresses stability, orderliness and conservatism. Both types attracted substantial feedback among peers. Failing Text C harbors inviting and accommodating, but vague values and failing Text D signals argumentative masculine leadership values. Find the positioning of first entries among 1. *Universalism;* 2. *Benevolence;* 3. *Conformity;* 4. *Security;* 5. *Power;* 6. *Achievement;* 7. *Hedonism;* 8. *Stimulation;* 9. *Self-direction.*

The deployed method for analyzing values was successful in generating spread of results. The

Figure 2. Hypothesized and analyzed first entries

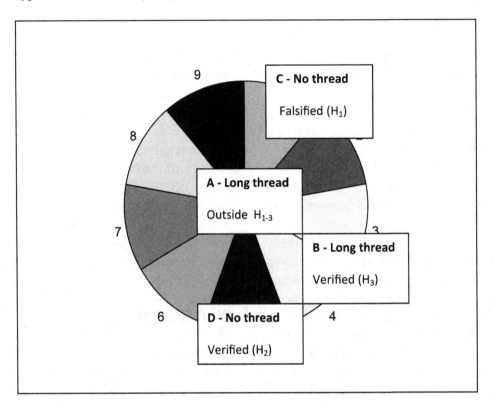

first phases of a SSM helped identify significant value orientations for all texts but for Text A. It seems as if low-profile moderate and vague values outscore extreme high-profile values as inspirational input to the studied interactions. Entries harboring vague values (Text A) and Conservative-Conforming values (Text B) attracted peer feedback in long threads. A first entry harboring universal-benevolent (Text C) or self-centered power (Text D) values failed to attract feedback because in times of change (new role as student), innovative e-learning environments (unfamiliar web procedures) and relations (with strangers), the student teachers search out, balance and stick to familiar values. The deployed analytical framework enables for understanding of the student teachers' preferred values. This is so because Openness to change parallels a flexible personality and the opposing value direction Conservatism matches a stable identity, both of which are necessary for portraying national values and attracting long threads. The result suggests that Self enhancement parallels instrumental push by a publicist approach to communication and the opposing Self transcendence matches dialogical relation building through pull.

The applied SSM was successful in revealing strategies and attitudes for a limited number of cases. Productive interlocutor entries seem to express traditionally held values in an allegedly value-neutral LMS-forum. Future research will benefit from applying a refined method on a comprehensive corpus of subjects. But the question remains: Is there socio-metric network exploration at work, suggesting that those who know and like each other at a rather superficial level put their effort to establishing virtual relations. An alternative explanation – as suggested in this article – is that people's willingness to respond to an entry is related to their appreciation of embedded values.

The conclusion indicates that web-based interlocutors would first read values into their peers' curricular entries and then – depending on how the values match their own ideals – respond to some values and stay clear of others.

REFERENCES

Alderman, C. (1996). *Sathya Sai Education in Human Values, Book 1, Ages 6-9*. Pinner, UK: Sathya Sai Education in Human Values Trust.

BKWSU. (1995). *Living Values: A Guidebook*. London: BKWSU.

Brusling, C., & Strömqvist, G. (Eds.). (1996). *Reflektion och praktik i läraryrket (Reflection and practice in the teacher profession)*. Lund, Sweden: Studentlitteratur.

Buber, M. (1988). *The Knowledge of Man. Selected Essays*. Atlantic Highlands, NJ: Humanities Press International Inc.

Byrne, D. (1966). *An Introduction to Personality. A Research Approach*. Englewood Cliffs, New Jersey: Prentice Hall Inc.

Checkland, P. (2000). Soft systems methodology: a thirty year retrospective. *Systems Research and Behavioral Science, 17*(11), 11–58. doi:doi:10.1002/1099-1743(200011)17:1+<:AID-SRES374>3.0.CO;2-O

Checkland, P., & Scholes, J. (1990). *Soft Systems Methodology in Action*. Chichester, UK: John Wiley & Sons, Inc.

Coutaz, N., Crowley, J., Dobson, S., & Garlan, D. (2005). Context is key. *Communications of the ACM, 48*(3), 49–53. doi:doi:10.1145/1047671.1047703

Dysthe, O. (2003). Dialogperspektiv på elektroniska diskussioner (A dialogical perspective on electronic discussions). In Dysthe, O. (Ed.), *Dialog, samspel och lärande (Dialogue, collaboration and learning)* (pp. 295–320). Lund, Sweden: Studentlitteratur.

Ess Edunet. (2007). *Values*. Retrieved October 2007 from http://essedunet.nsd.uib.no/opencms.war/opencms/ess/en/topics/1/

Festinger, L. (1957). *A Theory of Cognitive Dissonance*. Stanford, CA: Stanford University Press.

Gardner, H. (2000). *The Disciplined Mind: Beyond Facts and Standardized Tests, The K-12 Education that Every Child Deserves*. New York: Penguin Books.

Gaunt, D., & Löfgren, O. (1984). *Myter om svensken* (Myths about Swedes). Stockholm, Sweden: Liber förlag.

Gilligan, C. (1983). Do the social science have an adequate theory of moral development? In Haan, N., Bellah, R., Rainbow, P., & Sullivan, W. (Eds.), *Social Science as Moral Inquiry*. New York: Columbia University Press.

Gilligan, C., & Attanucci, J. (1988). Two moral orientations: gender differences and similarities. *Merrill-Palmer Quarterly, 34*, 223–237.

Goffman, E. (1959). *The Presentation of Self in Everyday Life*. London: Penguin Books.

Habermas, J. (1978). *Knowledge and human interests*. London: Heinemann.

Habermas, J. (1987). *The Theory of Communicative Action: Lifeworld and Social System (2)*. Boston: Beacon Press.

Hansson, T. (2000). *Heart of Learning Organizations. Exploring Competence for Change in Schools*. Luleå, Sweden: Luleå University of Technology.

Hansson, T. (2006). Workplace logics, kinds of knowledge and action research. *Systemic Practice and Action Research, 19*(2), 189–200. doi:doi:10.1007/s11213-006-9011-y

Hansson, T. (2008). Communication and Relation Building in Social Systems. T. Hansson (Ed.), *Handbook of Research on Digital Information Technologies: Innovations, Methods and Ethical Issues.* Hershey, PA: Information Science Reference. IGI Global.

Hansson, T. (2010). Co-construction of learning objects: Management and structure. S. Wallis (Ed.). *Cybernetics and Systems Theory in Management. Tools, Views and Advancements.* New York: Information Science Reference. IGI Global. 229-251.

Herrscher, E. (2006). What is the systems approach good for? *Systemic Practice and Action Research, 19*, 409–413. doi:doi:10.1007/s11213-006-9032-6

Hirschheim, R., Klein, H., & Lyytinen, K. (1995). *Information Systems Development and Data Modelling: Conceptual and Philosophical Foundations.* Cambridge, UK: Cambridge University Press.

Hofstede, G. (1984). *Culture's consequences: international differences in work-related Values.* London: Sage.

Isling, Å. (1974). *Vägen mot en demokratisk skola. Skolpolitik och skolreformer i Sverige från 1880- till 1970-talet (The road towards a democratic school).* Stockholm, Sweden: Prisma.

Kirschenbaum, H. (1977). *Advanced Values Clarification.* La Jolla, CA: University Associates.

Kohlberg, L. (1981). *The Philosophy of Moral Development: Moral Stages and the Idea of Justice.* London: Harper & Row.

Kvale, S. (1997). *Den kvalitativa forskningsintervjun (The Qualitative Research Interview).* Lund, Sweden: Studentlitteratur.

Levin, T., & Wadsmanly, R. (2008). Teachers' views on factors affecting effective integration of information technology in the classroom: Developmental scenery. *Journal of Technology and Teacher Education, 16*(2), 233–263.

Lickona, T. (1993). The return of character education. *Educational Leadership, 51*(3), 6–11.

Lovat, T., Schofield, N., Morrison, K., & O'Neill, D. (2002). Research dimensions of values education: A Newcastle perspective. In Pascoe, S. (Ed.), *Values in Education: College Year Book 2002.* Deakin West, Australia: Australian College of Educators.

Malle, B., & Edmondson, E. (2007). *What are Values? A Folk-Conceptual Investigation.* Eugene, OR: University of Oregon. Retrieved October 2007 from http://hebb.uoregon.edu/04-01tech.pdf

Munro, I. (1999). Man-machine systems: People and technology in OR. *Systemic Practice and Action Research, 12*(5), 513–532. doi:doi:10.1023/A:1022469607464

Ngwenyama, O., & Lee, A. (1997). Communication richness in electronic mail: critical social theory and the contextuality of meaning. *Management Information Systems Quarterly, 21*(2), 145–167. doi:doi:10.2307/249417

Pesendorfer, E.-M., & Koszegi, S. (2006). Hot versus cool behavioral styles in electronic negotiations: The impact of communication mode. *Group Decision and Negotiation, 15*, 141–155. doi:doi:10.1007/s10726-006-9025-y

Russell, B. (1952). *Menneskeheden paa skillevejen (New Hopes in a Changing World).* Copenhagen, Denmark: Berlingske forlag

Schwartz, S. H. (1992). Universals in the content and structure of values: Theory and empirical tests in 20 countries. In Zanna, M. (Ed.), *Advances in Experimental Social Psychology* (*Vol. 25*, pp. 1–65). New York: Academic Press.

Shea, V. (2007). *Netiquette*. Retrieved October 2007 from http://www.albion.com/netiquette/book/index.html

Visschers-Pleijers, A., Dolmans, D., Wolfhagen, I., & Van Der Vleuten, C. (2005). Student perspectives on learning-oriented interactions in the tutorial group. *Advances in Health Sciences Education: Theory and Practice, 10*, 23–35. PubMed doi:10.1007/s10459-004-9348-x

This work was previously published in the International Journal of Information Technologies and Systems Approach, Volume 3, Issue 2, edited by Frank Stowell and Manuel Mora, pp. 1-16, copyright 2010 by IGI Publishing (an imprint of IGI Global).

Chapter 13

Business Innovation and Service Oriented Architecture:
An Empirical Investigation

Bendik Bygstad
Norwegian School of Information Technology,
Norway

Tor-Morten Grønli
Norwegian School of Information Technology,
Norway

Helge Bergh
Norwegian ASA, Norway

Gheorghita Ghinea
Brunel University, UK

ABSTRACT

Recent research suggests that a strong link exists between business innovation and service oriented IT architectures: modern IT architecture enables business to quickly create new services. However, the relationship between IT capabilities and business performance is not always straightforward. How does SOA support fast innovation in practice, and under which conditions is it effective? In this paper, the authors investigate these issues and ask: How can a SOA architecture like the Enterprise Service Bus support business innovation? This paper investigates this question through a case study at an airline company. Analyzing the relationship between innovation and IT architecture in the company over time, the authors offer the following conclusion: ESB gives strong support to business innovation, under two conditions. First, the implementation of ESB has to be comprehensive, that is, it should include the core processes of the business. Second, the top management (and partners) need to understand the principles of ESB.

1. INTRODUCTION

Recent research suggests that there is a link between business innovation and service oriented IT architectures (SOA). It is assumed (and promised) that modern IT architectures have the capability to provide businesses with a real-time flexibility in a turbulent and competitive environment (Taylor et al., 2009). The key to this promise is that IT should not only *align* with business to support existing processes, but also contribute to a business transformation. In practice this implies that the SOA architecture enables new business services at a speed that matches the needs of the fast-changing corporation.

DOI: 10.4018/978-1-4666-1562-5.ch013

From past experiences both IS researchers and IT practitioners have learned to be wary regarding such grand promises. In particular, we have learned that the relationship between IT capabilities and business performance is not always straightforward. Although it has been shown that IT capabilities tend to increase business performance (Bharadway, 2000), it is also well documented that exploiting these capabilities depend on a number of factors, and that bandwagon behaviour often leads to mindless innovation (Swanson & Ramiller, 2004). We have also learnt that *context* plays a larger role in IS innovations than often assumed (Sharma & Yetton, 2003); what works in for example the retail may not work in education, and what works in a start-up company may not work in a mature organisation. The basic idea of SOA supporting business innovation, however, is attractive and exciting, and deserves to be investigated empirically.

But in order to so it is necessary to narrow down the scope of investigation. SOA is a relatively broad concept, and the same applies to business innovation. In this paper we have chosen to focus on a particular implementation of SOA called the Enterprise Service Bus architecture, and its practical use in a company. The ESB concept was introduced in 2002 (Chappell, 2004) as a part of the Service Oriented Architecture (SOA) paradigm. The ESB is an IT architecture that aims at being able to support two seemingly contradictory features: it integrates a network of business partners at a transactional level, enabling real-time systems to communicate seamlessly. At the same time the components are loosely coupled; it is possible to add or subtract business partners at short notice, without affecting the daily running of operations. In principle, this is indeed an architecture to support business innovation.

The bus architecture is an attractive idea, which has received much attention over the past few years. However, the ESB concept is primarily a technical architecture, and many issues remain much less known. In particular, the more direct relationship between IT infrastructure and innovative capability is not described in the ESB literature.

How should a company organize this in practice? The purpose of this research is to undertake an exploratory, but in-depth investigation of this issue, where we go beyond the promises of technology, and assess the practical implementation and use of SOA, and assess the interplay of technology and business innovation in practical setting. Our research question, then, is how can a SOA architecture such as the ESB support business innovation?

We proceed by reviewing the concepts and practices of business innovation, SOA and ESB. Then we present our method, and our case company. We describe the technical solution in some detail, before analyzing how this solution enabled the company to introduce a number of innovative services in very short time, and to exploit them successfully in a turbulent competitive environment. Finally we discuss the conditions for our approach to be viable.

2. REVIEW

In this section we offer a brief review of business innovation, service oriented architecture and the enterprise service bus.

2.1 Business Innovation and Agility

The innovation of new services has transformed several industries over the past decade, for example travel services, banking, gaming and the music industry (Tidd & Hull, 2003). This development has been heavily dependent on IT, in particular Internet technology, to such a degree that we should conceptualise these innovations not as "business/IT alignment", but as the results of a mutual reinforcement process: technology opens a space of possibilities, which spurs the creation of new services. The new services increase the space of possibilities, which again spurs the creation of new services (Bygstad, 2009).

The vision of technological flexibility in the development process was described by the agile software development community in the early 2000s (Beck, 2001; Larman, 2004). The agile project promises this through short product iterations, continuous communication between user and developer and a reliance on talent and skill, rather than formal processes. The aim is to deliver business value, not software components (Schwaber, 2004).

This capability is obviously dependent on more than technology; it also requires a certain amount of *business agility*. Agility is not primarily connected to strategy and aims, but rather to resources and capabilities. To be able to act with agility, it certainly takes financial, human and technical resources. Just as importantly, it also takes a number of capabilities, such as the ability to understand changes early, to assess the opportunities and to implement new solutions quickly (Mathiassen & Pries-Heje, 2006).

This mode of operating is particularly demanding, because it implies that the changes must happen *on the fly*. Productivity and quality must be maintained while new services are added. There is no time for year-long development projects with gradual deployment of solutions (Mathiassen & Pries-Heje, 2006). Thus, one important aspect of agility is to include resources from outside partners, at relatively short notice, fully integrated into the IT infrastructure. Obviously, these requirements put an unprecedented strain on the IT organization. One of the most promising responses to these challenges is service oriented IT architectures.

2.2 Service Oriented Architecture (SOA)

Since the term SOA was coined in 1996, it has become the state-of-the-art of software architecture thinking, and all large software vendors today offer various frameworks and implementations of SOA (Rosen et al., 2008). SOA is a framework for designing flexible and loosely-integrated services, in distributed environments. The main goal of SOA is to the address the following challenge: How should a corporate IT architecture support organizational innovation and agility in an unstable global environment? Included in the challenge are such issues as, how can the architecture support both *flexibility* (the ability to include both new and old systems into a distributed but seamless whole), *efficiency* (the ability to run the operation 24/7 at acceptable costs) and *reuse* (sharing components over the whole organization and even outside it)?

In practice, the application of the SOA principles must be a compromise between short and long term efforts, because most companies have large portfolios of existing systems and solutions. This is addressed in the practical implementation of SOA.

2.3 Enterprise Service Bus

One popular solution to implementing SOA is the Enterprise Service Bus. In some of the literature ESB is described as a product, a middleware software. Following Rosen et al. we will view ESB as an *architectural pattern* with existing products to be implementations of this pattern. Well known implementations are for example MULE (Sward & Whitacre, 2008) and Open ESB (Rosen et al., 2008).

An ESB allows for seamless integration and communication between different systems inside and outside an organization. This is enabled by the bus middleware, which allows for loose coupling at the business level. It is illustrated below, very simplified, in Figure 1.

The main features of ESB are (Rademakers & Dirksen, 2009):

Connectivity: The ESB connects any application with another, without coupling the message sender and the message receiver.

Figure 1. The ESB architecture

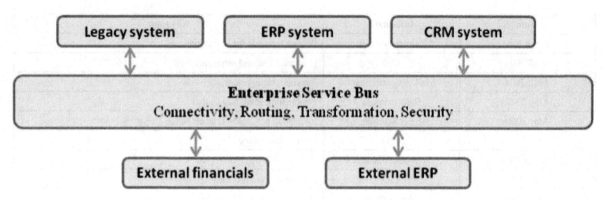

Routing: The ESB must identify the end destination of an incoming message. It must also be able to assess the integrity of the message, and (if needed) adding the necessary information.

Transformation: The bus should be able to integrate seamlessly applications with different protocols, such as HTTP, JMS, SMTP and TPC. The bus must also be able to transform a message from one format to another.

Security: Standard security mechanisms must be available, such as authentication, authorization and encryption. This is important both to prevent malicious use of the bus, and to ensure that outgoing messages comply with the requirements of external partners.

3. METHOD

We conducted an in-depth case study (Miles & Huberman, 1994), building on a critical realist ontology (Archer, 1995; Sayer, 2000; Easton, 2010), and focusing on the relationship between IT architecture and innovation. The general approach was process-oriented (Langley, 1999); taking a longitudinal view we were looking for explanations of events. Data collection was conducted during a period of eighteen months of 2008 and 2009.

The case company, Norwegian Corp, was chosen for two reasons. First, it was a young and successful company, with a reputation for innovation. Second, the company was expanding its initial successful IT infrastructure of booking services into new ICT-based services, thus constituting a fruitful case to study the relationship between innovation and IT architecture.

Ten managers and specialists were interviewed, each circa 2 hours, some of them twice. See Table 1. In addition a large volume of technical documentation (business plans, project plans, contracts, technical architecture documents) was collected.

Data analysis was conducted in the following three steps (Pettigrew, 1985). First, a time line was established, and important events were identified. We used the technique of *forward-chaining* to understand the intentions of key stakeholders and the subsequent projects and results. Then *backward-chaining* analysis was conducted, in order to find explanations, in particular for unexpected outcomes.

Second, a comprehensive analysis of architecture development and business innovation was done, focusing particularly on the interplay between these dimensions. As shown in the Discussion section we tracked and analysed in detail how a particular service innovation was directly linked to the IT architecture. For example, we analysed in detail some self-reinforcing mechanisms of the innovation process, such as the "NAPI" interface.

Table 1. Informants at Norwegian

Date	Informant	Key topic
March 2008	Business developer	Business models for Norwegian
April 2008	CIO	IT architecture and innovation
April 2008	Marketing consultant	Revenue management
May 2008	Bank manager	Establishing Bank Norwegian
May 2008	Sales manager	Innovation processes, internet sales
July 2008	CIO	Culture and management
August 2008	IT project manager	Project culture in Norwegian
Sept 2008	CIO	Call Norwegian project
Oct 2008	IT dept. manager	IT architecture and Call Norwegian project
Oct 2008	Project manager	Call Norwegian project and portal architecture
Jan 2009	Systems Director	IT architecture
May 2009	Systems Director	IT architecture and Call Norwegian
Dec 2009	CIO	Call Norwegian, business development

This was a service interface that Norwegian offered to partners, for example travel agencies. When agencies started to use it they proposed that, in addition to booking information, it should also be possible to exchange economic transactions the same way. This triggered the development of an extension, which enabled the partners to do economic clearing through a service from SAP.

Third, to ensure internal validity the preliminary findings were discussed with informants. For example, we conducted a full session with a technical specialist in order to confirm the correctness of our initial analysis of the role of the ESB. Finally, paper drafts were sent to key informants for comments.

3.1 The Case

Norwegian Corp is a privately owned company registered on the Oslo stock exchange. Led by the charismatic former jet fighter pilot Bjørn Kjos, the *Norwegian* airline company grew from virtually zero in 2002 to become the largest low-cost carrier in Scandinavia in 2009. Today Norwegian operates a total of 176 routes to 86 destinations in Europe (see Figure 2), and carried 9.1 million passengers in 2008. The company has 1400 employees and revenues in 2008 were 6.2 bn. NOK ($900 M.) Profits, however, have been moderate.

The company has achieved this growth through an aggressive pricing and an agile business culture, with the following attributes.

First, there is a strong entrepreneur culture. The respondents of the case study were all asked to characterize the culture, and were quite unanimous in their views. There is still a strong entrepreneur culture, with innovation in small teams, flat organization, empowered employees and a strong determination to succeed.

Second, there are no "IT projects", only business projects. New ideas come along as business proposals. They are evaluated on the sole criterion of financial benefits. If approved the involved units will co-operate to accomplish the necessary work, small changes in an informal group; larger initiatives in formal projects. This way, the people who design a solution will also operate it.

Third, there is no clear hierarchy. Employees are empowered to a large degree, with clear business accountabilities. A middle manager commented: "As long as I reach the company objectives I am free to choose my actions. This includes the

Figure 2. Norwegian's routes

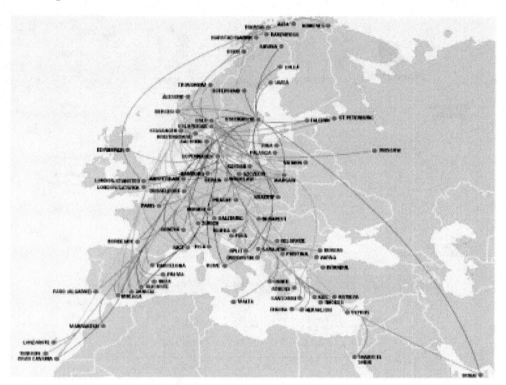

right to propose and implement changes in the computer systems. Of course, this does not mean that Norwegian is a flat organization, but it gives you the feeling that it is. The reason is that a good idea is never rejected for hierarchical reasons."

4. NORWEGIAN ESB

As a new entrant into the very competitive airline market, Norwegian started in 2002 with a very basic IT solution. As the company expanded quickly, the need for an IT architecture was acknowledged, and a CIO and two IT architects were hired from one of the competitors.

They had rather clear ideas on what to do (which they had not been allowed to develop at their former employer), and started in 2003 to experiment with a bus architecture. The aim was to develop a quite simple service bus, enabling later business development through reuse of components. The ESB was developed in 2004, and expanded gradually the following years.

The enterprise system architecture was created as an enterprise service bus architecture, rather similar to the ideas and structures used by i.e. the openESB initiative (Jennings, 2008). An overview is offered in Figure 3.

Figure 3 gives an overview of the enterprise architecture and positions the in the middle as the core system. As with most other architectures, different components communicate through a set of layers. One advantage of using the ESB structure is a loose coupling between enterprise components. The different layers are more easily maintained separately. We will further explore each of the layers in the ESB architecture more thoroughly.

Figure 3. Norwegian architecture – an overview

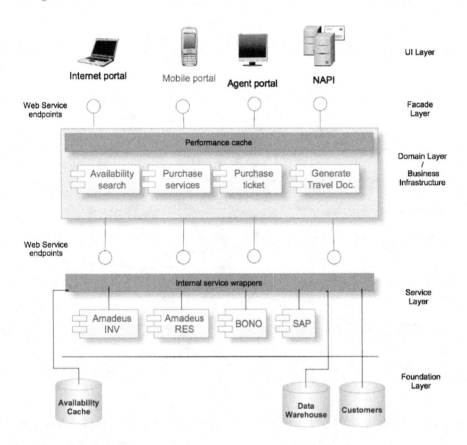

4.1 User Interface Modules

The enterprise system contains several modules developed for communication with external partners and customers. These modules range from: Norwegian' web page for reservations, mobile portal, agent portal, and the public available Norwegian Application Programming Interface (NAPI) (see UI layer in Figure 3). All these modules connect to the internal system by connecting to Web Service endpoints on the ESB. Data are exchanged as XML through standard communication protocols.

All modules have separate points of contact, each offering a public file describing the available business methods. The majority of the interface modules are designed and programmed in Microsoft.Net technology. Figure 3 shows the outline of the system highlighting the separation of concerns through modularization and interfaces. The possibility to communicate across technologies, such as Microsoft.Net and Oracle's Java, is another strength made possible by the ESB and common formats for data exchange.

4.2 Business Service System

The main module in the enterprise is described as the 'core' system, illustrated in the box in centre of Figure 3. This application suite controls business process management and flow of control between services.

This is a Java based system which runs in a clustered environment on a load balanced, multi-core, machines (JBoss servers). The system has a front facade layer which handles all requests from external partners, based on individual service contracts through the interface endpoints.

A Norwegian Application Interface (NAPI) is offered to partners needing individually tailored interfaces.

During sales campaigns the number of searches may approach 1 million per day. To increase performance a cache is implemented on top of traditional server load balancing functionality up front. This ensures that all calls are handled here before being redirected to the internal (core) modules.

The core system is driving all processes in the business, in addition to handling requests from external sources. The requests may as well origin from other internal applications in the enterprise. Examples of internal business processes the core system component handles are: Availability searches, ticket purchases, service purchases (extra luggage, custom requests etc) and module synchronization.

The 'core' component is designed as a stand-alone component and is currently not based on any public enterprise service bus architecture components such as Mule (Sward and Whitacre 2008). The reasons are partly that it was designed before the ESB architecture paradigm emerged, and partly based on a need of to be in control of each business process effectuation. This supports early adoption and implementation of new ideas.

A problem often seen in components evolving and growing over time is the temptation to keep loads of business process data in the core. Instead, this is solved by utilizing components further down in the hierarchy more suited for such work. Deploying stateless components increases the ability to handle a large number of simultaneous requests.

Aiming for as loose coupling as possible between the ´core´ and other modules a service and foundation layer is included. Web services in this layer process communication and output from other modules. Within each web service these technical modules then enables event handling

to data storages as well as retrieving data and performing message calls.

One feature of standard enterprise service bus systems is a security module. In this solution security and authorization is quite complex since the number of modules and external systems are high. The problem is addressed by using standard open source security modules, which are adapted and wrapped by custom tailored code to ensure sustainability of the application suite.

4.2.1 Facade Modules / Technical Wrappers

Facade modules and technical wrappers, illustrated as *Internal service wrappers* in Figure 3, wrap technical services and create abstraction by introducing a private programming interface. This approach enables programming interfaces between application modules, thereby enabling an easy plug-in of new modules. A wrapper module may have additional tasks such as performing multiple updates, performing caching services and executing message services. These modules and technical wrappers, though small components, are nonetheless key parts of this architecture to be able to sustain a viable ESB.

4.2.2 Data Store Modules

The underlying persistence foundation in the architecture (illustrated in the bottom of Figure 3) includes Data warehouses, Amadeus booking system (Amadeus Reservation and Amadeus Inventory), those Norwegian legacy back office system (BONO) and SAP. These storages are separate applications, but due to facade modules and technical wrappers they can also be exploited as mere data storages. This highlights the strength of ESB, enabling the architecture to use other large systems as sources of information rather than having these system setting constraints on ESB.

5. ANALYSIS

From 2003 Norwegian introduced a number of new ICT-based services in order to establish a strong position in the home market, and to grow in Europe. In this section we describe and analyze how Norwegian exploited the flexibility of their ESB architecture in order to innovate new services. The services were developed in close cooperation between the top management group and the IT senior executives. For each innovation we discuss the role of the ESB architecture, presented in the previous section.

2004: Internet Portal

After establishing the ESB architecture in 2003, the solution was set into production in 2004. The main challenge at the time was how to make customer book on the Internet, and not at travel agents (which were quite expensive for a low-cost airline).

The first new services on the ESB were SMS booking and, most importantly, an Internet portal. The portal used the full features of the ESB from the start, enabling easy online bookings. In addition, the layered structure of the architecture allowed for parallel teams in development, speeding up delivery.

Role of ESB architecture: The portal was enabled and supported by the ESB. Due to highly adaptable data formats, both the SMS and Internet portals could use the same facade endpoints. Data could be restructured after retrieval, facilitating for quick, tailored responses.

2005: The Low-Price Calendar

A major obstacle for low-price passengers at the time was how to find the cheap tickets, which used to be hidden inside a complex pricing structure. Capitalizing on their new ESB architecture Norwegian solved this problem in 2005 when the low-price calendar was introduced, which showed the cheapest flights to any chosen destination. The low-price calendar was on outstanding success, increasing the number of bookings substantially. It was internationally patented, although later copied by many other airlines.

Role of ESB architecture: The low-price calendar was mainly a result from innovation in the UI layer, made possible by the services in the façade layer. To avoid response time, the availability cache (building on existing processes) enabled complex searches with fast responses.

2005: The NAPI Interface to Partners

To expand their distribution, agencies and search engines were now given full access to Norwegian services, through the Norwegian Application Interface (NAPI).

Role of ESB architecture: SAP was connected to the ESB, providing clearing with partners.

2006: Electronic Dialogue with 90% of Customers

This dialogue included email and web marketing, on-line sales, booking and check-in. This was enabled by the easy use of the Internet portal and the performance of ESB.

Role of ESB architecture: These innovations in the service layer emerged as the result of CRM and ERP systems now being used as sources of information rather than isolated systems. Inventory was now moved to Amadeus, enabling a more seamless access to pricing data. High performance was enabled by load balancing in front (performance cache), and by load balancing in back (technical facade layer). The design of the domain layer allowed for quick response time, with up to one million searches each day.

2007: Bank Norwegian

In 2007 the company decided to enter the banking market with Bank Norwegian. From the outset, CEO Bjørn Kjos stated that: "Today we have one of the most visited web pages in Norway, with 2-3 million visitors each month. We aim at coupling this traffic towards bank services." The establishment of the bank was done during 6 months, serving 50.000 customers in 2008.

Role of ESB architecture: Bank Norwegian was linked to the ESB, as services in the foundation layer allowed for new systems to be used as pluggable parts of the system architecture. Each booking generates an XML message to bank Norwegian, and customer collects frequent flyer points in Bank Norwegian.

2008: Call Norwegian Portal

The aim of the mobile portal was to allow for easy airline booking, and to offer mobile broadband on the airport and (in 2009) during flight.

Role of ESB architecture: Booking and ticket are using the services on the ESB. The web server routes the calls to mobile server, and presents simple html GUI. The call Norwegian Portal was made possible by innovation over an existing service foundation in the Service layer as well as technical wrappers in the facade layers.

2008: Fly Nordic Merger

In 2008 Norwegian also bought the Swedish airline FlyNordic. It was fully integrated into the Norwegian network, including scheduling and booking.

Role of ESB architecture: With the ESB, conversion of data and integration was done in 3 months.

2009: Bar Code Ticket on the Mobile Phone

The mobile solution was extended in 2009, when the possibility of having a bar code ticket on the mobile phone was introduced.

Role of ESB architecture: The mobile portal for sales uses the ESB in much the same way as the internet portal, needing only new GUIs. The overall design and continuous innovation and adaption of services elsewhere in the ESB over the recent years led to the implementation being a small effort.

Summing up this section we argue that there is a mutually reinforcing process between an agile business organization and an ESB architecture: the ESB enables an agile organization to innovate new services, while the agile organization increases the options of the ESB by adding more services and components. Or, in the words of the IT architect of Norwegian: "The ESB makes services available that enable and support creativity at front-end. Service innovators need only relate to the defined services in the ESB facades".

6. DISCUSSION

While we do think that there are important lessons to learn from the Norwegian experience, we would like to emphasize that there are conditions which need to be satisfied in order to succeed with the approach described in this paper. In addition, we acknowledge that there are limitations to our research approach.

Through our analysis of Norwegian, we have identified two important conditions for the approach to work. *First, the implementation of ESB has to be comprehensive,* i.e. it should include the core processes of the business. This is crucial for achieving the desired flexibility, because the effect of a minor or partial ESB implementation is bound to be very limited. It is also a very demanding condition, because it means that a company with many legacy applications may find it excruciatingly difficult to redesign them in order to work on the ESB. In our case, Norwegian was in a lucky position, building their IT architecture more or less from scratch.

Keeping the architecture "clean", i.e. avoiding direct communication between services (without going through the ESB) is essential for the sustainability of the solution. The pressures of project deadlines is obviously a threat to this aim, and the IT architect of Norwegian emphasized that "my first and top priority is protecting the integrity the ESB structure, no matter how important a project deadline is".

Second, the top management (and partners) needs to understand the principles of ESB. It is often said that the IT people should understand the needs of the business. We definitely subscribe to this view, but would also add that in order to succeed the business people should also understand the principles of the ESB. Why? The reason is that IT-based business innovation is inherently dependent on understanding and exploiting the resources of the company. We believe that one interesting finding of the Norwegian case is that the quick innovation and deployment of new services was the result of very close co-operation between the business and IT side of the company. Often in projects, business people of Norwegian would comment, "OK, let' solve that problem in the bus".

The essence of this condition is that managers need to understand the reinforcement mechanisms of business innovation and the ESB. A flexible IT architecture provides resources which the business people may innovate on. As long as the architecture is kept clean (i.e. adhering to the principles of the ESB), the new services on the ESB not only increase the income of the company, but also increase the spectrum of possibilities for new innovations.

6.1 Limitations to Findings

We acknowledge that there are limitations to our findings. These limitations are strongly associated to our research design, which is a process case study. As characterized by Langley (1999), such studies are strong on accuracy and depth, but weaker on generalization.

Our findings then, have relevance as an *example* of how an organization may capitalize on the ESB architecture, and the conditions for the approach to work. The area of usefulness is likely to be similar modern business organisations with a highly skilled IT department.

7. CONCLUSION

Our research question was, how can a SOA architecture – such as the ESB - support business innovation. We researched this question through a longitudinal case study in an international airline.

We found that ESB gives strong support to business innovation, through a flexible and modularized architecture that integrates seamlessly at transaction level. In terms of *service innovation* we found that the ESB architecture supports the design and implementation of new services by combing internal and external IT resources. In terms of *business agility* we found that the ESB architecture enables the deployment of such services within short time spans, in windows of opportunity.

We have identified two conditions for the approach to be viable. First, the implementation of ESB has to be comprehensive, i.e. it should include the core processes of the business. Second, the top management and business partners needs to understand the principles of ESB.

Our findings were based on a single case study. Further research should broaden the scope of investigation to include more organisations in other lines of business. In particular, we think that the area of e-Government, which is in need of both service innovations and loose couplings between various actors, is a relevant field.

ACKNOWLEDGMENT

We thank the Norwegian Corp for engaging in the case study. We also thank the anonymous reviewers of the International Journal of Information Technologies and Systems Approach.

REFERENCES

Archer, M. S. (1995). *Realist Social Theory: The Morphogenetic Approach*. Cambridge, UK: Cambridge University Press. doi:10.1017/CBO9780511557675

Beck, K. (2000). *Extreme Programming Explained: Embrace Change*. Boston: Addison-Wesley.

Bharadwaj, A. S. (2000). A Resource-Based Perspective on Information Technology Capability and Firm Performance: An Empirical Investigation. *Management Information Systems Quarterly*, *24*(1), 159–196. doi:10.2307/3250983

Bygstad, B. (2009). Generative Mechanisms for Innovation in Information Infrastructures. In *Proceedings of the 17th European Conference on Information Systems (ECIS)*, Verona, Italy.

Chappell, D. (2004). *Enterprise Service Bus*. Sebastopol, CA: O'Reilly Media.

Easton, G. (2010). Critical realism in case study research. *Industrial Marketing Management*, *39*(11), 118–128. doi:10.1016/j.indmarman.2008.06.004

Jennings, F. (2008). *Building SOA-Based Composite Applications Using Netbeans IDE 6*. Packet Publishing.

Langley, A. (1999). Strategies for Theorizing from Process Data. *Academy of Management Review*, *24*(4), 691–710. doi:10.2307/259349

Larman, C. (2004). *Agile and Iterative Development: A Manager's Guide*. Boston: Addison-Wesley.

Mathiassen, L., & Pries-Heje, J. (2006). Business agility and diffusion of information technology. *European Journal of Information Systems*, *15*, 116–119. doi:10.1057/palgrave.ejis.3000610

Miles, M. B., & Huberman, A. M. (1994). *Qualitative Data Analysis*. Thousand Oaks, CA: Sage.

Pettigrew, A. M. (1985). Contextualist Research and the Study of Organizational Change Processes. In Mumford, E., Hirschheim, R., Fitgerald, G., & Wood-Harper, A. T. (Eds.), *Research Methods in Information Systems* (pp. 53–78). Amsterdam, The Netherlands: North-Holland.

Rademakers, T., & Dirksen, J. (2009). *Open-Source ESBs in Action*. Greenwich, CT: Manning Publications.

Rosen, M., Lublinsky, B., Smith, K. T., & Balcer, M. J. (2008). *Applied SOA: Service-Oriented Architecture and Design Strategies*. New York: Wiley Publishing.

Sayer, A. (2000). *Realism and Social Science*. London: Sage Publications.

Schwaber, K. (2004). *Agile Project Management with Scrum*. Microsoft Press.

Sharma, R., & Yetton, P. (2003). The Contingent Effects of Management Support and Task Interdependence on Successful Information Systems Implementation. *Management Information Systems Quarterly*, *27*(4), 533–555.

Swanson, E. B., & Ramiller, N. C. (2004). Innovating Mindfully with Information Technology. *Management Information Systems Quarterly*, *28*(4), 553–583.

Sward, R. E., & Whitacre, K. (2008). A multi-language service-oriented architecture using an enterprise service bus. In *Proceedings of the 2008 ACM Annual International Conference on SIGADA*.

Taylor, H., Yochem, Y., Phillips, L., & Martinez, F. (2009). *Event-Driven Architecture: How SOA Enables the Real-Time Enterprise*. Boston: Addison-Wesley.

Tidd, J., & Hull, F. M. (2003). *Service Innovation. Organizational Responses to Technological Opportunities & Market Imperatives*. London: Imperial College Press.

This work was previously published in the International Journal of Information Technologies and Systems Approach, Volume 4, Issue 1 edited by Frank Stowell and Manuel Mora, pp. 67-78 copyright 2011 by IGI Publishing (an imprint of IGI Global).

Chapter 14
An Open and Service-Oriented Architecture to Support the Automation of Learning Scenarios

Ângels Rius
Universitat Oberta de Catalunya, Spain

Jordi Conesa
Universitat Oberta de Catalunya, Spain

Francesc Santanach
Universitat Oberta de Catalunya, Spain

Magí Almirall
Universitat Oberta de Catalunya, Spain

Elena García-Barriocanal
Universidad de Alcalá, Spain

ABSTRACT

The specifications of automated learning scenarios can lead to advantages for virtual learning environments and important benefits for organizations, although research in this e-learning area has not addressed this issue. To achieve this goal, one requirement is to have an infrastructure able to support the execution of specifications of learning scenarios. This paper presents an open service-oriented architecture based on the Open Services Interface Definition (OSID) specifications proposed by the Open Knowledge Initiative (OKI) and other normative specifications. The architecture is used as a technological infrastructure in a virtual learning environment with more than 40,000 students enrolled and has been tested as the infrastructure of a tool to automate specifications of learning scenarios. A case study has been used to test the suitability of the architecture and describe such a tool for the future.

INTRODUCTION

Research in e-learning technology with respect to the concept of reusable learning objects and their standardization has evolved in recent years, however, research on the learning scenario concept and its automation has not been so successful.

The automation of the specifications of business processes has been very successful in the Business Process Management (BPM) area and has brought about important benefits for enterprises and organizations. In a similar way, the automation of specifications of learning processes could provide important advantages to the e-learning

DOI: 10.4018/978-1-4666-1562-5.ch014

area and those organizations that focus its activity on the LMS. Some of these advantages are: (1) the establishment of a valid set of primitive learning scenarios for any organization, (2) the creation of a catalogue of learning scenarios and the possibility to customize them according to an organization's features, procedures and rules, (3) the possible certification of learning processes that permits the implementation of learning scenarios as the first step to future standardization, (4) the optimization and innovation resulting from a deeper knowledge of learning scenarios and finally, (5) the taking on of a given role by the LMS could free a participant of those tasks that can be mechanized, thus providing time for carrying out others of a more added-value nature.

The IMS Learning Design (LD, 2003) specification provides recommendations about the learning process design and some tools related to the execution of learning scenarios, which have been developed to test the IMS LD specification. The RELOAD editor (JISC, 2006) to author learning designs in IMS LD format, the CooperCore Design Engine (Vogten, 2004; Vogten & Martens, 2005) to automate the scenario of the delivery of learning activities and finally, the LAMS (LAMS Foundation, 2005) to provide teachers with an intuitive visual authoring environment to create sequences of learning activities. In addition, there are other tools like the TELOS editor (Technologies Copigraph Inc., n.d.) to validate and design learning scenarios using an ontology-driven and service-oriented architecture. However, there is a lack of tools that facilitate the specification and posterior execution of automated learning scenarios does not exist.

In fact, learning scenarios may be executed by: 1) using a LMS and 2) programming the learning scenarios from scratch. Since using a LMS may constrain the possibilities of learning scenarios, which will have to be written using the rules of the LMS instead of the rules of the organization, we believe the second option is more interesting.

Hence, a framework to support the LMS specifications is needed.

The goal of this paper is facilitating the specification and execution of learning scenarios by means an open-source framework that permits interoperability among specifications and its reusability in the distributed learning environment. Thus, the proposal of this paper is to present an architecture that is able to support a tool capable of automating teachers' tasks that usually occur in a learning environment from its specifications, and not only those related to the learning process design. The technological infrastructure proposed matches with the results of the Campus Project (Open University of Catalonia, 2006) of the Open University of Catalonia (UOC). The UOC is a pioneer virtual university in Spain with more than 43,000 students enrolled during the academic course 2008-2009. The Campus Project has the aim of evolving the e-Learning Platform created 10 years ago according to an open and service-oriented approach. Nowadays, the presented architecture is being effectively used in the virtual Campus of the UOC.

This paper is composed of six sections, dealing with: the introduction and motivations of this work, the concept of a learning scenario, the requirements of the infrastructure to support the automation of specifications of learning scenarios, the proposal of our architecture, a case study that illustrates the feasibility of the automation of a learning scenario using the proposed architecture and, the conclusions and future work.

Learning Scenarios

The learning scenario concept used by IMS LD is that given by Fowler in (Fowler, 2000): "A scenario is a sequence of steps describing interactions between the user and the system (...)" in reference to the kind of scenarios considered which are related to the learning process design only.

From the point of view of computer science engineering, a learning scenario is a flexible tool for the system's design that has no single form or way of using it (Toffolon, 2006). This definition allows for the consideration of learning scenarios as a first draft of the system's behavior and sees them as a link between the LMS functionality and the learning processes or between the architecture and its implementation components. However, there are other definitions like those given by authors like Tood (Todd, 1999), which deals with scenarios from a pedagogical point of view, or Fahey (Fahey, 1997) that describes scenarios from an organizational perspective. Thus, there exists some semantic heterogeneity among the different learning scenarios definitions which are dependent of the authors' discipline.

In this paper, a learning scenario is considered as a function that occurs in an LMS and its boundaries with the aim of achieving goals related to learning in a broad sense. From a more detailed point of view, a learning scenario must be understood as a sequence of interactions among participants of a learning environment that collaborate to achieve a goal related to learning, whether it is before, during or after learning. Thus, a learning scenario can be as simple as an interaction or so complex as to be described in terms of sequences of reusable learning scenarios. Examples of complex learning scenarios could be the preparation of a course or the preparation of the learning activities for such a course; both include other simpler scenarios like searching for teaching materials in a repository or sending/receiving of messages for instance. Later, in the case study section, the description of the Preparation of Leaning Activities (LA) of a course scenario is presented (see Figure 3) and afterwards described in terms of a sequence of reusable learning scenarios.

Infrastructure Requirements

The architecture requirements proposed it this paper is based three main points: the need of specifications' interoperability, the autonomy of participants involved in each learning scenario and the reusability of specifications of learning scenarios. A more detailed explanation about each of them is given next:

- **Interoperability**: a learning scenario should be useful for any LMS with platform-independence. This goal implies achieving almost real interoperability between all the possible e-learning platforms and the tool. It involves normative descriptions like ADL SCORM (ADL, 2004) and IMS Common Cartridge specifications (CC, 2008) to provide portability, the LOM standard for defining metadata of learning resources (IEEE, 2002) or the OSID-OKI specifications (Open Knowledge Initiative, 2004) to define interfaces for component interaction and so on, in order to guarantee the integration of the tools and systems and the exchange of information independently of the medium of transmission. Thus, the infrastructure that supports such a tool must be based on normative descriptions to assure interoperability.

- **Platform independence**: it will result in fostering the autonomy of the participants involved in the different learning scenarios. The learning scenarios considered a set of interactions in a distributed environment that implement the communication of autonomous components of the system or other systems in the achievement of a given goal require a Service Oriented Architecture (SOA). The SOA is defined as "a paradigm for organizing and utilizing distributed capabilities that may be under the control of different ownership domains. It provides a uniform means to offer, discover, interact with and use capabilities to produce the desired effects and which are consistent with measurable preconditions and expectations" (MacKenzie et al., 2006). This kind of technological infrastructure based on web services was also proposed by Stojanovic (Stojanovic et al., 2001) and other specifications like CEN-LORI (Simon et al. 2005) and IMS_DRI (DRI, 2003) due to the distributed nature of the learning environment and the required collaboration between components involved in learning scenarios.

- **Promoting the reusability of specifications of learning scenarios**: This purpose requires the existence of some elemental specifications of learning scenarios which must be catalogued and called primitive scenarios in order to use them in other more complex scenarios. Thus, the learning scenarios as components of other learning scenarios must have a defined pattern of behavior that determine their functionality and facilitate their reuse, in a similar way of workflow patterns (Van der Aalst, 2003). Therefore, an architecture to support executable descriptions of learning scenarios must foster the reusability of learning scenarios and must permit the broadening of LMS functionalities even for the system's adaptation.

To sum up, the required architecture must promote interoperability, the loose coupling between the involved components, the reusability of learning scenarios and the broadening of LMS functionalities.

The Architecture of the UOC Campus Project

The Campus Project comes under the Digital University program fostered by the Catalan Government STSI Department. The Universitat Oberta de Catalunya (UOC) is in charge of coordinating and leading the project, which is carried out using the knowledge and experience of each associated university. Each member, therefore, contributes tools and resources to the project, which is orga-

nized according to a development community in open source.

The aim of the Campus Project is to develop a technological infrastructure with open source tools to provide online training. The project requirements are: (1) open code and open standards, (2) user-centered design, (3) interoperability between tools and with other systems, (4) scalability of the solution, (5) high concurrence of users and processes, (6) OKI OSIDs specifications (Open Knowledge Initiative, 2004) as a mechanism of interoperability, which can be executed and integrated into Moodle's and Sakai's platforms and is founded on a service-based architecture.

Furthermore, such architecture is designed to pursue a two-fold objective: (1) to share the UOC e-learning tools with other institutions and (2) to integrate and use e-learning tools from other institutions at the UOC. Therefore, the design of the architecture starts from the assumption that real interoperability relies on adopting a service-oriented approach in order to promote the interoperability of the system.

The Campus project's architecture follows a three-layered architectural model which the IMS-(Digital Repository Interoperability) (DRI, 2003) specifications recommend as can be seen in Figure 1. On the top layer, the modules corresponding to the tools and applications that extend the LMS functionalities are shown and on the bottom layer, the e-learning platform as the base of such an infrastructure. And just in the middle, the intermediate layer which acts as a bridge between the modules and the e-learning platform to extend the LMS functionalities of the system.

The desired interoperability has been considered during all the stages of the Campus project development. First of all, Moodle and Sakai, two open platforms have been included in the architectural model instead of a unique platform as can be seen in Figure 2.

Secondly, the two selected e-learning platforms have evolved in frameworks in order to solve some problems of integration with third party

Figure 1. The three-layered architecture of the UOC campus

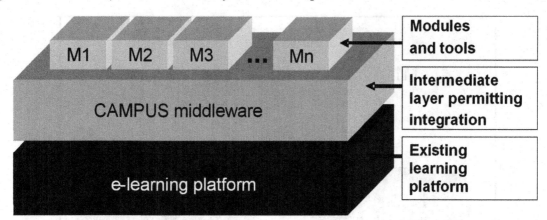

tools. A framework is the development of a platform which offers a set of APIs; mechanisms to incorporate plug-ins and other elements that enhance both the extensibility and personalization of the platform. This approach facilitates a loose coupling degree but is still not enough to achieve fine interoperability between systems and tools.

Thirdly, the service-oriented architectural model was adopted in order to go beyond the achieved interoperability. In SOA, the system is modeled around a set of modules with a public functionality and responsibility and a set of mechanisms that allow interaction between services (MacKenzie et al., 2006). If the services implement a very clear-cut interface, then it is possible to isolate the interaction mechanisms in a unique layer facilitating the control of loose coupling across the systems. It has been achieved through OKI, using the OKI Bus as part of the middleware. The mission of this OKI Bus is to solve all the problems related to the communication protocols, remote communication between applications, performance optimization measures, increasing communication quality and so on.

As each tool has its own architecture and the most appropriate technology to solve its business logic, an OKI Bus and an OKI gateway are needed in order to facilitate the communication between tools and platforms. The OKI gateway is an adapter that translates the requests of the basic services used by tools into calls to the specific API of each platform. Each platform has its own gateway, so in order to integrate a new platform; a new gateway must be used.

This architecture is based on the OKI proposal and the best way to see it is to think about a system of blocks or pieces that fit together as shown in Figure 2. Each piece is a black box that performs an activity within its limits and invisible to the rest. Consequently, each tool has its own internal architecture and the most appropriate technology to resolve its business logic.

As the implementation is based on a service-oriented architecture (SOA) the tools interact with the base platform using a set of basic services The criteria for deciding what these basic services should be are as follows: 1) the minimum, 2) they should be defined by OKI, 3) those that are indispensable for the system to work (authentication and authorization) an 4) those that allow the system to be administered and managed as though it were a single product (logging, locale, configuration and messaging). Thus, the tools developed communicate with the base platform using a maximum of six services:

1. **The authentication service** permits a new user to be registered in a system or to find out if a user is connected to it. It is an indis-

Figure 2. Three-layered architecture using OKI in the middleware

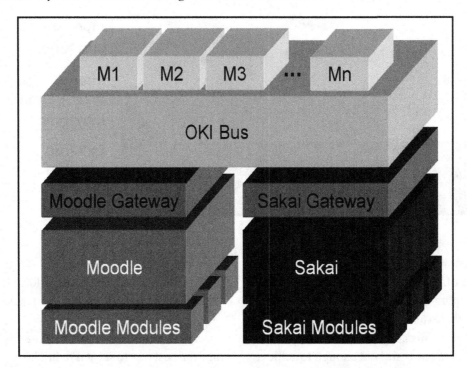

pensable service in any computer program with user registration.

2. **The authorization service** permits it to be known if a user is authorized to access to a function or resource. It is indispensable in any system where the users perform different roles.

3. **The logging service** allows data on the activity carried out by the program to be stored. It is very useful for finding out what is happening in a system and how it is working.

4. **The locale service** permits the language of a program to be changed or new languages to be added.

5. **The configuration service** permits the configuration of the parameters of a computer application to be created or changed.

6. **The messaging service** permits communication among users within the system. It is an indispensable service in any system based on a distributed architecture.

From all of this, it is easy to realize that the OKI proposal plays an important role in the architecture of the UOC Campus. Furthermore, the OKI-OSID specification is essential for the automation of specifications of learning scenarios since the definition of recommended web service interfaces are addressed specially to the higher education community which fosters interoperability, integration and is suitable for the SOA architectural model as will be seen in the following sections.

The Case Study

This section relates how the suitability of the proposed architecture as an infrastructure to support the automation is tested using a specific learning scenario that occurs frequently in every course in the UOC Campus. First of all, the specific learning scenario is described and secondly, some considerations regarding its implementation using OKI service interfaces are presented.

Figure 3. The BPM diagram of the Preparation of Leaning Activities (LA) of a course

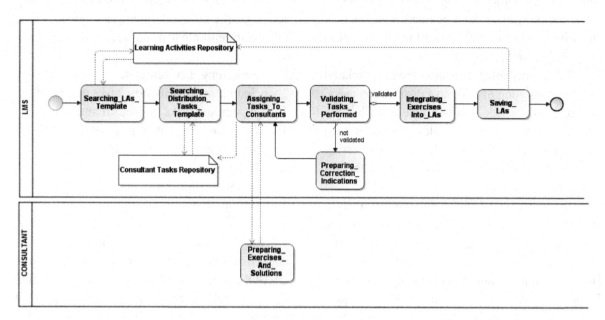

Learning Scenario Description

This case study scenario consists in preparing learning activities (LA) for a given course for the Computer Science, Multimedia and Telecommunication Departments in the UOC.

In Figure 3, the description of such a learning scenario in terms of a sequence of reusable learning scenarios is depicted using a BPMN diagram (Object Management group, 2006). The two pools of the figure correspond to both participants in this scenario: 1) the LMS assuming the role of the coordinator instructor and 2) the consultant as the teacher being able to interact with students during the course. For those who do not know the UOC learning methodology and the learning organization figures associated to such a pedagogical model, it would be recommended to read (Rodríguez et al., 2006) before going on.

The preparation of learning activities for a given course is shared by usually several virtual classes at the UOC Campus. Each group of students enrolled in each virtual class has its own consultant, who guides the learning process of students and

responds the students' doubts. Coordinating the consultancy tasks and taking care of the learning quality is the responsibility of the teacher, who is a member of the academic staff and is ultimately responsible for the subject matter in question. In this case, we are interested in those tasks related to the preparation of activities of the course, such as the distribution of tasks or their assignation and validation. As a result of the execution of this learning scenario, all of the activities of the course are going to be saved in a repository with its established format and structure for future use.

The course has four theoretical learning activities and two practical learning activities. Each of them is formed by a set of exercises with a specific learning objective and contributes to the final result of the learning activity where it is included. The LA template is a learning resource that describes the structural content of each LA, its learning objectives and the competences that it develops; the number of exercises that are composed in the LA activity, their type, objectives and their assessment criteria. This information must be annotated using the LOM metadata. Each learning activity has its own solution which is prepared by a consultant in order to estimate the time needed by students to solve it and to check that all the information required is well provided.

The teacher must distribute the tasks related to the preparation of LAs, so a distribution tasks' template is needed. This template describes the tasks to be carried out, the roles played, the condition for the validation of the tasks, the testing points of the task and the procedure required to carry them out.

The consultants design new exercises, including their solution. When the deadline reaches, they send their proposal to be verified. If it is not validated, then a list of corrections is returned to the consultant creator in order to improve his/her proposal. When all the exercises of the LA proposal are validated, the next step is the integration of them. It must be repeated for each LA of the course. The learning scenario finishes when all the LA of such a course is prepared and saved in the LA repository.

As it can be seen in this case study, the teacher role in the preparation of the learning activities of the course is done by the system when possible.

Learning Scenario Implementation

As interoperability and reusability are key factors and a requirement for the tool that automate the specification of learning scenarios, the OKI service interface definition specification and the recognition of behavioral patterns have been used in this prototype. On the one hand, the achievement of interoperability is possible due to the OKI-OSID specification. Such web service interfaces have been very useful in order to automate the mapping from the participant interactions to calls to web services due to the SOA architecture of the e-learning platform. On the other hand, the reusability of leaning scenarios promotes the description of a learning scenario in terms of sequences of reusable learning scenarios, which are defined once and can be reused many times.

In this case, the Preparation of the learning activities' scenario is defined as a sequence of the following reusable learning scenarios:

1. Searching_LA_template
2. Searching_distribution_tasks_templates
3. Assigning_tasks_to_consultants
4. Preparing_exercises_and_solutions
5. Validating_tasks_performed
6. Integrating_exercises_and solutions_into_Las
7. Saving_LAs

Due to the limited extension of this paper, it is not possible to present a detailed analysis of the OKI-OSID services used in the implementation of the scenario. Instead of it, a brief description of each reusable learning scenario is done in terms of the OKI service interfaces used.

The OKI services used in this implementation are those referred in the previous section (authentication, authorization, logging, locale and user messaging) in addition to the repository service. The reason is that learning activities and the templates used in the Preparation of learning activities' scenario are considered to be stored in a Dspace1 repository and described with IEEE LOM metadata. Other OKI services like Scheduling Service and Assessment Service will be added to the architecture in the future to achieve a more automated and easy-to-use tool.

Before presenting Tables 1 to 7 to describe the OKI services used in each reusable learning scenario, it is important to point out common OKI services in all of them. This part refers to the Agent Service to take user profile information like the preferred language of the user, the Logging Service to notify tracking and monitoring information, the Locale Service to configure the user interface using the user's preferred language and the Id Service to get and to create unique identifiers.

It is vital, at the beginning of the process, to check that the participant who is going to execute an operation has the proper rights to do so. This

Table 1. The OKI services used in the Searching_LAs_template process

Searching_LAs_template

A user with the **Teacher** role executes this application functionality.
   1. Verify if the user is authenticated: **Authentication Service**.
   2. Verify if the user is granted permission to execute this application functionality: **Authorization Service**.
   3. The user fills in a search form. The form's fields are the metadata used to describe the Learning Activity templates. The form is generated using the RecordStructure and PartStructure OKI OSIDs. **Repository Service**.
   4. The system searches all the assets that its metadata matches with the search form fields. **Repository Service**.
   5. A result form is showed to the user and the user selects the appropriate learning activity template.
   6. The selected template is returned.

Table 2. The OKI services used in the Searching_Distribution_Tasks_template process

Searching_Distribution_Tasks_Template

A user with the **Teacher** role executes this application functionality.
   1. Verify if the user is granted permission to execute this application functionality: **Authorization Service**.
   2. The user fills in a search form. The form's fields are the metadata used to describe the distribution task templates for the consultancy of the course. The form is generated using the RecordStructure and PartStructure OKI OSIDs. **Repository Service**.
   3. The system searches all the assets that its metadata matches with the search form fields. **Repository Service**.
   4. A result form is showed to the user and the user selects the appropriate distribution task's template.
   5. The selected template is returned.

Table 3. The OKI services used in the Assigning_Tasks_To_Consultant process

Assigning_Tasks_To_Consultants

A user with the Teacher role executes this application functionality.
   1. Verify if the user is granted permission to execute this application functionality: Authorization Service.
   2. The user introduces the planning schedule of the subject and the system returns all the consultants that can be course instructors of this subject. **Agent and Group Service**.
   3. The subject is a Group and its members are the different courses of the subject. The course is also a Group and has its own members, with different roles.
   4. The user sends a message to each consultant describing the task to be done according to the learning activity template and the distribution task's template. Messaging/e-mail Service.

verification is required for each process implementing a new primitive scenario and consequently this part of the code could be considered as a reusable scenario given its transversal manner. Therefore, an authorization role of each participant is needed, so the Authorization service and the Authentication service will be used at the beginning of each learning scenario, independently of the learning scenario complexity.

In order to show a part of the implementation code, two typical processes related to the repository have been selected: The Searching_

LAs_Template and the Saving_LAs_Template. They are so generic to represent the use of OKI web service interfaces related to any repository, independently of the asset to search or save.

In the code presented in Figure 4, it is possible to observe that the Authorization Service is the first OSID Service needed to check that the teacher grants permission to search the templates related to the LA that is to be created. Then, once the search condition is formulated, the system presents a form to be filled in with all that information so that the corresponding metadata could

Table 4. The OKI services used in the Preparing_Exercises_And_Solutions process

Preparing_Exercises_And_Solutions
A user with the **Consultant** role executes this application functionality. 　1. Verify if the user is authenticated: **Authentication Service**. 　2. Verify if the user is granted permission to execute this application functionality: **Authorization Service**. 　3. The user reads the message sent by the Teacher and creates the exercises and the solutions according to the message indications. 　4. The user sends the exercises and the solutions indicating the corresponding subject and the semester. **Messaging/e-mail Service.** 　5. The systems send a message to the Teacher notifying that the consultant task is done. **Messaging/e-mail Service**.

Table 5. The OKI services used in the Validating_Tasks_Performed process

Validating_Tasks_Performed
A user with the **Teacher** role executes this application functionality. 　1. Verify if the user is granted permission to execute this application functionality: **Authorization Service**. 　2. The user validates the exercises and solutions sent by the consultants. 　3. The user can send a message to a specific consultant to request their assignments or can send a message asking questions. **Messaging/e-mail Service.** 　4. If the user rejects a consultant's assignment, then a message asking for a new assignment is sent. **Messaging/e-mail Service.** 　5. Once consultants' assignments are accepted by the Teacher, then the **Integrating_Exercises_Into_LAs** process is called using the list of exercises and solutions as input parameters.

Table 6. The OKI services used in the Integrating_Exercises_Into_LA process

Integrating_Exercises_Into_LAs
A user with the **Teacher** role executes this application functionality. 　1. Verify if the user is granted permission to execute this application functionality: **Authorization Service**. 　2. The user takes the list of exercises and solutions and creates learning activities according to the learning activity template and the distribution task's template. 　3. The system calls the **saving_LAs** process using the Learning Activities list as an input parameter.

Table 7. The OKI services used in the Saving_LAs process

Saving_LAs
A user with the **Teacher** role executes this application functionality. 　1. Verify if the user is granted permission to execute this application functionality: **Authorization Service**. 　2. For each learning activity in the list: 　　1. The user fills in a saving form. The form's fields are the metadata used to describe the Learning Activities. The form is generated using the RecordStructure and PartStructure OKI OSIDs. **Repository Service**. 　　2. AN OKI Asset is created using the learning activity as content and the form's metadata as an OKI OSIDs Records and Parts. **Repository Service.** 　　3. The new Asset is validated before being saved in the repository. **Repository Service**. 　3. All the learning activities are in the repository described with metadata, available to be used by other processes like the course scheduling for the students and others.

search those templates and return them. Thus, it implies the need to use the Repository Service and use metadata according to the LOM standard.

Furthermore, in the Saving_LAs process, after using the Authorization Service, the LA is described by means of its metadata and such metadata and the LA together make up an asset which is saved in the repository as can be seen in Figure 5.

CONCLUSION AND FUTURE WORK

This paper presents an open source architecture that is able to support the automation of learning tasks that usually occur in a learning environment from its specifications. The presented architecture has especially designed in order to promote both interoperability between different leaning organizations that may have different rules or ways of working, technological interoperability and reusability. The technological infrastructure has been integrated in the virtual campus of the Open University of Catalonia (UOC). Nowadays, the architecture gives service to over 40 thousand students. Hence, the architecture has been widely tested and validated and its usefulness and usability has been validated from a practical point of view.

The OKI-OSID recommendations have been used in the middleware of the architecture presented in order to construct an interface mechanism to implement interactions between the different components that take part in the scenarios within a distributed environment and furthermore, it provides interoperability and loose coupling thereby satisfying the tools' requirements.

The main contributions of this paper are: (1) an architecture based on the OKI-OSID proposal, (2) the identification of some weakness of the OKI-OSID specification and (3) a practical demonstration of using the OKI-OSID specification to design a common level for LMS independently of the system's platform.

During the study of the OKI-OSID specification some weakness has been detected. Maybe, the main weakness is that the generality of the OSID framework sometimes forces to do things in a way that is not the usual way in a learning institution. When so happens, the way in which the learning activity performs is adapted to OKI and therefore, the processes or the activities a given user is supposed to do may change, changing then the processes of the institution. Examples of these cases are the assignation of tasks among the consultants in the UOC environment. In OKI it should be done at course group level instead of the courseSection level, which is equivalent to the class level that is the UOC is used to work with in this activity. On the other hand, we observed that authorization is required at the beginning of every operation invoked through the web services in order to check whether the participants have the right permissions to carry out the activities in the learning scenario. As a learning scenario only have sense if its participants are identified, it would be more useful to refer them in the invocation of each service interface in order to reduce repeated parts of code. The OKI services used in the learning scenario presented in Table 7 and the code shown in the Figure 4 and the Figure 6 illustrates so.

Although our work has not been yet validated experimentally from an academic point of view, it has been validated from a practical perspective. The usefulness and the improvement of the proposed architecture against other architectures have been tested. In fact, the architecture proposed is being used in the UOC Campus, a campus used over 40 thousand students. The use of this architecture is really new, from one year ago, but its use has allowed to include in the campus several extra tools such as a new initial page with widgets, blogs, wikis and the reuse of Moodle tools within the campus. Also the automation of the preparation of learning activities' scenario has been done in the UOC learning-environment, so the architecture

Figure 4. The implementation of Searching_LAs_template process using OKI services

```
private void searching_LAs_template() {
    try {
        if (authZ.isUserAuthorized(idC.getId("ActivityPlanification"), idC.getId("instance"))) {
            log.trace("searching_LAs_template");


            //step2
            org.osid.repository.Repository repository = repoComp.getRepository(idC.getId("LAs_template_repository"));

            log.trace("Repository: " + repository.getDisplayName());

            // This implementation has only one RecordStructure for Type

            RecordStructure rs = (repository.getRecordStructuresByType(this.LOM_STRUCTURE_TYPE)).nextRecordStructure();

                // create a form using record structure

                LOMForm form = new LOMForm(rs);

                form.setTitle(locale.getEntry("LOM_FORM_TITLE") + ". " + repository.getDisplayName());

                form.setHelp(locale.getEntry("LOM_FORM_HELP"));

                // show the LOM form

                log.trace("LOM Metadata search form.");

                if (form.show()) {

                    // repository search

                        log.trace("search by LOM Metadata.");

                        AssetIterator                                          assetIterator                              =

                    repository.getAssetsBySearch(form.getLOMAsset(),this.SEARCH_BY_LOM_TYPE,new SharedProperties());

                        // show the assets - result screen

                        AssetListForm listForm = new AssetListForm(assetIterator);

                        listForm.setTitle(locale.getEntry("LIST_FORM_TITLE") + ". "+ repository.getDisplayName());

                        listForm.setHelp(locale.getEntry("LIST_FORM_HELP"));

                        log.trace("Asset List Form.");

                        if(listForm.show()) {

                            // take the selected Asset.

                            log.trace("LAs Template selected.");

                            this.LAsTemplateDocument = listForm.getSelectedAsset().getContent();

                        }
```

Figure 5. The implementation of Saving_LAs process using OKI services

```
private void saving_LAs() {

  try {

    if (authZ.isUserAuthorized(idC.getId("ActivityPlanification"), idC.getId("instance"))) {

        log.trace("saving_LAs");


        //step8

        org.osid.repository.Repository repository = repoComp.getRepository(idC.getId("LAs_repository"));

        log.trace("Repository: " + repository.getDisplayName());

        // This implementation has only one RecordStructure for Type

        RecordStructure rs =

                        (repository.getRecordStructuresByType(this.LOM_STRUCTURE_TYPE)).nextRecordStructure();

        // save all the learning activities into the repository

        while (learningActivities.hasNext()) {

                java.io.Serializable document = learningActivities.next();

                // create a form using record structure

                        LOMForm form = new LOMForm(rs);

                        form.setTitle(locale.getEntry("LEARNING_ACTIVITY_METADATA_FORM_TITLE") + ". " +

                                repository.getDisplayName());

                        form.setHelp(locale.getEntry("LEARNING_ACTIVITY_METADATA_HELP"));

                        form.addDocumentLink(locale.getEntry("LEARNING_ACTIVITY_TO_DESCRIVE"), document);

                        // show the LOM form

                        log.trace("Learning Activity Metadata form.");

                        if (form.show()) {

                                // repository save

                                log.trace("Save the new Asset.");

                                Asset  newLA  =  repository.createAsset(form.getDisplayName(),  form.getDescription(),

this.LOM_ASSET_TYPE);

                                newLA.updateContent(document);

                                newLA.copyRecordStructure(form.getLOMAsset().getId(), rs.getId());

                                // set the records.

                                if(repository.validateAsset(newLA.getId())) {
```

of the Campus has been proved as suitable as a technological infrastructure for a tool able to support the automation of learning scenarios based on the mapping of the primitive scenarios to calls to OSID services. A more automated and friendly tool could be possible by adding other services and standards to the LMS. Scheduling, workflow and other services, as well as QTI and SCORM (ADL, 2004) specifications for the exercises can be very useful for this purpose.

As part of our future work and in order to solve the lack of automated mapping, there is the need to develop a framework based on ontologies to specify learning scenarios formally. Such a new framework would act as a front-end of the presented architecture and will deal only with the specification, allowing mappings between the specification and the calls to OSID services that could execute them. We plan to create a case tool to represent graphical specifications of educational settings (Rius, 2010) in order to use them to automate the instantiation of such framework and obtaining formal descriptions to be used in partial implementations of such learning scenarios.

In addition, we plan to create a repository of elemental learning scenarios with the aim of constructing a reusable set of scenarios to be used to compound complex learning processes.

ACKNOWLEDGMENT

This work has been partially supported by the Spanish Ministry of Science and Innovation thru the following projects: TIN2008-00444 (GMC), PERSONAL (ONTO) ref TIN2006-15107-C02 and TSI-020301-2008-9 (SUMA).

REFERENCES

ADL. (2004). *Sharable Content Object Reference Model Version 1.3.1.* Retrieved from http://www. adlnet.org

CC. (2008). *IMS Common Cartridge Specification. Version 1.0.* Retrieved from http://www. imsglobal.org/cc/

DRI. (2003). *IMS digital repositories interoperability-core functions information model Version 1.* Retrieved from http://www.imsglobal.org/ digitalrepositories/driv1p0/imsdri_infov1p0.html

Fahey, L., & Randall, R. M. (1997). What is scenario learning? In *Learning from the Future: Competitive Foresight Scenarios* (pp. 3–21). New York: Wiley.

Fowler, M. (2000). *UML Distilled: A Brief Guide to the Standard Object Modeling Language* (2nd ed.). Reading, MA: Addison-Wesley.

IEEE. (2002). *LTSC WG12: Draft standard for learning object metadata.* Retrieved from http:// ltsc.ieee.org/wg12/files/LOM_1484_12_1_v1_ Final_Draft.pdf http://ltsc.ieee.org/wg12/files/ LOM_1484_12_1_v1_Final_Draft.pdf

JISC. (2006). *RELOAD. Reusable eLearning Object Authoring & Delivery.* Retrieved from http://www.reload.ac.uk/

LAMS Foundation. (2005). *Learning Activities Management System.* Retrieved from http://www. lamsfoundation.org/

LD. (2003). *IMS Learning Design Information Model. Version 1.0 Final Specification.* Retrieved from http://www.imsglobal.org/learningdesign/ ldv1p0/imsld_infov1p0.html

MacKenzie, C., Laskey, K., McCabe, F., Brown, P., & Metz, R. (2006). *OASIS reference model for service oriented architecture v.1.0.* OASIS.

Object Management Group. (2006). *Business Process Modeling Notation Specification. Final adopted specification.* Retrieved from http:// www.bpmn.org/Documents/OMG%20Final%20 Adopted%20BPMN%201-0%20Spec%2006-02-01.pdf

Open Knowledge Initiative. (2004). *Open Service Interface Definitions. Version 2.0.0.* Retrieved from http://www.okiproject.org/view/html/site/oki/node/1478

Open University of Catalonia. (2006). *The Campus Project.* Retrieved from http://www.campusproject.org/en/index.php

Rius, A., Conesa, J., & Gañán, D. (2010). *A DSL Tool to Assist Specifications of Educational Settings.* Paper presented at the 6th Semantic Web Services Conference of the 2010 World Congress in Computer Science, Computer Engineering, and Applied Computing, Las Vegas, NV.

Rodríguez, M. E., Serra, M., Cabot, J., & Guitart, I. (2006). Evolution of the Teacher Roles and Figures in E-learning Environments. In *Proceedings of the 6th IEEE International Conference on Advanced Learning Technologies* (pp. 512-514). Washington, DC: IEEE Computer Society.

Simon, B., Nassart, D., Assche, F.V., Ternier, S., & Duval, E. (2005). *Simple query interface specification.*

Stojanovic, L., Staab, S., & Studer, R. (2001). elearning based on the semantic web. In *Proceedings of the World Conference on the WWW and Internet (Webnet 2001)*, Orlando, FL (pp. 23-27).

Technologies Copigraph Inc. (n.d.). *IMS-LD Scenario editors.* Retrieved from http://www.cogigraph.com/Produits/IMSLDScenarioEditors/tabid/1099/language/en-US/Default.aspx

Toffolon, C. (2006). Learning management system scenario-based engineering. In *Proceedings of the 5th European Conference on e-Learning (ECEL 2006)*, Winchester, UK (pp. 397-406).

Tood, C., Klagholz, L., Sheschter, E., Doolan, J., Jensen, J., & Ngler, I. (1999). *Learning scenarios.* New Jersey Languages Curriculum Framework.

Van der Aalst, W., ter Hofstede, A., Kiepuszewski, B., & Barros, A. (2003). Workflow patterns. *Distributed and Parallel Databases*, *14*(1), 5–51. doi:10.1023/A:1022883727209

Vogten, H. (2004). *CopperCore, an Open Source IMS Learning Design Engine.* Retrieved from http://hdl.handle.net/1820/286

Vogten, H., & Martens, H. (2005). *CopperCore 3.0.* Retrieved from.http://www.coppercore.org

ENDNOTE

[1]   http://www.dspace.org/

This work was previously published in the International Journal of Information Technologies and Systems Approach, Volume 4, Issue 1, edited by Frank Stowell and Manuel Mora, pp. 38-52, copyright 2011 by IGI Publishing (an imprint of IGI Global).

Chapter 15
Analysis of Click Stream Patterns using Soft Biclustering Approaches

P. K. Nizar Banu
Narasu's Sarathy Institute of Technology, India

H. Hannah Inbarani
Periyar University, India

ABSTRACT

As websites increase in complexity, locating needed information becomes a difficult task. Such difficulty is often related to the websites' design but also ineffective and inefficient navigation processes. Research in web mining addresses this problem by applying techniques from data mining and machine learning to web data and documents. In this study, the authors examine web usage mining, applying data mining techniques to web server logs. Web usage mining has gained much attention as a potential approach to fulfill the requirement of web personalization. In this paper, the authors propose K-means biclustering, rough biclustering and fuzzy biclustering approaches to disclose the duality between users and pages by grouping them in both dimensions simultaneously. The simultaneous clustering of users and pages discovers biclusters that correspond to groups of users that exhibit highly correlated ratings on groups of pages. The results indicate that the fuzzy C-means biclustering algorithm best and is able to detect partial matching of preferences.

INTRODUCTION

The World Wide Web is a popular and interactive medium to disseminate information today. The web is huge, diverse, and dynamic and thus raises the scalability, multimedia data, and temporal issues respectively. Due to these situations, we are currently drowning in information and facing information overload (Maes, 1994; Chakraborty, Dom, Gibson, Kleinberg, Kumar, & Raghavan, 1999). Therefore, web mining becomes an active and popular research field. Web mining is the term of applying data mining techniques to automatically discover and extract useful infor-

DOI: 10.4018/978-1-4666-1562-5.ch015

mation from the World Wide Web documents and services (Nasraoui, Rojas, & Cardona, 2006; Etzioni, 1996; Zamir & Etzioni, 1998). Based on the several research studies we can broadly classify web mining into three domains such as web content mining, web structure mining and web usage mining. Web Content Mining is the process of extracting knowledge from the content of the web documents and their descriptions. Web Structure Mining is the process of inferring knowledge from the structure of data.

Web usage mining is the process of applying data mining techniques to the discovery of behavior patterns based on web data, for various applications. Usage patterns extracted from web data can be applied to a wide range of applications such as web personalization, system improvement, site modification, business intelligence discovery, usage characterization, and so on. The overall process of web usage mining is generally divided into two main tasks; data preparation and pattern discovery. The data preparation tasks build a server session file where each session is a sequence of requests of different types made by single user during a single visit to a site (Liu, Chen, & Song, 2002; Yan, Jacobsen, Garcia-Molina, & Dayal, 1996). Pattern discovery converge the algorithms and techniques from several research areas, such as data mining, machine learning, statistics, and pattern recognition. In Web Usage Mining research existing approaches are single sided approaches which discover either user cluster (Xiao, Zhang, Jia, & Li, 2001) or page cluster (Smith & Ng, 2003).

Recently, web usage mining techniques have been widely applied for discovering interesting and frequent user navigation patterns from Web server logs (Liu & Keselji, 2007). Most of these efforts have proposed using various data mining or machine learning techniques to model and understand web user activity. Of the existed methods, some are non-sequential, such as association rule mining and clustering; and some are sequential, such as sequential or navigational pattern mining (Perkowitz & Etzioni, 2000).

By analyzing the characteristics of the clusters, web designers may understand the users better and may provide more suitable, customized services to the users. In web usage mining, clustering algorithms can be used in two ways: usage clickstream clusters (Xiao et al., 2001) and page clickstream clusters (Song & Shepperd, 2006). User clustering and Page clustering algorithms cannot detect partial matching of preferences because their similarity measures consider the entire set of users or pages respectively. The simultaneous clustering of users and pages discovers biclusters which correspond to group of users which exhibit highly correlated ratings on groups of pages. In this paper, three Biclustering algorithms are proposed to extract user profiles by integrating user clustering and page clustering techniques. Therefore, this research explores a new user profiling method integrating user clustering and page clustering techniques.

Furthermore User clustering and page clustering algorithms cannot detect partial matching of preferences because their similarity measures consider the entire set of users or pages respectively.

The paper is organized as follows. The first section describes user and page clustering approaches for web usage mining. A brief introduction to the biclustering technique is presented. The proposed Biclustering algorithms to perform user and page clustering simultaneously is described. The experimental results are then presented and analyzed.

BACKGROUND

Regarding web usage clustering algorithm, there exist two main approaches: user clustering which clusters users based on their similarity and page clustering which creates page clusters based on similarity between pages. However both user and page clustering are one sided approaches, in the sense, that they examine similarities either only between users or only between pages separately. This way, they ignore the clear duality that exists between users and pages. This research paper proposes a method for integrating user clustering and page clustering techniques. Traditional clustering approaches generate partitions; in a partition, each pattern belongs to one and only one cluster. Hence, the clusters in a hard clustering are disjoint. The rough clusters resulting from the proposed algorithm provide interpretations of different navigation orientations of users present in the sessions without having to fit each object into only one group. Such descriptions can help web miners to identify potential and meaningful groups of users based on the similarity between pages. The theory of rough sets was introduced by Pawlak, in early 1980s, has recently emerged as another major mathematical tool for managing uncertainty that arises from granularity in the domain of discourse - that is, from the indiscernibility between objects in a set. The concept of a rough cluster was introduced in (Voges, Pope, & Brown, 2002), as a simple extension of the notion of rough sets.

The boundary of a bicluster is usually fuzzy in practice as users and pages can belong to multiple biclusters at the same time but with different membership degrees. A fuzzy set is a generalization of an ordinary set in that it allows the degree of membership for each element to range over the unit interval [0, 1]. Thus, the membership function of a fuzzy set maps each element of the universe of discourse to its range space, which, in most cases, is assumed to be the unit interval. The categorization criterion of existing approaches refers to the data they involve (users or pages) or the nature of the grouping they perform and which may concern a hard assignment, i.e., data is divided into distinct clusters, where each data element belongs to exactly one cluster, or a fuzzy one, i.e., data elements are assigned to one or more clusters with different membership levels. The relations between web users' and pages' clusters are quantified to reveal users' interest in the different web pages' clusters (Koutsonikola & Vakali, 2009). The idea of Fuzzy biclustering is to associate each user with their similarity of pages with every cluster using a membership function (Fu, Sandhu, & Shi, 2000).

BICLUSTERING APPROACH

Many data mining techniques have been designed to support knowledge discovery from session matrix which can be represented as Boolean matrix: the rows denote users and the columns denote pages (Pensal, Robardet, & Boulicaut, 2005). The biclustering process on a data matrix involves the determination of a set of clusters taking into account both rows and columns. Each bicluster is defined on a subset of rows and a subset of columns. Moreover, two biclusters may overlap, which means that several rows or columns of the matrix may participate in multiple biclusters. Another important characteristic of biclusters is that each bicluster should be maximal, i.e., it should not be fully contained in another determined bicluster (Nanopoulos, Papadopoulos, & Manolopoulos, 2006).

Bicluster

A bicluster consists of a pair of a row set and a column set, which will be further designated as the user set and the page set, i.e., a bicluster is a pair (U, P), where $U \subset \{u_1, u_2 \ldots, u_m\}$ is a subset of users and $P \subset \{p_1, p_2 \ldots p_n\}$ is a subset of pages. Biclustering can be applied whenever the data to analyze has the form of a real-valued matrix A, where the set of values a_{ij} represent the relation between its users i and its pages j. This approach allows clustering the users and pages simultaneously.

Rough Biclustering

A rough cluster is defined in a similar manner to a rough set that is with lower and upper approximation. The lower approximation of a rough cluster contains objects that only belong to that cluster. The Upper approximation of a rough cluster contains objects in the cluster, which are also members of other clusters (Peters, 2006; Han & Kambert, 2001). In Rough biclustering, lower approximation contains row objects and column objects that belong only to one bicluster. The Upper approximation of a rough bicluster contains row objects or column objects in the bicluster, which are also members of other biclusters. To use the theory of rough sets in biclustering, the value set (V_a) need to be ordered. This allows a measure of the distance between each object to be defined. Distance is a form of *similarity,* which is a relaxing of the strict requirement of indiscernibility outlined in canonical rough sets theory, and allows the inclusion of objects that are similar rather than identical. Biclusters of row objects and column objects are then formed on the basis of their distance from each other. An important distinction between rough biclustering and traditional clustering approaches is that, with rough biclustering, an object can belong to more than one bicluster. In this paper, rough sets are used to represent biclusters in terms of upper and lower approximations.

Fuzzy Biclustering

In contrast to traditional clustering, a biclustering method produces biclusters, each of which identifies a set of users and a set of pages under which these users behave similarly. However, in practice, the boundary of a bicluster is usually fuzzy for three reasons:

1. The weblog dataset might be noisy and incomplete,
2. The similarity measurement between users is continuous and there is no clear cutoff value for group membership, and
3. A user might behave similarly to User1 under a set of pages and behave similarly to another User2 under another set of pages. Therefore,

there is a great need for a fuzzy biclustering method, which produces biclusters in which users and pages can belong to a cluster partially and to multiple biclusters at the same time with different membership degrees.

Fuzzy biclusters provide richer information than regular biclusters as fuzzy biclusters associate with each User/Page a membership value.

Let $X = \{x_1 \ldots x_r\}$ be a set of unlabeled data points, $Y = \{y_1, \ldots, y_s\}$, a set of cluster centers and $U = [u_{pq}]$ be the fuzzy membership matrix. Often, central clustering algorithms impose a probabilistic constraint on memberships, according to which the sum of the membership values of a point in all the clusters must be equal to one:

$$\sum_{q=1}^{r} u_{pq} = 1.$$

RELATED WORK

For analyzing Web user behavior, we first establish a framework, called the usage data analysis model. In this model, the relationships between Web users and pages are expressed by a session matrix. On the basis of this data model, associations between Web pages and user sessions hidden in the collected Web log data, is obtained using K-Means biclustering, Rough Biclustering and Fuzzy Biclustering algorithms. The discovered user and page clusters are used to generate user profiles. Figure 1 shows the proposed framework for usage pattern mining process.

Data Preprocessing

Data preprocessing is applied to make data more suitable for data mining. In addition, as biclustering, groups users and pages simultaneously, it allows to identify sets of users sharing common preferences across subsets of pages. In our ap-

Figure 1. Usage pattern mining process

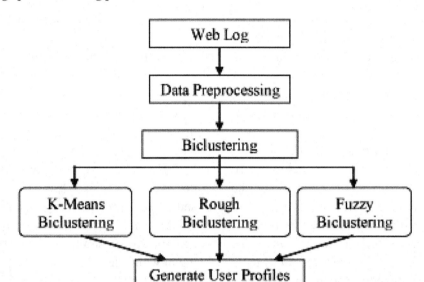

proach the main goal is to find the subsets of users who have visited pages. Therefore the binary values can be used to indicate the pages visited by the users. If the page is visited by the user then it is marked as "1" otherwise "0".

Extracting User Access Pattern Vectors

The base vector $B = \{P_1, P_2 \ldots P_n\}$ represents the access pattern of the users. For each User U, the session vector forms a binary input pattern vector PU, which is an instance of the base vector. The pattern vector maps the access frequency of each base vector element, URL_i, to binary values. It is of the form $UP = \{P_1, P_2 \ldots P_n\}$ where $1 \leq U \leq P$ and P_i is an element of UP having a value of either 0 or 1. Generated by the following procedure, the pattern vector is the input vector

    For each user U_i, $U = 1$ to Max_u
    For each element P_i in $\{P_1, P_2 \ldots P_n\}$
    Pattern vector P, $i = 1$ to Max_p
    1 if P_i is requested
    0 Otherwise
    End

Endwhere U stands for User and P stands for Page. Max_u is the maximum number of users; Max_p is the maximum number of pages.

The Biclustering Process

The biclustering process on a User access matrix involves the determination of a set of clusters taking into account both users and pages. Each bicluster is defined on a subset of users and a subset of pages. Moreover, two biclusters may overlap, which means that several users or pages of the session matrix may participate in multiple biclusters. Another important characteristic of biclusters is that each bicluster should not be fully contained in another determined bicluster. In order not to miss important biclusters, we allow overlapping. However, overlapping introduces a trade-off:

1. With few biclusters the effectiveness reduces, as several biclusters may be missed.
2. With a high number of biclusters efficiency reduces; as we have to examine many possible matching

The Proposed Biclustering Approach

In the first step, User access pattern Matrix is created. In order to provide recommendations, we have to find the biclusters containing users and pages with preferences that have strong partial similarity. A collection of interesting bisets denoted B has been extracted from User Access Pattern Matrix S beforehand. We are looking for k clusters of bisets $\{C_1, C_2...C_k\}$ ($C_i \subseteq B$).

A biset is an element $PU_j = (U_j, P_j) <U_j>$, $<P_j>=<u_{j1}, u_{j2}...u_{jm}>, <p_{j1}, p_{j2}...p_{jn}>$ Where $U_{jk}=1$ if $U_k \in U_j$ and $P_{jk}=1$ if $P_k \in P_j$

The K-Means Biclustering Algorithm

The K-Means Biclustering aims to cluster the users and pages with similar characteristics. This procedure consists of the following steps (Figure 2 and Figure 3).

Fuzzy Biclustering

This is a fuzzification of the K-Means algorithm, proposed by Bezdek in 1981. It partitions a set of N patterns $\{X_k\}$ into K clusters by minimizing the objective function

Figure 2. The K-Means Biclustering

Algorithm: The K-Means Biclustering

Step 1: Extract User Access Matrix from Web Log file

Step 2: Construct possible bisets B containing users and pages from User Access Matrix

Step 3: Let $Cent_1$, $Cent_2$...$Cent_k$ be the initial cluster centroids selected randomly. K is the number of clusters

Step 4: Distribute the bisets B among the K clusters as follows

$$d_E(x, y) = \sqrt{\sum_{i=1}^{n} (x_i - y_i)^2} \qquad (1)$$

$$x_i = u_i \cup p_i, y_i = u_i \cup p_i$$

where U_i User biset and P_i is Page biset

Step 5: Repeat

1. Assign each biset B to cluster C, such that $d(B, Cent_i)$ is minimal

2. Update the centroid of each cluster by using Eqn. (2)

$$z_j(k+1) = \frac{1}{N_j} \sum_{x \in C_j(k)} x \quad j=1, 2... K \qquad (2)$$

Where N_j is the number of samples in $C_j(k)$

Step 6: Otherwise go to Step 2

Figure 3. The Rough Biclustering

Algorithm: The Rough Biclustering

The Rough Biclustering aims to cluster the users and pages with similar characteristics. This procedure consists of the following steps.

Step 1: Extract User Access Matrix from Web Log file

Step 2: Construct possible bisets B containing users and pages from User Access Matrix

Step 3: Let $Cent_1$, $Cent_2$...$Cent_k$ be the initial cluster centroids selected randomly. K is the number of clusters

Step 4: Distribute the bisets B among the K clusters as follows

Step 5: Assign the bisets to the approximations.

(i) For a given biset X_n determine its closest mean m_h

$$d(X_l, m_h) = \min_{n,k} d(X_n, m_k) \Rightarrow X_l \in \underline{C_k} \wedge X_l \in \overline{C_k} \tag{6}$$

Assign X_n to the upper approximation of the cluster h $\quad X_n \in \overline{c_h}$

(ii) Determine the means m_t that are also close to X_n—they are not farther away from X_n than d $(X_n, mh) + \varepsilon$, where ε is a given threshold:

$$T = \{t : d(X_n, m_k) - d(X_n, m_h) \le \varepsilon \wedge h \ne k\} \tag{7}$$

- If $T \ne \phi$ (X_n is also close to at least one other mean m_t besides m_h)
  Then $\quad X_n \in \overline{C_t}, \forall t \in T$
- Else $\quad X_n \in \underline{C_h}$

Step 6: Compute new mean for each cluster U_i using the following equation

$$m_i = \begin{cases} w_{low} \dfrac{\sum x_k \in \underline{BU}_i X_k}{|\underline{BU}_i|} + wup \dfrac{\sum_{X_k \in (\overline{BU}_i - \overline{BU}_i)} X_k}{|\overline{BU}_i - \underline{BU}_i|} & if\ \overline{BU}_i - \underline{BU}_i \ne \phi, \\ \\ w_{low} \dfrac{\sum_{X_k \in \underline{BU}_i} X_k}{|\underline{BU}_i|} & Otherwise \end{cases} \tag{8}$$

Step 7: Stop.

$$J = \sum_{k=1}^{N} \sum_{i=1}^{c} (\mu_{ik})^{m'} \parallel X_k - m_i \parallel^2, \qquad (6)$$

where $1 \leq m' < \infty$ is the fuzzfier, m_i is the ith cluster center, $\mu_{ik} \in [0,1]$ is the membership of the kth pattern to it, and $\parallel . \parallel$ is the distance norm, such that

$$m_i = \frac{\sum_{k=1}^{N} (\mu_{ik})^{m'} X_k}{\sum_{k=1}^{N} (\mu_{ik})^{m'}}, \qquad (7)$$

and

$$\mu_{ik} = \frac{1}{\sum_{j=1}^{c} \left(\frac{d_{ik}}{d_{jk}} \right)^{\frac{2}{m'-1}}}, \qquad (8)$$

$\forall i$, With $d_{ik} = \parallel X_k - m_i \parallel^2$, subject to $\sum_{i=1}^{c} \mu_{ik} = 1$, $\forall k$. and $0 < \sum_{k=1}^{N} \mu_{ik} < N$, $\forall k$.

The algorithm proceeds as seen in Figure 4.

EXPERIMENTAL RESULTS

Data Source

The data set describes the page visits of users who have visited msnbc.com. The data is taken from Internet Information Server (IIS) logs for msnbc. com and news-related portions of msn.com for the entire day of September, 28, 1999 (Pacific Standard Time). Since this data is a Bench-Mark data available in the UCI Repository we applied the proposed algorithms to this bench mark web log data. Each sequence in the dataset corresponds to page views of a user during that twenty-four hour period. Each event in the sequence corresponds to a user's request for a page. Requests are recorded at the level of page category. The categories are "frontpage", "news", "tech", "local", "opinion", "on-air", "misc", "weather", "health", "living", "business", "sports", "summary", "bbs" (bulletin board service), "travel", "msn-news", and "msn-sports". Number of URLs per category ranges from 10 to 5000. For the purpose of evaluating the performance and the effectiveness of the proposed K-Means Biclustering, Rough Biclustering and Fuzzy Biclustering algorithms, experiments were conducted with preprocessed web access

Figure 4. The Fuzzy Biclustering

Algorithm: Fuzzy Biclustering

---

1. Pick the initial means m_i, i=1... c. choose values for fuzzfier m′ and $\in$ threshold

   Set the iteration counter t=1.

2. Repeat Steps 3-4, by incrementing t, until $\mid \mu_{ik}(t) - \mu_{ik}(t-1) \mid > \in$.

3. Compute μ_{ik} by   Eqn. (5) for c clusters and N bisets.

4. Update means m_i by   Eqn. (4)

---

logs of www.msnbc.com which is available in UCI repository.

In order to evaluate our proposed algorithms, we applied it to the Web log collected from msnbc. com by taking categories of pages visited by 250, 500, 750, and 1000 users.

User Profiles

User profiling on the web consists of studying important characteristics of the web visitors. The clustering process is an important step in establishing user profiles. Some of the discovered user profiles obtained using Fuzzy Biclustering algorithm, which is given in Figure 4, is summarized in Table 1 with the Fuzzy Membership Values. These user profiles are obtained by performing

Biclustering of pages visited by only 100 users from the web log file.

Validity Measures

We used two measures to evaluate the performance of the proposed Biclustering algorithm. Root Mean Square (RMSE) and Mean Absolute Error (MAE) (de Castro, de Franca, Ferreira, & Von Zuben, 2007):

Root Mean Square Error (RMSE)

$$RMSE = \sqrt{\frac{\sum (x - x')^2}{N}}$$

Table 1. User profile with fuzzy membership values

Cluster	Size	URLs/Profile	Fuzzy Membership values
1	56	'frontpage'	0.3981
		'news'	0.2283
		'sports	0.3736
2	73	'news'	0.0883
		'local'	0.3078
		'on-air'	0.2831
		'misc'	0.0883
		'weather'	0.2506
3	32	'opinion'	0.2173
		'msn-news'	0.2634
		'summary'	0.082
		'bbs'	0.2021
		'travel'	0.2352
4	15	local'	0.2762
		'msn-news'	0.2143
		'business'	0.2243
		'health'	0.071
		'living'	0.2142
5	24	'msn-sports'	0.7717
		'sports'	0.2283

Table 2. Comparison of performance measures for fuzzy biclustering

No. of Users	No. of Bisets	No. of Clusters	Root Mean Square Error	Mean Absolute Error
250	1190	17	0.0124	0.0134
500	1554	20	0.0060	0.0072
750	1980	23	0.0033	0.0040
1000	2442	25	0.0020	0.0025

Mean Absolute Error (MAE)

$$MAE = \frac{\sum |x - x'|}{N}$$

where x is the users with similar interest x' is the centroid of the cluster and N is the number of users with similar interest in a cluster.

Table 2 shows the experimental results for the RMSE and MAE validity measures for Fuzzy Biclustering. Table 3 shows the Performance of the K-Means Biclustering, Rough Biclustering and Fuzzy Biclustering Algorithm with two different Validity Measures. Figures 5 to 7 show RMSE and MAE values for K-Means Biclustering, Rough Biclustering and Fuzzy Biclustering

respectively. Figure 8 shows the optimal number of bisets generated by the proposed Biclustering algorithm for various datasets taken. Figure 9 and Figure 10 show the comparison of the proposed algorithms using the validity measures RMSE and MAE for various sizes of data sets respectively.

CONCLUSION

This paper has proposed an integrated model combining user and page clustering techniques for web page access prediction. The biclusters, contrasted with classical clustering, gives a much higher flexibility on dealing with data sets, as the clusterization is not restricted only to users, but involves the pages as well. In order to perform

Table 3. Performance of the K-Means Biclustering, Rough Biclustering, Fuzzy Biclustering algorithms

S. No	No. of Users	No. of Bisets	No. of Clusters	Proposed Biclustering Algorithms	Root Mean Square Error (RMSE)	Mean Absolute Error (MAE)
1	250	1190	17	K-Means Biclustering	1.0893	2.3733
				Rough Biclustering	0.5277	1.0381
				Fuzzy Biclustering	0.0124	0.0134
2	500	1554	20	K-Means Biclustering	1.0994	2.4175
				Rough Biclustering	0.4711	1.0054
				Fuzzy Biclustering	0.0060	0.0072
3	750	1980	23	K-Means Biclustering	1.0320	2.1301
				Rough Biclustering	0.4576	1.1303
				Fuzzy Biclustering	0.0033	0.0040
4	1000	2442	25	K-Means Biclustering	1.0346	2.1406
				Rough Biclustering	0.3364	0.6440
				Fuzzy Biclustering	0.0020	0.0025

Figure 5. RMSE and MAE values for K-Means Biclustering

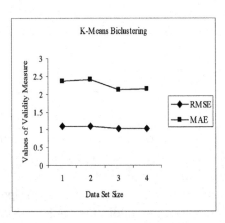

Figure 8. Optimal Number of Bisets

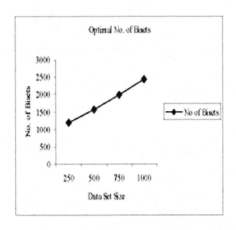

Figure 6. RMSE and MAE values for Rough Biclustering

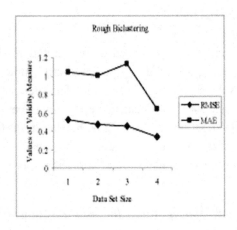

Figure 9. Comparison of RMSE

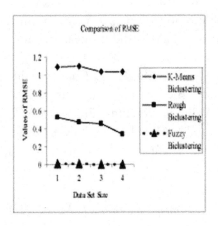

Figure 7. RMSE and MAE values for Fuzzy Bi-clustering

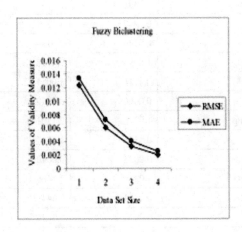

Figure 10. Comparison of MAE

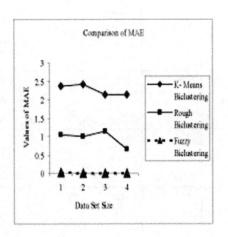

the generation of the biclusters, we proposed the K-Means Biclustering, Rough Biclustering and Fuzzy Biclustering that are capable of providing several diverse and high quality solutions. Diversity happens when there is little overlap among a set of biclusters, but this overlap is necessary as there are several groups that has some pages in common. Rough biclustering approach captures the overlapping user and page access patterns. Fuzzy biclustering approach captures the uncertainty that prevails in user access patterns and becomes more suitable for web page prediction. The Fuzzy integrated model has been demonstrated to be more accurate than Rough integrated model and conventional integrated model. These Biclustering approaches can be applied to find the user access patterns in any contemporary websites and web pages can be predicted easily.

REFERENCES

Chakraborty, S., Dom, B., Gibson, D., Kleinberg, J., Kumar, S., & Raghavan, P. (1999). Mining the link structure of the world wide web. *IEEE Computational Intelligence, 32*(8), 60–67.

de Castro, P. A. D., de França, O. F., Ferreira, H. M., & Von Zuben, F. J. (2007). Applying Biclustering to Perform Collaborative Filtering. In *Proceedings of the Seventh International Conference on Intelligent Systems Design and Applications* (pp. 421-426).

Etzioni, O. (1996). The World Wide Web: Quagmire or gold mine. *Communications of the ACM, 39*(11), 65–68. doi:doi:10.1145/240455.240473

Fu, Y., Sandhu, K., & Shi, M. (2000). Clustering of web users based on access patterns. In *Proceedings of the 1999 KDD Workshop on Web Mining* (LNAI 1836, pp. 21-38).

Han, J., & Kambert, M. (2001). *Data mining: Concepts and Techniques*. San Francisco: Morgan Kaufmann.

Koutsonikola, V. A., & Vakali, A. (2009). A fuzzy bi-clustering approach to correlate web users and pages. *International Journal of Knowledge and Web Intelligence, 1*(1-2), 3–23. doi:doi:10.1504/IJKWI.2009.027923

Liu, H., & Keselj, V. (2007). Combined mining of web server logs and web contents for classifying user navigation patterns and predicting users' future requests. *Data & Knowledge Engineering, 61*(2), 304–330. doi:doi:10.1016/j.datak.2006.06.001

Liu, L., Chen, J., & Song, H. (2002, June). The Research of Web mining. In *Proceedings of the 4th World Congress on Intelligent Control and Automation* (Vol. 3, pp. 2333-2337).

Maes, P. (1994). Agents that reduce work and information overload. *Communications of the ACM, 37*(7), 30–40. doi:doi:10.1145/176789.176792

Nanopoulos, A., Papadopoulos, A., & Manolopoulos, Y. (2006, August 20). Nearest Biclusters Collaborative Filtering. In *Proceedings of WEB-KDD'06*, Philadelphia.

Nasraoui, O., Rojas, C., & Cardona, C. (2006). A framework for mining evolving trends in Web data streams using dynamic learning and retrospective validation. *Computer Networks, 50*, 1488–1512. doi:doi:10.1016/j.comnet.2005.10.021

Pensal, R. G., Robardet, C., & Boulicaut, J. F. (2005). A Bi-Clustering framework for categorical data. In A. Jorge et al. (Eds.), *Proceedings of PKDD*, (LNAI 3721, pp. 643-650).

Perkowitz, M., & Etzioni, O. (2000). Towards adaptive web sites: Conceptual framework and case study. *Artificial Intelligence, 118*, 245–275. doi:doi:10.1016/S0004-3702(99)00098-3

Peters, G. (2006). Some refinements of rough k-means clustering. *Pattern Recognition, 39*, 1481–1491. doi:doi:10.1016/j.patcog.2006.02.002

Smith, K. A., & Ng, A. (2003). Web page clustering using a self-organizing map of user navigation patterns. *Decision Support Systems*, *35*(2), 245–256. doi:doi:10.1016/S0167-9236(02)00109-4

Song, Q., & Shepperd, M. (2006). Mining web browsing patterns for E-commerce. *Computers in Industry*, *57*, 622–630. doi:doi:10.1016/j.compind.2005.11.006

Voges, K. E., Pope, N. K. L., & Brown, M. R. (2002). Cluster analysis of marketing data examining online shopping orientation: A comparison of k-means and rough clustering approaches. In Abbass, H. A., Sarker, R. A., & Newton, C. S. (Eds.), *Heuristics and Optimization for Knowledge Discovery* (pp. 207–224). Hershey, PA: IGI Global.

Xiao, J., Zhang, Y., Jia, X., & Li, T. (2001) Measuring similarity of interests for clustering web-users. In *Proceedings of the 12th Australian Database Conference* (pp. 107-114).

Yan, T., Jacobsen, M., Garcia-Molina, H., & Dayal, U. (1996). From user access patterns to dynamic hypertext linking. In *Proceedings of the 5th International World Wide Web conference*, Paris.

Zamir, O., & Etzioni, O. (1998). Web Document Clustering: A Feasibility Demonstration. In *Proceedings of the 21st International ACM SIGIR Conference on Research and Development in Information Retrieval*, Seattle, WA.

This work was previously published in the International Journal of Information Technologies and Systems Approach, Volume 4, Issue 1, edited by Frank Stowell and Manuel Mora, pp. 53-66, copyright 2011 by IGI Publishing (an imprint of IGI Global).

Section 2
Security and Privacy

Chapter 16
Preventative Actions for Enhancing Online Protection and Privacy

Steven Furnell
University of Plymouth, UK

Rossouw von Solms
Nelson Mandela Metropolitan University, South Africa

Andy Phippen
University of Plymouth, UK

ABSTRACT

Many citizens rely upon online services, and it is certain that this reliance will increase in the future. However, they frequently lack a solid appreciation of the related safety and security issues, and can be missing out on an essential aspect of awareness in everyday life. Indeed, users are often concerned about online threats, but it would be stretching the point to claim that they are fully aware of the problems. Thus, rather than actually protecting themselves, many will simply accept that they are taking a risk. This paper examines the problem of establishing end-user eSafety awareness, and proposes means by which related issues can be investigated and addressed. Recognising that long-term attitudes and practices will be shaped by early experiences with the technology, it is particularly important to address the issue early and improve awareness amongst young people. However, the problem is unlikely to be addressed via the approaches that would traditionally be applied with adult users. As such, the paper examines information gathering and awareness-raising strategies drawing from qualitative methodologies in the social sciences, whose pluralistic approach can be effectively applied within school contexts.

INTRODUCTION

Many citizens in developed countries are now dependent on online services to some extent. Few individuals in any modern society would be able to 'survive' today without utilizing online services in one or other form on a regular basis. Our personal lives are controlled to a large extent by cellular communication technologies, email, and other Internet services. Few employees in the corporate and business worlds today would not be classified as information workers, meaning that

DOI: 10.4018/978-1-4666-1562-5.ch016

these employees are engaging with online systems to conduct their day-to-day tasks. The fact that users often have to manage dozens of user-IDs, passwords and PINs (Ross, 2003) to control access to various types of technology (e.g. websites, mobile devices, bank cards, personal and company PCs) demonstrates that most people today have a strong reliance upon online services.

As more world citizens are making use of online banking, Internet shopping and online social networking, more personal and financial details become accessible. In 2006 it was reported that 178 000 people in Britain alone fell victim to identity theft, with the problem of identity fraud costing in the order of £1.7 billion a year (Macintyre, 2007). These facts make it clear that online safety or eSafety is an international problem. It is not only a workplace problem, but a personal one too. As well as the adult population, children are introduced to online services at a very young age. Many children in the developed world have got a cellular phone and a bank card, with a large proportion also active on online social network sites where lots of information, including personal, is shared and exchanged daily. In addition, young people are more active in peer to peer file sharing than the older generations. If one considers the amount of illegal music and video files that are shared and distributed amongst young people, the situation is definitely of great concern (Mitropoulou & Triantafyllidis, 2008).

It is particularly concerning that the cavalier attitudes established at a young age might engender similar lax practices in later life. Once they develop into the working world, they are dealing with corporate, rather than personal, information, where significantly more is at stake. The corporate world has already reacted, as a study from 2006 pointed out that employers are less likely to hire such risky individuals, indicating that someone with "relaxed attitudes toward illegal downloads could put future job opportunities at risk" (Bush, 2006). Therefore, although more citizens are get-

ting more dependent on online services by the day, ignorance of eSafety and bad online habits can definitely inhibit the proliferation of secure online services and safe information sharing. It is imperative that education and awareness-raising efforts are made to increase the levels of eSafety by improving the behaviour of people using online services and systems. This appropriate behaviour should form part of an eSafe culture being cultivated amongst all online citizens. However, by the time users enter the workplace it may already be too late. Companies have realized that an increase in information security awareness and skills are not addressing the problem satisfactorily. Something is needed to change the behaviour of their future staff at an earlier stage. To quote the 2008 Information Security Breaches Survey from the UK's Department for Business Enterprise and Regulatory Reform: "Only when behaviour changes, do businesses realise the benefits of a security-aware culture" (PriceWaterhouseCoopers, 2008). The question is; *how can this be done effectively?*

PHYSICAL AND FINANCIAL SECURITY – AN ANALOGY

Most people, even children, have developed some customs to protect and secure their personal finances. People realize that money is an asset that needs to be protected. They also realize that many threats are looming that might result in financial harm to an individual. Therefore, most individuals act and behave in a certain manner to ensure their financial assets are properly protected. This secure way of behaviour is taught to youngsters by their parents or guardians from a very young age. Even small children will show some discipline and behave in a relatively secure manner to protect their personal funds. It is fair to suggest that most people have got some form of *financial* security culture. This culture is definitely carried over from one generation to another and normally the same principles that apply at a personal level are also carried over to the workplace and/or social environments. Such a financial security culture also dictates the behaviour and actions of individuals.

Similarly, most people have been taught to protect themselves and their belongings from physical damage or loss. People know how to act or behave so as not to put themselves, their personal belongings or those of some other party at risk. Again, this behaviour is passed on from one generation to another and adapted according to threats that change from time to time. Thus, some form of *physical* security culture also seems to be evident in most communities and individuals.

In both cases above it can be claimed that:

- Such cultures have developed over hundreds of years
- The culture might adapt from time to time as threats change
- The culture is definitely passed on from one generation to another
- Education and training do play a major role in cultivating such a culture and
- The concepts are transferable, and individuals normally apply the same principles in the workplace as they apply to their personal situations.

The idea is to cultivate an *information* security culture in the same manner. Unfortunately some barriers exist why the situation cannot merely be extrapolation onto an information security scenario. Some of the apparent reasons are:

- Information and communication technology is a very young discipline and no prevailing related security culture exist as yet
- The 'parent' generation of today is arguably less ICT literate than the younger generation and no culture exists as yet to pass onto the younger generation
- It seems as if individuals do not necessarily apply the same principles in the workplace as they apply to their personal situation.

The rest of this paper considers in more depth the reasons that may be preventing the effective online security and privacy practice, focusing in particular upon the situation amongst school children. In examining these issues, the paper draws upon a number of sources with which the authors have been involved:

1. The Trustguide project (Lacohee, Crane, & Phippen, 2006) which carried out a detailed qualitative exploration of attitudes toward Internet security and trust through focus group activities with 500 members of the public.

2. An end user survey study (Furnell, Bryant, & Phippen, 2007) of a population of 415 respondents within the UK that used a questionnaire to collect data about home security practice and beliefs.

3. A questionnaire based survey of school teachers (Phippen, Furnell, & Richardson, 2008), which assessed the confidence of educators in equipping young people with appropriate awareness of Internet safety issues.

4. The eSafety Ambassadors project (Atkinson, Furnell, & Phippen, 2009), an ongoing project, which examines the effectiveness of peer education on the education of Internet security and safety with young people. The work uses a mixed methodological approach to evaluate attitudes and assess impact. Key data collection techniques were focus groups and content analysis, as well as Internet based techniques to evaluate students involved in the project and their public online profiles.

Across these three projects there is strong complementary data to examining public perceptions of Internet protection with both the adult and youth population. While each project has published work related to findings specific to their datasets, a meta-analysis, as presented in the remainder of this paper, presents a strong case for the need for public education and potential techniques to achieve this.

EXAMINING ATTITUDES TO SECURITY AWARENESS

Having identified concerns about the current level of individual security culture, this section considers related evidence drawn from current users. At this stage, focus is given to the views and behaviours of the adult population, and as the first example suggests, a prevailing view is often confusion:

I have a virus check and it pops up and it says 'you are at risk from an incoming...' and what it means is that the application that I'm using is wanting to contact the Internet, you know it might be something perfectly harmless and innocuous or it might be that someone is trying to come in and read my keyboard and steal my password and my money, if I had any. But that's the thing, it's that ignorance and you don't know whether to say 'accept' or 'decline.

The above quotation is taken from the Trustguide project, which examined end user attitudes toward online engagement. The project carried out a large number of focus groups with a range of UK citizens, from those extremely experienced in online activities to complete novices. The project identified a number of alarming behaviour among end users when determining whether they wish to engage with an online service.

It would seem that factors such as perceived benefit and "informed" risk play a significant part in the engagement process. Prior to making a decision to engage with a service, the end user carries out a personal risk assessment. There are a number of factors that contribute to this assessment, such as familiarity/awareness of brand, likely impact of the transaction going wrong, the significance of personal benefit from engaging (for example, saving money in a financial transaction compared to an offline purchase). However, exploration of attitudes within the Trustguide project highlighted that the knowledge foundation from which many citizens build the online lives is extremely unstable. When exploring where people gained awareness regarding online engagement and IT security, the responses were generally around self-discovery, peers or media sources. There were few people within the Trustguide process that referred to any source of formal education, whether this was at school, or through post-school training courses or professional consultation.

I think, it's like when you were a kid, and your mother said don't touch the oven because it's hot, you still touched the oven just to find out if it is hot, and it is only when you burnt your fingers that you then think that next time I won't.

Looking beyond the Trustguide findings, it remains clear that the current adult population clearly has a long way to go with eSafety, and their security practices are often at odds with the claimed level of awareness. For example, a survey of 415 home users (conducted by the authors during 2006) revealed that while 99% claimed to understand the term 'virus' and 93% claimed to use anti-virus protection, only 63% indicated that they kept this protection up to date (Furnell et al., 2007). Thus, approximately one third of those who have taken then step to protect themselves have failed to follow things through properly. Similarly, only 38% claimed to keep their operating system updated; a factor that could very easily leave them open to exploitation, particularly in conjunction with outdated anti-virus protection. Although the survey did not specifically explore the reasons for this, they are likely to be a combination of ignorance (i.e. unawareness that the protection required updating) or neglect (i.e. recognising the issue but not having the inclination to address it, perhaps because they felt that they had spent enough time and effort on security already). These findings are by no means unique, and further supporting evidence can be found in a US study conducted by McAfee and the National Cyber Security Alliance (McAfee-NCSA, 2007). Rather than simply gauging user opinions, their approach took an interesting further step of auditing the protection being employed on the respondents' PCs. A total of 378 homes were surveyed, revealing some worrying disparity between the security measures that the users thought they were using and how well they are actually using it. As an example, while 70% believed they were using anti-spyware, only 55% actually had such protection installed. Moreover, even when protection existed on the systems, it was not necessarily being used or used properly. For instance, although 81% of systems had a firewall, it was only enabled on 64% of them. Similarly, while 94% had an antivirus package, many were effectively out-of-date, with only 51% having updated the signatures within the previous week. With thousands of new malware strains appearing each month, such infrequent update leaves a significant window of vulnerability.

Our research would suggest there is cause for serious concern in the security awareness of the adult population and the sources of education they use in developing their own knowledge. The concept of an over-confident population is something that comes out from both focus group and survey activity. Over 60% of the 415 respondents in our home user survey felt that they had the required knowledge to protect themselves from online threats. Yet, when asked about sources of security information and advice, they were almost as likely to ask a "friend or relative" (41%) as they were to consult an IT professional (43%) or an online information resource (43%). More worrying was that although online information resources were a significant source of knowledge for many people, the information on such sites was not valued. On average, only approximately a third of those respondents who had visited specified awareness-raising websites said they had found the information useful.

In a society where it would seem that security awareness is something that is acquired in an ad-hoc manner, rather than viewed as an essential life skill, the above findings highlight the power of the peer experience. Let us take the often used comparison between driving a car and using a computer; would we expect a similar approach to those learning to drive? Would a population who relied upon their peers to help them develop an understanding of how a motor vehicle operates, and how it can be driven safely; view this as an acceptable form of education? Yet, in the IT world one might argue that the environment is far less safe than the motoring one. While the environment in which a motor car exists is relatively stable (roads, behaviour of the machinery, signage, legislative control are all standardised and familiar to the road user) the IT environment, and the threats therein, are constantly changing.

THE AWARENESS OF THE NEW GENERATION

A recent report by Accenture (2008) examined attitude toward online life by what they referred to as "Millennials" (citizens aged between 17 and 27). The results showed that this generation is even more reliant on technology for communication that its predecessors and has less regard for the formal control of technology, and little education around its use in a workplace environment. The survey showed that 26% of working Millennials wrote openly about themselves and friends online, and 17% openly shared details of their life online. Concepts of privacy seem to be becoming eroded at exactly the same time as data exploitation threats (such as identity theft) are on the increase. The same study also revealed that the same users have a strong desire to make their own technology choices. For example, over 20% were dissatisfied with mobile technologies provided by their employers, and many consequently used their personal devices for work-related activities, (indeed 39% of 18–22-year-old respondents indicated that they used their own phones without employer support). The findings collectively paint a worrying picture, suggesting a tangible population of users that do not have an adequate appreciation of privacy and protection, and yet seek to select their own technology, on which they may then expose someone else's data.

The authors' research would certainly support the concerns of the Accenture report. Within the Trustguide work, it was interesting to observe that parents who attended the focus groups raised concerns for the behaviour of their children online:

There are people who are scared of computers and worried about doing stuff but I look at my daughter using a computer, no fear whatsoever, do anything and she's eight.

That's the trouble I have with my kids, they're not frightened of what they download.

Yet we have already identified a population that is ill at ease with their own online protection, let alone serving as role models for the next generation. This prompted further research, firstly examining attitudes of young people to their online behaviour, and then an examination of the education system that is expected to develop their life skills and make them ready to become adults in modern society.

The main source of data for the examination of young people's attitudes was further focus group activity with a series of school children aged between 13 and 18. Overall around 100 young people participated in these activities, which explored knowledge on online protection and attitudes toward the engagement with online services.

An initial activity with the young people worked through the scenario of signing up to a social networking site. There were some encouraging signs with this activity – many were aware of risks in posting up personal information, and some even developed their own strategies when registering, such as providing false information, or using multiple email addresses (one for personal communication, one for online services).

However, the activity also highlighted that this generation is less anxious about online engagement and has a somewhat lackadaisical attitude toward online identity. For example, many would have multiple profiles on the same social networking site, simply because they had forgotten their login credentials for a previous account.

Discussion around IT security concepts such as antivirus and pop-up blocking all suggested that while younger users were aware of the terms, the majority were not familiar with the consequences that the security safeguards sought to prevent. Moreover, they often appeared to underestimate the significance from their own perspective:

There is always the opportunity that somebody is going to hack into it and get what little personal information you have put on there. But so long as you are careful about what you do put there, then there is nothing they can do with it.

However, what was possibly most alarming was that in the event of potential harmful instances occurring, they seemed to have little regard for the severity of the threat, or what to do about it. From the discussions with around one hundred young people, we identified three cases of attempted grooming or stalking. However, in each of these cases, the subject of the stalking did not consider this to be a potentially vulnerable position – they acknowledged that they had accepted a friend request from someone they did not know, but still believed they were of similar age.

Every time I went on MSN, I found out she was very boring, so I didn't really talk to her and then 'Hello. How are you?' Oh God. Block her. She was a complete stalker. 'Oh we could meet up sometime.' No!

In each case the relationship was terminated through the blocking of an account, and in no instance was the behaviour reported to anyone other than (in one case) a parent. Perhaps most worryingly (and again a clear demonstration of the lack of perception among the older generation), the parent did not consider the behaviour serious enough to report to police, the child was simply told to ignore the person.

Having established various indications of their stance on eSafety and security, we also sought to determine where these young people had developed their knowledge about Internet threats, online security and the potential for harm. Perhaps unsurprisingly, the majority were self taught, or had learned from, and with, peers. In the majority of cases, participants said they could not turn to their parents for help, because they had less understanding about online issues than the young person themselves. However, more worrying, was that there did not seem to be much coverage within their formal education. The following response was typical:

You don't get any lessons about the Internet. It's just about work.

THE AWARENESS OF THE EDUCATORS

The work with young people has demonstrated a lack of formal education around Internet safety. This is, obviously, a major concern for those concerned with a secure online world, and we wished to formally investigate the trend we had identified in this lack of Internet awareness education. As such, a final layer of our research was to examine the understanding of Internet protection by the educators of the younger generation.

A survey was conducted amongst ICT teachers across a number of regions in the South West of the UK, with a focus on secondary (11-18) education (Phippen et al., 2008). As well as investigating how Internet awareness was taught in the classroom, this also examined the teachers' own security awareness and knowledge. While some aspects of security seemed familiar (e.g. virus

protection, where 85% stated they were confident in protection), others, such as ID theft (less than 50% confident), or botnets (26%) and pharming (27%), gave greater cause for concern. There were also varying levels of confidence between awareness and ability to protect where, in some cases, it would seem that respondents may have heard of terms, but had little depth of knowledge regarding protection.

In developing the research, we examined the coverage of security issues in the curriculum. Initial results showed some encouraging signs, such as mainstream aspects such as viruses, safe practice, information disclosure and identity theft, being covered in more the 60% of respondents' teaching. However, when examining teachers' beliefs about the coverage, we were met with something of a conflict, with more than 60% saying they felt that these subjects were not covered in enough depth:

The National Curriculum and our exam spec (DiDA) do not require us to address these issues. We teach personal protection as part of our own take on duty of care, but we're so pushed for time to cover everything else that if it is not required we don't do it.

It was commendable that, in some 46% of cases, teachers taught away from the curriculum in order to ensure that Internet protection was effectively covered. However, as an interesting aside, while most teachers believed that it to be the responsibility of the education system to cultivate Internet awareness, a significant minority (25%) believed that the responsibility lay with parents. Obviously this is cause for concern, given that our previous work had demonstrated that the parental generation was ill-equipped to protect themselves, let alone advise and guide their children.

The exploration of the attitudes of young people, and that of their teachers, has highlighted a fragmented, informal, inconsistent approach to the education of the Millennial generation. Yet, as the Accenture report has shown, this is a generation with less regard for Internet privacy, and less concern about online engagement (indeed, most expect it as a right). If we are proposing that security and online protection are essential life skills, in a similar way to learning to drive, how to cook and the like, there are not, as yet, effective practices in place to achieve this.

PURSUING NEW MODELS OF EDUCATION

In view of the issues observed thus far, it is clear that efforts are needed to ensure that eSafety engagement can occur at earlier stages. With this in mind, this section highlights the approaches that have been pursued by the authors.

The theoretical foundation for this work lies in the area of peer education. Tynes (2007) identifies the potential for working directly with young people to develop education around Internet safety. Further work by (Sharples et al., 2008) also supports the premise of working with young people, where their work in this area highlighted that this generation are well aware of the dangers yet frustrated that they are not engaged in the education of others.

Peer education has a substantial amount of literature around the social care and health education fields. Dodge and Prinstein (2008) cite "persistent findings in the social science literature" to show that peers have a positive impact on each other's behaviour due to common understanding and social contact. A youth project in the UK (Davies & Cranston, 2008) on behalf of the UK National Youth Agency suggests peer education and mentoring works with young people by providing reflective space within the learning experience.

By drawing upon the findings from our previous eSafety research, and underpinning this with a theoretical basis in peer education, materials have been developed to seed awareness-raising

activities with young people in the school context. Building upon existing relationships with schools in the South West of the UK we have invited participation in the development of a peer-education project aimed at developing e-safety resources for young people in the 14 to 16 age range. At the time of writing this has involved eight schools, and a series of further focus groups have been held aimed at observing young people's dialogue regarding online safety and security. A total of 202 participants were involved across these sessions, which sought to explore a number of issues relating to their current engagement with eSafety, including:

- How they currently perceive and understand their online risks;
- Good and bad practices when going online;
- Their understanding and utilisation of current resources and tools for limiting these risks;
- Identifying what resources might better support their e-safety learning.

Following each school visit, student representatives were invited to become 'eSafety Ambassadors' for their school, acting as the focal point for eSafety promotion and awareness-raising amongst their peers. The research team has worked with the Ambassadors in each school to develop their own resources and approaches for motivating and informing their peers about the issues surrounding eSafety. In addition, awareness-raising and information-sharing activities have been pursued via a project website and workshops in order to bring the Ambassadors from different schools together to enable them to share outputs and experiences.

Key factors of the approach are considered to be:

- Enabling a greater understanding of young people's attitudes toward online safety and security. The associated findings will feed into both the awareness activities within the project and into published materials arising from the work.

- By targeting the 14 to 16 age range the dissemination of Internet Safety practices into the younger years at the school can be more effective, because these are young people more likely to remain at the school for a period of time.

- The use of peer-education lends itself to more engagement from this age range in a fashion suited to their context and overcomes the perception of an unwelcome restrictive approach.

- A supportive environment can be provided not only between experts in the field of Internet safety, but also between other young people acting as e-safety Ambassadors within the South West area.

- The supportive environment will provide the opportunity for young people to initiate and take steps to protect themselves online, in addition to minimising known risks and educating young people in a manner which encourages positive and responsible use of the online environment.

Of course, the essence of the above approach has still placed reliance upon appropriate persons to initiate the dialogue and to speed the process with the Ambassadors. In the current project this role has been fulfilled by the researchers, but this would clearly be an impractical basis for large-scale deployment. As such, means are still required in order to ensure that teachers can assume a position of authority in this domain. Indeed, in the UK the Byron report has called for the Government to make eSafety a priority for the continuing professional development of teachers (Byron, 2008). However, the vision of Byron seems a long way off. If we are expecting schools to become the hub of eSafety knowledge within the community, then the research suggests that a

significant amount of effort needs to be invested even before a baseline of Internet awareness is prevalent within them.

Phippen (2009) worked with schools and eSafety policy and practice, and one clear finding was that eSafety provision was carried out at different stages in the education process, and in different subject areas (i.e. in some schools it was delivered as part of the ICT curriculum, in others it was deliver as part of "social" education, while some viewed it as "extra curricular"). In exploring practice among 62 different UK schools, it was apparent that while many staff felt that eSafety education was important, they did not know how to tackle it and or have the confidence to deliver effectively.

While the Byron review resulted in the formation of the UK Council for Child Internet Safety (http://www.education.gov.uk/ukccis/), which was expected to deliver the national coordination than many education professionals were asking for, the political influence over the body has meant the party politics has hampered any attempt for consistent delivery. Since the change of Government that resulted from the UK elections in May 2010, the organisation has not carried out any public facing activity. In addition, the intended change in the primary school curriculum that had been detailed by the previous Government was subsequently scrapped with no proposed alternative.

While this paper is not intended to be an exploration to educational policy in the UK it does highlight an issue facing those wishing to develop strategy to ensure a well informed and responsible end user population – public education efforts invariably rely on government intervention and the changes in party politics can severely hamper attempts to ensure consistent, research informed curriculum development. Indeed, the UK experience suggests that unlike other more established public awareness campaigns (e.g. road safety, drink driving, drugs, etc), online safety currently appears to be an issue whose perceived importance does not transcend political manifesto. As such it risks being sidelined or undermined by changes in policy, and related campaigns are consequently unable to have a sustained period of impact in order to effect a behavioural change.

CONCLUSION

From the perspective of most users looking to embrace the opportunities offered by IT and online services, security is a most unwelcome guest at the party. Indeed, having just bought a new PC or signed up for a new service, no-one wants to immediately have to start thinking about all the things that could go wrong with it. Nonetheless, security already represents an issue that users can ignore at their peril, and ensuring adequate awareness will be a key element of eSafety for the future. Moreover, the situation does not stand still and the threat landscape itself is still forming. As the technologies and services advance, so the users face new risks.

The lack of user awareness is a problem that cannot be solved via a single action. It requires a multi-pronged strategy that addresses both the next generation of users and those that are expected to educate them. Indeed, we find ourselves in a difficult transition phase in which our current educators have not grown up with the threats, but must become conversant with them in order to guide a generation that, without such support, will be poised to suffer significant problems. As such, we believe that an appropriate solution at this point is to encourage and enable young people to help themselves, and that (with appropriate seeding via core advice and material) a peer-led approach can help to embed an eSafe culture before users emerge into the workplace. At the same time, efforts need to be made to ensure that future generations of teachers are in a position to do the seeding work, and as such initiatives to increase the promotion of eSafety and security within teacher education programmes will place them in a better position to deliver such topics within the curricula.

ACKNOWLEDGMENT

The authors would like to acknowledge the work undertaken by Dr Shirley Atkinson and Ben Richardson, which contributed to some of the findings presented in this paper. This paper is based upon a development of work originally published by the authors in "Recognising and Addressing Barriers to eSafety and Security Awareness", which appeared in the Proceedings of IFIP TC 8 International Workshop on Information Systems Security Research (Cape Town, South Africa, 29-30 May 2009).

REFERENCES

Accenture. (2008). *"New-generation workers" want technology their way, Accenture survey finds.* Retrieved from http://newsroom.accenture.com/article_display.cfm?article_id=4767

Atkinson, S., Furnell, S. M., & Phippen, A. D. (2009, April 15-16). E-Safety and e-security: Raising security awareness among young people using peer education. In *Proceedings of the 8th Annual Security Conference*, Las Vegas, NV.

BERR. (2008). *2008 information security breaches survey (Tech. Rep. No. URN 08/788).* London, UK: Department for Business Enterprise & Regulatory Reform.

Bush, J. (2006). *Illegal downloads may deter future employers.* Retrieved from http://www.theeagleonline.com

Byron, T. (2008). *Safer children in a digital world: The report of the Byron review.* Retrieved from http://www.education.gov.uk/

Davies, T., & Cranston, P. (2008). *Youth work and social networking: Final research report.* Retrieved from http://blogs.nya.org.uk/ywsn/final-report.html

Dodge, K., & Prinstein, M. (2008). *Understanding peer influence in children and adolescents.* New York, NY: Guilford Publications.

Furnell, S. M., Bryant, P., & Phippen, A. D. (2007). Assessing the security perceptions of personal Internet users. *Computers & Security, 26*(5), 410–417. doi:10.1016/j.cose.2007.03.001

Lacohee, H., Crane, S., & Phippen, A. (2006). *Trustguide: Final report.* Retrieved from http://www.trustguide.org.uk/

Macintyre, B. (2007, November 24). *Do you need to change your PIN password, or just your attitude?* Retrieved from http://technology.timesonline.co.uk/tol/news/tech_and_web/the_web/article2933535.ece

McAfee-NCSA. (2007). *McAfee-NCSA online safety study – newsworthy analysis.* Retrieved from http://www.staysafeonline.org/

Mitropoulou, V., & Triantafylllidis, G. (2008). Primary school children's illegal Internet behaviour in Greece: A case study and suggestions. In *Proceedings of the World Conference on Educational Multimedia, Hypermedia and Telecommunications* (pp. 3838-3842).

Phippen, A. (2009). *E-safety policy: A survey of school e-safety policy and practice in the south west of the UK.* Exeter, UK: South West Grid for Learning.

Phippen, A., Furnell, S., & Richardson, B. (2008). *Sowing the seeds of eSafety.* Retrieved from http://www.bcs.org/server.php?show=ConWebDoc.22800&changeNav=8265

Ross, S. J. (2003). IS security matters: Identifier management. *Information Systems Control Journal, 3.*

Sharples, M. Graber., R, Harrison, C., & Logan, K. (2008). *E-Safety and Web 2.0.* Coventry, UK: Becta.

Tynes, B. M. (2007). Internet safety gone wild? Sacrificing the educational and psychosocial benefits of online social environments. *Journal of Adolescent Research, 22*(6). doi:10.1177/0743558407303979

This work was previously published in the International Journal of Information Technologies and Systems Approach, Volume 4, Issue 2, edited by Frank Stowell and Manuel Mora, pp. 1-11, copyright 2011 by IGI Publishing (an imprint of IGI Global).

Chapter 17

Minimising Collateral Damage:
Privacy–Preserving Investigative Data Acquisition Platform

Zbigniew Kwecka
Edinburgh Napier University, UK

William J. Buchanan
Edinburgh Napier University, UK

ABSTRACT

Investigators often define invasion of privacy as collateral damage. Inquiries that require gathering data from third parties, such as banks, Internet Service Providers (ISPs) or employers are likely to impact the relationship between the data subject and the data controller. In this research a novel privacy-preserving approach to mitigate collateral damage during the acquisition process is presented. This approach is based on existing Private Information Retrieval (PIR) protocols, which cannot be employed in an investigative context. This paper provides analysis of the investigative data acquisition process and proposes three modifications that can enable existing PIR protocols to perform investigative enquiries on large databases, including communication traffic databases maintained by ISPs. IDAP is an efficient Symmetric PIR (SPIR) protocol optimised for the purpose of facilitating public authorities' enquiries for evidence. It introduces a semi-trusted proxy into the PIR process in order to gain the acceptance of the general public. In addition, the dilution factor is defined as the level of anonymity required in a given investigation. This factor allows investigators to restrict the number of records processed, and therefore, minimise the processing time, while maintaining an appropriate level of privacy.

INTRODUCTION

Those who would give up essential Liberty, to purchase a little temporary safety, deserve neither Liberty nor Safety (Benjamin Franklin, 11 Nov 1755).

Since the September 11, 2001 many western governments have passed laws empowering public authorities with wider rights to gather operational data (Home Office, 2009; Swire & Steinfeld, 2002; Young, Kathleen, Joshua, & Meredith, 2006). For many years public opinion accepted the invasion

DOI: 10.4018/978-1-4666-1562-5.ch017

of personal privacy rights as the sacrifice needed to *fight the terror* (Rasmussen Reports, 2008). However, slowly, public opinion is shifting back to a state where such measures are considered unacceptable. This is shown by public opinion surveys, such as the one conducted by Washington Post in 2006 (Balz & Deane, 2006), where 32% of respondents agreed that they would prefer the federal government to ensure that privacy rights are respected rather than to investigate possible terrorist threats. This was an 11% increase from the similar survey conducted in 2003.

In the UK, the public authorities, including Police, request investigative data from third-parties on regular basis (Information Commissioner, 2008) and the data protection legislation allows for such requests, even without warrants (European Parliament, 1995; Home Office, 2007). Depending on the way these requests are performed, human and natural rights of the data-subject can be breached, and/or the investigation can be jeopardized (Kwecka, Buchanan, Spiers, & Saliou, 2008). A recent proposal by the UK government went further and recommended allowing the public authorities direct access to data held by Content Service Providers (CSPs), such as mobile telephony providers and Internet Service Providers (ISPs) (Home Office, 2009). According to the public consultation document, there were a few major motivating factors behind this proposal, these included: increasing access speeds to records; allowing for covert enquiries by anti-terror and national security agencies; lowering collateral damage to potential suspects under investigation; and enabling the analysis of data to facilitate the profiling of terrorists activities. In response, concerns were raised that if the proposal was implemented, it would thwart the privacy of Internet users around the globe, in order to increase the security of one nation. This research shows that most of the objectives set out in the proposal can still be achieved while maintaining high level of privacy. It is shown that an investigative system

can maintain the privacy of the data subjects and also preserve the confidentiality of investigations. However, both security and privacy must be built into the system at the design stage in order to achieve this (Swire & Steinfeld, 2002).

This paper gives an insight into use of Privacy Enhancing Technologies (PETs) in improving the current investigative data acquisition practices. The structure of this manuscript closely follows the methodology used to draw the final conclusions. First we provide a background to investigative data acquisition and to various privacy-preserving approaches to information retrieval. The analysis of the related research is presented and identifies an existing protocol, Private Equi-join (PE) that can facilitate efficient private database searching and information retrieval. It is also shown that the complexity of this protocol is lower that complexity of similar approaches, and for these reason the PE protocol is chosen as the base for the investigative data acquisition solution. This protocol is described and other commonly used privacy-preserving primitives that can be reused in order to build a platform suitable for investigative enquiries and the design considerations are discussed. The PE protocol is evaluated against the requirements derived from the literature described earlier. Finally, we describe the novelty of this paper – which are the three improvements needed to form an Investigative Data Acquisition Platform (IDAP) based on the PE protocol and the evaluation of IDAP is provided. IDAP is an efficient approach to maintain the secrecy, preserving the suspect's privacy and gaining the public's support for the PET technologies in digitalised investigative enquiries. The improvements include the introduction of the *dilution factor*, which is a numeric value that specifies the level of anonymity required for an investigation. Resultantly, the identity of a potential suspect can be hidden in a group smaller than the population, which permits the use of PIR systems with large databases. The second improvement is the technique for building complex privacy-preserving queries without affecting the complexity of the protocol. Finally, a semi-trusted proxy is introduced to the PE protocol, in order to ensure information theoretic privacy of data-subjects that are not the potential suspects.

BACKGROUND AND RELATED WORK

The background section is split into two parts. First the nature of public authorities' investigations is discussed together with the requirements for the way enquiries for data need to be handled. Then the second part of this section provides background to the private information retrieval protocols.

Data Acquisition

The public authorities are often required to carry out investigations based on data supplied by third parties. Such investigations may include fraud enquiries from Her Majesty Revenue and Customs (HMRC) tax office, solving a crime by Police, investigating alleged terrorism cases by Scotland Yard, or gathering health information about a patient at an Accident and Emergency (A&E) department (Home Office, 2009). The process of obtaining third party records is usually referred to as *data acquisition*. In the UK there are two major data acquisition legislations available to the public authorities, these are: the Data Protection Act 1998 (DPA) and The Regulation of Investigatory Powers Act 2000 (RIPA), but similar legislations can be found across Europe. Depending on the nature of the investigation, and the type of data required, the public authorities choose between the above legislations as grounds for their data acquisition requests. The main difference is that the voluntary disclosure mechanism of DPA can be used to gather general data records, while RIPA regulates requests for communica-

tion data. For any requests made under the DPA investigators need to provide justification for the acquisition requests and the dataholder can refuse providing data with no legal consequences if the request is not accompanied by a legal warrant (Spiers, 2009). Data acquisition notices served under RIPA do not need any form of justification and the dataholder will face a penalty if the relevant data is not provided to requesting public authority within two weeks. Still, the dataholder may choose to accept the penalty and refuse to provide the communication data (Home Office, 2007). Since, the searches of the communication data can be labour intensive, depending on the information system employed by a given CSP, the public authorities must make a contribution towards the costs incurred by the dataholder during fulfilling the data acquisition notice served under RIPA. Evidence handling guidelines suggest that any evidence collected may need to be presented in front of a court of law. If such requirement arises the electronic evidence must be provided as a true image of the data gathered (Association of Chief Police Officers, 2003). For these reason data acquired from third parties should be handled as potential evidence: no action taken should alter the data; and full audit trail needs to be kept for the processing of the data. Digital forensic literature suggests that in some cases there can be a number of suspects in a forensic inquiry and the enquiries may become complex (Palmer, 2001), thus a system for investigative data acquisition would need to accommodate for request with multiple interesting records and multiple selection criteria.

Retrieval of Private Information

Leaving the investigative context aside, the retrieval of information from a third-party in a private manner is a generic problem that has been researched for use in a variety of different scenarios. In the first instance, Private Information Retrieval (PIR) protocols were designed with a basic requirement of acquiring an interesting data record, from a dataholder (the *sender*) in a way that stops this dataholder from identifying which record is of interest to the requestor (the *chooser*). These protocols were not concerned with the secrecy of the records stored in the database, thus, in its least optimised state, a PIR could have been achieved by transferring the whole database from the *sender* to the *chooser*, as this would allow the *chooser* to retrieve the record in a private manner. Consequently, the main motivation behind PIR schemes is the achievement of minimal communicational and computational complexity (Ostrovsky & Skeith, 2007). A stronger notion than PIR is the *1-out-of-n* Oblivious Transfer (OT) primitive that allows the retrieval of a randomly-selected record from a dataset of *n* elements held by the *sender*, in a way that the *sender* cannot learn which record has been transferred, and the *chooser* cannot learn anything about other records in the dataset (Schneier, 1995). *1-out-of-n* OT protocols, that allow *chooser* to actively select a record to be retrieved, and that have linear or sub-linear complexity, can be referred to as Symmetric PIR (SPIR) protocols, as they protect the records of both parties during the information retrieval. These useful privacy-preserving data retrieval protocols can be employed in a variety of systems: electronic watch-lists of suspects (Frikken & Atallah, 2003); cooperative scientific computation (Du & Atallah, 2001; Goldwasser & Lindell, 2002); and on-line auctions (Cachin, 1999).

With the use of SPIR protocols a *chooser* would be capable of privately retrieving a record from the *sender's* database, by secretly referring to its index in this database. Such an index is expected to be publically available in an electronic catalogue or a directory (Aiello, Ishai, & Reingold, 2001; Bao & Deng, 2001). However, organisations, with large private databases, cannot be expected to maintain such freely available indexes. Also, it is expected that an investigator would normally refer to a suspect by a name, ID or phone number. For this reason, before the data can be received

using SPIR, a search would need to be performed by the *chooser* against the records in the *sender's* database. Such a private search operation requires a protocol that allows two parties to compare their values in a private manner. The protocols that are optimised to make comparisons for equality are referred to as Private Equality Test (PEqT) protocols, which are often based on commutative (Frikken & Atallah, 2003; Kwecka et al., 2008), or homomorphic, cryptosystems (Bao & Deng, 2001).

An interesting record can thus be located in a database using a *1-out-of-n* PEqT protocol and then retrieved with help of SPIR. Often each of these protocols would have a separate computationally expensive preparation phases, and such a solution would not be optimal. The exception to this rule is a range of protocols including: private intersection; private intersection size; and the PE defined in (Agrawal, Evfimievski, & Srikant, 2003). These protocols are based on commutative encryption, and thanks to the use of different properties of the underlying commutative algorithms, are capable of allowing for both private matching and private data retrieval. The operation of the PE is described previously together with a brief introduction of the cryptographic mechanisms used by this protocol, and other commonly used privacy-preserving primitives.

BUILDING BLOCKS

This section describes PE protocol that has been identified as suitable to facilitate private data acquisition enquiries. It relies on commutative cryptography, and thus some background for this is provided.

Commutative Cryptosystems

Many cryptographic applications employ sequential encryption and decryption operations under one or more underlying cryptosystems. The reasons to sequence (cascade) different crypto-graphic schemes together include: strengthening the resulting ciphertext; and achieving additional functionality, which is impossible under any given encryption scheme on its own (Shannon, 1949; Weis, 2006). A basic cascadable cryptosystem can consist of a number of encryption stages, where the output from one stage is treated as the input to another. In such a basic cascadable cryptosystem it is necessary to decrypt in the reverse order of encryption operations. However, a special class of sequential cryptosystems – commutative cryptosystems – allows for the decryption of a ciphertext in an arbitrary order. Thus, a ciphertext $c = e_b e_a(m)$ (c – ciphertext, m – plaintext, e – encryption operation under keys a and b), could be decrypted as either $m = d_b d_a(c)$ or as $m = d_a d_b(c)$. The advantages of such cryptosystems were widely promoted by Shamir (1980) and used in his, Rivest's and Aldman's, now classic, game of *mental poker*, employing the Three-Pass (3Pass) secret exchange protocol.

PH Encryption Algorithm

The most commonly used commutative crypto-system is based on the Pohling-Hellman (PH), asymmetric private key scheme (Pohling & Hellman, 1978). While the PH protocol influenced the design of the ever-popular Rivest-Shamir-Adleman (RSA) public key scheme (Rivest, Shamir, & Adleman, 1978), it has never become popular since it is asymmetric, and therefore, slow in comparison to other private key systems. The main strength of PH is that it is commutative for keys based on the same prime number, and that it allows for comparing the encrypted ciphertexts. Consequently, under PH the two ciphertexts $c_{ba} = e_b e_a(m)$ and $c_{ab} = e_a e_b(m)$ hiding the same plaintext m are equal (1), while this is not the case with ordinary encryption protocols, in which condition (2) is satisfied. The RSA shares these properties; however, it is unpractical and unsafe

to share the composite modulus of RSA between the communicating parties.

$$e_a e_b(m) = e_b e_a(m) \tag{1}$$

$$e_a e_b(m) \neq e_b e_a(m) \tag{2}$$

Thanks to these properties PH can be used in the 3Pass primitive that allows two parties to exchange data without exchange of keys, as well as to perform PEqT that permits private matching of data records.

Since, the popular public-key algorithm RSA is based on the PH scheme they are similar in operation, where the PH encryption and the decryption functions are shown in (3) and (4) respectively. In both PH and RSA the cryptographic operations are based on modular exponentiation, and different exponents (keys) are used for encryption (exponent e) and decryption (exponent d). However, in case of PH the operations are performed modulo a large prime number p, while the RSA uses a modulus made out of two prime numbers.

$$c = m^e \bmod p \tag{3}$$

$$m = c^d \bmod p \tag{4}$$

The encryption exponent e is chosen randomly from the range (5) and then it is used to calculate the decryption exponent d (6):

$$1 < e < p - 1 \tag{5}$$

$$de \equiv 1 \bmod(p-1) \Leftrightarrow d = e^{-1} \bmod(p-1) \tag{6}$$

Unlike it is the case with RSA in PH it is easy to calculate the decryption key knowing the modulus (prime p) and the encryption key, thus both keys should be kept secret. Hence, this is private key protocol. However, there is no harm in making the large prime p public. An adversary with the knowledge of the ciphertext c and the prime p would need to solve the following hard problem to break the PH protocol (Schneier, 1995):

$$e = \log_P C \bmod p \qquad (7)$$

It is also worth noting that both RSA and PH may leak some information about the plain text, i.e. its parity, and for these reason the inputs to these cryptographic operations should be almost random, such as secret encryption keys and hashed signatures.

Three Pass Protocol

The 3Pass protocol, shown in Figure 1, was intended to allow two parties to share a secret without exchanging any private or public key. The protocol was aimed at providing an alternative to public-key encryption and DH-like key negotiation protocols.

The operation of the protocol can be described using the following physical analogy:

1. Alice places a secret message m in a box and locks it with a padlock E_A.
2. The box is sent to Bob, who adds his padlock E_B to the latch, and sends the box back.
3. Alice removes her padlock and passes the box back to Bob.
4. Bob removes his padlock, and this enables him to read the message from inside the box.

There could be more parties, or encryption stages, involved in a 3Pass-like protocol, and this property makes it ideal for locking a plaintext message multiple times and then unlocking it in an arbitrary order.

Private Equality Test

PEqT protocols can be used to privately verify whether two secret inputs are equal or not. Agrawal, Evfimievski, and Srikant (2003) proposed one of the most scalable and flexible PEqT protocols for operations on datasets. The scheme is illustrated in Figure 2 and can be described in the following steps:

Figure 1. Three-pass secret exchange protocol. Three-Pass protocol allows for exchanging secrets without the requirement for the key exchange.

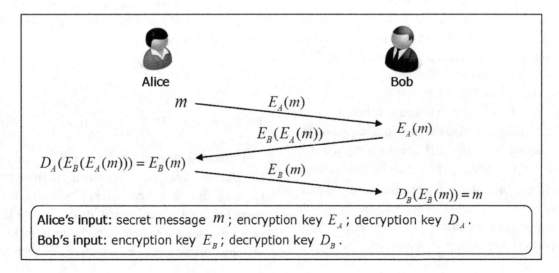

1. Alice encrypts her input and sends it to Bob.
2. Bob encrypts the ciphertext received from Alice and sends it back.
3. Bob encrypts his secret input and sends it to Alice.
4. Alice encrypts the ciphertext containing Bob's input.
5. Alice compares the two resulting ciphertexts, if they are equal then her and Bob's inputs are equal.
6. Alice may inform Bob about the result.

Private Equi-Join Protocol

PE protocol can enable two parties, the *chooser* and the *sender*, to privately compare their sets of unique values V_C and V_S, and allows the *chooser* to retrieve some extra information $ext(v)$ about records V_S, that match records V_C on a given parameter. The PE protocol involves the following steps:

1. Both parties apply hash function h to the elements in their sets, so that $X_C = h(V_C)$ and $X_S = h(V_S)$. Chooser picks a secret PH key E_C at random, and sender picks two PH keys E_S and E'_S, all from the same group Z_p^*.
2. Chooser encrypts entries in the set: $Y_C = E_C(X_C) = E_C(h(V_C))$.
3. Chooser sends to sender set Y_C, reordered lexicographically.
4. Sender encrypts each entry $y \in Y_C$, received from the chooser, with both E_S and E'_S and for each returns 3-tuple $\langle y, E_S(y), E'_S(y) \rangle$.
5. For each $h(v) \in X_S$, sender does the following:
   a. Encrypts $h(v)$ with E_S for use in equality test.
   b. Encrypts $h(v)$ with E'_S for use as a key to lock the extra information about v, $\kappa(v) = E'_S(h(v))$.

Figure 2. Private equality test. Private equality test allows two parties to test their inputs for equality, without revealing these inputs.

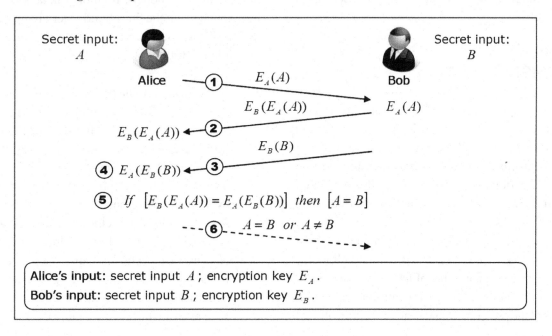

Alice's input: secret input A ; encryption key E_A.
Bob's input: secret input B ; encryption key E_B.

c.   Encrypts the extra information $ext(v)$: $c(v) = K(\kappa(v), ext(v))$ where K is a symmetric encryption function and $\kappa(v)$ is the key crafted in Stage 5b.

d.   Forms a pair $\langle E_S(h(v)), c(v) \rangle$. These pairs, containing a private match element and the encrypted extra information about record v, are then transferred to chooser.

6.   Chooser removes her encryption E_C from all entries in the 3-tuples received in Step 4 obtaining tuples α, β, and γ such that $\langle \alpha, \beta, \gamma \rangle = \langle h(v), E_S(h(v)), E'_S(h(v)) \rangle$. Thus, α is the hashed value $v \in V_C$, β is the hashed value v encrypted using E_S, and γ is the hashed value v encrypted using E'_S.

7.   Chooser sets aside all pairs received in Step 5, whose first entry is equal to one of the β tuples obtained in Step 6. Then using the γ tuples as symmetric keys it decrypts the extra information contained in the second entry in the pair $\langle E_S(h(v)), c(v) \rangle$.

The above protocol can perform the basic functions required for the purpose of investigative data acquisition. Its use in investigative scenarios described.

DESIGN

This section derives the requirements for an investigative data acquisition process from the literature discussed previously. The PE protocol has been initially selected as the most suitable base for the acquisition platform, thus, it is evaluated against these requirements and its shortcomings are identified.

According to the literature discussed, the protocol chosen for data gathering should allow for the retrieval of a number of interesting records at the time. If this is not the case multiple sequential runs of the protocol should bear low computational and communicational overhead. The protocol must leave the dataholder in control of the data, since the data retrieval can only be performed with the dataholder's consent. Taking into consideration that a dataholder has two weeks to provide the data under RIPA the computational complexity of the protocol can be reasonably large. However, shortening the time required by the data acquisition process is one of the main reasons that the government provide as a justification to the proposed modernisation of the process. Data records should be retrieved from the dataholder on a record-by-record basis, so that if only one of many records is required for the investigation, other records can be discarded. Otherwise the public authorities can end-up storing large amount of unnecessary data, and this can prove costly taking into consideration the level of security and auditing involved. Finally, the cost of the solution should be low as the public authorities will have to cover the costs of running the system. If the costs were not covered by the authorities, the dataholders would transfer the costs of handling the enquiries to the end-users and such a solution would be unacceptable.

A query, such as data acquisition request, made against a modern relational database can be mapped using the Structured Query Language (SQL). Thus, the operations required could be split into the following:

1.   Identification of the type of the information that is required. These could be h parameters that contain answers to investigator's questions, referred to as return parameters rp_{1-h}, for example DoB, address, location of a card payment, or the telephone numbers called by a given subscriber.

2.   Specification of any circumstantial request constrains, or l different input parameters, ip_{1-l}, with values ip_val_{1-l}, such as a time frame of the transactions being requested.

3.   Specification of the relevant data subject, such as by identifying the individual whose

data is to be retrieved, or by providing the mobile phone number of the suspect, and so on. This parameter is referred to as the record of the interest ri, with value of ri_val.

Then, if we refer to the dataset as the *source*, the request for investigative data could be mapped into the following SQL query:

SELECT rp_1, rp_2, ..., rp_h

FROM source

WHERE **ri=ri_val** *AND* ip_1=ip_val$_1$ *AND* ip_2=ip_val$_2$ *AND* ... *AND* ip_l= ip_val $_l$ (8)

In most cases the names of the return parameters, as well as the names of the input parameters, and values of these input parameters, can be openly communicated. But the value of the interesting record, *ri_val* is used to uniquely identify the suspect and must be hidden. This can be achieved by running a database query for the return parameters of all the records that satisfy the conditions defined by the input parameters, and then collecting the interesting record from the sender using the PE protocol. Consequently, the query that is actually run on the sender's database can be rewritten as:

SELECT **ri**, rp_1, rp_2, ..., rp_h

FROM source

WHERE ip_1=ip_val$_1$ *AND* ip_2=ip_val$_2$ *AND* ... *AND* ip_l= ip_val $_l$ (9)

The results of query (9) would then be an input to the PE that would enable the chooser to privately select only the record of interest that matches given *ri_val*.

Base Protocol

We discussed different types of protocols available that could enable the *chooser* to download a record from the *sender's* database maintaining the secrecy of the record selected. It also mentioned that most available protocols could not achieve the searches necessary for the acquisition protocol, and that a combination of two or more protocols is required. Such a combination typically results in high computational and communicational complexity, because each protocol usually requires its own preparation phase. The PE protocol was identified as the most suitable to become the base protocol for the data acquisition, since it can be used to for both private matching and SPIR, thus, has a low computational overhead. Table 1 illustrates the computational complexity of this protocol.

There are also other factors that make PE an ideal base protocol for the task at hand. It allows for acquiring more than one interesting record at the time, and adding more records to the enquiry increases the processing by negligible five asymmetric key operations and one symmetric operation per each extra interesting record in an enquiry. Use of the PE allows the dataholder to remain in full control of data, and to decide which data can be disclosed. In the PE protocol each record is processed separately and there are no chances of the records being mixed up by the privacy-preserving process. Thanks to this fact unnecessary, data of non-suspects could be discarded on reception by the authorities and still the encrypted interesting records received would form valid evidence for use in a court of law. The costs involved in building and deploying PE based solution to the private data acquisition are anticipated to be low since it is a software system and the architecture would be based on the protocol from the public domain.

The processing time required for the protocol to run is the main drawback of the PE protocol. If there are thousands of records in the database it only takes few minutes for the complete run of the protocol, however, the processing time is linear to the number of records in a dataset and data retrieval from a database with few million records would take few days to run on a typical PC. During an urgent enquiry, such as when the life of an individual is in danger, or where an individual can seriously endanger others, police should be able to get access to data within minutes. Such result could not be expected from the PE protocol if the database has more than a few thousand records. Additionally, even if the data requested is relatively small in size, for example 100kB per record, the results from a database of five million records would require more than 500MB of data to be transferred over the Internet. Clearly, there is a requirement for the PE to return a subset of the sender's database, rather than the whole database or another solution would need to be chosen.

Another issue is that the PE-based system allows for secure matching on a single value per record, for example an IP address, suspect's name, or a credit card number. In some scenarios it may be required to request records based on a number of secret input parameters. Consider scenario where Police has a profile of a suspect (e.g. sex, age, and ethnic origin) and would like to find individuals fitting this profile working in organizations in a neighbourhood to the crime scene, but revealing the profile to these organizations may harm the investigation and the individuals matching the profile. Currently the police would often have to delay their enquiries in order to protect the investigation, and the innocent individuals fitting the profile. For example, if the case being investigated had a public tension around it, and the suspect's profile matched individuals in a local minority group, an openly conducted enquiry could have serious consequences to the members of this minority.

Finally, the idea of a system that requires the legitimate dataholders to transfer data about all the records in the database to the third-party for investigative purposes is controversial. In PE the investigators can only read the data requested, still the records of all data subjects would require

Table 1. Computational Complexity of the PE Protocol

	Symmetric Crypto.	Asymmetric Crypto.	
	crypto. operation	key generation	crypto. operation
Step 1	-	$O(3)$	-
Step 2	-	-	$O(m)$
Step 4	-	-	$O(2m)$
Step 5	$O(n)$	-	$O(2n)$
Step 6	-	-	$O(2m)$
Step 7	$O(m)$	-	-
Total Complexity	$O(n + m)$	$O(3)$	$O(5m + 2n)$

The complexity of different steps of the PE protocol. Where n is the number of the data rows in the source, and m is the number of interesting records.

processing. This would not be normally allowed under the DPA. Also, it is likely that the general public would be concerned about trap-door, polynomial time secure, cryptographic technique protecting personal data. Consequently, there is a requirement for a control that would limit the possibility of exposure of the private records unrelated to the investigation.

NOVEL APPROACH TO DATA ACQUISITION - IDAP

The previous section has listed the design considerations for using PE as the base protocol for data acquisition in the investigative context. This section addresses the shortcomings of PE by three different correcting measures that modify the PE protocol into IDAP.

Allowing Multiple Selection Criteria

The PE protocol can be used to privately retrieve data if the data is identified by a single parameter, such as ID number, credit card number, IP address, and so on. However, this is not always the case. Consequently, if the protocol needs to be used to find a suspect based on circumstantial knowledge, or a suspect's profile, the PE protocol would need to be modified. Query (10) shows the way the request (9) would be modified for such enquiry, here sip_{1-j} stands for j secret input parameters:

SELECT sip_1, sip_2, ..., sip_j, rp_1, rp_2, ..., rp_h

FROM *source*

WHERE ip_1=ip_val$_1$ AND ip_2=ip_val$_2$ AND ...
AND ip_1=ip_val$_1$ (10)

A computationally expensive solution to this problem has been published by Kwecka, Buchanan, and Spiers (2010), who suggest that the symmetric encryption should be used to lock the return parameters and the symmetric keys should be secured with relevant commutative encryption keys that are unique to each value of the secret input parameter returned for the given row. Despite being computationally expensive, their solution has a unique benefit of allowing semi-fuzzy matching of the results if the underlying commutative protocol is ElGamal-based.

In this paper a simplified approach is proposed. Since, query (10) replaces the *ri* parameter with *j* different *sip* parameters, the list of these *j* parameters could be used as a complex *ri* in the improved IDAP protocol. Thus, in Steps B_2 and A_1 a list of all values for the *sip* parameters would be hashed together. In this way neither the security of the PE protocol, nor its complexity, are affected by this improvement.

Lowering Processing Time

We recommended minimising the processing time required for each run of the protocol in large databases, such as those belonging to ISPs and mobile telephony providers. Theoretically, in order to maintain the privacy of the suspect, the *chooser* needs to request all the records in the database to be included in a given run of the PE protocol. This is the only way that no information about interesting record is revealed and the correctness of this scheme can be proven. In its current form, the PE protocol would not be capable of processing any urgent requests due to the processing overhead. The mitigation for this could be to limit the numbers of records processed per enquiry by the *sender*. Privacy of the alleged suspect should be protected, but, if the probability of the *sender* guessing the ID of the interesting record is, for example 1:1000, and not 1:*n*, and the dataholder has no other information that could help infer any knowledge as to the identity of the suspect, then this research argues that the privacy of the suspect and the investigation is maintained. Police sources suggest that occasionally during traditional data gathering enquiries, this is face-to-face, investigators would use a concept of *diffusion* - hiding the suspect's identity by asking open-ended questions about a larger group of individuals rather than about a single person. This is a widely-accepted technique, however, in the digitalised environment, a system that would maintain privacy while providing answers to such general questions does not currently exist. Consequently, any attempts of investigators to *cast their net wide* during electronic investigations are prohibited and treated as *fishing* for evidence.

The problem is to decide on the technique of narrowing down the scope in a way that ensures interesting records are among the results returned. If the list of the record identifiers is public, such as the list of the Internet Protocol (IP) addresses or telephone numbers served by a given network operator, then the *chooser* could simply selected records to be processed at random from such a list. However, if such a list is not available, it would be possible to split PE protocol into separate parts: PEqT; OT; and an additional off-line preparation phase. In this way the initial off-line phase could be run against the whole database, but the information retrieval would be performed against a smaller set of records. Thus, the number of records requested per each interesting record can be defined as the *diluting factor – o*, and the modified PE protocol would operate as follows:

Phase A: Preparation

1. Sender applies hash function h to the elements in the input set V_S, so that $X_S = h(V_S)$.
2. Sender picks an encryption PH key E_S at random from a group Z_p^*, where p is a strong prime.
3. Sender encrypts each $h(v) \in X_S$ with the key E_S, the result is a list of encrypted identities $Y_S = E_S(X_S) = E_S(h(V_S))$

If more record need to be added to the set these can be processed using Steps A_1 (Step 1 of Phase A) and A_3, and then added to the list.

Phase B: PEqT

1. Following a request for data, sender provides chooser with a complete list of encrypted identities prepared during Phase A, reordered lexicographically.
2. Chooser applies hash function h to the elements in set containing the identities of the interesting records, so that $X_C = h(V_C)$.
3. Chooser picks a commutative cryptography key pair, encryption key E_C and decryption key D_C, at random from the same group Z_p^* that was used by sender in the Phase A.
4. Chooser encrypts entries in the set X_C, so that: $Y_C = E_C(X_C) = E_C(h(V_C))$.
5. Chooser sends to sender set Y_C, reordered lexicographically.
6. Sender encrypts with key E_S each entry $y \in Y_C$ received from chooser.
7. Sender returns a set of pairs $\langle y, E_S(y) \rangle$ to chooser.
8. Chooser decrypts each entry in $E_S(Y_C)$, obtaining
$$E_S(X_C) = D_C E_S(E_C(X_C)) = D_C E_S(Y_C).$$
9. Chooser compares each entry in $E_S(X_C)$ to the entries of Y_S received in the Step B_1. In this way the interesting records can be identified.

Phase C: OT

1. After identifying the interesting records in Y_S the chooser selects at random $o - 1$ other unique records from Y_S for each interesting record in V_C. These are the diluting records, that together with the records of interest,

form a shortlist for the enquiry. If the number of interesting records multiplied by o is greater than n, the size of the dataset V_S, then the complete Y_S is shortlisted.

2. Send the shortlist to sender.

3. Sender picks an encryption PH key E'_S at random from the group Z^*_p.

4. Sender identifies entries $h(v)$ from X_S that have been shortlisted and processes each shortlisted record in the following way:

   a. Encrypts $h(v)$ with E'_S to form the key used to lock the extra information about v, i.e. $ext(v)$, $\kappa(v) = E'_S(h(v))$.

   b. Encrypts the extra information using a symmetric encryption function K and the key $\kappa(v)$ crafted in the previous step: $c(v) = K(\kappa(v), ext(v))$

   c. Forms a pair $\langle E_S(h(v)), c(v) \rangle$.

5. The pairs formed in C4(c), containing a private match element and the encrypted extra information about record v, are then transferred to chooser.

6. Sender encrypts each entry $y \in Y_C$, received from chooser in Step B_5, with key E'_S to form set of pairs $\langle y, E'_S(y) \rangle$

7. Pairs $\langle y, E'_S(y) \rangle$ are then transferred to chooser.

8. Chooser removes the encryption E_C from all entries in the 2-tuples received in Step C_7 obtaining tuples α, β such that $\langle \alpha, \beta \rangle = \langle h(v), E'_S(h(v)) \rangle$. Thus, α is the hashed value $v \in V_C$, and β is the hashed value v encrypted using E'_S.

9. Chooser sets aside all pairs received in Step C_5, whose first entry is equal to one of the first entry of any two-tuples obtained in Step B_9. It then uses the appropriate β tuple associated with a given interesting record as a symmetric key to decrypt the extra information contained in the second entry in the pair received in C_5. This is performed for all the matching entries.

Figure 3 illustrates the processes involved in this improved version of acquisition protocol. It is worth noting that there is only five communication rounds required in this protocol. This is two rounds more than in the original PE protocol. Still, most of efficient SPIR protocols require considerably more rounds.

Reassuring the Public

Legal opinion about legality of the protocol that transfers large chunks of non-suspect data to the investigators is divided. Some consider this solution as acceptable as long as it can be proven that the public authorities are unable to decrypt any unsolicited data, while others suggest that anything that creates a privacy risk, however remote, requires the consent of the parties involved. Case law supports both of these opinions, thus, until such case is brought in front of court the matter cannot be answered. Clearly there is a need for a process that would further eliminate the privacy risk to the data records of non-suspects.

Sad quis custodiet ipsos custodies?

But who will watch the watchers? (Juvenal, Satires VI, 347)

It is likely that providing government agencies with encrypted records of innocent, non-suspected individuals would worry the general public. This is despite the data being encrypted in the way that would render the records unusable to the authorities. However, the public may worry that the government organisations have enough computing power to break the encryption used by PE. The solution proposed in this paper in order to reassure the public is to introduce a semi-trusted party into the protocol. This party would be a *proxy* between the investigators and the dataholder. The following modifications to the PE protocol are proposed:

Figure 3. IDAP process flow. Graphical representation of the improved PE protocol.

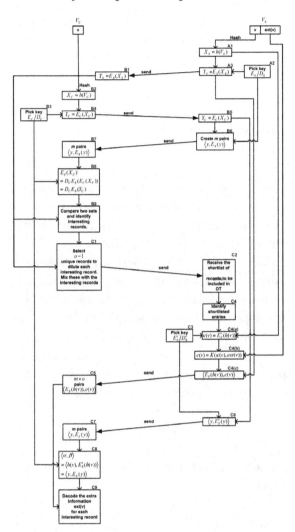

1. All communication between chooser and sender goes through proxy.

2. Chooser provides proxy with the identifiers of the interesting records encrypted by sender, $E_S(h(v))$. This is done over a secure channel, or with the use of the 3 Pass protocol, once the parties are authenticated.

3. At the stage where data is transferred from sender in Step C_4 (Figure 3), proxy filters the response and discards the records that were not specified by chooser's request, that is the records other than the ones identified in the step above.

The semi-trusted party should have no interest in finding out the objective of the investigation, or the content of the data records returned by the dataholder, for this reason it is suggested that the role of this party should be conducted by Information Commissioner's Office (ICO)[1] or its equivalent in other countries. The party that is chosen must not cooperate with the *sender*, or the protocol will be broken, since simple matching exercise would reveal the identities of the suspects.

EVALUATION

The technique for running queries with multiple selection criteria without affecting the computational complexity of the protocol was introduced. As a result the processing time is constant for enquiries with different number of selection criteria, if the time required for the database query is ignored. This is a large enhancement in comparison to the system presented by Kwecka et al. (2010) where the processing time increases linearly when adding more selection criteria.

Additionally, in the improved protocol the initial processing is dependent on the size of the dataset - n, but it needs to be performed only once in a given period of time, for example once per month, or once per year. The remaining operations are less processing savvy, as illustrated in Table 2.

The proposed method provides significant improvements to the processing time required for enquiries, if total number of records in the *sender's* database is higher than $o \times m$, that is higher than the number of interesting records m multiplied by the *diluting factor o*. This is illustrated in Figure 4. However, the true strength of this improvement is seen when multiple enquiries are run on the same database using a single encrypted catalogue of the records, compiled by the *sender* in Phase 1 (shown in Figure 5).

The introduction of the diluting factor o will allow real-life enquiries on large databases to be processed in minutes, rather than days as would

Table 2. Computational Complexity of IDAP

		Symmetric Crypto.	Asymmetric Crypto	
		crypto. operation	key generation	crypto. operation
Phase A (run periodically)	**Step 1**	-	-	-
	Step 2	-	$O(1)$	-
	Step 3	-	-	$O(n)$
Phase B (run per enquiry)	**Step 3**	-	$O(1)$	-
	Step 4	-	-	$O(m)$
	Step 6	-	-	$O(m)$
	Step 8		-	$O(m)$
Phase C (run per enquiry)	**Step 3**	-	$O(1)$	-
	Step 4(a)	-	-	$O(m \times o)$
	Step 4(b)	$O(m \times o)$	-	-
	Step 6	-	-	$O(m)$
	Step 8	-	-	$O(m)$
	Step 9	$O(m)$	-	-
Total Complexity for k enquiries, where $n < m \times o$		$O(km(o + 1))$	$O(2k + 1)$	$O(km(o + 5) + n)$
Cost (ms/operation)		**0.33**	**7**	**30**

The complexity of the different steps in the proposed improved solution. Where n is the number of the data rows in the source, m is the number of interesting records. Also the diluting factor o, as well as the number of the protocol runs k affects the processing time required by the protocol. Cost is the measured average time in ms to perform given cryptographic operation from managed C#.NET code on a Personal Computer with 1.6GHz CPU, 1GB of RAM, running Windows XP.

be the case if off-the-shelve SPIR solution would be employed in the data acquisition process.

In order for the IDAP to be introduced as the platform for investigative data gathering will first need to gain trust of the general public. In an ordinary SPIR protocol all the records are transferred from the *sender* back to the *chooser*. However, in IDAP thanks for introducing the concept of dilution the probability that investigators retrieve encrypted records of a particular individual that is not a suspect are small. Thus, for a dataset with *n* records, during investigation with *m* interesting records, and the *diluting factor o*, the probability of such event *A* can be defined as (11).

$$P(A) = \frac{(o - 1) \times m}{n - m} \qquad (11)$$

Consequently, for investigation with five interesting records, with a diluting factor of a thousand and dataset consisting a million records, the probability of this event occurring during a single run of the protocol would be less than 0.5%. This also means that the investigators would need to first break the encryption key used by the *sender* to hide identities (Phase A), before they could attempt to obtain the data about a specific individual that is not a suspect, otherwise the probability of the encrypted data being provided to them would be

Figure 4. Processing time per enquiry depending on the number of interesting records. This proposed modification of the protocol improves significantly the processing time required for the protocol to run for the cases where the product of the number of the interesting records m and diluting factor o is smaller that the number of the records in the database n. The graph drawn for n=1000 and o=100.

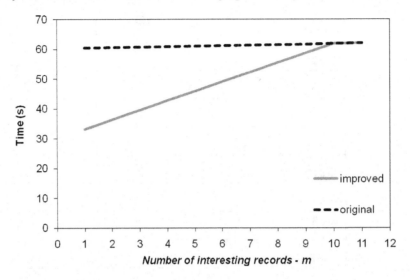

small. Additionally, if the identity of a data subject is never encrypted under the same key as the data records, investigators would need to successfully brute force two separate keys in order to make use of the retrieved encrypted records. Otherwise the information would be unintelligible.

The merits of the above discussion can improve the perception of the system; however, a key mechanism in IDAP is the semi-trusted *proxy*. Since, it has no incentives to find out the detail of the investigation, thus it is not going to purchase expensive cutting edge decryption technology to decode the data, nor it is going to cooperate with the *sender* in order to establish the identity of the suspect. On the other hand, if the need arises to verify the *chooser's* requests in a court of law, the *proxy* and the *sender* could work together to establish the identities of the records requested by the *chooser*. If an ordinary SPIR protocol is used to acquire investigative data this would shift the balance of the privacy protection from innocent individuals towards the suspect and the secrecy of investigation. Introduction of the semi-trusted third party into this protocol would

restore the natural order, where the rights of the data-subjects, ordinary citizens, are put ahead of the secrecy of the investigation. This is likely to benefit the general public's perception of PET based investigative systems.

CONCLUSION

This paper presented a platform for investigative data acquisition that preserves the privacy of the suspects and secrecy of the investigations. After a careful analysis of the related issues and research of available privacy-preserving primitives IDAP has been defined. The platform is based on PE protocol, a SPIR protocol based on commutative cryptography that allows retrieval of extra information about the records that are common between two datasets. Since, the features of the PE protocol closely match those required in retrieving investigative information from third parties, only three improvements were required to form IDAP from this protocol. These improvements are the contribution this paper makes to the PIR domain.

Figure 5. Processing time depending on the number of enquires. This proposed modification improves significantly the processing time required for the protocol to run for the cases where more than one enquiry is run against the same database. The graph drawn for n=1000, o=100, and m=10.

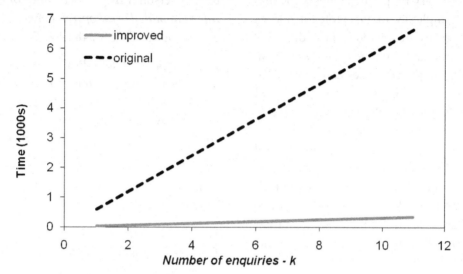

In this paper a view that in certain circumstances, hiding the objective of the PIR protocol by running the data retrieval protocol against only a subset of the dataset provides sufficient privacy protection is presented. This is certainly the case in the investigative data acquisition process. The number of records that are collected per every interesting record is specified by the *dilution factor o* introduced by this research. Since this factor can be changed before each protocol run, the investigators can dynamically chose the appropriate level of protection for the given investigation, the data subject, and the data controller. The protocol operates by creating a single encrypted table of identities held in the third party's database and allowing the investigators to privately match their suspects against this table. Once the investigators know the encrypted ID of the suspect a number of records are selected at random to make up a request of size *o*.

Consequently the data controller can then facilitate private data retrieval operating on a small subset of the database. In this way the processing time is significantly reduced and requests from large databases are feasible. Such technique could

be potentially risky if the same enquiry is made against few different data controllers, since the intersection of the requested results could help the cooperating controllers to identify the suspect. However, according to the Police it is not likely that data controllers will cooperate in such matters, especially if such cooperation would be forbidden by the letter of law. In the cases that the data is being retrieved from large databases that require use of the *dilution* technique during data retrieval process, the interesting records are usually identified by a mobile phone number, or an IP address. Phone numbers and IP addresses are often unique to the operators and their assignment can be obtained from the call and network routing tables. In this way, in most cases, the investigators only ask a single operator for information about a given identity. This fact makes most investigations are equivalent to a single database PIR allowing *dilution* to be applied, with no adverse affect on the privacy of the data-subjects.

A technique that enables investigators to perform complex database searches maintaining privacy is also provided in this paper. The investigators can create a list of values for every secret input parameter, and use this list in the same fashion an identifier of the interesting record would be used in the ordinary PE protocol. Consequently, neither the complexity of the protocol nor its security properties are altered in providing this additional functionality to the acquisition protocol.

Finally, this paper addresses concerns of the general public in employing encryption based PETs to handle sensitive data. People generally trust the security process more that they trust encryption. For this reason a semi-trusted third party is added to the protocol to act as a proxy. The entire communication between the investigators and the dataholders is thus done via this proxy. The key objective of the proxy is to filter out the records that were not requested by the investigators. This protocol is secure only as long as the *proxy* is trusted not to cooperate with the dataholder. For this reason a party whose main concern is privacy of the individuals should hold this function. Therefore, in the UK, ICO could handle such a function. This approach ensures that the balance between the privacy of the alleged suspect and the privacy of the innocent individuals are maintained after IDAP is introduced as a data acquisition technique. Such move is likely to improve the public's perception of the platform.

REFERENCES

Agrawal, R., Evfimievski, A., & Srikant, R. (2003). Information sharing across private databases. In *Proceedings of the ACM SIGMOD International Conference on Management of Data*, San Diego, CA (pp. 86-97).

Aiello, B., Ishai, Y., & Reingold, O. (2001). Priced oblivious transfer: How to sell digital goods. In B. Pfitzmann (Ed.), *Proceedings of the International Conference on the Theory and Application of Cryptographic Techniques* (LNCS 2045, pp. 119-135).

Asonov, D., & Freytag, J.-C. (2003). Almost optimal private information retrieval. In R. Dingledine & P. Syverson (Eds.), *Proceedings of the Second International Workshop on Privacy Enhancing Technologies* (LNCS 2482, pp. 239-243).

Association of Chief Police Officers. (2003). *Good practice guide for computer based electronic evidence (version 3)*. Retrieved from http://www.7safe.com/electronic_evidence/ACPO_guidelines_computer_evidence.pdf

Balz, D., & Deane, C. (2006, November 1). Differing views on terrorism. *The Washington Post*, p. A04.

Bao, F., & Deng, R. (2001). Privacy protection for transactions of digital goods. In S. Qing, T. Okamoto, & J. Zhou (Eds.), *Proceedings of the Third International Conference on Information and Communications Security* (LNCS 2229, pp. 202-213).

Cachin, C. (1999). Efficient private bidding and auctions with an oblivious third party. In *Proceedings of the 6th ACM Conference on Computer and Communications Security* (pp. 120-127).

Du, W., & Atallah, M. J. (2001). Privacy-preserving cooperative scientific computations. In *Proceedings of the 14th IEEE Workshop on Computer Security Foundations* (pp. 273-282).

European Parliament. (1995). European data protection directive 95/46/EC. *Official Journal of the European Union. L&C, L*(281), 31–50.

Frikken, K. B., & Atallah, M. J. (2003). Privacy preserving electronic surveillance. In *Proceedings of the ACM Workshop on Privacy in the Electronic Society*, Washington, DC (pp. 45-52).

Goldwasser, S., & Lindell, Y. (2002). Secure computation without agreement. In *Proceedings of the 16th International Conference on Distributed Computing* (pp. 17-32).

Home Office. (2007). *Acquisition and disclosure of communications data - code of practice.* Retrieved from http://security.homeoffice.gov.uk/ripa/publication-search/ripa-cop/acquisition-disclosure-cop.pdf?view=Binary

Home Office. (2009). *Protecting the public in a changing communications environment.* Retrieved from http://www.homeoffice.gov.uk/documents/cons-2009-communications-data?view=Binary

Information Commissioner. (2008). *Report of the interception of communications commissioner for 2008.* Retrieved from http://www.official-documents.gov.uk/document/hc0809/hc09/0901/0901.pdf

Kwecka, Z., Buchanan, W. J., & Spiers, D. (2010, July). Privacy-preserving data acquisition protocol. In *Proceedings of the IEEE Region 8 International Conference on Computational Technologies in Electrical and Electronics Engineering* (pp. 131-136).

Kwecka, Z., Buchanan, W. J., Spiers, D., & Saliou, L. (2008). Validation of 1-N OT algorithms in privacy-preserving investigations. In *Proceedings of the 7th European Conference on Information Warfare and Security.*

Ostrovsky, R., & Skeith, W. E., III. (2007). A survey of single-database PIR: Techniques and applications. In O. Tatsuaki & W. Xiaoyun (Eds.), *Proceedings of the International Conference on Public Key Cryptography* (LNCS 4450, pp. 393-411).

Palmer, G. (2001a). *A road map for digital forensic research* (Tech. Rep. No. DTR-T001-01). Utica, NY: Air Force Research Laboratory.

Pohlig, S., & Hellman, M. (1978). An improved algorithm for computing logarithms overGF(p) and its cryptographic significance. *IEEE Transactions on Information Theory, 24*(1), 106–110. doi:doi:10.1109/TIT.1978.1055817

Rasmussen Reports. (2008). *51% say security more important than privacy.* Retrieved from http://www.rasmussenreports.com/public_content/politics/general_politics/january_2008/51_say_security_more_important_than_privacy

Rivest, R. L., Shamir, A., & Adleman, L. (1978). A method for obtaining digital signatures and public-key cryptosystems. *Communications of the ACM, 21*(2), 120–126. doi:doi:10.1145/359340.359342

Schneier, B. (1995). *Applied cryptography: Protocols, algorithms, and source code in C.* New York, NY: John Wiley & Sons.

Shamir, A. (1980). On the power of commutativity in cryptography. In J. de Bakker & J. van Leeuwen (Eds.), *Proceedings of the 7th Colloquium on Automata, Languages and Programming* (LNCS 85, pp. 582-595).

Shannon, C. (1949). Communication theory of secrecy systems. *The Bell System Technical Journal, 28.*

Spiers, D. (2009). *Intellectual property law essentials.* Dundee, UK: Dundee University Press.

Swire, P., & Steinfeld, L. (2002). Security and privacy after September 11: The health care example. In *Proceedings of the 12th Annual Conference on Computers, Freedom and Privacy,* San Francisco, CA (pp. 1-13).

Weis, S. A. (2006). *New foundations for efficient authentication, commutative cryptography, and private disjointness testing.* Unpublished doctoral dissertation, Massachusetts Institute of Technology, Cambridge, MA.

Young, B. C., Kathleen, E. C., Joshua, S. K., & Meredith, M. S. (2006). Challenges associated with privacy in health care industry: Implementation of HIPAA and the security rules. *Journal of Medical Systems*, *30*(1), 57–64. doi:doi:10.1007/s10916-006-7405-0

ENDNOTE

[1]   ICO in the United Kingdom is a non-departmental public body which reports directly to Parliament and is sponsored by the Ministry of Justice. It is the independent regulatory office dealing with the Data Protection Act 1998 and the Privacy and Electronic Communications (EC Directive) Regulations 2003 across the UK.

This work was previously published in the International Journal of Information Technologies and Systems Approach, Volume 4, Issue 2, edited by Frank Stowell and Manuel Mora, pp. 12-31, copyright 2011 by IGI Publishing (an imprint of IGI Global).

Chapter 18
A Cross Layer Spoofing Detection Mechanism for Multimedia Communication Services

Nikos Vrakas
University of Piraeus, Greece

Costas Lambrinoudakis
University of Piraeus, Greece

ABSTRACT

The convergence of different network types under the same architecture offers the opportunity for low cost multimedia services. The main objective has been the high quality of the provided services. However, considering that older equipment with limited processing capabilities may be present in such environments, a tradeoff between security and service quality is inevitable. Specifically, low resource enabled devices cannot utilize state of the art security mechanisms, such as IPSec tunnels, integrity mechanisms, etc., and they simply employ HTTP Digest authentication. The lack of integrity mechanisms in particular raises many security concerns for the IMS infrastructures. Attacks such as Man in the Middle (MitM), spoofing, masquerading, and replay that can be launched in IMS environments, have been pinpointed in bibliography by various researchers. Moreover, an internal attacker may utilize his legitimate security tunnels in order to launch spoofing and identity theft attacks. This paper presents a cross-layer spoofing detection mechanism that protects SIP-based infrastructures from the majority of the aforementioned attacks without requiring an additional cryptographic scheme which would inevitably introduce considerable overheads.

1. INTRODUCTION

The provision of multimedia services over cellular and mobile devices is nowadays a necessity and not a special service. The need for better and contemporary services at low cost have forced the providers to widely deploy the IP Multimedia Subsystem (IMS) (3rd Generation Partnership Project, 2008) in order to introduce high quality services to the users of different network architectures. On the other hand, this universal infrastructure has to be flexible enough to cover the participating

DOI: 10.4018/978-1-4666-1562-5.ch018

entities that either come from technologically older network generations or low resource enabled devices. This fact comprises a special feature for the universality of the architecture and at the same time a major drawback for the security. More specifically, in order for all these obsolete devices to be satisfied, the security schemes have to include less resource demanding and eventually weaker encryption and authentication algorithms. Furthermore, the Session Initiation Protocol (SIP) (Rosenberg et al., 2002) is utilized in IMS as the main signaling protocol providing flexibility but also introduces threats as stated in many scientific works (Geneiatakis et al., 2006; Sher, Wu, & Magedanz, 2006; Walsh & Kuhn, 2005).

According to IMS specifications (3rd Generation Partnership Project, 2010) for all User Equipment (UE) that do not utilize a Universal Subscriber Identity Module/IP Multimedia Services Identity Module (USIM/ISIM), the authentication method has to be the SIP Digest (Franks et al., 1999). That implies that there is no integrity protection for the signaling messages or a tunneling between the UE and the Proxy-Call Session Control Function (P-CSCF). This raises many security and privacy concerns and introduces vulnerabilities and entry points to the IMS architecture (Abdelnur, Avanesov, & Rusinowitch, 2009; Hunter, Clark, & Park, 2007; Sher et al., 2006; Sher & Magedanz, 2007; Vrakas, Geneiatakis, & Lambrinoudakis, 2010).

Another important threat in such architectures comes from attacks that can be launched by internal users who have a legitimate subscription to the service. In these cases the attacker may bypass the security mechanism because he is able to authenticate the forged messages. Moreover, such an attacker may utilize his legitimate security tunnel when the AKA with IPSec (Kent & Atkinson, 1998) or TLS (Dierks & Allen, 1999) is employed as authentication method in order to launch identity theft and SIP signaling attacks (3rd Generation Partnership Project, 2010; Sisalem, Kuthan, Abend, Floroiu, & Schulzrinne, 2009).

The heavyweight employed security protocols between IMS core entities does not give the opportunity for another potential additional overhead. Thus, even though the employment of integrity mechanism such as S/MIME (Ramsdell, 1999) cannot deter the internal attacker (IA) from launching attacks, the utilization of public key encryption is rather heavy and resource draining for such devices.

Taking into account the restrictions imposed by the power and bandwidth limitations of UEs; we propose a cross-layer spoofing detection mechanism for VoIP/IMS infrastructures, without the use of any cryptographic protocols that would introduce an additional overhead to the network. The proposed detection method covers the majority of spoofing attacks against VoIP/IMS environments that utilize SIP as their signaling protocol, including MitM, masquerading and SIP signaling attacks from different network layers. It is worth noting that an accurate detection and prevention of spoofing attacks can reduce the need of an integrity mechanism and especially when SIP Digest is employed to reduce the number of required authentications.

The remaining of the paper is structured as follows: Section 2 presents the alternative threats faced by an IMS environment due to spoofing attacks. Section 3, provides a review of the detection mechanism presented by other researchers as well as a comparison, in respect to their efficiency in detecting attacks, with the proposed mechanism, while section 4 provides an extensive description of the proposed detection mechanism. Finally we conclude the paper with case study scenarios and some useful proposals for future work.

2. SPOOFING ATTACKS IN SIP/IMS ENVIRONMENTS

A malicious user can utilize many different techniques in order to hide his real identity. With the term *identity* we refer to either some hardware or to the person/subscriber. As far as the hardware, namely the UE, is concerned the identity can be the IP address in correlation with its unique MAC address. On the other hand, the identity of a user comprises the unique IMS Private Identity (IMPI) and IMS Public Identity (IMPU).

A malicious behavior of a user may compromise the authentication, integrity and confidentiality requirements, something which may also lead to denial of service (DoS) violating the availability requirements. The attacker can impersonate the user or a network element spoofing the hardware or user related information involved in a communication session. These attacks can be applied in different network layers of the protocol stack.

The absence of integrity mechanism when a UE lacks ISIM/USIM is not the only reason that makes such attacks successful. Next there are cases where an authenticated internal user can utilize his legitimate security tunnel in order to launch attacks.

SIP Signaling Attacks

A malicious user can launch DoS attacks by manipulating the SIP messages which are responsible for session handling (Geneiatakis et al., 2006; Sher & Magedanz, 2007). The main characteristic of these attacks is that the forged messages comply with SIP specification's (Rosenberg et al., 2002) rules and thus are difficult to detect.

CANCEL & BYE Request

The SIP BYE method terminates a session. A participant of a media session initiates such a message and forwards it to the P-CSCF requesting the termination of the session and the release of the allocated resources. An attacker by spoofing the headers "From" "Cseq" and "Call-id" with the corresponding of the victim is able to cause DoS tearing the session down illegally. When no integrity mechanism is employed (UE lacks USIM/ISIM) the attack can be launched without

much effort. However, an internal attacker can utilize his security tunnel in order to forward forged message to P-CSCF by spoofing these three headers. In many implementations a weak SIP parser would correlate these headers to the corresponding session causing its termination. It is worth noting that such a message can pass SA-SIP[1] correlation because the attacker has used his legal identity and IP.

Re-INVITE & UPDATE Requests

When a user wants to establish a session with another user or with a network entity in general (e.g. Media Resource Function Processor (MRFP) for call conferencing) he initiates an "INVITE" handshake. A second INVITE may be sent by a user in case where the former wants to modify the session parameters. This second in sequence invitation message is called re-INVITE and it is not a different request method than the conventional INVITE. An attacker utilizing such a request can cause DoS by turning it to mute or by changing the port numbers or event to redirect a call executing hijacking attack (Wu, Apte, Bagchi, Garg, & Singh, 2009). The UPDATE has exactly the same use but differs in the time frame where it can be sent. The UPDATE can modify an already established communication while the re-INVITE can modify the session parameters before the end of the handshake. The attack concept remains the same in both cases.

Spoofing / Identity Theft Attacks

An attacker may forward forged messages to the IMS core in order to charge the provided service to the victim. An internal attacker spoofs the public identity with the victim's one, executing an identity theft attack. The result is to overcharge the identity that corresponds to the victim instead of his account. After the allocation of an IP from the Getaway GPRS Support Node (GGSN), the attacker is able to utilize his legitimate security tunnel in order to launch such an attack in cases where IPSec or TLS is employed. In this case the attacker is also a subscriber (internal user) and initiates a registration procedure with his legitimate IDs (3rd Generation Partnership Project, 2010). After a successful registration, he forwards forged messages with stolen IDs launching an impersonation/identity theft attack.

Man in the Middle

One of the most harmful attacks in VoIP/IMS environments are the Man in the Middle attacks (Zhang, Wang, Farley, Yang, & Jiang, March 2009). The attacker utilizes Domain Name System (DNS) (Klein, 2007) and/or Address Resolution Protocol (ARP) poisoning (Wagner, 2001) techniques in order to act as an intermediate between two entities. This attack will enable attacking entities to gather the messages of a communication session.

Registration Expiration

Every registration is valid only for specific period. This period is defined in the first registration message and revalidated in the second one that takes place after the tunnel establishment (when IPSec or TLS is employed). The attacker acting as an intermediate is able to manipulate the header field "expires" of the first registration message, by

changing it to a zero value (Callegari, Garroppo, Giordano, Pagano, & Russo). The "contact" header which denotes the location of the user has to be exchanged with the asterisk symbol "*". This attack can cause the de-registration of the victim's UE and therefore leads to DoS. Normally, a UE uses such a message in cases where a user decides to switch off the utilized UE or to log out of the IMS server.

Bid Down

During the initiation of the registration handshake, the UE has to inform the Serving-CSCF (S-CSCF) about its capabilities and which cryptographic protocols are able to utilize for message authentication. The S-CSCF chooses the stronger one of the offered protocols for the rest of the authentication procedure and until the UE's de-registration. Executing a MitM attack (utilizing ARP or DNS poisoning techniques), a malicious user is able to manipulate the "Security-Client" field (included in "Authorization" header) of the first registration message of the victim's UE, removing the stronger cryptographic protocols (Sisalem, et al., 2009). A simplified example of a bid-down attack is depicted in Figure 1. Therefore the S-CSCF in such a negotiation will be forced to choose one of the offered weak-suites which the attacker can break more easily.

Figure 1. A simplified example of a bid-down attack. The attacker forces the selection of sip-digest instead of AKA with IPSec.

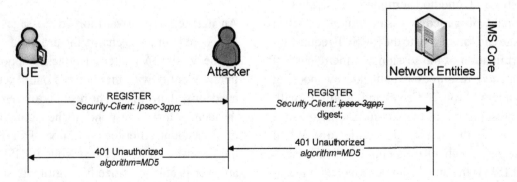

Generic / Authentication Abuse

Acting as an intermediate, the attacker can abuse the authentication scheme (Abdelnur, et al., 2009) especially when the SIP digest is employed as the authentication mechanism. The attacker impersonates the user and sends a registration message to the P-CSCF. The S-CSCF computes the challenge message (queering the Home Subscriber Server's (HSS) database) and forwards it to the attacker. The former impersonating the P-CSCF sends it to the user in order to authenticate it by inserting a valid response. The attacker gathers this authentication string and before the nonce expiration, uses it in order to authenticate the messages that he forwards to the P-CSCF.

Conference Interception

Another case of MitM attack is presented in (Vrakas et al., 2010). An internal attacker acting as an intermediate is able to manipulate SIP headers in order to illegally invite himself in a call conference without being identified by the other participants. The attacker must have a legitimate subscription to the IMS service in order to authenticate all the SIP requests initiated by him. Exploiting the lack of an integrity mechanism the attacker manipulates the "Refer-by" or "Refer-to" (depending the initiator of the invitation: the Media Resource Function Controller / Application Server (MRFC/AS) or user (3rd Generation Partnership Project, 2009) inviting himself to the conference instead of the intended user. After gathering the conference's URI initiates an invitation handshake with the MRFC (handles the signaling for media session establishment). The attacker joins the conference while the other participants will not notice the difference, especially in large conference rooms. Moreover the attacker makes the originating UE to believe that the REFER request has reached the legitimate/intended user while the core network knows the actual receiver of the request namely the attacker.

Masquerade in Layer 3

Even though the majority of attacking tools (Gayraud & Jaques, 2010; Guaci, n. d.; Ohlmeier, 2010) for VoIP environments implement application layer spoofing, an attacker may spoof his network layer IP address bypassing the security mechanisms. The SA-SIP correlation check performed in IMS environments detects the differences between SIP identities and IPs. Thus the attacker may also spoof the packet's IP (network layer) that has allocated from the GGSN in order to bypass this mechanism. The IP packet header may be spoofed by a malicious user (Tanase, 2003). Specifically, the header "Source Address" contains a 32 bit string that denotes the allocated IP address. The lack of integrity mechanism in IPv4 (Postel, 1981) gives the opportunity to the attacker to spoof this header field without being indentified.

Man in the Middle in Layer 2

Instead of DNS poisoning techniques that enable an attacker to act as intermediate and launch attacks as described in section 2.C, the former may also lunch similar attacks at the data link layer. The objective of ARP poisoning is to pass the traffic through the attacker who acts as a getaway for the communicating entities. The attacker floods the servers with ARP reply (Plummer, 1982) frames changing the correlation between MAC and IP address. Specifically, he forces the server to believe that the owner of the IP address does not correspond to user's MAC but to the attacker's MAC. Thus, the packet will be routed towards the attacker. The same has to be done on the user's side. The attacker floods the user's UE with ARP reply frames changing the IP-MAC correlation and thus forcing the packets to pass through the attacker. Achieving that, the attacker is able to launch the impersonation / MitM attacks at the application layer, as described above (see sections 2.B & 2.C), by spoofing the SIP messages.

RELATED WORK

Considering the bibliography and standards we can deduce that the majority of scientific works (3rd Generation Partnership Project, 2010; Abdelnur et al., 2009; Chen, Wu, Huang, & Chao, 2008; Geneiatakis & Lambrinoudakis, 2007) are focused on utilizing strong cryptographic protocols in order to provide integrity protection to the SIP messages. Such approaches can be considered heavy weight for the low resource enabled devices that may take part in these environments. Moreover, the employment of an integrity mechanism does not deter a legitimate subscriber to act maliciously trying to cause DoS or to launch identity theft (3rd Generation Partnership Project, 2010) and flooding attacks utilizing TLS or IPSec (Kent & Atkinson, 1997) tunnels. Under this context, we focused on developing a multilayer mechanism that detects spoofing attacks without the use of any cryptographic scheme that would introduce overhead to the system. Table 1 presents the comparison among the considered security mechanisms, in terms of their coverage against IMS threats. Note that the asterisk in layer 2 MitM attacks denotes that they can be partially prevented.

The authors of (Wu, Bagchi, Garg, Singh, & Tsai, 2004) present a cross protocol intrusion detection mechanism towards the mitigation of SIP flooding and SIP signaling attacks against VoIP infrastructures. This mechanism is based on application's layer obtained information by correlating the Real-time Transport Protocol (RTP) (Schulzrinne, Casner, Frederick, & Jacobson, 1996) and SIP protocols. The detection includes a case of re-INVITE (Wu et al., 2009) signaling attack that lead to call hijacking, the BYE attack and RTP flooding attacks. The call hijacking and re-INVTE attacks are detected by rules that catch orphan RTP streams based on the fact that the other participating member will not be notified about the session progress namely the session tear down (BYE attack) or call redirection (re-INVITE attack). Finally, the RTP flooding is detected by checking large gaps among the sequence numbers of two consecutive packets. According to the authors, flooding a UE with garbage flows may overflow their buffer and thus causing to crash.

Table 1. Security Mechanism Comparison

Layer	Thread Category	Attack	Proposed	Wu, Y	Wu, Y.(2)	Nassar, M.
Layer 5	SIP Signaling	BYE	✓	✓	✓	✓
		CANCEL	✓	X	✓	✓
		Re-INVITE	✓	✓	✓	X
		UPDATE	✓	X	X	X
	Masquerade / ID Theft (L5)	UE Impersonation (SIP IPs)	✓	X	X	X
		User Impersonation (SIP IDs)	✓	X	X	X
	Man in the Middle	Registration Expiration	✓	X	X	X
		Bid Down	✓	X	X	X
		Generic Authentication	✓	X	X	X
		Conference Interception	✓	X	X	X
	Replay	SIP Replay	✓	X	X	X
Layer 3	Masquerade (L3)	UE IP spoof	✓	X	X	X
Layer 2	Man in the Middle (L2)	ARP Poison	✓*	X	X	X

The specific approach cannot deter any other spoofing attacks except form BYE, re-INVITE.

In another work (Nassar & Niccolini, 2007) the authors propose a detection mechanism that is able to detect DoS flooding including some SIP signaling attacks. Specifically, they introduce a Honey Pot architecture in order to provoke attacker's interest and thus gathering useful data towards the detection of such attacks. Utilizing anomaly and signature based detection techniques; the mechanism creates profiles of "normal behavior" for users and network entities and signatures of known attacks. Any deviation from the normal behavior standards can be considered as an attack. An attack is detected by correlating different events through specific rules. For instance, the BYE signaling attack (Geneiatakis et al., 2006) can be detected by spotting orphan RTP flows after a period of time (only from one participant while the other has received the BYE message) utilizing the signature-based correlation with attack patterns. A similar detecting approach is presented in (Wu et al., 2004). However, a signature based mechanism cannot prevent MitM, replay and any masquerading attacks as well as any new or slightly modified attacks.

In Wu et al. (2009) an extended version of Wu et al. (2004) is presented. The mechanism utilizes rules in order to predicate about all the events in the architecture. A collection of events that corresponds to some rules triggers an alarm indicating an attack. The majority of the rules are based on an end to end matching rule which actually detects deviations in signaling flows. This extends the coverage of attacks from its predecessor including the MitM and billing fraud attacks. However, an attacker may bypass the rule by launching a layer 3 impersonation/spoofing attack. Finally, this approach does not offer protection against many MitM and signaling attack cases.

4. PROPOSED MECHANISM

In order to discourage and detect such attempts we propose a cross layer mechanism which relies on the information gathered from messages at different network layers of the protocol stack. All the information gathered is processed by the mechanism in order to decide about the originality of the messages. The main idea is based on the correlation of the application layer's authenticated messages and the information they bear in the very first registration of a UE, with the information derived from the IP packets and frames of the involved protocols.

The proposed mechanism can detect spoofed message attacks (refer to section 2) not only in cases where signaling messages lack authentication or integrity protection, but also in cases where the user establishes a security tunnel using IPSec or TLS with the corresponding server. For example, in cases where an internal malicious user utilizes his legitimate tunnel in order to forward to Core Network (CN), spoofed messages with stolen public IDs (see section 2.B) (3rd Generation Partnership Project, 2010) or forged messages at the application layer. Avoiding the utilization of any resource demanding cryptographic protocol, the deployment of such a lightweight mechanism can also decrease the number of required SIP authentications (e.g. only in registration messages) while it can detect spoofed messages and take decisions about their originality.

Monitoring Method

The monitoring system creates a unique binding between six values that can be gathered from layers 2, 3 and 5 of the network protocol stack. These values correlate a specific UE with a session, a set of IP addresses and the identities of the subscribers. For instance, the frames located at the data link layer (layer 2) bears the network or MAC address of the utilized UE. Furthermore, the bind among the IP address of the 3rd and 5th layer and the MAC address must be unique at a specific point of time.

Under this context, the proposed mechanism's monitoring system utilizes a table responsible for holding the values extracted from every involved layer. For every new incoming message a new tuple E_i, $\forall i \in \{0, ..., n\}$ is generated, where n is the number of incoming messages and $n \in N$. Thus, every new message has an i value larger than a previous one (Table 2).

In order to provide a more accurate and descriptive presentation of the proposed mechanism's detection procedure, we introduce the following sets for every network layer involved; M = {the set of MAC addresses}, I = {the set of IPs}, S = {the set of SIP-IPs}, D = {the set of IMPIs and IMPUs}, A = {the set of SIP methods}. Moreover, if R = {REGISTER} then $R \subseteq A$. Therefore, E_i = {m_i, i_i, s_i, a_i, d_i}, where $m_i \in M$, $i_i \in I$, $s_i \in S$, $a_i \in A$ and $d_i \in D$.

Also, C_i = {m_i, i_i, s_i, d_i} and $O = \bigcup_{i=1}^{n} C_i$ and finally $W = \bigcup_{i=1}^{n} E_i$.

An E tuple in order to be stored into the table has to be authenticated. The authentication is executed at the 5th layer utilizing the SIP digest mechanism. If the authentication procedure is successful and only then the MAC, IP, SIP IP and ids are bound and ready to be stored to the table. Therefore the first tuple (E_0) in the table that corresponds to a specific UE comes from a SIP registration message.

A registration request may also delete a tuple from the table removing all bindings among IPs and UEs, in the case where the subscriber logs-out or shuts down the UE (de-register). Note that there is no different request method for deregistration but the REGISTER request is utilized with a zero value in the "expires" header field (Rosenberg et al., 2002). The former description of the monitoring system is depicted in Figure 2.

Detection Method

Every new incoming message E_i is compared with all i-1 tuples (in the worst case scenario, where there is a new registration request or a spoofed message) in order to be correlated with a specific session or not (when the values of the specific tuple come from a spoofed message).

If $E_i \cap E_k = \varnothing$ with $a_i \in R$ and $d_i \notin E_k$, where $k \in \{0, ..., i-1\}$ then E_i corresponds to a new registration procedure, therefore there is no identical set in W. If the specific message has been authenticated and the $i_i = s_i$ (intra-packet check) then the corresponding tuple will be stored in the table denoting the first registration and the binding of the specific UE-subscriber for this specific period of time. If $d_i \in E_k$, then the message comes from a new registration request from a subscriber that has changed his UE and consequently a new IP has to be allocated.

Table 2. Proposed Mechanism's Cross-Layer Correlation Table

	UE	IP Address		IMPI/IMPU	Method
E_0	MAC_0	IP_0	SIP_0	ID_0	REGISTER
E_1	MAC_1	IP_1	SIP_1	ID_1	REFER
...	...	...	...	...	...
E_n	MAC_n	IP_n	SIP_n	ID_n	REGISTER
	Layer 2	**Layer 3**	**Layer 5**		

Figure 2. Proposed Mechanism's Monitoring Method

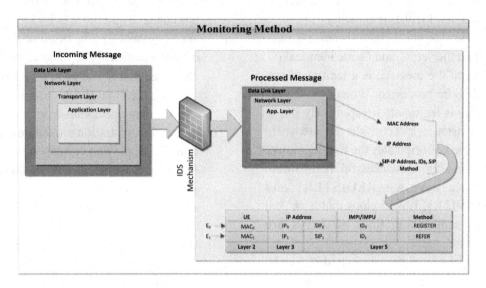

If $E_i \cap E_k = \varnothing$ and $a_i \notin R$, then there is no identical set in W thus the message has been spoofed and shall be dropped. The UE is actually not yet registered and this is derived from the fact that the two (E_i, E_k) sets do not have common elements.

If $E_i \cap E_k \neq \varnothing$, then at least one of the m_i, i_i, s_i, a_i, $d_i \in E_k$.

1. Let only $m_i \in E_k$, then i_i, s_i, a_i, $d_i \notin E_k$. Therefore the corresponding message shall not be processed because this corresponds to an identity theft attempt (see section 2.B) or the IP addresses have been spoofed.

2. Let d_i, $m_i \in E_k$, given that i_i, $s_i \notin E_k$. Then if $a_i \in R$ and $i_k = s_k$, the corresponding tuple shall be updated only when the message has been successfully authenticated. This registration message comes from a UE that has changed location and has been allocated a new IP address.

3. Let a_i, $m_i \in E_k$ given that i_i, s_i, $d_i \notin E_k$. If $a_i \in R$ then corresponding registration message has been initiated from the same UE but the subscriber has changed. After the successful registration the corresponding s_k has to be updated with the incoming s_i. For instance,

a user swaps the Universal Integrated Circuit Board (UICC) with another one utilizing the same UE and proceeds to a new registration procedure. The case where $a_i \notin R$ is covered in (1).

4. Let only s_i, $m_i \in E_k$, then there is application or network layer spoofing attempt and the corresponding message shall not be processed.

5. Let only the i_i, $m_i \in E_k$, then it is straightforward that $s_i \in E_k$ and thus there is an application layer replay or SIP signaling (refer to section 2.A) attack and the message shall be dropped. The attacker has reused a previously gathered SIP message from another subscriber. The attacker's objective is to bypass authentication mechanisms.

6. Let the i_i, m_i, $s_i \in E_k$, the message includes an IMPI/IMPU from another subscriber. This identity theft attempt (see section 2.B) comes from an internal attacker and the message shall be dropped. We can assume that the attacker is an insider because a registration for his UE already exists in the table (the only element that does not belongs to E_k is the d_i). This behavior may enable

the attacker to charge the provided service to the actual IMPI/IMPU owner.

7. Let the m_i, i_i, s_i, $d_i \in E_k$ then also m_i, i_i, s_i, $d_i \in C_k$. Then the sets C_i and C_k are identical ($C_i = C_k$) and the message is a legitimate one and shall be processed. When $C_i = C_k$, the message is legitimate irrespectively if $a_i \in E_k$. For instance, let's consider the case where a specific UE originates the first legitimate message after its successful registration. Then we have $a_0 = \{REGISTER\}$ and $a_1 = \{INVITE\}$. It is obvious that $a_0 \neq a_1$ but at the same time, both messages are legitimate.

8. Let only the $i_i \in E_k$ then m_i, s_i, a_i, $d_i \notin E_k$. The message that corresponds to this specific tuple is spoofed and shall be dropped.

9. Let the i_i, s_i, $d_i \in E_k$. If $a_i \in R$ then the corresponding shall be processed because it can be considered as a legitimate one. The subscriber has initiated a registration procedure utilizing a new UE and the tuple has to be updated (with the new MAC address) after a successful authentication. If $a_i \notin R$, then the IPs of both protocols (SIP and IP) are spoofed or there is an ARP poisoning attempt.

The correspondence between MAC and IP has changed and the sets $E_i \neq E_k$ and $C_i \neq C_k$.

10. We know that $C_k \subset E_k$ because $a_k \notin C_k$ then of course neither $a_i \notin C_k$. Therefore if $C_i \cap C_k = \varnothing$, given that $E_i \cap E_k \neq \varnothing$, it is derived that only $a_i \in E_k$. Then if the specific $a_i \in R$ and $i_i = s_i$ the message comes from a UE that has initiated a registration procedure for the first time. The tuple that corresponds to the specific E_i has to be updated ($i_i \rightarrow i_k$ and $m_i \rightarrow m_k$) and stored to the table after a successful authentication. Otherwise, if $a_i \notin R$ or $i_i \neq s_i$ the message is spoofed while an unregistered UE tries illegally to forward a message or to be registered with forged IP.

11. Let only the $s_i \in E_k$ then m_i, i_i, a_i, $d_i \notin E_k$. The message is spoofed at the application layer. This can be a replay attempt or a SIP signaling attack initiated from an external user. The deduction that the attacker comes from the outside is derived from the fact that none of m_i, i_i belong to E_k, thus the specific UE has not been registered until then.

The flow chart depicted in Figure 3 represents the detection method of the mechanism.

Figure 3. Proposed mechanism's detection method

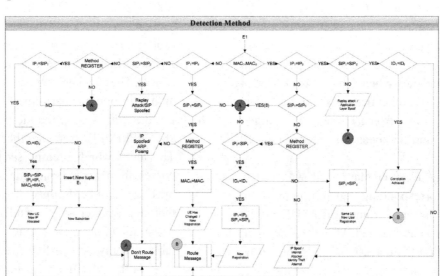

5. CASE STUDY

As described in Section 5.B the mechanism is able to detect the majority of spoofing attacks launched against VoIP/IMS infrastructures. Next, we can consider one indicative case of every attack category in order to present the detection phase clearly.

Let's consider the case of a call tear-down attack where the attacker utilizes the SIP BYE method. There are two different approaches for launching such an attack (refer to Figure 4), either by sending a spoofed BYE directly to the victim or to the P-CSCF while the former will forward it to the victim (Park, Patnaik, Amrutkar, & Hunter, 2008). After the session establishment the attacker spoofs the id and the IP addresses included in headers "From", "call-id" and "contact" and forwards this forged message. This attack falls in the (11) conditional test (refer to section 4.B). Moreover, as depicted in Table 3, the attacker's MAC and IP are not bound with any previously authenticated user/UE.

In identity theft attacks an internal attacker registers in the IMS with his legitimate account. Then he includes the ID of the victim, namely ID_{UE1}, into his messages in order to deceive the billing service by charging the victim's account. In such cases the attacker can be detected by the (6) conditional test because the information about the attacker's UE exists in the table but it has not bound with any authenticated message with this IMPU/IMPI.

Concerning MitM attacks an indicative example could be the conference interception attack. The attacker utilizing ARP poisoning techniques acts as an intermediate. This enables him to obtain the signaling messages and also to forward forge ones deceiving the participating entities. Let the UE has established a conference with MRFP and the UE2 has joined already. Afterwards the UE wants to invite UE3 to the conference utilizing the REFER SIP method. The attack methodology based on the fact that the UE believes that he has sent the Refer to UE3 but the attacker and the IMS core know that the actual receiver is the IA's UE. The IMS core sends the signaling messages pointing the IA while the former forges and forwards them to the unsuspected UE. The attacker having also a legitimate account is able to authenticate his SIP requests (Figure 5- step 8) but for the first time without launching APR and IP spoofing in order to "legally" join the conference. Afterwards the P-CSCF has to forward the (11) NOTIFY to the UE. The attacker on the other side has to launch the ARP poisoning attack in order to obtain the message and not to reach the UE. This attack though will fail because the server knows

Figure 4. BYE attack in IMS

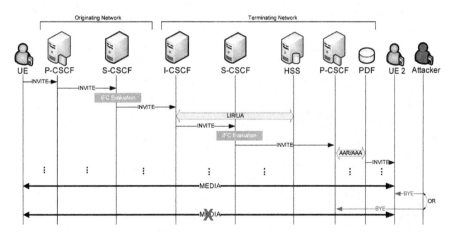

Table 3. Bye Attack Instance

	UE	IP Address		IMPI/IMPU	Method
E_1	MAC_{UE1}	IP_{UE1}	SIP_{UE1}	ID_{UE1}	REGISTER
E_2	MAC_{UE2}	IP_{UE2}	SIP_{UE2}	ID_{UE2}	REGISTER
...	...	...	...	...	...
E_{10}	MAC_{UE1}	IP_{UE1}	SIP_{UE1}	ID_{UE1}	INVITE
...	...	...	...	...	...
E_{14}	MAC_{UE1}	IP_{UE1}	SIP_{UE1}	ID_{UE1}	ACK
E_{15}	$MAC_?$	$IP_?$	SIP_{UE1}	ID_{UE1}	BYE
	Layer 2	**Layer 3**		**Layer 5**	

the correct binding between MAC/IP from the attacker's authenticated messages and consequently the (11) NOTIFY will reach UE. The former will parse the message without being able to correlate to a session because the header points the IA and not the UE's intended receiver namely the UE3.

6. CONCLUSION AND FUTURE WORK

The majority of the threats in VoIP/IMS environments come from the weak authentication methods and cryptographic schemes that are adopted in order to satisfy a large number of UEs that are not capable to handle state of the art security protocols. Moreover, the enormous amount of different specifications published from 3rd Generation Partnership Project and the involved protocols can inevitably introduce vulnerabilities to IMS environments due to possible misconfigurations in network entities. This fact may threaten the infrastructure even if security tunnels have been employed. An insufficient implementation may even render fragile a state of the art security protocol such as an IPSec tunnel. As described herein, spoofing-based attacks such as identity theft, MitM and replay may compromise the security requirements of the system.

Figure 5. Detecting conference interception / Layer 2,3,5 spoofing

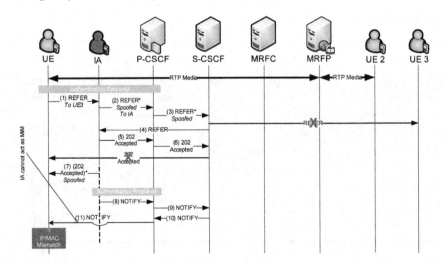

Considering the fact that an additional cryptographic scheme would introduce further delays to the session establishment and also that the low resource enabled devices would not be able to utilize it, we have designed and presented a cross-layer mechanism for preventing such attacks. This transparent mechanism is able to detect spoofing attacks by binding authenticated SIP messages with information from the other protocols that encapsulate these messages.

By extending this mechanism we may be able to reduce the number of the required authentication requests in SIP handshakes and consequently the session establishment delays. Moreover, the required resources may also be reduced while if we are able to detect spoofed SIP messages any additional integrity mechanism could be considered redundant.

REFERENCES

Abdelnur, H., Avanesov, T., & Rusinowitch, M. (2009). Abusing SIP authentication. *Journal of Information Assurance and Security, 4*(4).

Callegari, C., Garroppo, R. G., Giordano, S., Pagano, M., & Russo, F. (2009). A novel method for detecting attacks towards the SIP protocol. In *Proceedings of the 12th International Symposium on Performance Evaluation of Computer & Telecommunication Systems* (pp. 268-273).

Chen, C.-Y., Wu, T.-Y., Huang, Y.-M., & Chao, H.-C. (2008). An efficient end-to-end security mechanism for IP multimedia subsystem. *Computer Communications, 31*(18), 4259–4268. doi:10.1016/j.comcom.2008.05.025

Dierks, T., & Allen, C. (1999). *RFC 2246: The TLS protocol version 1.0*. Retrieved from HTTP://www.ietf.org/rfc/rfc2246.txt

Franks, J., Hallam-Baker, P., Hostetler, J., Lawrence, S., Leach, P., Luotonen, A., et al. (1999). *RFC 2617: HTTP authentication: basic and digest access authentication*. Retrieved from http://rfc.askapache.com/rfc2617/

Gayraud, R., & Jaques, O. (2010). *SIPp-SIP load generator*. Retrieved from http://sipp.sourceforge.net/

Geneiatakis, D., Dagiouklas, A., Kambourakis, G., Lambrinoudakis, C., Gritzalis, S., & Ehlert, S. (2006). Survey of security vulnerabilities in session initiation protocol. *IEEE Communications Surveys and Tutorials, 8*, 68–81. doi:10.1109/COMST.2006.253270

Geneiatakis, D., & Lambrinoudakis, C. (2007). A lightweight protection mechanism against signaling attacks in a SIP-based VoIP environment. *Telecommunication Systems, 36*(4), 153–159. doi:10.1007/s11235-008-9065-5

Guaci, S. (n. d.). *SIP Vicious*. Retrieved from http://code.google.com/p/sipvicious/

Hunter, M. T., Clark, R. J., & Park, F. S. (2007). Security issues with the IP multimedia subsystem (IMS). In *Proceedings of the Workshop on Middleware for Next-Generation Converged Networks and Applications* (p. 9).

Kent, S., & Atkinson, R. (1997). *RFC 2406: IP encapsulating security payload (ESP)*. Retrieved from http://www.ietf.org/rfc/rfc2406.txt

Kent, S., & Atkinson, R. (1998). *RFC 2401: Security architecture for the internet protocol*. Retrieved from http://www.ietf.org/rfc/rfc2401.txt

Klein, A. (2007). *BIND 9 DNS cache poisoning*. Retrieved from http://www.trusteer.com/docs/bind9dns.html

Nassar, M., & Niccolini, S. (2007). Holistic VoIP intrusion detection and prevention system. In *Proceedings of the 1ˢᵗ International Conference on Principles, Systems and Applications of IP Telecommunications* (pp. 1-9).

Ohlmeier, N. (2010). *SIP Swiss army knife.* Retrieved from http://sipsak.org/

Park, F. S., Patnaik, D., Amrutkar, C., & Hunter, M. T. (2008). A security evaluation of IMS deployments. In *Proceedings of the 2nd International Conference on Internet Multimedia Services Architecture and Applications* (pp. 1-6).

Plummer, D. (1982). *RFC 826: An ethernet address resolution protocol.* Retrieved from http://tools.ietf.org/html/rfc826

Postel, J. (1981). *RFC 791: IP: Internet protocol.* Retrieved from http://faculty.ksu.edu.sa/fantookh/RFC/rfc791.txt.pdf

Ramsdell, B. (1999). *RFC 2633: S/MIME version 3 message specification.* Retrieved from http://tools.ietf.org/html/rfc2633

3ʳᵈ Generation Partnership Project. (2008). *3GPP TS 23.228: IP multimedia subsystems (IMS): Third generation partnership project, technical specification group services and system aspects.* Retrieved from http://www.quintillion.co.jp/3GPP/Specs/23228-870.pdf

3ʳᵈ Generation Partnership Project. (2009). *3GPP TS 24.147: Conferencing using the IP multimedia (IM) core network (CN) subsystem: Technical specification group core network and terminals.* Retrieved from http://ftp.3gpp.org/specs/html-info/24147.htm

3ʳᵈ Generation Partnership Project. (2010). *3GPP TS 33.203: 3G security: Access security for IP-based services (Release 10): Third generation partnership project, technical specification group services and system aspects.* Retrieved from http://www.3gpp.org/ftp/specs/html-info/33203.htm

Rosenberg, J., Schulzrinne, H., Camarillo, G., Johnston, A., Peterson, J., Sparks, R., et al. (2002). *RFC 3261: SIP: Session initiation protocol.* Retrieved from http://www.ietf.org/rfc/rfc3261.txt

Schulzrinne, H., Casner, S., Frederick, R., & Jacobson, V. (1996). *RFC 1889: RTP: A transport protocol for real-time applications.* Retrieved from http://www.ietf.org/rfc/rfc1889.txt

Sher, M., & Magedanz, T. (2007). Protecting IP multimedia subsystem (IMS) service delivery platform from time independent attacks. In *Proceedings of the Third International Symposium on Information Assurance and Security* (pp. 171-176).

Sher, M., Wu, S., & Magedanz, T. (2006). *Security threats and solutions for application server of IP multimedia subsystem (IMS-AS).* Retrieved from http://www.diadem-firewall.org/workshop06/papers/monam06-paper-28.pdf

Sisalem, D., Kuthan, J., Abend, U., Floroiu, J., & Schulzrinne, H. (2009). *SIP Security.* New York, NY: John Wiley & Sons. doi:10.1002/9780470516997

Tanase, M. (2003). IP spoofing: An introduction. *Security Focus, 11.*

Vrakas, N., Geneiatakis, D., & Lambrinoudakis, C. (2010). A call conference room interception attack and its detection. In *Proceedings of the 7th International Conference on Trust, Privacy & Security in Digital Business* (pp. 38-44).

Wagner, R. (2001). *Address resolution protocol spoofing and man-in-the-middle attacks.* Reston, VA: The SANS Institute.

Walsh, T. J., & Kuhn, D. R. (2005). Challenges in securing voice over iP. *IEEE Security and Privacy, 3*(3), 44–49. doi:10.1109/MSP.2005.62

Wu, Y., Apte, V., Bagchi, S., Garg, S., & Singh, N. (2009). Intrusion detection in voice over IP environments. *International Journal of Information Security, 8*(3), 153–172. doi:10.1007/s10207-008-0071-0

Wu, Y., Bagchi, S., Garg, S., Singh, N., & Tsai, T. (2004). Scidive: A stateful and cross protocol intrusion detection architecture for voice-over-IP environments. In *Proceedings of the International Conference on Dependable Systems and Networks*, Firenze, Italy (p. 433).

Zhang, R., Wang, X., Farley, R., Yang, X., & Jiang, X. (2009, March). On the feasibility of launching the man-in-the-middle attacks on VoIP from remote attackers. In *Proceedings of the 4th ACM Symposium on Information, Computer and Communications Security* (pp. 61-69).

ENDNOTE

[1]   The S-CSCF checks the correlation between the IP and the given public ID of the messages from the Security Associations (SAs) which have been established during the AKA registration procedure.

APPENDIX

Acronyms and their definitions

AS	(Application Server)
CLF	(Connectivity Session Location & Repository Function)
GGSN	(Gateway GPRS Support Node)
HSS	(Home Subscriber Server)
IFC	(Initial Filter Criteria)
IA	(Internal Attacker)
IMPI	(IMS Private Identity)
IMPU	(IMS Public Identity)
IMS	(IP Multimedia Subsystem)
ISIM	(IP Multimedia Service Identity Module)
MRFC	(Media Resource Function Controller)
MRFP	(Media Resource Function Processor)
P-CSCF	(Proxy Call Session Control Function)
PDF	(Policy Decision Function)
S-CSCF	(Serving Call Session Control Function)
SIM	(Subscriber Identity Module)
UE	(User Equipment)
UICC	(Universal Integrated Circuit Card)
URI	(Uniform Resource Identifier)
USIM	(Universal SIM)

This work was previously published in the International Journal of Information Technologies and Systems Approach, Volume 4 Issue 2, edited by Frank Stowell and Manuel Mora, pp. 32-47, copyright 2011 by IGI Publishing (an imprint of IGI Global).

Chapter 19
Cryptographic Approaches for Privacy Preservation in Location–Based Services:
A Survey

Emmanouil Magkos
Ionian University, Greece

ABSTRACT

Current research in location-based services (LBSs) highlights the importance of cryptographic primitives in privacy preservation for LBSs, and presents solutions that attempt to support the (apparently) mutually exclusive requirements for access control and context privacy (i.e., identity and/or location), while at the same time adopting more conservative assumptions in order to reduce or completely remove the need for trust on system entities (e.g., the LBS provider, the network operator, or other peer nodes). This paper surveys the current state of knowledge concerning the use of cryptographic primitives for privacy-preservation in LBS applications.

INTRODUCTION

In the era of mobile and wireless communication technologies, recent advances in remote sensing and positioning technologies have altered the ways in which people communicate and interact with their environment. In the not-so-far future, *Location-Based Services* (LBS) that take into account the location information of a user, are expected to be available anywhere and anytime. Such services will be highly personalized and accessible even by resource-constrained mobile devices. A classification of the most popular services includes:

a) *point-of-interest* or "pull" services where a user sporadically queries an LBS provider to receive a nearby point of interest (Konidala et al., 2005; Candebat et al., 2005; Hengartner, 2006; Solanas & Balleste, 2007; Kohlweiss et al., 2007; Ghinita et al., 2008; Solanas & Balleste, 2008; Hengartner, 2008; Olumofin et al., 2009; Ardagna et al., 2009; Ghinita et al., 2009); b) *people-locator* services, where a watcher asks the LBS provider for the location of a target (Hauser & Kabatnik, 2001; Rodden et al., 2002; Bessler & Jorns, 2005; Jorns et al., 2005, 2007; Zhong et al., 2007; Sun et al., 2009); c) *notification-based* or "push'" services,

DOI: 10.4018/978-1-4666-1562-5.ch019

where location-based alerts or notifications are sent to a user (Zhu et al., 2003; Kolsch et al., 2005).

A typical scenario involves a user with a handheld device connecting through a mobile communication network to an external third party that provides an LBS service over the Internet. As with many aspects of ubiquitous computing, there is an inherent *trade-off* between access control and user privacy in LBS applications (Hauser & Kabatnik, 2001; Langheinrich, 2001; Rodden et al., 2002; Duckham & Kulik, 2006; Ardagna et al., 2007). On one hand the system typically needs to be protected from unauthorized access and misuse. On the other hand mobile users require the protection of their context information (e.g., location and/or identity information) against privacy adversaries (e.g., big-brother type threats, user profiling, unsolicited advertising) (Hauser & Kabatnik, 2001; Gruteser & Grunwald, 2003; Duckham & Kulik, 2006; Ardagna & Cremonini, 2009). The privacy issue is amplified by the requirement in modern telematics and location-aware applications for real-time, continuous location updates and accurate location information (e.g., traffic monitoring, asset tracking, location-based advertising, location-based payments, routing directions) (Gruteser & Liu, 2004; Kulik, 2009; Ghinita, 2009).

Recent research highlights the importance of *cryptography* in privacy preservation for LBSs, and presents solutions that attempt to support the (apparently) mutually exclusive requirements for access control and context privacy, while at the same time adopting conservative assumptions in order to reduce or completely remove the need for trust on system entities (e.g., the LBS provider, the network operator, or even the peer nodes). While a number of recent survey papers (Ardagna et al., 2007; Solanas et al., 2008; Ardagna & Cremonini, 2009; Kulik, 2009) cover aspects of access control and privacy, to the best of our knowledge there has been no thorough survey of the use of cryptographic techniques for privacy-preservation in LBS services.

Our Contribution

This paper surveys the current state of knowledge concerning the use of cryptographic primitives for achieving privacy-preservation in LBS services. Specifically, we categorize current research into three groups, based on the trust assumptions between parties involved in LBS schemes: TTP-based approaches, semi-distributed schemes, and TTP-free approaches. For each category, we review and evaluate the current literature in terms of privacy, security and efficiency.

DESIGN CONSIDERATIONS

Privacy Requirements

In general, privacy-preserving systems for LBS services are expected to satisfy some or all of the basic properties below (Pfitzmann & Kohntopp, 2000; Hauser & Kabatnik, 2001; Beresford & Stajano, 2003; Gajparia et al., 2004; Ardagna et al., 2007; Jorns et al., 2007; Kohlweiss et al., 2007; Solanas & Balleste, 2008; Hengartner, 2008; Ardagna & Cremonini, 2009):

- **Location privacy**: The protocol does not reveal the (exact) user's location information to the LBS provider. More generally, no unauthorized entity (or a coalition of unauthorized entities) should have access to the location data of the user, past or current.
- **Identity privacy (untraceability)**: The LBS provider is not able to find the identity of the user, based on the location information received during the user access. More generally, no unauthorized entity (or a coalition of unauthorized entities) should be able to trace the real identity of the user.
- **Tracking protection (unlinkability)**: The LBS provider is not able to link two or more successive user positions. More

generally, no unauthorized entity (or a coalition of unauthorized entities) should be able to link different sessions of the user.

Security Requirements

Access control in LBS involves satisfying some or all of the following security properties (Hauser & Kabatnik, 2001; Konidala et al., 2005; Candebat et al., 2005; Jorns et al., 2007; Kohlweiss et al., 2007; Ardagna & Cremonini, 2009; Saroiu & Wolman, 2009):

- **Mutual authentication**: Communication messages between system entities should be authenticated and integrity-protected. For example, an LBS provider will require user authentication in order to prevent service abuse, while users may also require identifying the LBS provider, in order to protect themselves from spoofing attacks.
- **Database secrecy**: The querying user should obtain no more than the requested information from the LBS provider. For example, from the LBS provider's perspective, returning a large number of points-of-interest in response to a cloaked location query would be against the provider's interests (Ghinita et al., 2009).
- **Location-Based Access Control (LBAC)** (also known as *context authentication*: The user may be required to prove her/his location in order to have access to a service or resource. This requirement is specific only to some location-aware applications, where a user may have an incentive to lie about her/his location.
- **Accountability**: Given the possibilities of abuse (e.g., illegal actions, abnormal access pattern of the user or when a credential is linked to an unlawful act), an option could be to have a mechanism for revoking the anonymity of a specific credential and tracing the identity of a real user, in

order to establish accountability. Typically, anonymity revocation will be an off-line protocol, where an LBS provider and a *Trusted Third Party* (TTP), given credential and transaction information, will be able to trace the identity of a user. The provider can then take appropriate measures, e.g., blacklisting a user. However it should not be easy to abuse this capability (e.g., in order to impersonate a user).

- **Non-repudiation**: A related requirement is non-repudiation, under which it should be possible to produce evidence regarding an entity participating to a transaction, in order to protect against a user's false denial of having participated to a transaction.

In the following we assume that an adversary will not exploit weaknesses in the underlying cryptographic primitives, and that when needed, a Public Key Infrastructure for certificate management is in place. Furthermore, while a typical threat model contains an adversary that will also attempt to read, modify or replay messages in order to impersonate users, set up man-in-the-middle attacks or disrupt the network in other ways, we do not emphasize on trivial uses of encryption to provide secrecy, integrity and authentication for the communication channel: this can be offered by classical techniques (Kaufman et al., 2002).

Efficiency Requirements

Any privacy-preserving scheme for LBS services should be efficient, mainly for the resource-constrained mobile user, in terms of:

- **Computation**: User registration and service access should be efficient, with as few public operations as possible.
- **Storage**: Users obtain and store a minimum necessary amount of credential information.

- **Communication**: The number of passes and bits that are communicated should be kept as low as possible.

A HIGH-LEVEL CATEGORIZATION OF CRYPTO-BASED LBS PRIVACY MODELS

A traditional approach for privacy is to move the users' trust from the LBS provider to a *fully-trusted* third party (TTP), in the form of an *online* application broker or proxy that mediates between the user and the LBS provider, guarantees identity and/or location privacy and is usually assumed not to conspire with the adversary (Rodden et al., 2002; Gruteser & Grunwald, 2003; Gajparia et al., 2004; Kolsch et al., 2005; Gedik & Liu, 2005; Konidala et al., 2005; Candebat et al., 2005; Mokbel et al., 2006; Khoshgozaran & Shahabi, 2007). Alternatively, the TTP may be an *offline* authority, whose role may include: certificate management, group key management, dispute resolution, credential revocation and accountability (Jorns et al., 2005, 2007). The different roles of a TTP in various models are depicted in Figure 1.

The strongest form of privacy can be achieved when any party receiving part of the communication is considered as untrusted. For example, the most conservative threat model considers a polynomial-time adversary that monitors all communications within the network to trace/track users, may compromise the LBS provider(s) and/or the network operator(s) and/or other peers and extract their logs to infer private information. The level of assumed trust can thus be used to classify the literature for privacy preservation (Figure 2). Indeed, we consider *TTP-based, semi-distributed* and *TTP-free* approaches:

- **TTP-based schemes:** Most schemes within this category adopt a centralized model for privacy. Here are included approaches that employ online and/or offline TTPs for: a) protecting the location information of users i.e., *TTP spatial k-anonymity* (Gruteser & Grunwald, 2003; Gedik & Liu, 2005; Mokbel et al., 2006), *TTP cloaking/obfuscation* (Ardagna et al., 2007; Hengartner, 2008; Khoshgozaran & Shahabi, 2007); b) protecting the link between location and user identity i.e., identity privacy with *simple pseudonyms* (Hauser & Kabatnik, 2001; Rodden et al., 2002; Konidala et al., 2005; Candebat et al., 2005) or *multiple pseudonyms* (Kolsch et al., 2005; Jorns et al., 2005, 2007).
- **Semi-distributed schemes:** This category, lies between TTP-based and TTP-free categories. To relax the need for a single trust-

Figure 1. Different roles of a TTP in LBS privacy models

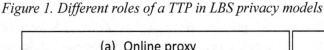

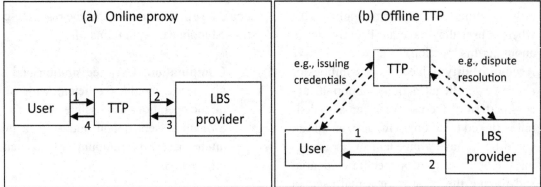

Figure 2. A categorization of crypto-based LBS privacy models

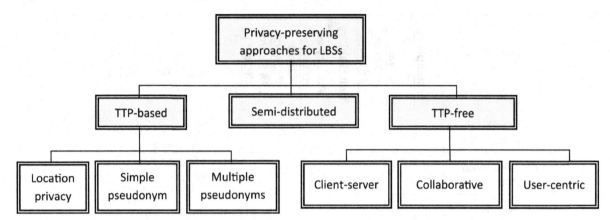

ed party, it has been proposed that trust should be distributed on a set of (two or more) non-colluding authorities that guarantee the privacy or the users (Kolsch et al., 2005; Kohlweiss et al., 2007; Zhong & Hengartner, 2008, 2009). Or, a semi-trusted authority could be trusted on some but not all aspects of user privacy: this authority could be the network operator, the LBS provider (Hauser & Kabatnik, 2001) or an external authority (Zhong et al., 2007).

- **TTP-free schemes:** In TTP-free solutions, trust assumptions are very weak or completely removed. The category contains *client-server* architectures (Ghinita et al., 2008; Olumofin et al., 2009; Ghinita et al., 2009), where communication takes place between a user and an untrusted LBS provider, as well as fully-distributed or *collaborative* settings (Solanas & Balleste, 2007,2008; Ghinita et al., 2007; Zhong et al., 2007; Ardagna et al., 2009; Rebollo-Monedero et al., 2009), where trust is distributed among a set of system peers that form ad-hoc networks and collaborate to achieve privacy against a set of untrusted entities (i.e., the LBS provider, and/or mobile peers or even the network operator). This change of paradigm may also exploit the hybrid nature of current mobile net-

works and the capabilities of modern handheld devices that are equipped with both WLAN and cellular interfaces (Solanas & Balleste, 2008; Solanas et al., 2008; Ardagna et al., 2009). Finally, this category also includes user-centric location privacy approaches where users control access to their location information without the need of any TTPs (Sun et al., 2009; Yiu et al., 2009).

Figure 3 summarizes the typical privacy and efficiency properties for the different categories of recent cryptographic schemes for privacy-preserving LBS services. Finally, another stream of research concerns *Location-Based Access Control* (LBAC) systems (Denning & MacDoran, 1998; Bardram et al., 2003; Zhang et al., 2005; Al-Muhtadi et al., 2006; Cho et al., 2006; Ardagna et al., 2007; Atallah et al., 2007; Saroiu & Wolman, 2009), that authenticate the physical location of a network entity before granting access to a service.

TTP-BASED APPROACHES

Location Privacy

Typically location privacy is suitable for applications where users' identities are required for the

Figure 3. The basic privacy models and their (typical) core properties

Properties / Models	Trust assumptions	Identity privacy	Location privacy	Unlinkability	Privacy vs accuracy	Client efficiency	LBS Server efficiency	Examples from academic literature
TTP spatial k-anonymity	√	X	√	X	√	√	√	Gruteser & Grunwald, 2003; Gedik & Liu, 2005; Mokbel et al, 2006
TTP cloaking/ obfuscation	√	X	√	X	√	√	√	Ardagna et al, 2007; Khoshgozaran & Shahabi, 2007; Hengartner, 2008
Simple pseudonym	√	√	X	X	X	√	√	Hauser & Kabatnik, 2001; Rodden et al, 2002; Konidala et al, 2005; Candebat et al, 2005
Multiple pseudonyms	√	√	X	√	X	X	√	Jorns et al (2005, 2007); Kolsch et al, 2005
Semi-distributed protocols	√	X	√	X	X	√	X	Kohlweiss et al, 2007; Zhong et al, 2007; Zhong & Hengartner (2008,2009)
PIR protocols	X	X	√	√	X	X	X	Ghinita et al (2008, 2009); Olumofin et al, 2009
Collaborative protocols	X	X	√	X	√*	X	√	Solanas & Balleste* (2007,2008); Zhong et al, 2007; Ardagna et al, 2009;
User-centric	X	X	√	X	X	X	√	Sun et al, 2009; Yiu et al, 2009

provision of a service, while at the same time the resolution of the location information can be reduced without severely degrading the service offered.

For example, in order to protect location privacy, the user's location information submitted to the LBS provider is *cloaked* by a TTP i.e., by sufficiently reducing its resolution in terms of space and/or time (Khoshgozaran & Shahabi, 2007). By adapting the well-known *k*-anonymity technique (Sweeney, 2002) to the spatial domain, the most popular approach has been to reduce the resolution of location information to an anonymity set of *k* users (Gruteser & Grunwald, 2003; Gedik & Liu, 2005; Mokbel et al., 2006). Or, location data may be perturbed/obfuscated by the TTP (Duckham & Kulik, 2005; Hoh & Gruteser, 2006; Ardagna et al., 2007; Lin et al., 2009) without severely degrading the offered service.

A cryptographic way to control access to location information, using simple public-key cryptography, is described in (Gajparia et al., 2004). In the proxy-based approach of Gajparia et al. (2004), an online Location Information Preference Authority (LIPA) is a trusted party that examines user-chosen constraints and makes decisions about the distribution of location information (LI) and accompanying constraints to the entity requesting the location information (i.e., an LBS provider or other users). To ensure that only the LIPA has access to users' LI and constraints, an online Location Gatherer (LG) constructs an LI token that contains the LI and constraints encrypted with the public key of the LIPA. The token also contains information which helps to identify the LI subject and the LIPA (from a list of available LIPAs). For access control, all information is digitally signed by the LG. Once the LBS provider wishing to use LI receives an LI token, verifies the signature, establishes the identity of the LI subject and submits the token to the appropriate LIPA, who checks if access to the LI is permitted for the requesting LBS provider.

A hardware-based approach for location privacy is proposed in (Hengartner, 2008), where a Trusted Computing (TC) module receives the user's location data encrypted with its public key. The module then queries the LBS database to retrieve the requested information, but for privacy it hands over location information to the LBS platform only if the platform is configured to implement an outlined privacy policy (e.g., the LBS does not learn location information). The module then signs and encrypts the LBS's response with the public key of the cellphone operator. In Hengartner (2008) software-based active attacks (i.e., query modification/injection) by the LBS provider are thwarted by using a *secure logging* approach, i.e., an auditing mechanism that stores logging information to the trusted module.

Evaluation Remarks

Schemes within this category typically achieve adequate access control assurances, since the user identity does not need to be secret. However, solutions based on location *k*-anonymization and spatiotemporal perturbation/obfuscation usually introduce a *privacy vs. accuracy* trade-off and may not be able to meet the high position accuracy requirements of modern location tracking applications (Gruteser & Liu, 2004; Kulik, 2009). Furthermore, in *k*-anonymous protocols, a sufficiently large number of users must be connecting at the same time to the same service. When user density is low, other solutions need to be examined (e.g., PIR-based privacy, or location perturbation/obfuscation). In addition, most of the above approaches typically involve sporadic queries that are executed at an LBS provider and may not be able to protect continuous paths (Ghinita et al., 2008; Bettini et al., 2009).

Another disadvantage that applies in general to TTP-based approaches is that the TTP is both a bottleneck and a single point of attack (Ghinita et al., 2007, 2008; Solanas & Balleste, 2008): the TTP must process all location updates of all the system users; in addition, if an adversary gets access to the TTP's data, then the privacy of system users is destroyed. Furthermore, users are not necessarily satisfied about completely trusting proxies and intermediaries (Rebollo-Monedero et al., 2009). Although TTPs are considered trusted entities, in reality, if a single authority is able to trace a user's identity, this power may be abused and privacy be violated; or, active (impersonation) attacks against system users could also be possible. Where there is only a single TTP, a trusted module could also be used to implement this trust, as in (Hengartner, 2008). On the other hand, the need for the acquisition of a specialized tamper-resistant module could also be seen as a drawback.

Current research focuses on approaches for *k*-anonymity and cloaking techniques that capture strong privacy guarantees while maintaining high data accuracy (Hoh et al., 2007), as well as on location privacy approaches that reduce (Zhong & Hengartner, 2008, 2009) or completely remove trust from any internal or external system entity (Solanas & Balleste, 2007, 2008; Ardagna et al., 2009).

Identity Privacy with Pseudonyms

This sub-category includes cryptographic methodologies based on pseudonyms to destroy the link between location information and the user identity. Specifically, in order to preserve privacy in location-based services that cannot be accessed anonymously (i.e., they require identification) but do not require a true identity either (Beresford & Stajano, 2003; Candebat et al., 2005). An advantage of the identity privacy setting is that location information can be kept as accurate as possible, which is often required in LBSs applications that offer high-quality information services (Gruteser

& Liu, 2004; Kulik, 2009), but the link to the real identity of a user is protected, in order to establish untraceability (Pfitzmann & Kohntopp, 2000).

The pseudonym-based approach was first used in (Hauser & Kabatnik, 2001) for a people-locator service and is based on public-key cryptography. In Hauser and Kabatnik (2001) a watcher digitally signs a query concerning a target and submits the signed query to the LBS provider. The query is accompanied with an authorization certificate, issued by the target, i.e., digitally signed by the target's private signature key, where the corresponding public key plays the role of the target's pseudonym for the specific service and is used as a reference with which the watcher can address the target. The certificate also lists the explicit permissions for the location data of the target. The watcher does not ever learn the target's pseudonym, as the pseudonym is encrypted with the public key of the LBS provider, who is also not aware of the real identity of the targets.

Another early approach was proposed in (Rodden et al., 2002). In their security model for location-tracking services, the user generates a random number X to be used as a pseudonym for communicating with an LBS provider T, and registers X to a trusted broker as $(T, Enc(K_T, X))$ where K_T is a symmetric encryption key provided by T to prevent unauthorized access to location information by other providers. The pseudonym X is used to communicate with T, only for the duration of the provision of the service. At any given time, a user may have a number of active pseudonyms. At some time the provider T queries the broker to find out the location of the user X. The broker is trusted on not revealing the real identity of the user. The LBS provider can keep querying the user's location, until the user decides to change pseudonym. All information is symmetrically encrypted, in order to deal with external observers. As shown in (Rodden et al., 2002), for people locator services the pseudonym can be securely passed to a group of watchers

that are approved by the user, while the broker is trusted on managing group membership.

Another scheme (Candebat et al., 2005) for point-of-interest LBSs assumes a proxy-based PKI and employs *identity-based encryption* [1] (Baek & Zheng, 2004) and threshold cryptographic principles [2]. For privacy preservation, each user owns one private key for decryption and signatures, while multiple pseudonyms are used as the corresponding public keys to communicate with the LBS provider. In addition, each user's private key is split between the user and an online *semi-trusted* mediator (SEM) who simplifies key management by validating the user credentials and acts as a proxy to request an LBS service on behalf of the user, under the different pseudonyms. The SEM carries out cryptographic operations in conjunction with the user to decrypt messages and generate identity-based signatures. The SEM assists the decryption (respectively, signing) process provided that the security credentials of the recipient (signer) have not be revoked. As a result, this mediated architecture makes credential revocation easier.

Evaluation Remarks

Approaches that combine simple pseudonyms with exact location information do not capture a strong notion of privacy. For example, an adversary (e.g., it could the provider or an adversary that analyses traffic) could trace the identity of a query by linking the physical location data to a particular individual. In addition, untraceability by itself may not be enough: if a set of distinct credentials can be linked to the same anonymous entity, then a customer profile can be built and this is considered a privacy violation. In this case, and in order to completely undermine privacy, the adversary will only have to trace one particular link of this chain (e.g., after the customer uses a credit card, with use of a camera, physical pursuit etc).

Finally, research for identity privacy in the LBS context may have something to gain from the literature on *anonymous credentials* (Camenisch & Lysyanskaya, 2001, 2002, 2004; Camenisch et al., 2006; Belenkiy et al., 2008), which build on top of early works on pseudonym systems (Chaum, 1985; Lysyanskaya et al., 2000). Here, a user proves to a service provider possession of a set of credentials without revealing anything other than this fact. However, state-of-the-art protocols for anonymous credentials in their present form induce high costs for both the user and servers, and so they should be carefully evaluated before adoption in the LBS context.

Multiple Pseudonyms for Unlinkability

As the use of traditional pseudonymity with long-term pseudonyms is not enough for strong privacy (Beresford & Stajano, 2003), sometimes privacy can be enhanced by destroying the link between successive user positions, mainly from the point of view of the LBS provider (Beresford & Stajano, 2003; Jorns et al., 2007). The pseudonym systems of the previous category were not designed with unlinkability as a key goal, although they could be modified to provide it (Hauser & Kabatnik, 2001; Rodden et al., 2002).

The provision of unlinkability is also closely related to an aspect of privacy that is also referred to as *path privacy* or *historical privacy* (Beresford & Stajano, 2003; Gruteser et al., 2004; Ardagna et al., 2007; Bettini et al., 2009; Ghinita, 2009). Here, the goal is to protect the privacy of mobile users in LBS applications against correlation attacks, e.g., to prevent the disclosure of the path followed by a mobile user who walks or travels in an urban area. A typical scenario may be a mobile user that sends continuous queries to LBS applications, e.g., "report the nearest restaurant while I move". LBSs of this type have also been called as *continuous LBSs* (Kulik, 2009).

In Beresford and Stajano (2003) it was argued that access to an LBS can be controlled by using a validated list of multiple, frequently changed pseudonyms that conceal the actual identity of a node. The use of untraceable and unlinkable pseudonyms to support privacy has also been extensively studied in location-aware applications for vehicular ad-hoc networks (VANETs) (Raya & Hubaux, 2005, 2007; Sampigethaya et al., 2005; Rahman & Hengartner, 2007; Sun et al., 2007). For example in Raya and Hubaux (2005, 2007), these pseudonyms are untraceable and unlinkable public keys for verifying digital signatures. Such solutions, if adopted in the LBS context, should be carefully designed to avoid increasing the complexity of user registration and the computational, storage and communication cost for the handheld devices.

The scheme in (Kolsch et al., 2005) considers a notification-based LBS, where the user gets allergy warnings based on weather conditions in the environment. Communication is encrypted, authenticated and integrity-protected with public-key encryption and signatures. A trusted location broker mediates between the LBS provider and the mobile operator. For every new LBS, a user creates a "fresh" pseudonym to interact with the operator and a different pseudonym to interact with the LBS provider, while each pseudonym is of the form of a public/private key pair for encryption and signature. For untraceability, signature data are never sent to the LBS provider; instead, warnings are sent to the user through an anonymous communication channel, opened by the user in cooperation with the broker. Mutual authentication between the LBS and the broker is performed through a *zero-knowledge proof* system[3]. The broker can link the different pseudonyms together and is aware of the user's location, but cannot trace the user. On the other hand, the mobile operator is aware of the true identity of the user and his/her location, but cannot learn the specific LBS that was used by the user.

In the people-locator service of (Jorns et al., 2007), users employ different transaction pseudonyms for different service requests, and these pseudonyms cannot be linked to each other by the LBS provider, although linking can be done by a trusted network operator. Watchers first establish a trust relation with a target, and then the network operator acts as a trusted proxy that assists users in pseudonym management and credential generation, and mediates initial handshaking between watchers and targets. Specifically, the operator, which shares a secret pw_A with a user A (the watcher), sends to A the initial element of a *hash chain* of elements (Lamport, 1981) i.e., an anchor value $h_0 = anchor_B$ that corresponds to the location of the target user B. Then, the list of n pseudonyms for a watcher A that subscribes to B's location[4] are generated by hashing the previous chain element together with the shared secret pw_A, that is: $h_i = HMAC(h_{i-1}, pw_A)$, $1 \leq i \leq n$, where HMAC could belong for example to the SHA family of functions (NIST, 2008). These pseudonyms are unlinkable by the LBS provider and are used by the watcher as authentication tokens to ask the location of the target from the provider. The provider will forward a token to the operator, who will act as a broker and return the target's location. The scheme is a successor of PRIVES (Jorns et al., 2005; Bessler & Jorns, 2005).

Evaluation Remarks

The mere use of multiple pseudonyms is not always sufficient for location privacy against a global observer that performs traffic analysis (Beresford & Stajano, 2003; Gruteser & Grunwald, 2003; Gruteser et al., 2004). For example, when the true identity could be directly or indirectly inferred by the location of the person, or when the adversary is able to correlate historical information i.e., spatial and/or temporal information about a mobile user (Beresford & Stajano, 2003; Raya & Hubaux, 2005; Buttyan et al., 2007; Bettini et al., 2009) in order to link two or more user transmissions. As a result, for path privacy a user may have to update a pseudonym at points where the spatial and temporal resolution is decreased e.g., within a MIX

zone[5] (Beresford & Stajano, 2003; Buttyan et al., 2007; Freudiger et al., 2009) or a junction (Gruteser et al., 2004; Burmester et al., 2008). Indeed, most related work for historical/path privacy attempts to decrease the spatiotemporal information that is revealed to an adversary, between successive locations (Beresford & Stajano, 2003; Gruteser & Grunwald, 2003; Gruteser et al., 2004; Buttyan et al., 2007; Hoh et al., 2007, 2008; Freudiger et al., 2009; Bettini et al., 2009; Ghinita, 2009). We refer the reader to (Ardagna et al., 2007; Bettini et al., 2009; Ghinita, 2009) for a survey and assessment of recent approaches for path privacy preservation in location-based services. Other attacks include a compromised LBS provider that links two different pseudonyms to the same set of personal preferences at the service level (Beresford & Stajano, 2003), or tracing/linking that may take place at the physical or MAC layers (Gruteser & Grunwald, 2005; Rasmussen & Capkun, 2007).

We also note that there may be cases where unlikability may be impossible or undesirable, as in reputation-based systems (Wakeman et al., 2007). Or, LBS providers may need to link information for supporting infotainment or value-added, personalization services. In such cases, the linkage may or may not necessarily require tracing the real identity, e.g., the simple pseudonym approach could be used instead (Duckham & Kulik, 2006).

A final remark is that solutions based on both simple and multiple pseudonyms can be counted as TTP-based: in reality, in order to establish accountability or non-repudiation a trusted system entity may have to keep a record of the issued pseudonyms, location data and/or the corresponding real identity of the device[6].

THE SEMI-DISTRIBUTED SETTING

At a high level, the semi-distributed approach can be seen as a trivial extension of the TTP-based privacy model. It relaxes trust assumptions by not requiring full trust on a single party but instead moving trust to a suitable set of (typically, two or more) non-colluding entities. In addition, we choose to include in this category schemes which employ one or more third parties that are trusted on some (but not all) aspects of user privacy and/or security.

For example in Zhong and Hengartner (2008, 2009), a distributed k-anonymity protocol is proposed, and privacy is based on the existence of a set of servers, each deployed by a different organization (i.e., they are assumed not to collude). A number of *location brokers* track the location of a different subset of registered users. Each location broker learns the location and number of users that have registered with this broker but not the total number of users in this cell, as some users may have been registered with another broker. Furthermore there are a number of secure *comparison servers*, where a server informs the user whether there are at least k users who have registered the user's current cell as their current location across all brokers. Similarly, the comparison server learns neither the user's location, nor the exact number of users in a cell. The solution in (Zhong & Hengartner, 2008) uses the *additively homomorphic* property of several probabilistic public key encryption schemes[7] (Okamoto & Uchiyama, 1998; Paillier, 1999), where for example there is an operation $\oplus$ on the message space and an operation $\otimes$ on the cipher space, such that the "product" of the encryptions equals the encrypted "sum" of the messages, i.e., $E(M_1) \otimes E(M_2) = E(M_1 \oplus M_2)$. To learn whether there are k users in his/her query area, the user interacts with each authoritative location broker and obtains the numbers of registered users within the user's cell, encrypted with the public key of the comparison server. The user uses the additively homomorphic property of the encryption scheme to calculate the encrypted sum of numbers, and randomizes (re-encrypts) the encrypted results, in order to hide the total num-

ber of users from the comparison server. Finally, the user interacts with the comparison server to learn whether this number is greater than k, without the server ever learning or infering k. In Zhong & Hengartner (2009) this is achieved by using a protocol (Blake & Kolesnikov, 2004) based on the *oblivious transfer* primitive[8] (Rabin, 1981).

Another scheme (Kohlweiss et al., 2007) assumes the existence of an online proxy P, an offline trustee T (an independent party without any commercial interests) and a number ℓ of LBS providers, with ℓ being a security parameter. The proxy, who has a financial relationship with the user, knows the user's location and mediates between the user and the LBS providers. In a data retrieval phase, the proxy runs a protocol with every LBS provider, and obtains an encrypted result. Using the additively homomorphic property of the generalized Paillier cryptosystem (Damgard & Jurik, 2001), the proxy combines the partial messages into a single encrypted result, which only the user (and not the proxy) is able to decrypt. The assets that are protected are: the user's location (against the LBS providers), the user's subscription (against the proxy) and the database contents of the providers (against the user and the proxy), apart from the location-based information that the user retrieves. By introducing the privacy trustee, the protocol assures that the LBS providers do not even learn whether a user is accessing their service or not, even if they cooperate with the proxy; this privacy assurance was named *service unobservability* (Kohlweiss et al., 2007). The above properties are achieved at the cost of using a number of cryptographic primitives, including zero-knowledge proofs[2], oblivious transfer[7], homomorphic encryption[6], and 3-out-of-3 *threshold encryption*[8]. However, the protocol is efficient for the mobile users, since only a single public-key decryption per user is required.

In the Louis privacy-preserving protocol for buddy-tracking applications (Zhong et al., 2007) Alice considers Bob nearby if he is within a circle of some radius centered around Alice. Trent is a semi-trusted third party that helps Alice and Bob decide whether they are nearby, but Trent does not learn any other location information concerning Alice or Bob. The only thing Trent learns is Alice's identity. The Louis protocol also exploits the homomorphic property of the Paillier public-key cryptosystem (Paillier, 1999). Alice encrypts and sends her coordinates to Bob, who "adds" his coordinates (using the additively homomorphic property of Paillier), and randomizes the result with a salt that only Trent can remove (i.e., the salt is encrypted with Trent's public key). The protocol terminates when Trent notifies Alice whether Bob is nearby.

Evaluation Remarks

Semi-distributed trust assumptions are considered weak as long as the set of non-colluding entities is sufficiently large, as in Zhong and Hengartner (2008, 2009), or when their interests is colluding. Note that the set of these entities can be well-known and so the risk of trusting a dishonest entity may be small (Rebollo-Monedero et al., 2009). Related to this is the notion of a *semi-honest* (also known as *honest but curious*) authority, proposed in the context of privacy-preserving data mining by Pinkas (2002), under a less conservative threat model: semi-honest adversaries are legal participants that follow the protocol specification, behave the way they are supposed to, do not collude or sabotage the process, but instead try to learn additional information given all the messages that were exchanged during the protocol. On the other hand, the assumption of a semi-honest adversary has also been seen as a strong assumption (Kargupta et al., 2007). Indeed, if the (assumingly, non-colluding) authorities misbehave and collude, then deprivatisation of a user privacy is trivial. For these reasons it is preferable that third parties are trusted on some (but not all) aspects of user privacy.

TTP-FREE SCHEMES

Recently a new paradigm of privacy for LBS applications has also emerged where network operators, LBS providers and even network peers are viewed as potential adversaries. As a result, a number of *TTP-free* solutions for enhanced location privacy in LBS services have been proposed (Solanas & Balleste, 2007, 2008; Ghinita et al., 2007, 2008; Zhong & Hengartner, 2008, 2009; Solanas et al., 2008; Ardagna et al., 2009). Such schemes relax or completely remove the need for unrealistic trust assumptions. Three main subcategories are the client-server approach, the collaborative approach and the user-centric approach. In most TTP-free approaches, it is implicitly assumed that mobile clients autonomously compute their own location (e.g., with GPS positioning) or else unnecessary trust assumptions should have to be made.

Client-Server Communication

Cryptography can help towards building client-server LBS architectures that are TTP-free. The use of identification mechanisms based on zero-knowledge proofs (Goldreich et al., 1991), was first discussed in (Duckham & Kulik, 2006) as a promising step towards balancing privacy with access control in location-aware computing. Since then, a number of privacy-preserving schemes have been proposed (Hengartner, 2006; Ghinita et al., 2008, 2009; Ghinita, 2008, 2009; Olumofin et al., 2009), and most of them are based on the theoretical work on *Private Information Retrieval* (PIR) (Chor et al., 1995; Kushilevitz & Ostrovsky, 1997; Chor & Gilboa, 1997). Schemes of this category introduce a new privacy model, depicted in Figure 4.

The new location privacy model is described in (Ghinita et al., 2008), building upon the *computational PIR* (cPIR) protocol introduced in (Kushilevitz & Ostrovsky, 1997). Specifically, the LBS provider holds a database that is coded as an n-item ordered array $X[1..n]$. The query of

Figure 4. A client-server model for privacy in LBSs

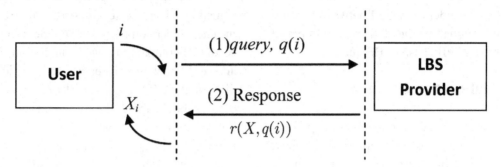

a user is transformed to a query-by-index, i.e., the user wants to easily retrieve the i-th item $X[i]$ in a way that is computationally infeasible for the LBS provider to find out the value of i (in the LBS setting, this could reveal for example the user's location). When initiating a query, the user creates an encrypted query object $q(i)$; the LBS provider computes privately, using a mathematical transformation, the result $r(X,q(i))$ and sends the result back to the user. An extension of PIR, *Symmetric PIR* (SPIR) (Mishra & Sarkar, 2000) establishes database secrecy by assuring that no information, other than what is relevant to the current location, is leaked to the querying user. At a high level, the SPIR primitive can be seen as a generalization of the oblivious transfer primitive (Rabin, 1981) -please also refer to Olumofin et al. (2009) for an overview and historical perspective of the PIR approach.

In Ghinita et al. (2008) PIR is used by a client to query an LBS provider for a nearby point of interest. The cost in Ghinita et al. (2008) is acceptable by letting the user retrieve a small fraction of the LBS database. The approach was extended in Ghinita et al. (2009), where the user locations are hidden inside a cloaked region, and then a PIR protocol is run between the client and the LBS provider in order to disclose an optimally small number of points-of-interest, for database protection.

The hardware-based architecture in Hengartner (2006) uses Trusted Computing (TC) technolo-gies to ensure that a compromised LBS provider does not access user location information, and a PIR technique to ensure that the user only learns information about his/her current location and that the provider cannot infer the location of a user by observing which location-specific data sets are retrieved by the user. The PIR algorithm is implemented within the TC module, at the LBS provider's premises. The TC module also acts as a trusted proxy and (securely) obtains the user's location data, submits queries and forwards the responses, encrypted with the user's public key.

Evaluation Remarks

PIR-based approaches provide the strongest privacy assurances with the weakest trust assumptions, as it is computationally untractable to reveal the link between the user and location data, while on the other hand the user only learns information relevant to his/her location. In Ghinita et al. (2008) and Ghinita, (2009) it is also shown how the PIR framework, in contrast to k-anonymous cloaking, could protect LBS users against correlation attacks (path privacy), by not revealing any spatial information.

A challenge is to design computationally efficient and practical solutions that reduce the processing overhead of the early schemes, in view of the low-computing and resource-poor end devices, and some recent approaches seem promising towards this direction (Ghinita, 2008;

Olumofin et al., 2009; Ghinita et al., 2009). Such approaches consider a tradeoff between privacy and computational overhead in order to improve performance in PIR-based LBS queries.

The Collaborative Setting

The fully distributed or collaborative privacy model (Figure 5) does not rely on centralized trusted entities, but trust is distributed among system peers that may also form ad-hoc networks and collaborate to achieve privacy against a set of untrusted entities (e.g., other mobile peers, the LBS provider, or even the network operator (Solanas & Balleste, 2007, 2008; Ardagna et al., 2009).

In the TTP-free approach of Solanas and Balleste (2007, 2008) a user U interacts with $k-1$ companions, requests their location information and computes a k-anonymized location, as the centroid of the current locations in the cloaked area (a similar approach was also taken in (Ghinita et al., 2007), where users also shared their location prior to computing a k-anonymized location). In Solanas and Balleste (2008), the masked location is then sent to the LBS provider and to U's companions. To deal with the threat that a malicious user learns the exact location of her/his companions and violates their privacy, an extended second scheme is also proposed in Solanas and Balleste (2008). The scheme exploits the additively homomorphic property of probabilistic public-key encryption. Specifically, users possess

the public key of an untrusted LBS provider, signed by a Certificate Authority. Then, a user U initiates a location request in cooperation with a set of $k-1$ companions: each companion encrypts and sends back to U its encrypted location coordinates, then U "combines" the encrypted coordinates and computes the encrypted aggregate. In this second scheme, stronger privacy is established under the assumption that the users will not trust each other (Solanas & Balleste, 2008). In this version, location privacy is guaranteed even against collisions of other peers with the LBS provider.

Another scheme, the Lester scheme in Zhong et al. (2007) implements a nearby-friends service in a collaborative manner. In the Lester scheme, users learn information about their friend's location only if this friend is actually online. Specifically, Alice and Bob execute a secure two-party protocol and jointly compute, in two communication steps, whether their positions are near to each other, without learning their exact positions. The protocol uses the homomorphic encryption property of a variation[6] of the ElGamal scheme (Cramer et al., 1997).

Another collaborative k-anonymity scheme for hybrid network architectures is presented in Ardagna et al. (2009), where the threat model views the network operator and other peers as potential adversaries. The scheme considers a hybrid network architecture, where users possess handheld devices that are equipped with both

Figure 5. A distributed model for privacy in LBSs

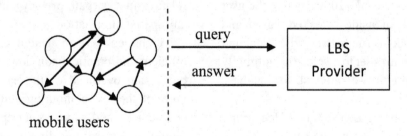

WLAN (e.g., WiFi or Bluetooth) and WWAN (e.g., GSM/3G) capabilities. Locally, mobile peers are able to establish ad-hoc connections (point-to-point or broadcast) with each other. At the same time, a user u belongs to a cellular network and is able to receive and send signals to a cellular network operator o in order to access services provided by an Internet-connected LBS provider. The scheme in Ardagna et al. (2009) works as follows: during a key setup phase, the sender u establishes a symmetric key SK with s. At some time in the future, u specifies a message M and a preference k, then splits M in k packets $\{m_1, m_2, ..., m_k\}$, encrypts each packet m_i with the key SK and then appends a message identifier mid, that is: $\bar{m}_i = E_{SK}(m_i) \parallel mid$, for each $i \le k$. The user then randomly selects $k-1$ peers in his/her range, and sends a different packet to each of them. Packets are distributed to the neighboring peers using a random forwarding distribution algorithm (Ardagna et al., 2009). Eventually the peers will forward the packets to the server s through the operator o, who will see packets from k different users, so k-anonymity is preserved. The server s can also reply to u, by encrypting a message reply with the key SK, and then transmitting the result to all k peers, through o. Only u will be able to receive and decrypt the message.

Evaluation Remarks

With collaborative protocols privacy is based on much less strong assumptions (even in cases when users trust each other), while the bottleneck of the TTP-based approaches is removed. In addition, such protocols can achieve higher fault tolerance and resilience against privacy and security attacks. However, the cost for the above advantages is usually higher communication and computation for the low computing, resource-constrained system clients.

User-Centric Model

Some very recent approaches employ cryptographic methods in order to give the user control over who is allowed to access her/his location information, and in some cases with which granularity. Typically, such properties are useful in people-locator services (Cox et al., 2007; Sun et al., 2009; Yiu et al., 2009). Since no trust assumptions concerning privacy are made, protocols of this category can be considered as TTP-free.

For example in Sun et al. (2009) each target defines and controls a group of entities that are allowed to access its encrypted location information, and group decryption keys are established and distributed to the members of the group. The proposed system also allows the user to define the granularity with which different group members have access to location information. For relatively small groups, the user will generate her/his own location information, encrypt it and then directly distribute the keys to the other members, by running a *group-key management* protocol (Rafaeli & Hutchison, 2003; Sun et al., 2009) such as Diffie-Hellman group key exchange (Diffie & Hellman, 1976; Kim et al., 2000).

In Yiu et al. (2009) users decide which trusted friends can perform spatial queries on their location data, using an untrusted LBS provider. A user transforms her/his spatial information using conventional (e.g., AES) symmetric encryption. A query is evaluated through a distributed, multiple round protocol between the user and the LBS provider.

Evaluation Remarks

Scalability is the key factor determining whether schemes of this category will flourish. Current schemes impose high costs in terms of computation and communication. For large groups, it seems inevitable that there will also be a third party, trusted or semi-trusted, that at a minimum will handle group management. In Sun et al. (2009)

for example, when larger groups are considered, the user needs to build a trust relationship with a server of the network. In (Sun et al, 2009) the user encrypts and uploads the location information into a Location Server (LS); on demand, the LBS provider requests the location from the LS and sends it to a trusted Group Server who manages the group keys (e.g., key distribution, re-keying and key updating) by using a *hierarchical key tree* structure (Sun et al., 2009). The idea is to hierarchically conceal location data with different keys, where each key corresponds to a particular granularity, and distributes the decryption keys to group members with the necessary permissions.

Location-Based Access Control

Another increasingly important issue for location-aware security services, is how to authenticate the physical location of a network entity before granting access to a service or resource (Zhu et al., 2003; Bardram et al., 2003; Al-Muhtadi et al., 2006; Cho et al., 2006; Atallah et al., 2007; Saroiu & Wolman, 2009). The notion of Location-Based Access Control (LBAC) is not new (Denning & MacDoran, 1998) and in the recent past a number of cryptographic mechanisms have been proposed to facilitate LBAC (Zhang et al., 2005; Cho et al., 2006; Al-Muhtadi et a.l, 2006). With context authentication, there are schemes that authenticate either the exact location information (Zhang et al., 2005) or an approximation of location information, such as the areas enclosed within a set of access points (Cho et al., 2006).

In Zhang et al. (2005) for example, LBAC is established among static sensor nodes in a distributed sensor network, and location is used as a node's identity when communicating with other nodes. In Zhang et al. (2005) sensor nodes are localized by mobile, GPS-enabled robots that securely pass to each sensor a location-based key (LBK) i.e., a symmetric key that corresponds to a node's geographic location. Based on the principle of identity-based public-key cryptography[1], LBKs

are later used to derive public keys and perform mutually authenticated key establishment with neighboring nodes, while security of the key establishment is based on the bilinear Diffie-Hellman assumption (Boneh & Franklin, 2001).

The work of Al-Muhtadi et al. (2006) for pervasive computing environments (PCEs) introduces *location-based encryption*: resources are stored in an encrypted form and they can be decrypted only when the requestor is at the correct location. In Hengartner (2006), it is argued that location-based encryption can be used for implementing a people-locator LBS, where the LBS provider could encrypt its information with location-dependent symmetric keys and make the encrypted data publicly available by using a distributed hash table, while the network operator would provide decryption keys to customers based on their current location. In Atallah et al. (2007) a key management technique for geo-spatial access control is described, where the access control policy assigns to a user a specific geographic area, and every user obtains access only to her/his area of information.

In Cho et al. (2006) access to a WLAN is granted only if a mobile node is located within the shared areas covered by multiple access points (APs). The protocol authenticates location claims and establishes shared session keys for each node/AP pair using Diffie-Hellman key exchange. Finally in Saroiu and Wolman (2009) the identities of mobile clients and the local infrastructure components (e.g., APs) are represented by public keys: clients send to the infrastructure a signed request for a location proof, to enable a mobile location-aware application or service. The AP validates the request, then signs and sends to the client a location proof with a current timestamp.

Evaluation Remarks

Schemes of this category give an emphasis not on privacy, but on security for access control. Clearly, privacy can be challenging when exact locations are used, or when users are granted access rights to a specific area. Under this view, the privacy of mobile clients in LBAC systems could be enhanced with pseudonym-based techniques. Future research could also build on recent results for TTP-free and collaborative solutions that reduce the trust assumptions of third parties. The goal may be to fill the need for high-quality LBAC systems while establishing privacy for the end users. Issues and challenges for privacy in LBAC systems are also given in Ardagna et al. (2007), Ardagna and Cremonini (200), and Saroiu and Wolman (2009).

CONCLUSION

Current research focuses in the inherent *trade-off* between user privacy and access control in LBS applications: On one hand the system typically needs to be protected from unauthorized access, on the other hand mobile users require the protection of their context information from unauthorized access. This paper surveyed the state-of-the-art in cryptography-based solutions for achieving privacy-preservation in LBS services. Specifically, we categorized current research into three groups, based on the trust assumptions between parties involved in LBS schemes: TTP-based approaches, semi-distributed schemes, and TTP-free approaches. For each category, we reviewed and evaluated the current literature in terms of privacy, security and efficiency.

REFERENCES

Al-Muhtadi, J., Hill, R., Campbell, R., & Mickunas, M. (2006). Context and location-aware encryption for pervasive computing environments. In *Proceedings of the 4th Annual IEEE International Conference on Pervasive Computing and Communications Workshops* (pp. 283-288). Washington, DC: IEEE Computer Society.

Ardagna, C. A., Cremonini, M., Capitani di Vimercati, S. D., & Samarati, P. (2007). Privacy-enhanced location-based access control. In Gertz, M., & Jajodia, S. (Eds.), *The handbook of database security: Applications and trends* (pp. 531–552). Berlin, Germany: Springer-Verlag.

Ardagna, C. A., Cremonini, M., Capitani di Vimercati, S. D., & Samarati, P. (2009). Access control in location-based services. In C. Bettini, S. Jajodia, P. Samarati, & X. S. Wang (Eds.), *Proceedings of Research Issues and Emerging Trends in Privacy in Location-Based Applications* (LNCS 5599, pp. 106-126).

Ardagna, C. A., Jajodia, S., Samarati, P., & Stavrou, A. (2009). Privacy preservation over untrusted mobile networks. In C. Bettini, S. Jajodia, P. Samarati, & X. S. Wang (Eds.), *Proceedings of Research Issues and Emerging Trends in Privacy in Location Based Applications* (LNCS 5599, pp. 84-105).

Atallah, M., Blanton, M., & Frikken, K. (2007). Efficient techniques for realizing geo-spatial access control. In *Proceedings of the 2nd ACM Symposium on Information, Computer and Communications Security* (pp. 82-92). New York, NY: ACM Press.

Baek, J., & Zheng, Y. (2004). Identity-based threshold decryption. In F. Bao, R. Deng, & J. Zhou (Eds.), *Proceedings of Public Key Cryptography* (LNCS 2947, pp. 262-276).

Bardram, J., Kjær, R., & Pedersen, M. (2003). Context-aware user authentication–supporting proximity-based login in pervasive computing. In A. K. Dey, A. Schmidt, & J. F. McCarthy (Eds.), *Proceedings of the 5th International Conference on Ubiquitous Computing* (LNCS 2864, pp. 107-123).

Belenkiy, M., Chase, M., Kohlweiss, M., & Lysyanskaya, A. (2008). P-signatures and noninteractive anonymous credentials. In *Proceedings of the 5th Conference on Theory of Cryptography* (pp. 356-374).

Beresford, A. R., & Stajano, F. (2003). Location privacy in pervasive computing. *IEEE Pervasive Computing / IEEE Computer Society and IEEE Communications Society*, *2*(1), 46–55. doi:10.1109/MPRV.2003.1186725

Bessler, S., & Jorns, O. (2005). A privacy enhanced service architecture for mobile users. In *Proceedings of the Third IEEE International Conference on Pervasive Computing and Communications Workshops* (pp. 125-129). Washington, DC: IEEE Computer Society.

Bettini, C., Mascetti, S., Wang, S., Freni, D., & Jajodia, S. (2009). Anonymity and historical-anonymity in location-based services. In C. Bettini, S. Jajodia, P. Samarati, & X. S. Wang (Eds.), *Proceedings of Research Issues and Emerging Trends in Privacy in Location Based Applications* (LNCS 5599, pp. 1-30).

Blake, I. F., & Kolesnikov, V. (2004). Strong conditional oblivious transfer and computing on intervals. In P. J. Lee (Ed.), *Proceedings of the 10th International Conference on the Theory and Application of Cryptology and Information Security* (LNCS 3329, pp. 515-529).

Boneh, D., & Franklin, M. (2001). Identity-based encryption from the Weil pairing. In *Proceedings of the 21st Annual International Cryptology Conference on Advances in Cryptology* (pp. 213-229).

Burmester, M., Magkos, E., & Chrissikopoulos, V. (2008). Strengthening privacy protection in VANETs. In *Proceedings of the IEEE International Conference on Wireless & Mobile Computing, Networking & Communication* (pp. 508-513). Washington, DC: IEEE Computer Society.

Buttyan, L., Holczer, T., & Vajda, I. (2007). On the effectiveness of changing pseudonyms to provide location privacy in VANETs. In F. Stajano, C. Meadows, S. Capkun, & T. Moore (Eds.), *Proceedings of the Fourth European Workshop on Security and Privacy in Ad hoc and Sensor Networks* (LNCS 4572, pp. 129-141).

Camenisch, J., Hohenberger, S., Kohlweiss, M., Lysyanskaya, A., & Meyerovich, M. (2006). How to win the CloneWars: Efficient periodic n-times anonymous authentication. In *Proceedings of the 13th ACM Conference on Computer and Communications Security* (pp. 201-210). New York, NY: ACM Press.

Camenisch, J., & Lysyanskaya, A. (2001). An efficient system for non-transferable anonymous credentials with optional anonymity revocation. In B. Pfitzmann (Ed.), *Proceedings of the International Conference on the Theory and Application of Cryptographic Techniques* (LNCS 2045, pp. 93-118).

Camenisch, J., & Lysyanskaya, A. (2002) Dynamic accumulators and application to efficient revocation of anonymous credentials. In M. Yung (Ed.), *Proceedings of the 22nd Annual International Cryptology Conference on Advances in Cryptology* (LNCS 2442, pp. 61-76).

Camenisch, J., & Lysyanskaya, A. (2004). Signature schemes and anonymous credentials from bilinear maps. In M. Franklin (Ed.), *Proceedings of the 24th Annual International Cryptology Conference on Advances in Cryptology* (LNCS 3152, pp. 1-6).

Candebat, T., Dunne, C., & Gray, D. T. (2005). Pseudonym management using mediated identity-based cryptography. In *Proceedings of the Workshop on Digital Identity Management* (pp. 1-10). New York, NY: ACM Press.

Chaum, D. L. (1981). Untraceable electronic mail, return addresses, and digital pseudonyms. *Communications of the ACM*, *24*(2), 84–90. doi:10.1145/358549.358563

Chaum, D. L. (1983). Blind signatures for untraceable payments. In *Proceedings of Advances in Cryptology* (pp. 199-203).

Chaum, D. L. (1985). Security without identification: Transaction systems to make big brother obsolete. *Communications of the ACM, 28*(10), 1030–1044. doi:10.1145/4372.4373

Cho, Y. S., Bao, L., & Goodrich, M. (2006). Secure access control for location-based applications in WLAN systems. In *Proceedings of the 2nd IEEE International Workshop on Wireless and Sensor Networks Security* (pp. 852-857). Washington, DC: IEEE Computer Society.

Chor, B., & Gilboa, N. (1997). Computationally private information retrieval (extended abstract). In *Proceedings of the Twenty-Ninth Annual ACM Symposium on Theory of Computing* (pp. 304-313). New York, NY: ACM Press.

Chor, B., Goldreich, O., Kushilevitz, E., & Sudan, M. (1995). Private information retrieval. In *Proceedings of the Annual IEEE Symposium on Foundations of Computer Science* (pp. 41-50). Washington, DC: IEEE Computer Society.

Cox, L. P., Dalton, A., & Marupadi, V. (2007). Smokescreen: Flexible privacy controls for presence-sharing. In *Proceedings of the 5th International Conference on Mobile Systems Applications and Services* (pp. 233-245). New York, NY: ACM Press.

Cramer, R., Gennaro, R., & Schoenmakers, B. (1997). A secure and optimally efficient multi-authority election scheme. *European Transactions on Telecommunications, 8*(5), 481–490. doi:10.1002/ett.4460080506

Damgard, I., & Jurik, M. (2001). A generalisation, a simpli.cation and some applications of Paillier's probabilistic public-key system. In K. Kim (Ed.), *Proceedings of the 4th International Workshop on Practice and Theory in Public Key Cryptography* (LNCS 1992, pp. 119-136).

Denning, D., & MacDoran, P. (1996). Location-based authentication: Grounding cyberspace for better security. *Computer Fraud & Security,* (2): 12–16. doi:10.1016/S1361-3723(97)82613-9

Desmedt, Y. G. (1994). Threshold cryptography. *European Transactions on Telecommunications, 5*(4), 449–457. doi:10.1002/ett.4460050407

Diffie, W., & Hellman, M. (1976). New directions in cryptography. *IEEE Transactions on Information Theory, 22*(6), 644–654. doi:10.1109/TIT.1976.1055638

Duckham, M., & Kulik, L. (2005). A formal model of obfuscation and negotiation for location privacy. In H.-W. Gellersen, R. Want, & A. Schmidt (Eds.), *Proceedings of the 3rd International Conference on Pervasive Computing* (LNCS 3468, pp. 152-170).

Duckham, M., & Kulik, L. (2006). Location privacy and location-aware computing. In Drummond, J., Billen, R., Forrest, D., & Joao, E. (Eds.), *Investigating change in space and time.* Boca Raton, FL: CRC Press.

ElGamal, T. (1985). A public key cryptosystem and a signature scheme based on discrete logarithms. *IEEE Transactions on Information Theory, 31*(4), 469–472. doi:10.1109/TIT.1985.1057074

Even, S., Goldreich, O., & Lempel, A. (1985). A randomized protocol for signing contracts. *Communications of the ACM, 28*(6), 647. doi:10.1145/3812.3818

Freudiger, J., Shokri, R., & Hubeaux, J. (2009). On the optimal placement of MIX zones. In I. Goldberg & M. J. Atallah (Eds.), *Proceedings of the 9th International Symposium, Privacy Enhancing Technologies* (LNCS 5672, pp. 216-234).

Gajparia, A., Mitchell, C., & Yeun, C. (2004). The location information preference authority: Supporting user privacy in location based services. In *Proceedings of the 9th Nordic Workshop on Secure IT-Systems* (pp. 91-96).

Gedik, B., & Liu, L. (2005). Location privacy in mobile systems: A personalized anonymization model. In *Proceedings of the 25th IEEE International Conference on Distributed Computing Systems* (pp. 620-629). Washington, DC: IEEE Computer Society.

Ghinita, G. (2008). Understanding the privacy-deficiency trade-off in location based queries. In *Proceedings of the SIGSPATIAL ACM GIS International Workshop on Security and Privacy in GIS and LBS* (pp. 1-5). New York, NY: ACM Press.

Ghinita, G. (2009). Private queries and trajectory anonymization: A dual perspective on location privacy. *Transactions on Data Privacy, 2*(1), 3–19.

Ghinita, G., Kalnis, P., Kantarcioglu, M., & Bertino, E. (2009). A hybrid technique for private location-based queries with database protection. In N. Mamoulis, T. Seidl, T. B. Pedersen, K. Torp, & I. Assent (Eds.), *Proceedings of the 11th International Symposium on Advances in Spatial and Temporal Databases* (LNCS 5644, pp. 98-116).

Ghinita, G., Kalnis, P., Khoshgozaran, A., Shahabi, C., & Tan, K. (2008). Private queries in location based services: Anonymizers are not necessary. In *Proceedings of the ACM SIGMOD International Conference on Management of Data* (pp. 121-132). New York, NY: ACM Press.

Ghinita, G., Kalnis, P., & Skiadopoulos, S. (2007). PRIVE: Anonymous location-based queries in distributed mobile systems. In *Proceedings of the 16th International Conference on World Wide Web* (pp. 371-380). New York, NY: ACM Press.

Goldreich, O., Micali, S., & Wigderson, A. (1991). Proofs that yield nothing but their validity or all languages in NP have zero-knowledge proof systems. *Journal of the ACM, 38*(3), 690–728. doi:10.1145/116825.116852

Gruteser, M., Bredin, J., & Grunwald, D. (2004). Path privacy in location-aware computing. In *Proceedings of the MobiSys Workshop on Context Awareness*.

Gruteser, M., & Grunwald, D. (2003). Anonymous usage of location-based services through spatial and temporal cloaking. In *Proceedings of the 1st International Conference on Mobile Systems, Applications and Services* (pp. 31-42). New York, NY: ACM Press.

Gruteser, M., & Grunwald, D. (2005). Enhancing location privacy in wireless LAN through disposable interface identifiers: A quantitative analysis. *Mobile Networks and Applications, 10*(3), 315–325. doi:10.1007/s11036-005-6425-1

Gruteser, M., & Liu, X. (2004). Protecting privacy, in continuous location-tracking applications. *IEEE Security & Privacy, 2*(2), 28–34. doi:10.1109/MSECP.2004.1281242

Hauser, C., & Kabatnik, M. (2001). Towards privacy support in a global location service. In *Proceedings of the IFIP Workshop on IP and ATM Traffic Management* (pp. 81-89).

Hengartner, U. (2006). *Enhancing user privacy in location-based services (Tech. Rep. No. CACR 2006-27)*. Waterloo, ON, Canada: University of Waterloo.

Hengartner, U. (2008). Location privacy based on trusted computing and secure logging. In *Proceedings of the 4th International Conference on Security and Privacy in Communication Networks* (pp. 1-8). New York, NY: ACM Press.

Hoh, B., & Gruteser, M. (2006). Protecting location privacy through path confusion. In *Proceedings of the 1st International Conference on Security and Privacy for Emerging Areas in Communications Networks* (pp. 194-205). Washington, DC: IEEE Computer Society.

Hoh, B., Gruteser, M., Herring, R., Ban, J., Work, D., Herrera, J. C., et al. (2008). Virtual trip lines for distributed privacy-preserving traffic monitoring. In *Proceedings of the 6th International Conference on Mobile Systems, Applications and Services* (pp. 15-28). New York, NY: ACM Press.

Hoh, B., Gruteser, M., Xiong, H., & Alrabady, A. (2007). Preserving privacy in GPS traces via uncertainty-aware path cloaking. In *Proceedings of the 14th ACM Conference on Computer and Communications Security* (pp. 161-171). New York, NY: ACM Press.

Jakobsson, M., Juels, A., & Syverson, P. (2004). Universal re-encryption for mixnets. In *Proceedings of the RSA Conference Cryptographers Track* (pp. 163-178).

Jorns, O., Bessler, S., & Pailer, R. (2005). An efficient mechanism to ensure location privacy in telecom service applications. In Gaiti, D., Galmes, S., & Puigjaner, R. (Eds.), *Network control and engineering for QoS, security and mobility, III* (pp. 57–68). New York, NY: Springer. doi:10.1007/0-387-23198-6_5

Jorns, O., Quirchmayr, G., & Jung, O. (2007). A privacy enhancing mechanism based on pseudonyms for identity protection in location-based services. In *Proceedings of the 5th Australasian Symposium on ACSW Frontiers* (pp. 133-142).

Kargupta, H., Das, K., & Liu, K. (2007). A game theoretic approach toward multi-party privacy-preserving distributed data mining. In *Proceedings of the 11th European Conference on Principles and Practice of KDD - PKDD*, Warsaw, Poland.

Kaufman, C., Perlman, R., & Speciner, M. (2002). *Network security: Private communication in a public world* (2nd ed.). Upper Saddle River, NJ: Prentice Hall.

Khoshgozaran, A., & Shahabi, C. (2007). Blind evaluation of nearest neighbor queries using space transformation to preserve location privacy. In *Proceedings of the 10th International Conference on Advances in Spatial and Temporal Databases* (pp. 239-257).

Kim, Y., Perrig, A., & Tsudik, G. (2000). Simple and fault-tolerant key agreement for dynamic collaborative groups. In *Proceedings of the 7th ACM Conference on Computer and Communications Security* (pp. 235-244). New York, NY: ACM Press.

Kohlweiss, M., Faust, S., Fritsch, L., Gedrojc, B., & Preneel, B. (2007). Efficient oblivious augmented maps: Location-based services with a payment broker. In N. Borisov & P. Golle (Eds.), *Proceedings of the 7th International Conference on Privacy Enhancing Technologies* (LNCS 4776, pp. 77-94).

Kolsch, T., Fritsch, L., Kohlweiss, M., & Kesdogan, D. (2005). Privacy for profitable location based services. In D. Hutter & M. Ullmann (Eds.), *Proceedings of the Second International Conference on Security in Pervasive Computing* (LNCS 3450, pp. 164-178).

Konidala, D. M., Yeun, C. Y., & Kim, K. (2005). A secure and privacy enhanced protocol for location-based services in ubiquitous society. In *Proceedings of the Global Telecommunications Conference* (pp. 2164–2168). Washington, DC: IEEE Computer Society.

Kulik, L. (2009). Privacy for real-time location-based services. *SIGSPATIAL Special*, *1*(2), 9–14. doi:10.1145/1567253.1567256

Kushilevitz, E., & Ostrovsky, R. (1997). Replication is not needed: single database, computationally-private information retrieval. In *Proceedings of the 38th Annual Symposium on Foundations of Computer Science* (pp. 364-373). Washington, DC: IEEE Computer Society.

Lamport, L. (1981). Password authentication with insecure communication. *Communications of the ACM, 24*(11), 770–772. doi:10.1145/358790.358797

Langheinrich, M. (2001). Privacy by design-principles of privacy-aware ubiquitous systems. In G. D. Abowd, B. Brumitt, & S. Shafer (Eds.), *Proceedings of the International Conference on Ubiquitous Computing* (LNCS 2201, pp. 273-291).

Lin, D., Bertino, E., Cheng, R., & Prabhakar, S. (2009). Location privacy in moving-object environments. *Transactions on Data Privacy, 2*(1), 21–46.

Lysyanskaya, A., Rivest, R., Sahai, A., & Wolf, S. (2000). Pseudonym systems. In H. Heys & C. Adams (Eds.), *Proceedings of 6th Annual International Workshop on Selected Areas in Cryptography* (LNCS 1758, pp. 184-199).

Magkos, E., Kotzanikolaou, P., Sioutas, S., & Oikonomou, K. (2010). A distributed privacy-preserving scheme for location-based queries. In *Proceedings of the IEEE International Symposium on a World of Wireless Mobile and Multimedia Networks* (pp. 1-6). Washington, DC: IEEE Computer Society.

Mishra, S. K., & Sarkar, P. (2000). Symmetrically private information retrieval. In B. Roy & E. Okamoto (Eds.), *Proceedings of the 1st International Conference in Cryptology* (LNCS 1977, pp. 225-236).

Mokbel, M. F., Chow, C. Y., & Aref, W. G. (2006). The new Casper: Query processing for location services without compromising privacy. In *Proceedings of the 32nd International conference on Very Large Data Bases* (pp. 763-774).

National Institute of Standards and Technology. (2008). *FIPS PUB 180-3: Secure hash standard (SHS)*. Gaithersburg, MD: National Institute of Standards and Technology.

Okamoto, T., & Uchiyama, S. (1998). A new public-key cryptosystem as secure as factoring. In K. Nyberg (Ed.), *Proceedings of the International Conference on the Theory and Application of Cryptographic Techniques* (LNCS 1403, p. 308).

Olumofin, F., Tysowski, P., & Goldberg, I. (2009). *Achieving efficient query privacy for location based services (Tech. Rep. No. CACR 2009-22)*. Waterloo, ON, Canada: University of Waterloo.

Paillier, P. (1999). Public-key cryptosystems based on discrete logarithms residues. In J. Stern (Ed.), *Proceedings of the International Conference on the Theory and Application of Cryptographic Techniques* (LNCS 1592, pp. 223-238).

Pfitzmann, A., & Kohntopp, M. (2000). Anonymity, unobservability, and pseudonymity- A proposal for terminology. In *Proceedings of the Workshop on Design Issues in Anonymity and Unobservability* (pp. 1-9).

Pinkas, B. (2002). Cryptographic techniques for privacy-preserving data mining. *SIGKDD Explorations Newsletter, 4*(2), 12–19. doi:10.1145/772862.772865

Rabin, M. (2009). *How to exchange secrets by oblivious transfer* (Tech. Rep. No. TR-81). Boston, MA: Harvard University.

Rafaeli, S., & Hutchison, D. (2003). A survey of key management for secure group communication. *ACM Computing Surveys, 35*(3), 309–329. doi:10.1145/937503.937506

Rahman, S., & Hengartner, U. (2007). Secure crash reporting in vehicular ad hoc networks. In *Proceedings of the 3rd International Conference on Security and Privacy in Communication Networks* (pp. 443-452). New York, NY: ACM Press.

Rasmussen, K. B., & Capkun, S. (2007). Implications of radio fingerprinting on the security of sensor networks. In *Proceedings of the 3rd International Conference on Security and Privacy in Communication Networks* (pp. 331 - 340). Washington, DC: IEEE Computer Society.

Raya, M., & Hubaux, J. P. (2005). The security of vehicular ad hoc networks. In *Proceedings of the 3rd ACM Workshop on Security of Ad Hoc and Sensor Networks* (pp. 11-21). New York, NY: ACM Press.

Raya, M., & Hubaux, J. P. (2007). Securing vehicular ad-hoc networks. *Journal of Computer Security, 15*(1), 39–68.

Rebollo-Monedero, D., Forne, J., Subirats, L., Solanas, A., & Martınez-Balleste, A. (2009). A collaborative protocol for private retrieval of location-based information. In *Proceedings of the IADIS International Conference on e-Society*, Barcelona, Spain.

Rodden, T., Friday, A., Muller, H., & Dix, A. (2002). *A lightweight approach to managing privacy in location-based services* (Tech. Rep. No. CSTR-07-006). UK: University of Nottingham, Lancaster University, and University of Bristol.

Sampigethaya, K., Huang, L., Matsuura, K., Poovendran, R., & Sezaki, K. (2005). CARAVAN: Providing location privacy for VANET. In *Proceedings of the 3rd Embedded Security in Cars Workshop*.

Saroiu, S., & Wolman, A. (2009). Enabling new mobile applications with location proofs. In *Proceedings of the 10th Workshop on Mobile Computing Systems and Applications* (pp. 3-9). New York, NY: ACM Press.

Shamir, A. (1984). Identity-based cryptosystems and signature scheme. In *Proceedings of Advances in Cryptography* (pp. 47-53).

Solanas, A., Domingo-Ferrer, J., & Martınez-Balleste, A. (2008). Location privacy in location-based services: Beyond TTP-based schemes. In *Proceedings of the 1st International Workshop on Privacy in Location-Based Applications* (p. 397).

Solanas, A., & Martınez-Balleste, A. (2007). Privacy protection in location-based services through a public-key privacy homomorphism. In J. Lopez, P. Samarati, & J. L. Ferrer (Eds.), *Proceedings of the 4th European PKI Workshop on Theory and Practice* (LNCS 4582, pp. 362-368).

Solanas, A., & Martınez-Balleste, A. (2008). A TTP-free protocol for location privacy in location-based services. *Computer Communications, 31*(6), 1181–1191. doi:10.1016/j.comcom.2008.01.007

Sun, J., Zhang, C., & Fang, Y. (2007). An ID-based framework achieving privacy and non-repudiation in vehicular ad hoc networks. In *Proceedings of the Military Communications Conference* (pp. 1-7). Washington, DC: IEEE Computer Society.

Sun, Y., La Porta, T. F., & Kermani, P. (2009). A flexible privacy-enhanced location-based services system framework and practice. *IEEE Transactions on Mobile Computing, 8*(3), 304–321. doi:10.1109/TMC.2008.112

Sweeney, L. (2002). k-anonymity: A model for protecting privacy. *International Journal of Uncertainty Fuzziness and Knowledge Based Systems, 10*(5), 557–570. doi:10.1142/S0218488502001648

Wakeman, I., Chalmers, D., & Fry, M. (2007). Reconciling privacy and security in pervasive computing: The case for pseudonymous group membership. In *Proceedings of the 5th International Workshop on Middleware for Pervasive and Ad-Hoc Computing* (pp. 7-12). New York, NY: ACM Press.

Yiu, M. L., Ghinita, G., Jensen, C. S., & Kalnis, P. (2009). Outsourcing search services on private spatial data. In *Proceedings of the 25th International Conference on Data Engineering* (pp. 1140-1143). Washington, DC: IEEE Computer Society.

Zhang, Y., Liu, W., Lou, W., & Fang, Y. (2005). Securing sensor networks with location-based keys. In *Proceedings of the Wireless Communications and Networking Conference* (pp. 1909-1914). Washington, DC: IEEE Computer Society.

Zhong, G., Goldberg, I., & Hengartner, U. (2007). Louis, Lester and Pierre: Three protocols for location privacy. In N. Borisov & P. Golle (Eds.), *Proceedings of the 7th International Symposium on Privacy Enhancing Technologies* (LNCS 4776, pp. 62-76).

Zhong, G., & Hengartner, U. (2008). Toward a distributed k-anonymity protocol for location privacy. In *Proceedings of the 7th ACM Workshop on Privacy in the Electronic Society* (pp. 33–38). New York, NY: ACM Press.

Zhong, G., & Hengartner, U. (2009). A distributed k-anonymity protocol for location privacy. In *Proceedings of the International Conference on Pervasive Computing and Communications* (pp. 1-10). Washington, DC: IEEE Computer Society.

Zhu, F., Mutka, M., & Ni, L. (2003). Splendor: A secure, private, and location-aware service discovery protocol supporting mobile services. In *Proceedings of the 1st IEEE International Conference on Pervasive Computing and Communications* (pp. 235-242). Washington, DC: IEEE Computer Society.

ENDNOTES

[1] With identity-based encryption, first proposed in Shamir (1984), key management is simplified as users are not required to exchange digital certificates of their public keys, but instead they are allowed to use their identity as their public key.

[2] In a typical setting, a set of system entities share a private key in a threshold public-key encryption system (Desmedt, 1994), and there is only one public key corresponding to the shared private key. The user submits an encrypted message with the public key of the authorities, and only a qualified set of honest entities are able to combine their shares and decrypt the message.

[3] Such proofs are prover-verifier interactive protocols, where the prover proves a statement to the verifier and the verifier learns nothing from the prover that he could not learn by himself, apart from the fact that the prover knows the proof (Goldreich et al., 1991).

[4] As noted in Jorns et al. (2007), a user may also subscribe as a watcher to his/her own location (e.g., in a GPS navigation service).

[5] Analogously to MIX nodes in communication networks (Chaum, 1981), a MIX zone is a spatial area where a user can enter and exit anytime, in a way that it is not possible for an observer to link a user position *before* entering the zone, with a position *after* exiting the zone.

[6] In a scheme for VANETs (Rahman & Hengartner, 2007), for example, each public key (pseudonym) is validated by a system entity, using *blind signatures* (Chaum, 1983) (the cryptographic equivalent of signing carbon paper-lined envelopes). The issued certificate also contains the real identity of the vehicle, encrypted with the public key of a trusted third party.

[7] The idea was first conceived in the context of privacy-preserving Internet elections (Cramer et al., 1997). The scheme in Cramer et al. (1997) uses a homomorphic variation of the ElGamal encryption scheme (ElGamal, 1985), with addition as group operation of the message space. Specifi-

cally, a message m is encrypted by choosing a random number $r \in Z_q$ and computing two values $(R,S) = g^r, y^r g^m$, where $y = g^s$ is the public key of the receiver, g is generator of Z_q and all operations are modulo p. Encryption functions of this type also allow for *universal re-encryption* (Jakobsson et al., 2004), e.g., randomization by calculating (R', S') where $R' = Rg^{r'}$ and $S' = Sy^{r'}$, where $r' \in Z_q$ is a random number.

In a trivial example of the oblivious transfer primitive (ElGamal, 1985), Bob has two secrets S_0, S_1 and Alice is able to learn exactly one secret S_i, while Bob will not know number i, i.e., which of the two secrets Alice got.

8

Chapter 20
Deploying Privacy Improved RBAC in Web Information Systems

Ioannis Mavridis
University of Macedonia, Greece

ABSTRACT

Access control technology holds a central role in achieving trustworthy management of personally identifiable information in modern information systems. In this article, a privacy-sensitive model that extends Role-Based Access Control (RBAC) to provide privacy protection through fine-grained and just-in-time access control in Web information systems is proposed. Moreover, easy and effective mapping of corresponding components is recognized as an important factor for succeeding in matching security and privacy objectives. Such a process is proposed to be accomplished by capturing and modeling privacy requirements in the early stages of information system development. Therefore, a methodology for deploying the mechanisms of an access control system conforming to the proposed Privacy Improved Role-Based Access Control (PIRBAC) model is presented. To illustrate the application of the proposed methodology, an application example in the healthcare domain is described.

INTRODUCTION

The evolution of information and communication technology (ICT) has significantly increased security and privacy concerns. A common practice with potential impact on citizens' privacy is that Web application data are likely collected, stored and processed without any consent of data subjects. However, in case such data are characterized as personal information a number of privacy issues are raised for data subjects, which usually are individuals or consumers.

Privacy awareness is increasing from the practice of modern organizations that utilize Web applications to collect, store and process private information of users, usually gathered from monitoring their behaviour, in order to provide more personalized and competitive services. Moreover, modern organizations, which are likely utilising ICTs to provide goods and services, aim to build

DOI: 10.4018/978-1-4666-1562-5.ch020

trust based on good privacy practices, and finally utilize privacy as a differentiating factor for their brand names and a way to attract more customers (Powers, 2002).

In the literature, capturing and modeling privacy requirements in the early stages of information system development is proposed as essential to provide privacy protection especially to consumer data (He & Anton, 2003). Privacy protection can be achieved by enforcing privacy policy rules within online and offline data processing systems of an organization. Nowadays, most organizations have a privacy policy posted on their websites. Due to separation of duties in an organization between security and privacy staff, privacy policies are usually defined as high-level natural language descriptions by the organization's privacy officer. Similarly, a security policy is usually defined by the security officer as a set of rules and procedures that regulate how the organization manages and protects enterprise data. Practical security is primarily related to access control policies and mechanisms that govern authorizations of users to gain access to stored application data. However, high-level natural language privacy policy descriptions are difficult to be enforced directly via access control. Furthermore, privacy requirements are often not reflected in the design and implementation of access control policies. As a result, a gap exists between security and privacy protection that is exacerbated by conflict of interests between stakeholders, system developers and administrators, and consumers.

Privacy is defined as "the claim of individuals, groups, or institutions to determine for themselves when, how, and to what extent information about them is communicated to others" (Westin, 1968). Analyzing this definition, the following words or terms can be isolated and further analyzed: "when", "how" and "to what extent". "When" introduces a situation or process that takes place in a particular time period and aims to the accomplishment of a specific purpose. "How" focuses

on the operations running during and after access to data, either requested by the data user or imposed by the system, as well as the conditions under which private information is accessed. The term "to what extent" refers to the amount of data accessed in order to form the private information that is finally communicated to others.

The important roles of purposes, conditions and obligations in developing efficient systems for privacy protection in modern information systems, are pointed out in the proposed by Powers (2002) elements of a privacy policy. Specifically, these elements are data users, operations, data types, purposes, conditions and obligations. Data users are the individuals that are requesting to access data. Operations are used to define access control rules specifying permitted actions on data objects. Data types are likely concerned as high-level definitions of data collections, such as patient insurance information. Purposes are the reasons for which data accesses are requested and actually represent the goals to be accomplished by performing particular organizational tasks, as for example sending a special offer by email. These goals are likely expressed by high-level processes or applications, e.g. marketing. Conditions are prerequisites to be met in order for an operation to be performed. Obligations are additional operations to be performed after a particular access is permitted.

It is widely acceptable that neither the classic access control approaches of Mandatory Access Control (MAC) and Discretionary Access Control (DAC) nor the nowadays commonly applied Role-based Access Control (RBAC) were intended to support privacy protection. According to Wang et al. (2007), the main difficulty arises from the fact that traditional access control models are focusing on which subject, either identified by its identity or classified by its attributes (rank, roles, etc), is allowed to perform which operation on which data object. However, privacy protection requires taking care of which type of data is accessed under which conditions and possibly imposed obligations in order to be further used for which purposes. To our opinion there is no significant difference between the viewpoint of privacy that is concerned with the potential usage after access, and that of security as can be expressed in properly extended access control approaches. Such an effort to extend the traditional view of access control can be strengthened by adopting the principles defined in (Powers, 2002) for privacy management and enforcement. These principles involve consideration of data subjects, business purpose and obligations incurred by data usage that must be justified.

Based on the elements of a privacy policy and the principles for privacy management, the definition of privacy rules can follow a structure of the following form (Powers, 2002): "ALLOW data user TO PERFORM Operation ON data type FOR purpose PROVIDED condition. Carry out [Obligation]". Aiming at implementing such a structure of privacy rules, the central role of access control technology in achieving trustworthy management of personally identifiable information (PII) is recognized.

Access control systems can provide privacy protection, given their support for fine-grained and just-in-time control (Mavridis, Mattas, Pagkalos, Kotini & Ilioudis, 2008). Fine-granularity of access control permits the development of mechanisms to efficiently check access requests against individual preferences and compliance with enacted privacy laws. Just-in-timeliness enforces the application of the principle of least-privilege (Saltzer & Schroeder, 1975) through the utilization of dynamic administration mechanisms. Furthermore, extending access control systems in order to provide mechanisms that support purpose, condition and obligation elements, as well as determining purpose assertions in an automatic (or semi-automatic) and data user-independent fashion, is also needed.

RELATED WORK

In the literature, there are similar approaches that recognize the need for extending RBAC to include privacy protection capabilities while retaining the simplicity of access control policy administration.

Byun and Li (2008) discuss on the significant role of the notion of purpose in privacy-centric access control models and propose the development of an RBAC-based access control model that introduces the process of purpose compliance and the notion of conditional roles. Specifically, an approach to purpose management, as the basis for the development of the so-called purpose-based access control is proposed. An important distinction is that between the notion of intended purposes, which are associated with data and regulate accesses by specifying the intended usage of data objects, and the notion of access purpose, which is determined by the system during run-time and reflects the purpose for which a data object is requested to be accessed. Additionally, besides the hierarchy of roles in RBAC, the intended and access purposes for a given organization are suggested to be developed also with hierarchical structures. Conditional roles are used to identify sets of users based on the values of role and system attributes that are in effect. These sets of users are then authorized for specific access purposes. The final access decision is made based on the compliance between the asserted access purpose and relevant intended purposes in the purpose tree. Intended purpose associations to data are proposed to be made with four methods of different granularity levels: relation-base, attribute-based, tuple-based and element-based. A specific encoding schema for efficient storing and processing of the purpose tree and a method based on query modification are also proposed. However, besides the fact that the proposed privacy-preserving access control model is an extension of RBAC, there is not a clear placement of the notion of purpose in the RBAC entity-relationship diagram.

A framework for modeling privacy requirements in an RBAC-based access control system is presented in (He & Anton, 2003). The framework is composed of a context-based data model and a goal-driven role engineering process. Specifically, the authors propose the use of two different kinds of purposes in enforcing purpose binding privacy requirements: consented by consumers data purpose that express how the corresponding collected data can be used, and business purposes that are the actual objectives for business tasks or applications. On the one hand, data purposes are high level and limited in number. Business purposes, on the other hand, are defined more specifically and according to organization's business processes. For example, the data purpose "contact" may be divided into three business purposes "phone/fax contact", "postal contact", and "email contact". Data purposes are connected with business purposes through the use of purpose hierarchies that represent partial ordered relations. Business purposes are the leaves (lowest level) of a hierarchy.

In Ni, Lin, Bertino, and Lobo (2007) and Ni, Trombetta, Bertino, and Lobo (2007) a family of Privacy-aware Role Based Access Control (P-RBAC) models that extend the RBAC family of models to support privacy policies is proposed. The proposed family involves the Core, Hierarchical, Conditional and Universal P-RBAC models. In the entity-relationship diagram of the Core P-RBAC model, the notions of purpose, condition and obligation are placed as entities that are bound to the traditional entity of permission in order to form the proposed composite notion of privacy data permissions. As a result, privacy policies are expressed as assignments of privacy data permissions to roles. An important point is that P-RBAC conditions are clearly separated from RBAC constraints. Nevertheless, treatment of constraints in P-RBAC is deferred to future work of authors. Conditions are expressed using context variables with a variety of languages, from the simple LC_0 to more complex LC_1 and

LC_2. However, in the presented examples the context variables of owner consent and parental consent are found, which represent no contextual (e.g. environment or system related) information but directly associated to stored application and privacy data. For example, the consent of an owner could be considered to be stored as metadata along with the intended purposes and the associated application data, which are characterized as her PII. Another questioning point is the assignment of internally to organization identified roles to privacy data permissions that include conditions expressed using externally provided owner and parental consents. Apparently, parents do not usually care about the internal organization of an enterprise, and, moreover, for its role-based access control system. P-RBAC is proposed as a solution for enforcing privacy policies in an organization, but it lacks a mechanism for mapping privacy requirements (e.g. high level types of data users) into the proposed components (e.g. corresponding organization roles) of the model. The use of hierarchies for roles, purposes and data is also suggested in P-RBAC to decrease the complexity of metadata management.

Another privacy-sensitive extension of RBAC is proposed by Masoumzadeh and Joshi (2008), which is called the Purpose-aware Role-Based Access Control (PuRBAC) and is composed of a hierarchy of models. In this approach, the notion of purpose is represented in the model's entity-relationship diagram as an intermediary entity between the entities of roles and permissions. Such placement is based on the recognition of a close relation between the notion of purpose in privacy policy and the notion of role in RBAC. More specifically, the authors observe the relation between the modeling of user responsibilities with a role and the modeling of associated tasks for fulfilling the corresponding responsibilities with a (business) purpose. In the PuRBAC model, constraints and obligations are defined as conditions on assignments of permissions to purposes. Additionally, hierarchies are defined for roles, purposes and permissions. A permission hierarchy is actually a data (aggregation) hierarchy for the same action. Purpose hierarchies support generalization and specification concepts during assertions. Role hierarchies are utilized not only for permission inheritance but for purpose inheritance too. During build-time, permissions are conditionally assigned to purposes, introducing constraints and imposing obligations. At run-time, conditional exercise of permissions for specific purposes is supported. Purpose assertion is provided by the data user and is limited to the purposes assigned to the activated roles. However, the utilization of conditional assignments in combination with the existence of hierarchies can lead to complex situations for the access control system administration. As a solution, the use of hybrid hierarchies for roles and purposes is proposed.

In all the above approaches it is the data user (subject) requesting access to a data object that is expected to specifically assert the purpose of accessing by including it in her data access request. However, the success of such an approach depends on the trustworthiness of data users. The main motivation of this research work is to address this problem by proposing a privacy-sensitive access control model that automatically determines purpose assertion and provides fine-grained and just-in-time control on accessing data in Web information systems.

THE PIRBAC MODEL

The proposed Privacy-Improved Role-Based Access Control (PIRBAC) model is based mainly on the DARBAC model (Mattas, Mavridis, & Pangalos, 2003; Mavridis, Mattas, Pagkalos, Kotini, & Ilioudis, 2008), which in turn awards priority to the administration of access control during run-time in order to provide fine-grained and just-in-time access control in Web application environments. The augmented for privacy protection PIRBAC model encompasses additional mechanisms and methods for mapping privacy policy elements to access control components. Specifically, the PIRBAC model assumes a Web-based information system wherein a number of application instances are in progress. Application instances can be conceived as groups of tasks that are accomplished by teams of users. An overview of the PIRBAC model that comrises the corresponding elements of privacy policy and their mappings to PIRBAC entities is shown in Figure 1.

In Figure 1, the continuous lines denote assignments that are defined during the build-time of the access control system. Thin dashed lines mean bindings and participations that are established during run-time. Thick dashed lines represent mappings of privacy policy elements to corresponding PIRBAC entities. The PIRBAC model consists of six sets of entities: users, organization-roles, application-roles, permissions, applications and constraints.

A user is a subject that uses Web-applications (e.g. stored procedures) to send requests for exercising actions on data objects. Permissions are pairs of data objects and actions that users can exercise on data objects. Data objects are formed according to the particular technologies and systems used, e.g. relational database systems. An action can vary from a simple operation, like read or write, to an abstract operation as, for example, a credit or a debit carried out by a process (an executable image of a program) that is executed on behalf of a user. For minimizing the administrative workload, the use of abstract operations is assumed. The types of actions depend on the technologies and the systems in which the application system's code was developed and deployed.

The PIRBAC model adopts the use of roles as defined in the RBAC family of models (Ferraiolo, Sandhu, Gavrila, Kuhn, & Chandramouli, 2001; Sandhu, Coyne, Feinstein, & Youman, 1996; American National Standards Institute, 2004). However, PIRBAC's roles are distinguished between organization-roles and application-roles. On the one hand, organization-role activation

Figure 1. PIRBAC model and corresponding elements of privacy policy

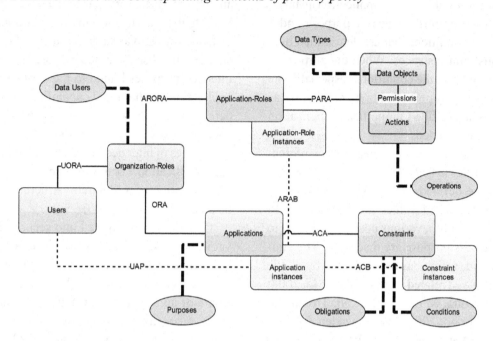

is utilized for determining application-instance participation. On the other hand, permission exercising to access data objects is controlled on the basis of application-roles activated during application-instance participation. Application-roles are grouped into organization-roles that in turn are assigned to users. Organization-roles are also assigned to applications creating so an assignment path from data to applications that serves as a way to bind data objects with intended (business) purposes. An application-role can be activated only in the time frame of an application instance, while organization-roles are activated in the discretion of each one individual user. An organization-role corresponds to a job title within an organization along with associated semantics regarding the authority and responsibility conferred on the user that is member of the organization-role. Organization-roles are also used for grouping users and associating them with particular applications. An organization-role should be activated by a user in order to subsequently ask for participation in a proper application instance. Application-roles are groups of permissions that are intended to

be exercised for specific purposes. Thus, they are assigned to applications through assigned organization-roles. More specifically, application-roles are fine-grained collections of permissions and are temporarily activated or delegated to other application-roles only in the frames of dedicated application instances. Application-roles are used as an intermediary between organization-roles and permissions and provide the ability to ensure that permissions are exercised only in the limited context of an application instance.

In PIRBAC, the authorization schema of users is determined not in the context of sessions, as in other RBAC-based approaches, but in that of application instances, which are more suitable for Web-based information systems. An application is a group of processes or tasks that can be carried out by a team of users, which are members of properly assigned organization-roles. The structure of an application is defined by the ORA assignments and represents a temporary project team organization that seems that of an adhocracy organization (Shim & Park, 2002); for a finite period of time the users-members of a project team are acting in the context of an application instance in order to accomplish a specific purpose under pre and post conditions that are determined by a set of constraint instances. When the purpose is accomplished and the conditions (especially the actions imposed by post conditions, also known as obligations) are fulfilled, the particular application instance is terminated.

A critical point in introducing privacy protection capabilities in PIRBAC is the way that access purposes are defined and by which method the relevant domains of values are determined. In Byun and Li (2008), various possible methods to identify access purpose are discussed. The simplest method, which has been adopted by all the above discussed related works (Byun & Li, 2008; Ni, Lin, Bertino, & Lobo, 2007; Ni, Trombetta, Bertino, & Lobo, 2007; Masoumzadeh & Joshi, 2008; He & Anton, 2003), is to let users to assert the purpose of data usage along with their access request. However, this method requires complete trust on the users. In a second method, the system determines automatically and dynamically the access purpose of an access request by reasonably inferring from the current context. Similarly, such a method is expected to be difficult to accurately determine the access purpose. A third method, which is adopted in the PIRBAC model, is to bind each one application with one or more purposes.

In our approach, the notions of intended purposes and access purposes, as defined by Byun and Li (2008) and further specialized by He and Anton (2003), are adopted. Specifically, data and business purposes are handled as further specializations of intended purposes. However, instead of associating intended purposes directly with data, an assignment path from data to applications through organization-roles and application-roles is utilized to bind data with applications that are actually expressing corresponding business purposes. The purpose for which a data object is accessed is called access purpose and is determined by the specific application instance that is used for. Thus, the decision on whether to allow or not

an access request for a particular access purpose has actually been taken at the time the application instance was activated; validating so the compliance of all subsequent access purposes with the intended purposes bound to the application. For applications with limited capabilities it is easy to determine the actions that users can exercise on data objects, which can thus be limited into the boundaries of intended purposes that were tagged to the application. For more complex applications, the utilization of a hierarchy structure seems to be an effective solution.

Constraints are divided into security and privacy ones. A security constraint is defined during build-time and controls the participation of users and the use of access control components in the frame of an application instance. The notion of privacy constraints is merely based on that of context, as defined in (Thomas, 1997), but is used in a broader sense. A privacy constraint is defined during run-time and is comprising of two conditions: a pre-condition and a post-condition. Pre-conditions control the start of participation (check-in) of a user in an application instance prior to check the access request against the permission set assigned to him via application-roles. Post-conditions control the end of participation (check-out) of a user in an application instance and actually are used to implement obligations in the form of conditional imposed actions that have to be performed after the access request is allowed. Privacy constraints are defined using contextual parameters that are evaluated occasionally for particular application instances. A context variable may include the particular target or resource of an application; for example, the payment of a check concerns a particular data object that is identified by serial number of the check. In general, a context variable may be checked against values of time intervals, object identities, and other contextual information that contributes to specify a restricted range to exercise generally applied permissions.

The following definitions provide some formalization to the above discussion.

Definition 1: Entities

- U, P, A, C, OR, AR stand for sets of users, permissions, applications, constraints, organization-roles and application-roles, respectively
- A_i, AR_i and C_i, are an application instance, an application-role instance and a constraint instance, respectively.

Permissions are assigned to application-roles with a many-to-many Permission to Application-Role Assignment relation (PARA). An application-role can have many permissions and the same permission can be assigned with many application-roles. Users are also related to organization-roles with a many-to-many User to Organization-Role Assignment relation (UORA). A user can own many organization-roles, and an organization-role can be assigned with many users. Furthermore, application-roles are assigned with organization-roles through a many-to-many Application-Role to Organization-Role Assignment relation (ARORA). Constraints are assigned to applications with a many-to-many Application to Constraint Assignment relation (ACA). The set of skills needed for an application to accomplish its goal is specified through many-to-many Organization-role to Application Assignment relation (ORA), where each organization-role refers to an autonomous activity of the application.

During run-time, users with sufficient administrative permissions can define and bind an instance of a privacy constraint to an instance of an application through a one-to-many Application instance to Constraint instance Binding relation (ACB). However, the same privacy constraint instance cannot be bound to more than one instances of the same application, as a result of the uniqueness of its definition that is be made using particular values of a set of context variables. Activated instances of application-roles are bound to holding application instances through a many-to-many application-role instance to application

instance binding relation (ARAB). In addition, when a user participates in an application instance, a new entry is added to the many-to-many User to Application instance Participation relation (UAP).

Definition 2: Relations

- PARA $\subseteq$ P $\times$ AR, is a many-to-many permission to application-role assignment relation
- UORA $\subseteq$ U $\times$ OR, is a many-to-many user to organization-role assignment relation
- ARORA $\subseteq$ OR $\times$ AR, is a many-to-many organization-role to application-role assignment relation
- ACA $\subseteq$ A $\times$ C, is a many-to-many application to constraint assignment relation
- ORA $\subseteq$ OR $\times$ A, is a many-to-many organization-role to application assignment relation
- ACB $\subseteq$ A_i $\times$ C_i, is a one-to-many application instance to constraint instance binding relation
- ARAB $\subseteq$ AR_i $\times$ A_i, is a many-to-many application-role instance to application instance binding relation
- UMP $\subseteq$ U $\times$ A_i, is a many-to-many user to application instance participation relation

Two types of constraints can be defined by security and privacy officers: security and privacy ones.

Definition 3: Security Constraints

Separation of Duty (SDC) and Join of Duty (JDC) security constraints (Mavridis, Mattas, Pagkalos, Kotini, & Ilioudis, 2008) are enforced during run-time to determine users' participations in application instances. SDC imposes the rule that a user cannot participate in an application instance with more organization-roles than specified. JDC rules that a user, who is a member of a given organization-role, can participate in an application instance, subject to participation of a second user, who is a member of another organization-role.

SDC: *is expressed as a set of pairs (rs, n). A set rs includes the organization-roles that are assigned to applications (as defined in ORA) and also are in separation of duties. SDC imposes the rule that no one user can participate in an application instance with n or more organization-roles from the set rs.*

Let SDC_a be the set of pair $(rs, n) \subseteq (2^{OR} \times N)$, which is defined for application $a \in A$, where $rs \subseteq \{r \in OR \mid (r, a) \in ORA\}$, $n \in N$, $|rs| \geq n \geq 2$. Let also sr_u be a subset of organization-roles in rs ($sr_u \subseteq rs$) that the same user may activate, via a particular Web application, when participating in the same instance of application $a \in A$. Then, the cardinality of sr_u (the number of organization-roles that the user can activate to participate in the instance of application a) cannot exceed the value of n:

- $\forall (rs, n): SDC_a, \forall sr_u \subseteq rs \bullet \mid sr_u \mid < n$

JDC: *is expressed as a set of triples $(r_1, r_2, \oplus)$, where $r_1, r_2 \in OR$ and $\oplus$ is a symbol meaning that a user with organization-role r_2 can participate in an application instance, only if another user with organization-role r_1:*

- is already participating, regardless when the user with organization-role r_1 will stop participating in the same application instance ($\oplus$ is replaced by symbol $\triangleright$), or
- is not concurrently participating ($\oplus$ is replaced by symbol #), or
- is concurrently participating ($\oplus$ is replaced by symbol $\|$).

Let JDC_a be the set of triples defined for application $a \in A$. Let also DT_{r_i} be the period of

participation of a user with role $r_i \in OR$, i=1, 2… N, in an instance of application a. Then, for any instance of application a, each one replacement of symbol $\oplus$ is defined as follows:

- $\forall (r_1, r_2, \triangleright): JDC_a \bullet DT_{r_1} \cap DT_{r_2} \subseteq DT_{r_1}$
- $\forall (r_1, r_2, \#): JDC_a \bullet DT_{r_1} \cap DT_{r_2} = \varnothing$
- $\forall (r_1, r_2, \|): JDC_a \bullet DT_{r_1} \cap DT_{r_2} = DT_{r_2}$

Definition 4: Privacy Constraints

A privacy constraint is expressed as a logical expression that is formed against context variables with values from various domains and takes one of the values "allow", "deny" and "notapply" (Ribeiro, Zuquete, Ferreira, & Guedes, 2001) in order to decide on allowing check-in or check-out of a particular user to and from an application instance, respectively. The syntax format of a constraint's logical expression is composed of two particular logical binary expressions. The first one defines the domain of applicability and the other decides on the acceptability of the current event. The domain and decide expressions are also expressed against context variables and use the logic operators "&", "|" and "~", respectively for conjunction, disjunction and negation, the equality/inequality operators "<", "=<", "=", "!=", ">", ">=", and the special values "true" and "false". A constraint's logical expression can be composed of particular logical expressions using the logic operators "AND", "OR" and "NOT", respectively for conjunction, disjunction and negation, and according to a specific tri-value algebra defined by Ribeiro, Zuquete, Ferreira, and Guedes (2001).

Common cases of privacy constraints are identity-based inclusions and exclusions of data users for participating in a particular application instance, which are expressed with User-Application Constraints (UAC). For example, let consider a patient who consents access to his medical data only for particular doctors and nurses, thus excluding all the rest healthcare personnel. By default, all users with appropriate organization-roles can participate in an instance a_i of application $a \in A$ if constraints SDC_a and JDC_a are satisfied, unless specified differently in a UAC_{a_i} constraint, as shown in Box 1.

The goal of such a rule is to provide a decision on accepting ("true") or denying ("false") an event. The implicit parameter "ce" is used to represent the current event upon which the rule is applied.

DEPLOYING PIRBAC FOR PRIVACY MANAGEMENT

According to Powers (2002), the definition of a privacy policy stating the rules about the collection and use of PII is the first step in implementing a privacy management solution in an organization. However, the organization privacy policy does not refer to technical issues and solutions provided by proper IT systems. On the contrary, the organization privacy policy is defined by the privacy officer in order to articulate in a conceptual manner a set of requirements that are derived from national and international regulations and law, as well as the business strategy in force. More specifically, security and privacy officers work in the regulatory context of the specific organization and in accordance to the overall high level security

policy (HLSP) to specify the security and privacy requirements of the organization's information system (Katsikas & Gritzalis, 1996).

Based on these requirements, the access control policy and the privacy policy are produced. An access control policy is comprised of a set of rules that regulate accesses in the form of requested actions on particular data objects based on the credentials of requesting users. A privacy policy is consisting of a set of rules that are specified on the aforementioned elements (Powers, 2002) of data users, data types, operations, purposes, conditions and obligations. Apparently, there is a gap between the objectives of privacy policy rules on the one hand and access control policy rules on the other. Therefore, a critical task is to map the privacy policy elements to access control policy components and deploy a properly configured access control system. The success of this task is dependent mainly on the selection of the access control model to be used. In the rest of this section, the PIRBAC access control model is adopted.

Afterwards, the security officer, along with the software developers, deploys the organization's privacy policy to the PIRBAC-based access control system of the Web-based information system. Attempting to adjust the structure of a privacy policy rule, as presented in (Powers, 2002), to the components of the PIRBAC model, one can conclude in the following form of access control rules to be supported by the deployed access control system: "ALLOW [Organization-role] to perform [Action] on [Data Object] for [Application] provided [Constraint]".

The effective completion of the deployment task will enable the PIRBAC-based access control system to resolve subsequent data access requests with the defined in the privacy policy rules. In more detail, the deployment task is performed according to the following methodology during the initial development or any subsequent maintenance software life-cycle (Sommerville, 2006) of an information system:

Box 1.

```
//The author of the event
user author;
//Group of users included
user set InclGroup;
//Group of users excluded
user set ExclGroup;
PreCondition:
(InclGroup != {} &
ce.author NOT IN InclGroup) |
ce.author IN ExclGroup
          :: false;
```

- Role engineering and mapping to data users
- Data decomposition and mapping to data types
- Permission definition and mapping to operations
- Application specification and mapping to business purposes
- Constraint specification and mapping to conditions and obligations

In the following subsections a brief demonstration of deploying an organization's privacy policy through the definition, naming and construction of the components of a PIRBAC-based access control system according to the proposed methodology is presented.

ROLE ENGINEERING AND MAPPING TO DATA USERS

The process of role engineering in general comprises the definitions of roles, permissions, role hierarchies and constraints, and the assignments of permissions to roles (Coyne, 1996). Applying methods and techniques that are found in the literature (Neumann & Strembeck, 2002; Epstein, 2002; Epstein & Sandhu, 2001; Crook, Ince, & Nuseibeh, 2002), the role engineering process results in an initial derivation of organization-roles based on organizational structures and security requirements. However, such a process does not aim in addressing privacy requirements. In our approach, is assumed that a preliminary work is accomplished by the security officer in order to specify and describe the organization-roles based on a set of requirement specifications for the application subsystem under consideration. These organization-roles can be categorized and associated with corresponding applications, according to the specified blocks of activities that characterize the type of the specific organization.

The determined organization-roles are then mapped to the data users that are defined in the privacy policy as types of individuals requesting and consuming data.

DATA FRAGMENTATION AND MAPPING TO DATA TYPES

The combination of privacy and security requirements results in the derivation of a set of data constraints. Based on the specified data constraints and the data subjects' opt-in and opt-out choices, a structured decomposition of the relational data scheme is performed. Such a process results in a set of disjoint data objects that are not further decomposable; in the sense that the access window of a role cannot be defined over a subset of a data object.

We distinguish between three basic types of data constraints (Pernull, 1994):

- Simple data constraints that define vertical subsets of data tables to restrict users from accessing certain attributes of the data scheme,
- Content-based data constraints that define horizontal subsets of data tables to express access restrictions based on the content of certain tuples,
- Complex data constraints define horizontal subsets of data tables depending on the values of attributes of different tables, in order to express access restrictions that span several tables.

Additional types of data constraints are defined in Thuraisingham (2005) and include the following:

- Event-based data constraints that define subsets of data tables based on the occurrences of real-world events,

- Association-based data constraints that define subsets of associations between data,
- Release-based data constraints that define subsets of data tables based on previously released information,
- Aggregate data constraints that define subsets of collections of data,
- Logical data constraints that specify implications,
- Data constraints that have conditions attached to them,
- Level-based data constraints that define subsets of data tables based on the privacy level of some data,
- Fuzzy data constraints that assign fuzzy values to their classifications.

  In the following of this paper, the first three types of data constraints (simple, content-based and complex) are utilized. More specifically, each one type of data constraint causes a corresponding kind of data fragmentation, as follows:
- A simple data constraint causes a vertical fragmentation, which is the projection of the relational schema onto a subset of its attributes,
- A content-based data constraint causes a horizontal fragmentation, which is a subdivision (selection) of a relation into a subset of its tuples, and
- A complex data constraint causes a derived-horizontal fragmentation, which is a subdivision (selection) of a relation into a subset of its tuples.

The resulting fragmentation schema can be considered as a set of data objects. The general scope data types that are defined in the privacy policy are then mapped to the specified data objects. These mappings may result in multiple data objects that are tagged with the same data type, as well as a single data object tagged with multiple data types.

PERMISSION DEFINITION AND MAPPING TO OPERATIONS

The decision making process in traditional access control systems is performed on the basis of simple actions, like read and write, which are dependent on the technology being used for the development of applications. However, permissions in RBAC-based access control systems are usually defined for abstract actions, like credit and debit transactions. In the PIRBAC model, the exercise of abstract actions that are carried out by basic processes executing on behalf of users is assumed.

Privacy policies are usually defined in terms of operations that are not dependent on specific technologies or systems used by the information technology (IT) infrastructure. These operations are characterized either as low level ("anyone in the company can create a customer record, but only certain data users are allowed to read that record" or as high level "doctors may use protected health care information for the purposes of treatment and diagnosis" (Powers, 2002)). However, in both cases the operations should be considered along with the business purposes that are intended behind the access.

In order to map the privacy policy's operations to groups of permissions defined in a PIRBAC-based access control system, the assignments of such groups of permissions to roles have to be refined first. Therefore, the security officer is co-operating with the application developers to derive the need-to-know requirements of data users and then to specify the collections of permissions that should be assigned to proper application-roles. More specifically, for each one organization-role, the part of the relational data scheme where it needs to have access in order to accomplish a number of tasks is recorded in the form of permissions that are going to be assigned to the role. The refinement of organization-roles may result in the definition of new roles, providing so an adequate level of granularity for fine-grained access control. The resulting set of application-roles is then structured in an application-role hierarchy.

APPLICATION SPECIFICATION AND MAPPING TO BUSINESS PURPOSES

The security officer along with the application developers specifies the applications as combinations of basic processes and other applications. Applications are associated with each other with a partial ordered relation in order to constitute an application hierarchy.

The intended purposes defined in the privacy policy are actually data purposes, which have to further be refined, based on the business strategy of the organization, into business purposes and finally constitute a hierarchy of purposes.

Subsequently, the privacy officer along with the security officer defines the mappings between applications (higher levels of the application hierarchy) and business purposes (lowest level of the purpose hierarchy).

CONSTRAINT SPECIFICATION AND MAPPING TO CONDITIONS AND OBLIGATIONS

Constraints in PIRBAC are defined by the security and the privacy officers in order to address security and privacy requirements for application participation and access control management.

Specifically, a privacy constraint comprises of two optionally specified parts: precondition and postcondition. A precondition is likely used to control data user participation in an application instance. A postcondition specifies the enforcement of required execution of particular actions in order for an application instance to be completed.

APPLICATION EXAMPLE

In this section, an example is described to illustrate the application of the proposed methodology for deploying an efficient and flexible PIRBAC-based access control system for privacy protection in the healthcare domain. More specifically, the application example concerns a part of a healthcare information system (HIS) for prescriptions (editing) and treatments.

Initially, the specific functional specifications of the healthcare application subsystem are recorded in a SADT diagram (Marca & McGowan, 1987), which represents applications and involved organization-roles that run these applications (Figure 2).

In the rest of this example, the organization roles Head Nurse (HN), Nurse (NU), Physiotherapist (PH) and Research Doctor (RD) are only considered. Furthermore, we assume that the need-to-know requirements of these roles are defined on a part of the database that includes the following data tables:

- PAtient, with attributes: PAcode, PAname, PAaddress, PAphone, PAsocialcode, PAsex, PAbirthday, PAbloodcode, PAvipflag
- Prescription, with attributes: PRcode, PRPAcode, PRclinic, PRdoctor, PRdisease, PRdatefrom, PRdateto, PRtype, PRdescription, PRcareinstructions

Subsequently, a set of security and privacy requirements for the specific healthcare institution can be defined, as follows:

- Medical (e.g. prescription) data may be accessed by health officials for prescription and treatment purposes only.
- A subset of patient and medical data can be accessed for research in aids (HIV) purposes only.

Figure 2. SADT diagram representing applications and involved organization-roles

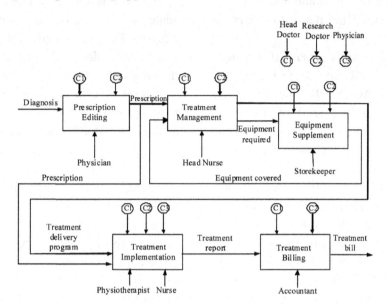

- Personally identifiable information of patients characterized as very important persons (VIP), may be accessed by head health staff (e.g. head nurses) only.

Then, a set of data constraints is defined in Table 1, for each one organization-role. Based on these data constraints, a fragmentation process is performed for each data table, as follows:

- **PA:** Organization roles NU and PH cause a vertical fragmentation of table PA onto data objects (fragments) PA1 (columns with personally identifiable data) and PA2 (columns with no personally identifiable sdata), as well as a horizontal fragmentation of data object PA1 onto data objects PA11 (for PAvipflag='VIP') and PA12 (for PAvipflag≠'VIP'). Role RD causes a vertical fragmentation of data object PA2 onto data objects PA21 (PAcode) and PA22 (all attributes, except PAcode). Role RD causes a derived horizontal fragmentation of data object PA22 onto data objects PA221 and

Table 1. Set of data constraints for organization-role

Organization-role	Data constraints
HN	PA, PR: none
NU	PA: PAname, PAaddress, PAphone, PAsocialcode, PAvipflag for PAvipflag = 'VIP' PR: all attributes for PRtype ≠ 'pharmacy'
PH	PA: PAname, PAaddress, PAphone, PAsocialcode, PAvipflag for PAvipflag = 'VIP' PR: all attributes for PRtype ≠ 'physiotherapy'
RD	PA: PAname, PAaddress, PAphone, PAsocialcode, PAvipflag for PRdisease = 'HIV' PA: all except PAcode for PRdisease ≠ 'HIV' PR: all attributes for PRdisease ≠ 'HIV' PR: PRcode, PRPAcode, PRclinic, PRdoctor, PRdisease for PRdisease = 'HIV'

PA222, based on the evaluation of predicate PRdisease='HIV' defined on data table PR.

- **PR:** Role RD causes a vertical fragmentation of table PR onto data objects PR1 (PRcode, PRPAcode, PRclinic, PRdoctor, PRdisease) and PR2 (rest of columns). User role RD causes a horizontal fragmentation of data object PR1 onto data objects PR11 and PR12 based on the evaluation of predicate PRdisease='HIV'. Organization roles NU and PH cause a horizontal fragmentation of data objects PR11, PR12 and PR2 to PR111, PR121 and PR21 based on the evaluation of predicate PRtype= 'pharmacy', and PR112, PR122 and PR22 based on the evaluation of predicate PRtype= 'physiotherapy', respectively.

The resulting fragmentation schema is represented with a data object hierarchy as shown in Figure 3. The data object hierarchy is a tree, which is a partial order on data objects such that each data object has at most one immediate ancestor.

Afterwards, the access windows (permissions to be assigned) of organization-roles are defined, as shown in Table 2. The common parts (overlaps) of access windows of roles HN, NU and PH are represented in Figure 4. The refinement of all the organization-roles results in the definition of application-roles: HNT, NUT, PHT, RDT and NPT.

As a result of the previous refinement, an application-role hierarchy is constructed, as shown in Figure 5. Senior (high level) application roles of the hierarchy inherit permissions from their child nodes, e.g. roles NUT and PHT inherit permissions from role NPT.

Figure 3. Fragmentation schema represented with data object hierarchy

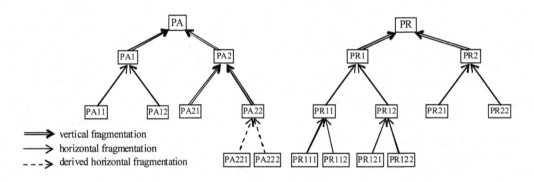

Table 2. Definitions of access windows of the organization-roles

Organization-role	Data objects
HN	PA, PR
NU	PA12, PA2, PR111, PR121, PR21
PH	PA12, PA2, PR112, PR122, PR22
RD	PA21, PA221, PR11

Figure 4. Common parts of access windows

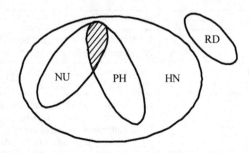

Figure 5. Application role hierarchy

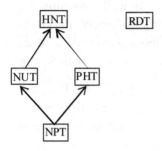

Figure 6. SADT diagram of business purposes of treatment management

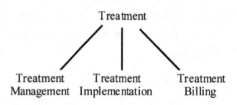

Apparently, for the data type of treatment data (e.g. schedule, drugs, doses, etc), the main data purpose to be associated is treatment. However, the three involved applications (Treatment management, Treatment implementation, Treatment billing) can be used for different business purposes. Therefore, the business purposes of treatment management, treatment implementation and treatment billing are mapped to the corresponding applications, which are depicted in the SADT diagram of Figure 6.

Privacy constraints resulting from additional privacy requirements, e.g. "health care workers should have access only to medical data of the patients they have the duty to care for", can be expressed with corresponding $UACa_1$ constraints and proper definitions of the InclGroup and/or ExclGroup sets of data users for explicitly specifying proper exclusions or inclusions of users for participating in application instances.

CONCLUSION

In this paper, the PIRBAC privacy-sensitive access control model that extends RBAC to provide privacy protection through fine-grained and just-in-time access control in Web information systems was proposed. As an important factor for succeeding in matching security and privacy objectives easy and effective mapping of corresponding components was suggested. Therefore,

a methodology for deploying the mechanisms of an access control system, which conforms to the proposed privacy enhanced access control model, during the initial development or any subsequent maintenance software life-cycle of an information system, was presented. Important aspects of our approach were demonstrated in an application example from the healthcare domain. A key feature of the proposed PIRBAC model is that purpose assertion is not made by subjects requesting access, as with other approaches, but through the binding of each one application with one or more business purposes.

REFERENCES

American National Standards Institute. (2004). *ANSI INCITS 359-2004: Information technology role-based access control*. Retrieved from http://webstore.ansi.org/RecordDetail.aspx?sku=ANSI+INCITS+359-2004

Byun, J.-W., & Li, N. (2008). Purpose based access control for privacy protection in relational database systems. *Very Large Data Bases Journal, 17*(4), 603–619. doi:10.1007/s00778-006-0023-0

Coyne, E. J. (1996). Role engineering. In *Proceedings of the 1st ACM Workshop on Role-Based Access Control*, Gaithersburg, MD.

Crook, R., Ince, D., & Nuseibeh, B. (2002). Towards an analytical role modelling framework for security requirements. In *Proceedings of the 8th International Workshop on Requirements Engineering: Foundation for Software Quality*, Essen, Germany.

Epstein, P. A. (2002). *Engineering of role/permission assignments*. Unpublished doctoral dissertation, George Mason University, Fairfax, VA.

Epstein, P. A., & Sandhu, R. (2001, December). Engineering of role/permission assignments. In *Proceedings of the 17th Annual Computer Security Applications Conference*, New Orleans, LA (pp. 127-136).

Ferraiolo, D. F., Sandhu, R., Gavrila, S., Kuhn, D. R., & Chandramouli, R. (2001). Proposed NIST standard for role-based access control. *ACM Transactions on Information and System Security*, 4(3), 224–274. doi:10.1145/501978.501980

He, Q., & Anton, A. I. (2003). A framework for modeling privacy requirements in role engineering. In *Proceedings of the International Workshop on Requirements Engineering for Software Quality*, Klagenfurt, Austria (pp. 137-146).

Katsikas, S., & Gritzalis, D. (1996). High level security policy guidelines. In SEISMED Consortium (Eds.), *Data security for health care, vol. II: Technical guidelines*. Amsterdam, The Netherlands: IOS Press.

Marca, D. A., & McGowan, C. L. (1987). *SADT: Structured analysis and design technique*. New York, NY: McGraw-Hill.

Masoumzadeh, A., & Joshi, J. (2008). PuRBAC: Purpose-based role-based access control. In R. Meersman & Z. Tari (Eds.), *Proceedings of the Confederated International Conference of On the Move to Meaningful Internet Systems* (LNCS 5332, pp. 1104-1121).

Mattas, A. K., Mavridis, I., & Pangalos, G. (2003). Towards dynamically administered role-based access control. In *Proceedings of the 14th International Workshop on Database & Expert Systems Applications*, Prague, Czech Republic (p. 494).

Mavridis, I., Mattas, A., Pagkalos, I., Kotini, I., & Ilioudis, C. (2008). Supporting dynamic administration of RBAC in Web-based collaborative applications during run-time. *International Journal of Information and Computer Security*, 2(4), 328–352. doi:10.1504/IJICS.2008.022487

Neumann, G., & Strembeck, M. (2002). A scenario-driven role engineering process for functional RBAC roles. In *Proceedings of the 7th ACM Symposium on Access Control Models and Technologies*, Monterey, CA (pp. 33-42).

Ni, Q., Lin, D., Bertino, E., & Lobo, J. (2007). Conditional privacy aware role based access control. In *Proceedings of the 12th European Symposium on Research in Computer Security*, Dresden, Germany.

Ni, Q., Trombetta, A., Bertino, E., & Lobo, J. (2007). Privacy aware role based access control. In *Proceedings of the 12th ACM symposium on Access Control Models and Technologies*, New York, NY.

Pernull, G. (1994). Database security. *Advances in Computers, 38*.

Powers, C. S. (2002). Privacy promises, access control, and privacy management. In *Proceedings of the 3rd International Symposium on Electronic Commerce* (pp. 13-21).

Ribeiro, C. N., Zuquete, A., Ferreira, P., & Guedes, P. (2001). SPL: An access control language for security policies with complex constraints. In *Proceedings of the Network and Distributed System Security Symposium*, San Diego, CA.

Saltzer, J. H., & Schroeder, M. D. (1975). The protection of information in computer systems. *Proceedings of the IEEE, 63*(9), 1278–1308. doi:10.1109/PROC.1975.9939

Sandhu, R. S., Coyne, E. J., Feinstein, H. L., & Youman, C. E. (1996). Role-based access control models. *IEEE Computer, 29*(2), 38–47.

Sommerville, I. (2006). *Software engineering* (8th ed.). Reading, MA: Addison-Wesley.

Thuraisingham, B. (2005). Privacy constraint processing in a privacy enhanced database management system. *Data and Knowledge Engineering Journal, 55*(2), 159–188. doi:10.1016/j.datak.2005.03.001

Wang, Q., Yu, T., Li, N., Lobo, J., Bertino, E., Irwin, K., & Byun, J.-W. (2007). On the correctness criteria of fine-grained access control in relational databases. In *Proceedings of the 33rd International Conference on Very Large Data Bases*, Vienna, Austria (pp. 555-566).

Westin, A. (1968). *Privacy and freedom*. Cambridge, MA: Atheneum Press.

This work was previously published in the International Journal of Information Technologies and Systems Approach, Volume 4, Issue 1, edited by Frank Stowell and Manuel Mora, pp. 70-87, copyright 2011 by IGI Publishing (an imprint of IGI Global).

Compilation of References

3D Berlin, S. (2008). Retrieved from http://www.3d-stadtmodell-berlin.de

3rd Generation Partnership Project. (2008). *3GPP TS 23.228: IP multimedia subsystems (IMS): Third generation partnership project, technical specification group services and system aspects.* Retrieved from http://www.quintillion.co.jp/3GPP/Specs/23228-870.pdf

3rd Generation Partnership Project. (2009). *3GPP TS 24.147: Conferencing using the IP multimedia (IM) core network (CN) subsystem: Technical specification group core network and terminals.* Retrieved from http://ftp.3gpp.org/specs/html-info/24147.htm

3rd Generation Partnership Project. (2010). *3GPP TS 33.203: 3G security: Access security for IP-based services (Release 10): Third generation partnership project, technical specification group services and system aspects.* Retrieved from http://www.3gpp.org/ftp/specs/html-info/33203.htm

A Guide to the Project Management Body of Knowledge PMBoK Guide. (2000). Newtown Square, PA: Project Management Institute (PMI).

Abdelnur, H., Avanesov, T., & Rusinowitch, M. (2009). Abusing SIP authentication. *Journal of Information Assurance and Security, 4*(4).

Abdelwahab, H. M., Guan, S. U., & Nievergelt, J. (1988, November). Shared workspaces for group collaboration - an experiment using internet and unix interprocess communications. *IEEE Communications Magazine, 26*(11), 10–16. doi:10.1109/35.9125

Abrahamsson, P., Salo, O., Ronkainen, J., & Wartsa, J. (2002). *Agile Software Development Methods: Review and analysis.* Oulu, Finland: VTT Electronics.

Accenture. (2008). *"New-generation workers" want technology their way, Accenture survey finds.* Retrieved from http://newsroom.accenture.com/article_display.cfm?article_id=4767

Ackoff, R. L., & Emery, F. E. (2006). *On purposeful systems.* New Brunswick: Aldine Transaction.

ADL. (2004). *Sharable Content Object Reference Model Version 1.3.1.* Retrieved from http://www.adlnet.org

Agar, M., Ali, F., Bhasin, S., Kota, N., Landa, R., & Linares, G. L. (2007). *IT Assessment: Final Report.* Dallas, TX: University of Dallas.

Agrawal, R., Evfimievski, A., & Srikant, R. (2003). Information sharing across private databases. In *Proceedings of the ACM SIGMOD International Conference on Management of Data*, San Diego, CA (pp. 86-97).

Aiello, B., Ishai, Y., & Reingold, O. (2001). Priced oblivious transfer: How to sell digital goods. In B. Pfitzmann (Ed.), *Proceedings of the International Conference on the Theory and Application of Cryptographic Techniques* (LNCS 2045, pp. 119-135).

Alderman, C. (1996). *Sathya Sai Education in Human Values, Book 1, Ages 6-9.* Pinner, UK: Sathya Sai Education in Human Values Trust.

Al-Muhtadi, J., Hill, R., Campbell, R., & Mickunas, M. (2006). Context and location-aware encryption for pervasive computing environments. In *Proceedings of the 4th Annual IEEE International Conference on Pervasive Computing and Communications Workshops* (pp. 283-288). Washington, DC: IEEE Computer Society.

Alonso, G., Casati, F., Kuno, H., & Machiraju, V. (2004). *Web Services: Concepts, Architectures and Applications.* New York: Springer.

Alonso-Ríos, D., Vázquez-García, A., Mosqueira-Rey, E., & Moret-Bonillo, V. (2010). Usability: A Critical Analysis and a Taxonomy. *International Journal of Human-Computer Interaction*, 26(1), 53–63. doi:10.1080/10447310903025552

Alreck, P. A., & Settle, R. B. (1985). *The Survey Research Handbook*. Homewood, IL: Irwin Publishers.

Alter, S. (2010). Viewing Systems as Services: A Fresh Approach in the IS Field. *Communications of the Association for Information Systems, 26*(1). Retrieved June 23, 2010, from http://aisel.aisnet.org/cais/vol26/iss1/11

Ambler, S. (2002). *Agile Modeling*. John Wiley & Sons.

American National Standards Institute. (2004). *ANSI INCITS 359-2004: Information technology role-based access control*. Retrieved from http://webstore.ansi.org/RecordDetail.aspx?sku=ANSI+INCITS+359-2004

Anagol, A. (2004). *J2EE Web Services on BEA WebLogic*. Upper Saddle River, NJ: Prentice Hall.

Andrade, J., Ares, J., Garcia, R., & Pazos, J. (2004). A Methodological Framework for Viewpoint-oriented Conceptual Modeling. *IEEE Transactions on Software Engineering, 30*(5), 282–294. doi:10.1109/TSE.2004.1

Andrienko, N., & Andrienko, G. (2004). Interactive visual tools to explore spatio-temporal variation. *AVI'04: Proceedings of the working conference on Advanced visual interfaces*.

Anon., (1988, August 1). A close-up of transmission control protocol internet protocol (TCP/IP). *Datamation, 34*(15), 72–72.

Archer, M. (1995). *Realist social theory: the morphogenetic approach*. Cambridge: Cambridge University Press.

Archer, M. (1998). Introduction: realism in the social sciences. In M. Archer, R. Bhaskar, A. Collier, T. Lawson, & A. Norrie (Eds.), *Critical realism: essential readings* (pp. 189-205). London: Routledge.

Archer, M. (2000). *Being human: the problem of agency*. Cambridge: Cambridge University Press.

Archer, M. S. (1995). *Realist Social Theory: The Morphogenetic Approach*. Cambridge, UK: Cambridge University Press. doi:10.1017/CBO9780511557675

Ardagna, C. A., Cremonini, M., Capitani di Vimercati, S. D., & Samarati, P. (2009). Access control in location-based services. In C. Bettini, S. Jajodia, P. Samarati, & X. S. Wang (Eds.), *Proceedings of Research Issues and Emerging Trends in Privacy in Location-Based Applications* (LNCS 5599, pp. 106-126).

Ardagna, C. A., Jajodia, S., Samarati, P., & Stavrou, A. (2009). Privacy preservation over untrusted mobile networks. In C. Bettini, S. Jajodia, P. Samarati, & X. S. Wang (Eds.), *Proceedings of Research Issues and Emerging Trends in Privacy in Location Based Applications* (LNCS 5599, pp. 84-105).

Ardagna, C. A., Cremonini, M., Capitani di Vimercati, S. D., & Samarati, P. (2007). Privacy-enhanced location-based access control. In Gertz, M., & Jajodia, S. (Eds.), *The handbook of database security: Applications and trends* (pp. 531–552). Berlin, Germany: Springer-Verlag.

Arlow, J., & Neustadt, I. (2002). *UML and the Unified Process*. The Object Technology Series. Addison Wesley.

Arnott, D., & Pervan, G. (2008). Eight key issues for the decision support system discipline. *Decision Support Systems, 44*(3), 657–672. doi:10.1016/j.dss.2007.09.003

Aronson, E., & Patnoe, S. (1997). *The jigsaw classroom: Building cooperation in the classroom* (2nd ed.). New York: Addison Wesley Longman.

Arthur, W. B. (1994). *Inductive Reasoning and Bounded Rationality*. American Economic Association Annual Meetings.

Arvola, M. (2006). Interaction design patterns for computers in sociable use. *International Journal of Computer Applications in Technology, 25*(2-3), 128–139. doi:10.1504/IJCAT.2006.009063

Asonov, D., & Freytag, J.-C. (2003). Almost optimal private information retrieval. In R. Dingledine & P. Syverson (Eds.), *Proceedings of the Second International Workshop on Privacy Enhancing Technologies* (LNCS 2482, pp. 239-243).

Association of Chief Police Officers. (2003). *Good practice guide for computer based electronic evidence (version 3)*. Retrieved from http://www.7safe.com/electronic_evidence/ACPO_guidelines_computer_evidence.pdf

Atallah, M., Blanton, M., & Frikken, K. (2007). Efficient techniques for realizing geo-spatial access control. In *Proceedings of the 2nd ACM Symposium on Information, Computer and Communications Security* (pp. 82-92). New York, NY: ACM Press.

ATHENA. (2007). *ATHENA Integrated Project.* Retrieved from http://www.athena-ip.org/

Atkinson, S., Furnell, S. M., & Phippen, A. D. (2009, April 15-16). E-Safety and e-security: Raising security awareness among young people using peer education. In *Proceedings of the 8th Annual Security Conference*, Las Vegas, NV.

Avgeriou, P., & Tandler, P. (2006). Architectural patterns for collaborative applications. *International Journal of Computer Applications in Technology, 25*(2-3), 86–101. doi:10.1504/IJCAT.2006.009062

Avgerou, C., Ciborra, C., & Land, F. (2004). Introduction. In C. Avgerou, C. Ciborra & F. Land (Eds.), *The Social Study of Information and Communication Technology: Innovation, Actors, and Contexts* (pp. 1-14). Oxford: Oxford University Press.

Avgerou, C., Ciborra, C., Cordella, A., Kallinikos, J., & Smith, M. L. (2005). *The role of information and communication technology in building trust in governance: toward effectiveness and results.* Washington, D.C.: Inter-American Development Bank.

Avison, D. E., & Gregor, S. (2009). An exploration of the real or imagined consequences of information systems research for practice. In S. Newell, E. Whitley, N. Pouloudi, J. Wareham, & L. Mathiassen (Eds.), *Proceedings of the 17th European Conference on Information Systems*, Verona, Italy (pp. 1780-1792).

Avison, D. E., Lau, F., Myers, M., & Nielsen, P. A. (1999, January). Action Research. *Communications of the ACM.*

Avison, D. E., & Fitzgerald, G. (1988). Information systems development: Current themes and future directions. *Information and Software Technology, 30*(8), 458–466. doi:10.1016/0950-5849(88)90142-5

Avison, D. E., & Fitzgerald, G. (2003). Where now for Development Methodologies? *Communications of the ACM, 46*(1), 79–82. doi:10.1145/602421.602423

Avison, D. E., & Fitzgerald, G. (2006). Developing and Implementing Systems. In Currie, W., & Galliers, R. (Eds.), *Rethinking MIS* (pp. 250–278). Oxford, UK: Oxford University Press.

Baek, J., & Zheng, Y. (2004). Identity-based threshold decryption. In F. Bao, R. Deng, & J. Zhou (Eds.), *Proceedings of Public Key Cryptography* (LNCS 2947, pp. 262-276).

Bahill, A. T., & Gissing, B. (1998, November). Re-evaluating systems engineering concepts using systems thinking. *IEEE TSMC Part C-Applications and Reviews, 28*(4), 516–527.

Baker, B., & Verma, D. (2003). Systems Engineering Effectiveness: a Complexity Point Paradigm for Software Intensive Systems in the Information Technology Sector. *Engineering Management Journal, 15*(3), 29–25.

Balz, D., & Deane, C. (2006, November 1). Differing views on terrorism. *The Washington Post*, p. A04.

Bao, F., & Deng, R. (2001). Privacy protection for transactions of digital goods. In S. Qing, T. Okamoto, & J. Zhou (Eds.), *Proceedings of the Third International Conference on Information and Communications Security* (LNCS 2229, pp. 202-213).

Barber, B. (1983). *The logic and limits of trust.* New Brunswick: Rutgers University Press.

Bardram, J., Kjær, R., & Pedersen, M. (2003). Context-aware user authentication–supporting proximity-based login in pervasive computing. In A. K. Dey, A. Schmidt, & J. F. McCarthy (Eds.), *Proceedings of the 5th International Conference on Ubiquitous Computing* (LNCS 2864, pp. 107-123).

Baschab, J., & Piott, J. (2007). *The Executive's Guide to Information Technology* (2nd ed.). New York: Wiley.

Basili, V. (1992). The experimental paradigm in software engineering. In D. Rombach, V. Basili, & R. Shel (Eds.), *Experimental Software Engineering Issues: Critical Assessment and Future Directives.* Springer-Verlag.

Beck, K. (2005). *Extreme Programming Explained: Embrace Change* (2nd ed.). Addison-Wesley.

Beck, K., Beedle, M., van Bennekum, A., Cockburn, A., Cunningham, W., Fowler, M., et al. (2001). *The Agile Manifesto*. Retrieved May 1, 2010, from http://agilemanifesto.org/

Beck, K. (2000). *Extreme Programming Explained: Embrace Change*. Boston: Addison-Wesley.

Befani, B. (2005). The mechanisms of suicide: a realist approach. *International Review of Sociology, 15*(1), 51–75. doi:10.1080/03906700500038504

Belenkiy, M., Chase, M., Kohlweiss, M., & Lysyanskaya, A. (2008). P-signatures and noninteractive anonymous credentials. In *Proceedings of the 5th Conference on Theory of Cryptography* (pp. 356-374).

Bénaben, F., Touzi, J., Rajsiri, V., Trupril, S., Lorré, J. P., & Pingaud, H. (2008). Mediation Information System Design in a Collaborative SOA Context through a MDD Approach. In *Proceedings of the First International Workshop on Model Driven Interoperability for Sustainable Information Systems* (pp. 89-103).

Beresford, A. R., & Stajano, F. (2003). Location privacy in pervasive computing. *IEEE Pervasive Computing / IEEE Computer Society and IEEE Communications Society, 2*(1), 46–55. doi:10.1109/MPRV.2003.1186725

Berlin 3D. (2008). Retrieved August 27, 2008, from 3D RealityMaps: http://www.realitymaps.de

BERR. (2008). *2008 information security breaches survey (Tech. Rep. No. URN 08/788)*. London, UK: Department for Business Enterprise & Regulatory Reform.

Bertolino, A. (2007, May 23-25). Software Testing Research: Achievements, Challenges, Dreams. In *Proceedings of the 2007 Future of Software Engineering -- International Conference on Software Engineering* (pp. 85-103). Washington, DC: IEEE Computer Society.

Bessler, S., & Jorns, O. (2005). A privacy enhanced service architecture for mobile users. In *Proceedings of the Third IEEE International Conference on Pervasive Computing and Communications Workshops* (pp. 125-129). Washington, DC: IEEE Computer Society.

Bettini, C., Mascetti, S., Wang, S., Freni, D., & Jajodia, S. (2009). Anonymity and historical-anonymity in location-based services. In C. Bettini, S. Jajodia, P. Samarati, & X. S. Wang (Eds.), *Proceedings of Research Issues and Emerging Trends in Privacy in Location Based Applications* (LNCS 5599, pp. 1-30).

Bharadwaj, A. S. (2000). A Resource-Based Perspective on Information Technology Capability and Firm Performance: An Empirical Investigation. *Management Information Systems Quarterly, 24*(1), 159–196. doi:10.2307/3250983

Bhaskar, R. (1978). *A realist theory of science* (Second ed.). Sussex: The Harvester Press Limited.

Bhaskar, R. (1998a). Philosophy and scientific realism. In M. Archer, R. Bhaskar, A. Collier, T. Lawson & A. Norrie (Eds.), *Critical realism: Essential readings* (pp. 16-47). London: Routledge.

Bhaskar, R. (1998b). *The possibility of naturalism: a philosophical critique of the contemporary human sciences* (Third ed.). London: Routledge.

Bhaskar, R. (2002). *From science to emancipation: alienation and the actuality of enlightenment*. Delhi: Sage Publications India Pvt Ltd.

Bhatnagar, S. (2004). *E-government: from vision to implementation*. London: Sage Publications Ltd.

BKWSU. (1995). *Living Values: A Guidebook*. London: BKWSU.

Blackburn, S. (1998). Trust, cooperation, and human psychology. In V. Braithwaite & M. Levi (Eds.), *Trust and Governance* (pp. 28-45). New York: Russell Sage Foundation.

Blake, I. F., & Kolesnikov, V. (2004). Strong conditional oblivious transfer and computing on intervals. In P. J. Lee (Ed.), *Proceedings of the 10th International Conference on the Theory and Application of Cryptology and Information Security* (LNCS 3329, pp. 515-529).

Boar, B. H. (1999). *Constructing Blueprints for Enterprise IT Architectures*. Wiley.

Boehm, B. (2000). Spiral Development: Experience, Principles, and Refinements. In W. J. Hansen (Ed.), *Spiral Development Workshop*.

Boehm, B. (2006, May, 20-28). A View of 20th and 21st Century Software Engineering. In *Proceedings of the International Conferences on Software Engineering '06*, Shanghai, China (pp. 12-30). New York: ACM.

Boehm, B. (1981). *Software Engineering Economics*. Upper Saddle River, NJ: Prentice Hall.

Boehm, B. (1998). A Spiral Model for Software Development and Enhancement. *Computer*, *21*(5), 61–72. doi:10.1109/2.59

Boneh, D., & Franklin, M. (2001). Identity-based encryption from the Weil pairing. In *Proceedings of the 21ˢᵗ Annual International Cryptology Conference on Advances in Cryptology* (pp. 213-229).

Booch, G., Rumbaugh, J., & Jacobson, I. (1999). *The Unified Modeling Language User Guide*. Object Technology Series, Addison-Wesley.

Booch, G., Rumbaugh, J., & Jacobson, L. (1999). *The Unified Modeling Language User Guide*. Reading, MA: Addison-Wesley Longman.

Booth, D., Hass, H., McCabe, F., Newcomer, E., Champion, I. M., Ferris, C., et al. (2004). *Web Services Architecture*. Retrieved from http://www.w3.org/TR/2004/NOTE-ws-arch-20040211/

Braithwaite, V. (1998). Communal and exchange trust norms: their value base and relevance to institutional trust. In V. Braithwaite & M. Levi (Eds.), *Trust and Governance* (pp. 46-74). New York: Russell Sage Foundation.

Brambilla, M., Ceri, S., Fraternali, P., & Manolescu, I. (2006). Process modeling in Web applications. *ACM Transactions on Software Engineering and Methodology*, *15*(4), 360–409. doi:10.1145/1178625.1178627

Brewin, B. (2010). *Glitch prompts VA to Shut Down e-health data exchange with Defense*. Retrieved April 27, 2010, from http://www.nextgov.com/site_services/print_article.php?StoryID=ng_20100304_9977

Brinkkemper, S. (1996). Method Engineering: Engineering of information systems development methods and tools. *Information and Software Technology*, *38*, 275–280. doi:10.1016/0950-5849(95)01059-9

Brooks, S., & Whalley, L. (2005). A 2D/3D hybrid GI system. In *Proc. of the 3rd intern. conf. on Computer graphics and interactive techniques in Australasia and South East Asia*. ACM.

Brooks, F. P. (1975). *The Mythical Man-Month*. Reading, MA: Addison-Wesley.

Brooks, F. P. (1987). No silver bullet: Essence and accidents of software engineering. *IEEE Computer*, *20*(4), 10–19.

Brusling, C., & Strömqvist, G. (Eds.). (1996). *Reflektion och praktik i läraryrket (Reflection and practice in the teacher profession)*. Lund, Sweden: Studentlitteratur.

Brynjolfsson, E., & Hitt, L. (2003). Computing Productivity: Firm-level Evidence. *The Review of Economics and Statistics*, *84*(4),

Buber, M. (1988). *The Knowledge of Man. Selected Essays*. Atlantic Highlands, NJ: Humanities Press International Inc.

Bunge, M. (2004a). Clarifying some misunderstandings about social systems and their mechanisms. *Philosophy of the Social Sciences*, *34*(3), 371–381. doi:10.1177/0048393104266860

Bunge, M. (2004b). How does it work? The search for explanatory mechanisms. *Philosophy of the Social Sciences*, *34*(2), 182–210. doi:10.1177/0048393103262550

Burbeck, S. (2000). *The tao of e-business services: The evolution of Web applications into service-oriented components with Web services*. Retrieved from http://www.ibm.com/developerworks/library/ws-tao/

Burmester, M., Magkos, E., & Chrissikopoulos, V. (2008). Strengthening privacy protection in VANETs. In *Proceedings of the IEEE International Conference on Wireless & Mobile Computing, Networking & Communication* (pp. 508-513). Washington, DC: IEEE Computer Society.

Bush, J. (2006). *Illegal downloads may deter future employers*. Retrieved from http://www.theeagleonline.com

Buttyan, L., Holczer, T., & Vajda, I. (2007). On the effectiveness of changing pseudonyms to provide location privacy in VANETs. In F. Stajano, C. Meadows, S. Capkun, & T. Moore (Eds.), *Proceedings of the Fourth European Workshop on Security and Privacy in Ad hoc and Sensor Networks* (LNCS 4572, pp. 129-141).

Bygstad, B. (2008, December 14-17). *Information infrastructure as organization: a critical realist view.* Paper presented at the International Conference on Information Systems, Paris.

Bygstad, B. (2009). Generative Mechanisms for Innovation in Information Infrastructures. In *Proceedings of the 17th European Conference on Information Systems (ECIS),* Verona, Italy.

Byrne, D. (1966). *An Introduction to Personality. A Research Approach.* Englewood Cliffs, New Jersey: Prentice Hall Inc.

Byron, T. (2008). *Safer children in a digital world: The report of the Byron review.* Retrieved from http://www.education.gov.uk/

Byun, J.-W., & Li, N. (2008). Purpose based access control for privacy protection in relational database systems. *Very Large Data Bases Journal, 17*(4), 603–619. doi:10.1007/s00778-006-0023-0

Cachin, C. (1999). Efficient private bidding and auctions with an oblivious third party. In *Proceedings of the 6th ACM Conference on Computer and Communications Security* (pp. 120-127).

Callegari, C., Garroppo, R. G., Giordano, S., Pagano, M., & Russo, F. (2009). A novel method for detecting attacks towards the SIP protocol. In *Proceedings of the 12th International Symposium on Performance Evaluation of Computer & Telecommunication Systems* (pp. 268-273).

Camenisch, J., & Lysyanskaya, A. (2001). An efficient system for non-transferable anonymous credentials with optional anonymity revocation. In B. Pfitzmann (Ed.), *Proceedings of the International Conference on the Theory and Application of Cryptographic Techniques* (LNCS 2045, pp. 93-118).

Camenisch, J., & Lysyanskaya, A. (2002) Dynamic accumulators and application to efficient revocation of anonymous credentials. In M. Yung (Ed.), *Proceedings of the 22nd Annual International Cryptology Conference on Advances in Cryptology* (LNCS 2442, pp. 61-76).

Camenisch, J., & Lysyanskaya, A. (2004). Signature schemes and anonymous credentials from bilinear maps. In M. Franklin (Ed.), *Proceedings of the 24th Annual International Cryptology Conference on Advances in Cryptology* (LNCS 3152, pp. 1-6).

Camenisch, J., Hohenberger, S., Kohlweiss, M., Lysyanskaya, A., & Meyerovich, M. (2006). How to win the Clone Wars: Efficient periodic n-times anonymous authentication. In *Proceedings of the 13th ACM Conference on Computer and Communications Security* (pp. 201-210). New York, NY: ACM Press.

Candebat, T., Dunne, C., & Gray, D. T. (2005). Pseudonym management using mediated identity- based cryptography. In *Proceedings of the Workshop on Digital Identity Management* (pp. 1-10). New York, NY: ACM Press.

Carlsson, S. A. (2004). Using critical realism in IS research. In M. E. Whitman & A. B. Woszczynski (Eds.), *The hanbook of information systems research* (pp. 323-338). Hershey: Idea Group Inc (IGI).

Carlsson, S. A. (2003). Advancing information systems evaluation (research): a critical realist approach. *Electronic Journal of Information Systems Evaluation, 6*(2), 11–20.

Carter, B., & New, C. (Eds.). (2004). *Making realism work: realist social theory and empirical research.* Oxfordshire: Routledge.

Cartwright, N. (2003). *Causation one word many things.* London: Centre for Philosophy of Natural and Social Science.

Cartwright, N. (2004). From causation to explanation and back. In B. Leiter (Ed.), *The Future for Philosophy* (pp. 230-245). Oxford: Oxford University Press.

Cater-Steel, A., & Toleman, M. (2007). Education for IT service management standards. *International Journal of IT Standards and Standardization Research, 5,* 27–41.

CC. (2008). *IMS Common Cartridge Specification. Version 1.0.* Retrieved from http://www.imsglobal.org/cc/

Chakraborty, S., Dom, B., Gibson, D., Kleinberg, J., Kumar, S., & Raghavan, P. (1999). Mining the link structure of the world wide web. *IEEE Computational Intelligence*, *32*(8), 60–67.

Chappell, D. (2004). *Enterprise Service Bus*. Sebastopol, CA: O'Reilly Media.

Charette, R. N. (2005, September). Why Software Project Fails. *IEEE Spectrum*, 42-49. Retrieved October 2006 from www.spectrum.ieee.org

Chaum, D. L. (1983). Blind signatures for untraceable payments. In *Proceedings of Advances in Cryptology* (pp. 199-203).

Chaum, D. L. (1981). Untraceable electronic mail, return addresses, and digital pseudonyms. *Communications of the ACM*, *24*(2), 84–90. doi:10.1145/358549.358563

Chaum, D. L. (1985). Security without identification: Transaction systems to make big brother obsolete. *Communications of the ACM*, *28*(10), 1030–1044. doi:10.1145/4372.4373

Chaves, F., Wilbois, T., & Grinberg, E. (2005). *IT-Konzept für die Erstellung eines KFÜ-Portals*. Karlsruhe, Germany: Fraunhofer IITB.

Checkland, P. (1981). *Systems Thinking, Systems Practice*. London: Wiley.

Checkland, P. (2000). Soft systems methodology: a thirty year retrospective. *Systems Research and Behavioral Science*, *17*(11), 11–58. doi:doi:10.1002/1099-1743(200011)17:1+<:AID-SRES374>3.0.CO;2-O

Checkland, P., & Scholes, J. (1990). *Soft Systems Methodology in Action*. Chichester, UK: John Wiley & Sons, Inc.

Checkland, P., & Winter, M. (2006). Process and Content: two ways of using SSM. *The Journal of the Operational Research Society*, *57*, 1435–1441. doi:10.1057/palgrave.jors.2602118

Chen, H. M., Perry, O., & Kazman, R. (2009, August 12-15). An Integrated Framework for Service Engineering: A Case Study in the Financial Services Industry. Paper presented at ICEC '09, Taipei, Taiwan.

Chen, L. D., & Skelton, G. W. (2005). *Mobile Commerce Application Development.* Cyber Tech Publishing.

Chen, T., Yu, H., Feng, C., & Wei, H. (2006). A New Security Architecture for Mobile Communication, In R. Wamkeue (Ed.), *Proceedings of the 17th IASTED International Conference on Modeling and Simulation: International Association of Science and Technology for Development* (pp. 424-429). Anaheim, CA: ACTA Press.

Chen, X., & Sorenson, P. (2007, November). Toward TQM in IT Services. In *Proceedings of the ASE Workshop on Automating Service Quality*, Atlanta, GA (pp. 42-48).

Chen, C.-Y., Wu, T.-Y., Huang, Y.-M., & Chao, H.-C. (2008). An efficient end-to-end security mechanism for IP multimedia subsystem. *Computer Communications*, *31*(18), 4259–4268. doi:10.1016/j.comcom.2008.05.025

Chen, H. M., Kazman, R., & Garg, A. (2006). BITAM: An Engineering Principled Method for managing misalignments between Business and IT architectures. *Science of Computer Programming*, *56*, 5–26.

Cho, Y. S., Bao, L., & Goodrich, M. (2006). Secure access control for location-based applications in WLAN systems. In *Proceedings of the 2nd IEEE International Workshop on Wireless and Sensor Networks Security* (pp. 852-857). Washington, DC: IEEE Computer Society.

Chor, B., & Gilboa, N. (1997). Computationally private information retrieval (extended abstract). In *Proceedings of the Twenty-Ninth Annual ACM Symposium on Theory of Computing* (pp. 304-313). New York, NY: ACM Press.

Chor, B., Goldreich, O., Kushilevitz, E., & Sudan, M. (1995). Private information retrieval. In *Proceedings of the Annual IEEE Symposium on Foundations of Computer Science* (pp. 41-50). Washington, DC: IEEE Computer Society.

Churchman, C. W. (1972). *The design of inquiring systems: Basic concepts of systems and organizations*. New York: Basic Books.

Ciborra, C. (1996). The Platform Organization: Recombining Strategies, Structures, and Surprises. *Organization Science*, *7*(2), 103–118. doi:10.1287/orsc.7.2.103

Ciborra, C. (1998). Notes on Improvization and time in Organizations. *Journal of Accounting. Management and Information Technology*, *9*, 77–94. doi:10.1016/S0959-8022(99)00002-8

Clark, R. W., & Maurer, R. (2006). Visual terrain editor: an interactive editor for real terrains. *J. Comput. Small Coll., 22*(2).

Collier, D., Seawright, J., & Munch, G. L. (2004). The quest for standards: King, Keohane, and Verba's designing social inquiry. In H. E. Brady & D. Collier (Eds.), *Rethinking social inquiry: diverse tools, shared standards* (pp. 21-50). Lanham: Rowman & Littlefield Publishers, Inc.

Conger, S. (2011b). *Finding the Sweet Spot in ITIL Implementation.* Paper presented at the Pink Elephant IT Management Conference, Las Vegas, NV.

Conger, S., & Landry, B. L. J. (2009, May 19-24). Problem Analysis: When established techniques don't work. In *Proceedings of the 2nd Annual Conf-IRM Conference*, Al-Ain, UAE.

Conger, S., & Picus, B. (2009). Sustainable Certification using ISO/IEC 20000. In *Proceedings of the American Society for Quality's Quality Management Forum* (pp. 14-19).

Conger, S., & Pollard, C. (2009, December 14). Servitizing the Introductory MIS Course. In *Proceedings of the AIS Special Interest Group on Services (SIG SVC) Workshop*, Phoenix, AZ.

Conger, S. (1994). *The New Software Engineering.* New York: Thomson Publishing.

Conger, S. (2009). Information Technology Service Management and Opportunities for Information Systems Curricula. *International Journal of Information Systems in the Service Sector, 1*(2), 58–68.

Conger, S. (2010). IT Infrastructure Library ITIL v3. In Bigdoli, H. (Ed.), *The Handbook of Technology Management* (Vol. 1, pp. 244–256). New York: John Wiley & Sons.

Conger, S. (2011a). *Process Mapping and Management.* New York: Business Expert Press.

Conger, S., & Schultze, U. (2008). *IT Governance and Control: Making sense of Standards, Guidelines, and Frameworks.* Chicago: The Society for Information Management International, Advanced Practices Council.

Conger, S., Venkataraman, R., Hernandez, A., & Probst, J. (2009). Market Potential for ITSM Students: A Survey. *Information Systems Management, 26*(2), 176–181. doi:10.1080/10580530902797573

Conti, G., & De Amicis, R. (2008). New generation 3d web-based GI systems - The importance of integrated infrastructures for territory management. In *proceedings of Webist,* Madeira, Portugal.

Conti, G., Andreolli, M., Piffer, S., & De Amicis, R. (2008). A 3D web based GI system for regional planning. In *proceedings of Webist,* Madeira, Portugal.

Cook, K. S., Hardin, R., & Levi, M. (2005). *Cooperation without trust?* New York: Russell Sage Foundation.

Cook, R. W., & Flynn, M. J. (1970). System design of a dynamic microprocessor. *IEEE T Comput C, 19*(3), 213. doi:10.1109/T-C.1970.222899

Coughlin, J., Cuff, S., & Krause, N. (2008). SERVIR Viz: A 3D data access and visualization system for mesoamerica. *Directions Magazione Worldwide Source for Geospatial Technology.*

Coutaz, N., Crowley, J., Dobson, S., & Garlan, D. (2005). Context is key. *Communications of the ACM, 48*(3), 49–53. doi:doi:10.1145/1047671.1047703

Cox, L. P., Dalton, A., & Marupadi, V. (2007). Smokescreen: Flexible privacy controls for presence-sharing. In *Proceedings of the 5th International Conference on Mobile Systems Applications and Services* (pp. 233-245). New York, NY: ACM Press.

Coyne, E. J. (1996). Role engineering. In *Proceedings of the 1st ACM Workshop on Role-Based Access Control*, Gaithersburg, MD.

Cramer, R., Gennaro, R., & Schoenmakers, B. (1997). A secure and optimally efficient multi-authority election scheme. *European Transactions on Telecommunications, 8*(5), 481–490. doi:10.1002/ett.4460080506

Crook, R., Ince, D., & Nuseibeh, B. (2002). Towards an analytical role modelling framework for security requirements. In *Proceedings of the 8th International Workshop on Requirements Engineering: Foundation for Software Quality*, Essen, Germany.

Culnan, M. J. (2007). The dimensions of perceived accessibility to information: Implications for the delivery of information systems and services. *Journal of the American Society for Information Science American Society for Information Science, 36*(5), 302–308. doi:10.1002/asi.4630360504

Cuyler, T., & Schatzberg, L. (2003). Customer service at SWU's Occupational Health Clinic. *Journal of Information Systems Education, 14*(3), 241–246.

Damgard, I., & Jurik, M. (2001). A generalisation, a simplication and some applications of Paillier's probabilistic public-key system. In K. Kim (Ed.), *Proceedings of the 4th International Workshop on Practice and Theory in Public Key Cryptography* (LNCS 1992, pp. 119-136).

Danermark, B., Ekstrom, M., Jokobsen, L., & Karlsson, J. C. (2003). *Explaining society: critical realism in the social sciences*. London: Routledge.

Davies, T., & Cranston, P. (2008). *Youth work and social networking: Final research report.* Retrieved from http://blogs.nya.org.uk/ywsn/final-report.html

De Amicis, R., Witzel, M., & Conti, G. (2007). Interoperable networked service-based infrastructure for interactive. In *Proceedings of Proceedings of the NATO-OTAN Workshop on Development of a Prototype System for Sharing Information related to Acts of Terrorism to the Environment, Agriculture and Water systems,* Venice.

de Castro, P. A. D., de França, O. F., Ferreira, H. M., & Von Zuben, F. J. (2007). Applying Biclustering to Perform Collaborative Filtering. In *Proceedings of the Seventh International Conference on Intelligent Systems Design and Applications* (pp. 421-426).

de Vreede, G. J. (1995). *Facilitating Organisational Change; The participative application of dynamic modeling*. Doctoral Dissertation, Delft University of Technology, Delft.

Deloitte. (2002). Achieving, Measuring, and Communicating IT Value. *CIO Magazine*. Retrieved from http://www.cio.com/sponsors/041503dt/complete.pdf

DeLone, W. H., & McLean, E. R. (1992). Information Systems Success: The Quest for the Dependent Variable. *Information Systems Research, 3*(1), 60–95. doi:10.1287/isre.3.1.60

DeLone, W. H., & McLean, E. R. (2003). The DeLone and McLean Model of Information Systems Success: A Ten-Year Update. *Journal of Management Information Systems, 19*(4), 9–30.

DeMarco, T. (1978). *Structured analysis and system specification*. Upper Saddle River, NJ: Prentice Hall.

DeMarco, T., & Plauger, P. J. (1979). *Structured Analysis and System Specification*. Upper Saddle River, NJ: Prentice Hall.

den Haan, J. (2009). *The Science of Model-Driven SOA*. Retrieved from http://www.theenterprisearchitect.eu/archive/2009/04/14/the-science-of-model-driven-soa

Denning, D., & MacDoran, P. (1996). Location-based authentication: Grounding cyberspace for better security. *Computer Fraud & Security*, (2): 12–16. doi:10.1016/S1361-3723(97)82613-9

Desmedt, Y. G. (1994). Threshold cryptography. *European Transactions on Telecommunications, 5*(4), 449–457. doi:10.1002/ett.4460050407

Dierks, T., & Allen, C. (1999). *RFC 2246: The TLS protocol version 1.0*. Retrieved from HTTP://www.ietf.org/rfc/rfc2246.txt

Diffie, W., & Hellman, M. (1976). New directions in cryptography. *IEEE Transactions on Information Theory, 22*(6), 644–654. doi:10.1109/TIT.1976.1055638

Dobson, P. J. (2002). Critical realism and information systems research: why bother with philosophy? *Information Research, 7*(2).

Dobson, P. J., Myles, J., & Jackson, P. (2007). Making the case for critical realism: examining the implementation of automated performance management systems. *Information Resources Management Journal, 20*(2), 138–152.

Dodd, J. L., & Carr, H. H. (1994). Systems development led by end-users. *Journal of Systems Management, 45*(8), 34.

Dodge, K., & Prinstein, M. (2008). *Understanding peer influence in children and adolescents*. New York, NY: Guilford Publications.

Doran, T. (2000, October 25). Compliance Frameworks: Software Engineering Standards. In *Proceedings of the NDIA Systems Engineering & Supportability Conference*, Washington, DC. Retrieved from http://sce.uhcl.edu/helm/SENG_DOCS/compliance_framework.pdf

Dorgan, S. J., & Dowdy, J. J. (2004). When IT lifts productivity. *The McKinsey Quarterly*, *4*, 13–15.

Doyle, K. G., Wood, J. R. G., & Wood-Harper, A. T. (1993). Soft systems and systems engineering: on the use of conceptual models in information system development. *Information Systems Journal*, *3*(3), 187–198. doi:10.1111/j.1365-2575.1993.tb00124.x

DRI. (2003). *IMS digital repositories interoperability-core functions information model Version 1*. Retrieved from http://www.imsglobal.org/digitalrepositories/driv1p0/imsdri_infov1p0.html

Du, W., & Atallah, M. J. (2001). Privacy-preserving cooperative scientific computations. In *Proceedings of the 14th IEEE Workshop on Computer Security Foundations* (pp. 273-282).

Dubie, D. (2002). *Procter and Gamble touts IT services model, saves $500 million*. ComputerWorld Management.

Duckham, M., & Kulik, L. (2005). A formal model of obfuscation and negotiation for location privacy. In H.-W. Gellersen, R. Want, & A. Schmidt (Eds.), *Proceedings of the 3rd International Conference on Pervasive Computing* (LNCS 3468, pp. 152-170).

Duckham, M., & Kulik, L. (2006). Location privacy and location-aware computing. In Drummond, J., Billen, R., Forrest, D., & Joao, E. (Eds.), *Investigating change in space and time*. Boca Raton, FL: CRC Press.

Dulaney, K. (2003, December). *Predictions 2004: Mobile and Wireless* (ID: AV-21-5094). Gartner Inc.

Dunleavy, P., Margetts, H., Bastow, S., & Tinkler, J. (2006). *Digital era governance: IT corporations, the state, and e-government*. Oxford: Oxford University Press.

Dysthe, O. (2003). Dialogperspektiv på elektroniska diskussioner (A dialogical perspective on electronic discussions). In Dysthe, O. (Ed.), *Dialog, samspel och lärande (Dialogue, collaboration and learning)* (pp. 295–320). Lund, Sweden: Studentlitteratur.

Easton, G. (2010). Critical realism in case study research. *Industrial Marketing Management*, *39*(11), 118–128. doi:10.1016/j.indmarman.2008.06.004

Eberlein, A., & Sampaio do Prodo Leite, J. C. (2002, September). Agile requirements definition: A view from requirements engineering. In *Proceedings of the International Workshop on Time-Constrained Requirements Engineering (TCRE'02)*.

E-gif. (2005). *E-government Interoperability Framework*. Retrieved from http://www.e.govt.nz/standards/e-gif/e-gif-v-3-3/

Eisenhardt, K. M. (1989). Building theories from case study research. *Academy of Management Review*, *14*(4), 532–550. doi:10.2307/258557

Eisenhardt, K. M. (1989). Building Theories from Case Study Research. *Academy of Management Review*, *14*, 532–550. doi:doi:10.2307/258557

ElGamal, T. (1985). A public key cryptosystem and a signature scheme based on discrete logarithms. *IEEE Transactions on Information Theory*, *31*(4), 469–472. doi:10.1109/TIT.1985.1057074

Encarnação, J., De Amicis, R., Conti, G., & J., R. (2008). Beyond FOSS 3D gis technologies: a chance for developing countries. In *proceedings of FOSS4G 2008 - Free and Open Source Software for Geospatial Conference*, Cape Town, South Africa.

Epstein, P. A. (2002). *Engineering of role/permission assignments*. Unpublished doctoral dissertation, George Mason University, Fairfax, VA.

Epstein, P. A., & Sandhu, R. (2001, December). Engineering of role/permission assignments. In *Proceedings of the 17th Annual Computer Security Applications Conference*, New Orleans, LA (pp. 127-136).

ESDIS. (2008). *The earth science data and information system project*. Retrieved from http://esdis.eosdis.nasa.gov

Espinal, R., Hartlyn, J., & Kelley, J. M. (2006). Performance still matters: explaining trust in government in the Dominican Republic. *Comparative Political Studies*, *39*(2), 200–223. doi:10.1177/0010414005281933

ESRI - Environment System Research Institute. (2008). Retrieved from http://www.esri.com

Ess Edunet. (2007). *Values*. Retrieved October 2007 from http://essedunet.nsd.uib.no/opencms.war/opencms/ess/en/topics/1/

Etzioni, O. (1996). The World Wide Web: Quagmire or gold mine. *Communications of the ACM, 39*(11), 65–68. doi:doi:10.1145/240455.240473

European Parliament. (1995). European data protection directive 95/46/EC. *Official Journal of the European Union. L&C, L*(281), 31–50.

Even, S., Goldreich, O., & Lempel, A. (1985). A randomized protocol for signing contracts. *Communications of the ACM, 28*(6), 647. doi:10.1145/3812.3818

Ewusi-Mensah, K. (2003). *Software development failures: anatomy of abandoned projects*. Boston: MIT Press.

Fahey, L., & Randall, R. M. (1997). What is scenario learning? In *Learning from the Future: Competitive Foresight Scenarios* (pp. 3–21). New York: Wiley.

Fay, B. (1994). General laws and explaining human behaviour. In M. Martin & L. C. McIntyre (Eds.), *Readings in the Philosophy of Social Science* (pp. 91-110). Cambridge, Massachusetts: The MIT Press.

Fenn, J., & Linden, A. (2004). *Gartner's Hype Cycle Special Report* (ID: AV-23-0877). Gartner Research.

Ferguson, G. T., & Pike, T. H. (2001). Mobile Commerce – Cutting Loose. *Accenture Outlook, 1*, 64–69.

Ferraiolo, D. F., Kuhn, D. R., & Chandramouli, R. (Eds.). (2007). *Role Based Access Control* (2nd ed.). Boston: Artech House.

Ferraiolo, D. F., Sandhu, R., Gavrila, S., Kuhn, D. R., & Chandramouli, R. (2001). Proposed NIST standard for role-based access control. *ACM Transactions on Information and System Security, 4*(3), 224–274. doi:10.1145/501978.501980

Festinger, L. (1957). *A Theory of Cognitive Dissonance*. Stanford, CA: Stanford University Press.

Feurer, R. C. K., Weber, M., & Wargin, J. (2001). *Aligning Strategies, Processes, and Information Technology: A Case Study*. In J.M. Myerson, (Ed.), *Enterprise Systems Integration* (pp. 11-28).

Fitzgerald, B., & Fitzgerald, G. (1999, June 23-25). Categories and Contexts of Information Systems Development: Making Sense of the Mess. In J. Pries-Heje, C. U. Ciborra, K. Kautz, J. Valor, E. Christiaanse, D. Avison, et al. (Eds.), *Proceedings of the Seventh European Conference on Information Systems,* Copenhagen, Denmark (pp. 194-211).

Fleetwood, S. (2001). Causal laws, functional relations and tendencies. *Review of Political Economy, 13*, 201–220. doi:10.1080/09538250120036646

Forrester, J. W. (1994). System Dynamics, Systems Thinking, and Soft OR. *System Dynamics Review, 10*(2-3), 245–256. doi:10.1002/sdr.4260100211

Fountain, J. E. (2001). *Building the virtual state: information technology and institutional change*. Washington, D.C.: Brookings Institution Press.

Fowler, M. (2000). *UML Distilled: A Brief Guide to the Standard Object Modeling Language* (2nd ed.). Reading, MA: Addison-Wesley.

Franks, J., Hallam-Baker, P., Hostetler, J., Lawrence, S., Leach, P., Luotonen, A., et al. (1999). *RFC 2617: HTTP authentication: basic and digest access authentication.* Retrieved from http://rfc.askapache.com/rfc2617/

Freudiger, J., Shokri, R., & Hubeaux, J. (2009). On the optimal placement of MIX zones. In I. Goldberg & M. J. Atallah (Eds.), *Proceedings of the 9th International Symposium, Privacy Enhancing Technologies* (LNCS 5672, pp. 216-234).

Frikken, K. B., & Atallah, M. J. (2003). Privacy preserving electronic surveillance. In *Proceedings of the ACM Workshop on Privacy in the Electronic Society*, Washington, DC (pp. 45-52).

Frye, C. (2005). *QUESTION & ANSWER The role of composite applications in an SOA*. Retrieved from http://searchsoa.techtarget.com/news/interview/0,289202,sid26_gci1109080,00.html

FTK - Research Institute for Telecommunication. (2008, May 30). European ICT manifesto for the regions. Dortmund.

Fu, Y., Sandhu, K., & Shi, M. (2000). Clustering of web users based on access patterns. In *Proceedings of the 1999 KDD Workshop on Web Mining* (LNAI 1836, pp. 21-38).

Fukuyama, F. (1995). *Trust: the social virtues and the creation of prosperity*. London: Penguin Books Ltd.

Furnell, S. M., Bryant, P., & Phippen, A. D. (2007). Assessing the security perceptions of personal Internet users. *Computers & Security, 26*(5), 410–417. doi:10.1016/j.cose.2007.03.001

Gajparia, A., Mitchell, C., & Yeun, C. (2004). The location information preference authority: Supporting user privacy in location based services. In *Proceedings of the 9th Nordic Workshop on Secure IT-Systems* (pp. 91-96).

Gallagher, M., Link, A., & Petrusa, J. (2005). *Measuring Service Sector Research and Development*. Washington, DC: National Institute for Science and Technology. Retrieved May 1, 2010, from http://www.nist.gov/director/prog-ofc/report05-1.pdf

Galup, S., Dattero, R., Quan, J., & Conger, S. (2009). An Overview of IT Service Management. *Communications of the ACM, 52*(5), 124–128. doi:10.1145/1506409.1506439

Gambetta, D. (1988). Can we trust trust? In D. Gambetta (Ed.), *Trust: making and breaking cooperative relations* (pp. xi-xiv). New York: Basil Blackwell, Inc.

Gambetta, D., & Hamill, H. (2005). *Streetwise: how taxi drivers establish their customers' trustworthiness*. New York: Russell Sage Foundation.

Ganesan, D., Estrin, D., & Heidemann, J. (2003). Dimensions: Why do we need a new data handling architecture for sensor networks? *SIGCOMM Comput. Commun.* (pp. 143–148).

Gardner, H. (2000). *The Disciplined Mind: Beyond Facts and Standardized Tests, The K-12 Education that Every Child Deserves*. New York: Penguin Books.

Garrido, J. L. (2003). *AMENITIES: Una metodología para el desarrollo de sistemas cooperativos basada en modelos de comportamiento y tareas*. Unpublished doctoral dissertation, University of Granada, Granada.

Gaunt, D., & Löfgren, O. (1984). *Myter om svensken* (Myths about Swedes). Stockholm, Sweden: Liber förlag.

Gayraud, R., & Jaques, O. (2010). *SIPp-SIP load generator*. Retrieved from http://sipp.sourceforge.net/

GDI3D. (2008). *Spatial data infrastructure for 3d-geodata*. Retrieved from http://www.geographie.uni-bonn.de/karto/hd3d/webstart.en.htm

Gedik, B., & Liu, L. (2005). Location privacy in mobile systems: A personalized anonymization model. In *Proceedings of the 25th IEEE International Conference on Distributed Computing Systems* (pp. 620-629). Washington, DC: IEEE Computer Society.

Geneiatakis, D., Dagiouklas, A., Kambourakis, G., Lambrinoudakis, C., Gritzalis, S., & Ehlert, S. (2006). Survey of security vulnerabilities in session initiation protocol. *IEEE Communications Surveys and Tutorials, 8*, 68–81. doi:10.1109/COMST.2006.253270

Geneiatakis, D., & Lambrinoudakis, C. (2007). A lightweight protection mechanism against signaling attacks in a SIP-based VoIP environment. *Telecommunication Systems, 36*(4), 153–159. doi:10.1007/s11235-008-9065-5

George, A. L., & Bennett, A. (2005). *Case studies and theory development in the social sciences*. Cambridge, Massachusetts: MIT Press.

George, J. A., & Schlecht, L. E. (1993). The NAS hierarchical network management-system. *IFIP Trans C, 12*, 301–312.

GEOSS - Global Earth Observation System of Systems. (2008). Retrieved from http://www.epa.gov/geoss

Gerring, J. (2007). *Case study research: principles and practices*. New York: Cambridge University Press.

Gershon, N., & Eick, S. (1997). *Information visualization applications in the real world*. IEEE.

Ghinita, G. (2008). Understanding the privacy-deficiency trade-off in location based queries. In *Proceedings of the SIGSPATIAL ACM GIS International Workshop on Security and Privacy in GIS and LBS* (pp. 1-5). New York, NY: ACM Press.

Ghinita, G., Kalnis, P., & Skiadopoulos, S. (2007). PRIVE: Anonymous location-based queries in distributed mobile systems. In *Proceedings of the 16ᵗʰ International Conference on World Wide Web* (pp. 371-380). New York, NY: ACM Press.

Ghinita, G., Kalnis, P., Kantarcioglu, M., & Bertino, E. (2009). A hybrid technique for private location-based queries with database protection. In N. Mamoulis, T. Seidl, T. B. Pedersen, K. Torp, & I. Assent (Eds.), *Proceedings of the 11ᵗʰ International Symposium on Advances in Spatial and Temporal Databases* (LNCS 5644, pp. 98-116).

Ghinita, G., Kalnis, P., Khoshgozaran, A., Shahabi, C., & Tan, K. (2008). Private queries in location based services: Anonymizers are not necessary. In *Proceedings of the ACM SIGMOD International Conference on Management of Data* (pp. 121-132). New York, NY: ACM Press.

Ghinita, G. (2009). Private queries and trajectory anonymization: A dual perspective on location privacy. *Transactions on Data Privacy*, *2*(1), 3–19.

Gianluigi, O. (2006). Mathematics as a Quasi-Empirical Science. *Foundations of Science*, *11*(2), 41–79. doi:10.1007/s10699-004-5912-3

Giddens, A. (1990). *The consequences of modernity*. Stanford: Stanford University Press.

Gilligan, C. (1983). Do the social science have an adequate theory of moral development? In Haan, N., Bellah, R., Rainbow, P., & Sullivan, W. (Eds.), *Social Science as Moral Inquiry*. New York: Columbia University Press.

Gilligan, C., & Attanucci, J. (1988). Two moral orientations: gender differences and similarities. *Merrill-Palmer Quarterly*, *34*, 223–237.

GMES - Global Monitoring for Environment and Security. (2008). Retrieved from http://www.gmes.info

Goffman, E. (1959). *The Presentation of Self in Everyday Life*. London: Penguin Books.

Goldenstern, C. (2010). *Closing the 21st Century Service Capability Gap*. Retrieved April 28, 2010, from http://www.tsia.com/secure/whitepapers/Closing_the_21st_Century_Service_Capability_Gap.pdf

Goldreich, O., Micali, S., & Wigderson, A. (1991). Proofs that yield nothing but their validity or all languages in NP have zero-knowledge proof systems. *Journal of the ACM*, *38*(3), 690–728. doi:10.1145/116825.116852

Goldwasser, S., & Lindell, Y. (2002). Secure computation without agreement. In *Proceedings of the 16th International Conference on Distributed Computing* (pp. 17-32).

Google Earth. (2008). Retrieved from http://earth.google.com

Gopinath, C., & Sawyer, J. E. (1999). Exploring the Learning from an Enterprise Simulation. *Journal of Management Development*, *18*(5), 477–489. doi:10.1108/02621719910273596

Gorla, N., & Lin, S.-C. (2010). Determinants of software quality: A survey of information systems project managers. *Information and Software Technology*, *52*(6), 602. doi:10.1016/j.infsof.2009.11.012

Grasso, V., & Singh, A. (2008). *Advances in space research*. Elsevier.

Grasso, V., Cervone, G., Singh, A., & Kafatos, M. (2006). Global environmental alert service. *American Geophysical Union, Fall Meeting*.

Gregor, S. D. (2006). The nature of theory in information systems. *MIS Quarterly*, *30*(3), 611–642.

Groff, R. (2004). *Critical realism, post-positivism and the possibility of knowledge*. London: Routledge.

Grønmo, R., Skogan, D., Solheim, I., & Oldevik, J. (2004). Model-driven Web Service Development. *International Journal of Web Services Research*, *1*(4), 1–13.

Gruteser, M., & Grunwald, D. (2003). Anonymous usage of location-based services through spatial and temporal cloaking. In *Proceedings of the 1ˢᵗ International Conference on Mobile Systems, Applications and Services* (pp. 31-42). New York, NY: ACM Press.

Gruteser, M., Bredin, J., & Grunwald, D. (2004). Path privacy in location-aware computing. In *Proceedings of the MobiSys Workshop on Context Awareness*.

Gruteser, M., & Grunwald, D. (2005). Enhancing location privacy in wireless LAN through disposable interface identifiers: A quantitative analysis. *Mobile Networks and Applications, 10*(3), 315–325. doi:10.1007/s11036-005-6425-1

Gruteser, M., & Liu, X. (2004). Protecting privacy, in continuous location-tracking applications. *IEEE Security & Privacy, 2*(2), 28–34. doi:10.1109/MSECP.2004.1281242

Guaci, S. (n. d.). *SIP Vicious.* Retrieved from http://code.google.com/p/sipvicious/

Guimaraes, T., Armstrong, C. P., & Jones, B. M. (2009). A New Approach to Measuring Information Systems Quality. *The Quality Management Journal, 16*(1), 42–55.

Gupta, D. (2008, September 14-16). *Servitizing Applications.* Paper presented at the 3rd Academic Forum at the itSMF-USA Conference, San Francisco.

Gutiérrez, F. L., Penichet, V., Isla, J. L., Montero, F., Lozano, M. D., Gallud, J. A., et al. (2006). Un marco Conceptual para el Modelado de Sistemas Colaborativos Empresariales. In *Proceedings of the VII Congreso de Interacción Persona Ordenador* (pp. 269-278).

Gutiérrez, F. L., Isla, J. L., Paderewski, P., Sánchez, M., & Jiménez, B. (2007). An Architecture for Access Control Management in Collaborative Enterprise Systems Based on Organization Models. *International Journal of Science of Computer Programming, 66*(1), 44–59. doi:10.1016/j.scico.2006.10.005

Habermas, J. (1978). *Knowledge and human interests.* London: Heinemann.

Habermas, J. (1987). *The Theory of Communicative Action: Lifeworld and Social System (2).* Boston: Beacon Press.

Haist, J., & Korte, P. (2006). Adaptive streaming of 3d gis geometries and textures for interactive visualisation of 3d city models. *9th AGILE Intern. conf. on Geographic Information Science.*

Han, J., & Kambert, M. (2001). *Data mining: Concepts and Techniques.* San Francisco: Morgan Kaufmann.

Hansson, T. (2008). Communication and Relation Building in Social Systems. T. Hansson (Ed.), *Handbook of Research on Digital Information Technologies: Innovations, Methods and Ethical Issues.* Hershey, PA: Information Science Reference. IGI Global.

Hansson, T. (2010). Co-construction of learning objects: Management and structure. S. Wallis (Ed.). *Cybernetics and Systems Theory in Management. Tools, Views and Advancements.* New York: Information Science Reference. IGI Global. 229-251.

Hansson, T. (2000). *Heart of Learning Organizations. Exploring Competence for Change in Schools.* Luleå, Sweden: Luleå University of Technology.

Hansson, T. (2006). Workplace logics, kinds of knowledge and action research. *Systemic Practice and Action Research, 19*(2), 189–200. doi:doi:10.1007/s11213-006-9011-y

Hardin, R. (2002). *Trust & trustworthiness.* New York: Russell Sage Foundation.

Hardin, R. (2004). Distrust: manifestations and management. In R. Hardin (Ed.), *Distrust* (pp. 3-33). New York: Russell Sage Foundation.

Hardin, R. (1993). The street-level epistemology of trust. *Politics & Society, 21*(4), 505–529. doi:10.1177/0032329293021004006

Hardin, R. (1996). Trustworthiness. *Ethics, 107*(1), 26–42. doi:10.1086/233695

Harmon, P. (2007). *Business Process Change: A Guide for Business Managers and BPM and Six Sigma Professionals* (2nd ed.). San Francisco, CA: Morgan Kaufman Publishers.

Harré, R. (1999). Trust and its surrogates: psychological foundations of political process. In M. E. Warren (Ed.), *Democracy and Trust* (pp. 249-272). Cambridge: Cambridge University Press.

Hauser, C., & Kabatnik, M. (2001). Towards privacy support in a global location service. In *Proceedings of the IFIP Workshop on IP and ATM Traffic Management* (pp. 81-89).

He, Q., & Anton, A. I. (2003). A framework for modeling privacy requirements in role engineering. In *Proceedings of the International Workshop on Requirements Engineering for Software Quality*, Klagenfurt, Austria (pp. 137-146).

Heeks, R. (1999). Reinventing government in the information age. In R. Heeks (Ed.), *Reinventing government in the information age: international practice in IT-enabled public sector reform* (pp. 9-21). London: Routledge.

Hengartner, U. (2008). Location privacy based on trusted computing and secure logging. In *Proceedings of the 4th International Conference on Security and Privacy in Communication Networks* (pp. 1-8). New York, NY: ACM Press.

Hengartner, U. (2006). *Enhancing user privacy in location-based services (Tech. Rep. No. CACR 2006-27)*. Waterloo, ON, Canada: University of Waterloo.

Herrscher, E. (2006). What is the systems approach good for? *Systemic Practice and Action Research, 19*, 409–413. doi:doi:10.1007/s11213-006-9032-6

Hetzler, E. G., & Turner, A. (2004). Analysis experiences using information visualization. *IEEE Computer Graphics and Applications, 24*(5), 22–26. doi:10.1109/MCG.2004.22

Hevner, A. R., March, S. T., Park, J., & Ram, S. (2004). Design Science in Information Systems Research. *Management Information Systems Quarterly, 28*(1), 75–105.

Hirschheim, R., Klein, H., & Lyytinen, K. (1995). *Information Systems Development and Data Modelling: Conceptual and Philosophical Foundations*. Cambridge, UK: Cambridge University Press.

Hochstein, A., Tamm, G., & Brenner, W. (2005, May 26-28). Service-Oriented IT Management: Benefit, Cost and Success Factors. In D. Bartmann, F. Rajola, J. Kallinikos, D. Avison, R. Winter, P. Ein-Dor, et al. (Eds.), *Proceedings of the Thirteenth European Conference on Information Systems,* Regensburg, Germany (pp. 911-921).

Høegh, R. T. (2006, November 20-24). Usability problems: do software developers already know? In J. Kjeldskov & J. Paay (Eds.), *Proceedings of the 18th Australia Conference on Computer-Human interaction: Design: Activities, Artifacts and Environments (OZCHI '06),* Sydney, Australia (pp. 425-428).

Hofstede, G. (1984). *Culture's consequences: international differences in work-related Values*. London: Sage.

Hoh, B., & Gruteser, M. (2006). Protecting location privacy through path confusion. In *Proceedings of the 1st International Conference on Security and Privacy for Emerging Areas in Communications Networks* (pp. 194-205). Washington, DC: IEEE Computer Society.

Hoh, B., Gruteser, M., Herring, R., Ban, J., Work, D., Herrera, J. C., et al. (2008). Virtual trip lines for distributed privacy-preserving traffic monitoring. In *Proceedings of the 6th International Conference on Mobile Systems, Applications and Services* (pp. 15-28). New York, NY: ACM Press.

Hoh, B., Gruteser, M., Xiong, H., & Alrabady, A. (2007). Preserving privacy in GPS traces via uncertainty-aware path cloaking. In *Proceedings of the 14th ACM Conference on Computer and Communications Security* (pp. 161-171). New York, NY: ACM Press.

Home Office. (2007). *Acquisition and disclosure of communications data - code of practice*. Retrieved from http://security.homeoffice.gov.uk/ripa/publication-search/ripa-cop/acquisition-disclosure-cop.pdf?view=Binary

Home Office. (2009). *Protecting the public in a changing communications environment*. Retrieved from http://www.homeoffice.gov.uk/documents/cons-2009-communications-data?view=Binary

Honour, E. (2004). Understanding the Value of Systems Engineering. In *Proceedings of the 14th International INCOSE Symposium*, Toulouse, France (pp. 1-16).

Hornbuck, G. D., & Ancona, E. I. (1970). lx-1 microprocessor and its application to real-time signal processing. *IEEE T Comput C, 19*(8), 710. doi:10.1109/T-C.1970.223021

Hosman, L., Fife, E., & Armey, L. E. (2008). The case for a multi-methodological, cross-disciplinary approach to the analysis of ICT investment and projects in the developing world. *Information Technology for Development, 14*(4), 308–327. doi:10.1002/itdj.20109

Houston, S. (2001). Beyond social constructionism: critical realism and social work. *British Journal of Social Work, 31*(6), 845–861. doi:10.1093/bjsw/31.6.845

Hunter, M. T., Clark, R. J., & Park, F. S. (2007). Security issues with the IP multimedia subsystem (IMS). In *Proceedings of the Workshop on Middleware for Next-Generation Converged Networks and Applications* (p. 9).

Hürster, W., et al. (2007). A Web Portal for Early Warning and Risk Management. In M. Khosrow-Pour (Ed.), *Managing Worldwide Operations and Communications with Information Technology, Proceedings of the 2007 IRMA International Conference,* Vancouver, BC, Canada (pp. 497-501). Hershey, PA: IGI Global.

Hürster, W. (2005). Remote Monitoring of Nuclear Power Plants in Baden-Württemberg, Germany. In Hilty, L., Seifert, E., & Treibert, R. (Eds.), *Information Systems for Sustainable Development* (pp. 333–341). Hershey, PA: IGI Global.

Hürster, W. (2006). A Web Portal for the Remote Monitoring of Nuclear Power Plants. In Tatnall, A. (Ed.), *Encyclopaedia of Portal Technology and Applications* (pp. 1151–1156). Hershey, PA: IGI Global.

IBM. (2003). *The Rational Unified Process. Version 2003.06.00.65.* Rational Software Corporation.

IDABC. (2004). *European interoperability framework for pan-European egovernment services, version 1.0.* Brussels, Belgium: Author.

IDEAS. (2002). European IST-2001-37368 project IDEAS: Interoperability Developments for Enterprise Application and Software - Roadmaps.

IEEE Std.1471-2000 (2000). *IEEE Recommended Practice for Architectural Description.*

IEEE. (2002). *LTSC WG12: Draft standard for learning object metadata.* Retrieved from http://ltsc.ieee.org/wg12/files/LOM_1484_12_1_v1_Final_Draft.pdf http://ltsc.ieee.org/wg12/files/LOM_1484_12_1_v1_Final_Draft.pdf

Information Commissioner. (2008). *Report of the interception of communications commissioner for 2008.* Retrieved from http://www.official-documents.gov.uk/document/hc0809/hc09/0901/0901.pdf

InfoSecurity.com. (2009). *Companies Invest in IT but Do Not Measure It.* Retrieved May 1, 2010, from http://www.infosecurity-us.com/view/3046/companies-invest-in-it-but-do-not-measure-it-value/ ISO/IEC. (1995). *ISO/IEC 12207:1995 Standard for Information Systems Life Cycle Processes.* Washington, DC: International Organization for Standardization and International Electrotechnical Commission (ISO/IEC).

INSPIRE. (2008). Retrieved from http://inspire.jrc.ec.europa.eu

Intergraph SG&I - Geospatially Powered Solution. (2008). Retrieved from http://www.intergraph.com/sgi/default.aspx

Isling, Å. (1974). *Vägen mot en demokratisk skola. Skolpolitik och skolreformer i Sverige från 1880- till 1970-talet (The road towards a democratic school).* Stockholm, Sweden: Prisma.

ISO/IEC. (2002). *ISO/IEC 15288:2002. Standard for Systems Engineering.* Washington, DC: International Organization for Standardization and International Electrotechnical Commission (ISO/IEC).

ISO/IEC. (2005). *ISO/IEC 20000-1: 2005 Standard for Information Technology – Service Management, Part 1: Specification.* Washington, DC: International Organization for Standardization and International Electrotechnical Commission. (ISO/IEC).

ISO/IEC. (2008). *ISO/IEC 12207:2008 Systems and software engineering -- Software life cycle processes.* Washington, DC: International Organization for Standardization and International Electrotechnical Commission (ISO/IEC).

ISO/IEC. (2010). *ISO/CD 9241-210:2010: Ergonomics of human- Part 210: Human-centred interactive systems.* Washington, DC: International Organization for Standardization and International Electrotechnical Commission (ISO/IEC).

IT Governance Institute. (2003). *Board Briefing on IT Governance* (2nd ed.). Retrieved January 18, 2006 from http://www.isaca.org/Content/ContentGroups/ITGI3/Resources1/Board_Briefing_on_IT Governance/26904_Board_Briefing_final.pdf

Ives, M. (2005). Identifying the Contextual Elements of Project Management within Organizations and their impact on Project Success. *Project Management Journal, 36*(1), 37–50.

Jackson, M. A. (1975). *Principle of Program Design.* New York: Academic Press.

Jackson, M. C. (2003). *Systems thinking: Creative holism for managers.* Chichester, UK: John Wiley & Sons, Inc.

Jacobson, I., Booch, G., & Rumbaugh, J. (1999). *Unified Software Development Process.* Reading, MA: Addison-Wesley.

Jakobsson, M., Juels, A., & Syverson, P. (2004). Universal re-encryption for mixnets. In *Proceedings of the RSA Conference Cryptographers Track* (pp. 163-178).

JBoss. (2008). *jboss.org: community driven.* Retrieved from www.jboss.org

Jennings, F. (2008). *Building SOA-Based Composite Applications Using Netbeans IDE 6.* Packet Publishing.

Jiménez, B., Sánchez, M., Gutiérrez, F. L., & Medina, N. (2007). Task Models Representation of a Collaborative System Using Hypermedia Networks. In *Proceedings of the 3rd International Conference on WEBIST* (pp. 113-120).

JISC. (2006). *RELOAD. Reusable eLearning Object Authoring & Delivery.* Retrieved from http://www.reload.ac.uk/

JOGL. (2008). Retrieved from Java binding for the opengl api: https://jogl.dev.java.net

Johnson, W. J., Leach, M. K., & Liu, A. H. (1999). Theory Testing Using Case Studies in Business to Business Research. *Industrial Marketing Management, 28*(3), 201–213. doi:10.1016/S0019-8501(98)00040-6

Jokela, T., Iivari, N., Matero, J., & Karukka, M. (2003, August 17-20). The standard of user-centered design and the standard definition of usability: analyzing ISO 13407 against ISO 9241-11. In *Proceedings of the Latin American Conference on Human-Computer interaction*, Rio de Janeiro, Brazil (Vol. 46, pp. 53-60). New York: ACM.

Jones, J. C. (1992). *Design Methods* (2nd ed.). New York: John Wiley & Sons.

Jorns, O., Quirchmayr, G., & Jung, O. (2007). A privacy enhancing mechanism based on pseudonyms for identity protection in location-based services. In *Proceedings of the 5th Australasian Symposium on ACSW Frontiers* (pp. 133-142).

Jorns, O., Bessler, S., & Pailer, R. (2005). An efficient mechanism to ensure location privacy in telecom service applications. In Gaiti, D., Galmes, S., & Puigjaner, R. (Eds.), *Network control and engineering for QoS, security and mobility, III* (pp. 57–68). New York, NY: Springer. doi:10.1007/0-387-23198-6_5

Jørstad, I., Dustdar, S., & Van Thanh, D. (2005). Service Oriented Architecture Framework for collaborative services. In *Proceedings of the 14th IEEE International Workshops on Enabling Technologies: Infrastructure for Collaborative Enterprise* (pp. 121-125).

JRC - Joint Research Centre. European Commission. (2006). *Report of international workshop on spatial data infrastructures, cost-benefit / return on investment,* Italy: Ispra.

Jugdev, K., & Muller, R. (2005). A Retrospective Look at Our Evolving Understanding of Project Success. *Project Management Journal, 36*(4), 19–31.

Kahneman, D. (2003). Maps of Bounded Rationality: a Perspective on Intuitive Judgment and Choice. *Nobel Prize Lecture*, 8 December 2002, also in *The American. Economic Review, 93*(5), 1449–1475. doi:10.1257/000282803322655392

Kaikkonen, A., Kallio, T., Kekäläinen, A., Kankainen, A., & Cankar, A. (2005). Usability Testing of Mobile Applications: A Comparison between Laboratory and Field Testing. *Journal of Usability Studies, 1*(1), 4–16.

Kaisler, S. H. (2005). *Software Paradigms.* John Wiley & Son.

Kalakota, R., & Robinson, M. (2002). *M-business: the race to mobility.* McGraw Hill.

Kallinikos, J. (2004). The social foundations of the bureaucratic order. *Organization, 11*(1), 13–36. doi:10.1177/1350508404039657

Kaner, C. (2001). *NSF grant proposal to lay a foundation for significant improvements in the quality of academic and commercial courses in software testing.* Retrieved April 27, 2010, from http://www.testingeducation.org/general/nsf_grant.pdf

Kaner, C. (2003). *Measuring the Effectiveness of Software Testers.* Retrieved April 27, 2010, from http://www.testingeducation.org/a/mest.pdf

Kaplan, S., & Kaplan, R. (1982). *Cognition and Environment: Functioning in an Uncertain World.* Praeger.

Karakostas, B., & Zorgios, Y. (2008). *Engineering Service Oriented Systems: A Model Driven Approach.* Hershey, PA: IGI Global.

Karakostas, B., Zorgios, Y., & Alevizos, C. C. (2006). Automatic derivation of BPEL4WS from IDEF0 process models. *Software and Systems Modeling, 5*(2), 208–218. doi:10.1007/s10270-006-0003-2

Kargupta, H., Das, K., & Liu, K. (2007). A game theoretic approach toward multi-party privacy-preserving distributed data mining. In *Proceedings of the 11th European Conference on Principles and Practice of KDD - PKDD*, Warsaw, Poland.

Katsikas, S., & Gritzalis, D. (1996). High level security policy guidelines. In SEISMED Consortium (Eds.), *Data security for health care, vol. II: Technical guidelines.* Amsterdam, The Netherlands: IOS Press.

Kaufman, C., Perlman, R., & Speciner, M. (2002). *Network security: Private communication in a public world* (2nd ed.). Upper Saddle River, NJ: Prentice Hall.

Kazi, M. A. F. (2003). *Realist evaluation in practice: health and social work.* London: Sage Publications.

Keil, M. (1995). Pulling the Plug: Software Project Management and the Problem of Project Escalation. *Management Information Systems Quarterly, 19*(4). doi:10.2307/249627

Keil, M., & Carmel, E. (1995). Customer-developer links in software development. *Communications of the ACM, 38*(5), 33–44. doi:10.1145/203356.203363

Kent, S., & Atkinson, R. (1997). *RFC 2406: IP encapsulating security payload (ESP).* Retrieved from http://www.ietf.org/rfc/rfc2406.txt

Kent, S., & Atkinson, R. (1998). *RFC 2401: Security architecture for the internet protocol.* Retrieved from http://www.ietf.org/rfc/rfc2401.txt

Kersting, O., & Doellner, J. (2002). Interactive 3d visualization of vector data in gis. *Proc. of the 10th ACM intern. symp. on Advances in geographic information systems* (pp. 107–112). ACM.

Khoshgozaran, A., & Shahabi, C. (2007). Blind evaluation of nearest neighbor queries using space transformation to preserve location privacy. In *Proceedings of the 10th International Conference on Advances in Spatial and Temporal Databases* (pp. 239-257).

Kim, Y., Perrig, A., & Tsudik, G. (2000). Simple and fault-tolerant key agreement for dynamic collaborative groups. In *Proceedings of the 7th ACM Conference on Computer and Communications Security* (pp. 235-244). New York, NY: ACM Press.

King, J. (2009). *IT's top tier: Strong and steady leadership.* Retrieved June 23, 2010, from https://www.computerworld.com/s/article/print/344381/IT_s_top_tier_Strong_and_steady_leadership?taxonomyName=Management&taxonomyId=14

Kirschenbaum, H. (1977). *Advanced Values Clarification.* La Jolla, CA: University Associates.

Klein, A. (2007). *BIND 9 DNS cache poisoning.* Retrieved from http://www.trusteer.com/docs/bind9dns.html

Klein, H. K., & Myers, M. D. (1999). A set of principles for conducting and evaluating interpretive field studies in information systems. *MIS Quarterly, 23*(1), 67–94. doi:10.2307/249410

Kljajić, M. (1994). *Theory of system.* Kranj, Slovenia: Moderna organizacija.

Kljajić, M. (2000). Simulation Approach to Decision Support in Complex Systems. In M. Daniel (Ed.), *Proceedings of the Third International Conference on Computing Anticipatory Systems (CASYS '99) International Journal of Computing Anticipatory Systems*, Hec Liege, Belgium. Liege, Belgium: CHAOS.

Kljajić, M. (2008). Significance of simulation and systems approach methodology in development of complex systems. Lasker, G., Kljajić, M., Mora, M., Gelman, O. and Paradice, D. (eds.). Symposium on Engineering and Management of IT-based organizational systems, Baden-Baden, Germany, *Engineering and management of IT-based organizational systems: a systems approach*. Tecumseh, Ontario: The international institute for advances studies in system research and cybernetics, 34-38.

Kljajić, M., & Farr, J. (2008). The role of systems engineering in the development of information systems. *International Journal of Information Technologies and Systems Approach, 1*(1), 49–61.

Kohlberg, L. (1981). *The Philosophy of Moral Development: Moral Stages and the Idea of Justice*. London: Harper & Row.

Kohlweiss, M., Faust, S., Fritsch, L., Gedrojc, B., & Preneel, B. (2007). Efficient oblivious augmented maps: Location-based services with a payment broker. In N. Borisov & P. Golle (Eds.), *Proceedings of the 7th International Conference on Privacy Enhancing Technologies* (LNCS 4776, pp. 77-94).

Koller, D., et al. (1995). Virtual gis: A real-time 3d geographic information system. *Proc. of the 6th conf. on Visualization* (pp. 94–9).

Kolsch, T., Fritsch, L., Kohlweiss, M., & Kesdogan, D. (2005). Privacy for profitable location based services. In D. Hutter & M. Ullmann (Eds.), *Proceedings of the Second International Conference on Security in Pervasive Computing* (LNCS 3450, pp. 164-178).

Konidala, D. M., Yeun, C. Y., & Kim, K. (2005). A secure and privacy enhanced protocol for location-based services in ubiquitous society. In *Proceedings of the Global Telecommunications Conference* (pp. 2164–2168). Washington, DC: IEEE Computer Society.

Koutsonikola, V. A., & Vakali, A. (2009). A fuzzy bi-clustering approach to correlate web users and pages. *International Journal of Knowledge and Web Intelligence, 1*(1-2), 3–23. doi:doi:10.1504/IJKWI.2009.027923

Kraft, T. (2009). *Business Process Alignment for Successful IT Project Management*. Saarbrücken, Germany: VDB Publishing House Ltd.

Kreger, H. (2003). Fulfilling the Web services promise. [-ff.]. *Communications of the ACM, 46*(6), 29. doi:10.1145/777313.777334

Kuhn, T. (1996). *The structure of scientific revolutions* (3rd ed). University of Chicago Press.

Kulik, L. (2009). Privacy for real-time location-based services. *SIGSPATIAL Special, 1*(2), 9–14. doi:10.1145/1567253.1567256

Kushilevitz, E., & Ostrovsky, R. (1997). Replication is not needed: single database, computationally-private information retrieval. In *Proceedings of the 38th Annual Symposium on Foundations of Computer Science* (pp. 364-373). Washington, DC: IEEE Computer Society.

Kvale, S. (1997). *Den kvalitativa forskningsintervjun (The Qualitative Research Interview)*. Lund, Sweden: Studentlitteratur.

Kwecka, Z., Buchanan, W. J., & Spiers, D. (2010, July). Privacy-preserving data acquisition protocol. In *Proceedings of the IEEE Region 8 International Conference on Computational Technologies in Electrical and Electronics Engineering* (pp. 131-136).

Kwecka, Z., Buchanan, W. J., Spiers, D., & Saliou, L. (2008). Validation of 1-N OT algorithms in privacy-preserving investigations. In *Proceedings of the 7th European Conference on Information Warfare and Security*.

Lacohee, H., Crane, S., & Phippen, A. (2006). *Trustguide: Final report*. Retrieved from http://www.trustguide.org.uk/

Lakatos, I. (1977). *The Methodology of Scientific Research Programmes: Philosophical Papers*. Volume 1, Cambridge University Press.

Lamport, L. (1981). Password authentication with insecure communication. *Communications of the ACM, 24*(11), 770–772. doi:10.1145/358790.358797

LAMS Foundation. (2005). *Learning Activities Management System*. Retrieved from http://www.lamsfoundation.org/

Land Baden-Württemberg. (2004). *Das Corporate Design im Internet, Styleguide für das Landesportal und die Ministerien-Websites, mit allgemeinen Regelungen zur Gestaltung weiterer Auftritte (Stand 07/2004)*. Stuttgart, Germany: Land Baden-Württemberg.

Langheinrich, M. (2001). Privacy by design-principles of privacy-aware ubiquitous systems. In G. D. Abowd, B. Brumitt, & S. Shafer (Eds.), *Proceedings of the International Conference on Ubiquitous Computing* (LNCS 2201, pp. 273-291).

Langley, A. (1999). Strategies for Theorizing from Process Data. *Academy of Management Review, 24*(4), 691–710. doi:10.2307/259349

Larman, C. (2004). *Agile and Iterative Development: A Manager's Guide*. Boston: Addison-Wesley.

Latour, B., & Woolgar, S. (1988). *La vie de laboratoire: la production des faits scientifiques*. Editions La Découverte, Paris.

Lawson, T. (2004). A conception of ontology. University of Cambridge: Faculty of Economics.

Lazanski, T. J., & Kljajić, M. (2006). Systems approach to complex systems modeling with special regards to tourism. *Kybernetes, 35*(7-8), 1048–1058.

LD. (2003). *IMS Learning Design Information Model. Version 1.0 Final Specification*. Retrieved from http://www.imsglobal.org/learningdesign/ldv1p0/imsld_infov1p0.html

Lee, V., Schneider, H., & Schell, R. (2004). *Mobile Applications: architecture, design, and development*. Upper Saddle River NJ: Prentice Hall PTR.

LeMoigne, J.-L. (1994). *Sur la capacité de la raison à discerner rationalité substantive et rationalité procédurale*. In Frydman (Ed.), Quelles hypotheses de rationalité pour la science économique? L'Harmattan, Paris.

Levi, M. (1998). A state of trust. In V. Braithwaite & M. Levi (Eds.), *Trust and Governance* (pp. 77-101). New York: Russell Sage Foundation.

Levi, K., & Arsanjani, A. (2002). A goal-driven approach to enterprise component identification and specification. *Communications of the ACM, 45*(10), 45–52. doi:10.1145/570907.570930

Levinson, M. (2003, October 1). How to Conduct Post-Implementation Audits. *CIO Magazine*. Retrieved March 10, 2010, from http://www.cio.com/article/29817/How_to_Conduct_Post_Implementation_Audits

Levin, T., & Wadsmanly, R. (2008). Teachers' views on factors affecting effective integration of information technology in the classroom: Developmental scenery. *Journal of Technology and Teacher Education, 16*(2), 233–263.

Lewis, J. R. (1995). IBM Computer Usability Satisfaction Questionnaires: Psychometric Evaluation and Instructions for Use. *International Journal of Human-Computer Interaction, 7*(1), 57–78. doi:10.1080/10447319509526110

Li, Z. (2006). *Enterprise Goes Mobile: A Framework and Methodology for Creating a Mobile Enterprise*. Doctoral Dissertation, Lawrence Technological University, Michigan, USA.

Lickona, T. (1993). The return of character education. *Educational Leadership, 51*(3), 6–11.

Lin, D., Bertino, E., Cheng, R., & Prabhakar, S. (2009). Location privacy in moving-object environments. *Transactions on Data Privacy, 2*(1), 21–46.

Liu, L., Chen, J., & Song, H. (2002, June). The Research of Web mining. In *Proceedings of the 4th World Congress on Intelligent Control and Automation* (Vol. 3, pp. 2333-2337).

Liu, H., & Keselj, V. (2007). Combined mining of web server logs and web contents for classifying user navigation patterns and predicting users' future requests. *Data & Knowledge Engineering, 61*(2), 304–330. doi:doi:10.1016/j.datak.2006.06.001

Lovat, T., Schofield, N., Morrison, K., & O'Neill, D. (2002). Research dimensions of values education: A Newcastle perspective. In Pascoe, S. (Ed.), *Values in Education: College Year Book 2002*. Deakin West, Australia: Australian College of Educators.

Lu, W. P., & nd Sundareshan, M. K. (1989, October). Secure communication in internet environments - a hierarchical key management scheme for end-to-end encryption. *IEEE T Commun, 37*(10), 1014-1023.

Luhmann, N. (1979). *Trust and power: two works by Niklas Luhmann.* Avon: John Wiley & Sons Ltd.

Luhmann, N. (1988). Familiarity, confidence, trust: problems and alternatives. In D. Gambetta (Ed.), *Trust: making and breaking cooperative relations* (pp. 94-108). Oxford: Basil Blackwell, Ltd.

Lukosch, S., & Schümmer, T. (2008). The role of roles in collaborative interaction. In *Proceedings of the 13th European Conference on Pattern Languages and Programs, EuroPLoP.*

Luthi, H. P., Almlof, J., Storm, W., & Kalinoski, R. (1992). TIMS/DADS - a project to develop a system of linking national and international repositories of multimedia information. *Ifla J-Int Fed Libr, 18*(3), 223–227.

Lynch, C. G. (2006, March 6). Most Companies Adopting ITIL® Practices. *CIO Magazine.*

Lyotard, J.-F. (1979). *La condition postmoderne.* Paris, Editions de Minuit.

Lysyanskaya, A., Rivest, R., Sahai, A., & Wolf, S. (2000). Pseudonym systems. In H. Heys & C. Adams (Eds.), *Proceedings of 6th Annual International Workshop on Selected Areas in Cryptography* (LNCS 1758, pp. 184-199).

Lyytinen, K., & Robey, D. (1999). Learning Failure in Information Systems Development. *Information Systems Journal, 9*, 85–101. doi:10.1046/j.1365-2575.1999.00051.x

MacEachren, M. (2005). *Moving geovisualization toward support for group work. Exploring geovisualization.* Elsevier.

Macintyre, B. (2007, November 24). *Do you need to change your PIN password, or just your attitude?* Retrieved from http://technology.timesonline.co.uk/tol/news/tech_and_web/the_web/article2933535.ece

MacKenzie, C., Laskey, K., McCabe, F., Brown, P., & Metz, R. (2006). *OASIS reference model for service oriented architecture v.1.0.* OASIS.

Maes, P. (1994). Agents that reduce work and information overload. *Communications of the ACM, 37*(7), 30–40. doi:doi:10.1145/176789.176792

Magkos, E., Kotzanikolaou, P., Sioutas, S., & Oikonomou, K. (2010). A distributed privacy-preserving scheme for location-based queries. In *Proceedings of the IEEE International Symposium on a World of Wireless Mobile and Multimedia Networks* (pp. 1-6). Washington, DC: IEEE Computer Society.

Malle, B., & Edmondson, E. (2007). *What are Values? A Folk-Conceptual Investigation.* Eugene, OR: University of Oregon. Retrieved October 2007 from http://hebb.uoregon.edu/04-01tech.pdf

Manoharan, T., Taylor, H., & Gardiner, P. (2002). A collaborative analysis tool for visualisation and interaction with spatial data. *Proc. of the 7th Int. Conf. on 3D Web technology* (pp. 75–83).

Mansourian, A., Rajabifard, A., & Zoej, J. (2005). *Development of a web-based gis using sdi for disaster management.* Springer.

Mao, J.-Y., Vredenburg, K., Smith, P. W., & Carey, T. (2005). The state of user-centered design practice. *Communications of the ACM, 48*(3), 105–109. doi:10.1145/1047671.1047677

Marca, D. A., & McGowan, C. L. (1987). *SADT: Structured analysis and design technique.* New York, NY: McGraw-Hill.

Marcos, E., Papazoglou, M. P., Piattini, M., de Castro, M. V., Vela, B., Caballero, I., et al. (2009, November 6). Forward. In *Proceedings of the First International Workshop on Model Driven Service Engineering and Data Quality and Security (MoSE+DQS 2009),* Hong Kong.

Markus, M. L., & Keil, M. (1994). If We Built It, They Will Come: Designing Information Systems that People Want to Use. *Sloan Management Review, 35*(4), 11–25.

Marrone, M., & Kolbe, L. M. (2010a, February 23-25). Providing more than just operational benefits: An empirical research. In M. Schumann (Ed.), Proceedings of Multikonferenz Wirtschaftsinformatik 2010 (pp. 61–63). Göttingen, Germany.

Marrone, M., & Kolbe, L. M. (2010b, June 6-9). ITIL and the creation of benefits: An empirical study on benefits, challenges and processes. In *Proceedings of the European Conference on Information Systems (ECIS)*, Pretoria, South Africa.

Martin, J. (1991). *Rapid Applications Development*. New York: Macmillan.

Martins, N. (2006). Capabilities as causal powers. *Cambridge Journal of Economics*(Advance Access).

Masoumzadeh, A., & Joshi, J. (2008). PuRBAC: Purpose-based role-based access control. In R. Meersman & Z. Tari (Eds.), *Proceedings of the Confederated International Conference of On the Move to Meaningful Internet Systems* (LNCS 5332, pp. 1104-1121).

Mathiassen, L., & Nielsen, P. A. (1989). Soft Systems and Hard Contradictions - Approaching the Reality of Information Systems in Organizations. *Journal of Applied Systems Analysis, 16*.

Mathiassen, L., & Pries-Heje, J. (2006). Business agility and diffusion of information technology. *European Journal of Information Systems, 15*, 116–119. doi:10.1057/palgrave.ejis.3000610

Mattas, A. K., Mavridis, I., & Pangalos, G. (2003). Towards dynamically administered role-based access control. In *Proceedings of the 14th International Workshop on Database & Expert Systems Applications*, Prague, Czech Republic (p. 494).

Mavridis, I., Mattas, A., Pagkalos, I., Kotini, I., & Ilioudis, C. (2008). Supporting dynamic administration of RBAC in Web-based collaborative applications during run-time. *International Journal of Information and Computer Security, 2*(4), 328–352. doi:10.1504/IJICS.2008.022487

Mayer, F., Schroeder, A., & Koch, N. (2008). MDD4SOA: Model-Driven Service Orchestration. In *Proceedings of the 12th International IEEE Enterprise Distributed Object Computing Conference.*

McAfee-NCSA. (2007). *McAfee-NCSA online safety study – newsworthy analysis*. Retrieved from http://www.staysafeonline.org/

McDavid, D. W. (1999). A standard for business architecture description. *IBM Systems Journal, Enterprise Solutions Structure, 38*(1).

Meckler, M., & Baillie, J. (2003). The truth about social construction in administrative science. *Journal of Management Inquiry, 12*(3), 273–284. doi:10.1177/1056492603257724

Melone, N. P. (1990). A Theoretical Assessment of the User Satisfaction Construct in Information Systems Research. *Management Science, 36*(1), 76–86. doi:10.1287/mnsc.36.1.76

Melville, N. P. (2010). Information Systems Innovation for Environmental Sustainability. *Management Information Systems Quarterly, 34*(1), 1–21.

Merton, R. K. (1967). *On theoretical sociology: five essays, old and new*. New York: The Free Press.

Miles, M. B., & Huberman, A. M. (1994). *Qualitative Data Analysis*. Thousand Oaks, CA: Sage.

Miller, A., & Listhaug, O. (1999). Political performance and institutional trust. In P. Norris (Ed.), *Critical citizens: global support for democratic government* (pp. 204-216). Oxford: Oxford University Press.

Miller, J., & Mukerji, J. (Eds.). (2001). *OMG Model Driven Architecture*. Retrieved from http://www.omg.com/mda

Milosevic, D., & Patanakul, P. (2004). Standard Project Management may Increase Development Project Success. *International Journal of Project Management, 23*, 181–192. doi:10.1016/j.ijproman.2004.11.002

Mingers, J. (2004c). Re-establishing the real: critical realism and information systems. In J. Mingers & L. P. Willcocks (Eds.), *Social Theory and Philosophy for Information Systems* (Vol. 372-406). Sussex: John Wiley & Sons Ltd.

Mingers, J. (2000). The contribution of critical realism as an underpinning philosophy for OR/MS and systems. *The Journal of the Operational Research Society, 51*(111), 1256–1270.

Mingers, J. (2001). Combining IS Research Methods: Towards a Pluralist Methodology: Towards a Pluralist Methodology. *Information Systems Research, 12*(3), 240–259. doi:10.1287/isre.12.3.240.9709

Mingers, J. (2004a). Critical realism and information systems: brief responses to Monod and Klein. *Information and Organization, 14*(2), 145–153. doi:10.1016/j.infoandorg.2004.02.003

Mingers, J. (2004b). Paradigm wars: ceasefire announced who will set up the new administration? *Journal of Information Technology, 19*(3), 165–171. doi:10.1057/palgrave.jit.2000021

Mingers, J. (2004d). Real-izing information systems: critical realism as an underpinning philosophy for information systems. *Information and Organization, 14*(2), 87–103. doi:10.1016/j.infoandorg.2003.06.001

Mingers, J. (2008). Pluralism, Realism, and Truth: The keys to knowledge in information systems research. *International Journal of Information Technologies and Systems Approach, 1*(1), 79–90.

Mishra, S. K., & Sarkar, P. (2000). Symmetrically private information retrieval. In B. Roy & E. Okamoto (Eds.), *Proceedings of the 1st International Conference in Cryptology* (LNCS 1977, pp. 225-236).

Mishra, P. P., Sanghi, D., & Tripathi, S. K. (1993). TCP flow-control in lossy networks - analysis and enhancement. *IFIP Trans C, 13*, 181–192.

Mitroff, I., & Linstone, H. (1994). *The Unbounded mind: Breaking the chains of traditional business thinking.* Oxford, UK: Oxford University Press.

Mitropoulou, V., & Triantafyllidis, G. (2008). Primary school children's illegal Internet behaviour in Greece: A case study and suggestions. In *Proceedings of the World Conference on Educational Multimedia, Hypermedia and Telecommunications* (pp. 3838-3842).

Mokbel, M. F., Chow, C. Y., & Aref, W. G. (2006). The new Casper: Query processing for location services without compromising privacy. In *Proceedings of the 32nd International conference on Very Large Data Bases* (pp. 763-774).

Molina, A. I. (2006). *A methodology for the development of groupware user interfaces.* Unpublished doctoral dissertation, Universidad de Castilla-la Mancha (UCLM).

Moon, M. J. (2003). *Can IT help government to restore public trust? Declining public trust and potential prospects of IT in the public sector.* Paper presented at the 36th Hawaii International Conference on System Sciences, Hawaii.

Mora, M., Gelman, O., Moti, F., Paradice, D. B., Cervantes, F., & Forginonne, G. A. (2008). Toward an interdisciplinary engineering and management of complex IT-intensive organizational systems: A systems view. *International Journal of Information Technologies and Systems Approach, 1*(1), 1–24.

Morton, P. (2006). Using critical realism to explain strategic information systems planning. *Journal of Information Technology Theory and Application, 8*(1), 1–20.

Moßgraber, J. (2005). *Entwicklungshandbuch für Web-Genesis (Version 7.10).* Karlsruhe, Germany: Fraunhofer IITB.

Munro, I. (1999). Man-machine systems: People and technology in OR. *Systemic Practice and Action Research, 12*(5), 513–532. doi:doi:10.1023/A:1022469607464

Myers, G. J. (1979). *The Art of Software Testing.* New York: John Wiley & Sons.

Nanopoulos, A., Papadopoulos, A., & Manolopoulos, Y. (2006, August 20). Nearest Biclusters Collaborative Filtering. In *Proceedings of WEBKDD '06,* Philadelphia.

NASA. (2008). *World Wind.* Retrieved from http://worldwind.arc.nasa.gov

Nasraoui, O., Rojas, C., & Cardona, C. (2006). A framework for mining evolving trends in Web data streams using dynamic learning and retrospective validation. *Computer Networks, 50,* 1488–1512. doi:doi:10.1016/j.comnet.2005.10.021

Nassar, M., & Niccolini, S. (2007). Holistic VoIP intrusion detection and prevention system. In *Proceedings of the 1st International Conference on Principles, Systems and Applications of IP Telecommunications* (pp. 1-9).

National Institute of Standards and Technology. (2008). *FIPS PUB 180-3: Secure hash standard (SHS).* Gaithersburg, MD: National Institute of Standards and Technology.

Nelson, R. R., Todd, P. A., & Wixom, B. H. (2005). Antecedents of information and system quality: an empirical examination within the context of data warehousing. *Journal of Management Information Systems, 21*(4), 199–235.

Neumann, G., & Strembeck, M. (2002). A scenario-driven role engineering process for functional RBAC roles. In *Proceedings of the 7th ACM Symposium on Access Control Models and Technologies*, Monterey, CA (pp. 33-42).

Ngwenyama, O., & Lee, A. (1997). Communication richness in electronic mail: critical social theory and the contextuality of meaning. *Management Information Systems Quarterly, 21*(2), 145–167. doi:doi:10.2307/249417

Ni, Q., Lin, D., Bertino, E., & Lobo, J. (2007). Conditional privacy aware role based access control. In *Proceedings of the 12th European Symposium on Research in Computer Security*, Dresden, Germany.

Ni, Q., Trombetta, A., Bertino, E., & Lobo, J. (2007). Privacy aware role based access control. In *Proceedings of the 12th ACM symposium on Access Control Models and Technologies*, New York, NY.

Nielsen, J. (1994). *Using discount usability engineering to penetrate the intimidation barrier.* Retrieved June 8, 2010, from http://www.useit.com/papers/guerrilla_hci.html

Nielsen, J. (2005). *Ten Usability Heuristics.* Retrieved April 27, 2010, from http://www.useit.com/paper s/heuristic/heuristic_list.html

Nielsen, J. (2000). *Usability Engineering.* San Diego, CA: Kaufmann.

Norman, D. A. (1998). *The Design of Everyday Things.* New York: Basic Books.

Norris, P. (Ed.). (1999). *Critical citizens: global support for democratic government.* Oxford: Oxford University Press.

Nourbakhsh, I., Sargent, R., Wright, A., Cramer, K., McClendon, B., & Jones, M. (2006). *Mapping disaster zones* (Vol. 439). Nature.

NVAC. (2008). *National visualization and analytics center.* Retrieved from http://nvac.pnl.gov

OASIS. *Web Services Composite Application Framework (WS-CAF).* Retrieved from http://www.oasis-open.org/committees/ws-caf/charter.php

Object Management Group. (2006). *Business Process Modeling Notation Specification. Final adopted specification.* Retrieved from http://www.bpmn.org/Documents/OMG%20Final%20Adopted%20BPMN%201-0%20Spec%2006-02-01.pdf

Obrecht, R. (2002). KFÜ BW - Erneuerte Kernreaktorfernüberwachung in Baden-Württemberg. In Mayer-Föll, R., Keitel, A., & Geiger, W. (Eds.), *Projekt AJA, Anwendung JAVA-basierter Lösungen und anderer leistungsfähiger Lösungen in den Bereichen Umwelt, Verkehr und Verwaltung – Phase III 2002 (Wissenschaftliche Berichte FZKA-6777).* Karlsruhe, Germany: Forschungszentrum Karlsruhe.

OGC - Open Geospatial Consortium. (2008). Retrieved from www.opengeospatial.org

OGC - Open Geospatial Consortium. (2008a). *Web map service.* Retrieved from Open geospatial consortium: http://www.opengeospatial.org/standards/wms

Ohigashi, M., Guo, Z. S., & Tanaka, Y. (2006). Integration of a 2d legacy gis, legacy simulations, and legacy databases into a 3d geographic simulation. In *Proc. of the 24th annual conf. on Design of communication* (pp. 149–156). ACM.

Ohlmeier, N. (2010). *SIP Swiss army knife.* Retrieved from http://sipsak.org/

Okamoto, T., & Uchiyama, S. (1998). A new public-key cryptosystem as secure as factoring. In K. Nyberg (Ed.), *Proceedings of the International Conference on the Theory and Application of Cryptographic Techniques* (LNCS 1403, p. 308).

Olumofin, F., Tysowski, P., & Goldberg, I. (2009). *Achieving efficient query privacy for location based services (Tech. Rep. No. CACR 2009-22).* Waterloo, ON, Canada: University of Waterloo.

OMG (2007). *OMG Unified Modeling Language Specification.* Version 2.1.2.

Open Geospatial Consortium. (2008). *Web processing service.* Retrieved from Open geospatial consortium: http://www.opengeospatial.org/standards/wps

Open Knowledge Initiative. (2004). *Open Service Interface Definitions. Version 2.0.0.* Retrieved from http://www.okiproject.org/view/html/site/oki/node/1478

Open University of Catalonia. (2006). *The Campus Project*. Retrieved from http://www.campusproject.org/en/index.php

Ordnance Survey. (2006, September). *Geographic information strategy*. Retrieved from http://www.ordnancesurvey.co.uk/oswebsite/aboutus/reports/gistrategy/gistrategy.pdf

Orlikowski, W. J., & Baroudi, J. J. (1991). Studying information technology in organizations: research approaches and assumptions. *Information Systems Research, 2*(1), 1–28. doi:10.1287/isre.2.1.1

Orriens, B., Yang, J., & Papazoglou, M. P. (2003). *Model Driven Service Composition Service-Oriented Computing*. Paper presented at ICSOC 2003.

Ostrovsky, R., & Skeith, W. E., III. (2007). A survey of single-database PIR: Techniques and applications. In O. Tatsuaki & W. Xiaoyun (Eds.), *Proceedings of the International Conference on Public Key Cryptography* (LNCS 4450, pp. 393-411).

Paillier, P. (1999). Public-key cryptosystems based on discrete logarithms residues. In J. Stern (Ed.), *Proceedings of the International Conference on the Theory and Application of Cryptographic Techniques* (LNCS 1592, pp. 223-238).

Palmer, G. (2001a). *A road map for digital forensic research* (Tech. Rep. No. DTR-T001-01). Utica, NY: Air Force Research Laboratory.

Papazoglou, M. P., Traverso, P., & Dagstuhl, S. (2006). Service-Oriented Computing Research Roadmap Seminar. In *Proceedings of the Service Oriented Computing (SOC) Conference*. Retrieved from http://drops.dagstuhl.de/opus/volltexte/2006/524 April 2006

Parasuraman, A., Zeithaml, V., & Berry, L. L. (1988). SERVQUAL: A Multiple-item Scale for Measuring Consumer Perceptions of Service Quality. *Journal of Retailing, 64*(1), 12–37.

Parasuraman, A., Zeithaml, V., & Berry, L. L. (1994). Reassessment of Expectations as a Comparison Standard in Measuring Service Quality: Implications for Further Research. *Journal of Marketing, 58*(1), 111–125. doi:10.2307/1252255

Park, F. S., Patnaik, D., Amrutkar, C., & Hunter, M. T. (2008). A security evaluation of IMS deployments. In *Proceedings of the 2nd International Conference on Internet Multimedia Services Architecture and Applications* (pp. 1-6).

Park, K. S. (1997). Human Error. In Salvendy, G. (Ed.), *The Handbook of Human Factors and Ergonomics* (2nd ed.). New York: John Wiley & Sons.

Paterno, F. (1999). *Model-based Design and Evaluation of Interactive Applications*. Berlin: Springer Verlag.

Pawson, R., & Tilley, N. (1997). *Realistic evaluation*. London: SAGE publications Ltd.

Penichet, V. (2007). *TOUCHE (Task-Oriented and User-Centred Process Model for Developing Interfaces for Human-Computer-Human Environments): A process model and a methodology for the development of groupware applications from the requirements gathering up to the implementation stage*. Unpublished doctoral dissertation, Universidad de Castilla-La Mancha (UCLM).

Pensal, R. G., Robardet, C., & Boulicaut, J. F. (2005). A Bi-Clustering framework for categorical data. In A. Jorge et al. (Eds.), *Proceedings of PKDD*, (LNAI 3721, pp. 643-650).

Perkowitz, M., & Etzioni, O. (2000). Towards adaptive web sites: Conceptual framework and case study. *Artificial Intelligence, 118*, 245–275. doi:doi:10.1016/S0004-3702(99)00098-3

Pernull, G. (1994). Database security. *Advances in Computers, 38*.

Pesendorfer, E.-M., & Koszegi, S. (2006). Hot versus cool behavioral styles in electronic negotiations: The impact of communication mode. *Group Decision and Negotiation, 15*, 141–155. doi:doi:10.1007/s10726-006-9025-y

Peters, G. (2006). Some refinements of rough k-means clustering. *Pattern Recognition, 39*, 1481–1491. doi:doi:10.1016/j.patcog.2006.02.002

Petkov, D., Edgar-Nevill, D., Madachy, R., & O'Connor, R. (2008, January-June). Information Systems, Software Engineering, and Systems Thinking: Challenges and Opportunities. *International Journal of Information Technologies and Systems Approach, 1*, 17–19.

Petkov, D., Edgar-Nevill, D., & O'Connor, R. (2008). Information systems, software engineering, and systems thinking: Challenges and opportunities. *International Journal of Information Technologies and Systems Approach, 1*(1), 62–78.

Petter, S., Delone, W., & Mclean, E. (2008). Measuring information systems success: models, dimensions, measures, and interrelationships. *European Journal of Information Systems, 17*(3), 236–263. doi:10.1057/ejis.2008.15

Pettigrew, A. M. (1985). Contextualist Research and the Study of Organizational Change Processes. In Mumford, E., Hirschheim, R., Fitgerald, G., & Wood-Harper, A. T. (Eds.), *Research Methods in Information Systems* (pp. 53–78). Amsterdam, The Netherlands: North-Holland.

Pfitzmann, A., & Kohntopp, M. (2000). Anonymity, unobservability, and pseudonymity- A proposal for terminology. In *Proceedings of the Workshop on Design Issues in Anonymity and Unobservability* (pp. 1-9).

Phippen, A., Furnell, S., & Richardson, B. (2008). *Sowing the seeds of eSafety.* Retrieved from http://www.bcs.org/server.php?show=ConWebDoc.22800&changeNav=8265

Phippen, A. (2009). *E-safety policy: A survey of school e-safety policy and practice in the south west of the UK.* Exeter, UK: South West Grid for Learning.

Pinkas, B. (2002). Cryptographic techniques for privacy-preserving data mining. *SIGKDD Explorations Newsletter, 4*(2), 12–19. doi:10.1145/772862.772865

Plummer, D. (1982). *RFC 826: An ethernet address resolution protocol.* Retrieved from http://tools.ietf.org/html/rfc826

Pohlig, S., & Hellman, M. (1978). An improved algorithm for computing logarithms over GF(p) and its cryptographic significance. *IEEE Transactions on Information Theory, 24*(1), 106–110. doi:doi:10.1109/TIT.1978.1055817

Pollard, C., & Cater-Steel, A. (2009). Justifications, Strategies, and Critical Success Factors in Successful ITIL Implementations in U.S. and Australian Companies: An Exploratory Study. *Information Systems Management, 26*(2), 164–172. doi:10.1080/10580530902797540

Popper, K. R. (1959). *The Logic of Scientific Discovery.* London: Hutchinson.

Popper, K. R. (1972). *Objective Knowledge, An Evolutionary Approach.* Oxford University Press.

Postel, J. (1981). *RFC 791: IP: Internet protocol.* Retrieved from http://faculty.ksu.edu.sa/fantookh/RFC/rfc791.txt.pdf

Potgieter, B. C., Botha, J. H., & Lew, C. (2005, July 10-13). Evidence that use of the ITIL framework is effective. In *Proceedings of the 18th Annual Conference of the National Advisory Committee on Computing Qualifications*, Tauranga, New Zealand.

Powers, C. S. (2002). Privacy promises, access control, and privacy management. In *Proceedings of the 3rd International Symposium on Electronic Commerce* (pp. 13-21).

Pratschke, J. (2003). Realistic models? Critical realism and statistical models in the social sciences. *Philosophica, 71*(1), 13–38.

Prescott, M., & Conger, S. (1994). Information technology innovations: A Classification by IT locus of impact and research approach. *Database, 26*(2-3), 20–42.

Priestley, M. (2005). *The Logic of Correctness in Software Engineering.* CAiSE Workshops.

Rabin, M. (2009). *How to exchange secrets by oblivious transfer* (Tech. Rep. No. TR-81). Boston, MA: Harvard University.

Rademakers, T., & Dirksen, J. (2009). *Open-Source ESBs in Action.* Greenwich, CT: Manning Publications.

Rafaeli, S., & Hutchison, D. (2003). A survey of key management for secure group communication. *ACM Computing Surveys, 35*(3), 309–329. doi:10.1145/937503.937506

Rahman, S., & Hengartner, U. (2007). Secure crash reporting in vehicular ad hoc networks. In *Proceedings of the 3rd International Conference on Security and Privacy in Communication Networks* (pp. 443-452). New York, NY: ACM Press.

Rajabifard, A., & Williamson, I. (2004). *SDI development and capacity building.* Retrieved from http://www.geom.unimelb.edu.au/research/SDI_research/

Ramsdell, B. (1999). *RFC 2633: S/MIME version 3 message specification.* Retrieved from http://tools.ietf.org/html/rfc2633

Rasmussen Reports. (2008). *51% say security more important than privacy.* Retrieved from http://www.rasmussenreports.com/public_content/politics/general_politics/january_2008/51_say_security_more_important_than_privacy

Rasmussen, K. B., & Capkun, S. (2007). Implications of radio fingerprinting on the security of sensor networks. In *Proceedings of the 3rd International Conference on Security and Privacy in Communication Networks* (pp. 331 - 340). Washington, DC: IEEE Computer Society.

Raya, M., & Hubaux, J. P. (2005). The security of vehicular ad hoc networks. In *Proceedings of the 3rd ACM Workshop on Security of Ad Hoc and Sensor Networks* (pp. 11-21). New York, NY: ACM Press.

Raya, M., & Hubaux, J. P. (2007). Securing vehicular ad-hoc networks. *Journal of Computer Security, 15*(1), 39–68.

Rebollo-Monedero, D., Forne, J., Subirats, L., Solanas, A., & Martınez-Balleste, A. (2009). A collaborative protocol for private retrieval of location-based information. In *Proceedings of the IADIS International Conference on e-Society*, Barcelona, Spain.

Reichheld, F. F. (2003, December 1). The One Number You Need to Grow. *Harvard Business Review.* Retrieved April 28, 2010, from http://harvardbusinessonline.hbsp.harvard.edu/b02/en/common/item_detail.jhtml?id=R0312C&referral=2340

Reimers, K., & Johnson, R. B. (2008, December 14-17). *The use of an explicitly theory-driven data coding method for high-level theory testing in IOIS.* Paper presented at the International Conference for Information Systems, Paris.

Ribeiro, C. N., Zuquete, A., Ferreira, P., & Guedes, P. (2001). SPL: An access control language for security policies with complex constraints. In *Proceedings of the Network and Distributed System Security Symposium*, San Diego, CA.

Rius, A., Conesa, J., & Gañán, D. (2010). *A DSL Tool to Assist Specifications of Educational Settings.* Paper presented at the 6th Semantic Web Services Conference of the 2010 World Congress in Computer Science, Computer Engineering, and Applied Computing, Las Vegas, NV.

Rivest, R. L., Shamir, A., & Adleman, L. (1978). A method for obtaining digital signatures and public-key cryptosystems. *Communications of the ACM, 21*(2), 120–126. doi:doi:10.1145/359340.359342

Rodden, T., Friday, A., Muller, H., & Dix, A. (2002). *A lightweight approach to managing privacy in location-based services* (Tech. Rep. No. CSTR-07-006). UK: University of Nottingham, Lancaster University, and University of Bristol.

Rodríguez, M. E., Serra, M., Cabot, J., & Guitart, I. (2006). Evolution of the Teacher Roles and Figures in E-learning Environments. In *Proceedings of the 6th IEEE International Conference on Advanced Learning Technologies* (pp. 512-514). Washington, DC: IEEE Computer Society.

Rombach, D., Ciolkowski, M., Jeffery, R., Laitenberger, O., McGarry, F., & Shull, F. (2008). Impact of research on practice in the field of inspections, reviews and walkthroughs: learning from successful industrial uses. *SIGSOFT Software Engineering Notes, 33*(6), 26–35. doi:10.1145/1449603.1449609

Ron, A. (2002). Regression analysis and the philosophy of social science. *Journal of Critical Realism, 1*(1), 119–142.

Rorty, R. (1979), *Philosophy and the Mirror of Nature.* Princeton: Princeton University Press.

Rosenberg, J., Schulzrinne, H., Camarillo, G., Johnston, A., Peterson, J., Sparks, R., et al. (2002). *RFC 3261: SIP: Session initiation protocol.* Retrieved from http://www.ietf.org/rfc/rfc3261.txt

Rosen, M., Lublinsky, B., Smith, K. T., & Balcer, M. J. (2008). *Applied SOA: Service-Oriented Architecture and Design Strategies.* New York: Wiley Publishing.

Ross, S. J. (2003). IS security matters: Identifier management. *Information Systems Control Journal, 3.*

Royce, W. (1998). *Software Project Management. A Unified Framework.* Addison-Wesley.

Royce, W. W. (1970). Managing the Development of Large Software Systems: Concepts and Techniques. *Proceedings of Western Electronic Show and Convention* (WesCon) August 25-28, 1970, Los Angeles

Rumbaugh, J., Booch, G., & Jacobson, I. (1999). *The Unified Modeling Language Reference Manual*. Object Technology Series, Addison-Wesley.

Russell, B. (1952). *Menneskeheden paa skillevejen* (New Hopes in a Changing World). Copenhagen, Denmark: Berlingske forlag

Saltzer, J. H., & Schroeder, M. D. (1975). The protection of information in computer systems. *Proceedings of the IEEE, 63*(9), 1278–1308. doi:10.1109/PROC.1975.9939

Sampigethaya, K., Huang, L., Matsuura, K., Poovendran, R., & Sezaki, K. (2005). CARAVAN: Providing location privacy for VANET. In *Proceedings of the 3rd Embedded Security in Cars Workshop*.

Sandhu, R. S., Coyne, E. J., Feinstein, H. L., & Youman, C. E. (2006). Role-based access control models. *IEEE Computer, 29*, 38–47.

SAP. (2005). *Developing composite applications with SAP composite application framework*. Retrieved from http://sdn.sap.com

Saroiu, S., & Wolman, A. (2009). Enabling new mobile applications with location proofs. In *Proceedings of the 10th Workshop on Mobile Computing Systems and Applications* (pp. 3-9). New York, NY: ACM Press.

Sayer, A. (2000). *Realism and Social Science*. London: Sage Publications.

Schekkerman, J. (2005). *Trends in Enterprise Architecture*. Institute For Enterprise Architecture Developments.

Schlachter, T. (2006). Environmental Portals of the federal states of Baden-Wuerttemberg and Saxony-Anhalt with access to the administrative environmental information. In Tatnall, A. (Ed.), *Encyclopaedia of Portal Technology and Applications*. Hershey, PA: IGI Global.

Schmidt, F. (2002). KFÜ-ABR – Weiterentwicklung des Dienstes Ausbreitungsrechnung in der Kernreaktor-Fernüberwachung Baden-Württemberg. In Mayer-Föll, R., Keitel, A., & Geiger, W. (Eds.), *Projekt AJA, Anwendung JAVA-basierter Lösungen und anderer leistungsfähiger Lösungen in den Bereichen Umwelt, Verkehr und Verwaltung – Phase III 2002 (Wissenschaftliche Berichte FZKA-6777)*. Karlsruhe, Germany: Forschungszentrum Karlsruhe.

Schneier, B. (1995). *Applied cryptography: Protocols, algorithms, and source code in C*. New York, NY: John Wiley & Sons.

Schulzrinne, H., Casner, S., Frederick, R., & Jacobson, V. (1996). *RFC 1889: RTP: A transport protocol for real-time applications*. Retrieved from http://www.ietf.org/rfc/rfc1889.txt

Schwaber, K. (2004). *Agile Project Management with Scrum*. Microsoft Press.

Schwaninger, M., & Grösser, S. (2008). System Dynamics as Model-Based Theory Building. *Systems Research and Behavioral Science, 25*, 447–465. doi:10.1002/sres.914

Schwartz, M. F. (1993). Internet resource discovery at the University of Colorado. *Computer, 26*(9), 25–35. doi:10.1109/2.231273

Schwartz, S. H. (1992). Universals in the content and structure of values: Theory and empirical tests in 20 countries. In Zanna, M. (Ed.), *Advances in Experimental Social Psychology* (*Vol. 25*, pp. 1–65). New York: Academic Press.

Seligman, A. B. (1997). *The problem of trust*. Princeton: Princeton University Press.

Sessions, R. (2007). *A comparison of the top four enterprise architecture methodologies*. Microsoft Developer Network Architecture Center.

Shadish, W. R., Cook, T. D., & Campbell, D. T. (2002). *Experimental and quasi-experimental designs for generalized causal inference*. Boston: Houghton Mifflin Company.

Shamir, A. (1980). On the power of commutativity in cryptography. In J. de Bakker & J. van Leeuwen (Eds.), *Proceedings of the 7th Colloquium on Automata, Languages and Programming* (LNCS 85, pp. 582-595).

Shamir, A. (1984). Identity-based cryptosystems and signature scheme. In *Proceedings of Advances in Cryptography* (pp. 47-53).

Shannon, C. (1949). Communication theory of secrecy systems. *The Bell System Technical Journal, 28*.

Sharma, R., & Yetton, P. (2003). The Contingent Effects of Management Support and Task Interdependence on Successful Information Systems Implementation. *Management Information Systems Quarterly, 27*(4), 533–555.

Sharples, M. Graber., R, Harrison, C., & Logan, K. (2008). *E-Safety and Web 2.0.* Coventry, UK: Becta.

Shea, V. (2007). *Netiquette.* Retrieved October 2007 from http://www.albion.com/netiquette/book/index.html

Sher, M., & Magedanz, T. (2007). Protecting IP multimedia subsystem (IMS) service delivery platform from time independent attacks. In *Proceedings of the Third International Symposium on Information Assurance and Security* (pp. 171-176).

Sher, M., Wu, S., & Magedanz, T. (2006). *Security threats and solutions for application server of IP multimedia subsystem (IMS-AS).* Retrieved from http://www.diadem-firewall.org/workshop06/papers/monam06-paper-28.pdf

Sherman, D. K., Mann, T., & Updegraff, J. A. (2006). Approach/Avoidance Motivation, Message Framing, and Health Behavior: Understanding the Congruency Effect. *Motivation and Emotion, 30*(2), 165–169. doi:10.1007/s11031-006-9001-5

Shneiderman, B. (2000). Universal Usability. *Communications of the ACM, 43*(5), 84–91. doi:10.1145/332833.332843

Shneiderman, B. (2004). *Designing the User interface: Strategies for Effective Human-Computer Interaction* (4th ed.). Reading, MA: Addison-Wesley.

Shumilov, S., Thomsen, A., Cremers, A. B., & Koos, B. (2002). Managment and visualization of large, complex and time-dependent 3D objects in distributed gis. *Proc. of the 10th ACM international symposium on Advances in geographic information systems* (pp. 113–118). ACM.

Silverman, B. (1995). Knowledge-based Systems and the Decision Sciences. *Interfaces, 25*(6), 67–82. doi:10.1287/inte.25.6.67

Silverman, B. (in press). Systems Social Science. *Intelligent Decision Technologies.*

Silverman, B., Bharathy, G., Nye, B., & Eidelson, R. (2007). Modeling factions for 'effects based operations': part I – leaders and followers. *J. Computational & Mathematical Organization Theory, 13*(4), 379–406. doi:10.1007/s10588-007-9017-8

Silverman, B., Bharathy, G., Nye, B., & Smith, T. (2008). Modeling factions for 'effects based operations': part II – behavioral game theory. *J. Computational & Mathematical Organization Theory, 14*(2), 120–155. doi:10.1007/s10588-008-9023-5

Silverman, B., Johns, M., Cornwell, J., & O'Brien, K. (2006a). Human behavior models for agents in simulators and games: part I – enabling science with PMFserv. *Presence (Cambridge, Mass.), 15*(2), 139–162. doi:10.1162/pres.2006.15.2.139

Silverman, B., O'Brien, K., & Cornwell, J. (2006b). Human behavior models for agents in simulators and games: part II – gamebot engineering with PMFserv. *Presence (Cambridge, Mass.), 15*(2), 163–185. doi:10.1162/pres.2006.15.2.163

Simon, B., Nassart, D., Assche, F.V., Ternier, S., & Duval, E. (2005). *Simple query interface specification.*

Simon, H. A. (1983). Models of Bounded Rationality. Cambridge: MIT Press.

Simon, H. A. (1991). *Rationality in Political Behaviour.* Working paper of Carnegie Mellon University, 1991.

Simon, H. (1957). *Administrative Behavior; a Study of Decision-Making Processes in Administrative Organisation.* New York: Macmillan.

Simon, H. (1967). *Model of Man* (5th ed.). John Wiley and Sons, Inc.

Singer, E. A. (1959). *Experience and Reflection.* Philadelphia: University of Pennsylvania Press.

Sisalem, D., Kuthan, J., Abend, U., Floroiu, J., & Schulzrinne, H. (2009). *SIP Security.* New York, NY: John Wiley & Sons. doi:10.1002/9780470516997

Skelton, G. W. (2003). *Wireless Application Development,* Boston, MA: Course Technology.

Skyttner, L. (2006). *General Systems Theory: Problems, Perspective, Practice*. Hackensack, NJ: World Scientific Publishing Company. doi:10.1142/9789812774750

Sliuzas, R. (2003). Governance and the use of gis in developing countries. *Habitat International, 27*(4), 495–499. doi:10.1016/S0197-3975(03)00002-X

Smith, K. A., & Ng, A. (2003). Web page clustering using a self-organizing map of user navigation patterns. *Decision Support Systems, 35*(2), 245–256. doi:doi:10.1016/S0167-9236(02)00109-4

Smith, M. L. (2006). Overcoming theory-practice inconsistencies: critical realism and information systems research. *Information and Organization, 16*(13), 191–211. doi:10.1016/j.infoandorg.2005.10.003

Sol, H. G. (1982). *Simulation in information systems development*. Doctoral dissertation, University of Groningen, Groningen.

Sol, H. G. (1988). Information systems development: a problem solving approach. *Proceedings of the Symposium and Systems Analysis and Design,* Atlanta, USA.

Solanas, A., & Martınez-Balleste, A. (2007). Privacy protection in location-based services through a public-key privacy homomorphism. In J. Lopez, P. Samarati, & J. L. Ferrer (Eds.), *Proceedings of the 4th European PKI Workshop on Theory and Practice* (LNCS 4582, pp. 362-368).

Solanas, A., Domingo-Ferrer, J., & Martınez-Balleste, A. (2008). Location privacy in location-based services: Beyond TTP-based schemes. In *Proceedings of the 1st International Workshop on Privacy in Location-Based Applications* (p. 397).

Solanas, A., & Martınez-Balleste, A. (2008). A TTP-free protocol for location privacy in location-based services. *Computer Communications, 31*(6), 1181–1191. doi:10.1016/j.comcom.2008.01.007

Sommerville, I. (2006). *Software engineering* (8th ed.). Reading, MA: Addison-Wesley.

Song, Q., & Shepperd, M. (2006). Mining web browsing patterns for E-commerce. *Computers in Industry, 57*, 622–630. doi:doi:10.1016/j.compind.2005.11.006

Sowa, J. F., & Zachman, J. A. (1992). Extending and Formalizing the Framework for Information Systems Architecture. *IBM Systems Journal, 31*(3).

Spiers, D. (2009). *Intellectual property law essentials*. Dundee, UK: Dundee University Press.

Stainton, R. S. (1984). Applicable Systems Thinking. *European Journal of Operational Research, 18*, 145–154. doi:10.1016/0377-2217(84)90180-2

Stearns, J., Chinnici, R., & Sahoo. (2006, May). *Update: An introduction to the java ee 5 platform*. Retrieved from Java ee at a glance: http://java.sun.com/developer/technicalArticles/J2EE/intro_ee5/

Steed, A. (2004). Data visualization within urban models. In *Proc. of the Theory and Practice of Computer Graphics* (pp. 9–16). IEEE.

Steen, M. W. A., Akehurst, D. H., ter Doest, H. W. L., & Lankhorst, M. M. (2004). Supporting Viewpoint-Oriented Enterprise Architecture. *Proc. of 8th IEEE Intl Enterprise Distributed Object Computing Conf. (EDOC 2004)*. IEEE.

Steenkamp, A. L., & Li, Z. (2006). An Approach to Developing IT Architectures – Enterprise Mobility Viewpoint. *Open Group IT Architecture Practitioners Conference*, Lisbon, Portugal.

Steenkamp, A. L., Li, Z., & du Plessis, E. (2004). Strategic Planning for Small IT Business. *Proceedings of AMCIS2004 Conference*, New York.

Stojanovic, L., Staab, S., & Studer, R. (2001). elearning based on the semantic web. In *Proceedings of the World Conference on the WWW and Internet (Webnet 2001)*, Orlando, FL (pp. 23-27).

Suchman, L. A. (1983). Office procedure as practical action: models of work and system design. *ACM Transactions on Information Systems, 1*(4), 320–328. doi:10.1145/357442.357445

Sumner, M. (2000). Risk factors in Enterprise Wide Information Management Systems. In *Proceedings of the AMC SIG CPR Conference*, Evanston, IL (pp. 180-188).

Sun, J., Zhang, C., & Fang, Y. (2007). An ID-based framework achieving privacy and non-repudiation in vehicular ad hoc networks. In *Proceedings of the Military Communications Conference* (pp. 1-7). Washington, DC: IEEE Computer Society.

Sun, Y., La Porta, T. F., & Kermani, P. (2009). A flexible privacy-enhanced location-based services system framework and practice. *IEEE Transactions on Mobile Computing, 8*(3), 304–321. doi:10.1109/TMC.2008.112

Swanson, E. B., & Ramiller, N. C. (2004). Innovating Mindfully with Information Technology. *Management Information Systems Quarterly, 28*(4), 553–583.

Sward, R. E., & Whitacre, K. (2008). A multi-language service-oriented architecture using an enterprise service bus. In *Proceedings of the 2008 ACM Annual International Conference on SIGADA*.

Sweeney, L. (2002). k-anonymity: A model for protecting privacy. *International Journal of Uncertainty Fuzziness and Knowledge Based Systems, 10*(5), 557–570. doi:10.1142/S0218488502001648

Swire, P., & Steinfeld, L. (2002). Security and privacy after September 11: The health care example. In *Proceedings of the 12th Annual Conference on Computers, Freedom and Privacy*, San Francisco, CA (pp. 1-13).

Tanase, M. (2003). IP spoofing: An introduction. *Security Focus, 11*.

Tarasewich, P., Nickerson, R.C., & Warkentin, M. (2002). Issues in Mobile E-Commerce, *Communication of the AIS, 8*(41).

Taylor, H., Yochem, Y., Phillips, L., & Martinez, F. (2009). *Event-Driven Architecture: How SOA Enables the Real-Time Enterprise*. Boston: Addison-Wesley.

Technologies Copigraph Inc. (n.d.). *IMS-LD Scenario editors*. Retrieved from http://www.cogigraph.com/Produits/IMSLDScenarioEditors/tabid/1099/language/en-US/Default.aspx

Tesch, D., Kloppenborg, T. J., & Stemmer, J. K. (2003). Project Management Learning What the Literature Has to Say. *Project Management Journal, 34*(4), 33–39.

Thayer, A., & Dugan, T. E. (2009, July 19-22). Achieving design enlightenment: Defining a new user experience measurement framework. In *Proceedings of the 2009 IEEE International Professional Communication Conference*, Waikiki, HI (pp. 1-10).

The Apache Software Foundation. (2008). *Tomcat*. Retrieved from http://tomcat.apache.org

The Open Group. (2009). *TOGAF (The Open Group Architecture Framework) Version 9 "Enterprise Edition"*. Available from http://www.opengroup.org

Thuraisingham, B. (2005). Privacy constraint processing in a privacy enhanced database management system. *Data and Knowledge Engineering Journal, 55*(2), 159–188. doi:10.1016/j.datak.2005.03.001

Tidd, J., & Hull, F. M. (2003). *Service Innovation. Organizational Responses to Technological Opportunities & Market Imperatives*. London: Imperial College Press.

Toffolon, C. (2006). Learning management system scenario-based engineering. In *Proceedings of the 5th European Conference on e-Learning (ECEL 2006)*, Winchester, UK (pp. 397-406).

Toffolon, C., & Dakhili, S. (1999). Requirements Elicitation Process: An Iterative Approach based on the Spiral Model. In *Proceedings of the XVIth International Symposium on Information and Computer Sciences (ISCIS'99)*, Izmir, Turkey.

Tolbert, C., & Mossberger, K. (2006). The effects of e-government on trust and confidence in government. *Public Administration Review, 66*(3), 354–369. doi:10.1111/j.1540-6210.2006.00594.x

Tolcher, D. J. (1989). Project admiral - the management of services on an internet. *Brit Telecom Technol, 7*(1), 20–24.

Tood, C., Klagholz, L., Sheschter, E., Doolan, J., Jensen, J., & Ngler, I. (1999). *Learning scenarios*. New Jersey Languages Curriculum Framework.

Tsoukas, H. (1989). The validity of idiographic research explanations. *Academy of Management Review, 14*(4), 551–561. doi:10.2307/258558

Tsouvalis, C., & Checkland, P. (1996). Reflecting on SSM: The Dividing line Between 'Real World', and 'Systems Thinking World'. *Systems Research, 13*(1), 35–45. doi:10.1002/(SICI)1099-1735(199603)13:1<35::AID-SRES73>3.0.CO;2-O

Turner, A. (2006). *Introduction to Neogeography.* O'Reilly Media.

Tynes, B. M. (2007). Internet safety gone wild? Sacrificing the educational and psychosocial benefits of online social environments. *Journal of Adolescent Research, 22*(6). doi:10.1177/0743558407303979

University of Bonn. (2008). *Heidelberg 3D.* Retrieved August 27, 2008, from 3D GDI Heidelberg: http://www.gdi-3d.de

Valecich, J., George, J., & Hoffer, J. (2009). *Essentials of Systems Analysis and Design* (3rd ed.). Upper Saddle River, NJ: Prentice-Hall.

Van Bon, J. (2007). *IT Service Management: An Introduction.* London: itSMF International.

van den Heuvel, W.-J., Zimmermann, O., Leymann, F., Lago, P., Schieferdecker, I., Zdun, U., et al. (2009, May 18-19). Software Service Engineering: Tenets and Challenges. In *Proceedings of PESOS'09* Vancouver, BC, Canada.

Van der Aalst, W., ter Hofstede, A., Kiepuszewski, B., & Barros, A. (2003). Workflow patterns. *Distributed and Parallel Databases, 14*(1), 5–51. doi:10.1023/A:1022883727209

van Meel, J. W. (1994). *The Dynamics of Business Engineering. Reflections on Two Case Studies within the Amsterdam Municipal Police Force.* Doctoral Dissertation, Delft University of Technology, Delft, The Netherlands.

Varshney, U., & Vetter, R. (2001). Mobile Commerce: Framework, Applications, and Networking Support. *Mobile Networks and Applications, 7*(3), 185–198. doi:10.1023/A:1014570512129

Visitacion, M. (2006). *What Successful Organizations Know about Project Management.* Retrieved from www.forrester.com

Visschers-Pleijers, A., Dolmans, D., Wolfhagen, I., & Van Der Vleuten, C. (2005). Student perspectives on learning-oriented interactions in the tutorial group. *Advances in Health Sciences Education: Theory and Practice, 10,* 23–35. PubMed doi:10.1007/s10459-004-9348-x

Voges, K. E., Pope, N. K. L., & Brown, M. R. (2002). Cluster analysis of marketing data examining online shopping orientation: A comparison of k-means and rough clustering approaches. In Abbass, H. A., Sarker, R. A., & Newton, C. S. (Eds.), *Heuristics and Optimization for Knowledge Discovery* (pp. 207–224). Hershey, PA: Idea Group Publishing.

Vogten, H. (2004). *CopperCore, an Open Source IMS Learning Design Engine.* Retrieved from http://hdl.handle.net/1820/286

Vogten, H., & Martens, H. (2005). *CopperCore 3.0.* Retrieved from.http://www.coppercore.org

Volkoff, O., Strong, D. M., & Elmes, M. B. (2007). Technological embeddedness and organizational change. *Organization Science, 18*(5), 832–848. doi:10.1287/orsc.1070.0288

Vrakas, N., Geneiatakis, D., & Lambrinoudakis, C. (2010). A call conference room interception attack and its detection. In *Proceedings of the 7th International Conference on Trust, Privacy & Security in Digital Business* (pp. 38-44).

W3C (2005, January 7). The Synchronized Multimedia Integration Language (SMIL 2.0) (2nd ed.). Presented at the *World Wide Web Consortium (W3C).* Retrieved November 19, 2009 from http://www.w3.org/AudioVideo/

W3C. (2002). *Web Services Description Language (WSDL), World Wide Web Consortium (W3C), Web Services Description Working Group.* Retrieved November 19, 2009 from http://www.w3.org/2002/ws/desc/

Wagner, R. (2001). *Address resolution protocol spoofing and man-in-the-middle attacks.* Reston, VA: The SANS Institute.

Wakeman, I., Chalmers, D., & Fry, M. (2007). Reconciling privacy and security in pervasive computing: The case for pseudonymous group membership. In *Proceedings of the 5th International Workshop on Middleware for Pervasive and Ad-Hoc Computing* (pp. 7-12). New York, NY: ACM Press.

Walsh, T. J., & Kuhn, D. R. (2005). Challenges in securing voice over iP. *IEEE Security and Privacy, 3*(3), 44–49. doi:10.1109/MSP.2005.62

Wang, Q., Yu, T., Li, N., Lobo, J., Bertino, E., Irwin, K., & Byun, J.-W. (2007). On the correctness criteria of fine-grained access control in relational databases. In *Proceedings of the 33rd International Conference on Very Large Data Bases*, Vienna, Austria (pp. 555-566).

Warren, M. E. (2004). Trust in democratic institutions. In F. Ankersmit & H. te Velde (Eds.), *Trust: Cement of Democracy* (Vol. 49-69). Leuven: Peeters.

Warren, M. E. (Ed.). (1999). *Democracy and trust*. Cambridge: Cambridge University Press.

Wautelet, Y. (2008). *A Goal-Driven Project Management Framework for I-Tropos Multi-Agent Iterative Software Development*. PhD thesis, Louvain School of Management, Université catholique de Louvain, Louvain-la-Neuve, Belgium.

Wautelet, Y., Schinckus, C., & Kolp, M. (2008). A Modern Epistemological Reading of Agent Orientation. *International Journal of Intelligent Information Technologies, 4*(3), 46–57.

Weber, R. (2004). Editor's comments: the rhetoric of positivism versus interpretivism: a personal view. *MIS Quarterly, 28*(1), iii–xiii.

Weis, S. A. (2006). *New foundations for efficient authentication, commutative cryptography, and private disjointness testing*. Unpublished doctoral dissertation, Massachusetts Institute of Technology, Cambridge, MA.

West, D. M. (2005). *Digital government: technology and public sector performance*. Princeton: Princeton University Press.

Westin, A. (1968). *Privacy and freedom*. Cambridge, MA: Atheneum Press.

White, D., & Fortune, J. (2002). Current Practice in Project Management – an Empirical Study. *International Journal of Project Management, 20*. Retrieved from www.ebsevier.com. doi:10.1016/S0263-7863(00)00029-6

Wilbois, T., & Chaves, F. (2005). *Fachkonzept für die Erstellung eines KFÜ-Portals*. Karlsruhe, Germany: Fraunhofer IITB.

Winniford, M. A., Conger, S., & Erickson-Harris, L. (2009). Confusion in the Ranks: IT Service Management Practice and Terminology. *Information Systems Management, 26*(2), 153–163. doi:10.1080/10580530902797532

Wireless Center. (2008), Mobile Application Architectures. Available from http://www.wireless-center.net/Mobile-and-Wireless/Mobile-Application-Architectures.html

WoS Expanded. (2009). *Tecumseh, Ontario: The international institute for advances studies in system research and cybernetics, 2008* (pp. 34-38). Retrieved October 28, 2009 from the world wide web.

Wu, M. C., & Unhelkar (2008). Extending enterprise architecture with mobility. *IEEE Vehicular Technology Conference*. VTC. Available from http://ieeexplore.ieee.org

Wu, Y., Bagchi, S., Garg, S., Singh, N., & Tsai, T. (2004). Scidive: A stateful and cross protocol intrusion detection architecture for voice-over-IP environments. In *Proceedings of the International Conference on Dependable Systems and Networks*, Firenze, Italy (p. 433).

Wu, Y., Apte, V., Bagchi, S., Garg, S., & Singh, N. (2009). Intrusion detection in voice over IP environments. *International Journal of Information Security, 8*(3), 153–172. doi:10.1007/s10207-008-0071-0

Xiao, J., Zhang, Y., Jia, X., & Li, T. (2001) Measuring similarity of interests for clustering web-users. In *Proceedings of the 12th Australian Database Conference* (pp. 107-114).

Yan, T., Jacobsen, M., Garcia-Molina, H., & Dayal, U. (1996). From user access patterns to dynamic hypertext linking. In *Proceedings of the 5th International World Wide Web conference*, Paris.

Yin, R. K. (2003). *Case Study Research: Design and Methods* (3rd ed.). Thousand Oaks, CA: Sage Publications.

Yiu, M. L., Ghinita, G., Jensen, C. S., & Kalnis, P. (2009). Outsourcing search services on private spatial data. In *Proceedings of the 25th International Conference on Data Engineering* (pp. 1140-1143). Washington, DC: IEEE Computer Society.

Young, B. C., Kathleen, E. C., Joshua, S. K., & Meredith, M. S. (2006). Challenges associated with privacy in health care industry: Implementation of HIPAA and the security rules. *Journal of Medical Systems, 30*(1), 57–64. doi:doi:10.1007/s10916-006-7405-0

Yourdon, E., & Constantine, L. L. (1975). *Structured Design*. New York: Yourdon Press.

Yu, E. (1995). *Modeling Strategic Actor Relationships for Business Process Reengineering*. Unpublished doctoral dissertation, University of Toronto, Department Computer Science.

Yu, X., Zhang, T., Wang, L., Hu, J., Zhao, J., & Li, X. (2007). A model-driven development framework for enterprise Web services. *Information Systems Frontiers, 9*, 391–409. doi:10.1007/s10796-007-9042-7

Zamir, O., & Etzioni, O. (1998). Web Document Clustering: A Feasibility Demonstration. In *Proceedings of the 21st International ACM SIGIR Conference on Research and Development in Information Retrieval,* Seattle, WA.

Zhang, R., Wang, X., Farley, R., Yang, X., & Jiang, X. (2009, March). On the feasibility of launching the man-in-the-middle attacks on VoIP from remote attackers. In *Proceedings of the 4th ACM Symposium on Information, Computer and Communications Security* (pp. 61-69).

Zhang, Y., Liu, W., Lou, W., & Fang, Y. (2005). Securing sensor networks with location-based keys. In *Proceedings of the Wireless Communications and Networking Conference* (pp. 1909-1914). Washington, DC: IEEE Computer Society.

Zhang, P., Galletta, D., Li, N., & Sun, H. (2007). Human-Computer Interaction. In Huang, W. (Ed.), *Management Information Systems*. Beijing, China: Tsinghua University Press.

Zhong, G., & Hengartner, U. (2008). Toward a distributed k-anonymity protocol for location privacy. In *Proceedings of the 7th ACM Workshop on Privacy in the Electronic Society* (pp. 33–38). New York, NY: ACM Press.

Zhong, G., & Hengartner, U. (2009). A distributed k-anonymity protocol for location privacy. In *Proceedings of the International Conference on Pervasive Computing and Communications* (pp. 1-10). Washington, DC: IEEE Computer Society.

Zhong, G., Goldberg, I., & Hengartner, U. (2007). Louis, Lester and Pierre: Three protocols for location privacy. In N. Borisov & P. Golle (Eds.), *Proceedings of the 7th International Symposium on Privacy Enhancing Technologies* (LNCS 4776, pp. 62-76).

Zhu, F., Mutka, M., & Ni, L. (2003). Splendor: A secure, private, and location-aware service discovery protocol supporting mobile services. In *Proceedings of the 1st IEEE International Conference on Pervasive Computing and Communications* (pp. 235-242). Washington, DC: IEEE Computer Society.

Zipf, A. (2008). Small island perspectives on global challenges: The role of spatial data in supporting a sustainable future. *GSDI 10 Conference Proceedings*.

Zucker, L. G. (1986). Production of trust: institutional sources of economic structure, 1840-1920. *Organizational Behavior, 8*, 53–111.

About the Contributors

Frank Stowell is Professor of Systems and Information Systems at the University of Portsmouth (UK). Before moving to Portsmouth, he was Director of Campus at De Montfort University at Milton Keynes. He has a PhD in organizational change and is an expert in systems thinking and practice. He has published papers and texts in the field and presented papers at a number of international conferences in Europe and the United States. He has supervised a large number of research projects and continues to supervise and examine PhD research. He has been a specialist reviewer for the Quality Assurance Agency for Higher Education within the UK. He is Co-Chair of the Systems Practice for Managing Complexity project (http://spmc.open.ac.uk/), past President of the UK Academy of Information Systems and board member for 9 years. He is Vice President of the UK Systems Society (http://www.ukss.org.uk/) and responsible for external relations. Prior to his academic career, he was a consultant in a central government sponsored management systems development group and has experience in defining and developing IT supported management information systems. His area of interest includes the application of systems ideas to the development of IT supported information systems. His present research is in the development of ways, in which the client can lead and control the development of their information system (http://www.ciiis.port.ac.uk/index.htm).

* * *

Magí Almirall works in the Open University of Catalonia (www.uoc.edu). He is director of the Learning Technologies' department (http://learningtechnologies.uoc.edu). His team receives the IGC (Internet Global Congress) innovation award 2006 and the IMS Gold ?Best Mobile Learning Solution? 2008. Since 1995 he has worked in the IT department leading the development of the virtual campus platform. His current work focuses on two themes; tools for e-learning platforms and new formats of learning contents. These projects focus on standardization, accessibility for people with disabilities, usability and open source development. Magí has a science graduate degree from the University of Barcelona.

P.K Nizar Banu is now working as a Lecturer in M.C.A at Narasu's Sarathy Institute of Technology, Salem. She received M.Sc and M.Phil degrees in Computer Science from Periyar University, Salem, Tamil Nadu, India. Also she received M.C.A degree from the Same University. She is a University Rank Holder in M.Sc and University Gold Medalist in M.Phil. Her research interests are Rough Sets, Fuzzy Systems Web Mining, and Image Processing.

Helge Bergh is the Systems Director at the Norwegian Corp, the largest Scandinavian low price air carrier.

William Buchanan is a Professor in the School of Computing at Edinburgh Napier University. He currently leads the Centre for Distributed Computing, Networking and Security, and works in the areas of security, e-Crime, intrusion detection systems, digital forensics, e-Health, mobile computing, agent-based systems, and simulation. He has published over 26 academic books, and over 100 academic research papers, along with awards for excellence in knowledge transfer. Presently, he is working with a range of industrial/domain partners, including with the Scottish Police, health care professionals and the FSA.

Bendik Bygstad is Professor of Information Systems at the Norwegian School of Information Technology. His main research interest is IT based service innovation.

Fernando Chaves holds a degree in Computer Science from the University of Karlsruhe, Germany. He joined Fraunhofer IITB in 1987 and his current position is Leader of the Working Group "Information and Knowledge Management Systems". His research interests include open service platforms for environmental information systems supporting large, distributed and heterogeneous communities. He is currently involved in design, development and support for applications based on WebGenesis®. National projects comprise risk and crisis management systems together with T-Systems: Web-Portals for monitoring nuclear power plants and for providing support to crisis squads in several Federal States of Germany.

Jordi Conesa is an assistant professor of Information Systems at Universitat Oberta de Catalunya, Barcelona, Spain. His research interest concerns the areas of Conceptual Modeling, Ontologies, Semantic Web, Knowledge-Based Systems and e-Learning. His long-term goal is to develop methodologies and tools to use ontologies effectively in several application domains, such as conceptual modelling, software engineering and e-learning. He received his M.S. and Ph.D. in Software Engineering from the Technical University of Catalonia.

Sue Conger, PhD is the author of *The New Software Engineering* (1944) and *Planning and Designing Effective Web Sites* (1997), and *Process Mapping & Management* (2010) and is beginning a book on *IT Service Management*. She is on the University of Dallas faculty where she manages both Information Technology and IT Service Management (ITSM) programs. She is the VP of Chapters for the Association of Information Systems, President of special interest group on IT Services, member of the Academic Executive Committee for the ITSMF-USA, manages the ITSMF-USA Research Subcommittee, and helps host the ITSMF-USA Academic Forum. She is on five editorial boards and the program and planning committees for several conferences.

Giuseppe Conti works as Senior Scientist at Fondazione Graphitech since 2003. In 2002 he received a PhD degree at the University of Strathclyde, Glasgow, UK on the implementation of a Virtual Reality (VR) system for urban planning. During his working experiences he has been working for various engineering firms in Italy and abroad. He has been active in a number of European, local and industrial projects in the field of Geographical Information Systems and web services for Geographical Information. His current research interests are in SDIs, the application of VR technology to GIS and 3D Geobrowsers.

Raffaele De Amicis is the General Manager of GraphiTech. Furthermore, he is member of the Board of Trustees of the INI-GraphicsNet Foundation (www.inigraphics.net) and Chairman of the INI-GraphicsNet Steering Committee. Since 2005 he belongs to Experts Board Member Panel for Mathematics and Information Technology and Industrial and Information Engineering of the CIVR, Italian Committee for Evaluation of Research of the Ministry of Education (www.civr.it). His research interests are in computer aided design, virtual reality, advanced 3D interaction techniques, multimodal interactions and shapes semantic. More details about can be found at the following web site www.graphitech.it.

Steven Furnell is professor of Information Systems Security at the University of Plymouth, with research interests including user authentication, intrusion detection, usability, and security culture. Prof. Furnell is active within three working groups of the International Federation for Information Processing (IFIP) – namely Information Security Management, Information Security Education, and Human Aspects of Information Security & Assurance. He is the author of over 210 papers in refereed international journals and conference proceedings, as well as books including Cybercrime: Vandalizing the Information Society (2001) and Computer Insecurity: Risking the System (2005). Further details can be found at www.plymouth.ac.uk/cscan.

Elena García-Barriocanal obtained a university degree in Computer Science from the Pontifical University of Salamanca in Madrid (1998) and a PhD from the Computer Science Department of the University of Alcalá. From September 1998 to February 1999 she worked as a lecturer in the Computer Languages and Information Systems Department of the Pontifical University, and in 1999 she joined the Computer Science Department of University of Alcalá as assistant professor. Starting from 2001, she is associate professor at Computer Science Department of the University of Alcalá and she is a member of the Information Engineering Research Group of this University. Her research interests mainly focus on topics related to the role of knowledge representation in fields like human-computer interaction and learning technologies; concretely she actively works on ontological aspects both in e-learning and in usability and accessibility. She supervises several phD works in those areas.

Gheorghita Ghinea a Reader in the Department of Information Systems and Computing at Brunel University, United Kingdom. Dr. Ghinea has over 100 publications in peer-reviewed journals.

Tor-Morten Grønli is a PhD student at Brunel University, and a lecturer at the Norwegian School of Information Technology. His main research interest is mobile technology.

Thomas Hansson is Associate Professor (Dozent) in Education/Pedagogy at Blekinge Institute of Technology, School of Management (MAM). Major research interests are on reflective practices related to teaching and learning, e.g. how educators understand, explain and describe operations on thinking and doing, especially in contexts related to Information and Communication Technology. TH is currently editing a publication on didactics for vocational teachers and another publication exploring the influence of learning objects on the interplay between individual and collective influences on human behaviour.

Walter Hürster holds a degree in Physics from the University of Freiburg / Germany. After his research work in nuclear and elementary particle physics, Dr. Hürster became responsible for the system design and the executive management of application projects in various fields: Air Space Surveillance, Air Traffic Control, Aeronautical Telecommunication Networks, Simulation Systems, Environmental Information Systems, Coastal Protection, Early Warning and Risk Management Systems. Besides his membership with the Coordination Committee for the Development of Environmental Information Systems with the Ministry for Environment, State of Baden-Württemberg, Germany, he has been repeatedly invited as a consultant for Risk Management Systems by the Commission of the European Union and by the ISDR Initiative of the United Nations. His current position is Private Researcher and Independent Consultant.

H. Hannah Inbarani is now working as an Associate professor in the Department of Computer science, Periyar University, Salem. She received M.Sc degree in Computer science from Bharathidasan University, Trichy, India, M.Phil degree from M.S University, Tirunelveli, India and M.Tech Degree from AAI deemed University, Allahabad, India. Her research interest lies in Rough sets, Fuzzy systems, Internet Technologies, Swarm Intelligence and Web mining. She has published five research papers in the areas like Web Usage Mining, Rough Sets and Ant Clustering.

Bill Karakostas is a senior lecturer with the Centre for HCI Design in the School of Informatics. City UIniversity, London, UK. He has also held posts with the universities of Manchester and Surrey in the UK. Bill holds a Masters in Computer Engineering and Informatics, from Patras University in Greece and an MSc and PhD in Software Engineering, both from UMIST, UK. He has acted as technical advisor to several organizations in the UK and to the IT research programmes of the European Union. He has a twenty plus year research track in areas such as service system engineering, business process management (BPM), simulation, modelling, redesign, workflow management), business object technologies, software reuse and component-based and model-based development. He is the author/co-author of over 120 scientific publications and of two books on system requirements and service engineering.

Vasilios Katos is Assistant Professor of Information and Communications Systems Security at the Department of Electrical and Computer Engineering of Democritus University of Thrace in Greece. He holds a Diploma in Electrical Engineering from the Democritus University of Thrace, an MBA from Keele University and a PhD from Aston University in the UK. Prior to his current post he was Principal Lecturer at the School of Computing at the University of Portsmouth where he participated in the development of the interdisciplinary Masters course MSc in Forensic IT. He has worked in the industry as a security consultant as an expert witness in information systems security and delivered invited presentations at professional conferences. His research interests are in information security, privacy, digital forensics and incident response.

Miroljub Kljajić graduated from the Faculty of Electronics, University of Ljubljana in 1970. He received his MS in 1972 and his PhD in 1974 at the same university. In 1970 he was employed at the Institute Jozef Stefan, Department for Biocybernetics and Robotics. Since 1976 he works at the Faculty of Organizational Sciences, University of Maribor as Professor of System Theory, Cybernetics, and Modeling and Simulation. He has been principal investigator of many national and international projects from modeling and simulation. As author and co-author he has published over two hundred scientific articles.

Manuel Kolp is a professor in Information Systems at the Université catholique de Louvain, Belgium where he is also head of the Information Systems Research Unit and Academic Secretary of Research for the Louvain School of Management. Dr. Kolp is also invited professor with the Universitary Faculties St. Louis of Brussels. His research work deals with agent-oriented and socio-technical architectures for e-business and ERP II systems. He was previously a Post Doctoral Fellow and an adjunct professor at the University of Toronto. He has been involved in the organization committee of international conferences and has chaired different workshops. His publications include more than 70 international refereed journals or periodicals and proceedings papers as well as three books.

Theresa Kraft teaches both Computer Science courses and Information Technology Courses for the University of Michigan Flint. She received her Doctorate in Management of Information Technology from Lawrence Technological University. Her graduate studies include a MBA from the University of Detroit Mercy and a Masters of System Engineering from Rensselaer Polytechnic Institute. Her recent articles on project management have been published in the Information Systems Education Journal and the Journal of Information Systems Applied Research. She has over thirty years of comprehensive industry experience in Manufacturing Engineering, Project Management and Information Technology.

Zbigniew Kwecka is a PhD Research Student in the School of Computing at Edinburgh Napier University and Senior Security Analyst for Secureworks. He is an active member of the Centre for Distributed Computing, Networking and Security. His main areas of interest are Privacy Enhancing Technologies, Data Acquisition, Digital Forensic and Covert Channels. He has won the British Computer Society prize at Scottish Young Engineer of the Year Awards, 2006 for work on Application Layer Covert Channels, and published at a number of European and international conferences.

Costas Lambrinoudakis holds a B.Sc. (Electrical and Electronic Engineering) from the University of Salford (1985), an M.Sc. (Control Systems) from the University of London (Imperial College -1986), and a Ph.D. (Computer Science) from the University of London (Queen Mary and Westfield College - 1991). Currently he is an Assistant Professor at the Department of Digital Systems, University of Piraeus, Greece. From 1998 until 2009 he has held teaching position with the University of the Aegean, Department of Information and Communication Systems Engineering, Greece. His current research interests are in the areas of Information and Communication Systems Security and of Privacy Enhancing Technologies. He is an author of more than 85 scientific publications in refereed international journals, books and conferences, most of them on ICT security and privacy protection issues. He has served as program committee chair of 5 international scientific conferences and as a member on the program and organizing committees in more than 60 others. Also he participates in the editorial board of two international scientific journals and he acts as a reviewer for more than 30 journals. He has been involved in many national and EU funded R&D projects in the area of Information and Communication Systems Security. He is a member of the ACM and the IEEE.

Zongjun Li holds the Doctor of Management in Information Technology degree from Lawrence Technological University, USA, and Master and Bachelor in Computer Science degrees from Huazhong University of Science and Technology, China. He is employed by the Ontario Government, Canada, and has provided several architecture solutions for Corporate Government, the Ministry of Health, and the

Ministry of Children and Youth Services. He has also provided mobile/non-mobile content distribution solutions and Web based J2EE architecture solutions for private and public companies in Canada, the United States and China. In recent years he has concentrated on Mobile Enterprise Architecture (MEA) completing his doctoral research in 2006 on "the Enterprise Goes Mobile".

Emmanouil V. Magkos received his first degree in Computer Science from the University of Piraeus, Greece, in 1997. In April 2003 he received his Ph.D. in Security and Cryptography from the University of Piraeus, Greece. Currently he is affiliated with the Department of Informatics, Ionian University, Corfu, Greece, where he holds the position of Lecturer in computer security and cryptography. His current research interests include security and privacy in distributed information systems and pervasive environments, key management in wireless ad-hoc networks, intrusion detection for malware propagation.

Ioannis Mavridis is Assistant Professor of Information Systems Security at the Department of Applied Informatics of University of Macedonia, Greece. He holds a Diploma in Computer Engineering and Informatics from the University of Patras, Greece and a Doctor's degree in Mobile Computing Security from the Aristotle University of Thessaloniki, Greece. He is a member of Working Group 11.3 on Database Security of International Federation for Information Processing (IFIP). He has participated in several research projects working on the area of IT security. His research interests include the areas of information security and assurance, privacy and access control.

Manuel Mora is an associate professor at the Autonomous University of Aguascalientes (Mexico) since 1995. He holds a doctorate in engineering from the Engineering Graduate School of the National Autonomous University of Mexico (UNAM). He also received his BS in computer systems engineering (1984) and his MSc in computer sciences with artificial intelligence as major area in 1989, both from the Monterrey Tech (ITESM). In the last six years, he has published and presented several papers in refereed international conferences in USA, Europe, and Mexico. He has also been a guest co-editor for special issues on DMSS for the *Information Resource Management Journal* and the *Journal of Decision Systems*. His current research interests are the organizational design and implementation of integrated decision making support systems and theoretical foundations of information systems, using the systems approach as the theoretical frame.

Andy Phippen is Professor of Social Responsibility in Information Technology at the School of Management, Plymouth Business School. He has carried out research for many years on the social implications of emerging technology working with academics, industrialists and policy makers on matters related to the responsibility of technology providers and educators to provide safe online environments. He is involved with young people and technology exploring issues of online engagement and the use/abuse of technology and protection measures, both social and technological. He writes and lectures on IT ethics and the role of the Internet as a research environment.

Stefano Piffer is a member of the technical staff at Fondazione Graphitech, where he works on issue related to high-quality interactive graphics in Geographical environment. He received the M.D. in Telecommunications Engineering in 2004 from the University of Trento, Italy with a work on the adaptive antennas synthesis, antenna design, adaptive signal processing and adaptive beamforming. His work covered a wide variety of computer graphics topics, including real-time simulation, general-purpose computation on GPUs and shading language. Nowadays he is working on NASA World Wind API and Virtual Terrain Project Tool for the fruition of Spatial Data Infrastructure in Public Administration context.

Patricia Paderewski Rodríguez, PhD in Software Engineering, Lecturer in the Software Engineering Department and Research Member of the Research Group in Specification, Development and Evolution of Software at the Department of Languages and Computer Systems, University of Granada, Spain. She is specialized in software architectures, software evolution and adaptation and software distributed agents for collaborative work environments and classroom work.

Àngels Rius is a lecturer of the Department of Computer Science, Multimedia and Telecommunication at the Universitat Oberta de Catalunya (U.O.C.), Barcelona, Spain. Since 1996 she is also part-time Assistant Professor of the High Engineering Polytechnic School at the Universitat Politécnica de Catalunya (UPC), Vilanova I la Geltrú, Barcelona, Spain. She received her B.Sc degree in Computer Science from the Facultat d'Informàtica de Barcelona (U.P.C.) and her M.Sc at the UOC University. Her research interest concerns the area of e-Learning, particularly in the technological and applied aspect. Recently, she is working on the automation of educational settings; this is from the formal description of educational settings provided by ontologies to its translation into executable process languages suitable for e-Learning environments.

Miguel Sánchez Román, Master Degree in Computer Science. Technician at the Computing Services and Communications Networks Centre, University of Granada, Spain. Member of the Research Group in Specification, Development and Evolution of Software at the Department of Languages and Computer Systems, University of Granada, Spain. His research focuses on the field of security in collaborative systems: security policies, access control models and definition of security patterns and their integration into software architectures.

Francesc Santanach has a Bachelor degree in Informatics Engineering from the Polytechnic University of Catalonia (UPC). He currently works in the Office of Learning Technologies of the Universitat Oberta de Catalunya (UOC). He is not only responsible for the design and technical architecture of the Campus Project (http://www.campusproject.org), but also for the development of the architecture of the UOC Virtual Campus. He also runs projects in the field of education contents, elearning tools and standards, such as SCORM, IMS QTI, videoconferencing, audio and video blogs, IMS LTI and OKI OSIDs. He has also been an author of learning materials and tutor for the UOC.

Christophe Schinckus is a postdoc fellow at the Univeristy of Québec at Montréal. He completed his PhD in financial economics at the University of Paris I Panthéon-Sorbonne. Economist and philosopher of science, Dr. Schinckus works on epistemological analysis of financial theory and especially econophysics. He has also a BSc in computer science and is interested in software engineering processes.

Bruno Simões was born in Ourém, Portugal in July of 1984. He is currently finishing the Master's Degree in Computer Science at University of Évora, Portugal and working as Software Developer on a 3D Geobrowser project at Fondazione Graphitech in Italy. In 2007 he worked as Junior Investigator in Bioinformatics at University of Évora and also in some free lancer projects. His research interests include all areas of Computer Graphics, advanced 3D interaction techniques and image processing. More details about him or his projects can be found at the following web site www.brunosimoes.pt.vu.

Matthew Smith received his PhD in Information Systems from the London School of Economics and Political Science. Matthew is currently a Program Officer with the Connectivity and Equity in the Americas program initiative at the International Development Research Centre in Ottawa, Canada. His central research interest is the use and impact of information and communication technologies for social, political, and economic development. Matthew has written on e-government, social science research, and human development and published in a variety of outlets including the Journal of Information Technology and Information and Organization.

A. L. Steenkamp is Program Director of the Doctoral Program in Management of Information Technology and Professor in Computer and Information Systems in the College of Graduate Management at the Lawrence Technological University, Southfield, Michigan. She holds a PhD in Computer Science specialized in Software Engineering. She teaches Enterprise and Information Technology Architectures, Information Technology Life Cycle Processes, and IT Research Methodology in the doctoral program, and has led a large number of projects in the field. She also directs a research program for doctoral students focused on enterprise architecture, knowledge management and approaches to process improvement in organizations. She has collaborated with industry on initiatives to improve the education and learning of IT professionals for more than 25 years.

Beatriz Jiménez Valverde, Master Degree in Computer Science. Technician at the Computing Services and Communications Networks Centre, University of Granada, Spain. Member of the Research Group in Specification, Development and Evolution of Software at the Department of Languages and Computer Systems, University of Granada, Spain. Her research focuses on the context of coordination models for representation of collaborative processes within the service-oriented software architectures.

Francisco L. Gutierrez Vela, PhD in Software Engineering, Lecturer in the Software Engineering Department and Research Member of the Research Group in Specification, Development and Evolution of Software at the Department of Languages and Computer Systems, University of Granada, Spain. He is specialized in interactive systems, user interface design and collaborative design systems. He is interested in the use of videogames and interactive systems applied to education. He is member of the Human-Computer Spanish Association.

Rossouw von Solms is a professor in the School of ICT and the Director of the Institute for ICT Advancement at Nelson Mandela Metropolitan University, in South Africa. He holds a PhD from the Rand Afrikaans University. He has been a member of the International Federation for Information Processing (IFIP) TC 11 committee since 1995 and is currently the vice chair. He has published many papers in international journals and presented numerous papers at national and international conferences in the field of Information Security Management.

Nikos Vrakas is a Ph.D candidate at the University of Piraeus. He has received his bachelor degree in Mathematics at the University of the Aegean and the M.Sc in Information and Communication Security where he received scholarship. He is also author of several papers and of chapter in a book in the field of IT Security. His research interests include availability, intrusion detection and prevention and privacy preserving mechanisms of the Session Initiation Protocol (SIP) in IP Multimedia Subsystem (IMS) of the Next Generation Networks (NGNs).

Yves Wautelet is an IT project manager and a postdoc fellow at the Université catholique de Louvain, Belgium. He completed a PhD thesis focusing on project and risk management issues in large enterprise software design. Dr. Wautelet also holds a bachelor and master in management sciences as well as a master in Information Systems. His research interests include aspects of software engineering such as requirements engineering, project management, software development life cycles, component-based development, epistemological foundations of SE and CASE-Tools but also information systems strategy.

Thomas Wilbois studied physics at the University of Mainz / Germany, followed by international research activities in the field of theoretical nuclear and elementary particle physics with the focus on hadronic and electromagnetic processes in few body meson-nucleon systems. In the following years, his main field of occupation changed to the design, development and operation of large integrated measurement network systems and environmental information, early warning and risk management systems. Concerning IT, the major domain is high availability in transaction processing oriented distributed systems. Beyond these technological issues, Dr. Wilbois is engaged in general questions concerning international emergency management. His current position is Senior Consultant at T-Systems.

Yannis Zorgios holds a PhD from the University of Manchester Institute of Science & Technology (UMIST), U.K. In 1998 joined CLMS (UK) LIMITED where he is the main architect and the product manager of the CLMS Enterprise Systems Management Platform, a service oriented platform that combines the latest research developments in systems engineering and business process management. His research interests focus on the provision of Contemporary Learning Management Systems and ontological frameworks that support large, complex and dynamic service oriented systems.

Index

U

User Clustering 212-214

V

Virtual Reality Mark-up Language (VRML) 156

W

waterfall model 9-10, 67

Web-Based Applications 157
Web Map Service (WMS) 158
Web Mining 212-213, 223
Web Services Composite Application Framework
   (WS-CAF) 93, 105
Web Usage Mining 212-213
WoS publications 40